NEW ERA CHALLENGES OLD PATTERNS

A World History, 1945-1960

Franklin D. Parker

UNIVERSITY
PRESS OF
AMERICA

Copyright © 1981 by

University Press of America, Inc.

P.O. Box 19101, Washington, D.C. 20036

ISBN (Perfect): 0-8191-1840-0
ISBN   (Cloth): 0-8191-1839-7

Library of Congress Catalog Card Number: **80-6296**

Dedicated to

Jennie Borden Parker

-- for her faith

and love of persons.

iv

ACKNOWLEDGEMENTS

The following copyrighted materials have been used with the permission of the copyright holders:

(1) On p. 312, a selection from Nathaniel Tarn's translation of The Heights of Macchu Picchu by Pablo Neruda (published by Farrar, Straus & Giroux, copyright 1967 by Nathaniel Tarn);

(2) On pp. 527-8, the hymn "How Great Thou Art" by Stuart K. Hine (international copyright secured, all rights reserved, copyright 1953, 1955 by Manna Music, Inc., 2111 Kenmere, Burbank, California 91504);

(3) On p. 537, a selection from Millar Burrows' translation of "The Manual of Discipline" in The Dead Sea Scrolls by Millar Burrows (published by Viking Press, copyright 1955 by Millar Burrows, permission received from E. G. Burrows);

(4) On pp. 788-9, a selection from Bernard Guilbert Buerney's translation of "Garden of Gethsemane" in Doctor Zhivago, written by Boris Pasternak and translated by Max Hayward and Manya Harari (published by Pantheon Books, copyright 1958 by Pantheon Books, A Division of Random House, Inc.).

The author acknowledges with appreciation the permissions granted by these holders of the respective copyrights.

OUTLINE OF THE VOLUME

A. Barriers between races, as important
as they have continued, nevertheless have become an anachronism on the world scene.
   B. Language problems remain very serious,
affecting nearly everyone; they involve both
prejudice and lack of understanding.
   C. Religious divisions, while becoming
less sharp, have left a tremendous cultural
prejudice behind them.
   Z. Some 20 racial groups, 100 languages,
and 20 organized religions are identified
here.

A. Nationalism, unlike race, language,
and religion, is a chiefly modern phenomenon.
   B. Most nation-states have come into
existence only since the widespread interest
in nationalism.
   C. Only a very few of the nation-states
can possibly provide a minimum of well-being
for their people without assistance from other
nations.
   Z. All the nations are identified as they
existed in 1940, and each placed in one of the
following (arbitrary) categories: the Orient,
Europe, the Americas, the Middle East, Sub-
Sahara Africa.

A. Democracy -- majority rule, the secret
ballot, freedom of information, proportional

representation -- is practiced or pretended by many nations, but in varying degree.

B. Socialism -- the public control of the means of production and distribution -- has become widely adopted, again in varying degree, though open opposition remains.

C. Democracy and socialism offer their own problems, and can serve only as harbingers of, not the essence of, a new age.

Z. A political spectrum is presented, with four divisions -- authoritarian socialist, democratic socialist, democratic private-enterprise, authoritarian private-enterprise -- and the roll call of nations fitted therein.

Z. The narrative begins, with a very brief review of the war year by year and a discussion of the political events of the time.

Y. Eight mini-biographies appear --Joseph Stalin, Winston Churchill, Tito, Eduard Benes, Harry Truman, Clement Attlee, Sukarno, Ho Chi Minh.

X. The political spectrum is updated to 1945.

1. India, Pakistan, Indonesia, Korea, the Philippines, Burma, Ceylon -- nearly one-fourth of the world's population.

2. With all its staggering problems, India alone of this group possessed the resources needed for continued viability.

1. Chiang Kai Shek and Mao Ze Dong (mini-biographies) establish performance-records and state their ideas; in the contest, Mao wins.

2. The Chinese Communist regime moved moderately at first, enacting reforms that modernized China without pushing it far into socialism.

terests.

       1. North Viet-Nam, Egypt, and Bolivia
-- the second led by Jamal Abd an-Nasir (mini-
biography) -- carried out revolutions without

opposition from the United States.
       2. Thus three depressed areas won a
new lease on life -- North Viet-Nam with communism, Bolivia with democratic socialism,
Egypt with a program yet to be determined.

       1. Modifications of the economic pano-
rama are presented.
       2. International financial assistance
is introduced.

       1. The Soviet Union intervened by force
in Hungary to halt the development of a more
democratic socialist regime.
       2. China and the Soviet Union gradually
worked their way into serious controversy
starting with the denunciation of Stalin by
Khrushchev.

       1. The United Kingdom, France, and Is-
rael entered into collusion to depose the
president of Egypt, and to change the status
of the Suez Canal.
       2. The United Nations, with the Soviet
Union and the United States agreeing, took
strong action to defeat the three-power move.

       1. The British, Belgians, and French
-- the last under Charles de Gaulle (mini-
biography) -- relinquished their hold upon
22 African nations.
       2. The new nations, lacking the re-

sources to stand alone, also faced the problem of great internal disunity.

     1. A revolution in Venezuela, carried
out by a coalition of parties, established
both democracy and socialism as its keywords.

     2. A revolution in Cuba, carried out
by Fidel Castro (mini-biography) and his band,
looked toward socialism but turned away from
democracy.

     1. After the Soviet intervention in
Hungary and a United States expedition to
Lebanon, some hope sprang from "the spirit of
Camp David" that tensions might relax.
     2. The incident of the U-2 plane shot
down in the Soviet Union shattered those possibilities for the remainder of the Eisenhower
presidency.

     1. National comparisons initiated ear-
lier are continued.
     2. National growth rates, 1950-60, are
examined.

PREFACE

This book offers no conclusion. It presents only the chief events -- political, economic, scientific, artistic, and religious -- of a short but very crucial time period in the history of one planet. The perspective is that of a person who lived through that brief epoch, whose early reading brought him a sincere appreciation of the past, and whose later contacts with the world caused him to anticipate with pleasure rather than pain the great changes that may arise in the future. The shape of those changes he leaves to the reader -- as well he must -- though he hopes that the accounts he unfolds in these pages will help produce wise judgements that the world so sorely needs.

The earlier chapters demand study beyond a mere reading if one is to share their full impact. Reader-composed charts and outlines (far superior to the published brand) will help make the message of these chapters subsist until it becomes useful for further reference. Here are presented the names and basic ideas -- some peculiar to the makeup of this publication -- upon which later discussions are frequently based. Even Chapter V, in its sections on the economy, science, art, and religion, contains a remnant of this early anticipatory approach.

A few maps at the reader's elbow will be useful to most persons, and essential to many. Of greatest importance is an up-to-date map of the entire world thirty inches or more in width, showing all the countries and the remaining dependencies. Because of name and administrative changes, a corollary map of the world as it existed in 1935 or 1939 will make a useful adjunct. Beyond these, maps showing the present political divisions of the world's four most populated countries -- China, India, the Soviet Union, and the United States -- will prove the most helpful, along with one of India before 1947.

A modest effort appears in these pages to treat all people alike. Some make more history than others, of course, and so receive more attention. Racial, linguistic, religious, and political groups are named, however, not on the basis of their familiarity in the author's home country but on the numbers involved in them or the uniqueness of their situations. Titles of distinguished persons are not capitalized; titles of "nobility" are left unmentioned.

Anglicizations of proper names have been allowed to stand where alterations might prove confusing. In other cases, decisions were made to move closer than usual to the original. The careful reader will soon find it convenient to remember that family names appear differently according to the language, and that many cultures use an individual's given name either by preference or exclusively. The custom followed for each name is clear to the reader only if he grants the matter a little special attention.

Controversy swirls over nearly all the sections of this book. In almost every instance, a variety of tomes may be found that handle the facts differently. I ask not that the reader take my version of any particular episode on faith, but only that if doubt arises he or she simply read as many books and articles as possible relating to that topic. I feel confident that those who approach the matter without a preconceived emotion will understand the reasonableness of the arguments here explained. The potential bibliography for the present work consists of an imaginary card catalog of all publications in the world since 1945. The author has used a wide variety of them. Some of the more important items are discussed in proper context.

The particular library that contained most of

the information gathered by the author, or that brought other materials in when they were needed, is the Walter Clinton Jackson Library of the University of North Carolina at Greensboro. I feel a very deep appreciation for the many facilities and favors extended to me by director James H. Thompson, assistant director John Thomas Minor, and all the Jackson Library staff. The two heads of my History Department during the course of the writing, Richard Bardolph and Ann P. Saab -- both of whose library studies are located close to my own -- granted continuing encouragement through recommendations for leaves and the provision of a harmonious departmental background.

My students and my family aided tremendously. The students, with whom I discussed the questions treated in the book long before the conception of this volume came to my mind, had a peculiar way of making me feel some aspects of the modern world whose drama could never have reached me fully through the medium of reading. Their very youth (increasingly notable as the years proceed) also helps me remember the vantage point of those who did not live through the time period this first volume describes. I owe a special debt of gratitude to graduate assistants who helped me in many ways. Among them, Alice North, Jane Eagle Lunsford, Charlotte Bennett Moore, and Michael Golnick read large sections of the manuscript, offering invaluable comment and criticisms. Margarita Townsend Throop, another able student, assisted in the same manner.

My two daughters Ginger Parker Collier and Jeannie Parker Blackwelder performed a special role as critics and advisers, Jeannie managing to cover the entire manuscript. I could never have completed the task if they and their mother had not, in times of physical distress, provided the encouragement and intellectual companionship I needed to keep me going. My wife Jennie Borden Parker, to whom the book is dedicated, served as my chief stimulator and critic through the entire process, typed the original typescript, and acted as co-proofreader and co-index builder on the final product. Mrs. Ginny Odum of Correspondence Center, Inc. (who will no doubt breathe some sigh of relief as she processes this last sentence) performed most capably the immense task of transforming the typescript into a neat packet resembling a book.

F.D.P.

May 27, 1981

I. THE SEPARATIONS OF MANKIND --

RACE, LANGUAGE, AND RELIGION

Homo sapiens is a name man gave himself. Homo means only man; some authorities contend there were others of him. Sapiens means intelligent, and the species of intelligent man includes all men now living. Men have become separated, however, as they wandered over the face of the globe. Biological, linguistic, and cultural divergences appeared as groups bred in isolation. Some of the manifestations of these, having evolved, re-mixed, evolved further, and re-mixed again into a veritable hodgepodge of ramifications, retain their place in the world and strongly affect its history since 1945.

Well-authenticated men and women -- who stood upright and were already very clever -- lived in southern Africa about a million years ago. Half a million years later persons related to them inhabited Java, China, and eastern Africa, and possibly Europe as well. Those of Java and China represented distinct branches of mankind. The Java branch seems for a very long time to have roamed southeastern Asia, Sumatra, and Java in search of game; eventually it moved onto nearby islands. Today its descendants, each mixed with a variety of other strains, are the frizzly-haired, brown-skinned, heavy-browed Melanesians of New Guinea and adjacent spots of land; the wavy-haired, brown-skinned, heavy-browed aborigines of Australia; and the curly-haired, brown-skinned, short-statured Negritos of Malaya, the Philippines, and the Andaman Islands. Few people have remained farther removed than these from the mainstream of history since 1945.

1

The persons who lived in China so long ago developed into one of the great modern sub-species of mankind. Mongoloid is the name of their progeny, with its straight hair, yellow skin, and epicanthic fold over the eyes. The Mongoloids seem to have developed in China alone for a very extended time, as they stalked the animals about them. But eventually they began to expand. As many of them moved into southeastern Asia, Madagascar, the East Indian islands, and the Philippines, they mixed with the previous inhabitants, and finally overshadowed them to form the straight-haired, dark-skinned Malayo-Indonesian population of those lands. Dramati-cally, another arm of Mongoloid expansion, after occupying Korea and Japan, reached into a huge New World for human habitation. Successive waves of migration from eastern Asia into North and South America, followed by new complexities of isolation and intermixing of the strains, pro-duced the vast variety of peoples known as Amer-ican Indians, also generally straight-haired and dark-skinned. The straight-haired, yellow-skinned Eskimo and their kin of eastern Asia and northern-most North America probably represent the most recent of the invasions of the New World from the Mongoloid sector of the Old.

The persons who lived in eastern Africa and possibly in Europe a half-million years ago are not so certainly the dominant ancestors of those who now live in the same areas. At later times, both eastern and northern Africa may have served as a bridge for the evolution of discernible present-day groups of man. One variety, quite possibly connected with the Mongoloids in its beginnings, seems to have developed somewhere in eastern or northern Africa, and to have main-tained importance for a time, only to become largely eclipsed in some subsequent era. Its modern descendents include the intensely curly-haired, brown-skinned, short-statured Bushmen and the related Hottentots of southern Africa. Some-how differentiating from the ancestors of the Bushmen, possibly by long isolation in western

Africa, there evolved a second great subspecies of modern man, the <u>Negroid</u>, with curly hair, brown skin, and full lips. Eventually, Negroids occupied all of central Africa and the west shore of Madagascar, developing a number of regional variations. The Pygmies of Zaire, who superficially resemble the Negritos of the Andaman Islands and the Philippines, are but a separate limb of the now widely distributed Negroid branch of mankind.

Europe, because of the off-and-on coldness of its climate until recent times, was one of the last parts of the Old World to become fully occupied by man. The cultural history of one race which lived there for an extensive period (the so-called Neanderthals) has received attention only in very recent times. Some persons whose appearance preceded that of the Neanderthals and others who occupied Europe in a more favored later time pertained to a third great subspecies of <u>homo</u> <u>sapiens</u>, the <u>Caucasoid</u>, with its wavy hair, light skin, and narrow nose. The first home of the Caucasoids may have been western Asia, where they still reside. Far back, their line may have associated with the one which produced the most ancient populations of Australia, New Guinea, and the Philippines, or with another which led to the bushy-haired, light-skinned Ainu of northern Japan. Through migration, not only all of Europe but northern Africa as well became part of their domain. The Basque people of Spain and France may be the oldest Caucasoids in this region who have maintained a separate identity. The Lapps, in the far north of Europe, seem to be among the latest to have become situated. Other distinguishable groups among European Caucasoids -- the brunette people living near the Mediterranean or the more blonde individuals of other climes (north and west or central and east) -- are in each case an amalgam of races that have come and gone.

The subcontinent of India like that of Europe was long ago occupied by Caucasoids. Those of

3

India, however, merged consequentially with other lines. Further change from inbreeding then produced the wavy-haired, generally brown-skinned, but very diverse Indo-Dravidians, whose life since 1945 remains vexed by the caste system, a sublimated form of a very old race problem.

Caucasoid and Mongoloid movements which began far back in the days when all men were hunters and gatherers of food have in some instances continued into most recent times. Caucasoid families who have come to Indo-Dravidian territory or Mongoloid families who have entered Malayo-Indonesian areas can often be identified after several hundred years. Equally visible, and even more sensational, are three other grand movements of people which began after the invention of farming. The Negroid peoples in one such foray have occupied most of southern Africa. The island-dwelling Indonesians and Melanesians have gone on across the Pacific as far as the Hawaiian Islands, Easter Island, and New Zealand, to evolve in that wide area into the wavy-haired, dark-skinned Polynesians of today. On Easter Island, they met American Indians expanding across the waters westward, thus completing a wide Pacific Ocean circle.

But most striking of all has been a movement of Europeans, in the last five hundred years, to every part of the globe, where their presence affected the pattern of life in hundreds of thousands of communities. In the New World, Europeans subdued most of the American Indians, and often brought in Africans as slaves; thereby establishing new blends of peoples (mestizo, mulatto, <u>zambo</u>, and three-way) and, in some places, creating tensions by raising legal barriers between them. In Africa, the Europeans established themselves as a favored minority, inviting trouble from the disadvantaged on every hand. In Asia, generally, they made but slight and temporary inroads -- except in India, where they stayed a few hundred years, and Siberia, where they filled in sparsely inhabited land. In much

4

of Oceania, as in India, they dominated other
peoples for a considerable time, and in Australia
and New Zealand erected constitutional fences
against penetration by their non-Caucasoid
neighbors.

Barriers -- and problems -- between races,
built upon differences in hair form, skin color,
or the shape of the body, perplex and bewilder a
considerable segment of mankind. In the fast-
moving world since 1945, nevertheless, they have
become an anachronism. The vast majority of
persons in the world today agree that race differences are of little significance alongside the
characteristics the races share in common. Because for a time the world seemed to be theirs
for the picking, Caucasoids of the nineteenth
century convinced themselves generally that there
existed great racial inequalities in intelligence
and drive. Various writers waxed eloquent to the
point of demanding, in effect, that the "super"
race of men be allowed to lead world progress,
and that the others follow. More careful observation has shown, however, that whatever differences can be discerned in intelligence and
drive are the products of culture and nutrition
rather than inherited biology. Without the sus-
taining power of the myth that one race or the
other is "naturally" inferior, twentieth-century
racial problems seem to have but one denouement
ahead. They will gradually disappear (as race
difficulties have in localized zones from time
immemorial) with the intermingling of the large
percentages of humans who find association with
members of other races more attractive than
repelling.

Linguistic differences of some sort between
groups of mankind are presumably as long-standing
as the biological ones. The most biologically
distinct of today's peoples also speak the most
disjunct tongues. This is not to say that their
languages in present-day form are the most ancient or the most primitive, but only that for a

5

very long time their evolution has proceeded along separate lines. The many languages spoken by Australian aborigines, the Papuan speech of the Melanesians on New Guinea and other islands, the Andamanese spoken by one group of Negritos, and the Ainu tongue of a small portion of Japan are all examples of very distinct speech developed in long isolation. So are the Khoisan languages, spoken by the Bushmen and their kin of Africa, whose use of implosive clicks has spread to others who live in their neighborhoods.

The Australian, Papuan, Andamanese, Ainu, and Khoisan lines of linguistic differentiation extend far back into the ages when all people subsisted as hunting and gathering nomads. The same may likely be said of one sizeable speech family, the Austroasiatic. Among its branches are the Munda languages of central India and a group of tongues heard in pockets from India to Viet-Nam, including the Khmer speech of a majority of the people of Norodom Sihanouk in the Khmer Republic, called Cambodia. Vietnamese itself, the language of Nguyen That Thanh, better known as Ho Chi Minh, and of Ngo Dinh Diem, Ho's adversary, fits in the Austroasiatic family, at least by influence. No one knows the history of the Austroasiatic languages. But it may be presumed that, long ago, they became separated by the infiltration of other peoples as well as by their own nomadism and the disturbances of geography.

Many other languages and groups of languages have become encircled and set apart in more recent times. Those saved for this paragraph and the next have been squeezed into their present localities only since the world advent of agriculture, or during the last ten thousand years. Most important of these by far is the Dravidian family of southern India, including the Telugu language of Andhra Pradesh, Tamil of Madras, Kannada of Mysore, and Malayalam of Kerala, the last the native tongue of Vengalil Krishnan Krishna Menon. In another part of Asia, there are the Kadai languages of southern China and nations to the south, especially those of Pibul Songgram of Thailand and Souvanna Phouma of Laos. In Africa, the so-called Sudanic family includes important branches along the upper Nile River (in Uganda and other lands) and in Sahara-related portions of Niger, Chad, and adjacent regions. Near the southwestern extremity of Europe there is the unique speech of the Basques; and in the mountainous southeastern corner the several languages of the South and North Caucasian families, the former including Georgian, the first tongue of Iosif Vissarionovich Dzhugashvili, or Joseph Stalin. In the New World, before the coming of the European and African, the Eskimoan tongues were very distinct, as well as those of the Tarascans in Mexico and of another Mexican linguistic group which included the Otomí.

In the last five hundred years, six of eight previously vigorous American Indian linguistic families have been reduced to small size, spoken now generally in isolated districts spaciously distributed over their former territories. Thus the course of fortune has run for languages associated with the Carib of tropical South America; with the Chibcha of Colombia; with the Nahuatl spoken by the Aztec of central Mexico; with the Algonkian of the eastern part of the United States; with the Siouan of the United States' Middle West; and with the Athapascan of western Canada. Only two American Indian speech families play a significant world role since 1945. The lesser of these comprises the several languages spoken by Maya peoples in southern Mexico and Guatemala; the other includes the very scattered Tupí-Guaraní of Brazil and Paraguay, the Aymara of Bolivia and Peru, and the extensive Quechua of Peru, Bolivia, and Ecuador.

Most modern world history has been made by persons attached to the seven major speech families yet to be mentioned. Each of these seven is larger in count of persons than any family so far outlined, with the exception of the Dravidian.

At the early dawn of farming, and continuing until most recent times, persons speaking certain "Afro-Asiatic" tongues have lived along the southern shores of the Mediterranean and in neighboring Asian and African lands. By far the most important branch of this family is that of the Semitic languages, including Amharic (the tongue of Tafari Makonnen, or Haile Selassie, of Ethiopia), Hebrew (the official speech of Israel), and the very extensive Arabic. Widely varying dialects of the latter were spoken by men such as Jamal Abd an-Nasir of Egypt, Ibrahim Abboud of Sudan, Muhammad Hassan of Morocco, Ahmad ben Bella of Algeria, Abd al-Aziz Al Saud of Saudi Arabia, Abdul Karim Qassim of Iraq, and Shukri al-Kuwatli of Syria. Related to their speech is that of other Afro-Asiatic branches, the so called Chad (including the Hausa of Abubakar Tafawa Balewa of northern Nigeria), the Cushitic (embracing Galla of southern Ethiopia and Somali of Somalia), and the Berber of pockets in northern Africa and the Sahara.

From fifteen to five hundred years ago, the Ural-Altaic family was one of the most active in world history, but since then has assumed a more quiescent attitude. Spreading from somewhere in central Asia, persons speaking these widely variant languages conquered or pushed aside a great number of others, making a deep impression on both Asia and Europe, but finally settling down. The extensive Turkic branch of this family is represented by languages as far east as western China and as far west as Europe, including Uzbek and Tatar in the Asian part of the Soviet Union, Azerbaijani reaching across the Soviet border into Iran, and most importantly Turkish itself, the language of the countrymen of Adnan Menderes. Other branches are the Ugric (containing the Hungarian of Janos Kadar in the middle of Europe), the Finnic of northern Europe (including the languages of the Lapps and of Estonia as well as the Finnish of Urho Kaleva Kekkonen), and the Mongol of faraway eastern Asia.

8

The Niger-Congo family is a very complicated one whose speakers, once restricted to western Africa, have during modern times occupied a great share of the territory in that continent south of the Sahara. The greater part of the expansion has been accomplished by peoples called Bantu who now occupy most of Zaire, Tanzania, Mozambique, and adjacent lands. The Bantu speak a great diversity of tongues; the best known of them are Swahili (used by Julius Kambarage Nyerere in Tanzania and Jomo Kenyatta in Kenya), Zulu-Xhosa-Swazi of South Africa and Swaziland, and Ruanda of Rwanda, Burundi, and nearby zones. Other branches of the Niger-Congo family besides that which includes the Bantu languages are the Kwa (embracing Yoruba and Ibo of southern Nigeria and the Akan tongue of Kwame Nkrumah in Ghana), the so-called West Atlantic (containing Fulani of northern Nigeria and adjacent lands), the Mande, and the Gur, all found in tangled patterns in the area running from Senegal to Cameroon. The spread of the Niger-Congo speech family correlates with the growing importance of the Negroid subspecies of mankind in the modern world.

Two large language families are associated with the Mongoloid expansion carried out over very long periods of time. To the southeast, the Malayo-Polynesian family has arisen, with its dominant Indonesian branch, including Javanese, Sundanese, and Madurese (all spoken on the island of Java); a separate Indonesian-Malay (which serves as the official language for both Indonesia and Malaysia); Bisayan and Tagalog of the Philippines (the latter the first speech of Ramón Magsaysay); and, far away, the Malagasy tongue of Philibert Tsiranana and the island of Madagascar. To the northeast, the Japanese-Korean family is very different, as the two branches (Japanese and Korean) are distinct one from the other. The Japanese language is that of Yoshida Shigeru; Korean is the tongue of the followers of Lee Sung Man, or Syngman Rhee, and of Kim Il Sung alike.

9

The second largest speech family of the globe is that called the Sino-Tibetan, at the heart of the Mongoloid world. Overwhelmingly represented in this grouping is the Chinese branch, including the Mandarin of northern and central China spoken by Mao Ze Dong (Mao Tse Tung) and hundreds of millions of others to make it the most used language in the world. Also contained in the Chinese branch are the Wu of Chekiang (first language of Chiang Kai Shek), the Cantonese of a large section of southern China, the Amoy of Fukien and Tai Wan, the Foochow of Fukien, and the Hakka of Kiangsi. Another branch, small only by comparison with the foregoing, includes the Burmese tongue spoken by U Thant, and the Tibetan. Of minor weight are two other possible Sino-Tibetan branches, one associated with the Miao of southern China and Laos, the other with the Karen languages of south Burma.

The 29 linguistic families so far enumerated, along with others too small to mention, include the speech habits of only half the world. The other half of the globe's inhabitants speak by preference one or another of the great assemblage of languages called Indo-European. This largest family of all, associated in its history with the wide spreading of Caucasoid peoples, has a traceable small beginning. From four to two thousand years ago it expanded both east and west from Asia Minor as far as Iran and Ireland (note the similarity in names) and beyond the first of those to India. Then, when the Europeans further spread over the face of the globe, especially in last five hundred years, their speech habits went with them. European languages are now accepted nearly everywhere in the Americas, and used for practical purposes in almost every land. In western Africa and the Caribbean, they have even merged with one another and with African and American Indian dialects to form new hybrid patterns.

The largest branch of the Indo-European family today is that called Indic, consisting of

10

related languages in central and northern India, Bangladesh, and Pakistan. Of these, Hindi, the official tongue of India, and Urdu, legally the language of Pakistan, form a double-pronged entity which stands as the third largest language of the world. (The two are written with different characters but spoken essentially the same.) Both India and Pakistan are troubled, however, by the fact that very large percentages of their inhabitants can comprehend neither Hindi nor Urdu. Bengali, another important Indic language, is used in West Bengal and Bangladesh. Marathi is found in Maharashtra, Punjabi in Punjab and part of Pakistan, Gujarati in Gujarat (this was the first tongue of Mohandas Karamchand Gandhi), Oriya in Orissa, Rajasthani in Rajasthan, Assamese in Assam, Magadhi in Bihar, and Sindhi in another part of Pakistan. The Sinhalese of Sirimavo Ratwatte Dias Bandaranaike of Sri Lanka, or Ceylon, the Nepali of Mahendra Bir Bikram of Nepal, and the Kashmiri spoken in Kashmir are three more of the better known members of the same Indic line. India's speech problems are typified by the fact that prime minister Jawaharlal Nehru, speaking Hindi, and his defense minister Krishna Menon, using Malayalam of the Dravidian family, understood each other best in the English they both learned in childhood.

English, the second most used of all the languages of the world, fits into the Germanic branch of the Indo-European family once localized in northwestern Europe. English in a British style, spoken by one such as Clement Richard Attlee of the United Kingdom, is used with some variation by the Australian countrymen of Robert Gordon Menzies, by most of the people of New Zealand, and by many in South Africa and Zimbabwe as well. Words from men like Harry Truman of the United States or Lester Bowles Pearson of Canada have a different ring. Many persons in former British colonies speak English, and one or another of its varieties may be heard in virtually every part of the world. The

11

German language, for which the Germanic branch is named, is spoken chiefly in the two parts of Germany (by such men as Konrad Adenauer and Walter Ulbricht), but is also the tongue of the countrymen of Kurt Waldheim of Austria and a majority of the inhabitants of Switzerland. Dutch, the speech of Willem Drees of the Netherlands, and Flemish, that of a majority of the people of Belgium, are variants of a single Germanic language. Other members of this branch are Swedish (the speech of Dag Hjalmar Agne Carl Hammarskjöld), Danish, Norwegian (spoken by Trygve Halvdan Lie), Afrikaans (used by Hendrik Frensch Verwoerd of South Africa), and Yiddish, a favorite with Jewish peoples in many lands.

The Romance languages, chiefly of southwestern Europe in their origins, constitute another Indo-European branch nearly the size of the Germanic. In the nineteenth century this subgroup of tongues probably outdistanced any other in the world excepting the Indic and the Chinese. The largest Romance language is Spanish, which places fourth on the entire globe. It was of course the language of Francisco Paulino Hermenegildo Teódulo Franco Bahamonde of Spain, but just as importantly that of men such as Adolfo Ruiz Cortines of Mexico, Juan Domingo Perón of Argentina, Alberto Lleras Camargo of Colombia, Manuel Prado y Ugarteche of Peru, Carlos Ibáñez del Campo of Chile, Marcos Pérez Jiménez of Venezuela, and Fidel Castro Ruz of Cuba. Altogether, Spanish covers most of Middle America and about half of South America as well. Brazil (the country of Getúlio Dornelles Vargas), covering most of the remainder of South America, speaks another Romance language, Portuguese, inherited from Portugal, the home of António de Oliveira Salazar. French, the tongue of France and of Charles-André-Joseph-Marie de Gaulle, is also used by a large minority of persons in Belgium, by many in Switzerland, by the inhabitants of a large linguistic pocket in Canadian Quebec, and as a widely spoken international language. The Italian of Amintore Fanfani and his countrymen, spoken likewise by sizeable minorities in various American lands, is the fourth of the large Romance languages. Of lesser size, but of the same branch, is the detached Romanian, speech of Gheorghe Gheorghiu-Dej and his nation. Still smaller are Provençal of southwestern France, Catalan of northeastern Spain, and the Haitian Creole of the Caribbean.

The fourth largest, but still very widespread, branch of the Indo-European family is that of the Slavic tongues found in central and eastern Europe. Russian, the chief language of Nikita Sergeyevich Khrushchev, is the most widespread of this branch and the fifth largest of the world. Besides blanketing much of the European part of the Soviet Union, it extends all the way across Siberia to the Pacific. In the southwestern part of Russia is found the distinct Ukrainian. Polish, the tongue of Wladyslaw Gomulka, stands along the western border of the Slavic region, as does the Serbo-Croatian tongue of Josip Broz, called Tito, of Yugoslavia. (Like Hindi-Urdu, Serb and Croatian are written differently but pronounced about the same.) Czechoslovakia is a country of two languages, the Czech, of Antonin Zapotocky, and the Slovak. The Bulgarian of Vulko Chervenkov and Belorussian on the western edge of the Soviet Union are two more members of the Slavic group of languages.

Six remaining branches of the Indo-European family complete this review of the more important languages of the world. The Iranian branch contains the Persian-Tajik language of Mohammad Reza Pahlavi and the people of Iran, and of a large minority in Afghanistan (including the ruler Mohammad Zahir); the Pashto of a majority in Afghanistan and a minority in Pakistan (Mohammad Ayub Khan was born in the Pashto region); and Kurdish, at the meeting place of Iraq, Iran, Turkey, and the Soviet Union. The Hellenic branch is largely confined to Greek, spoken by the countrymen of Georgios Andreas Papandreou. Tucked away in three corners of Europe are the Baltic

13

(Lithuanian and Latvian), the Armenian, and the Albanian divisions of the vast Indo-European family. Finally, there is the Celtic, once covering a wide area, but now pinched into small districts in France, Great Britain, and Ireland.

Language problems of some kind affect the life of every human being. No one expects that those peculiar to each individual will ever disappear. Those which are widely shared, however, can be solved, and solutions probably will be found for them with the passage of time, though the process may prove a very prolonged one. Group speech problems may be divided into three categories: First, a great number of languages in the world are too small to survive. There are about three thousand of them altogether, not counting dialects and lesser variations, but of that number only about a hundred can provide a modicum of the learning people need in the modern world. Second, large gaps in comprehension even among the favored hundred make more difficult every kind of cooperation among the peoples of the world. Third, both inside and between nations there have arisen sharp prejudices built along linguistic lines.

Some scholars argue that a group's culture is so tied to its language that the elimination of one leads inevitably to the destruction of the other. Yet Mandarin and English and Hindi-Urdu and Spanish and Russian are spoken today each one by an impressive variety of persons living an exciting diversity of lives. The eventual solution to worldwide linguistic problems will surely include the extinction of very many now-isolated tongues, with or without the loss of distinctions in culture which accompany them. Prejudices and misconceptions between other speech groups may persist until the day when all the peoples of the world decide to raise a new generation which can speak some agreed-upon second language. When that happens, the mutually unintelligible forms of writing will presumably also disappear.

Cultural differences between groups of homo sapiens, like those of race and language, extend far back into the dimmest pages of man's history. The long isolation of one group of persons from another is alone sufficient to explain any of them. From the viewpoint of modern man, however, cultural idiosyncracies remained slight compared to the peculiarities that developed in race and language, down to the time when men adopted quieter ways of living. Details of life for hunters and gatherers differed in response to the varieties of climate and availability of water, fruits, nuts, and game. But for those people the exigencies of remaining alive left little time for philosophizing; thus the bases for the world's primitive cultures, discussed in the following paragraph, remained essentially the same.

Early patterns of life that developed around the world carried close bonds with primitive religion. Seemingly every group of individuals in every land arrived at the conception of a world spirit or spirits with powers greater than man. Rituals were devised, including all of man's earlier art forms, to secure the aid of these spirits in projects at hand. The customs of the various tribes were designed by and large to invoke the pleasure or avoid the displeasure of the spirits, or gods. The rituals served as man's earliest "practice" of religion. Individual customs provided the beginnings of morality, as persons became judged as "good" or "bad" by the extent of their conformity to group ways of doing things. The customs taken together formed the culture of the clan. The very ancient tie-in between morality, religion, and culture continues into the modern world, affecting hundreds of millions of persons' lives.

Sharper cultural differences between peoples arose after the domestication of animals and the invention of farming. New tasks emerged for both earthlings and gods, and specialists now had time to construct theories for keeping alliances be-

15

tween the two going. A few individuals here and there found the leisure to speculate upon the whole nature of the universe and its relation to man. The new thought affected the complex of morality and culture. And as varying sets of ideas prevailed in different lands, the people grew apart rather than together. The advent of systems of writing (autochthonous in five regions) only hardened the lines of distinction, by providing authoritative texts which would last through the ages, until the world was left with the rather great religiocultural divergencies of modern times.

Nearly all the religious concepts of modern man received their first expression from three thousand to two thousand years ago. The earliest traditions at the base of today's structures emerged in India and Palestine. Those of India concerned themselves with spirits, those of Palestine more particularly with one spirit; though both systems put great stress on the theme of cooperation between man and his gods. With the passage of time, Hebrew prophets in Palestine expounded the one-god theme, extending it to include other nations, but restricting it by tying the god to Hebrew preoccupations with the fortunes of one people. A more complicated assemblage of tenets appeared in India, teaching means of deliverance from what many Indians had come to believe was a wheel of life into which persons' souls were continually reincarnated. In Iran, meanwhile, Zoroaster preached another doctrine of deliverance, effective at the end of one lifetime and one purging, whereby human beings might enter a happy and corporeal heaven. In China, philosophers like Confucius or the semi-legendary Lao Tzu drew their followers' attention to ethical or mystical ways of attaining contentment during one lifetime, without attempting to alter ancient conceptions of the gods.

Suddenly, about twenty-five hundred years ago, a new, well-defined religion appeared, the first of four which have spread internationally.

Siddhartha Gautama the Buddha, of northern India, preached a very strict and highly moral way of living by which men might attain the state of nirvana, or escape from the sadness of this world. Gautama himself, according to the most widely accepted line of traditional Buddhist doctrine, made the supreme sacrifice of renouncing nirvana to stay and help suffering mankind. As Gautama's faith captured the devotion of a very large number of Indians, it appealed to them in two separate ways. One, called Theravada (the School of the Elders) Buddhism, held to the older Indian concept that deliverance was possible only after a lifetime spent in activities associated with the priesthood. This school of thought commanded a minority following in India and eventually passed from the scene there, but became the faith of millions in Thailand, Burma, and other south Asian lands. The majority tradition, called Mahayana (Greater Vehicle) Buddhism, posed a departed Buddha himself as a savior god, seeking to draw all men (of whatsoever walk of life) to him, and portrayed other Buddhas and bodhisattvas (men striving to become Buddhas) who endeavored to deliver mankind from its disastrous ways. Mahayana Buddhism later virtually disappeared in India, like the Theravada branch, but became the religion of other millions in China, Japan, Korea, and Viet-Nam, evolving in a number of ways. The major sects of the Mahayana adherence are Vinaya, which stresses legalism; Zen, which emphasizes meditation; and the very popular "Pure Land," which attaches to a particular Buddha who maintains a more understanding attitude toward the imperfections of his people.

Jainism had its origins when Buddhism did, and subscribed to the same objectives. Extreme in austerity and asceticism, it nevertheless survives in its native land of India. The ideas of non-Buddhists and non-Jains of the same land coagulated about two thousand years ago into the system of belief called Hinduism. Here were incorporated old ways of living and of thinking about the gods; here also was stressed India's

17

caste system, built originally upon race lines
and opposed by Buddhists and Jains. Hindu types
of piety, however, enabled persons of all ranks
to work toward betterment in the next life or
no-life ahead. Hinduism teaches that release
from present states of being can come from good
deeds, love for the gods, and knowledge deriving
particularly from mystic exercise. Other religions, it says, are simply variants of emphasis on
these roads to better living. The Sikhism of
Punjab is a five-hundred-years-old adaptation of
Hinduism without caste, placing stress on the
principle of devotion to a single god.

Hinduism is one of the four religions which
spread far from the land where it was conceived.
For a thousand years (from fifteen hundred to
five hundred years ago) Indian gods were worshipped in southeastern Asia and the East Indies.
Even today, there are Hindu minorities in Bangladesh and a few faraway places to which Indians
have migrated. But for the most part, Hinduism
has retrenched into its native land, where it
remains the faith of the great majority. Other
large religions restricted chiefly to one country
are Confucianist and Taoist cults of China, which
have combined primitive beliefs with a few
thoughts from sophisticated followers of Confucius and Lao Tzu respectively; and the Shinto,
hero-venerating sects of Japan, now much influenced by Buddhism.

The easy tolerance of Hinduism and the multi-
farious adaptations of Buddhism contrast strikingly with an exclusiveness characteristic of two
remaining international religions, both of which
stem from origins already mentioned in Iran and
Palestine. The older of these is Christianity,
which nearly two thousand years ago sprang from a
background of Hebrew religious thought just as
the latter was absorbing the Iranian interest in
a very tangible heaven. Jesus the Christ, from
whom the new religion took its name, preached a
highly moral way of living as part of each individual's preparation for a kingdom of heaven

18

here on earth, though he laid down no strict set of rules as Gautama did. Jesus' supreme sacrifice, according to traditional Christian doctrine, was his crucifixion, substituting for ancient oblations to atone for the sins of the world. The bodily resurrection of Jesus taught by his disciples created evangelistic fervor, and the faith spread far and wide. Today approximately as many persons profess an attachment to Christianity as to the other three international religions combined.

Early Christians varied in their conception of Jesus' nature. After three hundred years, however, nearly all Christians agreed that Jesus, though fully human, was also fully divine, and that faith in his atonement constituted a requirement for anyone seeking to reach heaven. This accord among Christians remained remarkably unbroken for a millenium and a half. Power disputes nevertheless produced church schism. Most Easterners followed the lead of the archbishop of Byzantium, forming the so-called Orthodox branch of the religion, today broken into national churches in Russia, Romania, and elsewhere. The Coptic Christians of Africa (a residue resides in Ethiopia) became cut off from the rest, as did other small groups (often also separated in doctrine) from Syria even to China. The majority, on the other hand, remained loyal to the archbishop of Rome, and are today called Roman Catholics. They are now found in greatest numbers in Brazil, Italy, the United States, France, Mexico, Poland, Spain, West Germany, Argentina, the Philippines, and Colombia (in decreasing order). In Africa, their greatest concentration lies in Mozambique; on continental Asia, their largest community is in India.

Less than five hundred years ago large numbers of Lutherans in Germany, Anglicans in England, and Calvinists or "Reformed" in several countries separated from the Roman fold. In varying degrees -- the Lutherans were moderate, the Calvinists more extreme, the Anglicans ranged

19

through both attitudes -- their Protestant rebellion (some Anglicans did not accept this name)
shook off the accretions of the mother faith of
the millenium just past; it did not tamper with
the ancient formulas regarding the position of
Jesus. Lutherans, Anglicans, and Presbyterians
(Scotch Reformed) moved to the United States and
grew in numbers, but none so spectacularly as the
Baptists and Methodists who dissented from the
Church of England. A tremendous multiplicity of
Protestant sects related to these five are now
scattered throughout the world. So are other
Christian-based groups, such as the Mormons,
whose foundation is more recent and whose dogma
stands somewhat apart from the main stream of
Christian belief.

The followers of Hebrew lines of thought who
rejected Jesus, but who like the Christians accepted the idea of heaven as exported by Iran,
consolidated their own way of life and of thinking soon after Jesus' time into the group of
concepts known as Judaism. The Jewish people who
accepted these doctrines, though they moved to
nearly every country on earth, remained to an
amazing degree a group set apart from their surroundings. The greatest number of Jews in any
one country now live in the United States. Before 1940, the next highest concentrations existed in Poland and Russia; and thirty-five years
later (after the massacre of Jews in central Europe) Russia continued to serve as home for more
persons of this religious persuasion than the new
Jewish state of Israel.

The youngest of the great international religions, called Islam, like Christianity accepted
major elements of the ancient Hebrew and Iranian
heritages. Muhammad, the Arabian founder of this
creed, lived only thirteen hundred years ago; yet
his principles of faith have become the second
most widely accepted in the world. Muhammad
taught that the Christians had erred in identifying Jesus himself as a species of god, and that
his own Arabian people should cease their worship

20

of idols; beyond these matters, his stress lay on a very particular path for reaching a very sensuous heaven. Like that of Gautama, this way was paved with rules; like those of both Gautama and Jesus, it was highly moral. Muslims, the practitioners of Islam, are now found far spread in both directions from Muhammad's homeland. The Sunnite, or more traditional, branch of the faith has its greatest number of adherents in Indonesia, India, Pakistan, Bangladesh, the Soviet Union, China, Turkey, Egypt, Nigeria, and Afghanistan (in decreasing order); smaller states from Morocco to Iraq share the same devotion. In such distant and very Muslim countries as Indonesia, Bangladesh, and Pakistan, separate religious tendencies have begun to emerge; in the meantime, Saudi Arabia has returned, with its Wahhabi sect, to a very strict fundamentalist version. Iran is the chief home of the Shiites, who long ago separated from the Sunnites on a political basis, but who have become the freer of the two branches in doctrine. Other Shiites, scattered from Lebanon and Yemen to Bangladesh, are divided into several bands. From the Shiite background have arisen Ahmadiyah and Bahai, two sects which have put the narrowness of Christianity and Islam behind them and are striving toward an all-world religious union.

Religiocultural problems which face the world today are of two different kinds. One derives from the doctrinal intolerance of the world's two strongest faiths; neither in belief nor in practice have the vast majority of Christians and Muslims been willing to accept the validity of any religious approach save their own. The other, encompassing both religion and customs, stems from the great unwillingness of nearly all peoples to see virtue in other persons' ways of looking at things. The prejudice of a Muslim toward a Hindu has both doctrinal and cultural grounds; the prejudice of a Hindu toward a Muslim may lack the dogmatic basis, but with its roots in the mores of the people nevertheless emerge just as strong. For very large numbers of persons, especially those who do not read, these problems remain very difficult ones. For others, even for many who do little reading, they have begun very significantly to subside.

The lessening of religious tension began three hundred years ago in Europe, where at that time it was most needed. Until then, nearly all Christians had depised both Muslims and Jews; since the Protestant splitting, Christians had even scorned one another. Mellowing influences began in the Netherlands, spread to England, and by late eighteenth century developed in Germany and France. Among the intelligentsia, toleration led to an appreciation of other peoples' ways of living, and eventually to a restatement of Christian doctrine. Today millions of Christians no longer hold to the high singularity of their own religion. The requirement of a crucifix-centered atonement no longer appeals to them; in its place, for many, stands a this-worldly concern for the betterment of mankind, which seems close to the original teaching of Jesus. A few smaller sects such as the Unitarians have devoted themselves entirely to this change, but the great shift has transpired almost imperceptibly inside the larger groupings. Many Christians struggle against this tide. The older ideas reappear, winning favor for a time, in both conventional and new sophisticated clothing. But the new Christianity continues, and finds kinship with such basically Muslim sects as Bahai and Ahmadiyah, a Reform element among Jews, and recent modernist movements among Buddhists and Hindus.

Doctrinal barriers among the peoples of the world are falling. Old customs once associated with the doctrines remain, nevertheless, to the perplexity of almost all mankind.

II. THE SEPARATIONS OF MANKIND --

NATIONALISM

Race, language, and traditional religion
continue their divisive influences. They have
nevertheless assumed secondary roles as factors
in the disunity of mankind. As their hold on
men's self-images has slackened, a new force has
operated in their stead. The fresh element is
nationalism; in the twentieth century, whole
populations have done its bidding. The entire
world, most persons have come to believe, should
be partitioned into nation-states free to do
much as they please. Devotion to such states
has become the chief interest of many individuals, superseding earlier concern for reaching
nirvana or heaven.

Governments claiming the privilege of complete sovereignty are of course not new in the
world. The passionate following of such governments by the masses of their people, however, is
mainly a development of the last two hundred
years. Only a relative few of the present-day
nation-states themselves really antedate that
period, the epoch in which large numbers of people have learned to read. Through that time,
nation after nation has stressed the theme of
independence. Independence can indeed be an
important step in developing self-esteem. But
two global conflicts in the twentieth century
have convinced many persons that interdependence
must be the world's aim, with nation-states
having limits imposed upon their freedom.

This chapter seeks to present all the
"sovereign" states as they existed in the year
1940 of the Christian or common era. In that

year and the following one, a few nations moved far outward from their previous boundaries, re-defining their own sovereignty as they pleased. (Nation-states containing each more than 100,000,000 people are presented in two paragraphs, and those from 25,000,000 to 100,000,000 in one separate paragraph, as a rough population gauge.) Many regions of the world in 1940 lacked organization as nation-states; instead, they "belonged" to (that is, had come into the possession of or control by) a few countries that had extended their domains from the sixteenth to the nineteenth centuries. The dominated portion of the globe will also be reviewed here, to make the picture more complete. At the end of the chapter, man's efforts to establish some kind of regularized interdependence will be sketched to the same year of 1940.

For later convenience, the inhabited world is divided in this chapter into five portions, with somewhat arbitrary names. They are presented in order according to the number of people they contain. First, there is the Orient, the land of Asia and Oceania from Pakistan to Easter Island, excluding the Soviet Union. Second, there is Europe, the subcontinent often called a continent, including all of the Soviet Union. Third, there is the so-called Western Hemisphere, the land of the Americas. Fourth, there is Sub-Sahara Africa, including all the continent except the northern tier of lands bordering the Mediterranean Sea. Fifth and finally, there is the Middle East, the strip of African and Asian lands running from Morocco to Afghanistan not included in either Sub-Sahara Africa or the Orient.

The oldest and most populated country of the world today is China. Nearly one-fourth of the globe's inhabitants live there. The Mandarin-speaking portion of its population has a dynastic history extending back more than three thousand years. Empires waxed and waned during this long period; some of them attained considerable strength. In the last two millennia, they have usually included the people who speak the Wu, Cantonese, Amoy, Foochow, and Hakka tongues, as well as some of the Kadai languages and Miao. Able government in these empires was built upon Confucian precepts. Many of the people participated in the development of Confucian and Taoist cults, at the same time accepting Buddhist practices; other persons switched their loyalties to Islam. The Mongols became associated with Chinese empires seven hundred years ago, and the Tibetans have rounded out Chinese dimensions as they exist today for more than two centuries. With such a wide diversity of peoples incorporated under one government, China might have become a most powerful modern state. Within its boundaries, it contained both the natural and human resources to build a great land, a potential not shared by many nations. However, the ruling classes in China had not made a serious call for mass participation in government programs. China with all its advantages remained a nation-state only in name.

The Ching family, generally known as the Manchus, provided dynastic rule in China from 1644 to 1912. In the late nineteenth century, the Manchu potentates made great territorial and economic concessions to the British, French, Russians, Germans, and Japanese. Sun Yat Sen, who wanted to build a China designed more exclusively for the Chinese, inspired the revolution that overthrew the Manchus. Sun's hopes did not materialize before his death in 1925, however. Neither did his two best-known disciples, Chiang Kai Shek and Mao Ze Dong (Mao Tse Tung) realize them before 1940. Chiang established a Chinese republic ruled by his Kuo Min Tang party, with its capital at Nanking; Mao maintained a separate authority. While Chiang and Mao struggled against one another, Japan boldly invaded their land, in 1931 and again in 1937. In 1940, a Japanese puppet regime was

25

established in Nanking, while Chiang maintained his hold farther in the interior from the city of Chungking.

Japan in the 1930's had nearly one-sixth the population of China, but less than one-twenty-fifth China's area. The islands that constituted the Japanese homeland (and likewise that of a small pocket of Ainu) were a choice spot for the development of a vigorous national culture. The Japanese line of emperors can be traced back fifteen hundred years. The Buddhist faith arrived only a few centuries after the line of emperors began, and became much mixed with the Japanese religious practices known as Shinto. In the seventeenth and eighteenth centuries, military leaders called shoguns closed Japan off from nearly all outside influences. In 1867-8 the last shogun was deposed, while the emperor moved to the capital at Tokyo and a new group of military men began the task of building a modern Japan. A posture of aggressiveness toward others, spurred by the crowded conditions on the islands, formed part of the fresh concept of modernity. Wars with China and Russia brought Tai Wan (in 1895) and Korea (in 1910) as prizes. After emperor Hirohito began his reign in 1926, the Japanese seized Manchuria in 1931, making of it the puppet state of Manchu Kuo, and occupied further Chinese territory as mentioned above. Nationalism of an extreme sort developed to the point that expansion of living space had become a sacred cause. Japan thus achieved distinction as one of the more important nation-states of the twentieth century.

In all the Orient, only four nations in 1940 besides China and Japan remained free from the authority of another country. Thailand (named Siam until 1939), in very Buddhist southeastern Asia, had held its position as a kingdom for six hundred years, though much buffeted by neighbors and by Europeans on all sides. Nepal, nestled in the mountains between British India and China, was a kingdom containing a great variety

26

of people of mixed Hindu and Buddhist faith, pulled together under one monarchy in the eighteenth century. Australia and New Zealand were nineteenth-century-founded Britannias in Oceania, English-speaking and Protestant, though each held a native minority -- Australia its aborigines, New Zealand the Polynesian Maoris. These two former colonies became dominions under the British crown in 1901 and 1907 respectively, with a completely autonomous position defined in 1931.

British India, likewise tied to the crown worn in London, had not achieved autonomy by 1940, though passion for the building of one or two nation-states had built to great strength in the Indian area. Plans made in 1935 for a federation of British India and British-protected Indian states (Hyderabad, Mysore, Travancore, Jammu-Kashmir, Gwalior, Jaipur, Baroda, Jodhpur, and over five hundred others) were put aside in 1939 when Great Britain became involved in war.

The British in 1940 played an important role in many other parts of the Orient as well. Burma pertained to Britain, though it had been separated from India in 1937. Ceylon, the Straits Settlements, Hong Kong, Fiji, the Gilbert and Ellice Islands, and Pitcairn Island constituted British colonies. The Federated Malay States, five unfederated Malay states, and three states in Borneo were considered protectorates of Great Britain, as also the British Solomon Islands, the Maldive Islands, and Tonga. Bhutan and Sikkim lay under partial British guidance, and the New Hebrides under a British-French condominium.

Five outside powers besides the United Kingdom dominated parts of the Orient in 1940. The Netherlands administered the East Indies, including the nominal principalities of Surakarta and Jogjakarta on the island of Java. France held Indochina (comprising the colonies of Cochin China and Laos and the protectorates of

Tonkin, Annam, and Cambodia), five small colonies in India, and the colonies of French Oceania and New Caledonia, as well as sharing the Anglo-French condominium in the New Hebrides. The United States ruled the Philippines, Hawaii, Guam, American Samoa, and a few more islands. Portugal counted three colonies -- three tiny districts in India, including Goa; a part of the island of Timor; and the city of Macao. The Soviet Union held Tannu Tuva under its tutelage. Japan had annexed Korea and Tai Wan, and ruled Manchu Kuo as a puppet state, as has been explained. Papua constituted an external territory of Australia. Under League of Nations mandates, North-East New Guinea and nearby islands were assigned to Australia, Nauru Island likewise, Western Samoa to New Zealand, and the Mariana, Caroline, and Marshall Islands to Japan.

The Union of Soviet Socialist Republics ranked in 1940 as the second most populated country of the world. It covered all of northern Asia as well as a great part of the subcontinent of Europe, the very heartland of nationalism. The Soviet Union included the homeland of the Russian people along with the area dominated by them during the previous five hundred years. Russia, in Europe, could boast no antiquity to compare with that of China. When its people became Orthodox Christian believers, there existed a Russian language but no Russian state. The latter emerged when Mongol rulers were expelled in the fifteenth century. Continuing warfare against the Mongols brought a significant Tatar population under Russian rule. Expansion toward the west then brought in the Ukraine, Latvia, and Estonia, and later Belorussia and Lithuania, all in the seventeenth and eighteenth centuries. Persons speaking a variety of tongues in the Caucasus area -- South and North Caucasian, Armenian, Azerbaijani, and Kurdish -- became incorporated in the nineteenth century, along with the Poles and the Finns farther north and the Uzbeks in Asia. The Russians

28

themselves had in the meantime migrated into the vast, nearly empty stretches of Siberia. Russia had become a huge empire, with more than double the area of any other continuous territorial unit on earth. As in China, one majority language stood in the company of a variety of lesser tongues. Religious diversity existed also, with significant Muslim and Jewish populations living beside the Russian Orthodox. Like China again, the Soviet Union of truly formidable size held many advantages for life in the modern world, but until 1917 lacked the one important item of popular participation in its governmental programs.

The Romanovs (1613-1917), last of the Russian tsars, had not only maintained every prerogative for themselves but endeavored conspicuously to prevent the growth and spread of new ideas. One revolution in 1917 deposed them, and another in the same year brought in Vladimir Ilich Ulyanov, known as Lenin, as Russia's new person-in-authority. Lenin and his Communist party introduced a flood of ideas, including that of the founding of the Union of Soviet Socialist Republics, organized in 1922 with its capital in Moscow. At its outset, the Soviet Union represented the people and area of the old Russian Empire (less Poland, Finland, Lithuania, Latvia, Estonia, and parts of Belorussia and the Ukraine, lost in 1917-21). It gave its non-Russian people new dignity, however, and made provision for other groups which might choose to join the Union later. This was internationalism of an unprecedented sort; but when Lenin died in 1924, his successor Joseph Stalin (though himself a Georgian) thought in terms of an aggrandized Russia rather than a wider internationalism. While the people of many countries feared or disliked the Stalin regime, none spoke of it in more vituperative language than Adolf Hitler, the master of Germany. In 1939, thus, a shock wave swept the world when Hitler and Stalin agreed to lay their differences aside and to divide Poland between them. They accomplished the latter goal with no difficulty, after which the Soviet Union forcefully reincorporated Lithuania, Latvia, and Estonia, and acquired some territory from Finland. In the meantime, the Hitler-Stalin squeeze-play on Poland had started a major European war.

Germany became a nation-state only in 1871. The German people, roughly equal numerically to the Japanese, had long inhabited a plethora of small states in the middle of Europe. Some were Protestant, some Catholic, though their various customs and linguistic habits held much in common. The family named Hohenzollern busied itself for more than two centuries building a unified German state from its capital in Berlin, and eventually became the new country's ruling line of kaisers (1871-1918). The Germans after their defeat in World War I (1914-18) attempted to construct a republic looking toward accommodation with their neighbors. Adolf Hitler, who in 1933 destroyed this republic, liked to be called der führer (the leader); his support came from the National Socialist (Nationalsozialistische, or Nazi) party, for whom a very exaggerated form of nationalism served as the principal creed (despite the name, it had no connection with socialism). The Germans, like the Japanese, began to devote themselves to the cause of living-space expansion. Five years after gaining power, Hitler incorporated Austria and a part of Czechoslovakia into the German domain. The following year (1939) he carved up the remainder of Czechoslovakia to suit his whim, snatched the city of Memel from Lithuania, and (after the agreement with Stalin) took the free city of Danzig and the western two-thirds of Poland. With World War II then on his hands, Hitler moved boldly to take Denmark, Norway, the Netherlands, Luxembourg, Belgium, and France into German control by the end of 1940.

While Nazi troops emerged almost everywhere victorious, the United Kingdom of Great Britain and Northern Ireland stood in opposition, virtually alone. The island kingdom of Great Britain had been formed in 1707 through the union of England and Scotland. The people of both these states spoke English, save for small Celtic minorities, and had followed crowned monarchs for some nine hundred years. The island of Ireland was added to the association in 1801, bringing about the organization of the United Kingdom (with a capital in London), though only Northern Ireland remained tied after 1922. The largely Anglican or Presbyterian people of the United Kingdom spread far and wide, until under the house of Hanover (1714-1901) the British empire became the largest on the globe. The house of Windsor which followed (and which brought George VI to the throne in 1936) found it very difficult to maintain the empire's position. In fact, the British nation, with only two-thirds the population of Germany, began to feel concern for its own security in an increasingly hostile surrounding. The Conservative party leading the United Kingdom after 1935, however, seemed more worried about Stalin than about Hitler as a threat to British freedom and power. The nature of the Nazi threat became fully acknowledged only when Winston Churchill, a dissident Conservative, became the prime minister in May 1940.

Italy, in southern Europe, resembled Germany in its status as a very young nation-state, though the Italian people (largely Catholic) had inhabited the separate provinces of their peninsula for a long time. The house of Savoy, dominant in one corner of the land for eight centuries, accepted the throne of a united Italy in 1861, placing the capital in Rome nine years later. Victor Emmanuel III of this house began his rule in 1900. Control of Italy after 1922, however, lay in the hands of prime minister Benito Mussolini (il duce, also the leader), who brooked no dissidence as he and his Fascist party took the future into their hands. Italians felt national pride as they never had before when Mussolini in an open war of conquest an-

31

nexed African Ethiopia to its small empire in 1936, and when Italian armies seized nearby Albania in 1939. Though these conquests were not so extensive as those of Adolf Hitler, Mussolini and Hitler followed the same path, and caused no surprise when in 1940 they became war partners.

France, conquered but not completely obliterated in the occurrences of 1940, had a much longer history as a political entity than either Italy or Germany. Nominally, a government of largely Catholic France has operated from its seat in Paris for nearly one thousand years. Effectively, the kings of France controlled most of the present national territory (with its Provençal and Celtic minorities) for more than three centuries before one of them was deposed in 1792. Since that time, France has experimented with a very large number of governments, moving on restlessly from one to the other. A third French republic, organized during the early 1870's (the first had appeared in 1792-9, the second 1848-52), like the British monarchy ruled a very large round-the-world empire. When France itself was taken by Nazi armies in May-June 1940, some French persons including Charles de Gaulle fled the homeland to use parts of this empire for striking back against the enemy. With the third French republic ended, about four-fifths of the French people came under direct German control. The other fifth became subject to a German-sponsored regime in Vichy, southern France, headed by elderly Henri-Philippe Pétain.

Poland, caught in the German-Russian vise in 1939, had a national history extending back nearly as far as that of France, with an even more erratic quality. The old Catholic kingdom of Poland completely disappeared in a series of advances by three neighbors in the period 1772-95. An attempt to revive the state under the rule of Russian tsars (1815-30) resulted only in the incorporation of Poland into the

Russian domain. In 1918, with Russia having fared poorly in the First World War, Poland emerged again as a nation-state, its government a republic with the capital in Warsaw, its population including a minority of Yiddish-speaking Jews. An early war with Russia (1920-1) brought parts of Belorussia and the Ukraine into Polish territory. Under strong-men Jozef Pilsudski (1926-35) and Edward Smigly-Rydz, Poland continued the power game until crushed by its two larger neighbors in 1939. The Soviet Union in that year only regained what it had lost two decades earlier. A Polish refugee government in Paris, after all the Polish territory was gone, recognized Wladyslaw Sikorski as its premier and head.

Spain, seventh of the states of Europe in population in 1940, had earlier than its neighbors Great Britain and France experienced the lesson that national greatness can lead to exhaustion. Spain catapulted into fame when the marriage of the four-centuries-old crowns of Castile and Aragon coincided with the Spanish discovery of the New World. Spain built an empire in the Americas and the Philippines, only to see it lost by the Bourbon kings who ruled from Madrid during most of the period 1700-1931. Spain experienced much internal division also, not only through its proclivity toward provincial narrowness in outlook (emphasized especially by Catalan and Basque minorities) but also through its very Catholic stance which produced strong anti-Catholic, free-thinking sentiment. A second republic set up in 1931 (the first lasted only from 1873 to 1874) found itself in turmoil from the beginning. General Francisco Franco became the leader of forces which (with Fascist and Nazi help) fought to destroy the republic in the Spanish Civil War of 1936-9. Emerging victorious, Franco became chief of the state, commander of the army, and prime minister, with the three offices combined. His party, the Falange, now ran Spain along the same lines as those devised by

Mussolini for Italy, except that blood-stained Spain had no desire to enter World War II in 1939 or 1940. Later, one Spanish division assisted Germany; nothing more was needed to place the Franco regime in an anomalous position when the war terminated.

The Soviet Union, Germany, the United Kingdom, Italy, France, Poland, and Spain -- each, by virtue of size, enjoyed more justification than other European states for its being. In an older, less industrious and less populated world, their natural resources made them at least viable lands, though their viability became greatly upset whenever they jostled for advantage. Crowded Europe, however, contained 28 sovereign states, rather than 7, in the middle 1930's -- or, counting the very smallest ones, a total of 35. The smaller states, three or four times the number of those already named, could only with great difficulty stand alone, even in regard to their assets. In addition, they were unfortunately not exempt from the jostling, whenever it began. Yet to stand alone, in the nineteenth and early twentieth centuries, seemed often their greatest yearning.

Four of the smaller European lands appeared before modern times -- Denmark (of greater size in its beginnings than later) in the eleventh century; Portugal and German-speaking Austria in the twelfth; and Switzerland, as a confederation of German- and French-speaking districts, in the fourteenth. Denmark, which became Protestant, maintained loyalty to a king; the Swiss confederation, mixed Protestant and Catholic, developed into a republic in 1848; Catholic Portugal and Austria switched to republicanism later, Portugal in 1910, Austria in 1918. Three other lands, all Protestant, sprang from the Danish sovereignty -- Sweden in 1523, Norway in 1814, and Iceland in 1918. Sweden throughout its independent history had its separate king; Norway accepted Sweden's monarch until 1905, when it chose its own; Iceland (whose population in 1940

34

stood at about 120,000) maintained its allegiance to the Danish crown even after independence. Three states which seceded from a small miscellany of others were the mainly Protestant Netherlands, speaking Dutch; the chiefly Catholic Belgium, using the Flemish and French languages; and Catholic Ireland, familiar with English and its own Celtic tongue. The Netherlands (eventually a monarchy) broke from Spain in 1581; Belgium (since its beginnings a monarchy) from the Netherlands in 1831; and Ireland (at first a self-governing dominion, after 15 years a republic) from the United Kingdom in 1922.

Eleven more small national entities appeared in Europe in the nineteenth and twentieth centuries besides the four just mentioned. Four of them, all with kings, emerged from a decaying Ottoman Empire. These were Greece, Romania, and Bulgaria in 1832, 1861, and 1878 respectively, each with its own brand of Eastern Orthodoxy, and Albania in 1912, with its people chiefly Muslim. Four republics -- Protestant Finland, Catholic Lithuania, mainly Protestant Latvia, and Protestant Estonia -- freed themselves from a debilitated Russia in 1917-18. And in 1918 also, three nations cast aside former ties with Austria. They were Orthodox and Catholic Yugoslavia, speaking the Serbo-Croatian tongue, initially a monarchy; Catholic Czechoslovakia, a republic; and mainly Catholic Hungary, a kingdom without a king.

Jostling from 1938 through 1940 brought Austria, Czechoslovakia, Denmark, Norway, the Netherlands, and Belgium of these smaller 21 European states into the German fold. It also drove Lithuania, Latvia, and Estonia back into the hands of the Russians through their incorporation in the Soviet Union, and placed Albania under the rule of the Italians. Two of continental Europe's seven very smallest states (both of them German-speaking) also fell at that time to the Germans -- Danzig (population 400,000), a free city since 1920, and Luxembourg (300,000), a separate principality since 1839. The five others were the principalities of Liechtenstein (11,000) and Monaco (20,000), associated respectively with Switzerland and France; Vatican City (1,000), an enclave in the city of Rome ruled after 1929 by the Roman Catholic pope; and the miniscule republics of San Marino (15,000) and Andorra (5,000). The last-named spoke Catalan, and lay between Spain and France. San Marino, completely surrounded by Italy, boasted an independent history of 1,500 years, the longest of any "nation" in Europe. Such miniature states -- and for that matter, nearly all the other countries of the European subcontinent as well -- could survive in the twentieth century only upon the sufferance of others. Yet the existence of so many independent regimes, like the reiterations of the destructive collisions between them, stood as a distinctive mark of European nationalism in its full flower. In this part of the world, only the British colonies of Malta and Gibraltar remained outside the compulsive struggle to stand alone.

Only one other global region rivaled Europe in 1940 in the number of self-governing units it contained. This was the New World, the land of the Americas, of which the United States of America included the largest number of people, holding third place in population among the countries of the world. The United States stood as the oldest of the American nations also, having declared freedom from the British in 1776 and organized a republic in 1789, with its capital soon thereafter set in Washington. Most of the people of the United States had come from Europe; eventually they dispossessed from nearly all their lands the scattered tribes of American Indians associated linguistically with the Algonkians and the Sioux. A large percentage of the early newcomers spoke English, and those who came later spoke or learned to speak the same language as they put their various European nationalities aside. African people brought in as slaves perforce adopted English also. The Protestant faith became very strong among families deriving from both Europe and Africa, though the population also contained many Catholics and a smaller number of Jews.

For a century after independence, American people of this nationality (citizens of the United States of America) busied themselves in the occupation of great stretches of continental North American territory, from the Atlantic Ocean to the Pacific and embracing noncontiguous Alaska. Indian peoples related linguistically to the Athapascans of Canada and the Aztec of Mexico, like those associated with the Algonkians and Sioux, were either pushed out of the way or surrounded. In their place, the new nation built rapidly. In 1898, furthermore, it reached out to take Spanish-speaking Puerto Rico, Hawaii with a Polynesian tongue, and the faraway Philippines; five years later, it added (by lease) the Panama Canal Zone. The United States had suddenly grown not only to the status of a large nation but to the role of a world power, as its own sense of nationalism brought involvement in international quarrels. When large-scale wars began in Asia and Europe in the late 1930's, president Franklin Delano Roosevelt (who took office in 1933) pretended neutrality at first. But when the United Kingdom found itself without effective allies against Germany in 1940, Roosevelt made clear his determination that the British would not stand alone to the end.

Nearly half the inhabitants of South America in 1940 lived in the country named Brazil. (At that time, it was called the United States of Brazil, but for convenience in this study the designation United States will be saved for its North American counterpart whose name America, in a world history, proves awkward.) Brazil held less than one-third as many people as the United States, though the two countries covered roughly equal expanses of territory. The

37

Europeans who settled in Brazil spoke or soon learned the Portuguese language; Portugal lost their allegiance at the time of independence in 1822. Many Africans, sold into slavery in Brazil, learned Portuguese also. Indians related linguistically to the Caribs and the Tupí found themselves often pushed aside or absorbed, though a fair number of the latter group survived. More persons professed Roman Catholicism here than in any other country in the world. Men of the house of Braganza ruled independent Brazil at first as an empire. A republic inaugurated in 1889 set its capital at Rio de Janeiro. Getúlio Vargas, who admired the trappings of the Italian Fascist regime, acted as president of Brazil after 1930. Vargas became complete master of Brazil with his "new state" decreed in 1937. But through the year 1940 this strong man had not made up his mind to ally militarily with either the duce or the führer.

Twenty more nation-states complete the roster of the Americas in 1940. Of these, English-speaking, Protestant Canada (with a whole province of French-speaking Catholics and small minorities of Algonkian-related and Athapascan Indians and Eskimo) became a British dominion in 1867, conceded complete autonomy in 1931. Catholic Haiti, with its own language and a Negro-mulatto population, became the earliest to gain independence, in 1804 from France; eventually, it became a republic. The remaining 18 (all republics) spoke Spanish, at least officially, having once belonged to Spain, and continued largely Catholic in their traditions. Their people represented European, American Indian, or African physical heritages, or some mixture of the three, the ratio depending on the region and its history. Seven of them achieved national status in the wars of liberation from Spain, 1810-25. Of these, Mexico was largely a mestizo country, with Maya, Tarascan, Aztec-related, Sioux-related, and Otomí-related minorities. Argentina became (by immigration) almost entirely European. Colombia developed a chiefly mestizo population in the highlands, and mulatto in the lowlands, with only traces of the Chibcha languages remaining. Peru had more persons speaking Quechua than Spanish, and others using Aymara. Chile remained largely mestizo. Bolivia spoke both Quechua and Aymara very widely. Paraguay, though mostly mestizo, clung to Guaraní.

The states of Central America, free from Spain in 1821, became separated in 1838-9. The Maya persisted as the chief element in Guatemala, while Costa Rica emerged very European; El Salvador, Honduras, and Nicaragua developed a three-way mix of American Indian, African, and European peoples in every ratio. Five of the remaining Spanish-speaking countries were carved out from neighbors already mentioned. Predominantly European Uruguay began its existence in 1828 from land both Brazil and Argentina had claimed. Mestizo and mulatto Venezuela broke in 1830 from Colombia. Ecuador, where Quechua is widely spoken, did likewise. The Dominican Republic, largely mulatto, won its freedom from Haiti in 1844. Mestizo and mulatto Panama seceded from Colombia in 1903, just prior to leasing its Canal Zone to the United States. Cuba, European and mulatto, remained tied to Spain until its independence in 1898.

The Latin American states (those once ruled by Spain, Portugal, and France) had like those of Europe experienced much trouble trying to stand alone, even though the largest of them (Brazil, Mexico, and Argentina) barely held together in their early years. Still, their position of theoretical freedom was much envied by other American districts remaining in European hands. The British alone administered fourteen colonies in the Western Hemisphere: Jamaica, Trinidad-Tobago, British Guiana, Newfoundland, Barbados, the Leeward Islands, and four separate administrations in the Windward Islands, besides the Bahamas, British Honduras,

Bermuda, and the Falkland Islands. Guadeloupe, Martinique, French Guiana, and St. Pierre-Miquelon constituted colonies of France. The Dutch held Surinam and the colony of Curaçao (consisting of five and one-half islands); the United States controlled Puerto Rico and some of the Virgin Islands; Denmark possessed the colony of Greenland. With their very small populations, it is not easy to think of many of these as separate nation-states; yet in the years after 1940 several of them did become independent.

Africa would face the same problem on a much larger scale, with very many groups of people wanting to determine their own affairs. But in 1940 most of the nations of this continent had not yet entered the struggle for survival in the modern world. In Sub-Sahara Africa, there were only three nation-states in 1935. The Amharic-speaking kingdom of Ethiopia, whose Coptic Christian people had been cut off from the rest of Christendom by the Muslim conquest of Egypt far back in the seventh century, expanded in the 1850's to include persons of Galla speech and some fifty other languages of the Cushitic stock, but was itself conquered by Italian forces in 1936. (There are more than a dozen other Ethiopian languages, of either the Sudanic family or the Semitic stock.) The Union of South Africa became a British dominion in 1910, ruled by its people of European descent, guaranteed its autonomy in 1931. Some of the Europeans spoke English, while others of Dutch ancestry spoke Afrikaans. The great majority of South African people spoke Bantu languages, altogether eight of them, including especially the Xhosa and Zulu dialects; the Bushmen who also lived here spoke Khoisan tongues. Liberia organized as a republic on Africa's west coast in 1847, to harbor English-speaking Christian Africans returning from slavery in the United States of America. Its territory also included ten languages of the Mande and Kwa branches of the Niger-Congo family. Aside from Ethiopia, South

40

Africa, and Liberia, Sub-Sahara Africa lay under the control of Europeans -- the British, the French, the Belgians, the Portuguese, the Italians, and the Spaniards.

The United Kingdom ruled more Africans than all the other outsiders combined. The more important British colonies were Nigeria, the Gold Coast-Ashanti, Kenya, Southern Rhodesia, and Sierra Leone; others were Mauritius, Basutoland, Gambia, the Seychelles, and St. Helena. British protectorates other than some associated with the colonies included Uganda, Nyasaland, Northern Rhodesia, British Somaliland, Bechuanaland, Zanzibar, and Swaziland. As mandates from the League of Nations, Great Britain ruled Tanganyika and parts of the Cameroons and Togoland, while South Africa similarly governed South West Africa. The Sudan was held jointly by the United Kingdom and Egypt.

France administered the second greatest empire in Sub-Sahara Africa. The territory called French West Africa alone included seven colonies. Madagascar and the Comoro Islands constituted two more. French Equatorial Africa contained four colonies. There were also Réunion and French Somaliland, as well as a French share of the League of Nations mandates for the Cameroons and Togoland. Belgium ruled the Belgian Congo, much larger in population than any one French colony, and the mandate of Ruanda-Urundi. The Portuguese flag flew over five colonies, sizeable Mozambique and Angola and much smaller Portuguese Guinea, the Cape Verde Islands, and São Tomé-Príncipe. Italian East Africa came into being in 1936 to include Ethiopia with the former colonies of Italian Somaliland and Eritrea. Spanish Guinea, Spanish Sahara, and Ifní, three colonies of Spain, round out the 1940 tally of Sub-Saharan possessions in European hands. Sub-Saharan struggles for freedom from colonial rule and for some kind of sovereign standing constitute an important part of world history of the quarter-century following.

41

The Middle East in 1940 remained to a large extent an area emerging from the shadow of the old Ottoman Empire. As this empire declined for about three centuries prior to its demise in 1923, four European powers acted as midwives in the delivery of a numerous progeny from the weakening mother land. Not included in the Ottoman territory, however, were the eastern monarchies of Iran and Afghanistan. Iran, with a Persian majority and Azerbaijani and Kurdish minorities, stood as an ancient country revived in the sixteenth century; until 1935, it bore the name of Persia. Afghanistan, with a Pashto majority and Tajik minority, had a history of its own of only two hundred years. Both of these countries formed part of the religious world of Islam, as did the five other independent states of the Middle East in 1940.

Turkey, the very heart of the Ottoman Empire, made its transition to republican status in 1923, its boundaries drawn to include a Kurdish minority. Egypt secured autonomy from the Ottoman Turks in 1839, only to submit to British control (1882-1922) before solid foundation as a kingdom. Saudi Arabia was a monarchy put together in 1926 from pieces of the old Ottoman domain. Iraq constituted another such piece, a British mandate for twelve years, but after 1932 a full-fledged kingdom. The monarchy in Yemen, granted autonomy in the year 1913, established independence during World War I. All these previously Ottoman lands, with the exception of Turkey itself, spoke one style or another of Arabic; extreme southern Egypt also contained two languages of the Sudanic family.

Other Middle Eastern territories had not completed their transitions to freedom by the end of 1940. Morocco (though too far west as Iran and Afghanistan were too far east to have been included in the Ottoman Empire) constituted in large part a protectorate of France, the remainder a protectorate of Spain. Algeria tech-

42

nically formed a part of France itself, under special laws placing most Algerian people at a distinct disadvantage. Syria and Lebanon, mandates in French hands, in 1940 came into the control of the puppet French government at Vichy. Tunisia counted as one more French protectorate. In addition, Palestine and Transjordan were British mandates, Libya technically a part of Italy (but an Italian colony until 1939), and Cyprus a British colony. On the margins of the Arabian peninsula, Aden formed a combined British colony and protectorate, while Muscat-Oman, Kuwait, Bahrain, Qatar, and seven Arabian sheikhdoms collectively known as Trucial Oman accepted leadership from the United Kingdom as their guardian.

In all the world at the end of the year 1935, there existed 73 nation-states, for better or for worse theoretically free to do as they pleased -- 35 of them in Europe, 22 in the Americas, 7 in the Middle East, 6 in the Orient, and 3 in Sub-Sahara Africa. Thirty-five years later, the number had grown to 142 -- with 38 in Sub-Sahara Africa, 33 in Europe, 27 in the Orient, 26 in the Americas, and 18 in the Middle East. For one small globe -- made small by modern technological advances -- this total amounted to more than a sufficiency. Only a few of these states stood able by themselves to provide their people a minimum of economic and cultural well-being for life in the modern world. And yet, nation-enthusiasm, taught to virtually all who could read, came coupled more often than not in this brave, new world with the development of antipathy toward people of other lands. Resentments and prejudices have sprung from subtle distortions of history, and outright hostility from the beat of propaganda drums, resulting in a world communciations confusion that reaches far beyond the age-old difficulties generated by the great profusion of speech habits.

Most nation-states in the world, like most

languages, are simply too small to survive. Politically they are weak; economically and culturally they are impossible -- that is, they are utterly unable to stand apart on their own achievements. For this reason, mergers into larger entities have become favored topics for international bargaining. In the future, many such mergers will be arranged, though they present their own problems. The greatest dilemma of all is that in the very crowded globe of the twentieth century even the more nearly self-sufficient countries get in one another's way without trying. The greatest misdirection of recent times has been the continued kindling of nation-enthusiasm in the very face of these new realities.

Cold or hot battle lines built on national prejudices and misunderstandings have plagued the world through a succession of recent decades. It is but natural that the thinking of many persons would turn to possible antidotes for such malaise. International cooperation seems the obvious answer; but the questions remain -- on what basis and through what channels? Both Germany and Japan spoke in 1940 of large-scale international coordinations, each for its own part of the globe. Their plans were rejected by others because they clearly presupposed the "I-will-lead-and-you-shall-follow" basis, like those of earlier imperialistic design. The Union of Soviet Socialist Republics likewise had been joined by no other nation since its inception as an international body, in this case because other lands did not wish to merge into a political entity which relied upon narrow party channels in the making of major decisions. International cooperation of an effective sort would have to be on a more universal basis and through more democratic means.

An almost imperceptible foundation for democratic and universal internationalism arose in

1865, when specialists faced with a practical problem (that of round-the-world communication) founded the government-sponsored International Telegraph Union. A General Postal Union, organized ten years later for the same reason, soon became the Universal Postal Union, functioning nearly everywhere in the world. The International Meteorological Organization formed in 1878 became the third arrangement of the kind, though men who held government posts rather than governments themselves constituted the membership. The countries of the Americas, less Canada, formed a loose association in 1889 for greater economic and cultural cooperation in the hemisphere, a grouping later called the Pan American Union. A big step further was taken with the creation in 1899 of a Permanent Court of Arbitration, to settle quarrels between consenting nations of the entire world. An International Institute of Agriculture and an International Office of Public Health joined the list in 1908. But until the catastrophe of World War I, most persons remained unconvinced of the real importance of such programs.

The League of Nations was brought into being early in 1920 by leaders who hoped that worldwide conversations about threats to peace could prevent new outbursts of warfare. The seat of the League's activities lay in Geneva, Switzerland. At some time in its 20 years of active life, nearly every self-governing nation in the world participated as a member. Small Iceland and Europe's tiniest five remained exceptions, as did Nepal, Saudi Arabia, and Yemen, all at that time out of close touch with the modern world; and the United States of America, not out of touch but out of step, its population still subscribing to the doctrine that a nation which so desires can live serenely even while its neighbors are brawling. The Soviet Union did not receive permission to enter the League of Nations until 1934, however, and became expelled five years later when it attacked Finland, so that during three-fourths of the League's brief history it did not include the second and third largest countries in the world. Brazil gave notice of its withdrawal from membership in 1926. Japan and Germany did the same in 1933, Italy in 1937, and Spain in 1939. Clearly, the League came far from maintaining universal support. Furthermore, its constitutional stipulation that no substantive action might be taken if even one member expressed dissent made it unlikely that this organization would ever make major decisions in times of real crisis.

The chief value of the League of Nations thus remained the quiet labor of cooperation in less controversial spheres. Through such activity, the League laid groundwork for solving a variety of long-range problems and encouraged the habit of thinking in international terms. Its consideration each year of reports by mandate powers on their activities in mandated territories constituted an undertaking very new to the world. The League of Nations sponsored the world's first regularly-appointed judicial body, the Permanent Court of International Justice, founded in 1922 to examine points of international law whenever there appeared a call for its services. The International Labor Organization, founded in 1919, formed a working arrangement with the League. The International Organization for Intellectual Cooperation, which began to function in 1926, provided a new avenue for purposeful endeavor under general League of Nations auspices. The International Telegraph Union gave way in 1934 to a much broadened International Telecommunication Union, a forecast of the tremendous new wave of worldwide cooperation to come.

By 1934, however, the League of Nations was falling apart, and World War II was beginning to take form. Seven years later, when full war in Europe and Asia had become a hard fact, there appeared the first glimmerings of new structures for cooperation between peoples. New plans for collaboration were to prove both more plentiful and more individually adequate than ever before. But as people shuddered in the wake of World War II over the possibility of an approaching World War III, the question arose -- were they plentiful and adequate enough?

III. UNIFYING INFLUENCES --

DEMOCRACY AND SOCIALISM

Nationalism strode aggressively into the twentieth century, unmindfully splitting and re-splitting a world. Fortunately, however, for the planet thus divided, it is not the only modern enthusiasm. Two other ideas, those of democracy and socialism, have become popular, like nationalism, during the last two hundred years. They contrast with nation-love in that they tend to remind men not of their differences but of what they share in common.

Democracy is rule by the people. It contrasts with rule by one person or a few persons. Some Greeks took an interest in democracy two and a half millenia before 1945. The full-blown development of the idea, however, came with the wider ability of persons to read. In the year 1800 only a few nations even professed a faith in democratic procedures; but well before the year 2000, nearly every nation on earth had come either to practice the democratic doctrine (in varying degrees) or to pretend to practice it. Thus a grand tribute has been paid to a proposition much admired by modern man.

In nations, democracy is carried out by representative government of some kind. In every democratic regime, there is a legislature (assembly, congress, diet, parliament) elected by some or all of the adult people. Traditionally, as these bodies have evolved, a "lower" house or chamber (generally the larger of two) is the more immediately responsive to the wishes of the voters at large. In some countries, a chief executive or president is also selected by the people for a stipulated term. In others (where a president or monarch plays a very limited role) the executive power is wielded by a prime minister and cabinet responsible to the parliament or to its lower chamber. When through either revolution or evolution a country non-farcically adopts one of these plans, that nation may be said to have stepped over the threshold of democracy.

The world's most refined democracies have moved a very long way since stepping over that threshold. The experiences of no two of them have been identical. Yet there are four characteristics which have attracted wide attention as features of a democratically governed regime. First is the concept of majority rule, whereby half or more of the adults of a nation are permitted to decide the great issues that face them. There is no majority rule, of course, when the people are offered no alternative to an officially-developed line. Neither is there likely to be majority rule when on the basis of race, religion, sex, economic position, or illiteracy large blocs of people are prevented from voting. Majority rule, once adopted, offers no guarantee of a solution to a nation's problems, since majorities often think unwisely or wrong. But by mid-twentieth century, regardless of its inadequacies, most proponents of democracy tended to take this first principle for granted as a part of the democratic way of life.

The secret ballot is a technical feature of democracy which has become widely adopted. Voting must be done in secret, runs the argument for it, if persons are to be assured the privilege of speaking their own minds. Those who must not obtain sure knowledge of an individual's vote are his neighbor, his husband or wife, his political leader, most of all his employer -- or anyone in a position to withhold or hand out favors as a punishment or a prize. When voting is not done secretly, a minority of persons can much more easily dominate a majority. Indeed, countries which pretend rather than practice democracy are generally very familiar with voting in the open as a not-very-subtle means of control.

Freedom of information is a much-acknowledged characteristic of democracy which is nonetheless very frequently abridged. Abuses against this principle constitute a more devious, and often unnoticed, form of minority control. The individual in a working democracy needs as full access as possible to light on the controversies of his time. His own government is very likely, either daily or occasionally, to attempt to keep some of that light from him. Newspapers, magazines, radio outlets, and television stations very often serve as agencies of such obscurantism, with or without the direction of their governments. Even the bare existence of an intellectual climate hostile to new ideas, as they do become available, may prevent people from getting the stimulant necessary for thinking through their problems. Freedom of information is an ideal, as yet unrealized in most lands, but one which has gained significantly in recent decades.

In many democracies of the twentieth century, a fourth dimension has been added to the ideas of majority rule, the secret ballot, and freedom of information. The new dimension is proportional representation, a more accurate electoral design than the traditional ones, insuring that minority voices are not muffled when decisions are to be made. Minorities are sometimes right, runs the argument for proportional representation, and in any event the majority must not be permitted to ignore them. Their presence in the legislature in close ratio to their strength in the population at large is the lubrication needed to keep democratic machinery going. In practice, full-scale proportional representation encourages candidates to stand for office on the basis of what they genuinely

51

believe. With it, the necessary compromises of democracy are set after rather than before the elections. In its purest form, proportional representation had been adopted in only one nation, Ireland, by 1945; but half-way measures incorporating the principle, devised by many countries old and new, seemed definitely to constitute a trend in its favor.

Democracy is not exempt from problems. Voters make mistakes. Leaders seek fortune or power. Parties, organized to further ideologies, become corrupt. Whole nations plunge into war because that is their people's desire. Basically, of course, the weakness of the entire system lies in the shortcomings of the people. Only with time and effort will large expanses of popular ignorance, prejudice, and apathy disappear. But there are structural difficulties as well. Many are apparent in democracy's oldest working models, allowing the voters' management of affairs to be circumvented in devious ways. To patch up the faltering mechanisms, a number of newer practices have been constructed -- plural executives (a council to replace a president), "primary" elections (through which the people select party candidates), the initiative and referendum (the people at large participating in the legislative process), and the recall (the people changing their mind about an office-holder). Generally, though, these nineteenth-century repairs make poor substitutes for the new twentieth-century constitutional models.

Representative democracy, despite setbacks, does continue to improve its image. Among the self-contained problems it must yet solve are (1) how to convince its minorities that their problems can be solved through democratic channels; (2) how to prevent majorities who are not apathetic and not deeply ignorant from imposing an unfair will upon minorities in their own lands, in the belief that such a will works out to the majority's advantage; and (3) how to prevent leaders, even those most properly cho-

sen, from taking irretrievable steps that conduct whole nations into calamity. The answer
for all of these issues and for others similar
to them seems to lie in the direction of a more
nearly perfect global democracy, assigned specific powers, in which the minorities of one
country might have the backing of majorities in
others, and through which nations could be prevented from working themselves over toward catastrophe. In the third quarter of the twentieth century, most persons believed that the
world had a long road to travel to reach that
more nearly perfect global democracy.

Socialism is newer than democracy. To its
proponents, it is the natural extension of democracy into the economic sphere. Its principles were first defined in the early nineteenth
century. One hundred fifty years later, they
remained under serious challenge. Yet by then
socialism had become a great world ideology,
affecting the life of nearly every person.

The socialist doctrine is that the people
should control the industry of a country. It
contrasts with the laissez-faire doctrine, which
insists that private persons should control the
industry. Socialists argue that people's lives
are governed as fully by economics as by politics, and hence that economic as well as
political decisions should lie in the people's
hands. Some socialists prefer that industries
remain separated, each controlled by its own
group of laborers. Others hold to the efficacy
of large systems of cooperatives. But most are
interested in government management of enterprise, the government in each case being supposed to represent the entire population of the
land. Actually, as matters worked out in early
decades after World War II, only those socialist
regimes which denied political democracy moved
overwhelmingly into government-run enterprise.
Among others, it became common to speak of a
public (socialist) and a private (non-socialist)

53

sector in the economy of each nation.

A large segment of twentieth-century socialism derives from the teachings of one man, Karl
Marx (1818-83). Marx spoke of the desirability
of a classless society, the inevitability of a
classless society (replacing the bourgeois-led
society of his time), and the revolution whereby
the proletariat would bring about the classless
society in each country. Many of his followers
rejected his thoughts concerning abrupt revolution, preferring the quieter ways of democracy
instead. Non-Marxist socialists generally ignore his arguments about inevitability as well,
and often disagree with Marx on details of what
is desirable in the future. All socialists
cling to some sort of an ideal of a classless
society; but differences between the schools of
thought are so great they often refuse to
acknowledge one another as true proponents of
socialism.

"Democratic" socialists -- that is those,
either Marxist or non-Marxist, who strive
through the democratic processes -- are more
interested than the orthodox Marxists in demanding short-term socialist-oriented reform. Orthodox Marxists often warn that labor legislation short of socialism will only defer the time
of the revolution, by giving the workers a little of what they need. To democratic socialists, however, it has seemed important, before
the socialist economy is achieved, to work toward equality of opportunity and a redistribution of wealth whenever they can be had.
"Social security" measures for the laboring
classes were among the first they proposed.
Free or inexpensive medical care is one of their
major enthusiasms. The graduated income tax,
which charges the wealthy far more than the poor
for tax-channeled services rendered everyone,
fits very well with their design. Yet acceptance of these programs alone does not make one
a socialist. The democratic socialist calls for
an on-going government policy of placing at

least the industries that touch most persons'
lives out of the reach of private ownership and
profit.

Non-socialists in the twentieth century are
chiefly proponents of the economic system known
as private enterprise, free enterprise, or capitalism. Their thinking rests upon the base of
laissez-faire, the very antithesis of socialism,
the belief that entire populations will live as
well as nature will allow if private investors
are permitted to choose their own business ways
without interference. Competition is the key
word in their system, which holds that "laws"
such as that of supply and demand will operate
for everyone's maximum benefit if the business
world can operate without molestation from
outside. Raw laissez-faire doctrine has been
very little practiced. By the twentieth century, nearly everyone agreed that some government intervention in the business world was
needed. The argument as to just how much there
should be, and especially as to the nature of
its purposes, has produced sharp division in the
democratic non-socialist world.

Democratic non-socialist opinion is de-
scribed by the words <u>liberal</u> and <u>conservative</u>.
In the nineteenth century generally, the liberal
was one who favored political democracy and
championed laissez-faire. The conservative of
that time fought against the extension of political democracy. By the twentieth century, the
conservatives of many lands had conceded the
right of the masses to vote, and for their new
platform were moving over to defend private enterprise. Even here, they were willing to admit
that government should play a role in protecting
one industry from another, or in helping all
industry when it was passing through difficult
times. Twentieth-century liberals, on the other
hand, without renouncing their belief in private
enterprise as the best economic system, went
well beyond the conservatives in calling for
economic intervention by the government (called

social reform) to protect the people at large.

Three hundred years ago, all countries professed faith in some non-democratic, non-socialist form of one-man rule or absolutism. For this study, the small remnant of such regimes remaining in the world since 1945 will be placed in the extreme right (or fourth) quarter of an arc drawn to illustrate the global spectrum of politics. In the adjacent (third) quarter of the same spectrum will then fall the democratic non-socialist regimes, the conservatives ranging toward the right edge of this band, and the liberals toward the left, which is the center of the full spectrum. In the second quarter will be included those socialist governments (whether non-Marxist or Marxist) which preserve their dedication to political democracy. In the first, or extreme left, quarter will be placed those who in their push for socialism have sacrificed basic elements of the governmental democratic creed. All first-quarter regimes through 1958 were headed by persons professing some brand of devotion to Marxism.

The nineteenth century witnessed the birth of socialist parties fitting the first and second quarter of this spectrum. (A party may of course pertain to one quarter while the country in which it is located fits another.) The early twentieth century saw the development of the first socialist regimes -- again of both first- and second-quarter varieties. As a reaction to them, there then suddenly arose fascism, a stark negation of both socialist and democratic doctrine with an intense emphasis on nationalism. Fascism grew to fantastic proportions between the two world wars. Some fascists showed genuine worry about socialism; others may have become bewildered by the role of democracy in the world. Most younger people who adopted the creed, however, were looking for excitement rather than refuge. Fascism called for individual sacrifice for the advancement of the state;

56

its demands went so far that they merited the label <u>totalitarianism.</u> Fascists (after 1945 there <u>were fewer of</u> them again) occupy the fourth quarter of the global spectrum along with the remnant of absolutism. Their way is but a more skillful, streamlined version of rule by one man or a few, made less tolerable for many by the fact that the totalitarian way of life leaves even less room for individual freedom of movement than did most of the old-fashioned monarchies.

The spectrum thus delineated will be used as a frequent theme of reference in these pages. For convenience, the quarters will be designated (from left to right): (1) authoritarian socialism (or, through 1958, communism, the name generally applied to Russian-style Marxism and its derivatives); (2) democratic socialism; (3) democratic private enterprise; and (4) authoritarian private enterprise or fascism, including the mentioned diversity of anachronisms extant in recent times. To the questions (a) Shall there be democracy in government? and (b) Shall there be socialism in the economy? these are the responses of the four bands: (1) Communism says in effect no to the first, but yes to the second. (2) Democratic socialism says a hearty yes to both of them. (3) Democratic private enterprise says yes to the first, but no to the second. (4) Fascism answers in the complete negative, offering other attractions instead.

In the entire world at the end of the year 1940, in great contrast to the picture one decade later, only one regime fitted the first band of the spectrum. This was the Union of Soviet Socialist Republics, of Joseph Stalin and his party. Russia until 1917 had known only absolutism in its government, though after 1905 there existed a rudimentary parliamentary proceeding. When the Romanovs were overthrown, in March 1917, a wartime effort aimed to establish a democratic republic. But in November, when the Marxist party of Lenin took over the controls, the hope of many Russians for a genuine parliamentary regime had to be abandoned. Active on the margins of Russian political life starting in 1903, Lenin's party in 1918 began to call itself Communist; no other group has been permitted to share in Russian or Soviet political life since that time.

Karl Marx had taught the inevitability of socialist revolution in all nations, eliminating the employer classes and bringing the workers to power in their stead. The purported realization of such revolution in Russia led persons to expect the same elsewhere; but in 1918 and 1919, in the wake of World War I, only Germany and Hungary experienced brief (and unsuccessful) attempts to establish similar Marxist hegemony. A more solid move in that direction came with the establishment of a Communist International (Comintern) in 1919, dedicated to the fomenting of Communist party activity over the entire globe. The Comintern came into existence as the Third International of the socialist world, the First (1864-76) having been co-founded by Marx himself, and the Second (organized in 1889) holding a commitment to the principle of free parliaments. A German Communist party, member of the Comintern and the strongest communist body in the world outside of the Soviet Union, was extinguished by Adolf Hitler in 1933. A French Communist party gathered strength until it ranked as the third largest party of France before the Nazi conquest of 1940. But until that time, other communist groups organized in countries throughout the world remained small in their strength and impact.

Eight governmental regimes (4 in northern Europe, 2 in the Americas, 1 in the Middle East, and 1 in the Orient) occupied the second quarter of the spectrum at the beginning of 1940. The largest of these was Mexico, ruled by the Party of the Mexican Revolution founded in 1929 under another name. Mexico's revolution against an entire old order of society had begun in 1910. Its principles, enunciated in the constitution of 1917, were those of moderate democratic socialism. Political democracy in the usual sense, involving struggle between parties, remained slow in development in the new Mexico, the revolutionary emphasis being placed elsewhere. As far-going reforms occurred, however, especially during the presidency of Lázaro Cárdenas (1934-40), the bulk of the Mexican people supported the men who administered them. Mexico did not hesitate to develop its public sector at the expense of the private, which before 1910 had been dominated by a small minority of Mexicans and foreigners. But in so doing, it followed its own path without dependence upon the world of Marxism.

In the Middle East, Turkey became acquainted with socialism under an essentially democratic regime after the founding of its republic in 1923. One People's party provided the only vehicle for political activity, like the revolutionary party in Mexico, with little doubt that it represented the sentiments of a majority of Turkish people. The People's party was that of Mustafa Kemal, called Ataturk, president from 1923 until his death in 1938. Besides leading Turkey toward democratic ideals, he hoped to bring about rapid economic development in his country, and believed that state management of much enterprise was the avenue toward this goal. Socialism became one of the six "cardinal principles" of the Turkish constitution when it was amended in 1937.

Other second-quarter regimes paid as complete attention to political democracy as they did to socialism. Uruguay, led by the Colorado (Red, but not communist) party, had a socialist history longer than that of any other country, dating from 1911. The Social Democratic parties of Sweden and Denmark and Labor parties in Norway and New Zealand won power in the 1930's, in

each case moving like Mexico and Uruguay to en-
large the economy's public sector significantly.
Sweden, Denmark, and Norway at the same time were
champions of refined governmental democracy to
the extent of adopting proportional representation for political parties, and allowing some
voter choice within party lists. Finland adopted
socialist practices also, starting in the 1930's,
without the triumph of its Social Democratic
party, and went farther with proportional representation than the Scandinavian countries by
allowing voter choices crossing party lines.

Several countries contained political groupings that held second-quarter ideological aims
but had not achieved majority power. The largest was the Labor party of the United Kingdom,
founded in 1900. Very important were the Socialist groups of Spain and France, each one the
most popular single party of its nation before
the demise of democracy in those countries in
1939 and 1940. Also significant were the Labor
party of Australia, the Socialist of Belgium, and
the Social Democratic Labor grouping of the
Netherlands. The second-quarter parties in Europe, Australia, and New Zealand held Marxist and
non-Marxist membership in varying ratios, but
agreed on the necessity for peaceful persuasion
of the people toward their programs. Most of
them cooperated in the work of the Second International as it followed a faltering course between the two world wars.

Twenty-six governments (12 in Europe, 10 in
the Americas, 2 in Sub-Sahara Africa, 1 in the
Middle East, and 1 in the Orient) may be placed
in the third quarter of the spectrum at the beginning of 1940, though this classification is
clouded for some of them. Foremost of these by
far were the United States of America, the United
Kingdom of Great Britain and Northern Ireland,
and France. Many of the others equally or more
fervently devoted themselves to the cause of
political democracy; some, on the contrary,

though organized as democracies had not moved clearly away from minority control. None of the countries mentioned for this quarter, however, had moved into the orbit of socialism.

England, by far the most heavily populated part of the United Kingdom, may be said to have stepped over the threshold of democracy in 1689. It was then that a ruling king and queen, as they accepted their symbols of power, agreed for the first time to rule according to the statutes drawn by their parliament. The form accepted in 1689 became greater reality when the three crowned rulers who followed appointed ministers to serve for them as the actual chief executives of the land. Through the eighteenth century in Great Britain, there developed the principle that the support of the elected house of Parliament (the House of Commons) was essential for the continuation of a chief minister in office. As this house evolved to represent ever greater numbers of people in the entire United Kingdom, British democracy became more and more effective.

A non-elected House of Lords, nevertheless, continued to wield considerable power until 1911, and even then was allowed to hold on to the privilege of a two-year suspensive veto on nonfinancial matters. Archaic British electoral processes, with no hint of proportional representation, also limited democracy by making it possible for a minority to rule both the parliament and the country. The Conservative party, inheritors of the Tory tradition which dated back to the seventeenth century, constituted by far the strongest political organization in the United Kingdom in 1940. The Labor party ranked second in size, and the Liberal National a small third.

The United States and France stepped into the third quarter of the spectrum just one century after England. For the United States, the event was the inauguration of its first federal constitution in 1789. The quality of United States

61

democracy has been tempered by the very circumstances that its government is a federation (one
capital is not responsible for everything) and
that the nation is still ruled by a little-
changed eighteenth-century document. Nevertheless, through the action of both state and federal regimes, democracy has also grown greatly in
this country. Early state restrictions on voting
based on economic status or religion have largely
disappeared. A Senate once elected by state leg-
islatures, themselves often unrepresentative in
makeup, since 1913 has been chosen by the people
of the individual states, as have the presidents
of the country since the early nineteenth century. The hindrance of persons from voting
because of Negroid ancestry remained common in
1940 in some states, though it had diminished in
several and had never appeared in others. On
both state and federal levels, archaic electoral
practices persisted into mid-twentieth century;
far from showing concern about proportional representation, they even permitted minorities to
win control.

Neither of the country's two large parties
took an interest in electoral reform which might
encourage the growth of new political groupings. The Democratic party, in power in 1940,
had been founded in 1792, though it ran under the
name Republican during its first forty years.
The present Republican party was organized in
1854. By 1940, there existed little difference
between the two except that the Democratic ranks
included more liberals. Both Democrats and Republicans fitted the third quarter on the world
spectrum, and both spread from the moderate left
of that quarter to its very right extreme. Political compromises were made in the United
States before the elections rather than after
them, with a strong tendency for each party to
present as its platform what it thought the
people wanted.

France's experience with democracy after 1789
was much more tumultuous than that of the United

States. Its beginning lay in revolution against
an old regime whose monarchy remained absolute
though not altogether unpopular. The form as
well as the substance of French democracy varied
in the extreme, with the government a limited
monarchy at times and a republic at others. The
Third French Republic came into being in 1870 and
succeeding years only because a majority of monarchists could not agree on the choice of the
next king. The following half-century of
parliamentary life established the republican
tradition.

As in the United Kingdom, the French government included a prime minister and his cabinet
responsible to the parliament. Electoral practices, however, became less archaic in France,
the idea of a second ballot being introduced in
elections for the lower house, the Chamber of
Deputies. On this ballot, parties which had run
second and third could join forces against another which had run first but failed to gain a
majority, if they so chose. This device favored
a forthright stand by each party on the first
ballot for the principles it served, by allowing
compromises afterward. The provision was an
important one in this country which, by the
twentieth century, favored a multiplicity of
parties. Besides the Socialist and Communist
groups, the more important of these in 1939 were
the Radical and Radical Socialist party (to the
left on the third quarter of the spectrum, but
not really socialist) and the National Republican party, a conservative one. None of these
four functioned during the Nazi-sponsored Vichy
regime of 1940-3.

Egypt, Czechoslovakia, Argentina, Canada, and
South Africa made up five more, widely scattered regimes to which the ways of democracy were
known. Egypt, a limited monarchy starting in
1922, followed a rather erratic course. Party
life became disrupted from 1930 to 1934, but then
resumed. The Wafd, originally organized as a
nationalist movement against the British (the

63

name means Delegation, for a group that went to London), won nearly all the votes in 1934, but in 1938 lost its leading position in the lower house of parliament to the Liberal Constitutional (middle-of-the-third-quarter) party and the Saadists, a Wafd break-off named for an early Wafd leader. Czechoslovakia, flourishing as a parliamentary democracy between the two world wars, practiced proportional representation for its large number of political parties, though it offered no opportunity for the voters to choose candidates within each party. Argentina had pursued an ostensibly democratic course since 1862, though sixty years passed before the election of an opposition party became possible. Constitutional order, when broken in 1930, quickly stood repaired. In 1940, the Radical party (with a position like that of France) held the largest representation in Argentina, though the governing coalition consisted of the National Democratic (more conservative) and Radical Anti-personalista parties, the latter a split from the Radicals.

Canada as a self-governing dominion followed practices adopted from the United Kingdom. Before World War II, differences between its ruling Liberal and oppositionist Conservative parties remained minor. The Union of South Africa maintained the outward appearance of a neat democracy, though its United party ruled without opposition until 1939, when the People's party broke off to protest a declaration of war against Germany. Actually, most of its population were not allowed to vote, so that control lay in the hands of a Caucasoid minority.

Smaller nations fitting the third quarter of the spectrum early in 1940 included quite clearly Australia, the Netherlands, Belgium, Switzerland, Ireland, and Iceland as well as four of continental Europe's smallest six (Luxembourg, San Marino, Liechtenstein, and Andorra -- Danzig had been taken by the Germans in 1939.) Besides Labor, Social Democratic, and Socialist parties already mentioned for some of these, the United Australia (liberal) party, the Catholic parties of the Netherlands (liberal) and of Belgium (more conservative), the Anti-Revolutionary (conservative) party of the Netherlands, and the Fianna Fail (Warriors of Ireland) nationalist grouping in Ireland held significance. Electoral refinements in these lands included an alternative vote in Australia (like the second ballot in France, but marked simultaneously with the first); proportional representation for parties with some intraparty choice of candidates in the Netherlands and Belgium, and choices crossing party lines in Switzerland; and finally, in Ireland, complete proportional representation of the voters' sentiments, both within and between political parties or any interested groups.

There were other smaller nations of the third quarter in Latin America and Sub-Sahara Africa, though their democratic records stood less clear. In Latin America, Colombia enjoyed genuine, peaceful contention between Liberal and Conservative parties; Peru and Cuba subscribed to government by coalitions of elected parties; and Chile, Bolivia, Costa Rica, and Panama also followed the forms of democracy in 1940. Peru prevented most of its Quechua people from voting, however (on the basis of illiteracy); and of the entire number only Colombia, Chile, and Costa Rica had known at least one instance of peaceful transition from one party in power to another. Across the Atlantic, Liberia, with a restricted franchise and but one winning party, the True Whig (conservative), completes the roll of nations which at the commencement of World War II had at least some claim to the name "democratic."

In 1940 the fourth quarter of the spectrum weighed the heaviest of all. Before France fell to a fourth-quarter onslaught, there were already in this band 34 of the world's regimes (15 in Europe, 10 in the Americas, 5 in the Middle East, and 4 in the Orient), not counting recently subjugated Ethiopia, Austria, and Albania. The second, third, and fourth largest of these powers -- Japan, Germany, and Italy -- comprised the tripartite alliance often called the Axis which conducted the chief offensives in World War II from 1939 through 1941. China, the largest, lay severely wounded by Japan well before the year 1939. Others remained neutral in World War II or joined one or the other side; Lithuania, Latvia, and Estonia lost their sovereignty. Regardless of this scattering of sympathies and casualties, fascism went into the war strong and came out of it, in 1945, very weak. The fourth-quarter roll call is intended to emphasize this great change.

China under the rule of Chiang Kai Shek and the Kuo Min Tang was, despite its own great antipathy toward fascist Japan, the inheritor of the oldest non-democratic, non-socialist tradition in the world. Absolutism, either enlightened or unenlightened, had provided the keynote of its ancient regimes, lasting through the time of the Manchus. Sun Yat Sen hoped to move his nation into the second quarter of the spectrum, through programs devoted to popular government and the people's livelihood. But Chiang, whether through apathy toward these ideals (as would say his opponents) or through the confusion which plagued the land (as would argue his friends) did not move from 1925 to 1940 to implement Sun's democratic and socialist principles. In the 1930's, many outside observers believed that Communist Mao Ze Dong (Mao Tse Tung), who held a much smaller portion of Chinese territory, had under development a society closer to that envisaged by Sun.

Japan, unlike the republic of China, had attained a semblance of democracy before slipping completely into militaristic hands. Japan's constitution of 1889, carefully prepared after the revolution of 1867-8 against the shoguns, provided for parliamentary government with a restricted right to vote. Some parties grew to

66

positions of influence. The commencement of manhood suffrage in 1925 might have signaled the dawn of a genuine democratic era. Military leaders acted independently of the parliament, however, increasingly imposing their own will upon the nation. The parliament had little to do with the running of the country after 1936, and in 1940 lost out entirely as the old parties were dissolved and new councils planned to hold authority without elections.

Germany under Adolf Hitler and the Nazis could look back upon a short-lived democracy that had been repudiated. Even under the Hohenzollerns, before World War I, Germany had come close to stepping over the democratic threshold. Powerful parties arose, all the men could vote, and prime ministers paid much attention to the parliament even though they remained responsible to the kaisers. The republic fashioned in the city of Weimar in 1919 followed democratic practices including the system of proportional representation of parties. Politics in the so-called Weimar Republic ranged over the entire spectrum, each quarter being represented by at least one major political group. All parties except the National Socialist, which despite its name had nothing to do with socialism, were nevertheless declared illegal by Hitler within a half-year of his rise to power. Hitler ended Germany's presidency in 1934; his parliament, composed only of his followers, might as well have terminated also.

Constitutionally, Italy possessed a democratic orientation from its first emergence as a nation. Its government ran like that of the United Kingdom, excepting that parties tended to center around dominant personalities rather than ideas and that elections were often controlled, by subtle or non-subtle means. In 1919, for the first time, Italy seemed determined to breathe real life into its democratic framework. All males received the right to vote, following the party-list system of proportional representation. The Socialist and Popular (liberal) parties which quickly showed their strength under the new arrangements, however, encountered strong opposition from Mussolini and the Fascists, who captured the prime ministership in 1922 through the threat of force, and in 1928 made it impossible for any but their own candidates to be elected. Ten years later, the remaining step was taken, dispensing with elections entirely.

The nineteenth-century monarchy in Brazil approached democracy with greater gentility than that of Italy, but in the long run came no closer to the ideal. A seemingly significant step was taken in 1847, when the prime minister who had been responsible to the emperor was made accountable to the parliament. Actually, the emperor through non-violent means maintained virtually complete control of the legislative body until the 1880's, when his power deteriorated. The republic instituted in 1889 (and called the United States of Brazil) was modeled after that of the United States in North America, and from 1891 to 1930 functioned in somewhat the same fashion as its northern counterpart, though with considerable turbulence. More than half of the population -- largely that decended from Africans -- remained without a voice in the government because of their illiteracy. The rise of Getúlio Vargas to power entailed the use of force, with Vargas' following protesting fraud in an election count declaring him the loser. Four years later, in 1934, Vargas continued in office with a new constitution which allowed him to appoint part of the national legislature. Then, in 1937, still another document provided for a state of emergency under which the president simply ruled by decree.

Poland, like China and Brazil, constituted a fascist-type regime that did not adhere to the Axis. Poland's taste of democracy (1919-26) before the advent of its strong men Pilsudski and Smigly-Rydz proved full of friction and torment. Parliamentary forms continued, but without substance, under the guidance of these men who were only heads of the army. In the refugee government set up in 1939, Wladyslaw Sikorski served as prime minister as well as assuming the army position of Smigly-Rydz, but no parliament existed in London to back him.

Spain in 1939 found itself officially in sympathy with the Axis, which had provided important help during the Spanish civil war on behalf of the winning side. Many persons in Spain held democratic ideals, and three times in the nineteenth century democracy very briefly prevailed (1810-14, 1820-3, and 1873-4). From 1834 on, there was always a national parliament or Cortes, but a prime minister responsible to the queen or king actually picked its members, and at times a strong man from the military guided the entire governmental process. The second Spanish republic initiated in 1931 behaved like a democracy should, but had too much against it to survive. Its large Agrarian Populist party favored the old order of things rather than the new. Its equally popular Socialist party worried tradition-minded military men like Francisco Franco, whose revolt in 1936 brought about the dissolution of all parties except the Falange and the establishment of a provisional but long-lasting one-man regime.

The Middle Eastern lands of Iran and Afghanistan consituted examples of governments that had not yet pulled significantly away from old-fashioned absolutism by 1940. Both had constitutions, Iran since 1906 and Afghanistan since 1931, providing for parliamentary regimes. But the monarchs controlled the elections, and in neither was there a political party even in imitation of the custom elsewhere.

Yugoslavia and Romania in Europe and Thailand in the Orient, though also monarchies fitting the fourth quarter, had undergone some experiences of a newer fashion. Yugoslavia, organized as a constitutional regime, after ten

very difficult years passed in 1929 to a dictatorship under king Alexander. When Alexander was
killed in 1934, his cousin Paul ruled as first
regent, and elections continued to be controlled. Plans to move to a democracy in 1939
became thwarted by the war. Romania, theoretically a parliamentary regime after 1866, held its
first free elections in 1928, only to settle back
into a dictatorship by king Carol in 1930. Carol
ran a fascist-type regime, but made life
difficult for the Iron Guard, a fascist group
disloyal to him personally. When the tables
turned in 1940 and Romania fell into the Axis
orbit, Carol fled, his son Michael succeeded to
the kingship, and the Iron Guard became supreme. Thailand remained an absolute monarchy
until 1932, when it made a one-year attempt to
establish constitutional government, and then
settled for a council ruling for young king
Ananda Mahidol, who attended school abroad.

Smaller nations that also formed part of the
fourth quarter of the spectrum in 1940 included
Hungary, with its Party of Hungarian Life controlling the elections and joining the Axis;
Portugal, with a seven-year-old pure fascist
state which had been forced upon its republic;
Greece, with its parties and parliament dissolved since 1936; and Bulgaria, with no right
for a parliament to legislate since a coup in
1935. Among continental Europe's smallest six,
Monaco and Vatican City abided officially by
one-man rule. Latin American caudillos of
various styles governed in Venezuela, Haiti,
Guatemala, the Dominican Republic, El Salvador,
Honduras, Paraguay, and Nicaragua. One of the
eight had held power for eight years, two for
nine years, and two more for ten. Ecuador followed a junta that had risen to power by means of
a coup. In the remainder of the world, there was
monarchy run by a family other than the crowned
one in Nepal, monarchy controlling the country
through the parliament in Iraq, and unalloyed
old-fashioned absolutism in Saudi Arabia and
Yemen.

With the forces of fascism so strong at the beginning of World War II, both inside and out-side the Axis, it is understandable that fascism did not as a result of that war completely dis-appear. Individuals, some parties, and a few regimes maintained the old allegiances and awaited a resurgence of the old attitudes. No one could be sure in an unsettled world that there would be no return of fascism. But im-mediately after the defeat of the Axis, fascism seemed only a horrible dream, and those fascists who remained alive an absurd fringe on the poli-tics of the planet.

The great controversies continued to involve nationalism, fascism's chief positive ingredi-ent, to be sure; and at times world events showed no other determinant more clearly than nationalism. Nevertheless, most post-World War II conflicts emerged overlaid with arguments concerning democracy and socialism. These were, after all, the identifying marks of the first three quarters of the spectrum, from which came the might that defeated the Axis. It appeared that they were also the prime manifestations of a new age coming in, while an older age addicted to quarrelsome nationalism found itself seriously challenged.

If a new age was indeed dawning after 1945, its advent certainly did not indicate that the world would no longer run into problems. There existed, in fact, besides the host of perplexi-ties passed on from older times, an emerging list of concerns linked directly to democracy and socialism. The goal of these political and economic creeds was simply to set man free. Men are quite certain about what they want to be free from; in great numbers, they will no longer tolerate ancient tyrannies and exploitations. They seem less certain about what they want to be free for; at this point there arises the pos-sibility of a great emptiness in the new age.

71

Politics and economics have long served as the chief nuclei of action for mankind. With all their complexity, they are but sophisticated forms of exertions known throughout the animal kingdom. They will not disappear. But if the new age really dawns, they will very slowly fade into the background. People must then realize that science and art and religion, each one a distinctly human enterprise as far as life goes on this one planet, can provide the excitement once derived from gaining a fortune or seeking power over other persons.

Science has just begun; people a few hundred years into the new age will regard the knowledge of today as primitive. Art will discover new horizons, as people make contact with unknown worlds of touch, sight, and sound. Religion will acquire further profundity, as people more than ever before gain the capacity to philosophize. This study, while attempting to chronicle the post-1945 survival of problems connected with race, language, the older religion, and national-ism, and while seeking to show the tremendous new developments connected with the emergence of de-mocracy and socialism, will also do what it can to indicate man's efforts in science, art, and the newer religion. For true homo sapiens needs more than freedom from want and fear. He also craves freedom from boredom.

IV. A NEW WORLD DAWNS --

1941-1945

Boredom was no problem in late 1940, as nations flexed their muscles for the huge struggle ahead. The destruction of ten national regimes by the Germans, the termination of two by the Italians, and the occupation of a major part of China by Japan had composed but a prelude to the savagery that was to follow. In August, hordes of German planes bombed Great Britain in the beginning of an effort to break that nation's will. On September 2, the British received some comfort from a non-ally, when the United States agreed to provide ships Britain needed and to take over certain western-hemisphere naval and air bases. In September and October, Japan occupied French Indochina; Germany (with the assistance of Hungary) forced Romania to become its ally; and Italy invaded Greece. On September 27, the three Axis powers very openly and blatantly harmonized: "Japan recognizes and respects the leadership of Germany and Italy in the establishment of a new order in Europe. . . . Germany and Italy recognize and respect the leadership of Japan in the establishment of a new order in Greater East Asia. . . . Japan, Germany and Italy agree to cooperate in their efforts on the aforesaid lines." While the Axis cooperated, the British had no powerful allies; but the United Kingdom survived its siege of bombing.

Axis fighting forces emerged victorious everywhere they engaged in action in 1941. Bulgaria joined them in March, but was occupied by Nazi soldiers anyhow. The Germans took Yugoslavia, and joined the Italians in overcoming

73

Greece, in April. On June 22, Nazi armies entered the Soviet Union, discarding the Hitler-Stalin pact of 1939; in October, they laid siege to Moscow. The Finns united with the Germans in the attack on the Soviet Union. On December 7, the Japanese assaulted Pacific forces of the United States in the Philippine and Hawaiian Islands. The same month, Japan took Thailand (to rule as a puppet state) and Hong Kong.

The only bright spots for the opposition lay on the peripheries. The United States, not yet in the actual fighting, moved closer to Great Britain's side with the passage of a Lend-Lease Act March 11, 1941, providing a means whereby goods and services could be rendered to friends in need. In June, British troops intervened to keep the Germans out of Iraq. In June and July, the British aided by French individuals took Syria and Lebanon away from the control of the government in Vichy. In July, United States forces were sent to defend Iceland against possible invasion. In late July, the Soviet Union made its peace with the Polish regime of Wladyslaw Sikorski in London. In August and September, British and Russian invasion brought about the abdication of the ruling shah of Iran and the substitution of his more cooperative son, Mohammad Reza Pahlavi. In October, Washington helped to arrange a similar coup to assure friendly sentiment in strategic Panama. United States troops occupied Dutch Surinam, to avoid Nazi infiltration there, in November. British forces during the year cleared the Italians out of Italian East Africa, allowing the Ethiopian monarch to return home. Most important for the British, of course, was the new close association with two great allies, the Union of Soviet Socialist Republics in June, the United States of America in December. Declarations after December 7 aligned each of the three chief regimes on either side at war with all its counterparts on the other, with the exception of continued peace between the Soviet Union and Japan.

74

Little time remained available for ideology in 1941. August 14 of this year, however, was the day of the Atlantic Charter. In this document, president Franklin Roosevelt and prime minister Winston Churchill, speaking very nearly as though they had already become military companions, made themselves heard around the world. They opposed any aggrandizement of countries or territorial changes not desired by the peoples concerned. They stood for (1) the right of peoples to choose their own governments; (2) access by all states on equal terms to the trade and raw materials of the world; (3) international cooperation in the economic sphere; (4) "assurance that all the men in all the lands may live out their lives in freedom from fear and want;" (5) freedom of the high seas; and (6) a postwar abandonment of the use of force and a lightening of the burden of armaments. Nine other governments attacked by the Germans subscribed to these same principles on September 24, including the Soviet Union.

The year 1942 ran bitter. It began, on New Year's Day, with a "Declaration by United Nations" of determination to stay together until the Axis had come to its end. (Thus, in a wartime alliance, became initiated the name of man's greatest peacetime organization.) Signatories were the Soviet Union, the United States, and the United Kingdom, now joined by China, eight smaller European regimes, nine countries of Central America and the Caribbean, four British Commonwealth dominions, and British-controlled India. A few weeks later, an Inter-American Conference met in Rio de Janeiro to consult on defensive measures, agreeing that all members should sever diplomatic relations with the Axis, though only Mexico of those who had not done so already made a declaration of war before the end of this year.

Meanwhile, Japan took the Philippines, the Netherlands East Indies, Malaya, Burma, and for good measure British Borneo and Portuguese Timor. Further islands were seized as far east as Nauru and the Gilbert chain, and in the north even a few of the Aleutians in Alaska. German troops pushed hard into Russia, reaching all the way to Stalingrad. In November, finally, the Russians began to strike back successfully at Stalingrad, the Americans won a major naval battle in the Solomon Islands, and a British-American force landed in Vichy-controlled Morocco and Algeria -- though the latter step was followed by complete Nazi domination of the Vichy French regime. The United Nations remained a very long way from victory; at the end of 1942, they had only begun to stem the fascist tide.

The year 1943 was a critical one, though hardly yet decisive. Libya fell to the British, entering from Egypt, in January. Tunisia fell to the British and Americans, following their conquest of Morocco and Algeria, in May. When the same armies invaded Sicily, at Italy's toe, in July, Benito Mussolini resigned. The Italian successor government quit fighting when the war reached the mainland in September. The Germans fought on in Italy, however, with Mussolini behind their lines. The Germans also continued to do battle in Russia, though two large counter-offensives cleared them out of about half the Soviet territory which they had taken. In the Pacific, the Japanese remained firmly entrenched; at the end of the year, American forces continued the task of taking back from them the very-far-east Gilbert Islands.

Aside from the struggle, some important decisions were made this year on the United Nations side. In February, strong-man Getúlio Vargas of Brazil decided to cast his lot against the fascist regimes he had formerly admired; later in the year, Bolivia and Colombia also became allies. In May, Joseph Stalin dissolved the Comintern, easing a 24-year strain between the Soviet Union and every other government on earth. In Moscow in October, the leading United Nations (China, the Soviet Union, the United States, and the United Kingdom) spoke formally of end-of-the-war aspirations, including the establishment of a new organization to maintain international peace and security. For the United States, this amounted to an abrupt change from pre-World War II isolationist policy. In November, the first step in this direction came with the establishment of the United Nations Relief and Rehabilitation Administration to assist the millions of persons suffering from the war. And in November-December, the four leading nations' chief executives met -- Stalin, Roosevelt, and Churchill in Tehran, Iran; Chiang Kai Shek, Roosevelt, and Churchill in Cairo, Egypt -- stressing unanimity and agreeing on general strategy for the Pacific and Europe.

There were great differences in outlook between fourth-quarter regimes such as those of Chiang and Vargas, third-quarter governments like those of Roosevelt and Churchill, and a first-quarter state such as Stalin led. No one in 1943 expected cooperation among them to be easy. There is no reason, however, to suppose that any one of them spoke insincerely in the expression of desires for a new, more peaceful world where international machinery might develop real potential in determining relationships among people. That is not to say that any one of the leaders did not intend to preserve whatever advantage for his own nation he could. At the moment, with United Nations victory still far away, only small indications of each nation's tug for power had become visible. Four such indications, all of the year 1943, are given here separately, at the conclusions of four mini-biographies of men who played a role in them. All helped to set the stage for events of the post-war years:

(1) Sixty-four-year-old Joseph Stalin held the two most important positions in the Soviet Union in 1943. Since 1922, he

had served as secretary-general of the Central Committee of the Communist party; since 1941, also as president of the Council of People's Commissars, or prime minister. Stalin, originally Iosif Vissarionovich Dzhugashvili, was only one generation removed from serfdom. His father, a shoemaker of far-south tsarist Georgia, died when his son was only eleven. The financially destitute mother secured the lad's entrance into a seminary in Tiflis where for five years he trained for the Orthodox priesthood. But Stalin took more interest in adolescent merrymaking and instruction forbidden by the seminary, especially that in the literature of Marxism, and found himself expelled at the age of 19. He then became a full-time plotting and organizing revolutionary, determined to change the order of society; content to play his designated role in a master plan, even when having to submit to occasional arrest; eager to rise in authority, but able to bide his time. He met Lenin in 1905, and gradually came to that leader's attention as a hard-working and practical sort of man. Four years of exile in Siberia (1913-17) were followed by full-scale recognition of his merits, as he assumed a place on Lenin's first team.

There were those who opposed Stalin's taking the place of Lenin when Lenin died; particularly Leon Trotsky, whose disappointed followers around the world even formed a Fourth socialist International in competition with the Russian-led Third. By 1927, however, Stalin became the new master of the Soviet Union, and drove ruthlessly to establish communist principles, even in matters on which Lenin had compromised. Inside the Soviet Union, ruthlessness became terror for a very large number of people, though the popula-

tion as a whole made much material progress. In international affairs, Stalin
followed a peaceful course until 1939.
His policy indeed was one of cooperation
with third-quarter regimes when they found
themselves in conflict with fascism. Most
memorable was his expression of willingness to aid Czechoslovakia, if France as
she had promised would do likewise, when
Hitler was threatening Czechoslovakia's
ruin. The subsequent pact with Germany,
the occupation of eastern Poland, the territorial incorporation of Lithuania, Latvia, and Estonia, and the attack of 1939
on the borders of Finland seemed to indicate a new direction in Stalin's policy.
In doing these things, the Soviet Union
was recovering territory once governed by
the tsars, and claimed to be acting for
defensive purposes only. But had a new
communist era set in, when armed force
might supplement propaganda and plotting
in the furtherance of the revolutionary
cause? As Soviet armies marched successfully in 1943, probably no one, even
Stalin himself, knew the answer to that
question.

The idea nevertheless must have occurred to
him. Stalin felt very deeply throughout this
year that his people were conducting the war
against the Nazis without the help they deserved
from allies. Specifically, he favored the organization of a British-American "second front"
(the Russian being the first), not in North Africa or Italy but in France, across the English
Channel from the English-language bastion. At
times, he complained about this matter; in June,
he showed his bitterness at the final British-
American decision to wait until 1944 before
making the attempt. At other times, his attitude seemed more benevolent; it was obvious,
after all, that the more sacrifice the Russian
armies endured the greater would be the Soviet

Union's eventual advantage. In April 1943, Stalin interrupted the diplomatic relations he had developed two years earlier with the Polish refugee regime. Slowly, then, he began to work with some Poles in Russia in whom he felt more confidence than those led by Sikorski in London. This was no irretrievable decision in 1943. But Stanislaw Mikolajczyk, who succeeded Sikorski as Polish premier in London when Sikorski died in an airplane accident in July, was to learn within a few years how successful Stalin could be in looking for close East European co-operators and friends.

(2) Sixty-nine-year-old Winston Churchill, prime minister of the United Kingdom since 1940, had started life very differently from Joseph Stalin. Born in a palace, a son of the third son of the seventh duke of Marlborough, Winston attended private schools as a child of aristocracy, but did poorly in his studies. A military academy he attended in his teens fitted his interests better. When he graduated, high in his class, he served as an army officer in India, the Sudan, and South Africa until 1900. Next he entered politics, winning a seat in the House of Commons. Though a Conservative at the outset, and again much later on, Churchill stood for office as a Liberal for two decades after a switch in 1903, fighting particularly hard for Liberal principles in pre-World War I parliamentary battles.

In 1911 Churchill became first lord of the Admiralty in a Liberal cabinet. Four years later, with disaster dogging expeditions he had planned, he lost this position. For a time, later in World War I, he served as an infantry officer. Embroiled in politics again after that war, he showed clear antipathy toward the socialist doctrine then growing in England as

well as the "nameless beast," as he called it, of Russian communism. For five
years starting in 1924, a Conservative
government kept Churchill employed as
chancellor of the Exchequer. In the
1930's, however, he sat on the sidelines,
a Conservative criticizing the leadership
of his own party for its failure to show
alarm over the growing menace of Hitler-
ism. The day the United Kingdom declared
war in 1939, he became first lord of the
Admiralty again. And as prime minister
less than a year later, he served as his
own minister of defense, taking an active
hand in war planning.

Differences between London and Washington
concerning major war strategy were obvious almost
from the beginning. Washington favored military
action in France even in the year 1942. In a
series of conferences, however, the United States
agreed little by little that effective action
there should not be undertaken before May 1944.
Churchill proposed as an alternative, even until
the parley of 1943 in Tehran, a British-American
landing in Greece and Yugoslavia to accompany the
thrust against Italy. His plan, rejected by both
Roosevelt and Stalin, would if successful presumably have countered to some extent any postwar
Russian dominance in the Balkans. As matters
worked out, it held significance only in revealing the disposition of Churchill's mind. His
immediate prewar eminence had stemmed from his
warnings about the Nazi regime. His postwar
career might depend on how clearly he had
foreseen a new menace. The positions of partners
might change, but as Churchill envisaged the
future the world would go on with the same tug of
power politics it had known for centuries. The
problem was that such unimaginative ideas in
Churchill's mind encouraged others to think
equally traditionally.

(3) Fifty-one-year-old Josip Broz --
known by his boyhood diminutive of Tito --
became marshall of a new Yugoslavia and
president of its National Committee, or
prime minister, in late November 1943.
Tito was born in Croatia, the seventh of
15 children (only 7 of whom lived to
adulthood) of peasant parentage. Despite
a hard early life, he attended elementary
school for five years; for a time he
served as a Roman Catholic altar boy. In
1907, he left home and became an appren-
tice to a locksmith. Three years later he
lived in Zagreb, joining a metalworkers'
union and becoming a socialist. He held
several jobs, moving to Germany and then
to Vienna, Austrian capital of his own
Croatian land. In 1913 Tito began his
term of compulsory military service in the
Austrian armies; two years later, he lay
wounded on a Russian battlefield. As a
prisoner of war, he became enthusiastic
about the new communism; he remained in
Russia for five years before returning
home. Back in his new country of Yugoslavia, he became a revolutionary while
still a machinist. He spent six years
(1928-34) in prison; after that, he worked
full time for the illegal Yugoslav Communist party, becoming its secretary-
general in 1937.

The German occupation of Yugoslavia in April
1941 was preceded by the coming to power of 18-
year-old king Peter II, ending the regency of his
pro-Nazi uncle, prince Paul. Peter's government,
established in London after the Nazi seizure of
most of his country, continued relationships with
loyal forces in Yugoslavia, headed by Dragoljub
(called Draza) Mihajlovic, which at first fought
but later often collaborated with the German occupation troops. The common interest of Mihajlovic and the Germans lay in combating the strength
of Yugoslav Partisans organized by Tito and oth-

82

ers when the Nazis attacked the Soviet Union. As time went by, British and American sympathy for the cause of Mihajlovic declined, while their regard for the Partisans ran higher. They were already granting friendly aid to Tito when his Anti-Fascist National Liberation Committee on November 29, 1943, asserted its intention to rule Yugoslavia without the help of Peter. Tito's decision became memorable because he made it independently, without advice from the Soviet Union, the United Kingdom, or the United States. Tito remained a Communist with an unhidden attachment to Russia as a communist mother land; he had also been, from the beginning, a man who expected to deal with the strong powers without obeisance to any of them. The postwar world was to contain a large number of leaders of his kind.

(4) Fifty-nine-year-old Eduard Benes, president of a Czechoslovak refugee government in London since 1940, had been the president of Czechoslovakia for nearly three years beginning in 1935. He was one of eight children of a Bohemian farm couple who lived near the German-speaking people of Sudetenland. His father, a hard worker, sent his boys to school. Eduard left home to attend classes in Prague at the early age of eleven. He led a studious, sober life, but gave up his parents' Roman Catholicism. From 1904 to 1909, he lived in five cities (Prague, Paris, Dijon, London, and Berlin), studied in the universities of four of them, and earned two doctorates -- in international law, at Dijon, and in philosophy, at Prague. At the age of 25, he had already given careful attention to a wide range of European thought of his time -- a feat hardly matched by Stalin, Churchill, or Tito. As he began a long teaching career, a moderate, democratic socialism appealed to him as the path down which he would like his own nation to travel.

83

Teaching ended temporarily in 1915, as Benes left Prague for Paris again. He and his mentor, Tomas Masaryk, departed from home to work for the liberation of Czechs and Slovaks from the Austrian rule. When their work was finished in 1918, Masaryk became the president and Benes the foreign minister of the new Czechoslovak regime. For 17 years they retained these positions; and when Masaryk finally resigned, Benes succeeded him. His very democratic regime became the second to be taken over by the Nazis, in a quarrel ostensibly concerned with Sudetenland. The United Kingdom and France in effect gave Hitler permission to make this move; the Soviet Union, at the time, declared its willingness to back Czechoslovakia against Germany if France would. Benes resigned after this crisis, and for a time lectured on democracy at the University of Chicago.

In December 1943, as president of the refugee Czechoslovak regime, Benes made a trip to Moscow to sign a treaty of alliance with the Soviet government. Benes believed that his own nation could serve as a bridge between postwar first- and third-quarter states. He had reason for thinking that the Soviet Union might defend Czechoslovakia more readily than would the United Kingdom or France. Ideologically, also, he expected his own democratic socialist administration to represent a practical and beneficent compromise between two extremes. The trouble was that Benes and men like him in the postwar world often found it very difficult to survive.

The year 1944 stood as a very difficult one, but brought the assurance of victory to the United Nations side. Germany's long string of conquests terminated when Nazi soldiers occupied

Hungary in March, after three and a half years during which Germany and Hungary were allies. The other side now had its turn, the Russians pushing hard from the east, the Americans and British from the south (Rome was entered June 5), and finally American, British, and French armies from the west. Charles de Gaulle proclaimed himself president of a provisional government of France June 3, three days before the landings in France. The Germans surrendered Paris in August and Brussels, Belgium, in September. In the same two months, Soviet troops moved into Romania and Bulgaria. In October, Greek and British soldiers occupied Athens, Greece, while Yugoslav and Soviet forces entered Belgrade, Yugoslavia; in November, Axis troops evacuated Albania. Then, German lines held; and in December the Nazis made a last, mighty, but unsuccessful effort to resume the offensive. The Japanese were holding on much better. In January of this year the Americans began to take strategic points in the Marshall Islands administered by Japan; in June, they moved likewise into the Marianas; in October, they even reinvaded the Philippines. But Japan's forces remained entrenched in nearly all the territory they had conquered.

With the prospect of victory ahead, though the fighting had not been concluded, the United Nations in 1944 began serious planning for the postwar era. Three very important conferences were held in the United States, far from the anguished battlefields -- the first at Bretton Woods, a New Hampshire resort, in July; the others at Dumbarton Oaks, a mansion in the city of Washington, from August to October. At Bretton Woods 44 United and Associated Nations (the latter those who had broken diplomatic relations with the Axis without declaring war) signed two agreements, establishing the International Bank for Reconstruction and Development and the International Monetary Fund. The Bank came into existence to assist war-torn and less developed lands through foreign investment and loans; the Fund to promote monetary cooperation in the interests of an expanded world trade.

Spokesmen for the Soviet Union, the United States, and the United Kingdom conversed at Dumbarton Oaks more than a month; later, for nine days, delegations from China, the United States, and the United Kingdom did the same (preserving the nicety of the separation of two wars). At Dumbarton Oaks were stated the great powers' proposals for an ongoing United Nations organization to maintain international peace and security once these objectives came within reach. As principal organs, they suggested a General Assembly in which each member would have one vote, with important decisions to be taken only through the concurrence of two-thirds of those present and voting; a Security Council with five permanent and six non-permanent seats, its voting procedure yet to be determined; an International Court of Justice; and a Secretariat. An Economic and Social Council, they said, should be formed under the authority of the General Assembly. The five permanent Security Council seats would be allotted to the Dumbarton Oaks powers and France. No date was set for discussion of these plans with others of the United Nations -- there remained a difficult war to be won. During this entire year, only one additional country, Liberia, cast its lot on the United Nations side.

Bretton Woods and Dumbarton Oaks represented one kind of postwar planning. Winston Churchill and Joseph Stalin busied themselves in this year with a very different variety. Churchill, persisting in his interests in southeastern Europe, presumably with the object of limiting Soviet influence in that area, suggested to Stalin an agreement delimiting Soviet and British activities there. In May 1944, by mutual assent of the United Kingdom and the Soviet Union, but without consultation with the nations directly involved, Romania and Bulgaria were placed in the Russian orbit, while Greece and Yugoslavia were allotted to Britain. Kings Peter II of Yugoslavia and

George II of Greece both lived in London; Churchill hoped to reestablish them on their thrones. This agreement remained unformalized, however, and by October Churchill prepared to accept another instead. Now Romania, Bulgaria, and Hungary were to fall under major Russian influence, Greece to remain in the British sphere, and Yugoslavia to be considered open to the efforts of both the United Kingdom and the Soviet Union. Likewise, Churchill would not oppose the Russian plans for Poland, and Stalin would recognize a continuing British claim to Hong Kong. In plotting such bargains, Churchill thought in terms of a postwar balance of power, imitating policy followed by Great Britain ever since its acquisition of empire. He was also giving the Russians a go-ahead signal to manipulate affairs in Poland, Romania, Bulgaria, and Hungary as the British expected to manage the business of Hong Kong and Greece.

The Soviet plans for Poland had encountered great complications. The British and Americans recognized the Polish refugee government in London, headed since 1943 by premier Stanislaw Mikolajczyk. The Russians, having broken with that regime, in January 1944 entered the territory east of a line from Lvov to Vilna that had belonged to Poland 1921-39, but before 1921 had formed a part of Russia. The population of the district was chiefly Belorussian and Ukrainian; the Russians fully intended to reincorporate these people into the Soviet Union. Mikolajczyk and his cabinet, in the face of these realities, insisted that Poland could not agree to the Soviet incorporation of this region. In late July, after the Russian armies had pushed on into territory which was indisputably Polish, west of the Lvov-Vilna line, a Polish Committee of National Liberation formed in Lublin received recognition by Moscow as the administrative authority in lands retaken from the Germans on the western side of the line.

Other Polish forces in Warsaw, in partial

87

liaison with the regime in London, rose against the Germans on August 1, expecting to take over that city before the Soviet armies arrived. The Russians were not in a position to reach Warsaw quickly, and when the insurrection did poorly in the face of German power, the Soviet forces made little effort to rescue the Warsaw Poles. Many of the latter were killed; the remainder surrendered to the Nazis October 3. Nine days later, Mikolajczyk visited Moscow while Churchill was there, to see whether a better relationship between Russians and Poles could be devised. Most of the Polish regime in London remained committed to the idea that Poland must not lose the easternmost third of its territory, however, while Stalin remained adamant in his unwillingness even to discuss that matter, or to limit his own close attachment to the Committee in Lublin. Mikolajczyk resigned his premiership of the Polish refugee regime in London on November 24. On the last day of the year, the Russian-supported Committee of National Liberation declared itself the (sole) provisional government of Poland.

Soviet armies took Warsaw from the Germans on January 17, 1945. Budapest, Hungary, fell to the Russians in February; the city of Danzig in March (it was immediately incorporated into Poland); Vienna, Austria, in April; Prague, Czechoslovakia, in early May. Prague was really liberated by its own inhabitants; the Americans driving from the west could have arrived there before other outsiders, but abode by prior agreements with the Russians as to which territories each of the great powers should occupy. American, British, and Russian troops met amicably in Germany while the Nazi regime went through its final collapse in late April and early May. Sickening evidence of its sadistic nature came to light as millions of its prisoners were found dead or dying. News of the suicide of Adolf Hitler and of Joseph Goebbels, his propaganda chief and intended successor as chancellor, was broadcast

May 1, as Soviet troops marched into Berlin. Six days later, the last German armies surrendered.

Benito Mussolini, after a year and a half behind German lines, was captured (a second time) and killed by hostile Italians on April 29, bringing an end to Italy's contribution to the Axis. Japan alone remained to continue the struggle. In a bold, frontal approach to that country, but very selective in design, United States forces took the tiny Japanese island of Iwo Jima in February-March and the larger Japanese island of Okinawa in April-June. In February, the Americans took Manila in the Philippines; in May, the British entered Rangoon, Burma; in June, an Australian army invaded Borneo. No one on the United Nations side relished the prospect of having to push the Japanese out of all the lands they had occupied, nor could anyone anticipate with pleasure the bitter assault expected on the Japanese home islands. From May to July, tremendous air and naval bombardment of Japanese cities wrought great havoc there, but did not produce an offer of complete Japanese surrender, though many Japanese officials asserted their own readiness to desist from further warfare.

The war was nearly finished, though at the end of July no one could have foreseen that fact with certainty. Eventual United Nations victory had seemed sure, however, since very early in the year. President Roosevelt and prime ministers Stalin and Churchill met at Yalta in the Russian Crimea in February, focusing their attention mainly upon the postwar era. The Soviet Union promised to enter the struggle against Japan on condition that it be ceded the Japanese Kuril Islands and given back rights in Manchuria along with land on Sakhalin island lost by Russia in 1905. President Roosevelt was to seek concurrence on the Manchurian privileges from China's president Chiang. Russian entry into the Far Eastern theater of conflict would take place within three months after victory in Europe. The

89

remaining Yalta announcements all concerned arrangements postulated on victory.

Germany would have to pay reparations, the three powers said, in capital, goods, and labor. The amount would be worked out, but as an initial basis for discussion Stalin and Roosevelt proposed 20,000,000,000 dollars in capital and goods, with half to be paid to the Soviet Union. The liberated portion of Europe, on the other hand, was assured that the three powers wanted to help (and would help when they themselves found it necessary) in the reestablishment of internal peace, the relief of distressed peoples, and the formation through free elections of governments responsive to the popular will. Poland, the powers agreed at Yalta, should be ruled by a new Provisional Government of National Unity combining Poles living in Poland with Poles who had gone abroad, which in turn should hold "free and unfettered elections as soon as possible. . . ."

Yalta also moved the world a step closer to a permanent United Nations. For the projected Security Council the powers proposed that seven concurring votes be prescribed in the making of any decision, and that each permanent member retain the right to veto any item other than a matter of procedure. For the General Assembly, Churchill and Roosevelt agreed to support separate seats for two of the Soviet Union's constituent republics, the Ukraine and Belorussia. The three powers also decided to invite the other United Nations to a conference in San Francisco, California, where the new organization would be formed. March 1, 1945, was set as the deadline for a nation to declare war against the Axis in exchange for an invitation. Ecuador, Peru, Chile, Paraguay, Venezuela, Uruguay, Turkey, Egypt, Saudi Arabia, and newly independent Syria and Lebanon all declared war so that they might be included.

Invitations to participate in the United Nations organization conference went out on

March 5, China joining the Yalta three in extending them. France, because no French group had been invited to the Dumbarton Oaks talks, declined to join the sponsors. The 42 nations to whom invitations were sent included 21 who had signed the Declaration by United Nations on January 1, 1942, and another 21 who had signed since -- France, the United States-held Philippines, Ethiopia, occupied Iraq and Iran, and the others already mentioned as having declared war against the Axis. Of all the United Nations signatories, only Poland received no vote. Caught in the contention among the three Yalta powers, its new government failed to organize in time for the conference. The Ukraine and Belorussia received invitations as separate delegations after the meeting began. So did Denmark, which had not had a refugee government to sign against the Axis, and Argentina, the only one of the Latin American countries which had not tried to meet the deadline but which did declare war on the Axis March 27. There thus came to be 50 charter members of the new United Nations, or 51 including Poland, which was invited to sign. Four of them (India, the Philippines, Ukraine, and Belorussia) did not claim the status of sovereign countries.

The San Francisco conference met April 25-June 26. Everyone agreed there should be a postwar United Nations. Its purposes would be "to maintain international peace and security," "to develop friendly relations among nations," and "to achieve international co-operation in solving international problems of an economic, social, cultural, or humanitarian character, and in promoting and encouraging respect for human rights and for fundamental freedoms for all without distinction as to race, sex, language, or religion." But the means by which these ends were expected to be realized went only a few steps beyond levels already attained by the League of Nations. The new organization, like its predecessor, would be "based on the principle of sovereign equality of all its Members," and would not be authorized by its Charter "to intervene in matters which are essentially within the domestic jurisdiction of any state. . . ." Other states than the founding ones would be invited to join the gathering, once their applications for membership had been approved, with the understanding that they must be "peace-loving."

There were planned six principal organs rather than the four suggested at Dumbarton Oaks. The Economic and Social Council, though elected by the General Assembly, received separate status; to it would be entrusted the task of coordinating the work of specialized agencies to be established. A Trusteeship Council would take over the responsibilities formerly handled by the League's system of mandates. The roles of the International Court of Justice and the Secretariat were defined. The former would take the place of the Permanent Court of International Justice of the League of Nations period. The Secretariat would comprise a secretary-general and his staff.

Greater controversy arose over the makeup and functions of the proposed General Assembly and Security Council. The role of the latter seemed crucial. It was assigned "primary responsibility for the maintenance of international peace and security." United Nations members agreed "to accept and carry out the decisions of the Security Council in accordance with the present Charter." The Council might "investigate any dispute . . . which might lead to international friction. . . ." It was to "determine the existence of any threat to the peace, breach of the peace, or act of aggression," and then to make recommendations to the parties concerned; or, if these were not effective, to call upon United Nations members to apply measures short of war; or, if even those measures should prove inadequate, to "take such action by air, sea, or land forces as may be necessary. . . ."

The stronger powers had made plain their

intention to dominate the Security Council. Theirs was the chief responsibility for peace; theirs, they said, should be certain special prerogatives concerning decisions to commit strength against an aggressor. But Dumbarton Oaks and Yalta had left some major problems regarding the Security Council unresolved. One concerned the principle of big-power unanimity: How wide was the expanse of non-procedural matters to which the veto of the permanent members would apply? The five powers themselves finally announced (in San Francisco) that they would not use that privilege to prevent a problem from being discussed or a party to a dispute from being heard, but that after the discussion any vote as to whether a suggested move was procedural or non-procedural would itself remain subject to the veto. Another problem concerned the Security Council's authority: How tight a control should the Council exercise over regional defense arrangements less than world-wide in scope? The Dumbarton Oaks proposals had specified that regional groupings should take actions to enforce peace only upon the authority of the United Nations Security Council, an idea not now supported by the Dumbarton Oaks powers themselves. The new charter abandoned this requirement, pointing out instead certain instances when regional action without such authority would be justified.

The General Assembly was the only United Nations organ in which each member nation would have one vote. Here there would be no great-power dominance, but the contrary; the "Big Five," containing over half the population of 1945 in United Nations lands, would hold less than one-seventh of the General Assembly voting strength. The Assembly was authorized to discuss any matter it liked within the scope of the Charter, except that it should defer to the Security Council for action on matters within the latter's province. To ensure that the Council would not opt for non-action on such matters when the Assembly thought action was needed, the secretary-general was required, "with the consent of the Security Council," immediately to notify the General Assembly (or its members if it was not in session) when the Security Council ceased to deal with any matter regarding the maintenance of international peace and security. The Assembly would meet at least annually and control the budget.

The United Nations Charter was signed at San Francisco on June 26. Only three weeks passed before the Yalta powers whose forces had made the peacetime United Nations possible held another meeting of their chiefs of state, in Potsdam, a suburb of Berlin. Two important new personages entered the international scene at Potsdam:

(1) Harry Truman, 61 years of age, had become president of the United States when Franklin Roosevelt died April 12, 1945. His were responsibilities as serious as those of any person in the world from the day he entered office. Truman had come from southwestern Missouri, where his father farmed and traded in horses and mules. The son attended primary and secondary schools in Independence, Missouri, doing well despite difficulties with his eyes. At the time he graduated in 1901, his father had run into financial problems. Harry worked for six months as a timekeeper for railroad crews and for four years as a banking clerk in Kansas City. Then, from 1906 to 1915, he labored with his father on a farm he had known in childhood. When his father died, the farm occupied Truman's attention for two more years, after which he saw service in the United States army of World War I in France. He returned to Kansas City in 1919, getting married and settling down as part owner and salesman of a clothing store.

94

The store failed in 1922. Harry Truman turned to an army friend for a job, and thus became involved in politics. The friend was a nephew of Tom Pendergast, famed strong man of Democratic politics in the state of Missouri. Truman held his first county office under Pendergast sponsorship in 1923-5. Defeated at the polls, he worked for an automobile club, but in 1927 began an eight-year stretch as manager of his county's business. The Pendergast machine which pushed his election was notoriously corrupt; Truman, however, won a clear reputation for integrity and honesty.

In 1934, to his own surprise, Harry Truman became the Pendergast choice for United States senator from Missouri. The farm, the haberdashery, and the automobile club had given him scant training for such a position. Neither the county offices nor a desultory spare-time experience with law school seemed of much greater promise. Truman won twice and served ten years, however, showing that a good mind and hard work could surmount his lack of preparation. He supported the Roosevelt administration in everything except its prosecution of the Pendergast machine, through which he remained loyal to old friends, even when Tom Pendergast was consigned to the penitentiary. During World War II, Truman became known nationally as the head of a committee monitoring government wartime spending. Roosevelt chose him as his vice-presidential running mate in 1944 on the basis of his acceptability to both conservative and liberal wings of his party. The Democratic victory in the election made Roosevelt president for his fourth term and Truman vice-president for his first in January 1945.

The world wondered upon Roosevelt's death in April whether there would be a change in United States foreign policy. There is no reason to believe that Harry Truman desired any new direction in public affairs. Neither can there be any certainty as to what decisions Roosevelt might have made if he had continued to live. The most momentous questions immediately before Truman were whether to support the Soviet Union's claim for 10,000,000,000 dollars in reparations and whether to consider a request from Stalin for a 6,000,000,000-dollar loan. The whole thrust of United States propaganda from 1917 to 1941 had lain away from measures which might in any way assist the building of the only communist economy in the world. But Roosevelt had become the first president of the United States even to recognize the Soviet Union, and had gone far at Tehran and Yalta in an attempt to convince Stalin that Washington meant well toward his regime. His attitude on reparations and the loan might have run differently from that of the American public. Truman and the advisers Truman chose tended to lean, like the majority of their countrymen, against anything that might favor a communist country. The difficulty with this line of thought was that Truman and his advisers were in no position to hold down all of Stalin's aspirations in 1945.

(2) Clement Attlee, 62 years of age, became prime minister of the United Kingdom July 27, after a defeat of Winston Churchill's Conservative party at the polls. Unlike Truman, Attlee had actively sought his position as one of the chief architects of the postwar world. Clement Attlee came from the family of a distinguished lawyer of London. From the age of nine he attended preparatory school, then Haileybury College, and later University College at Oxford until the age of 21. Though his father was a Liberal, he counted himself as a Conservative at Oxford,

like the majority there. However, he took little interest in politics at that time, expecting to make a full career in regular practice of the law.

The year 1907 brought a distinct change in Attlee's life, when he assumed the management of a boys' club supported by his first college in the poor district of East London. There he became acquainted with the life of England's economically distressed peoples. He came to believe that the very structure of society was wrong, that the future required the most basic changes, and that socialism provided the philosophy for these alterations that simply had to come. He joined the Fabian Society, where he met the chief proponents of the British socialist movement. For seven years he accepted a miscellany of responsibilities within this movement and for the working-class people of East London. In 1912, he added a teaching position in the London School of Economics.

Clement Attlee was not a pacifist like some of his socialist friends. In World War I, he served the British army in Greece, Mesopotamia, and France. Back in East London at the old activities, he became mayor of his borough in 1919. In 1922, he took a seat in the House of Commons as a Laborite, winning the post from his district in all seven elections of the period 1922-45. His chance for higher leadership (second in command of the party) came when he survived the elections of 1931 in which Laborites generally did poorly. Four years later, Attlee moved on to the party's top position. In 1940, he joined Churchill's wartime coalition cabinet. A year later, he became deputy prime minister, serving as acting premier whenever Churchill himself was absent.

The election of July 5, 1945, was fought chiefly on British domestic issues. Both Conservatives and Laborites offered significant reform programs for the benefit of the masses. Churchill and his party, however, chose to emphasize what they called the freedom of the individual -- laissez-faire, the right of a man to choose for himself -- while Attlee and his group pounded away at the theme that what the Conservatives really meant was freedom for the rich and slavery for the poor. The Labor party won nearly 12,000,000 votes to the Conservatives' 9,000,000, and 393 of the 640 seats in the House of Commons. Attlee took Churchill's place in the middle of the conference at Potsdam. But Attlee had no more desire than Truman to make sharp changes in his nation's foreign policy. Like Churchill, Attlee believed the Russians were asking too much for reparations. Concerning loans, he had no decision before him as did Truman; before the year concluded the British government itself asked Washington for a low-interest line of credit.

Joseph Stalin met Winston Churchill, Clement Attlee, and Harry Truman at Potsdam July 17, Churchill having invited Attlee as an observer. Unlike Tehran and Yalta, the new conference assumed a two-sided aspect at once, with the Russians arguing one way, the British and Americans another. The flow of events in Poland, Romania, and Bulgaria had helped to produce this situation. The Polish Provisional Government of National Unity had finally been formed June 28, as planned at Yalta. Stanislaw Mikolajczyk, premier in London 1943-4, had joined it, as had others not formerly associated with the Lublin (later Warsaw) regime. But Stalin had driven a hard bargain, and the incoming group numbered only 5 in a 21-member cabinet. In Romania, Soviet occupation had been followed in March 1945 by the establishment of a coalition regime which excluded conservative elements. In Bulgaria as the Potsdam meeting began, a broader coalition expelled members less friendly to the Russians. In Hungary, Russian moves remained less advanced; but there and even in Czechoslovakia, wherever Soviet armies had moved in, the strong pressures toward regimes friendly to the Soviet Union were very much in evidence.

In Poland, Romania, Hungary, and Bulgaria, Stalin was only doing what Churchill had in 1944 recognized as Stalin's privilege. The British were also using force for their own purposes in Greece, with Stalin's consent, following the agreement he and Churchill had made. Yet none of the Russian actions in Poland, Romania, and Bulgaria fitted the promises that had been given by the three powers at Yalta that they would help liberated peoples form governments chosen by themselves. Actually, popularly elected governments in these three countries might turn out to be very anti-Moscow. Persons in the United States and the United Kingdom thought little of that fact, or of the Russians' feelings concerning security in the wake of wartime ravages in their land worse than any the world had ever known. Russian strong-arm action to spread communism was indeed what American and British people had been taught to expect all along, even if it had not appeared internationally until 1939. Truman, Churchill, and Attlee went to Potsdam expressing the spirit of their people, that the happenings in eastern Europe were evil. Whether for lack of conviction, or strength, or wisdom as to how to deal with the situation, however, they did not use Potsdam to counter Stalin's moves.

The conference lasted through August 2, with Churchill dropping out a week earlier and Attlee moving up from observer to British spokesman. There was a great deal of argument through its 16 days, and there were some significant decisions, but aside from questions in regard to Germany no real attempt to find a solid middle ground. Germany, the powers decided, would be occupied for the time being by armies of the Soviet Union,

99

the United States, the United Kingdom, and France. Each would have its own zone, though all were to share in the work of the Control Council which would meet in Berlin. The occupation intended to bring about "the complete disarmament and demilitarization of Germany" and would also serve "to convince the German people that they have suffered a total military defeat and . . . cannot escape responsibility for what they have brought upon themselves, . . . to destroy the National Socialist Party . . . , to dissolve all Nazi institutions, to ensure that they are not revived in any form," and "to prepare for the eventual reconstruction of German political life on a democratic basis." In carrying out these proposals, the three powers said, "so far as is practicable, there shall be uniformity of treatment of the German population throughout Germany." Specifically, in regard to all business matters, Germany was to be "treated as a single economic unit."

Nevertheless, in regard to reparations, there appeared a difference between zones. At Potsdam, Stalin had to give up his request for 10,000,000, 000 dollars. Both British and Americans now argued against a set amount, saying that Germans should be allowed to retain a European standard of living, requirements for which were difficult to foresee. Stalin agreed that reparations "should leave enough resources to enable the German people to subsist without external assistance." Russian and Polish claims, it was decided, would be met by removals of German equipment and goods from the Soviet zone of occupation, plus one-fourth of "such industrial capital equipment as is unnecessary for the German peace economy" from the three other occupation zones. All other United Nations claims would be satisfied from the American, British, and French zones. The surrendered German navy and merchant marine would be divided equally among the three powers represented at Potsdam.

For a legion of unsettled questions, the Potsdam conferees placed hope in a Council of Foreign Ministers, to include themselves with China and France, and to meet periodically in London. This Council would draw up peace treaties to submit to the United Nations, in addition to considering other matters. The world could already see, however, as the conference concluded at Potsdam, that no postwar honeymoon of good relations could be expected among the great powers that had been allies. Stalin was concerned about security and Russian economic recovery, and presumably interested as well in an East European spread of communism. Attlee felt concern about the Russian threat to an older balance of power in Europe, but took primary interest in his country's switch to socialism in the midst of worry about British economic recovery. Truman held economic power in his hand while his allies stood compassed about by ruin, but envisioned the power he held as an opportunity to assist sure friends rather than a means of influencing possible enemies. A loan to Moscow, as the Russians had proposed, to purchase goods manufactured in the United States, failed to come up for discussion at Potsdam, and from all appearances never received serious consideration by the Truman regime. Washington occupied itself instead in wrapping up the war in Europe and proceeding with the war against Japan.

When Truman and Churchill met at Potsdam, they had one important decision they chose not to share with Stalin, the Russians not being involved yet in the war in the Orient. That was whether to use against the Japanese people a new and terrible weapon which had been proved practicable just the day before. It was called the atomic bomb. Ancient peoples had spoken of "atoms" as the smallest particles into which the universe could be divided. Modern scientists had adopted the name, believing that all matter in the universe is composed of certain chemical elements or combinations of same and describing atoms as the smallest particles of these elements. Further study revealed that the postulated atoms themselves must have component parts, specifically in each case a structured nucleus surrounded by whirling electrons. The idea of indivisibility of the atom was shown to be wrong only in the twentieth century.

It had been suggested that the splitting of atomic nuclei, if it could be devised, would result in the actual transformation of matter to energy on a tremendous scale. This was accomplished in the American state of New Mexico on July 16, 1945, the rapid disintegration of a small amount of uranium in a test bomb providing power enough to destroy a small city -- or to serve more constructively in a variety of ways. Churchill and Truman agreed at Potsdam that the new device should be used against Japan, hoping thus to bring the war quickly to an end. They told Stalin about it a week later; he expressed no surprise. There seems little doubt that he already knew about the bomb, through the efforts of the Russian intelligence network, and that such knowledge contributed to the distrust he felt toward his western allies.

The atomic bomb was dropped on Hiroshima, Japan, August 6. A second fell on Nagasaki three days later. The carnage amounted to no more than that suffered by Tokyo and several other Japanese cities in June and July. But now there appeared instantaneous death for tens of thousands with the dropping of a single bomb, plus living torture for others who were burned. Not even the most determined Japanese leadership could withstand such odds, made even more ominous by the Soviet Union's invasion of Manchuria on August 9. Japan asked for peace on August 10, and five days later announced its surrender. The terms Japan signed on September 2 stipulated that it would give up conquests of the previous 50 years.

Unresolved lay the question of what forces would control the areas that the Japanese evacuated. Persons in Europe and America generally assumed that matters would revert roughly to their prewar status in the territories the Japanese had seized. Not everyone in the Orient agreed. Two nationalist leaders were particularly prepared to step in as the Japanese moved out. Their actions produced a great impact in many separated regions of the postwar world:

(1) Sukarno (Kusnasosro in his childhood), 44 years of age in 1945, was a native of eastern Java, the island which contained the capital and much of the urban sector of the Netherlands East Indies. His father participated as a schoolteacher in the Muslim culture of Java; his mother came from the Hindu-oriented island of Bali. As a young boy, Sukarno lived much with his father's parents, attending school, but particularly fascinated by the Javanese puppet-drama of ancient Indian origins. At 14, he moved to the home of a patron and entered a Dutch secondary school, where he became proficient in four European languages. At his new home he became acquainted with most of the leadership of the Indonesian nationalist movement, just beginning in those days, his patron being the chairman of the first Indonesian political party. Sukarno next attended college in Bandung, graduating in 1925 with a degree in civil engineering. In Bandung also, he married his landlady, older and wealthier than he; she remained his companion for 15 years.

As a young engineer, Sukarno helped design a new church and a new prison in Bandung. This kind of activity did not suit him, however. He turned instead to the more exciting and somewhat dangerous pastime of organizing Indonesian nationalist study clubs. In 1927, he combined many of them into an association to struggle for independence through evolutionary means; it became known as the Indonesian National party. In late 1929 Sukarno was arrested, tried on a charge of conspiracy to use force against the Dutch government of the Indies, and kept for two years in the prison he had helped to plan. Free then for a year and a half, he wrote a book describing mass action for the cause of independence, and became a very popular leader. In 1933 he was returned to his prison, this time without charges or trial; there followed exile to the island of Flores in 1934 and to Sumatra in 1938, with no more freedom of movement until the arrival of the Japanese in early 1942.

The Japanese in their occupation of the Indonesian islands decided to use the administrative services of some of the native leaders the Dutch had despised. Not all Indonesians were inclined to co-operate with the Japanese. Sukarno chose to do so, although with ulterior purposes; maintaining contact with friends who de-cided otherwise. In 1943 he became chair-man of an organization designed to rally support from Java and Madura for the Jap-anese war effort. The organization did gain strength, but aroused more interest in the Indonesian cause than in the Jap-anese. A reordering of affairs in 1944 left Sukarno the chairman of a new associ-ation under tighter control by the mili-tary authorities.

When the war was going very badly for them, in March 1945, the Japanese set up a committee to prepare for Indonesian independence. Sukarno, as a member, on June 1 made a speech that did much to unify his people. He outlined five principal points for a new nation: nationalism (one people from three thousand islands, all those ruled as part of the Netherlands Indies); internationalism (support for a family of nations, but not a homogeneous world); and in addition, representative government, social justice, and the principle of belief in one God. Sukarno's long exile had given him much time to read; he had emerged from it, like Eduard Benes from his long university career, a democratic socialist in creed. To him came the honor of proclaiming the Indonesian declaration of independence, in front of his own home in the capital of Jakarta on August 17, 1945. A day later, a provisional constitution appeared for the new regime. However, the Japanese had not yet left the islands, the Dutch expected to return, and a multitude of problems stood between Sukarno and the achievement of his objectives.

(2) Ho Chi Minh, orginally Nguyen Sinh Cung, in his teens Nguyen That Thanh, 55 years of age in 1945, was born in Annam, protectorate of French Indochina. His father held anti-French views, and although acquainted with the Chinese Confucian classics spent much of his life practicing herb medicine. The son received training from his father and in various schools, the last of which was a French <u>lycée</u> in Hue, the Annamese capital. For a short time, he taught in another lycée, organized by Vietnamese persons along French lines but without the marks of colonialism.

In 1911, Thanh left Indochina; he would not return for 30 years. First he worked on a French ship, visiting Africa and North America. He then settled in London, working as a pastry cook, only later to return to sea again. Next he chose Paris, where he supported himself by retouching photographs and joined the French Socialist party. In 1920 this organization split, its left wing becoming the Communist party of France. Nguyen That Thanh, now known as Nguyen Ai Quoc, went with the Communists for their uncompromising line on putting an end to colonialism. From this point on, his career became involved with international communist activities. Half of 1923 and most of 1924 he spent in the Soviet Union. In 1925, in Canton, China, he organized his own revolutionary movement for Vietnamese young people. After returning to Europe, Thanh showed up in Thailand in 1928, talking communism and independence to the Annamese. In Hong Kong in 1930, with his earlier effort dissolved, he organized the first Indochinese Communist party. Jailed by the British in that city for six months in 1931, he then traveled widely again for nearly a decade, studying in Russia during 1934-5 but spending most of his time in China. He often, but not always, received support from non-communist southern Chinese for his basically anti-French activities.

When the Japanese occupied French Indochina in 1940, Thanh finally returned to his home. There, in the following year, he helped to organize the Revolutionary League for the Independence of Viet-Nam, known in abbreviated form as the Viet-Minh. The Vietnamese nation as envisaged would include the former French protectorates of Tonkin and Annam and the former French colony of Cochin China. The Viet-Minh itself was a heterogeneous group, not as completely communist-oriented as Thanh and some of its other organizers. Thanh, returning to China again, now fell under arrest by Chinese who had formerly protected him, and spent 1942-3 in jail. Upon his release, he adopted the name by which he became famous, Ho Chi Minh, meaning One Who Enlightens, and put several older aliases aside.

106

After 1943, Ho and the Viet-Minh, struggling against the Japanese, maintained friendly contact with Chinese and Americans who were cooperating with Chiang. On August 19, 1945, the Viet-Minh occupied the Tonkinese capital of Ha Noi. On September 2, the day Japan surrendered, Ha Noi proclaimed the existence of the Democratic Republic of Viet-Nam. Its leader Ho Chi Minh would be faced with great problems, like Sukarno of Indonesia. The French planned to return to Indochina, and not all Vietnamese welcomed the regime that the Viet-Minh had designed. Ho, despite any change in name, was a Communist revolutionary; unlike Sukarno, he had yet to prove that his own people's nationalism constituted his first concern. Ho and Sukarno, nevertheless, had already set a pattern of independence-seeking which a great share of the colonial world would soon follow.

The stronger powers of the planet had in effect made Sukarno's and Ho's proclamations of independence possible, by defeating the Japanese. They themselves were busy after the war with a number of other objectives, and for the moment paid little attention to the new revolutionaries. Their first Council of Foreign Ministers, held September 11-October 2, 1945, resulted in an impasse as the Soviet Union raised objections to full participation by China and France on the matter of peace treaties. Only the Soviet Union, the United States, and the United Kingdom attended another meeting held in Moscow December 16-26. They laid beginning plans for treaties with Italy, Romania, Bulgaria, Hungary, Finland, and Japan. They also reached agreement on the establishment of a government in Korea, and recommended that the United Nations establish a commission for atomic energy control. By the time of the Moscow meeting, the postwar United Nations had become a reality, its charter coming into effect on October 24, 1945; the first meeting of its General Assembly was scheduled for January 10, 1946. In this body, eventually, the interests of the large powers and the small, the older states and the newer ones, were all to meet together, producing a most unprecedented tangle of surprises.

With the second great global conflict terminated, a new world did seem to be dawning. It was not, even in its earliest years, a world of peace, though the United Nations alliance had become a peacetime enterprise. Neither was it a world of freedom from fear and want, a goal of the Atlantic Charter. It was, rather, a world of new sources of power and of change more rapid than man had known before. The scientific development of energy made many material projects seem feasible for the first time, including even the prospect that man might leave his own planet and embark upon new quests in space. Even more immediately, however, there appeared a great postwar shaking up of people's minds by the ideas inherent in democracy and socialism. Most individuals, it is true, sensed no dawning of a new world, and intended to cling to their respective old worlds just as long as possible. Others knew that human society could never be the same after its nightmare of fascism, and stood ready to welcome a new and radically different order. But even those who wanted change often felt shocked or dismayed by the rapidity of it all, and by the very unpredictability of the newly released scientific and ideological forces.

Many -- not all -- of the postwar changes were tied directly to politics. Even before the end of the year 1945, the global spectrum had altered considerably. Five eastern European nations had moved from fascism to communism. Poland, Romania, and Bulgaria, though in each case only provisionally, had governments so much more approved by Moscow than by Washington or London that everyone expected them to become completely communist-dominated. Yugoslavia became a republic in November, completely under Tito's control and isolated from the possibility of return of the former king Peter. Albania, though a few months behind on its timetable, was likewise set to reject its monarchy and follow its own communist regime. Meanwhile, in eastern Asia, Mongolia declared its independence as a communist republic in 1945 (its territory that of the old and very Buddhist Outer Mongolia belonging to China but under Russian influence since the early 1920's); while the protectorate of Tannu Tuva became fully incorporated into the Soviet Union. Elections for a constituent assembly in France had furthermore revealed increased communist strength there, the Communist party winning more seats than any other, nearly one-fourth of the total.

The democratic socialist quarter of the spectrum also grew during the period 1941-45. The most important nation-state added here was the United Kingdom. Even in the year 1945, in their first few months in power, Clement Attlee and the Laborites showed that an identity with Washington on economic recovery and foreign policy did not entail a similarity of views on domestic matters. Measures introduced to indicate the new orientation included a bill to nationalize the Bank of England, a bill to establish government ownership of the coal mines, and a national insurance act to create new forms of social security.

The Labor party of Australia won victory there in 1943, two years earlier than its British counterpart. Austria, occupied like Germany by four powers, held elections nevertheless, choosing almost evenly between the Catholic People's party and the Socialists, but moving by mutual consent to the nationalization of property to keep it out of the hands of the Russians. Finland in 1945 kept its face turned in the same direction when well over half of the seats in its parliament were won by an alliance of democratic socialists and Finnish communists, all of them committed to abide by democratic procedures. The tiny republic of San Marino turned to democratic socialism when precisely the same electoral event occurred there. In the constituent assembly of 1945 in France, the Socialist party ranked third of three with major influence.

The most remarkable events in the democratic private-enterprise quarter were the re-entries into this band of Brazil and France, both in 1945. In Brazil, Getúlio Vargas announced the approaching end of his dictatorship in March, with elections to be held in December. He did not intend to participate, he said. Doubts arose, however, as the months passed by and voices were raised in Vargas' behalf. A revolution in October removed him from the presidency, to which Eurico Gaspar Dutra, Social Democrat, won election in his stead. Brazil's Social Democratic party, however, had no connection with socialism like others of its name; a tenant of the third quarter instead, it only dimly deserved to be called liberal.

The French postwar government emerged through the leadership of those who had left French home soil to fight the Axis. Charles de Gaulle, their leader, established his Committee of National Liberation in Algeria, June 1943. After changing its own status a year later to that of a provisional government, the group moved to Paris in September 1944, incorporating stay-at-home fighters against the Axis across the political spectrum. The elections for a constituent assembly sponsored by this government in October 1945, providing proportional representation for parties, brought little comfort to president de Gaulle, whose thinking remained that of a conservative. Besides the Communist and Socialist strength already mentioned, the second largest bank of seats went to the Popular Republican Movement, a new group, Catholic and moderately liberal in its sentiments.

Five nations besides Brazil and France may be said to have joined and one rejoined the third quarter of the spectrum during the war years, while a small member of this band changed its governmental form. Chief among these was Iran, whose pro-United Nations monarch Mohammad Reza Pahlavi worked toward changing his country's parliament from a farce into a reality after his accession in 1941. Hungary, though occupied by Russian armies, held free elections in 1945 which gave the victory to a liberal-conservative Smallholders (peasants) party. In Latin America, Guatemala ousted its dictatorship in 1944 with the objective of establishing democracy in government and more justice in society. Panama, whose constitutional government had been overthrown in the pro-Washington coup of 1941, held new elections in 1945. In the Middle East, Syria and Lebanon were recognized by the French forces as full-fledged republics in 1944, though French troops still occupied portions of their territory. Muslims predominated in the Syrian population, while that of Lebanon divided half and half between Christians and Muslims; each of the two new nations had its own Arabic dialect. Faraway Iceland, which already occupied a place in the third quarter, dropped its allegiance to the Danish king and became a republic in 1944.

The fascist quarter of the spectrum suffered heavily in 1945. Of its continuing large adherents, only Kuo Min Tang China stood on the winning side in the war, and even there victory was abridged by the powerful hold on the countryside maintained by the Communists. Chiang's regime faced great problems, including the disposition of Manchuria and Tai Wan, returned (after 14 and 50 years respectively) by the Japanese. Japan lay prostrate, its cities now occupied by United States forces completely in command. Germany remained divided among Soviet, American, British, and French armies of occupation, with its eastern portion cut off and granted unofficially to Poland. The previous capital Berlin, though itself shared by the four powers, lay no more at Germany's center, but buried deep in the eastern (Russian) zone. Italy found itself in somewhat better circumstances, due to late Italian cooperation in the wars against Germany and Japan. A pro-United Nations Italian provisional government ruled (Pietro Badoglio, premier 1943-4; Ivanoe Bonomi, 1944-5), but Italian national reorganization lay in the future.

Other nations large and small remained within the fourth quarter through the end of 1945. Only one, however, moved to that band during the war years. This was Argentina, where a military coup in 1943 led to the abolition of all political parties. The generals who ran the new state made no secret of their Axis sympathies. As the war ended, Spain outside and Argentina inside the United Nations stood almost alone as verbal defenders of fascism in a world where even the authoritarian rulers liked to pose on the democratic side.

Democracy, after all, was a principal theme of the new United Nations. Democracy in its broadest sense (the provision of equal opportunity for all people) provided the objective when the Food and Agriculture Organization of the United Nations began its existence in October 1945 and the United Nations Educational, Scientific and Cultural Organization (UNESCO) wrote its constitution in November. The former hoped to raise standards of nutrition and farming in a world not realizing the most from its physical resources. The latter planned to further justice and freedom through avenues of the mind and spirit. Three other, more specialized, agencies completed postwar plans by the end of 1945 -- the International Bank for Reconstruction and Development and the International Monetary Fund designed in Bretton Woods the previous year, and the International Labor Organization, continued from the pre-World War II period with a new tie to the United Nations. On a less-than-global basis, but also with democratic principles (among nations) in mind, eight Middle Eastern entities (Egypt, Saudi Arabia, Iraq, Syria, Yemen, Lebanon, Palestine, and Transjordan) founded a League of Arab States in 1945; and the countries

112

of the Americas (less Canada) decided to form a more effective regional organization for their hemisphere than the loose Pan American Union.

The stage was being set for highly significant levels of international cooperation. The question remained whether the nations, as they moved into their new world of change, would make great use of the new institutions they had established -- or would prefer to resort to the age-old tactics of unilateral pressures, intimidation, and violence.

V. A COLD WAR BEGINS --

1946-1950

The violence of the second great world conflict had taken many lives. The number of deaths in battle alone surpassed the level of 15,000,000. Chinese people made up over a million of these, Japanese individuals another million, and Germans more than three times that number. The two groups that suffered by far the most, however, were inhabitants of the Soviet Union and an aggregate of central European Jews. Six million Jews perished, not in battle but in a grim program for their extermination conceived by the Nazis. Six million Soviet citizens died in battle, and other millions behind the Soviet lines. Jewish and Russian wartime suffering produced strong reverberations in the pattern of world activities during the next five years.

Far more people remained living, however, than had died. Their total number lay at approximately 2,500,000,000. More than 500,000,000 of them in British India, the Netherlands Indies, and other Asian regions would win political freedom in the next five years. A similar number would undergo just as drastic a change with the transformation of mainland China from extreme right to extreme left authoritarianism. Two hundred million people who had supported the Axis would also experience sharp changes in regime, with the great majority of them moving or being moved from fascism to democratic private enterprise. And nearly 2,000,000,000 who had stood against the Axis were going to help decide just how much use they would make of their new United Nations. In the realm of world politics from 1946 to 1950, these were the most significant happenings, along with two more that carried very large shares of attention -- the creation of the state of Israel to relieve the oppression of the Jews, and the commencement of a new world struggle when Russians remembered better than most other people the Soviet distress of the wartime years.

Asian Independence

Freedom for British India and the Netherlands Indies came accompanied by the institution of self-government for Korea, the Philippines, Burma, and Ceylon. Altogether, this six-part to eight-part political liberation affected nearly one-fourth of human kind. Four out of five of the persons involved, however, lived in British India. It was one of the wonders of the world that such a large assemblage of people should be controlled by a kingdom of less than one-eighth their number, existing so far away. But the British had come only in modern times, during the period of extensive European expansion, and had not mastered virtually all of India for long.

The old India, before it became independent and partitioned, filled an entire subcontinent impressive in size, and separated by high mountains from its neighbors. It was large enough and isolated enough that at least one major racial group had evolved there. In the last four thousand years, the mingling of Caucasoids from Iran with people who already lived in India had produced the heterogeneous Indo-Dravidian race of today. People of differing physical appearance gradually fell into separate castes, or strata of society, tied in greater and greater degree to specific vocations. Religious literature supplied a divine origin for the system, but the fact remained that the lighter-skinned invaders occupied most of the room in the higher castes while the darker-skinned conquered people

116

provided most of the millions in the lower castes. As time went by, caste rules became very strict, to the point that a son had to follow his father's occupation, and marriage between the castes was forbidden. The harsh application of caste regulations penetrated Hinduism, but was not accepted by Buddhists and Jains. Buddhism did not survive in this land of its birth, however, and Jainism encompassed only a small percentage of the people.

From the northeastern district of Magadha, just two centuries after Siddhartha Gautama had lived there, armies went forth to establish a great Indian empire. All the northern and central parts of the subcontinent fell into their hands, except for primitive pockets of Munda-speaking peoples, who also lived in the northeast. The Buddhist builders of this empire, and of a lesser one over half a millenium later, are remembered through the Magadhi language still spoken in their home district.

As Buddhism slowly faded in India, a thousand years ago, the much younger faith of Islam sought to make its entry. Four kingdoms of that time left impressions for India's linguistic map, important for an understanding of recent Indian history. The Sindhi speech of today is the remnant of the old province of Sind of the northwest, taken and held by the Muslims centuries before any other Indian territory. Marathi and Rajasthani language districts of today represent the two Hindu monarchies which long held the Muslims at bay. Strongest of all of the kingdoms of that time, however, was one in far southern India, at first Buddhist but later Hindu in religion, whose district now uses the Tamil tongue.

In the very late twelfth century, Muslim armies broke through the resistance, conquering great stretches of northern and central India. Within two hundred years, three great nuclei of Muslim power developed -- a centrally-located

117

government at Delhi; a second state on the west coast, where Gujarati is spoken today; and a third in the important northeastern region where the language is now Bengali. Great masses of the Bengali people subscribed to Islam, while conversions elsewhere were neither numerous nor durable. Oriya-speaking people in the northeast held out against the Muslims, retaining their own Hindu regime. A greater bulwark of Hinduism lay in the southern regions, where persons of the present-day Telugu-speaking area managed a small but strong domain.

A new Muslim empire founded at Delhi in 1526 spread over much of India during the next two centuries. Its rise, and the parallel diffusion of one speech pattern, explains the fact that today about half the people of the subcontinent understand some form of either Hindi or Urdu. Other regimes remained active around the margins of this empire. Devotees of the new Sikh religion provided the chief opposition to Delhi for some time, seizing the reins of power among the people who spoke Punjabi. A separate Muslim government ruled the Kannada-speaking state of Mysore in the south. Travancore, at the very southern tip of India, remained under a Hindu family; its language was Malayalam.

Beginning in 1498, Europeans poured themselves and their ideas into this linguistic and religious mélange. The Portuguese came first, seeking commerce; acquiring coastal towns, they also introduced their Roman Catholic religion. The English and French who followed (in early and late seventeenth century, respectively) had farther-reaching ambitions in mind. Their interests clashed, however, and were eventually settled by warfare. In the 1750's and 1760's, the very time that the Muslim government at Delhi suffered near-mortal blows from its enemies on every side, the British defeated the French in India. The French had from this time forward to content themselves with some seaports, while the British took full advantage of the situation caused by the weakening of Delhi.

The British conquest of India took about one hundred years. A great part of the subcontinent came under direct British control. Borders were even extended, through the inclusion of Pashto-speaking people in the northwest and the Assamese in the northeast, the territory of the latter including people related linguistically to the Khmers of Cambodia. The Andaman Islands, partially inhabited by the Andamanese Negritos, were added as a penal colony. A lesser portion of India (45% of the land, but short of one-fourth of the population) remained nominally in the hands of separate Indian governments; in 1945, there remained 562 of them. The British handled the business of these states to whatever degree pleased the British. Most of them constituted new creations from the dust of the Delhi empire; their boundaries seldom followed linguistic lines.

Hyderabad, the most populated of the nominal Indian states, included persons speaking the Telugu, Marathi, and Kannada tongues, though covering only a portion of each of the three. A Muslim family ruled its largely Hindu population. Mysore constituted only a remnant of its former self, occupying part of the Kannada area; a Hindu dynasty ruled in Mysore. Travancore was its old, Malayalam-speaking entity, having survived intact by courting Britain's friendship as an ally. One-fourth of the population of Travancore became Christian. Jammu-Kashmir was a northern kingdom, long separate, which the British brought into India. Though ruled by a Hindu, its Kashmiri and other population maintained a loyalty to Islam. Gwalior constituted a part of the Hindi area. Jaipur and Jodhpur together occupied much of the Rajasthani-speaking district. Baroda lay in the region of Gujarati speech; other states also existed there. Gwalior, Jaipur, Baroda, and Jodhpur, all basically Hindu states, also followed the rule of Hindu people.

Central and northern India made a last great effort to dislodge the British in the years 1857-8. The effort failed, but led to a new conception of the subcontinent in the popular mind. Before, when the greater empires had arisen, they were secured by the dominance of one people over others. Now, a new image appeared of a great people united. The British themselves did much to encourage the new concept, both intentionally (by building railroads, for example) and unintentionally, making of themselves an adversary -- a temporary foe, to be sure, but one that all the Indians came to hold in common.

The organization of a British school system in India helped to introduce democratic precepts. Nevertheless, Indian men who graduated from the British schools had no opportunity to participate in a democratic government. In 1885 a number of them formed the All-India National Congress, an association providing a platform for criticism though it had no connection with government. The Muslim League, a society with similar purpose, was founded in 1906, the Muslim minority believing that separation would better protect their own interests. Both the Congress and the League argued vehemently that the Indian people stood ready and capable to handle their own national life. In the twentieth century, the British made concession after concession to that point of view, until finally British rule terminated.

First came the decision in 1909 to allow elected Indians to serve on provincial councils in areas ruled directly by Britain. Next, in 1919, the provincial councils were given complete control over certain internal affairs, and a new Indian parliament was created. The latter had very limited influence, but the British announced it as a step toward complete self-government. Some Indian leaders cooperated with the new order, while others in both Congress and League refused to do so. Those opposed to collaboration followed Mohandas Karamchand Gandhi, who began in 1920 to organize large campaigns displaying defiance to the British without a resort to violence. The British jailed Gandhi in 1922-4, 1930-1, and 1933. Each time his popularity increased with great masses of uneducated Indians, who became ready to die for the cause of independence if necessary. They called Gandhi Mahatma, or "Man of Great Soul."

In 1935, under this new pressure, the British stepped up their program to restructure the Indian government. They planned the federation mentioned in Chapter II to include protected states along with provinces. The provinces would be reorganized under the new regime and granted much autonomy. Reluctance on the part of the Indian princes prevented the federation from functioning successfully before 1939. Other British reforms did become realities. But Indian public opinion had moved well beyond interest in halfway measures. The All-India Congress would no longer accept any kind of self-government under the British flag. Further complicating matters in 1940, the Muslim League announced that its leadership would consent to nothing less than a separate Muslim state, to be called Pakistan.

During World War II, India officially joined the United Nations. The proclamation of war with the Axis, however, was sounded only by the British viceroy, and the Indians refused to engage in enthusiastic war effort. When the Japanese took Burma in early 1942, a special British mission sought to win Indian cooperation against the new threat by offering India dominion status upon the conclusion of the conflict. An Indian constituent assembly at the end of the war would not only select its own democratic practices, but might even sever ties with the United Kingdom if the Indian people so preferred. Individual provinces would also be free to secede from India upon their own decision. These British wartime concessions went very far; yet neither they nor the presumed Japanese threat made a strong impression. Subhas Chandra Bose, a one-time supporter of Gandhi, actually joined the Japanese. Gandhi and the leaders of the National Congress, refusing to cooperate with the British unless they simply abandoned India, inaugurated fresh campaigns of non-violent resistance. They were then arrested and detained, Gandhi for two years (1942-4) and many others for three years until the war was finished.

One of the men imprisoned was Jawaharlal Nehru. He had gone through the experience several times before. Born in the Hindi-speaking area in 1889, his aristocratic and very British childhood had not portended such a career. His father, a wealthy lawyer, had the boy tutored in English at home. Jawaharlal then went to England for seven years of preparatory school, college, and further study toward a career in law. Not long after he returned to India in 1912, he attended a session of the All-India National Congress. He became attracted to the cause of Gandhi in 1913 (when the latter was practicing non-violent resistance in South Africa), and slowly over the next seven years gave up his life of ease. His father also joined Gandhi's cause.

The Nehrus, father and son, were two among 30,000 persons sent to jail for agitation in India in 1921. Released after three months, the son immediately engaged in some picketing, and went to prison again for nearly a year. In 1923 he became mayor of his native city, Allahabad; the following year he received appointment as secretary of the All-India National Congress. In his position with the Congress, Nehru found himself occasionally at odds with Mohandas Gandhi. Gandhi had certain old-fashioned ideas, such as his preference for rustic over modern industry. Nehru fretted at what he regarded as the older Gandhi's impracticality. Through 1925, however, Jawaharlal Nehru had not developed a full-blown philosophy of his own.

Another trip abroad, lasting nearly two years, changed Nehru from a follower to a leader. His wife's poor health prompted the voyage early in 1926. The chief sojourn was in Switzerland, but Nehru by himself did some traveling, and spent a few days with his father in Moscow. His experience there and in other European capitals developed his interest in socialism. The Marxist theory of history appealed to him, and like Ho Chi Minh he felt impressed by the anti-imperialist strain of the Third International, not as evident in the Second. Nehru did not like all that had happened in Russia, and he remained devoted to the principles of democracy. Capitalism seemed to him, however, to embody criminal deeds, with one class permanently oppressing another, whereas communism he believed made only temporary use of criminal deeds, for momentary advantage. As he returned to India late in 1927, Nehru held relatively congealed views concerning the varieties of socialism. Gandhi took little interest in these matters.

Nehru now became a full-time activist, participating in trade union and youth league excitement, and getting beaten by policemen in the street. He served as president of the Congress in 1929, but was jailed twice in 1930 for a new period of 10 months in prison. Between his father's death early in 1931 and that of his wife five years later, he was held twice again -- for 20 months in 1932-3 and 19 in 1934-5. As president of the Congress in 1936, he disagreed with those Indians who favored cooperation with the British plan of the preceding year. In 1938, he traveled to Europe, visiting and sympathizing with the republican forces in the civil war in Spain. In late 1939, he argued before the All-India National Congress that the United Kingdom should show it was fighting for democracy by ending an undemocratic occupation of India.

Like so many others who took his uncompromising stand, Jawaharlal Nehru spent most of the war years in prison -- 13 months in 1940-1, and 34 more in 1942-5. He and his friends might have emerged embittered from so much political detention. But the world into which they finally stepped free was very different from the one they had known. The new Labor government in London favored complete self-government for India, as soon as it could be arranged. Now the leaders who had been held in prison so long faced large and immediate responsibilities, for the Indian leadership itself would have to deal with the princely states and the Muslim demand for a separate homeland. Unrest grew throughout the subcontinent as even humble people came to realize these questions would not wait long to be resolved.

A British mission in 1946 tried to persuade Indian leaders to work together to form initial plans. Failing in this objective, it recommended an Indian union to handle foreign, defense, and communications affairs, leaving other business to the states and provinces. The latter would be free, as suited their lesser purposes, to make associations among themselves; but there was no provision for a completely separate Pakistan. This suggested plan had its appeal, but became lost in bad feeling between the National Congress and the Muslim League. At first the Congress rejected the idea while the League accepted it. Later, the Congress decided to accept, but the League changed its mind also.

124

The British proceeded nevertheless with the appointment of a new interim government which included top members of both Congress and League. Nehru became minister of external affairs; Liaquat Ali Khan, secretary of the Muslim League, minister of finance. Nehru and Mohammed Ali Jinnah, president of the League, went to London in December for talks, but again no agreement appeared. The Muslims refused to participate in a constituent assembly in session at the end of the year.

British initiative forced the issues in 1947. Prime minister Attlee introduced a bill calling for two new dominions under the British crown. One would be India, governed from New Delhi; the other Pakistan, governed from Karachi in Sind. The large provinces of Bengal and the Punjab would be divided, the eastern part of the first and the western part of the second to constitute two areas of Pakistan seven hundred miles apart. The states ruled by princes were to be free to join either India or Pakistan or to remain independent. India and Pakistan thus began their separate history as dominions on August 15, 1947. While a Britisher served as first governor-general (representative of the British crown) in India, the first such official in Pakistan was Mohammed Ali Jinnah himself. No final bloodshed occurred between the British and the people of this subcontinent. Popular unrest nevertheless produced a great wave of violence as the transition took place, especially in the Punjab. There millions of Muslims moved from Indian territory to that of Pakistan while millions of Hindus and Sikhs migrated conversely. It took the best efforts of both Gandhi and Jinnah to calm the strong antagonistic sentiments.

Almost all of the states ruled by princes elected to become part of India; a few joined Pakistan, and three attempted for the time being to maintain positions of their own. In most cases, religion acted as the simple determining factor. Of the larger states, Jodhpur and Jaipur, situated the closest to Pakistan in the northwest, remained heavily Hindu in faith and subject to Hindu rulers. Both became part of a new Indian state of Rajasthan, matching the Rajasthani language area, to be ruled by the maharaja of Jaipur. The maharaja of Gwalior became the ruler of a larger state called Madhya Bharat (Middle India) while Baroda was incorporated with the still larger state of Bombay. Mysore and Travancore joined the Indian union as states, with the previous maharaja becoming the new governor of each. Vallabhbhai Jhaverbhai Patel, a powerful and relatively conservative figure in the Congress, arranged most of these rather large but smooth transfers of power. In centrally-located Hyderabad and far-northern Jammu-Kashmir, however, greater difficulties arose.

Most of the people of Hyderabad were Hindus. The ruler, called the nizam, pertained to a Muslim family that had governed for over two centuries. In 1947, the nizam announced Hyderabad would remain independent, though it quickly became clear that his territory would be completely surrounded by the new nation of India. An attempt was made to solve this problem peacefully, but talks between India and the nizam failed. In August 1948, Hyderabad complained to the United Nations Security Council of pressure from India to give up its independence. A month later, Indian troops invaded Hyderabad and incorporated it as an Indian state, with the nizam to serve as the first governor. The much smaller state of Junagadh, near Baroda, shared the situation and experience of Hyderabad, except that Junagadh lost its identity immediately upon incorporation in the union.

Jammu-Kashmir, with the largest area of the princely states, presented an even more difficult problem. This state held borders with Pakistan as well as India. Three-fourths of its people were Muslims, though a Hindu maharaja served as ruler. In August 1947 the maharaja made no move toward either India or Pakistan. In

126

October, however, when Pashto-speaking Pathan tribesmen from West Pakistan invaded Kashmir, the maharaja asked for help from India, and announced that Kashmir would join the Indian union.

As the leaders of India perceived matters, a Muslim majority in one large state could live as happily in their country as other Indian citizens, many of whom practiced the Islamic faith. India had not been founded along religious lines, although the great majority of its people were Hindus. Many Muslim people of Kashmir, on the other hand, saw matters in a different light. Their democratic vote, if they could have experienced one, would almost certainly have placed them with Pakistan. The feelings of these Kashmiri, in opposition to their own ruler, encouraged intervention in their behalf by the Pathans; and later (once Indian forces moved in) the Pakistani army as well. Fighting took place through the remainder of 1947-8, with bitter feeling on both sides. The United Nations Security Council finally managed to secure a cease-fire in January 1949. It recommended that a plebiscite be held to let the people decide their future, but India accepted the proposal only on the understanding that Pakistani troops would withdraw while Indian troops remained until the vote was taken. The Pakistanis did not agree on this point, of course, and the Kashmir affair continued unsettled, a persisting obstacle to friendship between two new countries.

Jawaharlal Nehru, prime minister of India from its beginning, was the man responsible for the use of force in Hyderabad and Kashmir. In the former instance, he countered the stand of one ruler; in the latter, he thwarted the sentiments of a people. Nehru, far from being a militarist, had long followed the teaching of Gandhi that non-violent resistance provided the best avenue to success, even in the most important problems. Like most men of his time, however, Nehru remained a nationalist, quite able to persuade himself that India behaved morally in

127

actions which he might have questioned had they proceeded from other governments.

Mohandas Gandhi died in January 1948 at the hands of an assassin. With independence assured, he had turned his attention to a campaign on behalf of Hindu "untouchables," the very lowliest group segregated by the caste system. Gandhi's teachings had exercised a tremendous influence on thought in his own and other countries. (See the further discussion in "Religion.") Persons like Nehru, who had sat at Gandhi's feet but wanted to move India more rapidly into the modern world than Gandhi ever would have, were the individuals who would build this new nation now that Gandhi had departed.

Nehru and his Congress party believed in a united India, and came as close as they could to that goal. Esteeming political democracy, they wrote for themselves (in a constituent assembly, 1946-9) a constitution for a democratic republic modeled on the British parliamentary pattern. They believed in social democracy as well, placing in the new document prohibitions on the practice of untouchability and on unequal treatment for persons on the basis of caste, sex, race, or religion. They also expressed hope for a rapidly developing India, a concept that had not excited Gandhi, though not all the leadership stood as convinced as Nehru that government intervention was essential to the development process. (Patel, the best known of the figures of the Congress who preferred the initiative of private enterprise, died in 1950.) Everyone agreed there was much to be done, since despite the richness of the land high proportions of the population remained illiterate and poverty-stricken. The tasks facing the new government might indeed best have been described as staggering.

The British had bequeathed the Indians their independent government, despite the long contention between the two peoples. The British by their own will accelerated the planning for freedom in 1947. They also brought democratic ideas to Indian and Pakistani minds, and contributed a wealth of constitutional niceties. An odd additional heritage was the English language, understood among educated people from Kashmir to Travancore. The government in New Delhi, having no other language to bind the states together, adopted English as a temporary Indian tongue. It could more readily put aside other reminders of British tutelage. In mid-1948, an Indian took the place of a Britisher as India's governor-general; and in January 1950 the new republic of India came into being, with no governor-general at all. On its own decision, however, India remained a member of the Commonwealth (formerly British Commonwealth) of Nations, containing the United Kingdom and all its autonomous dominions. Thus India, the second most populated state in the world (with about 345,000,000 inhabitants in 1947, including those of Hyderabad and Jammu-Kashmir) became launched through its own efforts and those of a faraway land on a separate but friendly way.

Pakistan, unlike India, remained for the time being a dominion. The Pakistani people (approximately 78,000,000 of them) were saddened at the outset of independence when their own Mohammed Ali Jinnah lived less than a month after becoming the first governor-general. Jinnah held the respect of the Muslim masses in the same way that Gandhi commanded that of the people of India. The smaller of the two nations would have profited from Jinnah's steadying hand. Liaquat Ali Khan continued as prime minister, however, to provide some tie between past struggles and those that lay ahead. Pakistan, the fifth most populated country in the world, prided itself on not being subject to India's caste problems in society. India's other great enigmas (language, illiteracy, poverty) belonged to Pakistan also, while the geographical disconnection between East and West Pakistan, with more people living in the East and the capital situated in the West, left the way open for difficulties unknown by any other country.

Indonesia, or the Netherlands Indies, had almost the same number of people as Pakistan (Indonesia about 75,000,000 in 1949). Only the four largest nations in the world -- China, India, the Soviet Union, and the United States -- greatly outnumbered either one of them. Approximately two-thirds of the Indonesians lived on the island of Java, though about three thousand islands stood at their disposal altogether. The Indonesians formed part of the Malayo-Indonesian racial group, created when large numbers of Mongoloids moved into this part of the world with other peoples already there. This process, though still continuing, constitutes but a minor factor in recent Indonesian politics. Other changes of the last two millenia, however, have left a strong impression.

Persons from India came to these islands two thousand years ago. Their first interest was trade, but after some time they also began to establish kingdoms. Sumatra and Java came under their dominion, as well as neighboring islands. Dynasties arose and fell for more than a thousand years; the stronger of them built grand Hindu and Buddhist structures. The greatest of the Hindu kingdoms had its base in eastern Java in the fourteenth and fifteenth centuries. It included the region of today's Madurese language along with the island of Madura. In western Java at the same time a lesser kingdom of Sunda flourished, leaving the Sundanese language as its heritage.

Trade was always important to the islanders. Most of the international commerce of the fifteenth century fell into the hands of Malays. Their language became widely spoken in port towns of Sumatra, Java, and Borneo, and the officially recognized Indonesian speech of today. The Muslim faith of Malaya became popular

130

also, spreading widely over the archipelago. In the sixteenth and seventeenth centuries, with Europeans already in the vicinity, Muslim monarchies gained the ascendancy in the greater part of the main islands. One of them continued the Sundanese predominance in western Java. The strongest, however, had its seat in central Java where the vigorous Javanese language is spoken today. A few Hindu princes held out for a very long time past this period; the smaller island of Bali remains Hindu-oriented to this day.

The Portuguese appeared on the Indonesian scene in 1512. Their interests were chiefly commercial, centering on the Moluccas or Spice Islands, far east of Bali and Java. The Dutch and the English followed them nearly a century later, and the Dutch founded Batavia on Java in 1619. The Dutch early defeated the British, who evacuated the region. The Portuguese also soon lost all their holdings except a portion of the island of Timor. Then the Dutch turned to subdue the native states one by one, a process not ended until the early twentieth century. The powerful western and central Javanese states were humbled in the eighteenth century, however, with the Dutch-controlled principalities of Surakarta and Jogjakarta set up in the central Javanese district in their stead.

The Dutch were the first to unify all of present-day Indonesia. While their wars continued, they gave little indication that they would allow Indonesians even to assist in the management of their homeland. In 1918, however, a new advisory council included some elected East Indies members. Four years later, this body became a legislature with veto power over new laws. In 1929, persons from the Indies fell heir to over half the seats of this legislature. However, such measures did not satisfy the yearnings of educated Indonesian people for a nation much more completely their own. Men such as Sukarno, who wanted independence, continually found themselves in trouble with the

Dutch. Sukarno's nine years of peacetime confinement (1933-42) typified the treatment these men experienced until the Japanese conquest of their islands. It is no wonder that some of them cooperated with Japanese leaders once they became personally liberated. (See Chapter IV for the life of Sukarno.)

In late 1942, the refugee Dutch queen spoke from London of a postwar union of all peoples in the prewar Dutch empire, under the Dutch monarch as their sovereign. However, the 75,000,000 people of Indonesia compared to 10,000,000 in the Netherlands itself, and less than 500,000 involved in this proposal elsewhere. Sukarno and his closest collaborators, as they declared independence for a new republic of Indonesia while the Japanese still held the area (August 17, 1945), did not intend to join in a Dutch union unless circumstances made that necessary.

British troops, more available than the Dutch army, were designated by the United Nations command to receive the surrender of the Japanese in these islands. The British held instructions to recognize only the Dutch claim to sovereignty. They occupied most of Indonesia except Java and Sumatra, and also gained several of the cities on these two islands, including the Dutch capital of Batavia or Jakarta. The infant Indonesian republic moved its headquarters from Jakarta to Jogjakarta, the capital of one of the two native principalities formerly under Dutch rule. Sukarno stood aside, however, as more moderate Indonesian leaders talked with the Dutch about a possible compromise.

The year 1946 remained one of probing by all sides. Leaders in both the Netherlands and the Indies disagreed as to the best path for the future. A great deal of violence transpired as Dutch forces moved in to replace the British. The Dutch outside of Java, Sumatra, and Madura began to organize their own United States of Indonesia, designed to fit into the union sug-

132

gested by the queen. They nevertheless stood willing to talk with republican leaders of Jogjakarta, who besides boasting much support in Java held a number of Dutch prisoners originally taken by the Japanese. In November, the two parties in Java agreed to a cease-fire and compromise incorporated in a statement drawn up in Linggadjati. By this pact, the Indonesian republic would control Java, Sumatra, and Madura; the republic would be joined with Dutch Borneo and the islands to the east in a greater United States of Indonesia; and the whole would be combined with the Netherlands and the remainder of its empire in a two-way (Netherlands-Indonesia) union. For a very short time, it appeared that the matter had been completely solved.

For a few years more, however, a large segment of the Dutch leadership remained unwilling to approve such an agreement. These men could not accept the idea that about two-thirds of the Indonesian people would soon be released from Dutch control. In the months that followed the meeting at Linggadjati, the Dutch sponsored friendly native state governments not only in Borneo and the eastern islands, but also in disaffected parts of Java, Sumatra, and Madura. In July-August 1947, after renewed quarrels, the Dutch army attacked the republican forces again, this time obliging them to retreat considerably. India and Australia took this disturbing turn of events to the United Nations Security Council. This body appointed a Committee of Good Offices, composed of Belgium, Australia, and the United States, which managed, aboard the United States ship Renville, to get a truce signed in January 1948. The chief new element in this agreement was that the people of Java, Sumatra, and Madura would decide by plebiscites whether they preferred the republic or Dutch-sponsored states in those islands. The Dutch meanwhile continued in control of the districts they had seized.

The plebiscites were not held. The Dutch

133

argued that even the area controlled by the republican army should vote; the Jogjakarta regime felt otherwise. The Netherlands government proceeded with its plans for a United States of Indonesia, but talks with the republican leadership broke down completely. On December 18, 1948, the Dutch-sponsored United States of Indonesia came formally into being, and on the same day the Dutch launched a new military offensive against the Jogjakarta republic. Sukarno and other leaders were captured the following day; their republic seemed to have terminated.

But those who had planned the most recent series of Dutch moves had not reckoned with the strength of Indonesian and world opinion. The December offensive produced a strong reaction in several critical places. Leaders in other Indonesian states who had cooperated with the Dutch resigned in protest over the new happenings. Seventeen Asian and two African nations held a conference in New Delhi to express disapproval of the action. The Security Council called for a Dutch back-down, for renewed talks with republicans, and for a new United States of Indonesia constituted by elections rather than by the Netherlands government. By February 1949, under the pressure of such opinion, the Dutch policies began to change.

The republican leaders were freed; from June, their republic functioned again. In August-November, representatives of the Netherlands, the Jogjakarta republic, and the Indonesian remainder met at the Dutch capital of the Hague. Sharp differences quickly surfaced, but this time there existed a desire to surmount them. The conferees agreed finally, as Sukarno had wanted all along, that the new Indonesia (all of it) would form a republic organized by its own people; that it would be accorded full sovereignty rather than having its hands tied; and that the changeover from Dutch rule would transpire before the end of the year.

134

In exchange, the Indonesians agreed to a cooperative union with the Netherlands, and to a series of transitional measures making matters easier for Dutch interests in the islands. There was also a postponement of a decision as to whether western New Guinea should continue under Dutch rule or become part of the new country. The combined Indonesian representation at the Hague submitted a provisional constitution for the new republic. When the conference concluded, delegates from all the Indonesian states chose Sukarno as provisional president. The new republic of the United States of Indonesia came into being on December 27, 1949.

Elections for an Indonesian constituent assembly did not materialize at once. Instead, in August 1950 the federal structure for the country envisaged at the Hague was put aside in favor of a strong central administration from Jakarta. Sukarno ruled for the time being with the aid of a cabinet and a legislature, both representing a wide variety of viewpoints. To reconcile many of those viewpoints with his own hopes for a democratic socialist regime would prove a formidable task. Yet it was to this work that Sukarno seemed prepared to dedicate himself as he held his very widely scattered Indonesian people together.

Korea, unlike Indonesia, possessed a compact territory and a long national history. Of Mongoloid derivation, situated between China and Japan, the Korean people maintained their own rule for over half a millenium until 1910. Even before the time of their kingdom, they had developed a distinctive Korean language and accepted the Mahayana Buddhist religion. Korean independence came precipitately like that of Indonesia, however, after its Japanese absorption of 1910-45, while Korea bore the additional burden of involvement in big-power conflicts.

The international troubles stemmed from the

decision that Soviet and United States troops were to divide occupation responsibilities upon the surrender of the Japanese, their zones separated by the 38th parallel of latitude. This agreement cut Korea roughly in half by area while placing two-thirds of the people in the American zone. The powers planned a four-nation trust (China, the Soviet Union, the United States, and the United Kingdom) until a provisional Korean regime could be established. Russian and American negotiating teams failed to agree on details for this scheme, however, in talks which ranged through many weeks in 1946-7.

In September 1947, the United States took the problem to the United Nations General Assembly, which set up a United Nations Temporary Commission on Korea to visit the land and organize elections, looking toward quick nationhood. The Soviet Union did not concur in this decision, and refused to permit the Commission to carry out its work in North Korea, the Russian zone. The Commission proceeded nevertheless to sponsor elections in the southern zone, through which partisans of Lee Sung Man (Syngman Rhee) won a plurality of seats in a constituent assembly. Rhee was well known as an enthusiast for Korean independence from Japan, though he maintained the outlook of a conservative. He held a doctorate in international law from Princeton University in New Jersey; for a long time, he resided in Hawaii. A Christian, he once spent a short time as a Methodist missionary to his own people. He held distinctly anti-communist views, and opposed the idea of the four-power Korean trusteeship. Now the constitutional assembly chose him to become South Korea's first president, August 15, 1948, with his capital in the city of Seoul. Among his problems was South Korean price inflation, the wildest of the world at this time, with prices more than quintupling during the quinquennium.

In the meantime, the northern zone took action of it own. Conferences held there attracted men from all over Korea who disliked the prospect of the presidency of Rhee. Some who attended held conservative views; most, however, stood on the left, and those in the ascendancy were communists. They prepared a constitution that pretended to speak for all of Korea as did the one written in the South; but that of the North took its pattern from constitutions then becoming fashionable in communist eastern Europe. Kim Il Sung of the North Korean Workers party (the following year general secretary of a combined Korean Workers Party), a veteran fighter against the Japanese but also a long-time communist with Russian war experience and training, became the premier of the new regime. It began its existence September 12, 1948, with its capital at Pyongyang. The Russians withdrew from North Korea (population 8,000,000) in December 1948, the Americans from South Korea (population 20,000,000) in June 1949. But with two governments claiming to speak for the whole country, there seemed a certainty of bad trouble ahead. (Korea's story is continued in "The Cold War," later in this chapter.)

Independence for the Philippines, Burma, and Ceylon arrived with less strain than that of Korea. The Philippine archipelago was an isolated region where even the anciently separated Negritos had survived. The Malayo-Indonesian racial group had long ago taken over most of the islands, however. They became subject to Muslim kingdoms in the thirteenth and fourteenth centuries. The Bisayan (central Philippines) and Tagalog (central Luzon) languages from dominant cultures of those days are still the most widely spoken, with Tagalog chosen officially as the language of the future. The Spaniards who came to the Philippines in 1565 brought the Roman Catholic faith, which was accepted by most of the inhabitants. The Spanish wars of conquest brought together for the first time the Philippine territory of today. Spain ceded the islands to the United States in 1898, after a war

137

in which Spain was defeated. In 1935, they were organized as a commonwealth with its capital at Manila, under the United States flag; and were further promised complete independence for July 4, 1946. Though World War II and the Japanese occupation intervened, the schedule remained unchanged.

The new Philippine government, ruling 18,000,000 people, changed little from commonwealth times. The Nationalist party of the commonwealth split in 1946 into Liberal and Nationalist factions, with no clear line between them. Presidents Manuel Roxas (1946-8) and Elpidio Quirino (from 1948) were Liberals. They had three chief problems: (1) The United States, while granting Philippine independence and aiding the Philippines considerably, did not relinquish all special privileges in the islands. Washington's insistence brought about the provision that United States businessmen would receive the same rights as Philippine citizens in developing the archipelago's natural resources. An agreement also provided that United States army, navy, and air forces might retain bases for 99 years on the Philippine Islands.

(2) A group of farmer-warriors called the Hukbalahaps constituted another of the government's problems. These men were veterans of World War II; under communist leadership, they had fought as the People's Army against Japan while others of their countrymen collaborated with the Japanese conquerors. After the war, the Hukbalahaps demanded extensive agrarian reform in the large section of Luzon where they had operated and where they now conducted their own government while the nearby regime in Manila remained powerless against them. (3) The third problem the Manila government faced was the character of its own officialdom. The Liberals who ruled took no interest in radical reform of the type favored by the Hukbalahaps. When the Liberals did introduce moderate reform programs of their own, their effectiveness amounted to near

zero as their administration became plagued by a plethora of corruption.

Freedom came for Burma and Ceylon in the wake of the changes in British India. In Burma, to the east, persons of Mongoloid stock had surrounded other groups -- especially speakers of Karen languages and linguistic relatives of the Khmers of Cambodia. The Mongoloids spoke their own Burmese language and followed the Theravada Buddhist religion. A unified Burmese kingdom arose in mid-eighteenth century, only to be conquered by the British in three wars, 1824-86. Incorporated at first with India, Burma in 1937 became a British colony. The Japanese occupied the land, and granted it a technical independence in 1943, receiving the cooperation of some of the Burmese. Toward the end of the war, the Anti-Fascist People's Freedom League declared itself against Japan but sought freedom from the British also. When important communist leaders of the League were expelled in 1946, the officers who remained gave the League a strong democratic socialist flavor.

British moves toward Burmese independence closely paralleled those in neighboring India. Burma's constituent assembly of 1947 consisted almost entirely of members of the People's Freedom League, who planned a republican government of the parliamentary style. Independence came January 4, 1948, Burma (population 18,000,000) going one step farther than India by declining to remain a member of the Commonwealth. Prime minister Nu of the Burmese regime (known at this stage of life as Thakin Nu, the name Thakin a title of respect) was a devout Buddhist with a Burmese university education, a confirmed socialist in outlook but enthusiastic about democracy. At first, Burmese freedom seemed a disaster. The Karen peoples took a military stand against the government, while communist and other extremist bands harried the country. But the government of Thakin Nu, though forced to fight the insurgents, took actions to make itself

139

popular as well, obtaining financial assistance from abroad, initiating agrarian reform, and nationalizing Burmese industries. Far more than the Philippines or Korea, which were just limping along, Burma seemed to be going somewhere as a country.

Ceylon held less than half the population of Burma (Ceylon 7,000,000 in 1948). The people of Ceylon were racially the same as those of India, and its Theravada Buddhist faith had come from India also, but the Ceylonese had their own Sinhalese language. The Portuguese conquered most of the island in the sixteenth century, the Dutch took it away from the Portuguese in the seventeenth, and the British finally took all of it in the late eighteenth. Ceylon formed a separate British colony, administered in its own way, which after 1931 meant a high degree of self-government on a democratic plan. On February 4, 1948, Ceylon took another step when it became a dominion of the British empire with complete autonomy. Its parliamentary life proved vigorous from the beginning, since the United National party in power lacked a majority of seats in the parliament. Ceylon contained linguistic and religious minorities, but they did not pose the immediate difficulties minorities had caused elsewhere.

The face of the Orient had changed. Self-rule had come to nearly all the people in an area where colonialism had run strong. Large numbers of persons remained under European rule in 1950 only in three portions of this wide region. In Indochina, the French were following a course reminiscent of that of the Dutch in Indonesia. In the Malay states and Straits Settlements, the British were reorganizing their dependencies. In Hong Kong, the British were holding tight.

There was little reason to think that the new entities aside from India were individually viable states. As in nations the world over of their size, their problems were too great, their resources too slight, for them to stand without aid in the modern world. Still, their moves to political independence formed an important step in their development. Without responsibility for their own affairs, they remained in poor position to negotiate the interdependence they and others needed. Their early history as twentieth-century sovereign peoples would consist of the many adjustments necessary before even a fragile network of interdependence would become possible.

Chinese Communism

China, the world's oldest and largest nation, needed sharp rehabilitation in 1945. Here lived move than one-fifth of all the earth's people. Their problems had accumulated under many generations of warfare and misrule. The Manchu dynasty had permitted foreigners and a class of favored landlords to exploit both the natural and human resources of this country. China's provincial warlords engaged in nearly perpetual striving, each of them bent upon increasing his own power. The people's sufferings were great, extending even to large-scale famine.

Sun Yat Sen was hailed by many as the man whose ideas would change China. He emphasized three principles: China for the Chinese, a genuine participatory democracy, and a decent livelihood for the people. When the Manchu dynasty fell in 1912, however, Sun's ideas did not prevail. First, Yuan Shih Kai, president 1912-16, tried to found a new authoritarian dynasty. Then came deep chaos, with one general after another seeking to establish his own authority. Sun's Kuo Min Tang party established in 1920 helped to bring about a semblance of order. But the Kuo Min Tang included revolutionaries of a wide range of opinion, some excited about socialism, some interested in the establishment of democracy, and many enthusiastic only about the prospects of nationalism. Two years after Sun's death the party became divided. In 1928, the majority wing, retaining the party name, organized its own government of China on the base of self-asserted prerogative, with Chiang Kai Shek at its head. Mao Ze Dong (Mao Tse Tung) and other leftists, expelled from the Kuo Min Tang, put their full effort into a Communist party, with Mao becoming its head. The credentials for leadership of both Chiang and Mao need to be carefully examined:

(1) Chiang Kai Shek was born in Chekiang province on the eastern coast of China in 1887. His father worked as a merchant for the government-controlled salt industry, but died before Chiang reached the age of ten. Chiang attended school thereafter, while he lived with city relatives. When he was 18, he entered a Chinese military academy, from which he went to Japan in 1907 to develop further proficiency in the arts of warfare. There he also learned Japanese and joined a Chinese society sponsored by Sun Yat Sen, dedicated to the removal of the Manchus.

Chiang returned to China in 1911 in time to participate in the overthrow of the imperial dynasty. He cooperated with anti-Yuan forces in the next four years, living in Shang Hai and later in Canton. Chiang left his military career when Yuan died, however, and entered the Shang Hai business world. He became independently wealthy, then lost his fortune, and by 1923 was ready to work full time in Sun's cause. Others about Sun argued as to whether the Kuo Min Tang should follow a conservative or socialist orientation. Chiang's emphasis lay on what seemed to him more practical matters -- how the Kuo Min Tang could win and hold all of China. Sun, too, came to believe that this outlook must take precedence.

Sun's cause needed outside help to make headway against warlords more interested in power than reform. In 1923 he turned to the Soviet Union, the only large nation that was interested. Sun sent Chiang to Russia for four months of study in that year. Communist advisers showed up at Sun's headquarters in Canton in 1924, assisting Chiang in the organization of a new military academy. By the end of 1926, Kuo Min Tang forces had fought into central China, establishing a provisional government at Hankow. Chiang, supreme general on the battlefield after the death of Sun, quarreled with the leaders in Hankow and set up his own center of power in Nanking. In March 1927 he made a personal break with Moscow, accepting the backing of the very wealthy society of Shang Hai. In April, disturbed by reports of anti-Chiang subversion in that city, he carried out a ruthless massacre of thousands. The Hankow authorities dismissed him from his post, which he left in August. He returned to Chekiang, the province of his childhood, and from there to Japan, where he married Soong Mei Ling, sister of the widow of Sun. As a general, however, Chiang had impressed many persons who felt his services were still needed. By the end of the year, the Kuo Min Tang had sent its Russian advisers back to Moscow (where the widow of Sun joined them), had expelled much of its own left wing, and stood prepared to ask Chiang to head its forces again.

Late in 1928, Chiang became president of nearly all of China. His next two years were occupied in suppressing new rebellions. At the end of this period, he became a convert to Christianity, the religion of his wife. At the same time, he began fresh military campaigns to eliminate pockets of Communist hegemony. When Japan attacked Manchuria in late 1931, Chiang made it plan that the presence of the Chinese Communists worried him more than that of the Japanese. Chiang's popularity momentarily declined, and he resigned his position as president, but was soon called upon to help manage the Chinese army again. By 1934, Chiang's influence seemed as strong as ever. Kuo Min Tang armies made life very hard for the hold-out Communists in that year, and finally the party launched a campaign at least ostensibly aimed toward the rehabilitation of China. Called the New Life Movement, the program stressed strict private morality in line with old Confucian or Christian themes, while ignoring the popular demand for radical social reform. Economic reconstruction and social justice would come later, Chiang said, once the Communist threat had been eliminated.

In 1935, Chiang became president of the executive branch of the government, or prime minister; he also retained the highest position in the army. As the Japanese continued their probing, however, demands arose that he resist the foreigners more determinedly. For two weeks in December 1936, he was actually held prisoner in Sian, Shensi province, by a general who wanted him to fight Japan. A few months after this episode, Chiang negotiated a truce with the Communists at Yen An, not far from Sian. The Japanese attacked in full force in July 1937 and took Nanking in December. The Chinese government withdrew far to the west to Chungking, where it remained for eight years. Chiang became the chairman of a defense council holding all political power, and in 1943 assumed the presidency again. At the conclusion of the war, he could justifiably

144

plead that his many years in power had been very troubled ones. But the programs he had sponsored during that period had not won the admiration of the people in such a manner as to evoke the general support that he needed.

(2) Mao Ze Dong was born in a village of southerly Hu Nan province in 1893. His father, a peasant, also traded in rice, and made a harsh disciplinarian; his mother, a devout Buddhist though illiterate, entertained dreams of young Mao's entering the priesthood. After elementary training in the home village, Mao left home at the age of 14 to attend another school. In 1911, he and a companion moved to Chang Sha, the capital of Hu Nan. After serving as a young soldier in the final uprising against the Manchus, Mao settled down with his friend in Chang Sha for nearly six years of teacher training. Mao cared little for what lay behind him -- the Confucian precepts he had once studied, the Buddhism he had learned from his mother, the militarism he had experienced in the army. He became fascinated instead by a new world of ideas now opening before his eyes. In 1914, he founded the New People's Study Organization, a student society devoted to exploring non-traditional themes.

In 1918, Mao graduated and traveled to Peking -- attracted by the university, where he obtained a workaday position in the library. But after a few months, he returned to Chang Sha to lead his four-year-old society, now open to anyone interested in a new China, or against warlords and old ways of doing things. Mao took interest, like Sun, in both socialism and democracy. His frustrations sprang from his realization that most Chinese

145

individuals in power cared very little for one or the other. Visitors to China from the Soviet Union in 1920 suggested new strategies for revolution, in Marxist-Leninist style. These ideas were accepted by men Mao admired, and by Mao himself as their follower. Mao and his friends did not steep themselves in Marxist theory; they searched only for a means through which they might operate to change the face of China. They founded China's Communist party in Shang Hai in 1921. Mao's wife, the daughter of a professor, seconded his new enthusiasm.

Mao undertook the organization of the Communist movement in Hu Nan as his first task for the new party. Aided by his previous connections, he attained eminent success. In early 1924, he joined the Kuo Min Tang as one of several Communist leaders interested in the Soviet-Kuo Min Tang alliance. Employed by both parties, he did propaganda work among Chinese peasants whose support the Kuo Min Tang coveted. Mao came sincerely to believe in the peasants as the backbone of the revolution for a new China. The Russian advisers took more interest in the urban poor, while many in the Kuo Min Tang simply wanted the backing of peasants without allowing them any real influence in the movement. A peasant rebellion of 1926 in Hu Nan, not directed by Mao, caused Chiang to denounce such spontaneous uprisings. Mao felt delighted, however, by this aspect of the new revolutionary ideology. Cut off from both Kuo Min Tang ties and Russian advice in 1927, he and men like him continued thinking for themselves. Mao retired to Hu Nan, where he could hide, when a wave of murders of Communists all over China followed the Chiang-ordered massacre in Shang Hai. In Hu Nan, for a year, Mao lived in the mountains gathering thousands

146

of armed men, ready for the first time to use violence whenever he felt it necessary. The Kuo Min Tang government executed Mao's first wife, and Mao married a second time.

In early 1929, Mao's people moved east from Hu Nan to Kiangsi province. Here they held on for five years, seeking to initiate in their small portion of China the kind of regime they proposed for all. Chiang gave them little rest after 1930, but the pocket survived anyhow, as did others led by men of similar persuasion. At a first meeting of the Communists so engaged from all over China in Kiangsi in 1931, Mao was chosen to head their central committee. In 1934, however, government pressure became so intense that Mao's group had to leave Kiangsi. They began a march far to the west, suffering many losses, after which they turned north to settle in Shensi province in 1935. Communists from other pockets joined them, but Mao emerged as supreme leader. In 1936, he established new Communist headquarters in the city of Yen An, having authority over the territory of China in that vicinity. In 1939, divorcing his second wife, Mao married a film actress later known as Jiang Qing (Chiang Ching).

Mao's rule from Yen An in the early years extended over more than 1,000,000 people. That of Chiang at the same time included over 450,000,000. Yet Mao's position was strong. In Shensi he showed both Chinese and foreigners what a benevolent peasant-centered communism could do. And while he cooperated with Chiang after 1937 in fighting the Japanese, Mao remained ever busy gaining new advantage. Well before the end of World War II, his one area of Communist strength had spawned

147

nearly a dozen others, and the number of persons under his direction had increased to more than 100,000,000.

Obviously, a contest lay in the offing, as soon as the Japanese retired. Two men would be struggling for the control of all China. The contention between them might involve renewed civil war or might be worked out through more peaceful channels. Either way, each leader would do what he could to influence Chinese minds toward an endorsement of his endeavor. Looking forward to these days, both men had put some of their ideas into writing. Chiang's best-known document, written in 1943, contrasted dramatically in both substance and style with a comparable effort of Mao produced two years later. Both referred constantly to Sun Yat Sen and his three principles. But from there, Chiang reached into the old-fashioned world of moral precepts which both he and Mao knew well, but which Mao had long ago put aside. Mao concentrated on new moral emphases which Chiang overlooked entirely.

Chiang wrote, "What we revolutionaries should above all pay attention to is the search for truth . . . and the clear understanding of words. . . . Confucius said: 'There are five major evils under heaven, not counting theft and robbery. They are . . . a treacherous and sinister mind; . . . mean and incorrigible behavior; . . . false and eloquent words; . . . a heart full of shameful memories along with the appearance of great learning; . . . a disposition to wrong doing with a cunning for whitewashing it. Any man having any one of these should not escape punishment by the upright. . . .'" The crux of Chiang's philosophy, all based on such subjective premises, appeared in his further advice, "Let no useful man voluntarily abandon himself to a meaningless life, or spend a single ounce of energy without purpose. For the sake of our country's good I hope that all will come with one will and one heart and unite under the Three Principles of the People and the Kuomintang." Such loyalty

148

would not develop easily, however, among those who had been expelled from the Kuo Min Tang 16 years before, those indeed who had seen many of their own friends murdered because no man guilty of "a treacherous and sinister mind" or of "false and eloquent words" should "escape punishment by the upright" like Chiang.

Mao felt less convinced than Chiang of the moral stance of leading elements in the Kuo Min Tang. "Why has . . . a grave situation arisen," he said, "under the leadership of the Kuomintang's chief ruling clique? Because that clique represents the interests of China's big landlords, big bankers and big compradors. . . . These people . . . say that 'the nation is above all', but their actions never conform to the demands of the majority of the nation." Nevertheless, Mao distinguished between this "clique" and the "large numbers of democratic people" also in the Kuo Min Tang. He said he wanted to ally with the latter to organize a new democracy for China. "It is only through democracy that socialism can be attained," ran his words. "It would be a sheer illusion to try to build socialism on the ruins of the colonial, semi-colonial and semi-feudal order . . . without the development of a new-democratic state, . . . private capitalist and co-operative enterprises, . . . a national, scientific and popular culture . . . , or . . . the individual initiative of hundreds of millions of people. . . ."

Mao then spoke specifically of Sun's proposition of "land to the tillers," calling it "a correct one for China's bourgeois-democratic revolution at the present stage. . . . The proposition . . . is . . . one . . . of all revolutionary democrats, and not of us Communists alone. What distinguishes us . . . is the fact that . . . we Communists . . . take this proposition with special seriousness. . . ." Until 1945, Mao's actions had shown no more faith in the principles of political democracy than those of Chiang, regardless of the prodemocratic slant

149

of his words. But his phrases concerning radical agrarian reform had all the ring of sincerity. Although Mao made it plain that the ultimate goal of Chinese communism lay beyond peasant ownership of the land, the new peasant proprietors in the areas he controlled had benefited considerably.

Neither physically nor ideologically, it soon became evident, could Chiang's regime hope to cope with Mao's, even though after the war Chiang again ruled most of China from Nanking. Chiang's government was recognized by the winning United Nations, including the Soviet Union. The British and French renounced their concessions in China in order to help Chiang. (The Germans had already relinquished theirs, to the Japanese.) The Russians occupied Manchuria at the end of the war, but promised to withdraw within a year. The Americans did more than anyone else to help Chiang, providing his forces with transportation as the Japanese withdrew and even occupying some regions themselves until the Nanking regime could get to them. But these advantages did not suffice to override the handicaps from which the Kuo Min Tang government suffered.

Washington attempted to build a base for averting a new civil war in China. Patrick Hurley, the United States ambassador during the latter part of the war, had conversed much with both Mao and Chiang, but failed to bring the two together with a feasible plan. George Catlett Marshall, chief of staff of the United States army throughout the war, followed Hurley in these efforts in December 1945. The Kuo Min Tang, the Communists, and several minor parties attended a January meeting in Chungking. They agreed to hold a national assembly in May to plan for a postwar regime. An interim coalition government would be headed by Chiang, and soldiers of both Mao and Chiang would remain in the areas they already controlled.

The agreement became upset when Soviet armies withdrew from Manchuria and both Chinese regimes rushed in to take their place. Marshall tried to renew meaningful negotiations through the remainder of the year, but found a high degree of recalcitrance on both sides. "The greatest obstacle to peace," he reported when he returned home in January 1947, "has been the complete, almost overwhelming suspicion with which the Chinese Communist Party and the Kuomintang regard each other. . . . They each sought only to take counsel of their own fears."

Chiang and Mao entertained more than suspicion, however. Both of them looked forward to a gamble. The stakes were all of China rather than part, and one might even hope for the complete obliteration of his competitor. Chiang decided to make his play by reorganizing the nation unilaterally. His own national assembly wrote a new constitution in December 1946, to take effect after a year. In April 1947, Chiang's defense council gave up its executive power, though Chiang remained interim president. The democratic constitution took effect in May 1948, but was immediately amended to give emergency powers to Chiang, once again chosen the president. Chiang resigned the presidency in favor of general Li Tsung Jen in January 1949, but remained as director-general of the Kuo Min Tang. Actually, none of these constitutional gestures succeeded. The initiative had passed into other hands.

In 1947, Mao concentrated on the seizure of Manchuria, even giving up the wartime capital at Yen An, though also taking the trouble to set up an autonomous region in Inner Mongolia, immediately south of Mongolia. In 1948, his forces retook Yen An, finished their take-over of Manchuria, and captured a substantial part of northern China. In 1949, one large city after another fell into the Communists' hands -- in January Peking, in April Nanking, in May Shang Hai, in October Canton. General Lin Biao (Lin Piao) conducted the successful operations against Manchuria, Peking, and Canton. Chiang's armies retired or surrendered until they were gone from the mainland; Tai Pei on the island of Tai Wan they declared the nation's capital. Some Chinese, like Hu Shih, chancellor of the university in Peking, moved to the United States while maintaining allegiance to Tai Pei. But there existed a big, new reality in their lives, a Communist regime governing all of mainland China from its capital in Peking. This People's Republic of China, officially proclaimed October 1, 1949, comprised a population of about 524,000,000, contrasted to the 7,000,000 on Tai Wan.

Mao Ze Dong acted as chairman of the new regime's Central People's Government Council, in charge of policy. Jou En Lai (Chou En Lai), who had served at Mao's side even before the long march to Shensi, now took the role of prime minister as head of the State Administration Council. Mao traveled to Moscow in December 1949, remaining two months and signing a Chinese-Soviet alliance. Close collaboration between the Soviet Union and China seemed in prospect when Russian advisers moved to China to help the Chinese, and when Mao's troops in late 1950 became involved in the warfare in Soviet-influenced North Korea. Mao's regime owed little to the Russians, however; its birth struggle had remained quite strictly Communist Chinese. Mao negotiated as a partner, not as a disciple. He and his friends intended to develop Chinese socialism as they pleased.

The new mainland government of China offered peace and change to a people desperately in need of both. The benefits of peace, it quickly became apparent, were not to be put aside by too rapid a program of change. Agrarian reform did not take place in the newly liberated areas until the pronouncement of a program on June 30, 1950, designed not to establish collectivization but to redistribute the land. Most peasant families received less than one acre; even for this small fortune in real estate, many farmers felt pleased. No nationalization of city industry was attempted through 1950, though some state indus-

tries were formed. Private-enterprise manufacturing and commercial companies did better
financially than they had for some time, and for
this their owners also tended to look favorably
upon the new regime.

Some programs originated in 1949-50 had been
planned by the Kuo Min Tang, though it never
implemented them on a large scale. Peking now
forbade childhood marriage; gave women equal
rights with men; encouraged women to enter the
government and professions, as well as to join
work brigades; expanded health services rapidly;
started teaching the working classes to read; and
for the first time treated large national
minorities with respect, while simultaneously
encouraging them to think of themselves as Chinese. Persons who had already acquired the capacity to read before the revolution, however --
particularly primary and secondary school teachers -- became obliged to engage in personal
"thought reform" to orient themselves toward the
socialism that lay in China's future.

Chinese communism constituted a new force in
the world. Its further developments were to
provoke much consternation, even in the other
communist states. Once in power, Mao gave little indication that he remembered the words he
had uttered concerning political democracy, despite the fact that members of eight parties of a
bourgeois nature received appointment to high
office. Mao did make it clear, however, that he
would change the face of China. This was a task
that Chiang, with his program built entirely on
personal-morality concepts, could hardly have
been expected to accomplish. The key to Mao's
success in 1949 lay in the fact that millions
(not necessarily hundreds or even tens of millions) of Chinese recognized this difference
between the two men, and understood that Mao's
regime, even if it proved a very authoritarian
one, had its base in a more comprehensive morality than that of Chiang. However, that did not
mean that Mao's government any more than the new

one in India could move ahead without staggering problems.

Post-Axis Democracy

The three chief members of the Axis had suffered complete defeat. The cause of fascism seemed thoroughly discredited in all of them. Nevertheless, their people stood divided in their wishes for the future. In each instance, a majority chose its path for the immediate postwar period through a vote to adopt governmental democracy. The Italians (45,000,000 of them in 1946) made the decision on their own; the West Germans (49,000,000 in 1949) with the cooperation of United States, British, and French armies; and the Japanese (76,000,000 in 1946) under the tutelage of the United States without its allies. Only the East Germans (18,000,000 in 1949), under a Soviet occupation, dissented, choosing left-wing authoritarianism instead.

The general policy by which Japan's surrender should be consummated was set up by a Far Eastern Commission of eleven members, approved at the conference of late 1945 in Moscow. The powers also set up a four-member Allied Council for Japan to advise in everyday decisions that would arise. A United States individual, however, the supreme commander of the allied forces in Japan, would serve as the chairman of the Allied Council. General Douglas MacArthur of Arkansas held the position through this five-year period. He in effect told the Japanese what they must do, in those features of life which mattered to his own country. Both the strengths and the weaknesses of major Japanese decisions in the early years may be attributed to him.

To MacArthur, and also to Washington at the time, it seemed desirable to convert Japan from an enemy to an ally. Certain internal changes were demanded. Fascism would have to be replaced

154

by democracy. Individual leaders would be punished for their prosecution of the war. (Some, such as prince Konoe Fumimaro who had opposed the war, committed suicide in 1945.) The financial apparatus that made the war possible would have to be dismantled. From the beginning, however, there existed no tendency to punish the entire nation, for the United States felt concern lest Japan become too hungry or poor. (The cost of living in Japan nearly quintupled during this time period.) Reparations would be paid someday, when the countries Japan had occupied requested them. Each government could bargain with Japan individually as peace treaties were signed. The United States would request no reparations, since its territory had not been occupied.

The peace treaties themselves were rather long in coming. The United States early stated its readiness to sign one, on terms drawn up in Washington. No difficulty would have been encountered in imposing these upon an exhausted Japan. The trouble lay instead with the Soviet Union, which wanted to prevent the kind of Japanese-American cooperation that seemed to lie in the offing. In addition, after 1949 the Chinese Communist regime expected to speak for China in any peace conference. Moscow and London supported its right to do so, while Washington demurred.

Regarding Japanese internal policy, on the other hand, the United States generally had its way. In the year of 1946, this meant a veritable revolution for Japan. On January 1, emperor Hirohito officially declined the Shinto definition of himself as a divine personage, and declared that contrary to the traditional teaching of Shintoism the Japanese people should not regard themselves as superior to others. In March, a new constitution appeared, sharply delimiting the position of the emperor and completely renouncing the use of war by Japan. A prohibition of the rebuilding of the armed forces emphasized the renunciation of warfare. As the fifth largest nation of the world thus turned officially pacifist, sentiment in both Japan and the United States approved. Americans remembered three years of tough fighting in the Pacific, initiated by Japan; the Japanese remembered the horror of all the bombings and the shock of defeat.

Japan's revolution continued in August, when a radical agrarian reform was adopted, and in September, when certain strong financial holdings were attacked. Japan's military machine had found its monetary support in the large fortunes of a very few families. The wealth derived from the near-monopolistic position these households held, through strategic combinations, in the Japanese economy. The income depended also upon a plentiful supply of cheap labor imported from the agricultural zones for city industry. The agrarian reform weakened the latter practice by making land and better living available to poor peasants. The occupation then liquidated the financial combinations, and forced some competition into the investment process. Some Japanese thought that the absentee landowners who lost their agricultural holdings and the wealthy families who lost their financial position should yield their interests to the nation without compensation. The American government thought otherwise, however, and the Japanese nation had to buy out these men before redistributing their properties.

The new constitution took effect on May 3, 1947. With it, Japan returned to a path it had forsaken, and instituted sharp democratic reform. Women could vote for the first time, and the votes of all the electorate would have meaning. Both houses of the national diet would be elected by the people. The prime minister and his cabinet would be responsible to the whole diet. The emperor would reign but the prime minister would rule, in effect. The councils of government used during World War II were eliminated altogether. Under the aegis of general

MacArthur, backed by the American forces, Japan had stepped over the threshold of democracy with considerable firmness.

The step over the threshold, nevertheless, did not guarantee the Japanese a late-model democracy. The British and United States practices, both of which served as models, failed in one important respect. Democracies fashioned in the twentieth century, in contrast to those from the eighteenth, generally used some system of proportional representation to meet their peoples' needs. The electoral procedures adopted for Japan did make some concession toward the idea. In three-member districts in elections for the diet, each voter would select one candidate rather than three. A sizeable minority might thus achieve representation without holding a majority anywhere. The vote totals would work out proportionately, however, only by the rarest of coincidences. The lack of genuine proportional representation in Japan left that country subject to the same minority frustrations felt in the United States and the United Kingdom.

A variety of postwar parties early emerged to seek the favor of the voters. The Liberal party soon proved itself the one most consistently able to win. Its emphasis on business interests and the principle of free enterprise gave it a nineteenth- rather than a twentieth-century flavor. Many of its organizers were jailed for their cooperation with wartime leadership. Yoshida Shigeru, Liberal prime minister 1946-7 and again in 1948, stood more conservative than the average in his party, but had not associated directly with the war effort. His policies seldom failed to please Washington. The People's Democratic party organized in 1950 maintained a more distinctly twentieth-century liberal outlook, and favored a foreign policy less oriented toward the United States. The Social Democratic party represented urban labor, favoring a moderate nationalization of industry and demonstrating great sincerity about pacifism. In the conflict

157

erupting between world communism and the United States, it favored a policy of neutrality. A Social Democrat held the prime ministership in 1947-8, but only by means of a coalition with other parties. The Communists, who did not participate in that coalition, made up the fourth party of Japan, at their greatest strength one-tenth the size of the Liberals.

Germany's occupation differed from that of Japan in that four armies had moved into German territory. In Germany, no supreme commander could pressure the entire nation toward his own preferences. Instead, an Allied Control Council consisting of the military governors -- one each from the Soviet Union, the United States, the United Kingdom, and France -- held control of the German territory. Berlin, the city where they met, was in itself divided into four sectors, surrounded by the Russian zone. A four-power municipal board handled the administration of Berlin. Both Berlin and Germany, according to original arrangements, would be administered as single entities; but quarrels between the occupying powers prevented unified action.

Differences appeared immediately in regard to local and state elections held in 1946. In the American, British, and French zones, free balloting provided great numbers of votes for the Christian Democratic (liberal-conservative) Union and the Social Democratic party, as well as minority representation for a small conservative group on the right and the Communists on the left. In the Soviet zone, under duress, the Social Democratic leadership agreed to a merger with the Communists. The resulting Socialist Unity party won majorities or near-majorities even in districts the least affected by coercion. But in Berlin, where all four powers had influence, the Social Democratic party alone won nearly half the vote, while Socialist Unity had to be satisfied with one-fifth.

In their attempt to fashion policy for Germany, the four powers disagreed vigorously upon almost every subject. They did decide unanimously, in an International Military Tribunal held at Nuremberg 1945-6, to execute twelve Nazi leaders and jail seven more, though they reached no accord on the punishment for others. (Of the twelve, Hermann Göring committed suicide; from 1939 until late in the war Hitler had considered Göring his successor.) Reparations proved the sorest point of conflict among the four occupying powers. The Soviet Union could take what it considered it deserved from its own zone, and started at once to do so. Its only problem there lay over the question whether industrial plants themselves should be moved to Soviet and Polish territory, or whether the plants should be left in Germany and their production taken instead. The United States, the United Kingdom, and France, however, had to lend their continuing assent for a successful implementation of the Potsdam agreement on materials from the other three zones. Good will between those powers and the Soviet Union became very rare in the post-World War II atmosphere, and Germany became a symbol of the winning powers' inability to work together harmoniously.

Many persons hoped that some kind of peace could be arranged for Germany in the year 1947. A four-power foreign ministers' meeting in Moscow during March and April provided the first opportunity. There was discussion in Moscow of a possible provisional regime to rule all of Germany, but no agreement as to details. The Soviet Union spoke for a strong central government for Germany, the United States and the United Kingdom for a federal system giving more power to the states, and France for a weak federation in which the states would assume most of the decision-making. When the Moscow conference failed, the Americans and British proceeded to unite their two zones economically, and to plan for their further union as well. Another four-power conference in London, in November-December, stalled on the centralization issue again, and fell completely apart as it attempted to deal with reparations. Four-power cooperation in dealing with Germany had come to an end even before it effectually reached its beginnings.

The Allied Control Council and the board to govern Berlin did not meet after March 1948. Each military zone and sector, from this point on, had to be administered separately. At this point, the French joined with the British and Americans in the moves toward the combination of zones. In October 1948, their three areas arranged an economic merger. In May 1949, they completed work on a poltical union, with the writing of a West German constitution. From June 1948 to May 1949, the Soviet Union tried unsuccessfully to cut off the three western sectors of Berlin from the three western zones of Germany. (Details are presented in "The Cold War.") In May-June 1949 the four powers met again, in Paris, but on the question of German unity only admitted their failure to come to any decision. West Germany then became a functioning state in September 1949, followed by East Germany in October. A comparable division took place in Berlin, with the western sectors adhering to West Germany despite the occupation agreement.

West Germany called itself the Federal Republic of Germany; its capital was set at Bonn. The West Germans had written their own constitution in debate lasting through three quarters of a year. The controlling body in government would be the Bundestag, or lower house of parliament. Its members would be chosen by the people through a mixed system of voting, some of them to be elected directly while others received seats by choice of their parties on a formula providing proportional representation for political groups. The Bundesrat, or upper house of parliament, represented the states, but the prime minister and his cabinet would be responsible to the Bundestag alone. Germany had experienced democracy before, during the short-lived Weimar Republic, and now by their own choice nearly three-fourths of the German people returned to democracy again.

Three political parties became immediately important in West Germany. The Christian Democratic Union, the largest of them, contained a mixed membership of liberals and conservatives and tended to defend the system of private enterprise. Konrad Adenauer, Christian Democratic prime minister, had passed his 70th birthday when he took office in 1949. A conservative and quiet practitioner of the law, he held the distinction of having been imprisoned twice by the Nazis. The Social Democratic party had followed a democratic Marxist point of view since its beginnings far back in 1863. By this postwar period, however, it had evolved into a moderate protest party, calling for a stronger central government and some nationalization of industry. The Free Democratic party, more consistently conservative than the Christian Democratic Union and only one-third its size, had to be included by the latter in its government to provide a majority in the Bundestag.

East Germany called itself the German Democratic Republic. Its capital lay nominally in Berlin, but policy for East Germany came very obviously from Moscow. When elections were held in East Germany the year after the regime was instituted, all parties were forced to accept an assignment of seats in advance of the voting. Socialist Unity and its allies received 70% of them. Walter Ulbricht, secretary-general of the ruling party, became the day-to-day master of the East German regime. Trained as a carpenter, Ulbricht had turned to communist organizing activity while young; long considered among the most faithful of the devotees of Moscow, he even imitated some of Lenin's personal mannerisms.

Konrad Adenauer, chosen by his people, had to maintain some popularity with them in order to

161

continue in his position. In his very first year, he managed to terminate most of the reparations program from the three western zones. He succeeded also in establishing a foreign policy of his own, though the three occupying powers had not intended that he should. Basically, of course, he remained very cooperative with Washington, London, and Paris, just as Ulbricht cooperated with Moscow. There existed a great difference, however, in that Adenauer ruled three occupation zones, not one, and that he could rightly claim to speak for his part of the German nation.

In Italy, far more than in Germany or Japan, postwar negotiations moved along in good order. Only Washington and London held voting representation on the Allied Commission to oversee Italian affairs. For two years before the war ended, an Italian provisional government had cooperated with these allies. Italy could not escape the penalty for having earlier formed a major part of the Axis. But this Mediterranean nation's most worrisome problems were internal ones.

Italy became the subject of major decisions in the year 1946. In May, King Victor Emmanuel III abdicated in favor of his son. Victor Emmanuel had worn the crown 46 years, during nearly half of which he associated with Mussolini. Many Italians felt that the monarchy had been compromised altogether. In June, a majority voted to institute an Italian republic, and the son followed the father into exile. The following month, a peace conference met in Paris to discuss treaties between the winners on one side and Italy, Romania, Hungary, Bulgaria, and Finland on the other. The conference ended in October; the Soviet Union, the United States, the United Kingdom, and France made the terms final in December; and they became official the following February.

Italy suffered from its peace treaty. It had to pay sizeable reparations bills to Yugoslavia, Greece, and the Soviet Union, and smaller ones to Ethiopia and Albania. Greece received islands in the Aegean Sea which had been held by Italy for 35 years. Border territories had to be given up to both France and Yugoslavia. The Italian city of Trieste was placed under United Nations management. The winning powers took over the portions of Africa that had been ruled by Italy until their future could be decided. Italy accepted these terms -- it had no other choice -- and prepared to make the most of its position. The greater part of the dire situation in which it now found itself, including even stark hunger in the countryside, remained more attributable to past internal policies than to the severity of its peace.

Though prices doubled during this quinquennium, Italy's hunger was unnecessary. It constituted the direct effect of the oppression of one class of people by another. The families in which wealth abounded had controlled Italy for some time. Indeed, the possibility that they might lose control formed the chief element that had brought on the scourge of fascism. To take power, Mussolini had had to eliminate the Italian socialist and liberal parties which the wealthy families feared. The very arbitrary nature of his regime converted many of the poorer people to communism. The shift of popular opinion in this direction mounted so steeply that Italian postwar politics revolved about the question whether communism, in a fair election, could win.

Actually, the Italian Communist party came in consistently second rather than first at the polls. The new Christian Democratic party held greater strength. The Christian Democrats included a variety of people. Some were wealthy and conservative, though ready to drop previous alliances with fascism; others wealthy and liberal, having come to believe that there must be change. Most, however, were middle-class and poor, their allegiance guaranteed by the intervention of the Roman Catholic priesthood. Some priests even taught that to vote other than Christian Democratic was to commit prejudicious sin. The United States of America seconded the attitude of the church, providing important financial encouragement to the party. The Christian Democratic ideology ran strongly anti-communist, pro-Roman Catholic, and pro-United States. But it did constitute a clear break with fascism.

Some Socialists aided the thrust of the pro-Soviet Communists for power in Italy. Socialists in general agreed with the Communists on major internal reforms, such as the nationalization of industries and redistribution of land, but disagreed on matters of procedure. A majority wing of the Socialist party decided to align with the Communists in seeking control, hoping that their combined strength might bring victory at the polls. A separated Socialist Party of Italian Workers, however, would have nothing to do with the Communists, and cooperated in Christian Democratic governments instead. In the turbulent Italian situation after World War II, new fascist groups arose also, with the intention of saving the land from communism as they thought Mussolini had done. The early stalwartness of the new republic, however, rested on its devotion to Christian Democracy, an attitude fostered by clerical zeal and United States money at election time, though the Christian Democrats gave no clear sign of their intentions in domestic policy.

A new constitution took effect on January 1, 1948. It changed nearly every aspect of the government except that an official tie to Roman Catholicism continued from the Mussolini regime. The prime minister and his cabinet would be responsible to the combined parliament, both of whose houses would be elected by the people. Proportional representation for parties would be achieved through the use of new electoral procedures. There would exist no simple method whereby a few persons could obtain dominance over many, as an elite of the wealthy had done before and during the time of Mussolini. In the first elections under the new provisions, in April 1948, the Christian Democratic party gained a majority in the lower house of parliament.

Alcide De Gasperi, the first prime minister of the Italian republic, was himself a sincere Roman Catholic; earlier in life he had taken an interest in philology, but later turned to politics. He spent his first 37 years in an Italian-speaking part of Austria ceded to Italy after World War I. Later, Mussolini held him in prison, as the Nazis had held Konrad Adenauer. De Gasperi faced many demands, most of all from those who needed land and those who disliked his attitude of obeisance toward the United States. He countered them through a show of force where he felt that was necessary -- or through token reform, as with his agrarian policy, providing enough change to offer some hope to the poor without reaching the point that it would disturb the rich people. Christian Democratic councils proved varied enough in sentiment that no one could be certain what to expect from them, except that they would not likely depart far from Washington's desires.

By 1950, it was clear that the three chief Axis powers had broken quite firmly with fascism. In West Germany, Italy, and Japan, pro-Washington private-enterprise democracy had become the order of the day. Neutrality-minded persons in West Germany and Japan criticized many of the governmental policies, as did also the Soviet-oriented persons of Italy. But protest and disagreement formed a regular part of democracy, and were sure to be intense in three countries that had recently suffered defeat on the world's battlefields. If the ruling hybrid parties of hopeful liberals and reluctant conservatives continued to maintain the fairness of

which they had shown themselves capable, three
nations stood poised to determine their own destinies in a manner none of them had very successfully employed before, through the free use
of the secret ballot.

United Nations Realities

The United Nations completed its Charter in
1945.   United Nations realities, however, remained to be determined. The beginning years of
the new peacetime organization would set precedents not easy to overcome. Both what the United
Nations chose to do and what it chose not to do
assumed importance, for this was man's loftiest
attempt at international cooperation in history.

Nine more nation-states joined the enterprise during the first five years. Of the nine,
Thailand, Afghanistan, Sweden, Yemen, and Iceland had all in one sense or another acted as
bystanders during World War II. The remaining
four -- Pakistan, Indonesia, Burma, and Israel --
all sought United Nations seats as new countries.   Other regimes applying for membership
failed to win approval, their eligibility forming another point of contention among the quarreling powers. After its conquest by the Mao
party, mainland China had no voice in the United
Nations, Tai Wan being permitted to retain the
Chinese seat.   Japan and Germany expected to
remain outside until the conclusion of their
peace treaties. The Soviet Union blocked Italy's
membership and that of seven smaller states, due
to the unwillingness of several countries to
admit five newly formed communist governments.
Nearly all members agreed to deny a seat to the
Franco administration in Spain.

More noteworthy than the list of countries
excluded, nevertheless, with the one exception of
the ostracism of Communist China, was the
register of nations already admitted. Especial-

166

ly, it made a great difference to the world that the two most powerful antagonists of the postwar period -- the Soviet Union and the United States -- had become active members. The Soviet Union had found itself barred from participation in the League of Nations through most of the time that organization existed. The United States refused to play a League of Nations role. After World War II, neither of the pair expected to permit the United Nations to set its foreign policy. But both had to respond in the United Nations, day after day, to questions about their intentions and activities. The experience proved beneficial to the two strongest powers in the world, and to a large number of others as well.

Smaller countries had always complained about the readiness of the stronger powers to use force in the pursuance of their policies. As the first item of business before the United Nations Security Council, on January 25, 1946, Iran accused Soviet troops stationed in its territory of making trouble for the Iranian government in its control of Azerbaijan. In March, Iran entered the additional complaint that the Soviet troops had stayed on past the deadline set for their evacuation in the wake of World War II. The Security Council heard the case argued, and agreed upon resolutions favoring Iran. The Soviet forces quietly withdrew, giving up an attempt to build a communist regime for the Iranian Azerbaijani. They did so not because a superior military force had told them they must, but because their not-very-subtle operation had come under the glare of world opinion. Syria and Lebanon spoke to the Council about unrequested British and French troops on their soil in February 1946, and these soldiers were withdrawn by June. A complaint from Egypt a year later about British forces in that country did not produce the same consequences; in this situation, however, there existed no abrogation of a promise or a treaty.

The problem of Indonesia occupied a far greater share of United Nations energy during the first five years. The Ukraine introduced this situation in February 1946 with a complaint about the actions of British troops in Indonesia. When the matter reached a new stage, with no foreseeable end to violence between the Dutch and the Javanese, the Security Council created its Committee of Good Offices on August 25, 1947. (See "Asian Independence.") When the Dutch angered world opinion through their actions in late 1948, the Security Council took a strong stand. Its resolution of January 28, 1949, led directly to the talks at the Hague and full independence for Indonesia. In the culmination of this problem as in those of Iran, Syria, and Lebanon, world opinion speedily asserted itself through the United Nations, bringing an end to the use of force by one people in another people's land.

Trieste and the Italian possessions in Africa constituted another type of United Nations problem. The Italian peace treaty provided that the Security Council should determine the future of the city of Trieste; generally, Trieste expected to be denominated a "free" city, like Danzig between the two world wars. Disposition of the African territories had been turned over to the four powers which had virtually written the Italian treaty, with the provision that if they could not agree they should accept the verdict of the General Assembly. Since the powers did not agree, the Assembly in 1949-50 decided that Italian Somaliland should become a trust territory of the United Nations, with Italy as its trustee, until it would gain its independence within ten years; that Libya should be made independent by 1952; and that Eritrea should federate with Ethiopia in 1952 after establishing its own local government. (The Eritreans were not granted the right to opt for independence by plebiscite.) The Security Council managed less efficiently with Trieste, postponing a decision, as the British and United States governments realized a free Trieste might become dominated by the communist Yugoslavs. On matters such as these, presented to the United Nations on some basis other than complaint or concern, the General Assembly with its two-thirds vote without veto obviously operated with greater dispatch than the Security Council, though not necessarily to the satisfaction of everyone.

During its first quinquennium, the United Nations acted on two great international quarrels without direct bearing on the powers holding the Council veto. One was the series of disputes involving India, Pakistan, Hyderabad, and Kashmir. United Nations efforts resolved none of these; the chief problem concerning Kashmir reached no solution at all beyond a cease-fire. In this case, the Security Council would have gone farther in accordance with its own non-partisan plan, but stood faced with the simple fact that India would not cooperate peacefully. The other great international controversy concerned the status of Palestine, where European Jews wanted to establish a state which Middle Eastern Arabs vehemently opposed. This problem occupied more United Nations attention during this half-decade than any other brought to its chambers. It even resulted in the calling of two special sessions of the General Assembly. (See "A Third Israel.") The Assembly on November 29, 1947, voted to establish a Jewish state covering part of Palestine, with a new Arab state occupying the remainder. Of the 33 votes in support of this plan, 13 came from European nations and 15 from the Americas. Every one of the nine Middle Eastern votes opposed the measure. Clearly, a situation had arisen in which outsiders were attempting to impose their will on a specific part of the world, not with the opposition of the United Nations but through the actual employment of its instruments. The Palestinian Arabs, who constituted a majority in their own territory, declined to cooperate in the designed program.

Quarrels between the stronger powers also

provoked a great deal of United Nations study, even though most of the disputes between them failed to reach United Nations channels. A whole series of accusations sprang from the troubles of Greece with its neighbors Yugoslavia, Bulgaria, and Albania; Greece was backed by the United Kingdom and the United States, the neighbors by the Soviet Union. The United Nations also heard complaints about the forcing of Czechoslovakia into communism, the isolation of Berlin by the Soviet Union, and the (largely presumed) Soviet interference in China in favor of a communist government there. The United Nations took no action on any of these questions except the Greek one, for which the General Assembly on October 21, 1947, set up a Special Committee on the Balkans.

By far the greatest problem directly affecting the big powers came before the Security Council on July 25, 1950. (See "The Cold War.") This was the invasion of the South Korean territory by the army of North Korea, premeditated and undertaken with the intent of complete conquest. The Council denounced the move quickly, as an aggression which ought to be repelled. It found itself able to do so only because the Soviet Union had absented itself (in a remarkable lack of communist coordination), declaring that it would not participate in Security Council discussions until the United Nations recognized the right of Peking to the seat of China. Nevertheless, the Council's move proved decisive. Full-scale aggression had run into disapproval from almost every state in the noncommunist world. When the Soviet Union returned to the Security Council without waiting for the entry there of Communist China, the United States (November 3) pushed a "Uniting for Peace" resolution through the General Assembly stating the readiness of that body to take needed action when the Council might be stymied by the veto. The real problems between Moscow and Peking on the one hand and London and Washington on the other were scarcely discussed by the United

Nations during this time. But one energetic performance of the United Nations had made it clear that no simple solutions of those problems would be achieved through the use of violence.

Further complaints to the United Nations included one from India about the treatment of persons of Indian origin in South Africa; others concerning the limitation of civil rights of religious people in Romania, Hungary, and Bulgaria; and one about a decision of the Soviet Union to make it difficult for Soviet women married to foreigners to emigrate to their husbands' countries. In none of these matters, regarded as domestic business by the regimes responsible, did the influence of the United Nations carry far or its resolutions really matter.

Three United Nations decisions proved the most sensational during the first five years: (a) the General Assembly vote of November 29, 1947, calling for a partition of Palestine into Jewish and Arab states; (b) the Security Council vote of January 28, 1949, opening the way for the independence of Indonesia; and (c) the Security Council vote of June 27, 1950, asking United Nations members to help South Korea. The Palestinian vote was 33-13, on an almost strictly regional basis, Europe and the Americas against the Middle East; the Indonesian 9-0, with both Moscow and Washington taking an affirmative stand; the Korean 7-1, without the participation of Moscow. The Korean decision involved the use of force; the United Nations could not go any farther. The Indonesian finding, fully as effective, required only good, clear language to make its point. The resolution in regard to Palestine had no immediate effect, because it ignored the wishes of the majority in the affected territory.

These three cases seemed to point to a simple definition of United Nations strength. The organization functioned well when it stood for the rights of an aggrieved majority, in South Korea and Indonesia; it ran into trouble when it ignored such rights, in Palestine. Such a simple definition did not hold, however, in a more precise accounting. The United Nations failed whenever nations argued that such-and-such constituted domestic policy; the nations had not agreed to surrender jurisdiction over this domain. It experienced frustration when a country became adamant in its international policy, even if the matter took on less than global consequences. Above all else, it lacked strength when it approached any matter of contention among the stronger powers; these perplexities remained too intertwined to permit an efficacious settlement of them one at a time. The United Nations further lacked the opportunity to strike at the world's crucial problems simply because the most knotty arguments of Cold War antagonists were generally kept away from this forum.

The United Nations displayed three political strengths: (1) It could handle in a most efficient style problems such as the disposition of colonial territories placed before it by all rather than by one of the stronger powers. (2) It could strike out in dramatic manner, in the presence of strong feeling and a considerable degree of unanimity, to assist entire nations when they fell into distress. (3) It could, through its encouragement of frank and full discussion of nearly every subject, prevent grievous acts from taking place against the climate of world opinion. From time to time, nations might seem to ignore world judgments on their policies in order to act entirely as they pleased. Yet the occasions upon which recent governments have silently taken world opinion into account have in all probability become innumerable.

The United Nations made virtually no progress at all when it attempted to negotiate in affairs of the military. The Charter provided

172

for a Military Staff Committee to organize standby national forces upon which the United Nations could call. The Committee began its talks early (February 1946) and proceeded with them regularly, but the members could not agree on the basic principles required. The General Assembly created an Atomic Energy Commission on January 24, 1946, to plan limitations on the use of atomic energy in weapons. The Commission quickly became deadlocked in disagreement between Washington and Moscow, each doubting the sincerity of the other. A Commission for Conventional Armaments established by the Security Council February 13, 1947, had major disarmament as its goal, but no better way of attaining its objective. The business of all three of these groups became even more difficult in 1950 when the Soviet Union withdrew from them to protest the presence of Tai Wan representatives in seats allocated to China. With or without either Moscow or Peking, however, the assignments handed these bodies seemed impossible until a greater harmony could prevail.

Other business of the United Nations could and did proceed despite the lack of harmony. A great share of its less publicized activities lay outside the political sphere. Everything the League of Nations had done, the United Nations now did better, its deliberations improved by its greater universality. Associated agencies of the United Nations -- the Food and Agriculture Organization; the Educational, Scientific and Cultural Organization; the Bank for Reconstruction and Development; the Monetary Fund; the Labor Organization; the Postal Union; the Telecommunication Union; the Civil Aviation Organization from 1947; the Health and Refugee Organization from 1948; the Meteorological Organization from 1950 -- carried on work in nearly every conceivable realm. But with all this, the United Nations reputation seemed likely to depend upon its usefulness in politics. By the end of 1950, it had shown itself capable of decisive action on the most crucial matters, though without the overtone of military authority. In its first five years, the United Nations had become a fitting symbol for a new age, even though later generations might think of it as a very primitive one.

A Third Israel

The first Israel was a man, according to traditional Jewish, Christian, and Muslim account, a patriarch of Palestine and progenitor of the Hebrew people. His father's father was named Abraham. Abraham had moved to Palestine from what is now Iraq. His god promised him this new home for his descendants, though other people already inhabited it. Abraham had several children, including two well-known sons. Abraham's wife's servant bore him Ishmael, the older of these two; eventually she and her child were forced to flee from Abraham's household. Abraham's wife bore Isaac, the younger of the two, at the unusual age of 100. Ishmael became the ancestor of the Arabs of Arabia. Isaac became the father of Jacob and Esau. Jacob, later renamed Israel, claimed the promise of the land inheritance made to Abraham as applying only to himself and his twelve sons.

The second Israel was a Hebrew kingdom which covered Palestine three thousand years ago. It consisted of twelve tribes, named for the first Israel's sons (or, to be more exact, for only ten of them and two of his grandsons). The kingdom held a mixed population, for the Hebrews had had to conquer the land, but the religion and the culture became dominantly those of the conqueror. The twelve-tribe unity, however, lasted only one century. After that, ten of the tribes stayed together for two hundred years more, retaining the name of Israel. Finally conquered by outsiders, they are often called "the lost ten tribes of Israel." Very likely, some of their physical heritage is to be found in nearly any "Palestinian Arab" of today.

The two tribes which separated from the kingdom of Israel after its first century of existence were those named for Judah and Benjamin. Their own smaller kingdom, named Judah, lasted nearly a century and a half longer than the larger one, and its people came to be called Jews. When other ancient people finally conquered Judah, and carried some of its people away, a part of them retained their religious and cultural identity, associating it with their former homeland. Jews eventually became widely dispersed in the world (they speak of the process as the diaspora, or scattering), but tended to think in terms of Palestine as their real home, once promised to Abraham. Their sentiments failed to take into account (a) the question of the validity of any such promise or the account containing it, on the first hand; (b) the lack of fairness involved in the neglect of Abraham's and Isaac's other children; and (c) the fact that even most of the descendants of the man Israel are not Jews but, more likely, Christian and Muslim "Arabs."

Muslim armies from Arabia conquered Palestine in the seventh century, very shortly after Muhammad died. Within a hundred years, their conquests extended from the northwestern borders of India to Spain. The Arabs could not people all this wide area, but they ruled it and gradually imposed upon it their religion and language. Not everyone in Palestine conformed; Jewish and other non-Muslim religious communities survived. But the great majority of the people, of mixed cultural and physical heritage, adopted the new faith and language and came to be counted Arabs. Arabs everywhere respected Hebrew traditions, incorporating them into their own, but insisted that the promise of Abraham included Ishmael, Abraham's first son.

For a very long time, Jewish communities of the diaspora fared better in Muslim than in Christian lands. Judaism reached new heights as

175

its people lived under Muslim rule in what are now Iraq, Syria, Egypt, and Spain. Western Christendom was then less erudite than Islam, and Christians generally less tolerant and more barbaric. The Christian crusades of the twelfth century, organized to take Palestine from the Muslims, also resulted in large-scale Christian massacres of European Jews. Later, four western European countries expelled all their remaining Jews -- first England, next France, later Spain and Portugal. Most of the German states made life miserable for their Jewish populations as well. By the sixteenth century, Poland, Russia, and various Muslim lands had accepted most of those who fled the western countries. Jews moving from Germany spread their own Yiddish language through the Jewish groups living in non-Muslim areas. When these particular groups talked of a future migration to Palestine, as they tended to do, they spoke of their aspirations in a Germanic rather than a Semitic language, and from an essentially European cultural background.

A Christian tolerance for Jews and Judaism finally began to be propagated in western Europe in late eighteenth century. The new thought did not extend to Poland and Russia, however, where most European Jews lived. Jewish people fared very poorly in both of these lands under their common Romanov rule in the nineteenth century. In Russia, their plight reached the same levels of massacre and persecution as in western Europe a half-millenium before. Those Jews who did not die yearned once again to move elsewhere. Many did reach the United States of America. Others remained attracted by the old idea of migration back to Palestine. They found friends in the sponsors of the Zionist Organization, established in Switzerland in 1897, which ten years later began providing money for Jewish acquisition of Palestinian land.

The year 1917 provided new impetus for the Zionist movement, though the political changes in

Russia brought an end to the persecutions there. As part of their operations against the Ottoman Empire in World War I, British forces entered Palestine. British foreign secretary Arthur James Balfour declared that the British government looked with favor upon the establishment of a Jewish national home in Palestine, though he said this must be accomplished without prejudicing the rights of non-Jewish people who lived there. This declaration became a part of the agreement of 1922 whereby the League of Nations assigned Palestine to the United Kingdom as a mandate. But the non-Jewish people of Palestine had no part in this decision, nor was there a single Arab in the League of Nations at that time to speak for them.

There was really no way of establishing a Jewish national home in Palestine without prejudicing the rights of non-Jewish people already there. The latter protested violently when Jews were encouraged to immigrate to Palestine. In 1922, a population of 591,000 Muslims, 84,000 Jews, and 73,000 Christians lived in the Palestinian territory. By 1939, the numbers had changed to 849,000 Muslims, 424,000 Jews, and 115,000 Christians. Clearly, if Jewish immigration continued on a large scale, the Jewish population would soon outnumber the Muslims and Christians combined. If this meant the establishment of a Jewish state, Muslim and Christian Arabs would have to accept the rule of a group which at the beginning of the mandate had constituted only one-ninth of the total. The British government, caught in its own dilemma, decided to decelerate Jewish immigration considerably in 1939. But this decision came in the very teeth of a new cry from central Europe for the relief of sorely oppressed Jewish people in that area.

The new anguish derived from systematic anti-Jewish policies devised by the Nazis. Adolf Hitler had made it plain that he hated the Jewish people well before his advent to power. As he saw the matter, though they were by nature inferior, they threatened the leadership role of his mythical north-European Aryan race. Before World War II, he persecuted them individually, segregating them where they were not so already, putting them at economic disadvantage, embarrassing them, and badgering them constantly with the uncertainty of what torment might come next. After World War II began, he decided to exterminate them on a scale no leader had attempted before. In Poland and other occupied lands, Jews were starved to death or gassed to death or tortured to death in a thoroughly deliberate, highly organized, extraordinarily ghastly program. Census reports from before and after the war confirm that six million Jews disappeared. Most of those still living in 1945 wanted desperately to get away from the scene of such atrocious behavior. Some went to the United States, some to Latin America, but others longed to live in Palestine. Here, after a few years of hardship and toil, there might appear genuine refuge from the wanderings of centuries, with Jews living in a state ruled by Jews for the first time in nearly two millenia. Jews already constituted nearly one-third of the population of Palestine in 1945, and in some Palestinian regions formed well over a majority.

London continued its administration of Palestine for three years after World War II, although its League of Nations mandate was not transformed into a United Nations trust territory. The British came under extreme pressure in 1946, as both the United States government and the Zionist Organization requested the admission of 100,000 extra Jews, while Palestinian Arabs argued that immigration should cease altogether. Bands of Jews and Arabs fought each other, as British forces tried in vain to preserve order. Illegal Jewish immigrants arrived, only to be arrested and detained. The United Kingdom attempted to persuade the opposing forces to agree on some compromise and to desist from terror. Its last attempt came in February

1947, when it proposed the entry of 100,000 more Jewish immigrants during an interim, while separate but temporary Jewish and Arab states would assume the task of working out their own arrangements for unity. Both Arabs and Jews rejected the idea.

In April 1947, the United Kingdom requested help from the United Nations. A special session of the General Assembly convened April 28 to discuss the matter. Arab delegations asked that this session discuss the termination of the British mandate and the independence of Palestine. The independence of Jordan (previously Transjordan) in 1946 had ended all other mandate rule in the vicinity. The Assembly snubbed the Arab proposal, however, as it set up a United Nations Special Commission on Palestine May 15, to "investigate all questions and issues relevant to the problem of Palestine." The Christian world of Europe and the Americas saw, or professed to see, a relationship between the Nazi torment and extermination of the Jews and the creation of a Jewish state in Palestine. The Muslim world of the Middle East denied any connection between what had happened in Europe and the proper future of Palestine. The Arabs regarded the situation as one in which a European people speaking a Germanic language wished to take over a district which even in 1947 remained predominantly Arabic in culture and Semitic in language.

The United Nations Special Committee on Palestine contained eleven members -- four from Europe and four from the Americas in addition to India, Iran, and Australia. The Committee unanimously approved part of its report of August 31, but another portion represented the accord only of a majority of seven. Everyone on the Committee agreed that the mandate should be ended and independence granted to Palestine, and called for the preservation of Palestinian economic unity. Three of the European and all four of the American representatives stated their preference for a partition of Palestine into three separate regimes which would agree to an economic union. India, Iran, and Yugoslavia preferred a federal government to cover all of Palestine, with the authority of Arab and Jewish component states restricted to local concerns. Australia decided at this level to abstain.

The proposal of the majority of seven won favor in the second regular session of the General Assembly. The Jewish state it envisaged, divided into three sectors, would encompass more than half the area of Palestine. The Arab state, similarly split, would along with Jerusalem contain more than half of the initial population. The city of Jerusalem, however, would have its separate regime, administered by the United Nations Trusteeship Council for ten years, to protect the religious interests of Judaism, Christianity, and Islam. The economic union, to cover all three regimes, would be compulsory for at least ten years, and would involve a common tariff and complete freedom of trade, a joint currency system, and provision for shared economic development. The representative of the Jewish leadership in Palestine, invited to express its views to the Assembly, spoke of its willingness to go along with this plan. The Arab leadership, on the other hand, expressed its complete rejection of the idea. The British government stated its own unwillingness to implement any solution that was not accepted by both sides in the conflict.

When the final vote on this measure was taken, on November 29, 1947, the 33 delegations in favor included 13 from Europe and 15 from the Americas as well as the Philippines, South Africa, Australia, New Zealand, and Liberia. The 13 in opposition comprised 9 Middle Eastern states along with India, Pakistan, Greece, and Cuba. Six Latin American countries, China, the United Kingdom, Ethiopia, and Yugoslavia abstained from voting. Though not all predominantly Christian countries stood in favor, every country voting for the resolution had a largely Christian population, at least until the advent of communism. Every predominantly Muslim country, on the other hand, stood opposed. The partition of Palestine thus constituted a very drastic step for the United Nations, seeking to establish an alien people on someone else's land -- against the wishes of the party most concerned (the Arab majority in Palestine) and contrary to the preferences of all their neighbors. It proved obvious from the beginning that the Palestinian Arabs would oppose the plan by violence, and that they could count on help from other Arabs.

The United Nations Palestine Commission, set up by the partition resolution, possessed no military backing for its task of implementing the plan. London declined to impose the United Nations decision upon the Arabs. The situation in Palestine became near-chaotic as Jews continued to arrive illegally, as Arabs joined forces to oppose the plan, as the most excited on both sides engaged in new acts of terror, and as the British announced their intention to give up the mandate and leave. By February 1948, the circumstances grew so difficult that the Commission threw up its hands. The United States government then decided to withdraw its support for immediate partition and to substitute a proposal for a trusteeship in Palestine. At Washington's initiative, the Security Council called for a second special session of the General Assembly. This session convened on April 16, 1948, but by then the initiative had slipped completely away from United Nations hands. The Palestinian events of the following year emphasized in extreme manner the political limitations of the new international organization.

The United Kingdom had chosen midnight of May 14-15, 1948, as the time when it would relinquish its Palestine authority. The United Nations, caught with its own decision that required force against the Palestinian majority, had neither the desire to carry out such a program nor the time to work out a better one. Obviously, the solution at this point lay in the hands of those who lived in Palestine, with whatever help they could get from outside. The Jews who resided there had long prepared for this moment, and with financial and moral support from abroad did not shrink from what they considered their responsibilities. On May 14, they announced the creation of the modern state of Israel, to function the moment British control terminated. The territory of Israel was drawn roughly to match that of the Jewish state proposed in the partition plan. The United States government quickly forsook its plan for buying time (the proposal for a trusteeship), and gave Israel immediate recognition and support. The Soviet Union waited only three days to extend its hand of friendship. But the League of Arab States, formed three years earlier in preparation for this moment, announced on the same May 14 its intention to organize a free, unitary Palestine; while troops of Egypt, Iraq, Syria, Jordan, Lebanon, and Saudi Arabia pushed into Palestinian territory, showing their eagerness to carry out this aim.

The General Assembly, overwhelmed by the turn of events, adjourned feebly on the day of the two announcements. To "promote a peaceful adjustment of the future situation," it appointed a United Nations mediator; little else remained that could be done. The mediator chosen six days later by a committee of the Assembly was count Folke Bernadotte of Sweden, who had presided over the Swedish Red Cross and helped to arrange the surrender of Germany in World War II. The efforts of count Bernadotte and the Security Council brought about a truce on June 11. Count Bernadotte then proposed a new idea for union between Israel and Jordan, with Jordan receiving Jerusalem and the non-Israeli part of Palestine but both sides conceding some territorial changes from the United Nations partition plan. Both sides rejected this proposal, and began fighting again July 8. After that, the combatants reached other truce agreements but broke each one in turn, until there seemed no way out of this conflict. Terrorists assassinated count Bernadotte himself on September 17. His successor, acting mediator Ralph Bunche of the United States, professor of political science and member of the United Nations Secretariat, attempted only to get the bloodshed stopped. He managed to do so with armistice agreements between Israel and its four neighbors -- first Egypt, then Lebanon and Jordan, finally Syria -- in February-July, 1949.

In the time before the armistices were arranged, Israel did well in the fighting. From original boundaries splitting its territory into three sectors and granting it somewhat over half of Palestine, its armies pushed the Arabs back until one compact state of Israel covered nearly four-fifths of Palestine and included part of Jerusalem. Furthermore, in the territory affected, both that suggested by the United Nations and that added later by the Israelis, most of the Arab population moved out, leaving a four-fifths majority of Jewish people. The Arabs relocated chiefly to a large section of land on the west bank of the Jordan River, under the jurisdiction of Jordan; and a small strip that included the city of Gaza in the southwest, administered by Egypt. There were about 800,000 of the Arab refugees altogether, afraid that their lives might be endangered in Israel (some of their kin had been killed needlessly), and in any event unwilling to live under an Israeli administration.

The new nation of Israel contained 800,000 inhabitants, of whom about 650,000 were Jewish; in January 1949, it began to organize itself as a modern republic. The people elected the parliament, a unicameral body, and chose Chaim Weizmann as president; the parliament selected David Ben-Gurion as prime minister. Israel wrote no constitution but adopted means of government

183

that provided a high degree of democracy. Proportional representation was provided for political parties, of which a large number flourished, representing a wide variety of both people and viewpoints. The largest parties had socialist programs; others catered to religious and ethnic minorities. The Mapai (Israeli Workers Party, moderate socialist) formed the first government in coalition with three other parties. David Ben-Gurion, prime minister and leader of the Mapai, had immigrated from Poland as David Gruen while Palestine still formed part of the Ottoman Empire. Forced to leave, he spent three years in the United States and traveled elsewhere, but returned after World War I; all genuine Jews, he believed, should seek to live in Palestine. Chaim Weizmann, a formerly British chemist (though born in Russia), had served 22 years (in two terms) as president of the Zionist Organization.

Of necessity, the Israel of prime minister Ben-Gurion faced up to a long period of austerity. The announcement that all Jews would be welcomed to Israel from every part of the world meant that provision had to be made for those who arrived. The first half-million came from 60 countries, and included significant numbers from Muslim Yemen and Iraq. Israel needed capital to develop its resources, and to provide subsistence for those who arrived without money. For this, there were many friends in Europe and America -- Jews who preferred not to move to Palestine but liked to send assistance instead, and Christians who believed that the new nation-state served a worthy purpose and deserved their support. Israel became a member of the United Nations in May 1949, before Jordan was admitted there; the new nation had indeed many friends. In its immediate geographic vicinity, however, only enemies existed, with no softening of implacable sentiments on the horizon; for the time being, with all the promise it seemed to hold for weary Jewish peoples, the third Israel had also to be accepted by them as the latest in a long world

184

series of predicaments.

The Cold War (Part I)

Hot war had reached a climax in 1939-45 from which everyone wanted to withdraw. Many persons hoped for at least an interlude of good will and civilization-building. Such an episode did not appear -- for the first five years, not even the glimmering of one. The new dissonance that emerged instead involved all the stronger powers. They had provided the might to win the war, at least in three of five instances. They received special prerogatives in maintaining the peace. Special responsibilities thus devolved upon them for wise planning in the postwar years.

The Big Five, as they were called, held the veto privilege in the United Nations Security Council. Their territorial and population strengths in 1945 indeed seemed to merit this special treatment. Armed forces of the United Kingdom guarded more than a fourth of the world by either of two counts, watching over 13,000,000 square miles and 540,000,000 people. The Soviet Union governed nearly 10,000,000 square miles and 190,000,000 inhabitants. France controlled nearly 5,000,000 square miles with more than 110,000,000 population. China and the United States contained roughly 4,000,000 square miles each, China holding 450,000,000 and the United States 160,000,000 residents. Upon the surrender of the Axis, no other power equaled these in at least the superficialities of global grandeur.

From the beginning, however, many persons found it realistic to speak not of the Big Five but of the Big Three. This custom spread, despite the assignation of the veto privilege, because China and France lacked the strength to match their size. The Chinese government had experienced difficulty through the war in hold-

185

ing even a portion of its own domain. Afterward, both during the internal conflict and under the Communist regime, China's concerns seemed separate and isolated until 1950. The French government had found it impossible during 1942-4 to maintain even a base on its home territory. The Fourth French Republic founded in 1946, though it played an important role in Europe, produced little immediate impact upon the world scene. Thus the United Kingdom, led by prime minister Clement Attlee; the United States, headed by president Harry Truman; and the Soviet Union, ruled by premier Joseph Stalin, constituted the real powers of the early postwar scene. Each of the three countries occupied a distinct place in the world political spectrum quite in keeping with its leader's personality and background. (Attlee, Truman, and Stalin were introduced in Chapter IV.)

Prime minister Attlee, a well educated man, was not as absorbed by nationalism as Stalin and Truman. His Labor government, elected in 1945, ruled the United Kingdom through this period. Some Laborites would willingly have cast their country in a third role, neither hostile nor overtly warmhearted to the United States or the Soviet Union. Labor's chief appeal to the British electorate, however, lay in its advocacy of moderate socialism. Preoccupied with this matter, with the shattering reduction in the British Asian empire, and with the economic necessity to preen commitments abroad, Attlee's government tended to plan its foreign policy in conjunction with that of Truman. There remained differences of opinion, as in regard to Palestine, but when Washington and Moscow glowered at one another London generally took Washington's side.

President Truman had not sought his first term in office, but in 1948 campaigned successfully for a second. His popularity, undimmed by a paucity of formal training, rested upon the plainspoken quality of his character -- in its

186

honest but often narrow simplicity not unlike that of many of his countrymen. In domestic policy, Truman walked in the footsteps of Franklin Roosevelt, whom he admired. In international bargaining, however, there existed few precedents for the issues Truman had to face. He and most United States citizens believed that they perceived an essential evil in communism. They took little note of the fact that the communist regimes so deeply committed to authoritarianism did often bring material sustenance to their people. United States opinion in the later 1940's saw communism as a diabolical plot, intended to drive as many persons as possible to their ruin. The Soviet Union, as mastermind of the plot, must be blocked in its pro-communist endeavors. Very few persons of either Republican or Democratic persuasion dissented from this general line of thinking, though differences emerged as to details of plans for action.

Premier Stalin continued in his position through this period without consultation with his people. After the war on the international scene as before the war only on the domestic front, he seemed to be attempting to prove all the worst stories about communism. Before 1939, the Soviet Union worried other nations only through propaganda and a little subversion. Now, obvious machinations followed in the wake of Soviet troops, bringing new peoples under communist domination. (Stalin even received attention for endeavors he did not undertake, such as the Communist seizure of China.) The Soviet government wished to spread communism, eventually -- such a goal remained part of its official intention. However, it had not prior to World War II used armed force in the enterprise. From 1943 to 1950, Stalin insisted that Soviet security was at stake in the political situations of eastern Europe. People in the United States did rapidly forget Russian sacrifices in the war effort, and quickly dealt in more friendly manner with the Germans and Japanese than with their former ally. Wounds opened by these actions would take

187

some time to heal. Stalin may have behaved the way he did because he felt his country threatened, or because he wanted to spread communism; probably no great distinction between the two causes existed in his mind.

In neither Europe nor Asia was the Cold War die cast in the year 1946. Decisions in that direction had not yet become irretrievable. Nor could one have discerned with certainty in that year that such a long-lasting strain would materialize. The Big Five Council of Foreign Ministers (but without China) met twice in 1946 to push on with European peace treaties. These two sessions (in Paris, May-July, and New York, November-December) came on either side of a Paris peace conference in which 25 nations participated, arranging terms for Finland, Bulgaria, Hungary, Romania, and Italy. Further talks, it seemed to many, would soon bring formal peace with Germany, Austria, and Japan. In some regions where the Soviet Union held great strength, there had not yet emerged clear evidence of a switch to communism. Klement Gottwald, a Communist, became prime minister in Czechoslovakia in 1946, but democratic socialist Eduard Benes continued as president and Jan (son of Tomas) Masaryk served as foreign minister. When Hungary instituted a republic in February, both its president and its premier came from the democratic private-enterprise Smallholders party. Moscow maintained its recognition of the Chiang regime as the legal government of China. Negotiations concerning a united Korea had not yet reached an impasse.

Nevertheless, a general feeling existed in the United States that communism was making catastrophic advances. Some of this attitude stemmed from the occurrences in Poland, Romania, and Bulgaria after the occupation of those countries by Soviet troops. Communist leadership had developed some popularity in Yugoslavia and Albania. The Communists led the field in multiparty races in France in 1945-6, and showed even

188

greater strength (while remaining a minority) in
Italy in 1946. Additional concern sprang from
the threatening situation in China. Persons who
did not comprehend the Chinese antipathy toward
Chiang tended to overrate Mao (along with his
presumed mentor Stalin) as a sort of superman, a
master of aggressive design. Further fear of
communism derived from United States confusion
over differences between first- and second-
quarter countries on the world spectrum. When
democratic socialist Czechoslovakia nationalized
its key industries, even though the United Kingdom had its own nationalization program, Washington reacted sharply, withdrawing economic aid.

President Truman and his people were not
completely mistaken about the intentions of communists in the world. Authoritarian socialism
remained primed to utilize every advantage. Nor
did the American citizenry fail to comprehend the
popularity of communism in specific instances.
Hungry and disadvantaged people more readily accepted communism than others; hence a necessity
to alleviate their plight. Most North Americans
grossly misgauged the world poverty problem, however, both as to its nature and its magnitude.
Instead of looking for allies who dealt with that
problem sympathetically and intimately, Washington tended to befriend those who shouted their
hatred for world communism or their friendship
for the United States. Government officials
often regarded nationalization of industry as
anti-United States as well as anti-private
enterprise. The resulting mental imbroglio meant
that no attempt could be made to retain the
friendship of Moscow or influence with communist
leaders, but that full attention had to be paid
to protecting the "free" world, as it was in-
accurately called, from further communist
incursions.

Three events of the year 1947 marked the
transition from the period of simple bad feeling
to the chronic trauma of the Cold War. The first

189

was the enunciation of the Truman Doctrine in the month of March. Its appearance came as an immediate reaction to the situation in Greece and Turkey. Greece had ostensibly returned to third-quarter democracy in 1946, ending the postwar interval when Great Britain controlled its situation. Elections produced a victory for the monarchist Populist party, which sponsored a plebiscite to bring back George II. Dissatisfied socialist and liberal parties, however, had refused to participate in the elections, stating that their candidates lacked freedom of movement. British military might countered armed resistance to the royal government by both the socialists and liberals. Assistance from Yugoslavia, Bulgaria, and Albania, however, enabled the revolutionary elements to continue.

Although not subject to turmoil similar to that of Greece, the people of Turkey also lived in a state of anxiety. In this case, the problem stemmed directly from attitudes of the Soviet Union. Russia had long been dissatisfied with its strategic situation on the Black Sea. The best ports of Russia could be entered only through the straits of the Bosporus and the Dardanelles. Great Britain and France perennially insisted that any agreement concerning these straits should include British and French signatures. Now, the Soviet Union proposed that Black Sea powers alone (the Soviet Union, Turkey, Romania, and Bulgaria) should determine a new accord which would remove the straits from control by Turkey. A Soviet newspaper campaign became so violent that the reluctant Turks felt an invasion might be imminent.

By early 1947, Clement Attlee's government felt the necessity to reduce its commitments abroad. London could not afford to keep even its old empire going, let alone the marginal interests previously considered vital to the empire. One of these was its influence in the Mediterranean area, designed to maintain the British "lifeline" past Gibraltar, Malta, and

Cyprus, and through the Suez Canal. If the British withdrew their support for Greece and Turkey, however, and if no other support appeared, communist influence in the region seemed certain to increase considerably. President Truman thus intervened to strengthen the hands of Greece and Turkey as the British concluded their chapter of aid. In doing so, he spoke of the "broad implications involved" in a United States decision to help nations such as these: "I believe that it must be the policy of the United States to support free peoples who are resisting attempted subjugation by armed minorities or by outside pressures. I believe that we must assist free peoples to work out their own destinies in their own way." The plain inference in Truman's announcement, buttressed by a remark concerning intimidation in Poland, Romania, and Bulgaria, was that the Soviet Union did not concur in this outlook toward the free peoples.

The formulation of the so-called Marshall Plan constituted the second and most determinative of the events of 1947 that signaled the commencement of the Cold War. Though not presented as such, this new program developed as a logical extension of the Truman Doctrine. George Kennan, a State Department adviser, suggested the idea, and United States secretary of state George Marshall bequeathed the plan his name when he delivered its basic ideas in a speech on June 5. The full character of the Marshall Plan became defined, however, by a statement of the Soviet foreign minister Vyacheslav Mikhaylovich Molotov, a month later.

Secretary Marshall simply presented Europe's postwar need, without drawing distinctions between communist and non-communist regions. "Europe's requirements for the next three or four years . . . are so much greater than her present ability to pay that she must have substantial additional help or face . . . deterioration of a very grave character," he said. "It is logical that the United States should do whatever it is

191

able to do to assist. . . . Such assistance . . . must not be on a piecemeal basis as various crises develop. Any assistance . . . should provide a cure rather than a mere palliative. . . . The initiative, I think, must come from Europe. . . . The program should be a joint one, agreed to by a number, if not all, European nations." Marshall spoke of his country's desire to cooperate with any government "willing to assist in the task of recovery." But he spoke for a nation which had already rejected a Soviet request for help (mentioned in Chapter IV), which blocked Soviet claims to German reparations, and which withdrew asssistance to Czechoslovakia when that country nationalized its industries. The United States, not Europe, had already taken the initiative in suggesting this idea, despite Marshall's words to the contrary. Did his speech mean that the United States would decide who was willing to assist in the task of recovery? Would the United States Congress approve this Plan if it included the communists?

Prime minister Stalin and foreign minister Molotov apparently experienced uncertainty in regard to these questions. Molotov traveled to Paris to confer with British and French counterparts there. The Cold War might have been prevented if he had agreed to make plans for a European recovery program to include all its peoples. At the least, if this was not what Marshall had intended, Moscow might thus have exposed a tremendous American bluff. Molotov, however, could not convince himself of the sincerity of the project insofar as it included the communists, but preferred to consider it as another means of attacking his country. Worst of all, from his point of view, was the thought of the advantage which would accrue to Germany, at whose hands the Soviet Union had suffered so much. Neither did the Soviet Union really want to join a plan which might conflict with its own hopes for the future. Impressed by the capitalist world's addiction to financial crises, communists in general believed that their own world could be constructed to eliminate economic depressions; close ties with non-communist economies might well vitiate such ideas. The Soviet government decided that neither it nor any other communist regime would participate, and thus set the character of the Marshall Plan. Nine months later, the United States Congress which passed it generally assumed its basic anti-Soviet character. Many North Americans indeed believed that the blockage of the Soviet Union's designs constituted the most important reason for helping a part of Europe to recover.

The conference at which most of non-communist Europe took over the initiative from secretary of state Marshall met in Paris in July. Nine third-quarter regimes (Italy, France, the Netherlands, Belgium, Greece, Switzerland, Ireland, Iceland, and Luxembourg) attended, along with six from the second quarter (the United Kingdom, Turkey, Sweden, Austria, Denmark, and Norway), and lone Portugal from the fourth. No invitation went to Spain; nor could non-organized West Germany attend, though Bonn's financial interests were included in the program. The decision against participation by Moscow produced similar negative replies from Poland, Yugoslavia, Romania, Hungary, Bulgaria, and Albania. Finland also declined to attend, pleading its anxiety to avoid quarrels. Czechoslovakia agreed to participate, but changed its mind after pressure from Moscow. The break between communists and non-communists, save for Finland, was a sharp one. The last conversations had ended, it seemed, and the battle lines had been drawn. Many people expected a hot war to emerge very soon, but the Cold War developed instead.

The 16 countries at Paris requested 22,000,000,000 dollars from the United States. During the next four years, they received 13,000,000,000 dollars in loans and grants, channeled through their Organization for European Economic Cooperation. European industrial recovery received a real boost, though the continent's living standards remained far below those of the benefactor. For the help they received, it cannot be said that the recipients gave away their national freedom, as Molotov had charged would happen. They did agree to monetary controls which most of them would have favored anyhow. Moderate socialists, however, remained free to carry out their programs in the United Kingdom and Scandinavia, or to campaign for the same privilege in most of the other countries. Even communists were allowed to remain active where they held strength, as in Italy and France. Western European countries did not become minions of the United States. But this does not mean that the communist regimes could have accepted the Marshall Plan without making greater sacrifices. It might have meant for them, indeed, a relinquishment of communist economic ideals in return for capitalist favors. The Soviet Union preferred to battle for its own recovery. Seven other governments, in view of their circumstances, decided to tag along. In January 1949, the Soviet Union, Poland, Romania, Czechoslovakia, Hungary, Bulgaria, and Albania formed their own Council for Mutual Economic Assistance, referred to in English as COMECON; East Germany joined them in 1950. They looked toward a coordinated development of their national economies and an acceleration of economic and technological progress.

A third event of 1947 starkly symbolized the advent of the Cold War, even before the European Recovery Program began. In September, representatives of the communist parties of the Soviet Union, Italy, France, Poland, Yugoslavia, Romania, Hungary, and Bulgaria met secretly in Poland. There they decided to establish a Communist Information Bureau, soon known as the Cominform, to encourage world communist cooperation. The Comintern had been abolished four years before, in the interests of good relations between allies. The new organization had little working significance, since communists had never

ceased cooperating, but provided a clear indication of premier Stalin's set of mind against
international good will. The Cominform, announced in October, established its headquarters
in Belgrade. Its chief propaganda magazine carried the title For a Lasting Peace, For a
People's Democracy!

The Hungarian sequence of events in 1947
indicated the wide gulf between people's
democracy as the phrase was used by communists
and democracy in the remainder of the world.
Free elections had been held in Hungary with the
presence of the Soviet army; indeed, they constituted the first real taste of democracy the
country had known. The Smallholders party chosen
for office, however, made up a most heterogeneous
entity, some of its leaders seeking radical social reform while others remained very conservative. Much of its support probably came from
persons who regarded it as the only anti-Soviet
vehicle available. The Smallholders in 1947
proved no match for the Soviet Union and its
local cooperators. Various outstanding members
of the party were accused of treason and purged;
even the premier decided to seek exile. Other
Smallholders continued in office, but lost the
allegiance of anti-Soviet voters. In new
elections in August, the Communist party won the
largest single vote (22%) while the Smallholders
remnant, now in coalition with the Communists,
dropped to third position. Two-fifths of the
vote continued in opposition, but the Communists
and their allies held a clear majority. From
this point on, the so-called people's democracy
replaced genuine democracy completely in Hungary, as those in control decided policy for the
nation under the apparent assumption that one
election constituted a perennial mandate.

The fourth meeting of the four-power Council
of Ministers (not counting China, which again did
not attend) took place in Moscow, March-April
1947. The fifth met in London in November-December. The ministers achieved no progress toward

the peace treaties with Germany and Austria. The London conference brought out clearly some essential differences between the Russians and their previous allies. Especially did the Russians emphasize German reparations; they had received only a small portion of what they had been asking. Molotov reverted in London to the figure of 10,000,000,000 dollars, first suggested at Yalta. But the other three powers had turned their backs on reparations to the Soviet Union from the western zones, counting on German production there as a part of their own European Recovery Program. They had in effect chosen West Germany as a new partner, rejecting the former ally whose economy the Germans had attempted to ruin. When the London meeting adjourned without any lessening of tension on these matters, neither time nor place was set when the ministers might meet again.

Cold War battle lines seemed more firm than ever when Czechoslovakia dropped fully into the Soviet orbit in February 1948. In this transition which the Russians so obviously desired, direct Russian intervention proved unnecessary. The people of Czechoslovakia had given more than one-third of their vote to the Communist party in elections of 1946. The premiership had remained Communist since then, the Communists and one other party holding a majority between them. With Eduard Benes (see Chapter IV) as president and Jan Masaryk as foreign minister, the nation set out on a course of friendship to all nations. This course became greatly disturbed when Washington withdrew financial assistance, and when Moscow in effect told Prague it could not participate in the European Recovery Program. The chief contention within Czechoslovakia, however, lay over the right of the Communist minister of the interior to put Communists in control of the police. Noncommunists in the cabinet demanded that the minister of the interior resign. When he refused, they did so themselves, on February 20, in a body, following the old-fashioned manner of asserting a grand protest. Premier Klement Gottwald called for their replacement, however, with Communists and some collaborators. Communist groups used force during the next few days to intimidate those who would not go along with them, taking control of most government agencies, communications centers, and newspaper plants. On February 25, Benes gave in to Gottwald's demands. The changeover became thus simply consummated.

Jan Masaryk, the only cabinet member not chosen by the Communists after February 25, continued as foreign minister. On March 10, Masaryk died; the Gottwald government said he committed suicide, while others have maintained he was murdered. On May 30, the new government sponsored communist-style elections with only one list of candidates, all approved by those in authority. A new constitution, prepared subsequently, followed communist models. President Benes resigned June 7 rather than sign the new document; on September 3, he too died. The noncommunist world, which respected Benes, thought he had made an error. Most people there took his career as evidence that one cannot do business with the communists and expect to win. This type of reasoning, however, put the communists in an impregnable and insuperable position, giving them credit for greater valor than the facts required. Benes had really only committed the error of behaving gentlemanly in a non-gentlemanly world. He lived by intellect and honor. Others, especially the large numbers in Czechoslovakia who had no respect for the strength of his position, simply did not understand the superiority of his way, not only for him but for them.

Marshal Tito of Yugoslavia was a less gentle, more arbitrary man. (Again, see Chapter IV.) Born in humble surroundings like Benes, he had learned raw activism and eschewed intellectual endeavor. These proved the traits Tito needed in 1948 for an operation the opposite of that in Prague. Tito admired the Soviet Union and disliked the other big powers, but Tito had never thought of himself as a puppet of the Soviet regime. As Hungary and Czechoslovakia knuckled under, in effect, to complete Soviet control, Tito's pride in an independent though allied position began to bother Moscow. Troubles arose concerning trade, Russian spies in Yugoslavia, and Yugoslav conversations with the United States, which had never ceased to be represented in Belgrade. On June 28, the Cominform (meeting in Bucharest rather than Belgrade) read Tito's party out of its membership. Stalin, who had come to despise the Yugoslav with a fury, believed that this would finish the man.

Anticipated rebellions against Tito, however, failed to materialize. The Yugoslav generals upon whom Stalin had counted found that Tito had the support of his people. Pressures of various kinds came from other communist regimes, including that of Albania. But the Soviet Union did not invade Yugoslavia, as many persons thought it would, and Tito continued in control of the country. The following year he gave up thought of renewing the old ties, and sought to establish good relations with non-communist governments. Tito was a hard man; everyone knew he ruled as a dictator. If he had ruled as a gentle man, he could hardly have survived in the world around him. Yet he dedicated his own willfulness to something other than absolute power for himself. Some realization of this fact may have prompted the Yugoslav citizenry to stand by him.

Still another happening of 1948 illustrated the limitations of Soviet power. In a sense, this one may rather be considered a newsworthy non-happening. Finland's position in relation to Moscow had run similar to that of Czechoslovakia. There lay some difference in the fact that the Finnish Communists did not control the prime ministership; they did occupy other positions in the cabinet, however, including the ministry of the interior. More significantly, many Czechs appreciated the Soviet Union's moral support against Hitler in 1938 and its end-of-the-war liberation of their country from the Nazis, while Finns were bound to remember the beginning-of-the-war attack on their country by Soviet troops. Finland and the Soviet Union entered into friendly treaty arrangements in April 1948. In May, nevertheless, when a crisis developed over the refusal of the minister of the interior to resign (the precise situation encountered three months earlier in Prague), the remainder of the cabinet forced him to do so. Communist groups began to organize violence, but quieted when a communist sympathizer received appointment as the new minister of the interior. Then, in free elections of early July, the Communist party and its closest ally suffered a considerable setback. Moscow had evidently thought that its partisans might win this election; it had even gone to the pain of cutting Finland's remaining reparations bill in half, in order to prove Russian good will just before the casting of the ballots. Moscow's failure to win Finland stemmed ultimately from its own confidence in the Soviet cause, the belief that its own collaborators were genuinely popular. The Finns' success in keeping Finland their own could not have transpired, however, without a remarkably careful control of Finnish strategy. In Finland, at least, politics remained the province of hard-working, hard-thinking, and clever gentlemen.

The action and non-action, respectively, of Yugoslavia and Finland received much less attention in 1948 than the Cold War battle for West Berlin. Here one strong power -- the Soviet Union -- tested its ability to strike at other nations of robust strength without physically coming to blows. The struggle developed into a long test of audacity and daring. The world slept uneasily as each day seemed to pose the real danger of another global conflict. But all the derring-do remained controlled, and after a full year of tension people breathed more easily as the situation again relaxed.

When Joseph Stalin decided to tighten his battle lines, Berlin must have constituted his sorest perplexity. By agreement not with the smaller neighbors who sometimes trembled at his authority, but with the only possessor of atomic weapons in the world and some of that nation's closest friends, he had allowed a bastion of non-communism on the very inside of his communist world. The three sectors of West Berlin (American, British, and French) were provided with good communications by highway, by rail, by canal, and by air lanes to tie them to the three zones of West Germany. Technically, no political connection existed, but ideologically there rapidly grew one, so that West Berlin became an island in a communist sea, well provided with lifelines for non-authoritarian living. Stalin's squeeze on West Berlin, in an effort to change all this, began on the last day of March 1948, soon after all attempts at four-power control of the city had ended.

For nearly three months, there was only interference with the free movement of men and supplies. Papers had to be checked where no inspection took place before. Border authorities turned some trains back and allowed others to proceed, but with only a part of their cargo. The controls became tighter and tighter, until only by air could the three powers count on getting through to their sectors in the city. Then, on June 18, the western occupation forces announced a currency reform in their zones and sectors which the Russians had not approved. Because of this, ostensibly -- though the whole crisis seems bound to have occurred anyhow -- the Soviet Union six days later stopped all traffic from West Germany to West Berlin by highway, railway, and canal. To emphasize the intentions, the East German regime cut off the West Berlin population from supplies of electricity and coal. The United States high command in Germany advised president Truman to authorize a push by armed convoy through to West Berlin. The president accepted more moderate advice, deciding along with prime minister Attlee to fly in all the goods that West Berlin needed.

The Berlin airlift, as the new proceeding was called, proved no simple operation. A new airport had to be built in Berlin. Large planes had to maneuver skillfully in previously negotiated airlanes. Potatoes and coal made strange freight for the airlines, though enough of both was hauled so that West Berliners could, through careful rationing, survive. The Russians even made difficulties for the planes as they flew over East Germany, at one point carrying on air war games which brought Soviet, American, and British air fighting equipment directly wing to wing. Stalin did not desire hot war with the United States, however; he only wanted a cheaper victory in Berlin. When he finally saw that would not be possible, in May 1949, he abandoned the effort more suddenly than it had started, and West Berlin had its communications again. The western powers thus triumphed, through a combination of determination and sagacity -- but unfortunately their victory did not mean the Cold War had ended.

Those who suffered most from the anxieties of the Berlin blockade were the people of western Europe, confronted by Russian might. Among ground elements of force in Europe, the Soviet government controlled a clear preponderance; only the existence of the American atomic bomb offered the non-communist peoples some security should the Soviet Union choose to attack. Five of the western nations -- the United Kingdom, France, the Netherlands, Belgium, and Luxembourg -- signed an alliance pact in Brussels in March 1948, though together they lacked sufficient resources to take on a strong enemy. Next they turned to other countries for consultation, notably faraway Canada and the United States. Italy was brought in, and Iceland and Portugal;

likewise Denmark and Norway, though not a hesi-
tant Sweden. Ireland took no interest; Spain
received no invitation. But the twelve who consented to enter negotiations did decide to write
an important treaty.

All of these countries with the exception of
Italy and Luxembourg held some coastline on the
North Atlantic Ocean. They thus decided to call
their agreement, signed April 4, 1949, the North
Atlantic Treaty; and the continuing association
therefrom the North Atlantic Treaty Organization,
or NATO. The treaty did not mention the Soviet
Union, but everyone understood that it was directed at that country -- provocatively so, said
the Russians; only for the obvious necessities of
defense, said those who favored NATO. The pact
contained a simple basic idea: "The Parties
agree that an armed attack against one or more of
them . . . shall be considered an attack against
them all; . . . each of them . . . will assist
the Party or Parties so attacked by taking . . .
such action as it deems necessary. . . ." NATO
rapidly moved beyond this mutual promise,
however, providing the actual forces that would
cooperate at the beginning of any emergency.

With NATO a reality, the peoples of western
Europe could breathe easier, though the Soviet
and American giants seemed to be breathing harder
all the time. Neither of the latter two, however, wished to push farther at once. The Berlin
blockade ended in May, the month after the signing of NATO. A sixth Council of Foreign Ministers met in Paris in May-June, making some
progress toward the peace treaty with Austria.
Perhaps nothing did more to still the existing
furor than the unannounced explosion in July of
the first Soviet atomic bomb. Moscow after four
years possessed a weapon to match that of the
United States, though for a while the Soviet
Union would lag behind in its production. Now,
however, the Soviet Union had less to fear from
the United States, and Stalin felt less need to
establish strong battle lines on the ground.

For nearly a year, no significant new step appeared in the Cold War. And then, when one did come with great suddenness, a small power rather than a big one was immediately responsible. On the early morning of June 25, 1950, world attention focused sharply on Korea, where invasion armies crossed the 38th parallel of latitude from north to south. The last occupation forces had left Korea a year earlier (see "Asian Independence"). After their departure, both Pyongyang and Seoul glowered at one another, each contending a right to speak for all Korea, and occasionally sending probes across the line that divided them. South Korean forces owed their training and equipment to the Americans, and North Korean troops theirs to the Russians, but neither lay demonstrably under a larger power's control. The action of June 25, 1950, differed from any on this line that had taken place previously. The North Koreans had prepared to strike all the way to the end of the peninsula; they expected South Korea to become theirs. The action amounted to simple all-out-aggression with the aim of complete conquest, the kind the world had experienced when World War II began.

The government of the United States, seconded by virtually the entire non-communist world, reacted very forcefully to this new crisis. Before the end of the day, the United Nations Security Council noted "with grave concern the armed attack upon the Republic of Korea by forces from North Korea," and called upon North Korea to withdraw its army to the 38th parallel. Nine countries voted for and none against this resolution; Yugoslavia abstained. The Soviet Union had absented itself from the Council since January, protesting the holding of the Chinese seat by Tai Wan. On June 26, president Truman decided to use United States naval and air forces against the invaders. Announcing this decision on June 27, he also stated that a United States fleet would protect Tai Wan from invasion from the Chinese mainland. Later that afternoon, despite this intermingling of two disputes, the

203

Security Council recommended to United Nations members that they "furnish such assistance to the Republic of Korea as may be necessary to repel the armed attack and to restore international peace and security in the area." The vote ran 7 to 1 (Yugoslavia casting the negative) with the Soviet Union still absent; the delegates of India and Egypt lacked instructions from home.

Forty-seven members of the United Nations sent communications supporting these resolutions. India joined this company, though Egypt opted to abstain. Five other Arab delegations spoke indirectly if at all about the resolution of June 27, while five communist members joined Yugoslavia in declaring the move illegal. (Only six votes had been cast in the affirmative, not counting that of Tai Wan, and the measure lacked the support of the Soviet Union and mainland China.) By the end of the year, 39 United Nations members and Italy had rendered some kind of help to South Korea. Fifteen of these dispatched military units to fight on Korean territory. The United States began sending in ground troops from Japan on June 30. On July 7, the Security Council asked the United States to provide a unified command. The following day, Douglas MacArthur was appointed the commanding general. One month and even two months later, the South Korean and United Nations forces found themselves holding only a small part of the Korean peninsula. But suddenly in September the picture changed, with a surprise landing farther north by United Nations personnel, and quickly the lines became redrawn near the 38th parallel.

There was now a major decision to be made. Should the North Korean armies be pursued into their own territory, their attack having been repelled? The United Nations had originally designed a plan for all Korea. Now that it stood triumphant on the battlefield, should it use the forces still at its command to further its own peacetime decisions? Communist China issued a warning that a foreign occupation of North Korea would bring intervention by Chinese forces. But few persons took Mao's regime seriously on this point, and few worried about the principles involved. It appeared in late September that a mop-up operation would suffice to bring North Korea to a full surrender. General MacArthur recommended this action, the United States accepted the proposal, and the United Nations agreed also. Of those who had assisted South Korea, only India expressed misgivings as the General Assembly on October 7 resolved that "all appropriate steps be taken to ensure conditions of stability throughout Korea."

The first non-Korean troops crossed into North Korea on October 8. South Koreans, also under United Nations (MacArthur's) command, had crossed the parallel a week earlier. Half of the new invasion army, driving from south to north, consisted of men from the United States, two-fifths of South Koreans, and one-tenth of soldiers contributed by 14 countries. After a week, "volunteers" began to cross over the Ya Lu River from Communist China to fight on the North Korean side. To avoid provocation of the Chinese, Washington had counseled general MacArthur to use only South Korean troops in areas close to the Chinese frontier. MacArthur failed to heed this advice, or to take the entire Chinese intervention seriously. On November 24, already in control of much of North Korea, MacArthur began an "end the war" offensive which he expected to conclude within a month. On November 26, Chinese troops counter-attacked in heavy numbers, tearing the United Nations position to shreds. Instead of victory within the month, as MacArthur had predicted, there came bitterness and chagrin. On December 28, Chinese and North Korean forces began once again an invasion of South Korea.

And so, as 1950 came to an end, the Cold War had smouldered into very hot war on the peninsula of Korea. The United States had made a mistake of crossing the 38th parallel in the direction of China; 14 members of the United

Nations had erred in following along. The Soviet Union, holding aloof from armed hostilities, resumed attendance in August at the meetings of the Security Council, speaking for North Korea there. If the Soviet Union did encourage the North Koreans to invade South Korea in the first place, as most non-communists assumed, then this was the greatest miscalculation of all. But few persons were admitting errors anywhere, least of all general Douglas MacArthur, who had behaved over-eagerly in command. With no one prepared to give in, even in the face of an expanded hot war, the Cold War would obviously carry over into the new decade.

The Political Spectrum

The spectacular political event of the first postwar quinquennium loomed larger than any of the headlines. Directly or indirectly, it took them all in, and held farther-reaching implications than all of them combined. This event was the very remarkable growth of the keynotes of the new age, democracy and socialism. There is no way of measuring private persons' devotions to these causes. A rough over-all analysis can be made, however, on the basis of the number of people involved in nations following one ideology or another. The counts used here (and henceforward in this study) include neither colonial territories nor those countries whose population totals reached less than half a million. In this chapter, numbers of inhabitants to the nearest million are given for individual countries as of 1950, with the exception of those whose populations were mentioned earlier in the treatment of this time period.

The measure of democracy is taken by adding the second and third quarters of the political spectrum together. At the end of 1945, even with the gains of that year, the democratic regimes indicated in Chapters III and IV included a little less than one-third of the world's population living in independent countries. At the end of 1950, well over half (about 57%) lived under democratic rule of one degree or another. Major additions to the ranks were several new countries -- India, Pakistan, Indonesia, the Philippines, South Korea, and Burma -- and the three principal Axis powers, Japan, West Germany, and Italy. Czechoslovakia constituted the most significant of the few losses from this massive category.

The extent of socialism is gauged by combining the first and second quarters. (Note that regimes of the second quarter are counted for both socialism and democracy, and those of the fourth quarter for neither.) At the end of 1945, even with the gains of that year and the previous one, the socialist regimes indicated in Chapters III and IV included an approximate one-fourth of the world's population living in independent countries. At the end of 1950, nearly three-fifths (about 59%) lived under socialist rule of one degree or another. The addition of China and India alone goes far toward explaining this great change, but the accession of Burma, East Germany, and Czechoslovakia also assumed significance. A few socialist parties in second-quarter regimes lost power when defeated in elections. The socialism they had introduced remained, however, so that no country deserted either part of the socialist half of the spectrum.

The increase in communist-ruled population was the most sensational of all the changes, communist countries (3 in the Orient, 9 in Europe) making up 36% of the world's non-colonial population in 1950. The growth of the first quarter came about largely because of the addition of the people of China. Many non-communist people seemed to feel that the Chinese nation in taking up communism had converted itself into a sort of pariah. Some non-communist countries recognized Mao's regime as the government of

China, but others proved very reluctant to do so. The United States particularly took the lead in non-recognition of "Red" China, continuing to act as though Chiang's government of Tai Wan were that of all China, as it pretended to be. In the United Nations, Mao's administration claimed the right to hold all the Chinese seats, including the permanent one on the Security Council. India, in September 1950, proposed that mainland China be accorded this right. Sixteen countries, including six communist regimes, India, Pakistan, the United Kingdom, and Burma, voted in favor of the resolution. The United States, 17 Latin American countries, and 15 others voted in the negative. France, Egypt, Argentina, and Canada abstained, as did six other delegations. When Chinese troops fought United Nations forces two months later in Korea, no one could argue that China should have chosen to meet over the conference table, since that mode of action constituted the very privilege Mao's government had sought and been denied.

North Korea and Mongolia, the remaining communist countries of the Orient, were similarly isolated, though for different reasons. North Korea has received attention in "Asian Independence" and "The Cold War." Mongolia (800,000 population in 1950) made a slow start in implementing Marxist theory (Marx had taken little interest in the pastoral pursuits which engaged many Mongolian people), but did organize a five-year plan starting in 1948.

Leadership in the communist world remained with the Soviet Union, with 180,000,000 people in 1950. Its 33 years of communist rule simply had no match among the other communist regimes, the oldest of which possessed only six years of experience. Moscow wanted to maintain its leading position, of course, and could do so only with rapid national recovery. Soviet people had died in large numbers during the war, probably as many civilians as soldiers, in the neighborhood of 12,000,000 altogether. Tens of thousands of population centers had been destroyed, millions of buildings smashed (including factories, libraries, and schools), tens of thousands of miles of railroad track obliterated, and many sources of electric power demolished -- though industrial districts in Siberia remained unharmed. The Soviet Union had to overcome these disadvantages, suffered in a common cause, largely without the assistance of its allies. The United States, best in a position to help, did not really wish to see the Soviet Union recuperate. Moscow, on the other hand, not only expected to recover the gains it had lost but to forge far ahead, proving to the world the advantages of communism.

The Soviet Union inaugurated a Fourth Five-Year Plan for the development of its economy in 1946, modeling after its first three which preceded the world conflict. The Five-Year Plan entailed the setting up of goals and definition of the means to attain them, the goals themselves remaining adjustable through the operation of the Plan. In heavy industry, which the Fourth Plan emphasized (as had the first three), specific quantities of production of such items as coal, oil, and steel were projected for the year 1950. The government hoped that by that year industrial output would exceed that of ten years earlier, before the German invasion. Without a loan from the United States, and without sizeable reparations from West Germany, but with the cooperation of other eastern European peoples engaged in the same enterprise, the Soviet Union did manage to forge ahead rapidly under its Fourth Five-Year Plan. Most of its original goals, indeed, were achieved in four years rather than five. Many persons outside the communist world failed to notice Soviet war damages, or to take this capability for self-recovery seriously. Even the Russian development of the atomic bomb in 1949 made little impression on these people, who remained convinced that socialist planning would never become that effective.

Prime minister Stalin could hardly have failed to feel enthusiastic about the accomplishments of the Fourth Five-Year Plan. His moves on the international scene had often run into frustration or been countered. His hopes at home nevertheless had materialized, and his position in the communist world seemed nearly undisputed. The defection of Yugoslavia could be counted an annoyance, counterbalanced by the almost complete servility of the remaining European communist regimes. Stalin's concept of leadership never became sophisticated. It was too much to expect this poorly educated son of a shoemaker to grasp all the intricacies of thought of a Lenin. In Stalin's manner of thinking, other nations performed wisely when they followed the Russian line. And his own people acted sensibly only when they followed him.

In the postwar world even more than formerly, Stalin's firm sense of self-wisdom on every subject branded him one of the world's most thorough-going dictators. In 1946, he directed campaigns not only to rid Soviet society of the large numbers of people who had taken advantage of war conditions for their own gain, but also to purify the country from all foreign influence. He criticized writers and musicians for susceptibility to alien ideology. He disciplined filmmaker Sergey Eisenstein for failure to portray the first Russian tsar as an unmitigated hero, banning release of the second part of Eisenstein's Ivan the Terrible. In 1948, he accused famed musicians Dmitry Shostakovich, Sergey Prokofiev, and Aram Khachaturian of the crime of composing in bourgeois style. Later in the same year, he took the side of biologist Trofim Denisovich Lysenko in a dispute over genetics, in effect choosing Lysenko's line of interest as the only legitimate field of inquiry. (Lysenko, interested in grains and transplants, taught the inheritance of characteristics acquired during the lifetime of seeds and plants.)

Official criticism and control in science and

the arts naturally had a dampening effect. This became balanced, however, to a considerable extent by the generous encouragement granted the more cooperative scientists and artists. Stalin prizes were set up for those who did follow the lead of the regime, but from whom a certain degree of quality was demanded. The Soviet Union launched an all-out "peace drive" in 1949-50, with trappings so very elaborately unsophisticated that Stalin himself might have planned them. (No less a personage than atomic scientist Frédéric Joliot-Curie headed a concomitant World Peace Movement.) The doves used as a symbol by Stalin seemed utter hypocrisy to those peoples who believed he had planned the Korean invasion. They probably seemed to Stalin himself a true expression of his own desire for a quieter world, drawn more on the Soviet pattern. They appealed to millions of persons in both communist and non-communist societies as an expression of Soviet simplicity, directness, and sincerity in a world that for them had become too complicated.

Poland, third largest of the communist-guided nations (its population dropped to slightly below 25,000,000 after World War II), proved one of the clearest examples of the servility imposed upon eastern European "satellite" regimes. The Polish Provisional Government of National Unity formed in 1945 lasted until elections of January 1947. Plebiscites held earlier ratified an agrarian reform and a drastic nationalization of industry. As the election approached, it became plain that one slate of candidates, submitted by the majority in power, would win, and that anyone who chose to have continuing influence might as well join the majority bloc. Stanislaw Mikolajczyk and others who were not comfortable with that bloc remained free to continue propaganda for their parties, but failed to get anywhere in the elections. A United Polish Workers (urban) party and a United Peasant party in coalition formed the overwhelming lead in the Polish parliament, with the

urban group making all decisions before the parliament acted. Mikolajczyk left the country by
stealth in October 1947, after the government had
persecuted his followers with terror and intimidation, leaving a small Democratic party, more
willing to cooperate, as the only represented
minority. A year later, Wladyslaw Gomulka,
secretary-general of the Workers party since
1943, lost his job after showing sympathy for
Tito. In 1949, a Russian general, Konstantin
Rokossovsky of Polish birth, became a Polish
citizen so that he could head the ministry of
national defense. In 1950, under president
Boleslaw Bierut and premier Jozef Cyrankiewicz,
each of whom had held office three years, Poland
gave every sign of complete readiness to do the
Soviet Union's bidding.

In East Germany, the similarly obeisant government of premier Otto Grotewohl and Communist
party secretary Walter Ulbricht agreed in 1950 to
the ceding of a large district of eastern Germany
to Poland. In Yugoslavia (16,000,000), on the
other hand, marshal Tito's communist regime
showed that, in a more fortunate combination of
circumstances, such humility was not really
necessary. The Yugoslav regime displayed as much
harshness as any, but in Tito's favor rather than
that of Moscow. It began its existence as a
republic with the trial and execution of Draza
Mihajlovic, who had once fought the Germans. In
the early years, Tito quarreled vehemently with
the royalist regime in Greece, with the United
States over downed airplanes, and with the United
Nations over Trieste. Once ousted by the Cominform, he directed his energies just as vigorously
against Yugoslav citizens showing continued
friendship for the Soviet Union. But Tito had
trouble on his hands. His own first five-year
plan (1947-51) faltered when one after another of
the communist bloc of nations refused to trade
with him. To save his own industrialization program, and his attempt to collectivize Yugoslav
agriculture, he turned to Moscow's enemies for
aid. London first and Washington later decided

212

to assist the man whom they had helped fight the Nazis, but whose aims had now changed considerably.

Romania (16,000,000) throughout this quinquennium moved steadily in the Soviet orbit. Premier Petru Groza had taken office in 1944; though not a Communist, he served equally well for carrying out the Russian intentions. Elections in 1946 were decided before they took place in favor of a Communist-dominated coalition of parties. Those who protested stood in danger of imprisonment or execution. King Michael himself abdicated in December 1947, and Romania became a republic four months later. Thenceforward, nationalization of industry and collectivization of agriculture became the order of the day. Czechoslovakia (12,000,000 -- see "The Cold War") followed much the same policy, under president Klement Gottwald and premier Antonin Zapotocky, though having to contend with the opposition of its Roman Catholic church.

The communist government of Hungary (9,000,000) after 1947 likewise became embroiled in controversy with the Catholic church. Here the strongest opposition came from Jozsef Mindszenty, the archbishop of Esztergom (27 miles from Budapest) and primate of the country, who became indignant when the state took over the Catholic schools, and who also supported most aspects of the previous Hungarian order of aristocratic society. Cardinal Mindszenty was arrested on charges of treason to the nation, and sentenced to life imprisonment in February 1949. Hungary by this time had come under the domination of the Hungarian Workers party, a merger of communists and other socialists, which "cooperated" with other small groups in the People's Front.

Bulgarian evolution went beyond that of Hungary, the switch to the Soviet line having occurred three years earlier. In Bulgaria (7,000,000), a republic replaced the monarchy in 1946; the Bulgarian Fatherland Front became an organization rather than a coalition, completely dominated by the Communist party. Albania (1,200,000), also organized as a republic in 1946, lay completely in the hands of prime minister Enver Hoxha, who served as secretary-general of the Communist party, renamed the Labor party in 1948. World communist hopes for the future also devolved to a considerable extent on the fortunes of the large Communist parties in Italy and France and the sizeable one in Japan.

The second -- democratic socialist -- quarter of the spectrum grew less sensationally in this period than the first quarter, but nevertheless also made dramatic gains. Democratic socialist countries (4 in the Orient, 6 in Europe, 2 in the Americas, 2 in the Middle East) made up 23% of the world's non-colonial population in 1950. This band's biggest accession by far was India. The determination of India's leaders to follow democracy ran strong, and contrasted sharply with the inattention to such matters in the neighboring republic of China. India maintained a philosophic and pragmatic dedication to socialism, eschewing the strident dogmatism of the communist countries. India's attention in its early years remained absorbed by problems of organization on democratic lines along with the conflict over Kashmir. When the Korean crisis came, India picked its way carefully, favoring the United Nations effort in South Korea but frowning upon the extension of that effort to North Korea. Here lay the beginnings of the development of a third position, sympathetic with neither side in the Cold War but too independent to be labeled simply "neutral." India, a new country, possessed a greater opportunity to lead in this position than the United Kingdom, weighed down as the British government was by history.

Burma under prime minister Nu made a firmer commitment than India to socialism, while the two remaining democratic socialist regimes of the

Orient were turning the other way. Both Australia (8,000,000 population) and New Zealand (2,000,000) voted Labor parties out of office in late 1949. In each instance, however, the succeeding party, professedly devoted to private enterprise, did not expect to reverse most of the steps toward socialism. Only the latest changes, such as the nationalization of banking in Australia which the winning Liberals did not wish to accept, became the subject of real inter-party controversy.

In Europe, the United Kingdom (50,000,000) moved rapidly to adopt socialism, the pressure for which had built gradually for some sixty years. (Beatrice and Sidney Webb, early leaders of the socialist Fabian society, died in 1943 and 1947 respectively; novelist Herbert George Wells, their rival in the society, in 1946; playwright George Bernard Shaw, their friend, in 1950.) The British socialist legislation came in the face of financial distress wrought by wartime devastation and the loss of the Asian empire. The year 1946 proved the most energetic one for the introduction of nationalization measures. The Laborite government took over the coal industry, the nation's bank, civil aviation, the telecommunications network, and surface transportation facilities aside from the railways. It also instituted an elaborate social insurance scheme, and initiated a free national health service. In 1947, electricity and the railways were added to the government's domain. In 1948 and 1949, the nationalization of the iron and steel industry was voted. Labor had proposed nothing more than this when it received its mandate in 1945. For good measure, however, in 1949 the parliament cut back the right of the oppositionist House of Lords to delay any of these programs (or any non-financial bill passed by the House of Commons) from a two-year to a one-year privilege.

New elections were held in Great Britain in February 1950. Attlee's party retained its majority, but only by a slim margin. Now, how-

215

ever, two or more moderate socialist parties existed in this country, in effect, rather than the Laborites alone. The Conservatives said they would reverse the iron and steel nationalization but would not disturb the other public enterprises. And on the other hand, Labor itself (except for the iron and steel) made no proposal to move farther at once. With party policies so nearly identical, the people chose among leaders instead. Winston Churchill, still the head of the Conservatives, received a large hearing when he stated that he would not have dissolved the empire as had Clement Attlee. The Conservative party, the National Liberal (formerly the Liberal National), and one other, voting together, forced Labor to remain united or to fall. Many Laborites disagreed with Attlee, however, in wanting to push nationalization more rapidly and preferring an independent stand toward the Cold War. Events that held the Laborites together were the attainment of Marshall Plan recovery objectives ahead of schedule in 1950 and the preparation of a new plan whereby the United Kingdom would aid in the development of southern and southeastern Asia.

Northernmost continental Europe, freed from Nazi influence and rule, resumed its general tendencies toward democratic socialism. Social Democratic rule took the place of a wartime coalition of parties in neutralist Sweden (7,000,000). Denmark (4,000,000) renewed its independent political life with an even balance between Social Democratic and private-enterprise parties. Finland (4,000,000), whose postwar reparations bills from the Soviet Union spurred a moderate growth of socialism and an immoderate wave of inflation (prices more than tripled), moved very little farther in the direction of socialism after 1948, when its democratic socialists refused to form new coalitions with the nation's Communists. Norway (3,000,000) returned to its prewar rule by the Labor party. Austria (7,000,000), south rather than north of Germany, continued its coalition of the People's (formerly Catholic People's) and Socialist parties, with its affairs dominated by the prolonged argument of the powers over its peace treaty.

Mexico, now third in size of the second-quarter regimes (26,000,000), continued its separate revolutionary course. The Party of the Mexican Revolution became the Institutional Revolutionary party in 1946, dedicated to the further development of programs that had already been initiated. The government sponsored a far-going literacy campaign and initiated a number of large public works projects. Mexico was turning to the right, some critics said, under the presidency of Miguel Alemán (from 1946), since Alemán encouraged private industry and talked little in terms of socialism. But Mexico had moved far to the left through the enlargement of its public sector a decade earlier, and did not intend to have matters otherwise. Uruguay (2,000,000) remained the only other Latin American second-quarter regime, a bastion of freedom alongside authoritarian Argentina.

Turkey, (21,000,000), while retaining its socialism, underwent a new experience in democracy when an opposition party won an election. Ismet Inonu, head of the Republican People's (formerly People's) party and president of the republic 1938-50, had decided to place Turkey close to the United States when his regime felt threatened by the Soviet Union. A Democratic party professing to hold liberal private-enterprise views, in keeping with those of the United States agents who arrived, campaigned hard and won overwhelmingly in elections of 1950, obtaining voting power in the parliament six times that of the Republican People's group. It became obvious at once, however, that the Democrats did not intend to dismantle the public sector in Turkey in favor of the private. Beleaguered Israel after its creation in 1948 joined Turkey as a second outpost of European democratic socialism in the Middle East.

217

The largest of the democratic socialist parties not in power during this quinquennium was the Social Democratic organization of West Germany. A new Labor party of Brazil, the Social Democratic of Japan, and the Socialist of France added significantly to second-quarter strength. In addition, the Socialist and Socialist Workers parties of Italy, a Labor (formerly Social Democratic Labor) party of the Netherlands, and the Socialist party of Belgium each held some strength in their respective countries. Many of these groups participated in fraternal meetings, but no immediate postwar reconstruction of the Second International took place. Neither did there exist any other second-quarter form of cooperation to compare with the first quarter's Cominform.

In quantity of people involved, the third -- democratic private-enterprise -- quarter of the spectrum gained as dramatically as the second. In the number of countries newly adhering, its gains were the most sensational of all. Democratic private-enterprise nations (11 in the Americas, 6 in the Orient, 8 in Europe, 5 in the Middle East, and 2 in Sub-Sahara Africa) made up 34% of the world's non-colonial population in 1950.

The third-quarter nation containing the most people (152,000,000 of them at the end of this period) remained the United States of America. Its stand for democracy ran strong, its wartime private-enterprise record impressive. Before the war, as its economy recovered from a major depression, its people had already achieved the highest living standard in the world. During the war, as other lands suffered, this one made new material gains. From 1940 to 1945, its gross national product per capita increased 44%, exclusive of the change in value of the inflated dollar. Many persons believed that such growth could continue into peacetime.

There remained two economic problems, however, which this nation had never resolved, and which the war experience exacerbated. One was the riddle of inflation, which rendered the false impression that the wartime gain in living standard amounted to 100% rather that 44%, and which everyone knew hurt the person with savings. The other was the fact that this best-fed and best-clothed population on earth still had to struggle, by and large, for a living. The nation contained not only a very poor segment -- the least prosperous 20% of persons received only 4% of the income -- but also the medium poor, a large share of the workers, who found it very difficult to move ahead financially. Many though far from all of the medium poor, represented by the American Federation of Labor and the Congress of Industrial Organizations, asked for higher wages as soon as the war terminated. Their demands, generally not willingly granted by the employers, led to mammoth strikes in 1946 against such giants as the automobile industry, the steel manufacturers, the soft coal mines, and the railroads. The unions won what they demanded, but in every instance the increase became swallowed by inflation. The per capita gross national product change from 1945 to 1950 amounted to a 7% loss as measured in constant dollars, to compare with the 44% gain during wartime. Members of the unions achieved nothing. Workers outside the unions often suffered severely.

The theory of private enterprise insisted that businessmen should set their own prices, since the laws of supply and demand and the effects of competition would keep prices at the proper level, at least during peacetime. In line with this reasoning, most wartime controls on prices were removed in 1946, resulting in a 33% rise during this quinquennium. Workers could ask for more, but the prices would go up accordingly, for the employers had the last word in setting prices. Except for rises in productivity per worker, not always easy to attain, private enterprise seemed to have no way out of this conundrum.

Worker initiatives for higher wages in 1946, which inconvenienced many non-union people who then tended to blame the workers for the inflation, helped the Republican party win control of both houses of Congress in that year. A coalition of Republicans and southern (conservative) Democrats pushed through legislation in 1947 to cut the power of the unions, making it illegal for them to demand a "closed shop" (open only to members of the union). To many people's surprise, however, Democratic president Harry Truman produced a comeback in the elections of 1948, carrying both houses of Congress with him as he was reelected to office. Truman had often talked of a Fair Deal, the equivalent of Franklin Roosevelt's New Deal for the workers, and although few of them had really gained during his first term, Truman could at least make out that he was trying in their behalf. Thomas Dewey, his Republican opponent from New York, possessed less of the common touch. Third-party candidates Strom Thurmond and Henry Wallace -- the former concerned because Truman displayed a sense of fairness to non-whites, the latter averring that Truman had acted unwisely toward the Soviet Union -- received relatively few votes. In 1950, however, the Democrats lost ground in the Congress again, so that the Republicans and southern Democrats together could dominate the assemblage. The United States thus edged toward the conservative right while much of the world looked in the opposite direction.

As the Cold War played upon people's nerves and minds, the intolerance that prevailed in the Soviet Union made a strong appearance in the United States also. People of conservative bent began to call liberals communists, or communist dupes (one hardly more complimentary than the other), just as liberals or conservatives were labeled fascists in the communist press. The wildest of the name-callers began to accuse

220

others of spying; persons who labeled themselves
ex-communists or ex-spies seemed particularly
adept at accusing others. Some spying took
place, of course, on both sides; and the work of
a few of the spies became uncovered. Many people accused of communist conspiracy, however, had
engaged in nothing of the kind. In the year
1950, senator Joseph McCarthy of Wisconsin
emerged as the worst name-caller of all, as he
made unsubstantiated claims that the Department
of State harbored many subversives. Many people
took McCarthy seriously, and the climate against
any kind of dissidence became stronger. Conservatives in both parties voiced their support of
McCarthy, while liberals often found themselves
obliged to argue from the defensive. The brand
of thinking which McCarthy espoused came depre-
catingly to be labeled McCarthyism. With its
acceptance even in high governmental circles, the
United States courted fascism more closely than
it realized. (See "Three Steps in Human
Dignity," Chapter VI, for a further discussion of
McCarthyism.)

Brazil (52,000,000), which had but recently
experienced fascism, showed real signs of development of its democratic processes during this
quinquennium. President Dutra served his five-
year term starting in early 1946. Neither he nor
his Social Democratic (liberal-conservative)
party did much to solve the nation's problems.
Workers became poorer than ever with new rises in
the cost of living. Dutra showed genuine
interest in democracy, however, as he helped
prepare a new constitution in 1946 and followed
it thereafter. The Social Democratic candidate
for president ran third in the elections of
1950. The nominee of the National Democratic
Union (conservative) came in second. The winner
was none other than Getúlio Vargas, the former
dictator. Vargas' associations had changed. His
support came from the Labor party, organized to
fight for social justice to the most impoverished people of Brazil. Vargas hoped, he said,
to make Brazil a socialist democracy like the

United Kingdom and the countries of Scandinavia. The difficulty lay in the fact that Vargas would not have the backing of his own parliament, since labor had come in third there, and neither Social Democrats nor National Democrats took any interest in his program. A fourth party of some size -- the Communist -- had been declared legal in 1945 and outlawed again in 1947; in 1948, the federal government expelled its delegates from both national and municipal bodies.

In Canada (14,000,000), democracy ran a tranquil course. Liberal prime minister William Lyon Mackenzie King retired in 1948 after 22 years of service, the last 13 of them consecutive. Louis St. Laurent, his liberal successor, received an overwhelming vote of confidence from the country the following year, with his chief opponents the Progressive Conservatives (formerly the Conservatives) doing poorly.

Colombia (11,000,000) moved into a very difficult period beginning in 1946. At that time, the Liberal party in power split. This group had moved from a nineteenth- to twentieth- century liberalism in the 1930's. Now, one wing of the party led by popular Jorge Eliécer Gaitán began to advocate moderate socialism. As the liberals struggled among themselves, Conservative Mariano Ospina Pérez won election as a minority president 1946-50, while ill feeling ran very high. Many Liberals held the Conservatives at least indirectly responsible when an assassin murdered Gaitán in 1948; the finger of suspicion pointed particularly at a nineteenth-century wing of the Conservative party led by Laureano Gómez. A fierce riot (called the bogotazo) took place in the capital Bogotá, and dreadful carnage broke loose in the countryside. The Liberals withdrew their candidate for president in 1949, though they retained a majority in the congress. Gómez became president in 1950 and suspended the congress, but could not stop the bloodshed. Until Gaitán, Colombia's democracy had never fully taken the masses into account. Now the masses in

222

their vast, inchoate way were registering an opinion. (See "Three Losses for Democracy," Chapter VI.)

Elsewhere in Latin America, the record of democracy remained rather desultory. Peru deserted the third for the fourth quarter. Chile (6,000,000) did better, despite a more-than-doubling of its cost of living, with a Radical president and left-wing coalition in Congress (which included Communists for a year, after which their party was outlawed). The so-called Authentic Revolutionary party governed Cuba (6,000,000), keeping the presidential succession regular but doing little of what it had promised for the people. (Again, see "Three Losses for Democracy," Chapter VI.) Guatemala (3,000,000) moved quietly to the left, holding to democracy while engaging in social reform opposed by foreign business interests. Bad feeling arose between Guatemala and the United States, when the ambassador from Washington showed solicitude for the financial situation of the companies while remaining insensitive to the needs of this country's majority, the Maya people. (See "Three Revolutions Interrupted," Chapter VI.)

In the meantime, Ecuador (3,000,000), after enduring a period of confusion marked by a doubling of prices in this period, emerged from the fourth quarter in 1948 with a freely elected, non-party president. Bolivia (3,000,000) saw its chief executive hanged on a lamp post in 1946, but chose another one without duress the following year, in the midst of the same inflation of prices that had hit Chile and Ecuador. Costa Rica (900,000) suffered a break in regularity when the party in power lost the election in 1948 but attempted to continue its rule. A group led by José Figueres prevented this attempt, and turned the presidency over to the man not of their party who had won. In Panama (800,000) a rather similar event occurred, as Arnulfo Arias (ejected by coup in 1941) won the election but had to resort to force to become president.

The bulk of the population increase in the third band came from the adherence of six Oriental nations. Of these, Japan and Ceylon maintained the best-developed political life, with parties reaching across three quarters of the spectrum. Pakistan and Indonesia held democratic intentions, but with their difficult geographical situations remained slow in getting organized. The Philippines government had its problems with corruption, while the South Koreans became involved in a war. In Europe, West Germany and Italy also constituted important additions to this band. Party life blossomed rapidly in both, the West German groupings remaining confined to the two democratic bands while those of Italy scattered across the entire spectrum.

France (42,000,000) contained a wide dispersion of parties also, though the most rightwing of them stayed clear of fascism. The Fourth French Republic, organized on a second try late in 1946 (the voters rejected the first constitution), promised to be as tempestuous as the Third. President De Gaulle resigned even before the first constitution was submitted, arguing that France needed a stronger executive than the document provided. Dissatisfaction over poverty at home became matched by France's difficulties abroad, particularly with the Asian part of its empire. Governing cabinets, which changed at least once each year, included all three of the largest parties at first, but after 1947 dropped the Communists. This left the Popular Republicans and Socialists in control along with smaller groupings, of which the Radicals assumed the most importance. The Republican Party of Liberty, strong for private enterprise, usually remained outside of the coalitions.

The Netherlands reached the 10,000,000 mark in population late in this time period. Wilhelmina of the house of Orange, who had acceded to the Dutch throne in 1890 while yet a child, abdicated the crown because of poor health in 1948, in favor of her daughter Juliana. Democracy at home contrasted sharply with Netherlands policies in Indonesia until the recognition of that country's independence. The Catholic People's (formerly Catholic) party and the Labor (formerly Social Democratic Labor) party shared the responsibilities of government at this time.

Third-quarter democracy in smaller European countries continued strong, though it demonstrated many ramifications. The Social Christian (formerly Catholic) and Socialist parties of Belgium (9,000,000) quarreled through most of the quinquennium as to whether king Leopold III, who had cooperated with the Nazis, should be allowed to keep his throne. The Socialists, after threatening civil war over the matter, won when Leopold abdicated in favor of his son Baudouin. Switzerland (5,000,000) steered a conservative and aloof course, not even making application to join the United Nations. Ireland (3,000,000), whose prime minister Eamon De Valera resigned in 1948 after more than ten years in office, separated itself more completely from former British ties in 1949 by dropping its membership in the Commonwealth. Greece (8,000,000), whose cost of living climbed to 15 times its former level (the most ruinous of any nation's inflation during this time period), suffered sharp division from 1946 until 1949, when Yugoslav aid to its insurgents stopped and the virtual civil war ended. Leftists had adequate representation in the parliament after new elections in 1950 that provided proportional representation for parties as well as some freedom of choice for the voters within the parties. The Populists remained the single largest group, but a coalition led by the Liberals ran the government.

Two Middle Eastern countries of this quarter had meaningful experiences with democracy. Eqypt (20,000,000) conducted elections in 1950 in which the opposition won. The chief Egyptian preoccupations after the war were the continued presence of British troops on Egyptian soil and the events in Palestine. The nationalist Wafd party, which had ruled for two years during the war but gave way again to the Saadists and Liberal Constitutionalists, conducted a lively campaign in 1949, promising popular reforms inside Egypt along with a strong stand in regard to the British and the situation in Palestine. A non-partisan government managed the election, which Wafd won easily, while only small minorities supported the other two parties.

There were also elections in Iran (16,000,000) in 1947, though no great change developed from them. Encouragement of democracy by the shah, however, led to the development of a Tudeh (Masses) party which favored drastic reform. Tudeh first attracted attention as a pro-Soviet organization; later, its announced program followed the orientation of democratic socialism. Tudeh, though outlawed in 1949, continued to maintain considerable popularity.

Three smaller Middle Eastern nations also belonged to the third quarter. Syria (4,000,000), organized as a parliamentary-style republic, suffered three coups in the one year of 1949, but returned again through free elections and a new constitution. Lebanon (2,000,000), with a Christian for president and a Muslim for premier, survived this period without any coups. Jordan (previously Transjordan, population 1,300,000) joined this quarter in 1946 upon the termination of its mandate. Jordan's king remained very friendly to the British, with whom he fashioned a close alliance, and Jordan's parliament proved equally cordial to its king. The Jordanese people spoke the Arabic language, and chiefly worshipped as Muslims, but the other Arab states did not approve Jordan's annexation of the eastern part of Palestine in 1950.

Sub-Sahara Africa during this quinquennium contained few independent countries and a dwindling amount of democracy. South Africa (12,000,000) lost an esteemed prime minister in 1948, as a result of elections, and headed down a trail certain to lead into a maze of problems. Jan Smuts had served as premier for 14 years, the last nine of them in succession, as leader of the United party favoring liberalism and cooperation with Great Britain. The National party, which won the most votes in 1948 (though not a majority), was the People's party renamed, the group that had opposed the declaration of war against Nazi Germany. Daniel Malan, its prime minister, proposed and began to implement a system of apartheid to remove nonwhites from whites as far as possible without the whites losing the non-whites' labor. Liberia (900,000), the other Sub-Saharan regime of this band, moved constitutionally to allow its True Whig president, very friendly to the United States, to succeed himself beyond a second term.

The fourth quarter of the spectrum lost as sensationally in numbers of people as the first quarter gained. Fascist-type countries (2 in Europe, 3 in the Orient, 1 in Sub-Sahara Africa, 9 in the Americas, and 4 in the Middle East) made up only 7% of the world's non-colonial population in 1950. The largest fascist country remaining in the world was Spain (population 28,000,000 in 1950). There, Francisco Franco and the Falange party continued to rule through this period despite the expressed unfriendliness of a great part of the outside world. The United Nations General Assembly recommended in 1946 that nations not maintain ambassadors in Madrid, and that Spain be barred from all United Nations-associated agencies. Monarchists within Spain maintained some opposition to the Franco regime as did a Spanish refugee government located in Mexico since the civil war of 1936-9. By insisting on his firm anti-communist record, however, Franco began to get more of a hearing. In 1950, the United States government granted a loan to his administration, and the General Assembly retracted its recommendations. Portugal (8,000,000), which had a fascist-type regime like that of Spain (its premier António de Oliveira Salazar had held office since 1932), remained outside the United Nations also, but only because of communist opposition; Portugal became a member of NATO from the beginning.

Thailand with 20,000,000 inhabitants (named Siam again 1945-9) passed through considerable turmoil during this five-year period, moving to the third quarter for a time but soon returning to the fourth. The young king, Ananda Mahidol, came back from his studies in late 1945. The following year he led the way to democracy under the (modified) constitution of 1932, providing for free elections and a bicameral assembly to which the premier and his cabinet would be responsible. In June the 20-year-old monarch was found dead with a bullet in his head, in circumstances suggesting murder. His still younger brother Bhumibol Adulyadej succeeded him while still in Switzerland for his education, and came home in 1950. Field marshal Pibul Songgram, who had cooperated with the Japanese from 1938 to 1944, led a coup in late 1947, bringing the democracy to an end. Further, he produced a second coup in 1948, after his party had lost an election, to place the power firmly in his own hands as premier. Thailand under the arbitrary rule of Pibul took a strong anti-communist stand at the time Mao's forces occupied mainland China, and thus won the friendly attention of the United States government.

Nepal (7,000,000) showed some signs of moving from the fourth quarter also, like Siam under the leadership of a king. One family had held the prime ministership in this land since 1846, and with that position absolute control of the country. In 1950, king Tribhuvan, who had held the symbols of authority since 1911, fled to India, receiving support there for a more democratic Nepali regime. Tai Wan, in effect becoming a separate country from China in 1949, moved in the opposite direction as Chiang Kai Shek resumed the presidency after acting president Li Tsung Jen traveled to the United States and refused to return. Tai Wan had been peopled chiefly by Amoy-speaking immigrants from Fukien province in the eighteenth and nineteenth centuries; its culture reflected that of China as modified by Japanese influences during 50 years.

Ethiopia (18,000,000) remained after the Second World War the largest of the old-fashioned monarchies. Haile Selassie, its emperor since 1930, had lived in London during the Italian occupation of his country 1935-41. Ethiopia possessed a parliament, but Haile Selassie appointed all its members. He took as his chief project after the war the prevention of an Italian return to Eritrea and Somaliland. In regard to the former, he had the satisfaction of seeing plans approved by the United Nations in 1950 for a federation of that colony with Ethiopia. A part of Eritrea had belonged to Ethiopia prior to 1882.

Of all the fourth-quarter regimes, Argentina (17,000,000) behaved most like a democracy at this time, though its similarity in some matters of behavior did not make it one. Juan Domingo Perón became president early in 1946 for a six-year term. He may well have been the choice of a majority, as the election results said. He had aimed his campaign to appeal to the laboring class, and an attack by the United States may also have increased his popularity. (An official paper from the United States dealt with the fascist sympathies of Perón during the war.) But Perón received the support also of the generals who had upset the constitutional order in 1943, with whom he himself had been associated. He now banded his followers together in a single Peronista party which won most of the seats in the congress. A small Radical minority continued to be elected also. Perón nationalized Argentina's banking, railroads, and airlines, and drew up a new constitution in 1949 promising great social change. He had no intention of socializing Argentina's economy, however, while inflation in Argentina in these five years raised prices to two-and-a-half times their former level. His party spent much of its time and energy preparing the way for extended Peronista rule, making it increasingly difficult for any opposition to raise its voice.

Of the smaller Latin American countries, Peru (8,000,000) and Venezuela (5,000,000) performed some meaningful maneuvering toward second-quarter ideas, only to be thrown back into the hands of their militaries. Peru's moderate president José Luis Bustamante, elected in 1945, had accepted the backing of a pragmatic democratic socialist party, the American Revolutionary Popular Alliance or APRA, led by Víctor Raúl Haya de la Torre. APRA had sought power in Peru since the early 1930's, and now set out to exploit its advantage. Other elements backing the Bustamante regime, however, opposed every move of APRA, and the country sank deeply into turmoil. A series of actions led to the termination of Peru's democratic regime in 1948 by conservative general Manuel Odría, who two years later made himself the president. Meanwhile, the Peruvian cost of living more than doubled during this quinquennium. Venezuela had undergone a revolution in late 1945 which led to the first democratic elections in the nation's history in early 1946 and late 1947. The leading party was Democratic Action, headed by Rómulo Betancourt. Its program called for renovation of the country along second-quarter lines, with the government to play a large role in a newly developing economy. In late 1948, however, these plans came tumbling down as a military junta took over the controls.

Nothing even so evanescently significant happened in six other Latin American countries of this band. The regime which ruled Haiti (3,000,000) during this period came in by coup in 1946 and went out the same way in 1950. The Dominican Republic (2,000,000) remained in the hands of Rafael Trujillo, in charge since 1930, pressures from more democratic regimes of the Caribbean area notwithstanding. El Salvador (2,000,000) had rid itself of a 13-year dictatorship in 1944, but failed to reach the point of free elections before a small group of men took power. Another coup in 1948 produced a more socially conscious but nevertheless arbitrary regime. The aging president of Honduras (1,400,000), Tiburcio Carías Andino, gave up the office he had held since 1933; a more progressive man of the same party succeeded him on January 1, 1949. Paraguay (1,400,000) ran through several rapid changes in leadership, winding up with one-party rule, while its prices more than quadrupled in five years. Anastasio Somoza García, in charge of Nicaragua (1,100,000) since 1937, experimented with puppet presidents but, dissatisfied, returned to the office of chief executive himself. Only Ecuador of this group managed to escape to the third quarter.

Neither were there dramatic happenings in the Middle Eastern contingent of fourth-quarter lands. Mohammad Zahir, who had succeeded to the throne in 1933, continued his reign in Afghanistan (12,000,000), undisturbed by thoughts of political parties or democracy; he remained preoccupied instead with the idea of an autonomous state of Pashtunistan to be carved out of his new neighbor Pakistan, to include the Pashto people who lived there. Afghanistan from the 1880's until World War II had been considered a buffer state between the Russians to the north and the British in India. After 1947, it constituted the only non-communist state besides Finland which had borders with the Soviet Union and no alliance with the United States.

Saudi Arabia (5,000,000), under the rule of Abd al-Aziz Al Saud (Ibn Saud) since 1926 (the country having been named for him) remained an absolute monarchy, but a very wealthy one, with the postwar development of the oil discovered in 1938. Iraq (5,000,000) developed a very adequate set of parties during this period, but muffled their activity as the government continued to

231

consist of a regent acting for a very young king, assisted by only one political leader. Yahya, already the ruler of Yemen (4,000,000) nine years before it became autonomous in 1913, was assassinated in 1948; one of his sons succeeded him.

Approximately 7% of the population of the entire world (some 23,000,000 more people than lived in fourth-quarter countries) remained under colonial rule of one kind or another in 1950. A small portion of them inhabited former League of Nations mandates now made over into United Nations trust territories. All of these territories stayed in the same hands, except Syria, Lebanon, and Transjordan, which had become independent; Palestine (see "A Third Israel"); South West Africa, which South Africa incorporated into its territory in 1949 over United Nations protest; and the formerly Japanese Mariana, Caroline, and Marshall Islands, which by a Trusteeship Council "strategic area agreement" were put into the hands of the United States.

Some changes took place during this period within the yet large British and French empires. The Straits Settlements, a British colony, became separated into its three parts in 1946, one of them now called the colony of Singapore, the other two joining with nine Malay states to form a new protected union of Malaya, labeled a federation in 1948. North Borneo and Sarawak, two of three protectorates on the Borneo coast, became British colonies in 1946. India took over the British role in both Bhutan and Sikkim in 1947. The British colony of Newfoundland became a part of Canada in 1949. In 1946, France incorporated as part of the home country (calling them "overseas provinces") the former colonies of Guadeloupe, Martinique, French Guiana, and Réunion. The parts of French West and French Equatorial Africa, along with French Oceania, New Caledonia, French Somaliland, and St. Pierre-

232

Miquelon, it labeled "overseas territories." Upper Volta, an eighth division of French West Africa, reached the status of an overseas territory in 1947, in company with the Comoro Islands.

Of the colonial areas still held in 1950, by far the most populated were British Nigeria and French Indochina, with about 34,000,000 and 29,000,000 inhabitants respectively. Indochina, when the French army returned in 1946, became affected by turbulence leading into open warfare. France recognized Laos (formerly a colony) along with Cambodia as a protectorate and associated state within a newly established French Union. The difficulty lay elsewhere, in the eastern part of Indochina, which Ho Chi Minh and his Viet-Minh following (introduced in chapter IV) called the Democratic Republic of Viet-Nam, but which the French described as the protectorates of Annam and Tonkin and the colony of Cochinchina. Early in 1946, as they prepared to renew their prewar controls, the French signed a tentative pact with Ho's political apparatus, recognizing its dominance of Tonkin and part of Annam but not its claimed status as an independent regime. Further negotiations broke down, chiefly over the quarrel as to the status of Cochinchina. However, besides the difficulty over this matter the French and Viet-Minh objectives differed radically.

Regular warfare between the two broke out in December 1946 and continued through the quinquennium. During all this time, Ho held the greater part of the territory, even in Cochinchina, and had the backing of a very large number of Vietnamese people. To counter the popularity of Ho, the French chose to deal with Nguyen Vinh Thuy (better known as Bao-Dai, or Keeper of Greatness), the former emperor of Annam under French protection, a man who had received his education in France, who liked French ways, and lived in France after resigning his position in 1945. Bao-Dai had previously enjoyed his own

233

species of popularity, but he was not a person to cope with revolutionary ferment for causes alien to his personality. In 1948, France announced the creation of its own Viet-Nam, territorially the same as that Ho claimed to rule. In 1949, Bao-Dai returned there to live and to act as the protected ruler. His Viet-Nam achieved the status, like Cambodia and Laos, of an associated state in the French Union. However, the Vietnamese people now showed little enthusiasm for Bao-Dai. The war went on, while communist governments began to recognize Ho's regime, the British and United States governments recognized that of Bao-Dai, and others like India and Indonesia refused to recognize either one.

Despite the Cold War and other troubles, international organization continued to grow during this period. The League of Arab States, created in 1945, held many meetings of its General Council, planning common action of its members, chiefly in regard to Palestine. Friction arose over the concept of a "greater Syria," to include Iraq and Jordan as well, which elements in these countries favored but Egypt opposed. Jordan stood alone on its annexation of eastern Palestine. A treaty of 1950 to create an Arab League Economic Council, a Joint Defense Council, and a Permanent Military Commission had little immediate effect.

The Ninth International Conference of American States met in Bogotá, Colombia, in 1948, before and during the time of the bogotazo. Its prime achievement was the creation of the Organization of American States, which took provisional effect immediately. The OAS, as the group became known in English, adopted the Pan American Union as its secretariat, and by 1950 organized its overall Council, an Inter-American Economic and Social Council, and an Inter-American Council of Jurists. It provided also for Meetings of Consultation of Ministers of Foreign Affairs, especially to handle complaints of disturbances

234

of the peace covered by an Inter-American Treaty of Reciprocal Assistance signed in Rio de Janeiro in 1947. Minor difficulties between Costa Rica and Nicaragua in 1948, Haiti and the Dominican Republic in 1949, and Haiti, the Dominican Republic, Cuba, and Guatemala in 1950 provided the OAS Council early opportunities for peacemaking.

In 1949, there came into being a new type of international body. This was the Council of Europe, in a very real sense representing all the people of the 10 to 13 countries included. The United Kingdom, Italy, France, the Netherlands, Belgium, Sweden, Denmark, Norway, Ireland, and Luxembourg constituted the original ten. Turkey, Greece, and Iceland joined the association later. The Committee of Ministers of the Council of Europe would represent its states, as in the OAS and the Arab League. The Consultative Assembly, however, would represent the parliaments of those states, and in the actual working of things (since all were practicing democracies) the parties in close proportion to their strength. This Council did not intend to deal with security matters; it aimed instead to do what it could to build unity among its members.

Five new specialized international agencies related to the United Nations appeared during this period, and two older ones contracted a tie with the United Nations. The latter two were the Universal Postal Union and the International Telecommunication Union. The others were UNESCO, which started functioning in 1946 (see Chapter IV); the International Civil Aviation Organization (1947); the World Health Organization and the International Refugee Organization (1948); and the World Meteorological Organization (1950), now with governments rather than government officials as its members. The International Refugee Organization had for its object to assist the millions of persons displaced by World War II and its aftermath. Along with the World Health Organization, it took over most of the responsibilities formerly assigned to the United Nations

235

Relief and Rehabilitation Administration, created in 1943 and dissolved in 1947. An International Trade Organization and an Inter-Governmental Maritime Consultative Organization passed through the planning stages but found trouble getting the ratifications needed.

The United Nations itself enjoyed effective leadership from its first secretary-general, Trygve Lie. Lie had served in the cabinet in Norway both before and after the German occupation; his background lay in the Norwegian Labor party. Under his guidance, the United Nations Secretariat became a real model of efficiency in presenting non-biased information to United Nations personnel and the people of the world. The United Nations accepted a gift of land in the heart of New York City as the site for its general headquarters, under construction in 1950. Of the vast amount of long-range work for peace and the betterment of mankind which took place in the meantime, the creation in 1947-8 of three Economic Commissions -- for Europe, for Asia and the Far East, and for Latin America, respectively -- held the greatest potential for the future. The Commissions came into existence to provide an avenue whereby nations could assist other nations in long-term developmental gains. Their mode would be not to force their way into situations, to carry out their own programs, but to work cooperatively with other agencies looking toward the same goals.

The United Nations General Assembly took a symbolic step on December 10, 1948, when it adopted a Universal Declaration of Human Rights, by a vote of 48 nations to 0. Other such declarations had appeared before, but only on the national level. This statement proved the most careful in language. It did not say that "all men are created equal," as had an American document of 1776, or that "men are born and remain free and equal in rights," as ran the improved French version of 1789, but that "all human beings are born free and equal in dignity and

236

rights." The delineation of the rights was a careful one also, argued out by the delegates of 56 nations. On separate roll-call votes, many articles finally passed unanimously, others with two or three abstentions, and three with eight or nine abstentions. Six communist regimes, South Africa, and Saudi Arabia felt dissatisfied enough to abstain on the document as a whole. Everyone knew, of course, that to declare such rights fell far short of observing or enforcing them. Nevertheless, as statements of purpose or belief, they seemed much better said than unsaid.

The Economic Panorama

"Everyone," read the Universal Declaration of Human Rights, "has the right to a standard of living adequate for the health and well-being of himself and of his family, including food, clothing, housing and medical care and necessary social services. . . ." In 1950, in the new country of India, such a standard remained difficult to achieve; the entire national income for the year amounted to only 55 United States dollars per person when imaginatively spread even. Elsewhere, some lands shared India's intense poverty, while others had moved farther ahead. The Japanese people, on the average, earned twice as much as those of India. The Brazilians and Italians acquired four times the Indian figure in a year. People of the United Kingdom, whose flag had recently flown in India, found themselves ten times as prosperous per capita. And persons in the United States, on the average, received nearly thirty times as much money as those of India for their personal comfort and well-being.

This is not to say that everyone in India was suffering, nor that everyone in the United States possessed an adequate standard of living. In all lands, there existed gradations in individual family incomes. In nearly all noncommunist

237

lands, these gradations remained severe. The millionaire and the pauper inhabited the same cities and towns. They usually saw each other every passing day. The poor in income very often worked hard for the others who enjoyed prosperity. Yet even in the world's most affluent country in the middle of the twentieth century, the rawest of poverty was often taken for granted, as a natural consequence of the process of development. In the more poverty-stricken regions, in Latin America, Africa, and Asia, persons with an adequate standard of living frequently formed a small minority, living the best they could at the expense of the downtrodden multitude about them.

There existed three chief causes for the poverty of people around the world: (1) More people lived in some districts than the land itself could support. Sometimes natural resources had been wasted until they no longer remained sufficient. In other instances, more blame attached to a rapid increase in population. The scientific conquest of some of man's worst plagues and diseases caused more persons to live long enough to raise large families, thus causing a "population explosion" which produced scarcities. (2) Many people lacked the ability to make the most of available resources. A lack of modern methods of agriculture and manufacturing still characterized many economies. (3) Persons' attitudes also made a difference. Many wealthy individuals thought of their fortunes protectively rather than expansively. Whether in the laissez-faire tradition or in an older landlord-serf relationship, they believed essentially that their own prosperity depended upon the degradation of others. Both in private-enterprise and socialist economies, many individuals had overcome such attitudes, and their wealth had come to be used for the permanent betterment of others. The residue of the older type of thinking, however, remained impressive.

Nearly three-fourths of the people in the

world made their living by farming. Agriculture has occupied the attention of the great majority of humans for the last few thousand years. In the modern world, however, especially in the last two centuries, farming has come to be recognized as one of the slowest ways to gather income. In the period following World War II, the predominantly agricultural nation came to be categorized as "underdeveloped" while the state that had moved on to other industry was considered a "semi-developed" or "developed" land. The expression "developing" came to be used also as a euphemism for "underdeveloped," though all nations moving ahead might properly be described as developing. There existed no reason, of course, why a whole nation specializing in agriculture should be regarded as backward in any sense. At this period in history, however, farming economies generally remained the poorer ones in terms of material income, and it was widely assumed (as a vagary of the time) that if a nation wished to prosper it must develop other forms of industry.

The large fraction of the world's population engaged in agriculture meant that three-fourths or more of the people in a very large number of nations worked at farming in 1950. Specific nations varied from the pattern, however, including some of the larger ones. In Brazil, about three-fifths of the people worked as agriculturists; in Japan, somewhat less than half; in Italy and the Soviet Union, approximately two-fifths. In the United States, only one-eighth of the population tilled the soil, and in the United Kingdom only one-twentieth. Thus the proportions shifted, not alone on the basis of the development of other industry, but also in keeping with such factors as the suitability of the land for farming, the density of population, and the availability of natural resources for manufacturing. There existed no precise inverse ratio between the percentage of farming and the per capita income; only in a worldwide and general sense were most farmers more impoverished than most other people.

To judge by the total amount of money persons were willing to pay to procure the various edible products of the soil, rice constituted the single most important agricultural commodity. Rice had been grown in both India and China for more than five thousand years. At the end of World War II, its cultivation lagged because of political disturbances in the larger countries of the Orient. China proved unable to cultivate the quantity produced in prewar years, but remained the largest grower of rice, followed by India, Pakistan, and Japan. Burma and Thailand provided over half of the world's rice exports. (In all the listings of agricultural commodities in this section, the major countries are given in order as they stood in averages of the years 1948-50, carried to a cut-off point of half of the total reported or estimated production or exports. The cut-off is extended to two-thirds of the production for rice, wheat, maize, and cotton. Nations with reported or estimated totals larger than 90% of the preceding one on the list are also mentioned as "near-ties".)

The second most valuable crop, wheat, stood first in terms of the acreage used in its production. Wheat had been cultivated for as long as rice, but in the Middle East rather than in the Orient. Rice-hungry people frequently turned to wheat in the immediate postwar years, since a great surplus of the one (in four countries little hurt by the war) balanced the considerable dearth of the other. The Soviet Union and the United States grew the most wheat, followed by China, Canada, France, Italy, India, Australia, and Argentina, the last two as near-ties. The United States and Canada exported more than half of the world's sale of wheat and wheat flour between nations. To avoid chaos in the wheat market as some of these lands accumulated wheat surpluses, arrangements were made in 1949 for a regular flow of world wheat trade, at prices actually lower than those obtainable at the time on the free market. Single-commodity agreements of this type, though generally very cumbersome and awkward, constituted one more recognition that unrestricted laissez-faire does not necessarily work to anyone's advantage.

Maize was the planet's third most coveted commodity. It too possessed an ancient history, like rice and wheat, but one restricted to the Americas until the opening of world contacts in the late fifteenth century. The United States, where it is called corn rather than maize, ranked far ahead of all other countries in the production of this crop after World War II, with China, Brazil, and the near-tie Soviet Union assuming second, third, and fourth position respectively. The United States and Argentina provided more than half of the world's maize exports.

Other cereals besides rice, wheat, and maize added significantly to the world's nutrition and economy. Millet and sorghum received considerable attention in the agriculture of China and India. Barley was raised in generous quantities in China, the Soviet Union, the United States, Canada, India, the United Kingdom, Japan, Turkey, and Spain, the last three included as near-ties. (The appearance of such a long list, usually counting in some near-ties, is of course a sign that the particular crop is more widely grown than others.) Oats held special importance in the United States and the Soviet Union. More than half of the world's rye came from the Soviet Union and Poland. These five grains formed a much smaller part of international trade than the three mentioned before them; they nevertheless assumed considerable significance to the domestic animals and people who consumed them.

The fourth commodity in value in the world picture was cotton, raised more for clothing than for food. One of the riddles of history is that cotton as another ancient crop appears to have made its way around the world before man did. In the nineteenth century, the cotton customs of the time produced severe poverty among Negro and mulatto slaves in the southern part of the United

States and among the fellahin or peasant class in Egypt. After World War II, with cotton in short supply, these two countries still accounted for more than half of the world's exports. The United States production of cotton amounted to more than one-third of the total, with the Soviet Union, China, India, Egypt, and Brazil following, the last two as near-ties. New, mechanized procedures for the cultivation of cotton made possible the dissociation of the cotton industry from poverty in the postwar world.

The remainder of the vegetable fibers of the world assumed far less total value than cotton, but continued important to individual peoples. More than half the world's supply of flax came from the Soviet Union. Pakistan and India specialized in the cultivation of jute. Significant quantities of hemp were raised in India, the Soviet Union, and Italy, while Tanganyika and Kenya produced sizeable amounts of sisal, Mexico of henequen, and the Philippines of abaca. More than two-thirds of the world's trade in silk, an animal rather than a vegetable fiber, came from Japan. (Exports of wool are mentioned later.)

Sugar, extracted from both cane and beets, ranked fifth in value among the world's crops. Cane sugar, grown in ancient India, became common in Europe after successful transplanting in the Caribbean area. Beet sugar became well known only in the nineteenth century. Cuba, which had more than doubled its cane harvests during the war, produced over one-sixth of the sugar raised in the immediate postwar world, and very nearly half of the total international exports. The United Kingdom exported the second largest quantity of sugar. In the production of this very widespread commodity, very often by a nation chiefly for its own use, Cuba was followed by the Soviet Union, the United States, Brazil, India, Puerto Rico, France, Australia, Hawaii, East Germany, and Poland, the last three as near-ties. International agreements to control the sugar trade dated from 1937; they had as their chief object the protection of producers against the threat of low prices from over-supply. Many Asian and Latin American countries used sweeteners more coarse than sugar. India's production of sugar and gur together exceeded the output of sugar by the Soviet Union.

Tobacco stood sixth in total value of the commodities of the world. Rice, wheat, maize, and sugar were eaten, and cotton was worn. Tobacco was smoked, chewed, or snuffed, with no beneficial effect save a certain mesmerization induced among its addicts. Only some American Indians had become acquainted with tobacco five hundred years ago, but its use spread very rapidly among other peoples, once it began. The United States both produced and exported far more tobacco than any other country in the postwar world. In production, chiefly for home usage, India, the Soviet Union, and China followed; in exports, the second ranking country was Turkey.

The livestock industry accounted for a large segment of postwar agriculture. Man from ancient times had bred certain species of animals for his own uses, and now there were roughly as many domesticated animals -- not counting pets and poultry -- as there were people in the world. Cattle and sheep existed in greatest numbers. India, the United States, the Soviet Union, Brazil, China, and near-tie Argentina led in numbers of cattle in 1950, while New Zealand and Denmark specialized in exports of butter, and Argentina and Australia in exports of beef and veal. Australia, the Soviet Union, Argentina, India, South Africa, New Zealand, China, and near-tie United States had the most sheep, while Australia and New Zealand led in exports of wool, and New Zealand alone exported more than half of the mutton and lamb in world trade.

There were fewer than half as many swine and goats as cattle and sheep. China, the United States, the Soviet Union, and near-tie Brazil together held well over half the swine, while the

243

largest numbers of goats were found in India, China, Turkey, the Soviet Union, Iran, Nigeria, and Ethiopia. Horses and mules, in lesser numbers still, were owned chiefly in the Soviet Union, Brazil, Argentina, China, the United States, and Mexico. India raised over half the world's buffaloes; China, Ethiopia, Mexico, Turkey, and Brazil had the most donkeys; Anglo-Egyptian Sudan, British Somaliland, Italian Somaliland, Ethiopia, and India reported the largest numbers of camels. In addition to these larger creatures, chickens were nearly universal, and ducks, turkeys, and geese widespread.

A not-so-ancient enterprise is the significant development of vegetable oils for the world's food and industrial markets. The extensive use of many of them corresponds to the relative wave of affluency which came to North America and Europe in the twentieth century. After World War II, the United States grew some of the associated crops rather than importing the oils as before. China and the United States together now cultivated almost all the world's soybeans, though India and China remained well ahead in groundnuts (peanuts). Cottonseed came from the United States and the Soviet Union, and linseed from the United States and Argentina, while more than half of the rapeseed was cultivated by China alone. Of the oils which could not be produced in the cooler climates, coconut oil came chiefly from Ceylon, the Philippines, and near-tie Malaya, and both palm oil and palm kernels from Nigeria and the Belgian Congo. Lesser products in this category included olive oil (Spain and Italy), sesame seed (China and India), sunflower seed (the Soviet Union and Argentina), and castor oil (India and Brazil).

A certain few beverages also stood much in demand in the postwar world, though their contribution to nutrition was rather limited. Coffee, originally developed in Arabia, led this field, with Brazil and Colombia its chief growers and Brazil alone providing over half the

244

exports. A Brazilian surplus accumulated during wartime became completely devoured in the early postwar years. Tea came in second, grown mostly in India and Ceylon. Cacao, used for both food and drink, though originally an American item was now produced also in Africa, with the Gold Coast harvesting the largest crop and Brazil the second.

Rubber obtained from the latex produced by certain plants forms a branch of agriculture all its own. Only early in the twentieth century, with the advent of automobiles and trucks, had the natural rubber industry become important. The Malay states and the Netherlands East Indies were the world's great producers of natural rubber before World War II. When the Japanese cut off these sources of supply from the United Nations, the latter developed a synthetic rubber to take the place of the natural. After the war, Malaya and Indonesia resumed their prewar role as world suppliers, but now with competition from the man-made product.

A wide variety of vegetables and fruits added further interest to the world's selection of foods. The best known of the vegetables in the postwar years were potatoes (grown chiefly in the Soviet Union, Poland, and West Germany), sweet potatoes and yams (China and Nigeria), cassava (Brazil, Nigeria, Indonesia, and near-tie Belgian Congo), tomatoes (the United States and the Soviet Union), beans (Brazil, China, the United States, and India), peas (China and the Soviet Union), and chick-peas (over two-thirds from India). The four most outstanding fruits were apples (France, the United States, and West Germany), oranges including tangerines (from the United States, Brazil, and Spain), bananas (Brazil, India, Venezuela, and near-tie Honduras), and grapes (France, Italy, the United States, and near-tie Spain).

Forestry and fishing constituted minor industries compared to the more important of the agricultural enterprises. During this period,

245

the Soviet Union, the United States, Brazil, and near-tie Canada led by far in cuttings of wood, that in Brazil serving chiefly for fuel, that in the other three countries going more for lumber and the production of pulp. Japan, the United States, the Soviet Union, Norway, the United Kingdom, and Canada were the major fishing nations of this time, together catching over half the fish that were caught, often far from these nations' coastlines.

Manufacturing and mining activity of some kinds goes back as far in history as agriculture and forestry, though not as far as fishing. Manufacturing has forged itself a very special place, however, in the last two hundred years, moving ahead sensationally in the very countries which secured a higher standard of living. It has come to be considered the mark of the more developed nations as contrasted to the less developed ones. Indeed, many people have come to believe that a strong manufacturing industry is essential for any nation which wishes to do more than survive. So tightly has the image come to be drawn that mining and manufacturing together are often labeled simply "industry," as though they possess a monopoly on the word.

Some of the manufactures of food and textiles are among the oldest industries of the world. The preparation of food and beverages for consumption or for storage has long occupied the attention of many people. It continues of great importance, and is done largely where the food crop is harvested or the animal to be slaughtered is raised. Textile manufacturing like food processing took place chiefly in the home for several millenia, not far from the sources of supply. By the eighteenth century, however, some nations in Europe imported cotton for the manufacture of clothes. Suddenly, with new inventions to speed up processes and provide a better power supply, first England and soon other nations built factories, taking the people out of their homes but greatly spurring the textile industry. From that day to this, textile manufacturing like the growing of cotton has generally carried an association with poverty. In the years following World War II, the United States held a big lead in the production of cotton yarn (pure and mixed combined), with the Soviet Union and India following. The United States, the United Kingdom, and France led in the output of wool yarn (likewise pure and mixed combined), and the United States alone made half of the world's supply of continuous rayon and acetate filament yarn. (In these and other listings of manufactures and products of mining which follow, the major countries are given in order as they stood in averages of the years 1948-50, as they were in the listings of agricultural commodities. The cut-off point remains at the half-way mark, with mention also of nations in near-tie. Coal, iron ore, and cement, however, are carried out to the two-thirds mark, and the items of crude petroleum and land motor vehicles to nine-tenths.)

Coal became important as a power supply at the same time the textile industry was so rapidly expanding. It remains very prominent, though there are now many competitors and the industry has had to face many problems. In the years 1948-50, the United States, the United Kingdom, the Soviet Union, and West Germany mined the most coal (two-thirds of it altogether), while East Germany, West Germany, and near-tie Soviet Union extracted large quantities of lignite. The United States, West Germany, and near-tie Soviet Union led in the production of metallurgical coke as a specialized fuel.

Petroleum has become significant to the world only during the last hundred years. The kerosene distilled from petroleum meant much to the developing nations of the nineteenth century. The gasoline and fuel oil partly derived from petroleum now seem almost indispensable for modern living. The production of crude petroleum grew

247

rapidly before World War II, and resumed its climb during the latter years of the conflict. In 1946, the United States led with two-thirds of the total; by 1950, its share had been cut nearly to one-half. Venezuela, whose yield (under the care of United States companies) tripled from 1943 to 1950, stood as the second ranking nation in petroleum. The Soviet Union placed third, though it had lost many oil wells during the war. In fourth, fifth, sixth, and seventh place, respectively, stood Iran, Saudi Arabia, Kuwait, and Mexico. The Anglo-Iranian Oil Company, representing British interests in Iran, developed that country's production at the same speed as that of Venezuela, tripling it from 1943 to 1950. The Arabian American Oil Company, founded by United States capital, put Saudi Arabia on the petroleum map during this quinquennium, developing wells that had been discovered just before the war. The same may be said of joint British-American interests in Kuwait, which had existed as a tiny Arabian desert sheikhdom unnoticed by nearly everyone except the British guardian, but now promised to become some kind of more-money-than-needed delight. Its population reached less than a fifth of a million.

Iron is the most important of modern manufacturing industry's raw materials. Objects have been made from iron for more than three thousand years. They remained very few in number, however, until the nineteenth century. Cast iron products then became very widespread, and brought on the demand for a stronger derivative of iron, which the invention of steel satisfied. Steel now provides the backbone for a large percentage of man's greatest structures and machines. In this time period, the United States mined over one-third of the world's output of iron ore (as measured by its content of iron) and produced more than one-third of the crude iron (including ferro-alloys) and crude steel. The Soviet Union held second place in all three of these categories, while France and near-tie Sweden placed third and fourth in the production of iron ore.

248

Many other metals served particular uses. Put together, their immediate postwar value was more than four times that of iron alone. Indeed, copper and gold each exceeded iron in worth of the total production. Copper had been used a thousand years before iron, and gold well before copper. The United States, Chile, Northern Rhodesia, and near-tie Canada mined the largest quantities of copper after the war, and South Africa and Canada over half the gold. The copper served for wires, in motors, and for a variety of other purposes; almost all of the gold had come to be held in monetary reserves to provide stabilization for paper currency. Lead (chiefly from the United States, Australia, and Mexico) had about half the production value of iron, gold, or copper; storage batteries and ammunition devoured much of the lead supply. Aluminum (derived from bauxite mined mostly in Surinam, British Guiana, and the United States) held great popularity in the postwar world for a variety of new uses, including several in the building industry. Zinc (from the United States, Canada, Mexico, and Australia) played a role in the iron industry and in combination with copper to make brass. Tin (Malaya and Bolivia) provided tinplate and was used in soldering. Manganese, valuable for the manufacture of steel, came chiefly from the Soviet Union, the Gold Coast, and India.

Mexico, the United States, Canada, and near-tie Soviet Union mined silver, utilized for money and photography, in largest quantities. Canada provided over three-fourths of the world's supply of nickel, employed also in the iron industry. Other highly useful metals were tungsten (China, the Soviet Union, and the United States), platinum (Canada and possibly the Soviet Union), antimony (Bolivia, Mexico, and South Africa), molybdenum (the United States), and titanium (commercialized only in 1947, from the United States and India). Mercury, liquid at ordinary temperatures, came from Italy and Spain.

Other minerals not of a metallic nature also held great value for postwar man. Cement, a powder made of a number of these, stood in greatest demand (even more than gold, copper, or iron), mainly for construction purposes. The largest amounts of cement were produced in the United States (nearly one-third), the United Kingdom, West Germany, the Soviet Union, France, Italy, Belgium, and Japan. The Belgian Congo provided more than half of the world's diamonds, famed for their beauty and hardness. Canada produced more than half of the asbestos, noted for its fire-resistant fibers. Salt, used both to season and to preserve food, came chiefly from the United States, the Soviet Union, and the United Kingdom. Phosphate rock (the United States and Morocco), provided phosphorus used mainly for fertilizer. Sulphur (over half from the United States, with by-product sulphur not counted) formed the base of sulphuric acid in one of the world's most important chemical industries.

The world's chemical and engineering industries, in a sense, sit on top of the awe-inspiring work done with coal, petroleum, iron, and all the other metals and minerals. Chemistry and engineering provide a majority of the products which make the lives of most twentieth-century people so very different from those of their ancestors. Both of these two remarkable realms of the manufacturing world broadened out considerably in the nineteenth century after following desultory courses theretofore. Their growth became very rapid in the twentieth century, each bringing out a variety of products that had scarcely been suggested earlier. The end of World War II came as a signal to them to construct a whole new world of surprises. The chemical industries produced certain basic chemicals in large quantities (sulphuric acid, soda ash, caustic soda, nitric acid), as it had for some time, but now also engaged in making chemical fertilizers, dye-stuffs, plastics, and synthetic rubber. The engineering industries

manufactured machine tools, agricultural, textile, and mining machinery, electric and electronic equipment (the latter including television
sets, only a few of which had been constructed
before the war), railroad locomotives, ships,
land motor vehicles, and aircraft.

There was scarcely a line of activity in all
the chemical and engineering industries in which
the United States of America did not lead. In
many of them, the lead was so commanding that
other countries seemed hardly to be competing.
Shipbuilding provided the most notable of the
exceptions, in which the United Kingdom held
first position in the non-communist world (the
Soviet Union and China did not publish statistics on this item). Several factors accounted
for the overall impressive leadership of the
United States: First, and very important for
this quinquennium, the productive capacity of
other countries engaged in manufacturing had been
damaged very badly by the war, while the
continent of North America remained practically
unshaken. Second, the United States possessed
the size and the wealth of natural resources to
enable it to gather together most of the ingredients for modern manufacturing industry
without having to pay other nations for them.
Third, the managers of United States industries,
whether under duress from labor unions and governments or by the imaginative force of creative
good will, had in a large number of instances
treated their employees and consumers well enough
that the people of the United States could
purchase the goods and services provided for them.

Two other reasons were often given for United
States leadership in manufacturing industry and
per capita income. Some persons asserted that
the United States, as an imperialist country,
built its own riches upon the poverty of others.
This argument contained some validity. United
States capital operating abroad often treated its
employees in ways that would not have been permitted at home. The United States purchased

251

other nations' products at prices generally far from commensurate with those charged for United States products going abroad. Nevertheless, it could hardly be argued that greater fairness in the international price structure or more altruistic policies by United States capitalists investing abroad would have made the United States notably poorer. Too great a share of the North Americans' wealth came from their own work and their own resources.

The other reason given for the advanced position of the United States was that it constituted a natural consequence of allegiance to the principles of private enterprise as against the doctrine of socialism. Certainly, the United States followed private-enterprise ideas more closely than many other postwar countries. Obviously, the extent of laissez-faire actually practiced had not prevented the good fortune that came. But private companies had often received assistance from the United States government, and on the other hand the United States economy had reached its leading position while there existed many restrictions on its free enterprise stemming from business as well as governmental policies. In some other countries that practiced laissez-faire more strongly, the masses of the people remained sunk in poverty.

Some nations hoped or expected to challenge the lead of the United States at least in some portion of the world market. In land motor vehicles, for instance (about three-fourths automobiles, one-fourth trucks), while the United States continued its commanding position of more than three-fourths of the world's production in 1948-50, output by the United Kingdom, Canada, and France had to be taken into account to reach the fraction of nine-tenths of the total, and that of the Soviet Union (mostly trucks) constituted a near-tie with that of France. The amazing recovery of western Europe and the Soviet Union, however (the first with and the second without Marshall Plan aid), did not mean that these countries could match the total United States accomplishments very soon. Aside from the Soviet Union, indeed, it appeared unlikely that they could ever reach that goal working singly. Neither the lands of western and central Europe nor most of those of Asia, Latin America, and Africa contained the resources to realize this achievement unaided.

Many other industries engaged the attention of people not involved in agriculture, forestry, fishing, manufacturing, or mining. The construction and maintenance of homes and other edifices, along with the provision of electricity, gas, steam, water, and sanitation for them, secured employment for many. In the immediate postwar period, Europe and North America alone, with one-third of the world's population, produced seven-eighths of the world's electricity, leaving virtually all the remainder of the world far behind.

The various branches of commerce -- trading, banking, insurance, real estate -- offered occupations for other people, as did the associated activities of transport, storage, and communication. Trade within countries held importance everywhere, though a great deal of variety existed in the manner of its accomplishment. In this quinquennium, India possessed three times as much railway freight traffic per capita as China, the Soviet Union about twenty-five times as much per person as India, and the United States two-and-a-half times as much per capita as the Soviet Union. North America and Europe together contained over nine-tenths of the world's telephones. Noncommunist societies used much costly advertising to stimulate demand, while communist regimes regarded the provision of consumer goods as a service for those who wanted them, unprovoked by sales appeals.

International trade like domestic trade existed everywhere, though often with startling differences in benefits to individual countries.

The "colonial" lands of the world, as one country after another declared itself independent politically, were those which remained highly dependent upon economic decisions made by foreigners. One company with its head offices in a more developed land might wield more strength than an entire nation with which it did business. Such relationships often went hand in hand with a set of prices in import and export trade that gave all the advantage to the nation which had more, and sorely oppressed the nation which had less. Nevertheless, virtually everyone traded across national lines, for to discontinue doing so meant too severe an isolation. Non-communist Europe sold almost four-twelfths of the world's internationally traded goods during this quinquennium, and the United States and Canada approximately three-twelfths, according to value based on the prices demanded. The total for the communist nations came near the mark of one-twelfth, while noncommunist Asia, Latin America, and Africa combined accounted for the four-twelfths remainder. A chiefly non-communist arrangement, the General Agreement on Tariffs and Trade (GATT), came into force in 1948 as the proposed International Trade Organization ran into difficulties, aiming to encourage world trade through the lowering of artificial barriers.

Large numbers of people provided services not attached to a particular industry. Some of these activities were person-to-person in nature, while others were associated with governments or communities. Here, as in the occupations already described, individual material gains varied tremendously. No one could measure the degree of monetary fortune of one person against another, because of the many intangibles involved. Neither national nor personal circumstances resembled one another sufficiently to provide comparisons. But everyone knew that most of the people had not enough to eat, to clothe themselves properly, or to obtain decent shelter from the sun, rain, or cold. The postwar generation would care more than any earlier generation about these conditions, and would debate vigorously as to what should be done about them.

Science

Hersey, Hiroshima . . the hydrogen bomb . . the synchrocyclotron and the synchrotron . . berkelium and californium . . the pion . . the Mount Palomar telescope . . the steady-state theory . . Einstein and the unified field theory . . Russell, Human Knowledge . . Wiener, The Human Use of Human Beings . . the transistor . . antibiotics from Streptomyces . . Vitamin B_{12} . . cortisone for arthritis . . cloud seeding . . the flying saucer phenomenon . . Chase, The Proper Study of Mankind . . Kinsey, Sexual Behavior in the Human Male . . abnormal hemoglobins in the study of races . . radiocarbon dating . . Mead, Male and Female . . Durant, The Age of Faith . . Brown, The Story of Maps . . Frazier, The Negro in the United States . . Deutscher, Stalin.

Homo sapiens came into the world, one might say, already equipped with a governmental structure and an economy. In his earliest days, the family served to preserve discipline and to organize food-gathering. Much of his history ever since then can be written in political and economic terms, involving ever-larger governmental units and business associations, continuing into the new era starting in 1945. There are, however, three other types of activity intelligent man has developed for himself. Essentially, this book takes as a theme, there are only three basically human activities -- science, art, and religion are their names -- not shared even in primitive form by plants and other animals. All three seem indispensable to man, and likely to occupy a greater share of his attention in the future over a long run of time, as smoother-working political and economic arrangements are devised and the excitement of politics and

255

economics subsides.

Science is an expression of man's mind. Man developed the ability to dominate his planet because he sought to understand the world about him. Curiosity led to retention of fact, or memory, in his superior brain, and retention of fact led to the desire to train one's children to understand also. As more and more facts accrued, over a very long period of time, man possessed the knowledge that was necessary for something more than bare survival. His thirst for new explanations continued, sometimes to obtain a more comfortable life for himself through a development of his technology, sometimes to carry out a self-perpetuating intellectual exercise which brought a sense of satisfaction with each bit of knowledge acquired but itself remained intact into the future. In the world after 1945, scientific enthusiasm led man to believe that he could solve all the problems of his planet if he tried, and that within a short time he would be able to explore planets other than his own.

To go to other planets, man needed power beyond that which he had previously mastered. The atomic bombs dropped on Hiroshima and Nagasaki, Japan, had shown the world one example of the possibilities ahead. For a while, many people felt a tendency to recoil in the face of the horrible damage. John Hersey in 1946 wrote a simple but devastating account called Hiroshima of six persons who survived the first nuclear blast. Miss Toshiko Sasaki, an office clerk; Dr. Masakazu Fujii, owner of a private hospital; Mrs. Hatsuyo Nakamura, a tailor's widow; Father Wilhelm Kleinsorge, a German priest; Dr. Terufumi Sasaki, a young surgeon; and the Reverend Mr. Kiyoshi Tanimoto, a Methodist pastor, provided the genuine characters in Hersey's non-invented plot. First came the atomic flash, seen but not heard by these witnesses; next the dreadful fire; later, a period during which convalescence accompanied speculation as to what had happened; but finally, a sickening after-math when persons who thought they were well or recovering learned that nearly all their number had been exposed to slower-working radiation illness. Hersey's witnesses, telling their own accounts, did not assume the stature of heroes; they remained very human beings, with all their strengths and weaknesses. The atomic bomb, how-ever, proved a new element in their lives, with which they found themselves totally unable to cope. More than fifty thousand other persons, facing the same machine of destruction, did not live into the convalescent stage, but simply died.

The argument raged, among readers and non-readers of Hiroshima, as to whether the bombs should have been dropped on the two Japanese cities. Many said that man's knowledge had out-run his morality, on the premise that both qual-ities engage in an ongoing developmental pro-cess. Man had learned new techniques to accomplish his desires, ran the idea, without developing the controls to ensure that they would yield more good than harm. Others pointed out that the two bombs had stopped the war, and thus that their justification lay in actually saving the lives of great numbers of other people who would have perished in a forced occupation of Japan. Might there have been a gigantic demon-stration of some kind, other than at the hearts of two cities, which could have brought the end of the war without the same human suffering? No one knew the answer, for the opportunity had passed.

In any event, the horror at Hiroshima and Nagasaki remained minor compared to the total of the preceding six years. Furthermore, there existed a chance that the possession of the weapon might prove a deterrent to further con-flict. Most people came to expect the continu-ing manufacture of the bomb, by both the United States and the Soviet Union. And most people accepted the thought that atomic weaponry would be developed to a point of destructive capabil-

257

ity far beyond that of the first apparati. Scientific reasoning led to the thought that a "hydrogen bomb," one in which destructive energy would be released through the transformation of hydrogen into helium, could be triggered by a uranium bomb acting as a fuse. A "cobalt bomb" seemed possible also, using a hydrogen bomb to render the cobalt radioactive, so that it might be carried by the winds to scorch the life of wide areas. The Soviet Union exploded its first uranium bomb in 1949. In early 1950, president Truman made it clear that the United States intended to develop a hydrogen bomb several times more powerful than the uranium bombs it had dropped. Without an announcement, the Soviet Union proceeded toward the same goal, surpassing the United States in preparations before the end of this year. In the meantime, scientists of several countries began studies to channel atomic energy toward more peaceful purposes.

Hydrogen bombs would become very formidable in destructive potential. The energy-releasing process to take place in them, however, involved only the tiniest particles known to man. Basically these were the electron, discovered in the nineteenth century; the proton of the atomic nucleus, detected early in the twentieth; and the neutron, also of the nucleus, encountered in 1932. Nuclear physics, the study of these and other subatomic particles, along with the new mathematics needed to understand their characteristics, rose on foundations laid early in the twentieth century, so that many of the founders of the two sciences (including all the persons mentioned below) remained active past World War II.

Max Planck of Germany (died 1947) led the way with his "quantum" theory of 1900, that energy can exist only in discrete quantities, or quanta, each some multiple of a tiny constant, later found to equal approximately

0.0000000000000000000000000066262 erg or
0.000000000000000000000000000000000066262 joule.
(One erg represents the acceleration of one gram
of mass at one centimeter per second for one
second; one joule represents the energy released
in one second by a current of one ampere through
a resistance of one ohm.) In 1905, Albert Einstein of Germany, then resident in Switzerland,
proposed that light is composed of quanta (later
called photons) which bear the behavior of both
matter and energy, and suggested that the amount
of energy (expressed in ergs) "stored" in a specific amount of matter may be determined by mul-
tiplying the amount of matter (expressed in grams
of mass) by the square of the velocity of light
in centimeters per second (the famous formula
$E = mc^2$, by which a kilogram of mass, approximately the equivalent of 2.2 pounds avoir-
dupois, equals 900,000,000,000,000,000,000,000
ergs or 90,000,000,000,000,000 joules). Niels
Bohr of Denmark, then resident in England, postulated in 1913 that an atom may exist only in
particular states of energy, and that radiation
of a specified amount is emitted by the atom when
it jumps from a higher state of energy to a lower
one.

Louis de Broglie of France in 1923 introduced the idea that electrons and other forms
of matter might possess wavelike properties
as do the forms of energy, placing them thus in
the same category as Einstein's dual-character-
istic photons. Werner Heisenberg (of Germany)
and Erwin Schrödinger (of Austria, living in
Switzerland) in 1925-7 rendered essential aid
in the development of the new mathematics of
"quantum mechanics," needed to deal with the
inner world of the atom. Heisenberg pointed out
the "indeterminacy principle," that a piece of
matter may not be described as occupying an exact
position and possessing an exact momentum at the
same time. Paul Adrien Maurice Dirac of England
showed in 1928 that the properties of an
electron could all be described in terms of four
wave functions represented by equations, and

predicted from one of them that a new atomic particle would be found with characteristics the reverse of those of an electron. The presence of an evanescent anti-electron, or positron, was first detected by a research team in 1932, as nuclear physicists began to speak of a possible universe, unknown to mankind, composed of such anti-matter. Linus Pauling of Oregon applied quantum theory to molecules in the 1930's, building upon the prior work of Lawrence Bragg (from Australia, living in England), who for two decades had studied crystal structure through x-ray diffractions. John von Neumann of Hungary, living in the United States, laid out the general principles of quantum mechanics in a book published in 1932. After the finding of the positron and the neutron in that year, the existence of the mu-meson, or muon, a short-lived atomic particle, was detected in 1936. Physicists postulated the neutrino and anti-particles for each of the particles during the 1930's, though their existence remained unconfirmed.

Another series of experiments in the same decade, coupled with the political exigencies of the time, led nuclear science into a new avenue of development. In 1934, Irène and Frédéric Joliot-Curie of France discovered that they could artificially produce radioactive phosphorus, nitrogen, and silicon from aluminum, boron, and magnesium respectively, by bombarding the latter three with helium atoms ("persuading" the nuclei to accept two protons each, thus raising them two places in the table of elements). Enrico Fermi of Italy, hearing of that performance, proceeded to produce other ra-dioactive elements by bombardment with neutrons. Fermi became the first to "split" the nucleus of the uranium atom (the process called "fission"), changing uranium, high in the table of elements, into two elements intermediate in the table, but did not immediately recognize what he had done. Otto Hahn of Germany and Lise Meitner of Austria in 1938, repeating these experiments, came to understand that the atomic nucleus had been split -- and that a new and frightening source of power had become available with the great release of energy the split atoms provided. Fermi, migrating to the United States in 1939, along with several colleagues assessed the possibility of a self-sustaining but controlled nuclear chain reaction which could be used as a bomb. They wrote a letter to president Franklin Roosevelt to recommend an attempt to construct such a bomb, and persuaded Albert Einstein, who had come to the United States in 1933, to sign it with them and to deliver it.

Enrico Fermi led the group of scientists who achieved the first man-initiated nuclear chain reaction in late 1942. J. Robert Oppenheimer of New York (whose first initial represented no name) was then appointed to direct the so-called Manhattan Project, to produce the bomb. Hans Albrecht Bethe, who had moved from Germany to the United States in 1934, headed the group of theoretical physicists advising the Manhattan Project. Lev Davidovich Landau, the most noted physicist of the Soviet Union, who like Oppenheimer had studied under some of the notables mentioned above, in the meantime devoted his attention to the behavior of atoms and molecules at very low temperatures, as Percy Williams Bridgman of Massachusetts had studied reactions at very high pressures since the first decade of the century. The difference in the emphases of Landau and Oppenheimer, as well as the migrations of Einstein, Bethe, and Fermi to the United States, provided examples of the manner in which personal decisions of men of science could influence the world of politics.

Proof of existence or "discovery" of the tiny particles within the atom did not mean that these bodies had actually been seen. The tracks they left behind when they moved, as discerned in various detecting devices, provided the data needed to describe them. Some of the particles traveled in alone from space, others from the high atmosphere. Still more were produced artificially, under carefully controlled processes. Machines built in the 1930's whirled available particles in an expanding circular path, accelerating them with quick flashes of electric current, eventually releasing them to attack atomic nuclei and uncover their secrets. The cyclotrons of the 1930's had their limits in that the particles so tremendously accelerated in speed actually increased in mass (as had been predicted in the late nineteenth century, though not completely verified until this time), thus developing a lag in speed which countered further acceleration.

Vladimir Iosifovich Veksler of the Soviet Union and Edwin Mattison McMillan of California, working separately, showed in 1945 that this difficulty could be overcome by a buildup of the accelerating force to synchronize with the augmentation of mass. Following their ideas, the University of California built the first synchrocyclotron in 1946, opening the way for greater and greater particle accelerations, resulting in an ever-more-complicated picture of the atomic nucleus. Neither the cyclotron nor the synchrocyclotron, however, served for the acceleration of electrons, far lighter in mass than the protons and neutrons. A "betatron" designed in 1940 (separated electrons are called "beta particles") accelerated electrons in a single circular path. A "synchrotron," or improved betatron, was built in England in 1946, and other synchrotrons for use with protons starting in 1947. The synchrotron showed more potential even than the synchrocyclotron for the future.

Besides particles, the cyclotrons and synchrotrons produced chemical elements man had not seen before. The detection of element number 61, promethium, among the products of the fission of uranium, rounded out the nineteenth-century periodic table of the elements only in 1945. Number 93, neptunium, the first with a mass greater than uranium, had appeared as a by-product of the fission process in 1940. Teams headed by chemist Glenn Theodore Seaborg of Michigan then discovered plutonium (94) in the same manner in 1941, and bombarded other atoms to produce curium (96) in 1944, and americium (95) in 1945. Other teams headed by Stanley Gerald Thompson of California and including Albert Ghiorso of California and Seaborg, all working at the University of California at Berkeley, made a memorial of the name of their institution when they produced berkelium (97) in 1949 and californium (98) in 1950. Plutonium, discovered in pitchblende from Belgium in 1950, proved the first transuranium element to be found in nature.

New particles from the atomic nucleus came into evidence during this period in profusion, to the extent that theory could not keep up with them. Only the mesons (mesotrons or particles of intermediate mass, much heavier than the electron, much lighter than the proton) were deciphered to some extent. The pi-meson or pion, found in 1947, provided a cohesive force for the nucleus, of which the muon of 1936 turned out to be only a short-lived derivative. Later, other mesons appeared as well as particles heavier than the proton whose functions remained to be defined.

In the field of astronomy, there was no technical breakthrough in the years immediately following the war to match that in nuclear physics. The reflector type of telescope, used since early in the twentieth century, brought a far greater vision of the sky than had the refractor type used earlier, but only because it made possible a larger lens. Systematic radio-canvassing of the heavens began in 1938, and rapidly proved a most valuable theorizing supplement. The dedication of the world's largest reflecting telescope in 1949, on Mount Palomar near San Diego, California, provided the most exciting development of this period. It opened a stupendous panorama to the astronomer's view. Before 1924, man had perceived only his own galaxy, the Milky Way. In

263

that year, he comprehended that some of the many nebulae already observed are actually other galaxies. Now, from Mount Palomar, he could see billions of galaxies. And now, scholars began to notice clusters of galaxies and to wonder if there might be clusters of clusters of galaxies, and so on.

Since the late 1920's, most astronomers had subscribed to the theory that the entire universe of galaxies is expanding. All the outer galaxies appeared to be receding from our own, to judge by the shift toward the red in their light spectra, and the more distant galaxies seemed to be receding most rapidly. The expansion of the universe led to the supposition that it must have originated in a "big bang" or tremendous explosion. Beyond that, the unassisted human mind found it difficult to travel, even with surmise. In 1948, astronomers Hermann Bondi and Thomas Gold (both born in Austria but resident in England), along with their colleague Fred Hoyle of England, suggested a "steady-state" theory of the universe. The recession of the most distant galaxies beyond earth's total vision as their increasing speed surpasses the speed of light (an event which might be described as their departure from "our" universe) is countered by the creation of new matter inside our universe, they speculated, so that the amount of matter within man's ken remains unchanged. The "big bang" proponents and those of the "steady-state" theory argued the merits of their respective stands, presenting the likelihood that their contention would lead to theoretical developments important to science. The underlying assumption made by many on both sides of the argument, however -- the assumption that our visible universe and the universe are identical -- seemed to lie in the realm of primitive geocentrism.

No one could say in 1950 whether astronomy and nuclear physics would continue to develop rapidly, or whether either one or both of them might reach some hard-to-leave plateau. Theorists in both realms had pointed out possible absolute limitations to man's knowledge. If distant galaxies, for instance, remained a part of the universe after their velocity exceeded that of their light as they sped away from man's part of the universe, would they not nonetheless disappear from man's vision without leaving a trace? Or if the very tiniest and most sensitive particles within the atom reacted violently to the slightest attempt to inspect them, how could one ascertain the aspect they assumed when no one was looking? Physicists particularly had come to the point that, baffled by the behavior of an occasional particle, they preferred to speak in terms of a statistical probability rather than a certainty that such-and-such would happen if a specific situation were posed. Werner Heisenberg presented the "interdeterminacy principle" in 1927 (see above), and Andrey Nikolayevich Kolmogorov of the Soviet Union described the basic principles of probability as related to measurement in 1929. Astronomers since 1905 had worked on the premise that there is no fixed point in space from which they can measure, and that consequently everything they say in regard to time and space must be taken as truth only in relation to the vantage point from which man observes.

Albert Einstein, who formulated this "special" theory of relativity in 1905, was one of several scientists who resisted the final authority of the indeterminacy principle after 1927. Einstein believed that ultimately the study of the universe would reveal concrete laws that govern all change and control all forces. In 1916, in his native Germany, he had published his "general" theory of relativity, describing gravity not as a mysterious mathematical force drawing bodies in space toward one another (as it had been considered since its first description in the seventeenth century) but as a kind of distortion-curve in a continuum proposed by Einstein to include both time and space. Observations scattered over several decades revealed

265

that the mathematics of Einstein's "curved space" matched actuality better than the older gravitation equation, suggesting that the general theory of relativity indeed held substance. In the United States in 1950, Einstein presented a "unified field" theory, attempting to establish a mathematical link between the world of gravitation on the one hand and the realms of electricity, magnetism, and light on the other, the latter three having already been brought together. Verification or refutation of this mathematical exercise would not likely appear for decades. In the meantime, despite the fame of the author, the theory did not spark enthusiasm.

Philosophers, including mathematician-philosophers who attracted special attention in the twentieth century, had long dealt with the theme of knowledge (what man can know and how best man can know the essence of things). Among philosophers and logicians in the non-communist world, three schools of thought on these matters attracted attention in mid-twentieth century. Famous early proponents of each remained active into the postwar era. John Dewey of Vermont, co-founder of the school of pragmatism popular in the United States, emphasized that ideas are instruments in the attainment of knowledge, which itself consists of man's total experience of credibility in regard to how well each idea functions. Bertrand Russell and Alfred North Whitehead, both of England (the latter moved to the United States and died in 1947) published Principia Mathematica in 1910-13, establishing the realm of mathematics on a basis of logical principles (to the extent that they could), and thus providing the groundwork for an entire structure of knowledge on the same bases. Their preoccupation dominated the thinking of those committed to the school of logical empiricism, or logical positivism, widespread in Europe. Ludwig Wittgenstein wrote a treatise concerning the importance of language in the search for reality, while serving in the army of Austria during World War I. Following the lead of Russell, Whitehead, and Wittgenstein, Rudolf Carnap of Germany and a circle of thinkers at the University of Vienna (of which Carnap was a member) served as the chief proponents of logical empiricism 1926-38, insisting that all meaningful discourse springs from logic, mathematics, and the sciences, to the total exclusion of both art and religion. In the 1930's, a third philosophy of "existentialism" emerged in Europe; reference to it appears in this chapter under the heading "Art," and more comprehensive discussions in "Religion," Chapters V and VII.

The increasing tendency of nuclear physicists to favor statements of probability over laws of absolute cause-and-effect meant that early-twentieth-century concepts of logical bases of knowledge stood in need of some overhauling. Bertrand Russell attempted this task in his book Human Knowledge: Its Scope and Limits, published in 1948. Russell reminded his readers that there are two kinds of probability which must be kept in mind in accepting new scientific proposals as established. One is the mathematical probability which physicists have adopted as part of their new knowledge -- the idea that things are not necessarily always thus-and-so, but that there is only one chance in a million that they will be otherwise. The other is the degree of credibility which a certain proposition may have. To make advances, scientists cannot "prove" everything along the way; they can only say, in effect, that for nine out of ten considerations of which they can think, thus-and-so seems a reasonable proposition, one with which they can work for a time. To this point, logical empiricism had had to bend toward pragmatism.

Russell, however, remained an enthusiast for, not a critic of, modern science. The main thrust of his book lay in the attempted establishment of certain logical postulates that he argued might be accepted though they are not themselves very precisely based upon experience, to serve as guidelines whereby science might safely infer new

267

knowledge from that which could in some manner be observed. The postulate of "quasi-permanence" stated that "it happens very frequently" that an event is matched by a "very similar" event nearby in time and space. The postulate of "separable causal lines" asserted that "it is frequently possible" that one or two events in a series will offer information about all the other events in that series. That of "spatio-temporal continuity" averred that a cause and its effect which remain at some distance one from the other must be connected by intermediate links. The "structural" postulate stipulated that structurally similar "complex" events ranged about a center in regions not widely separated "usually" all belong to causal lines having their origin in an event at the center. The postulate of "analogy" added that when cause-effect relationships are observed between two events, "it is probable" that if one is observed when there is no way of observing the other, the latter nevertheless does exist. These five postulates, themselves amounting to a kind of knowledge if Russell's argument is accepted, demanded a new explanation of what really constitutes knowledge. Russell, speaking now of the limitations of empiricism, only suggested a new answer, though in interesting detail, with the concept that knowledge, in the fullest sense the word can have for mankind, is but a refinement of what is called expectation in the lower animals.

A prime accomplishment of science in the eighteenth and nineteenth centuries was the development of machines to take the place of man's brawn. Only a few inventions before World War II -- the governor for a steam engine, the thermostat for heat control, the servomechanism first designed to control a ship's rudder -- took the place also of man's brain. Many guns and rockets developed during the war made use of the same brain-substitution principles, the most important of which is called "feedback." Feedback consists, in effect, of a message sent by a machine to itself that affects its own behavior -- or, by

268

analogy, a message sent by a living person to herself or himself which affects that individual's behavior. In the human being, the message is carried by the nervous system; in both the human being and the twentieth-century servomechanism or automaton, it is carried electronically.

Norbert Wiener of Missouri, associated with the Massachusetts Institute of Technology, and Arturo Rosenblueth, a physiologist in Mexico, collaborated during and after the war in the development of a new line of theory on messages. Theirs, they felt, constituted one of a number of borderline areas between established sciences that needed investigation not from one side or the other but by thinkers who would take a new approach. They chose the name cybernetics, from the ancient Greek word for steersman, as the name for their new science. Wiener wrote a book called Cybernetics, or Control and Communication in the Animal and the Machine, published in 1948. Two years later, he produced another entitled The Human Use of Human Beings: Cybernetics and Society. Wiener and Rosenblueth thus pioneered with concepts which spread very rapidly. The thinking machines they envisaged, on beyond the Electronic Numerical Integrator and Automatic Calculator (ENIAC) invented during the war and the Universal Analog Computer (UNIVAC) of 1950 (both built by John Presper Eckert of Pennsylvania and John William Mauchly of Ohio), could replace millions of thinking men. Wiener expressed considerable worry about the human factor involved in these developments, declaring that this "second industrial revolution" could bring more grief to workers than the great industrial changes of the eighteenth and nineteenth centuries. As for the very advanced machine of the future actually taking over man's place, however, a possibility that could lead only to dread, he believed no machine would ever dominate society unless society gave it the signal to go ahead. He did not explore the possibility that only a small segment of society might someday obtain a monopoly on the control of such a machine.

The science of electronics preceded the science of cybernetics by only fifty years. In the beginning, electronics formed a part of the area of physics, though its investigations later extended into the field of astronomy. When electronics experts developed radio after World War I and television after World War II, millions of persons, even many of the very poor, came to have new diversity in their lives. The vacuum tube, upon which both radio and television depended for a time, was invented early in the century to serve as a "rectifier" of electric current, from alternating to direct. Lee De Forest of Iowa in 1907 built a second variety serving as an "amplifier" of radio waves, giving them the strength necessary for satisfactory hearing or viewing. Edwin Howard Armstrong developed an electric circuit in 1918 that adjusted radio signals variably to lower frequencies, so that one dial knob would be all needed to tune in a transmission at its peak. In 1933, Armstrong demonstrated a new type of "frequency modulation" or FM radio, contrasting with the "amplitude modulation" or AM variety (the frequency of the radio wave acting rather than its intensity as the basic determinant of the sound), and eliminating most of the bothersome static. Others experimented with both black-and-white and color television in the 1930's. FM radio and black-and-white television became widely available in some areas soon after the war.

During World War II, it was realized for the first time that solid crystals could be devised that would serve as efficient rectifiers. Metals labeled semiconductors, because they conducted electric current less freely than others, would conduct with greater ease, it was learned, when treated with other metals. Germanium, one of the semiconductors, would conduct from "negative" to "positive" poles through a flow of "extra" electrons if mixed with a trace of arsenic,

270

for example, or would conduct in the same direction through a reverse flow of "spaces" in the atomic arrangement into which electrons could fit, if mixed with a trace of boron. Neither the germanium-arsenic mixture nor that of germanium-boron would conduct from positive to negative poles, but they neatly complemented one another in the other direction. The treatment of a crystal of germanium with both arsenic and boron, one at one end and one at the other with a resulting impasse or freedom for current to pass through, depending upon the momentary direction of the alternating current, transformed the semiconducting crystal into a rectifier. In 1948, William Bradford Shockley, Walter Houser Brattain, and John Bardeen of the United States (born in England, China, and Wisconsin respectively) fashioned crystals of a sandwich type (to follow the illustration, placing germanium-boron in a thin middle and germanium-arsenic at both ends). By speeding or slowing the flow of electrons, these new treated crystals would serve as efficient amplifiers. Both of the devices, called "transistors" because they transferred signals through metals which acted as resistors, rapidly found their way into commercial production, providing greater convenience in size and simplicity than the vacuum tubes they displaced.

The science of aeronautics developed at the same time as electronics. Orville Wright of Ohio, who with his brother Wilbur participated in the first (59-second) flight by airplane in 1903, died in 1948. Igor Sikorsky of Russia began a long career in the construction of airplanes in 1910, three years before Henry Ford of Michigan (died 1947) initiated the mass construction of automobiles. Charles Augustus Lindbergh, also of Michigan, encouraged the use of airplanes for regular passenger flights when he crossed the Atlantic Ocean alone, New York to Paris in 33-1/2 hours, in 1927. Sikorsky, now resident in the United States, demonstrated the helicopter in 1939, while others experimented with gas-turbine engines to drive the propellers, and with jet

271

propulsion to eliminate the propellers altogether. In 1947, piloted airplanes flew past the "sound barrier" for the first time, traveling faster than the speed of sound. (Pilotless planes had performed the experiment earlier.) In 1948, a jet-propelled air liner flew from the United Kingdom to Libya, and a United States air force plane made the first non-stop flight around the world (on a course covering 23,452 miles), taking on fuel four times during the long journey.

The science of bacteriology, on the border between biology and chemistry, is a century older than cybernetics, and a half-century older than electronics and aeronautics. Early bacteriologists found it difficult to convince the world of practicing medicine that bacteria really do exist. Identification of types of bacteria led to associations between them and various diseases. In the twentieth century, scientists began the attempt to synthesize drugs which would kill dangerous bacteria or inhibit their growth, allowing the organism attacked by the bacteria to survive. The sulfa drugs, manufactured in the 1930's, provided the first real success in these endeavors. Penicillin, isolated in 1941, was very quickly produced in large quantities. Penicillin came from a bread mold; it constituted the weapon, in effect, that the bacteria forming the mold used to kill other bacteria on contact. Man took the weapon out of the hands of the bread mold and used it for his own purposes. For the quantity he demanded, however, he would have to fashion the weapon for himself.

One find of the type early led to others, and to further necessities to synthesize. The new-style drugs were called "antibiotics," since they inhibited or destroyed (bacterial) life. The widespread genus of Streptomyces, dwelling mostly in the soil, proved the most helpful of all the bacteria on man's side in this quest. Intense study of Streptomyces followed the reasoning that, although all living things eventu-

272

ally return to the ground, the bacteria that cause so many of the deaths do not infest the earth to which all past creatures have fallen. Bacteriologists isolated several major antibiotics from the cultures of various species of Streptomyces during the late war and immediate postwar periods. Streptomycin, the first, appeared in 1943, and chloramphenicol in 1947. A group called the "tetracyclines" because of their four-ring molecular structure included several familiar trade names. These and a few other antibiotics provided man with an amazing new arsenal in his combat against disease. Put together, they attack a wide variety of dangerous bacteria, the even smaller organisms called rickettsiae, a few large viruses, and some other fungi. Unfortunately, they can kill friendly bacteria also; and less fortunately still, the enemy bacteria soon developed skill in fighting back, through their own breeding into antibiotic-resistant strains. In the warfare which continued, however, man and his friendly allies seemed to have a fair chance to win.

Enzymology like bacteriology lies on the borderline between biology and chemistry. Enzymology is the younger of the two, dating from only late nineteenth century. Its beginnings were actually inhibited by the development of bacteriology, physiologists by this time having come to believe that bacteria bore the responsibility for most or all of the diseases of man. Enzymes are proteins which serve as catalysts in the performance of particular body functions. A body malady, or disease, may be caused by the lack of a specific enzyme as readily as by the presence of a horde of bacteria. Research through the twentieth century has revealed not only the functions of a large number of enzymes, but also the complicated interplay between the enzymes on the one hand and various vitamins, minerals, and hormones on the other.

The vitamins began to be identified in the second decade of the twentieth century. They are

273

organic compounds, necessary for the chemical functioning of particular enzymes, but unlike the bulk of the enzymes are not produced by the body. This means that in most instances the vitamin is procured as part of a person's food supply. Specific food deficiencies, then, may mean vitamin deficiencies as well. One of the earlier vitamin substances to be isolated -- and called Vitamin B before its chemical composition became known -- later turned out to contain several separate compounds. Thus, there came to be Vitamin B_1, Vitamin B_2, and so on, as the various compounds became identified in the 1930's and 1940's. One of the more remarkable developments of this series proved to be the isolation of Vitamin B_{12}, or cyanocobalamine, accomplished in 1948 by Ernest Lester Smith in England and Illinois-born Karl August Folkers, working separately in the Merck Laboratories. Dorothy Mary Crowfoot Hodgkin of the United Kingdom, born in Egypt, then set out along with colleagues to study its atomic arrangement through x-ray diffraction. The disease associated with Vitamin B_{12} deficiency is the so-called pernicious anemia, involving a great decrease in the numbers of red blood cells. Cyanocobalamine is manufactured by friendly bacteria which dwell in the intestine. Persons who have pernicious anemia may have a normal supply of Vitamin B_{12}, but one that cannot escape through the intestinal wall to reach the blood stream. But cyanocobalamine, once it became synthesized, could be injected into the bloodstream, thus vanquishing one more of the physical troubles besetting man.

Hormones, unlike vitamins, are produced by the body itself. They serve as chemical messengers from one part of the body to another. Scientists had been able to identify a number of them since the work began early in the twentieth century, though they little understood the media through which they functioned. Hormones seemed to be enzyme-helpers rather than chemicals like the vitamins that enter into the enzymes. Nevertheless, their help is indispensable, so that hormone deficiencies can lead to serious difficulties. Epinephrine, the first hormone recognized, acts as a stimulant for the heart. Insulin, essential to the body's handling of carbohydrates, became isolated in the early 1920's, and put to work at once to counter diabetes. In the later 1920's, a new group of hormones of steroid (cholesterol-like) structure came under investigation. During World War II, a number of them were found to be secreted by the cortex of the adrenal gland. In 1949, Philip Showalter Hench of Pennsylvania, working at the Mayo Clinic, found one of the steroids named cortisone to be highly beneficial in treating the symptoms of rheumatoid arthritis -- though its particular body function had yet to be discovered. In the same year, ACTH or the adrenocorticotrophic hormone, product of the pituitary gland which stimulates the adrenal cortex to manufacture the cortisone, became recognized as having the same therapeutic value. It appeared that millions of people suffering from rheumatoid arthritis would soon gain great relief. Use of cortisone and ACTH, however, remained limited by the lack of understanding of the actual function of cortisone and its very complicated effects.

The science of meteorology had its beginnings in mid-nineteenth century, as the telegraph opened new means of communication. Two hundred years earlier, the first artificial clouds had been produced through the use of the first air pumps. Only in 1875 was it realized that water vapor condenses into clouds only when condensation nuclei such as dust (or sea salts or smoke) are available in the moist air. Precipitation, it was learned, comes about through the fall of larger rain droplets from rising, cooling air in the warmer climates, and through the fall of ice crystals formed by the clinging of rain droplets to tiny ice particles in the cooler climates. In 1946, Vincent Joseph Schaefer and Irving Langmuir at the General Electric Research Laboratories

found that pellets of frozen carbon dioxide dropped into a cloud in a deep-freeze box produced a
precipitation of ice crystals from the cloud.
(Both men came from New York; Langmuir had made
notable contributions to the study of matter at
the atomic level since early in the century.)
Their experiments showed that, when clouds have
reached a near-saturation point, especially with
water droplets as yet unfrozen in freezing temperatures, an injection of "dry ice" can cause
precipitation -- which, when lower atmosphere
temperatures are warm enough, strikes the earth
in the form of rain. Soon after this discovery,
pilots began to fly airplanes into promising
clouds to produce rain for needy farmers. Other
interested persons built fires of silver iodide
or lead iodide, to produce a fine-particle smoke
for use toward the same objective. Sometimes the
anticipated results materialized; oftentimes,
since the mechanisms of clouds remained poorly
understood, they did not. Further problems,
which early expressed themselves in law suits,
arose as the perception dawned that "cloud
seeding" providing a benefit to one family or
community might also prove a disadvantage to
others.

A strange phenomenon entered the experiences
of a variety of the earth's people after World
War II, encouraging them to report the sighting
of strange machines in the sky. The airships, if
such they were, seemed somewhat ghostlike in
quality, with an aspect dissimilar to that of
modern aircraft; many of the strange objects had
the appearance of a saucer in flight. Scattered
reports of unusual sightings in the sky extended
far back into history. During 1944-5, aviators
on both sides of the world conflict detected
unexplained objects on their radar screens. In
1946, a variety of postwar reports of sightings
originated in Denmark, Sweden, and the Baltic Sea
area. Many more instances reached the attention
of the world's press in 1947-8; they came from
widely scattered points on the planet, but

especially from the United States. The phenomenon nearly died out in 1949, but resumed with
considerable strength in 1950.

Many reports of "flying saucers" and other
objects originated, it seemed likely, from the
strong role played by suggestion in people's
minds. One "sighting" of a strange craft might
easily lead to a myriad of supposed sightings,
mounting into a whole wave of them during a short
interval of time -- until the press and the public tired of them, so that they ceased to attract
attention and the wave came to an end. Yet this
reverberation effect, which did become typical
with these reports, did not explain how the waves
began; nor did it account for scattered, individual reports originating nearly simultaneously
from distant points of the earth's surface. Many
persons attributed the appearances to weather
balloons of unfamiliar types -- balloons that
indeed were being used -- or pointed out that
new, secret aircraft might have been lofted by
some nation's military arm.

Some individuals suggested that man and his
planet might be under observation by intelligent
beings whose home lay elsewhere in the universe.
Mid-twentieth-century science generally accepted
the likelihood of the existence of life in the
universe aside from that found on earth. There
seemed to be good reason to think that some
civilizations elsewhere would have advanced much
farther than the one on this particular planet.
Earthbound science, however, took little interest
in flying saucers as possible evidence of the
existence of an extraterrestrial society, or of
any interest such a society might have in inspecting conditions on earth. Indeed, very few
scientists believed that the flying saucer epi-
demics merited any attention as a phenomenon,
preferring to categorize all reports as optical
illusions that could not readily be explained in
some other fashion.

The excitement surrounding synchrotrons, the world's largest telescope, the new cybernetics, transistors, tetracyclines, Vitamin B_{12}, and cortisone manifested the advance of natural science in this time period. The impressiveness of concrete developments in these areas precluded great scholarly interest in the intensely nebulous realm of flying saucers. What had the social sciences, dealing with the society of man, to offer that would compare in magnitude? The social sciences had developed chiefly in the last four hundred years. Organized study of them in the universities in most instances extended back less than a century. At the conclusion of World War II, many persons argued that greater attention to the social sciences could help prevent such calamities as war -- that, above all, man needed to understand man. But as with the natural sciences in their earlier years, there existed a dearth of ideas as to how to proceed.

Stuart Chase of New Hampshire, a popular author with the training of an economist, examined the social sciences in a book he called The Proper Study of Mankind . . . An Inquiry into the Science of Human Relations (1948). Chase counted the basic social sciences as five: cultural anthropology, social psychology, sociology, economics, and political science. Anthropology, he believed, had gone the farthest of the group, with the development of its concept of "culture." Through it, people are reminded that most of their actions fit patterns which their cultures seem to demand -- that, to this extent at least, man's behavior may be thought of as "determined." The other basic areas of study, particularly economics, Chase felt had suffered through their remaining oblivious to the culture concept and the corollary principle of cultural lag. The twin tendencies to theorize in a vacuum and to accept theories as verified truths, he believed, had resulted in the acceptance of a great deal of hypothesis as science, in such a manner as to prevent real progress. Though Chase did not discuss the point, the same might have been said of natural science in an earlier period.

The Proper Study of Mankind attempted more than mere criticism and the pointing out of shortcomings. It reviewed the very real accomplishments of social scientists, particularly during the war years. It noted that some of the most important projects had been carried out by teams of social scientists employed in various capacities. It suggested a list of great problems social scientists might be called upon to tackle, each one necessitating the talents of individuals from several disciplines. It called for the dropping of ideologies already shown to be insubstantial -- the Marxist theory of class struggle, for example, or the doctrine of laissez-faire -- and the substitution for them, in the universities, of instruction in processes as they exist. In effect, Chase called for a self-assessment by social science which could only lead to humility, but would provide a proper foundation for the future.

One of the social science projects that Stuart Chase thought significant had already gained unusual attention. Alfred Charles Kinsey of New Jersey and two Indiana University associates published its results under the title Sexual Behavior in the Human Male (1948). More correctly, they might have called it "Sexual Behavior in White Males of the United States." Kinsey had followed the career of zoologist, a specialist on wasps, before he undertook this study on the border between biology and sociology. He and his colleagues intended this as the first of a lengthy series of studies of human sex, the second of which would comprise a companion study of female behavior. Their report, based upon 5,300 personal interviews, drew attention because of its subject matter, of nearly universal appeal among educated people, but also because it established some facts in a field previously saturated with fancy.

In the Protestant, Catholic, and Jewish context from which most United States males derived, only one outlet for sexual energy met with full approval. Everyone expected men to engage in sexual intercourse in marriage, especially directed toward the procreation of children. Tradition-minded Christians and Jews regarded most other sexual practices as immoral. Addiction to any one of a number of them they considered unnatural and degrading -- in some instances, even leading to debility. Churches had taught the sinfulness of erotic self-stimulation; counselors for young people advised that such activity could lead all the way to insanity. Pre-marital heterosexual intercourse, though not described as unnatural or conducive to debility, remained categorized as spiritually deleterious regardless of the circumstances. Homosexuality came under the ban of proscription, to the point that Christians generally followed a taboo on mentioning the subject in public. Even sexual intercourse in marriage, in traditional Jewish and Christian mores, had severe restrictions thrust upon the manner of its accomplishment, inhibiting indulgence in body pleasure.

The first Kinsey report showed that high percentages of American males lived sexually at variance with the teachings that hovered in their backgrounds. Over 90% of white United States males engaged in self-stimulation leading to sexual orgasm before the age of 20. Indeed, such exercise accounted for over one-fourth of total male sex energy through the age of 40. Over 80% engaged in pre-marital heterosexual intercourse by the age of 25, and extra-marital intercourse provided an outlet for more than 5% of the married. Over 35% by the age of 20 participated in homosexual activity to the point of climax. In marital relations, oral stimulation of the female clitoris (in many states forbidden by law) occurred in nearly 60% of the case histories of males who had attended college, and large numbers of persons assumed positions in intercourse that ignored the restraints of custom. Marital intercourse, it is to be noted, continued to provide

85% of the outlet of sexual energy for married white United States males. The evidence did not indicate that the family was about to be discarded. Kinsey's team elicited a wealth of information concerning deviancy from the marriage standard, however, and in doing so provided substantial grounds for changes in education, medicine, psychology, and the law. Their study furthermore indicated that in one essential realm of life the world's most popular religion in its traditional form wielded considerably less influence than had been supposed. Some observers explained this development in terms of a significant change of emphasis in the Christian outlook; others believed that the faith had simply lost its attraction for people.

Biology made another contribution to social science in the late 1940's besides Kinsey's investigations of sex. This development gave support to anthropology in its effort to classify the races of man. Early efforts to catalog the earth's peoples followed the external physical characteristics of individuals -- the color of skin, the texture of hair, the presence of an epicanthic fold or full lips or a narrow nose. Though "primary" or general races could be thus discerned, allowing a very considerable margin of error, these attributes proved too superficial to be dependable. Human skeletons seemed to offer hope for a time, but the complexities of skeletal relationships proved unfathomable. Early in the twentieth century, new possibilities appeared with the discovery of the existence of blood types. Passed on from one generation to another intact, they could be used in the tracing of ancestry. However, too few blood types existed to perform the task of race classification throughout the world, and anthropologists again felt disappointed.

In the early 1940's, a new blood characteristic was discovered -- the rhesus or Rh factor, so named for rhesus monkeys used in the research. When scholars learned that the Basque people of northern Spain are distinctive in Rh factor from all other peoples of the world, the specification of the Basques as a distinct race seemed fully justified. Similar separations of race for a variety of peoples became possible when biologists took note of multiple variations in hemoglobin. Sickle-cell anemia, so called because the red blood cells of persons afflicted with the disease occur in the shape of a sickle rather than rounded, attacks Negroid persons frequently but seldom the Caucasoid or Mongoloid; its occurrence usually results in death. Sickle cells are inherited, like blood types and the Rh factor. But for some time after their discovery in 1910, no one knew how they were passed on by persons not afflicted with the disease, nor did anyone understand the manner in which they operated. In 1949, sickle cells were shown to be related to abnormal hemoglobin, and suddenly a variety of abnormal hemoglobins came to light. By themselves, they could not solve the racial riddles of mankind, complicated as they are through race-mixing. Their appearance alongside the other blood types and factors, however, gave greater substance to the quest.

Anthropology received yet another gift from natural science in 1948, in this case from the study of electronics. Before the war, scientists learned to use the known radioactive life-times of certain heavy elements to determine the age of rocks. After the war, with physicists splitting the atom, various radioactive isotopes of lighter elements became available for the first time. One of the most useful of these for a variety of reasons was carbon 14, often called radiocarbon, slightly heavier than the very common carbon 12. The importance of carbon 14 for the study of anthropology lay in its half-lifetime, extending roughly 5,600 years -- a given quantity of it will be reduced by one-half in that length of time through the process of radioactivity. Willard Frank Libby of Colorado and his students at the University of Chicago determined in 1946 that carbon 14 is contained in all organic life

282

and maintained at a certain level. When death comes -- as when early man cut a tree or killed an animal with a spearhead -- the level is no longer maintained, but the disintegration process ticks on regularly. An accurate Geiger counter (available since 1928), measuring the rate of radiation left, reveals the age of the object which is being studied, to the point at which the emissions are too weak to be read. Over five half-lifetimes of radio-carbon could be gauged, providing anthropologists with their first universal key to the chronology of the organic past (at least to the extent that the organic level of maintenance of carbon 14 remained constant through time). By 1948, Libby perfected the technique of dating by the radiocarbon method, which seemed destined eventually to make man's early history at least as clear as that of the earth's rocks.

Anthropology badly needed its new tools provided by biology and electronics. The human world it studied possessed far more intricacy than any other at hand. Earlier students of anthropology had found it necessary simply to pick away at the tremendous pile of evidence, though they did this on an amazingly grand scale. One of those who had gained prominence in the field in the late 1920's was Margaret Mead from Pennsylvania. Prior to World War II, she studied the people of Samoa, five groups on New Guinea and related islands, and the culture of Bali. Her books about Samoa and New Guinea caught the public interest. She wrote voluminously, in both scholarly and popular vein, comparing what she had found in Oceania with the culture she knew well at home.

In 1949, Margaret Mead published a new book on her earlier studies, summing up her impressions concerning male and female fulfillment in primitive and sophisticated societies. She called it Male and Female: A Study of the Sexes in a Changing World. "Anything that any of us can say about contemporary cultures is only a very little," said this student of society. "It is partial, inadequately formulated, incomplete -- as is all science, especially in its beginnings." Nevertheless, scholars should set out not only to describe societies but to show how such data could be applied. This book described how individuals of the two sexes learn their roles in the world under the rules that apply in their respective cultures. It showed how both men and women in the more primitive context could win self-esteem and self-assuredness through filling their simple roles. Men, the author argued, had gone on in the more civilized groups to learn new ways of achievement that take the place of such primitive accomplishments as skill with the bow and arrow. Women stayed behind, generally satisfied until recently to seek nearly all fulfillment through child-bearing. Women should not seek to emulate men, wrote Mead, but to do many things that they can do better. Included among these are intellectual pursuits, which require a sense of impersonal balance; pursuits for which motherhood grants an advantage, through its recognition of outside objects (such as newly born children) as different from one's self.

History, the oldest of the attempts to study society, is not usually counted a social science, due to its lack of complete commitment to modern scientific method. Proper historical research, however (regardless of how seldom it may be achieved), requires the same care and freedom from prejudice to which the ideal scientist subscribes. And while anthropologists have taken over the study of the world's history before the written word, and all of social science focuses upon the present, historians continue to be the chief expositors of that exciting part of human experience from today back to the invention of writing. That portion can be interpreted panoramically in a number of ways; Benedetto Croce, historian-philosopher of Italy, suggested in 1938 that it be considered the story of liberty. Important twentieth-century historiography consists of two kinds. One is the filling in, on a vast scale, of details of the record, which often correct distortions in the understanding of history accepted in previous times. The other is an attempt at integration, showing the unity of mankind, obliterating the old idea that one or a few peoples have been responsible for all that is interesting or worthwhile in civilization.

Will (William James) Durant, popular philosopher and historian of Massachusetts birth and French Canadian parentage, published one of the best known integrating accounts in 1950. It was called <u>The Age of Faith: A History of Medieval Civilization -- Christian, Islamic, and Judaic -- from Constantine to Dante: A.D. 325-1300</u>. Durant had composed three earlier volumes in his story of civilization, the first appearing in 1935. Unlike most popular and not-so-popular historians before him, Durant gave proper attention to the Muslim and Jewish cultures of medieval times, thus placing the dual Christian world (Byzantine and Roman) in proper context. He sought also to present all phases of each culture and of this age "in one total picture and narrative." Kings and conquerors had to take their place beside leaders of thought; the mighty had to live (as they did) with the humble. Durant portrayed this thousand years in the history of Europe and the Middle East as a time of achievement, not as an interlude. Medieval Europe conquered barbarism, and created a civilization in its stead. The Renaissance which followed, and would form the subject of his next book, stood in Durant's mind not as a repudiation but a fulfillment of the millenium through which Europe had climbed.

The filling in of the historical record requires operations of several kinds. Large numbers of postwar historians dedicated themselves to the writing of monographs, covering neglected corners in areas already traversed. Occasional attempts to describe a new area or to write from a new perspective, bringing out broad new truths, generally took on more significance when measured item by item. Lloyd Arnold Brown, a librarian from Rhode Island, covered a new era in The Story of Maps (1949). Brown went back to the beginning; modern maps, referring to latitude and longitude, entered his discussion only at the middle of the book. He also brought his narrative to the present, taking up the technical matters essential to the account while managing to remain completely readable. Here then lay a revelation of what had happened in one region of man's mind, from the most primitive to the most advanced ideas of cartography. Brown's study served likewise as a multi-faceted illustration of the scientific accomplishments of man through a period of twenty centuries.

The Negro in the United States, another publication of 1949, provided not a new area but a fresh historical perspective. Its author was Edward Franklin Frazier of Maryland, chairman of the Department of Sociology at Howard University. Frazier, himself of some African descent, wanted to present his own people as a part of American society rather than as a problem. He treated every aspect of their lives, starting like Brown from the very beginning. He put them in perspective not only with Europeans but also with Africans who had gone to other parts of the Americas, whose history Frazier had also studied. He faced the Negro difficulties of his day squarely, though he believed that there had been improvement. Five years earlier, Gunnar Myrdal, sociologist from Sweden, had written extensively about the racial situation in the United States, presenting it as the American dilemma, a contradiction between profession and practice. Persons of African ancestry received the treatment of inferiors, though the United States constitution specified that all persons be treated as equals. Frazier wrote not to argue these matters, though they formed a part of his book, but to remind his readers that Negroes too are people, with a fascinating history of their own.

Biography is a very special form of history;

well-balanced biographies are rare. The reason is simply that the writer very easily develops an emotional bias either for or against his subject. Most biographers know ahead of time what they want to do to the image of the person whom they have adopted as subject, and even if they set themselves the arduous goal of fairness the results often prove most dubious. A single biography of a notable person may teach something meaningful, and yet fail to give a comprehensive view. Isaac Deutscher, a Polish communist and journalist resident in England, managed to produce an unusual one, however, in 1949. He called it <u>Stalin: A Political Biography</u>, pointing out that Stalin's personal life remained very little known. Deutscher could write dispassionately about Stalin for two reasons. First, he both admired the man and felt distaste for him. Second, he tried with all his might to write impartially. Deutscher had followed Trotsky rather than Stalin in the feud that developed between the two leaders in the 1920's. This permitted him a sympathetic understanding of the communist revolution in Russia, without approval of all that followed. His own devotion to the task of preparing an extraordinary biography then led him to acknowledge Stalin's further contributions to the Soviet Union in the face of the disaster for freedom there. The developments in the Soviet Union as presented by Deutscher shaped a portrait of high idealism led conversely into tyranny; he believed that Stalin, half-Asian in his origins, made his land over into a half-Asian regime, following the principles of the revolution but changing the modus operandi. The worth of the biography, however, lay not with this theme, but with the description of a noted leader in hundreds of details as an individual subject to all the loves, hatreds, passions, and despairs that most persons find in their lives.

Isaac Deutscher, E. Franklin Frazier, Lloyd A. Brown, Will Durant, Margaret Mead -- all could be read with great profit by anyone who had acquired college-level understandings. Norbert Wiener and Bertrand Russell were more difficult, and appealed to a relative few. Most persons in mid-twentieth century, however, had not reached the college level of instruction. In specific countries, several of them large, many individuals could not read at all -- of those over ten years of age, more than half of Brazil's population and more than four-fifths of India's, for example. Programs to rid nations of illiteracy would become common in the post-war world. But a great gap existed between simply learning how to read and active participation in the world of science. Even the most educated nations did little to prepare most of their citizens for the new life after 1945 beyond the provision of economic needs. The world of unclaimed knowledge seemed large enough to accommodate new millions of interested people, nevertheless, whenever the appropriate educational programs could be created.

Art

Fanny Blankers-Koen in women's track . . Sweden in the Olympics . . Uruguay in soccer . . Copland, Third Symphony . . Prokofiev, War and Peace . . Ives, Third Symphony . . Messaien, Turangalila . . Britten, Peter Grimes . . Menotti: The Medium; The Consul . . García Lorca, La casa de Bernalda Alba . . O'Neill, The Iceman Cometh . . Fry, The Lady's Not for Burning . . Williams, A Streetcar Named Desire . . Miller, Death of a Salesman . . Eliot, The Cocktail Party . . Frisch, Die Chinesische Mauer . . Brecht, Der Kaukasische Kreidekreis . . Sartre, Les mains sales . . Camus, Caligula . . Ionesco, La cantatrice chauve. . . . Malraux, Psychologie de l'art. . . . Picasso, La joie de vivre . . Giacometti, Composition with Seven Figures and One Head . . the United Nations Secretariat building . . Rossellini: Roma città aperta; Paisan . . De Sica: Sciuscià; Ladri di biciclette . . Buñuel, Los olvidados . . Kurosawa, Rashomon . . Hamer,

Kind Hearts and Coronets . . Cocteau, Orphée . .
Auden, The Age of Anxiety . . Neruda, Canto general . . Stowe, While Time Remains . . Ward, The
West at Bay . . Laski, The American Democracy . .
Hersey, The Wall . . Paton: Cry, the Beloved
Country . . Camus, La peste . . Orwell, Nineteen
Eighty-Four.

   Art is an expression of man's spirit. Early
in his existence, perhaps when he found his first
spare time, he realized this second way of doing
something satisfying. There were many beauties of
sight and of sound which he could enjoy in the
world about him. There were also paintings he
could sketch, polished stones or figurines he
could shape, and music he could devise, once the
first concepts of these art-realms had occurred
to him. Eventually, there would be writing which
he could use to evoke new beauties beyond his
former imaginings. Probably, other impressive
sensations eluded him with his poorly developed
senses of taste, smell, and touch. As he developed the art faculties easiest for him,
nevertheless, he made significant strides in
understanding not available through science. In
the post-1945 world, artistic enthusiasm would
reach many people who had not possessed the time
for art activity before, and would carry society
through a restless experimentation with new
ideas. Some of the experiments showed hopeful
signs of leading on to delightful new horizons.

   The aesthetic sensibilities of man became
very early tuned to the gracefulness inherent in
music, dance, and games. Primitive peoples developed thousands of forms of each of them.
Games have constituted the most popular for of
art in modern times. The twentieth century ias
seen some of them organized internationally, even
on a global scale. Since 1896, Olympic games
have been held each four years, in partial imitation of the ancient Greek games held in Olympia,
to encourage world interest in sports and the
values of elegance and beauty that go with them.

War conditions caused the games to be cancelled in 1916 and again in 1940 and 1944. In 1948 they resumed, in Switzerland and England.

Fifty-nine countries and dependencies sent squads including a total of 4,468 athletes to participate in the "summer" games held in London, England. The Soviet Union did not send a team -- Russian athletes had not participated in the games since 1912, before the Russian communist revolution -- though groups did attend from the other communist states of eastern Europe. Japan and Germany also remained outside. Fanny (Francina) Blankers-Koen of the Netherlands at the age of 30 won three individual gold medals (for top position) in women's track events, in the 100-meters and 200-meters dash and the 80-meters hurdles, and another as a member of a team in the 400-meters relay. In the team sports, the winners of gold (first-place), silver (second-place) and bronze (third-place) medals were, respectively, groups from the United States, France, and Brazil in basketball; from Sweden, Yugoslavia, and Denmark in soccer; from India, the United Kingdom, and the Netherlands in field hockey; and from Italy, Hungary, and the Netherlands in water polo.

The Olympic games are officially contests between individuals or teams rather than between nations. In the twentieth-century nationalistic world, however, most people cheered with more strength for competitors from their own countries and kept track of results by nationality. Two-thirds of the medals awarded in London, on a weighted base allowing three points for gold, two for silver, and one for bronze, were won by persons from the following countries: the United States (171 points), Sweden (78), Italy (54), France (53), Hungary (51), the United Kingdom (40), Switzerland (38), Finland (34), and Denmark (34). On a per capita basis, however, a very different picture emerged. Athletes from Sweden performed by far the best in numbers of points on medals earned (11.3) for each million of its population. There followed, among the first ten, Finland (8.7), Switzerland (8.2), Denmark (8.1) in close company with one another; Hungary (5.6) and Jamaica (5.2); and Trinidad-Tobago (3.3), Australia (3.0), the Netherlands (2.8), and Norway (2.8). (The figure for Trinidad-Tobago is an inverted one, that colony having contained less than a million people.)

Twenty-eight nations sent 778 athletes to attend the "winter" games held in St. Moritz, Switzerland, for which the climates of many countries placed them at a disadvantage. Teams from Canada, Czechoslovakia, and Switzerland won the three medals (gold, silver, and bronze respectively) in ice hockey. One-half of the points according to medals earned (using the weighted system as for the summer games) were won by participants from only three countries: Sweden (with 21), Norway (19), and Switzerland (17). On the per capita basis, Norway (with 5.9 points for each million inhabitants) performed the best, with Switzerland (3.7), Sweden (3.0), and Finland (2.8) doing as well as any country of the first ten in the summer games.

All the players in the Olympics were supposed to be or considered to be "amateurs" who engaged in sport for motives other than money. Competition for the World Cup in soccer, the most popular variety of football, provided the chief international event of the quinquennium without reference to amateur status. Soccer had its origins in England, even before modern times, but spread to much of the world by late nineteenth century. Before World War II world cups had been awarded in 1930, 1934 and 1938. In the final rounds for the fourth Cup in 1950 in Brazil, Spain tied one game with Uruguay, for one point; Sweden defeated Spain, for two points; Brazil won over Sweden and Spain, for four points; and Uruguay defeated Brazil and Sweden and tied with Spain, for five points and the championship. A sensational aspect of Uruguay's achievement lay in the size of its population, far smaller than

291

that of any one of its competitors.

Until modern times, the art of dancing may have rated higher than games in popularity. It remains far from forgotten, though mass participation has declined. After World War II, three Latin American dances held international favor for a time. These were the rumba from Cuba, popular since early in the century; the samba from Brazil, spread during the war; and the mambo from Haiti, recently designed as a variation of the rumba. All three possessed deep roots in the Afro-American background. Older European styles and the jitterbug, danced in the United States since the 1930's, likewise commanded a large following.

Dance performances in many lands brought styles formerly seen only by the aristocracies to persons of a much wider public. Ballet, a European vogue for a few hundred years, had become fashionable even in countries very non-European in their backgrounds. And as interest in ballet spread, it became mixed with "modern dance" movements performed in the United States since the early 1900's and with a variety of folk dances from many regions. Vaslav Nijinsky, a leading ballet dancer of the tsarist court in Russia until 1917, in his own choreography rejected conventional forms late in his career (suffering a breakdown in 1919, he lived until 1950). Georgy Balanchivadze, or George Balanchine, moved from Russia to France and Denmark, and in 1948 organized the New York City Ballet, specializing in highly original dance patterns. Martha Graham of Pennsylvania choreographed modern dance movements in a far-reaching attempt to reveal inner emotions on the stage.

European-style music (with its emphasis upon melody and harmony and its use of a seven-tone scale) spread around the globe well before the Second World War. It went wherever Europeans traveled all through modern times, of course, and in the 1920's and 1930's became ever more popular through the influence of radio and motion pictures. There were really two kinds of European music, however -- that which had retained a strong appeal for the masses of people and that which had developed specifically for the concert stage. A great gulf had arisen between them, so that partisans of either kind would frequently not listen to the other, though both species after the sixteenth century used the same homophonic style of harmonic chords blending with a lead melody. In the Americas, the more popular European music had time to blend with African and American Indian influences before the twentieth century, producing an exciting diversity of musical customs known to the masses of the people. In Africa and Asia, traditions that did not recognize homophony have coexisted with the European style until the most recent times. After World War II, it seemed that the most distinct musical forms might gain the opportunity to get together.

The first steps in the amalgamation process came the easiest -- a recognition on the part of the composers of European concert music that popular music of their own lands had its own kind of fascination. Bela Bartok of Hungary (who lived until 1945), Manuel de Falla of Spain (until 1946), Jean Sibelius of Finland and Heitor Villa-Lobos of Brazil (the latter two composing through this quinquennium) all reached out for the music of their people before the war, and received worldwide acclaim for the happy results. Such activity continued after 1945 on a wide scale, with Ralph Vaughan Williams of England, Aaron Copland of New York, Roy Harris of Oklahoma, and Carlos Chávez of Mexico among the most noted of its practitioners. Copland's Third Symphony, presented in 1946, represented the North American personality in distinguished fashion.

While some masters of the concert reached toward the popular music, one brand of the latter, named jazz, made its own way to the concert stage. Interestingly, this development occurred in the United States rather than in the Soviet

Union, whose government officially encouraged the "people's music." Invented by the United States Negro community in the very late nineteenth century, jazz began in the late 1910's to bridge the gap between poor people's listening and that of sophisticated audiences without significant compromise. By the 1930's, jazz-influenced concert pieces spread widely. After World War II, Morton Gould of New York and a host of others continued to compose in the jazz idiom. The spontaneity of the recognition of jazz had no counterpart in revolutionary Russia. Dmitry Shostakovich and Sergey Prokofiev, the most recognized Russian composers of the immediate postwar period, tried to work with the people's music, but had their genuine roots elsewhere. War and Peace by Prokofiev, first performed in 1946, was a magnificent opera depicting the Russian will to survive when threatened by foreign armies. Aram Khachaturian came closer to catching the spirit of a people as he reflected the tastes of his own Soviet Armenia. But Shostakovich, Prokofiev, and Khachaturian all had to humble themselves before Stalin in 1948 for not staying close to the proletariat.

A majority of the sophisticated composers of this quinquennium remained uninterested in bridging any gap between themselves and the masses. They took the position, to the contrary, that the people should join them, and to a small extent they succeeded in achieving that objective. Some -- including Howard Hanson of Nebraska and Samuel Barber of Pennsylvania -- continued the nineteenth-century "romantic" trend of Schubert and Liszt. Richard Strauss of Germany, the twentieth-century apotheosis of the extremist romantic style of Wagner, himself lived until 1949. Other composers of this time period reverted to the later-eighteenth-century "classical" mode of artists like Mozart or the earlier-eighteenth-century "baroque" of persons like Bach. Igor Stravinsky, Russian resident in California, liked the style of Mozart; Paul Hindemith of Germany, living in Connecticut, preferred that of Bach. A stronger personal element entered the works of three noted French composers, Darius Milhaud, Arthur Honegger, and Francis Poulenc, all of them having reacted in their youth to the rules imposed even by romanticism. Charles Ives of Connecticut had very early broken the rules where he pleased, even in his most serious works. His Third Symphony, finished in 1904 but first played in 1947, was based upon New England hymn tunes, and ignored symphonic rules in an outrageously pleasant way.

Some groups of musicians dedicated themselves to new expressions in sound. A sizeable school followed the lead of Arnold Schoenberg, Austrian resident of California, and of Anton von Webern, another Austrian killed in 1945 in an aftermath of the war. These two men had developed a "twelve-tone" technique substituting new rules for old ones that required attention to a tonality tied to a chosen note. The new requirement, while setting the composer more free, continued to emphasize a particular arrangement of twelve tones chosen as the base for any one composition. Another school of musicians, led originally by Stravinsky and Prokofiev, not only abandoned the old tonality but declared themselves liberated rhythmically as well, setting the rules aside even more completely. Olivier Messaien of France in 1948 presented Turangalila (Hindi name for Turanga-performance, or performance of the celestial musicians) offering European listeners a mixture of their own music with that of the Orient. Carl Orff of Germany composed declaimed (rather than sung) operas in Latin and Greek. In France in 1948, "concrete music," produced on tape from everyday sounds, provided an electronic novelty going beyond all the other novelties.

Two of the most popular postwar composers wrote in several veins, choosing the mode according to the emotion that they wished to express. Their most noted efforts served as a reminder of how drastically concert music had changed, even within one person's lifetime. Now a writer could do as he pleased, if he had the talent, without leaving his audience horrified at his breaking with custom. These two men chose to write opera and other works which made them masters of the theater in addition to the musical art. They were Benjamin Britten of England, whose Peter Grimes of 1945 comprised the sad story of a lone fisherman unjustly believed guilty of a crime; and Gian Carlo Menotti of Italy, residing in the United States, who produced The Medium (1946) and The Consul (1950), macabre plots accompanied by entire kaleidoscopes of modern music. William Walton of England, William Schuman of New York, Leonard Bernstein of Massachusetts, and Walter Piston of Maine proved themselves adept in the same manner within the world of sound.

Theater does not extend as far back in history as music, dancing, and games. Neither has popular participation in theatrical activities ever been so widespread. Each of the nations of the world, however, has some kind of playhouse tradition. Old plays are often as well liked as new ones. After World War II, old plays constituted the regular fare in most countries. Notable dramatic creativity appeared chiefly in North America and non-communist Europe, where a fair amount of exchange took place. Most of it in this five-year period centered about a quality of despair in man. Much of it also revealed concern about the relationship between the drama and its audiences. Stage settings, though sometimes very simple in design, were contrived for their ambient effect upon the persons attending the play, in accord with the early-twentieth-century striving of Edward Gordon Craig of England, master of the art of theater who lived through this postwar quinquennium, and the preferences of George Bernard Shaw of Ireland (died 1950) and Gerhart Hauptmann of Germany (died 1946), two of the most noted playwrights of the century.

Three notable postwar productions reminded

their audiences of the prewar theater scene. Federico García Lorca of Spain had written La casa de Bernalda Alba (The House of Bernarda Alba) in 1936, shortly before a Falangist group killed him; the first performance took place in 1945. Recently widowed Bernarda Alba in this play attempts to enforce eight years of mourning upon her five unwed daughters, in the spirit of small-village Spanish mores, eventually driving the youngest of them to suicide. Eugene O'Neill of New York composed The Iceman Cometh in 1939, offering it to the public in 1946. A group of human derelicts await the visit of a generous traveling salesman (who has often regaled them with stories of his wife and an imaginary iceman with whom she makes love), only to learn when he arrives that the salesman's wife is dead -- indeed, that the salesman has killed her because he could not stand her virtuousness in the face of his own delinquency. The Lady's Not for Burning, completed and produced in 1948 by Christopher Fry of England as a sophisticated play in verse, offered some hope to Fry's countrymen of a revival of the superb theater that country had enjoyed in the sixteenth century. In the fifteenth-century plot, the young lady wrongly accused of witchcraft and sentenced to be burned reaches safety through the aid of a young man who, disenchanted by his previous experiences in life, has asked to be hanged for a murder he mistakenly believes himself to have committed.

Postwar theater generally, however, ran in other directions than these. "Tennessee" (Thomas Lanier) Williams of Mississippi contributed A Streetcar Named Desire in 1947. The daughter of a decadent and bankrupt aristocratic family rides a car by this name (which expresses her own sexual proclivities) to the address of her sister in New Orleans, Louisiana, where her involvements with men eventually result in her commitment to an institution. Arthur Miller of New York wrote Death of a Salesman in 1949, portraying the ignominious termination of life experienced by a husband and father whose goals have all remained

tied to a business career that did not materialize. Thomas Stearns Eliot of Missouri, a noted
poet who had settled in England and whose presence there bolstered English hopes for a literary
renaissance, produced The Cocktail Party, a drama
in verse, in 1949. The hostess, not present at
the party because she has become separated from
her husband, is advised by a psychiatrist (who
speaks for Eliot) to reunite with her spouse, so
that the couple may take what joy they can from a
dull, mediocre life (the play ends as another of
their cocktail parties begins) which for all its
shortcomings remains preferable to the violence
and greed about them. Meanwhile, the girl who
had come between the married couple, accepting
advice from the same source, offers her life in
martyrdom as a missionary to a primitive people,
thus achieving a spiritual fulfillment unavailable to ordinary persons, atoning (like Jesus)
for the sin that (in the outlook of non-traditional Eliot as in that of traditional Christianity) besets everyone.

Die Chinesische Mauer (The Chinese Wall,
1946) flowed from the very imaginative but pes-
simistic mind of Max Frisch of Switzerland as he
turned toward a career in drama. Literary and
historical figures from the time of the building
of the Great Wall in northern China to the present (a span of about 2,200 years) argue the respective merits of their roles in presentations
before the emperor who built the wall, while the
emperor, in a style resembling that of Hitler,
hears but does not heed the words of a twentieth-
century intellectual, who speaks for Frisch, contending that the world does not need leaders who
consider war unavoidable. The intellectual,
mockingly awarded a prize by the emperor for demonstrating the uselessness of rebellion against
the emperor's will, gives up, becoming mute, in
despair. Der Kaukasische Kreidekreis (The Caucasian Chalk Circle, 1948) was written by Bertolt
Brecht of Germany, who had produced "epic" theater for a quarter of a century, permitting the
audience to see the mechanisms of the stage, in

298

an effort to encourage the public to adopt a thoughtful rather than an emotional response to the play. Brecht, a Marxist, wishes in this instance to get across the point that material holdings should be awarded to those persons who will make best use of them. The play deals with a dispute over an agricultural valley in the Caucasus mountains of Soviet Georgia. The main action, however, comes from an ancient Chinese play-within-the-play, whereby the point for the settling of another dispute stems from a chalk circle drawn by an erratic judge, who calls for a tug of war between two women contending for a child, but awards the child to the one who refuses to enter the contest because she does not want to see the youngster harmed. Brecht wrote this play while in the United States (1941-7), a refugee from the Nazi regime, but produced it in Switzerland; in 1949 he moved to East Berlin.

Jean-Paul Sartre of France became known for his dramas and philosophical writings during the war period. An individualist Marxist, like Brecht, he described an atheistic outlook that he called "existentialism," borrowing vocabulary from but dropping most of the concepts of Christian existentialist doctrine of the nineteenth century. Man exists, asserted Sartre, only as he makes himself. He cannot be judged by rules, but only by his own sense of responsibility. He is responsible not only for himself, but for all mankind. (The existential outlook of Sartre is discussed further under the heading "Religion," in this chapter; Christian existentialism, in Chapter VII.) In Les mains sales of 1948 (Dirty Hands, also known as Crime passionnel and Red Gloves), Sartre portrays a communist party leader in an occupied European state during the war who in the judgment of "purists" within his own party soils his hands through collaboration with bourgeois parties against the foreign enemy. The purists plot to murder him, and one of them carries out the assassination (a task requiring bare hands rather than gloves). He does so, however, only after much hesitation because of his personal admiration of the virtues of his intended victim. As he is killed, the leader excuses the murder as a <u>crime passionnel</u>, since indeed he had carried on a very mild flirtation with the murderer's wife. At the end of the war, the party switches its line to approval of the successful policy of collaboration with bourgeois elements, and the now-dead man who carried it out is considered a martyr. In the strange blend of Marxist and Sartrean ideas found in this play, the murderer then finds his existentialist freedom as a real man by admitting the political motivation for his crime -- this decision being his act of "responsibility" to mankind -- while the victim in his turn is seen in history as a man who died -- once again "responsibly" -- for his (now correct) program, rather than simply dying "by accident."

The existentialist ideas of Sartre included the concept of the "absurdity" (lack of coherent meaning) of the world in which man lives. After the war, the theme of absurdity entered plays written by men who were impressed by Sartre's ideas. One writer, Albert Camus, born in Algeria of French and Spanish parentage, produced <u>Caligula</u> in 1945, indicating his respect for the "logic" in the consideration of the universe as absurd but his unwillingness to allow the theme to take over people's minds. Caligula, the ancient Roman emperor, comprehends the theme of absurdity and decides to seek his own happiness through a wild assertion of his own freedom, though he believes this must come at the expense of others. His opposition prefers a happiness coupled with security for the people, and Caligula -- after three years of cruelty and rapine -- finally decides that his own path to happiness leads nowhere. Eugène Ionesco of Romania, living in France, not only accepted the Sartrean theme of absurdity, but desired to express it theatrically. Thus he wrote <u>La cantatrice chauve</u> (rendered unfaithfully as <u>The Bald Soprano</u> or <u>The Bald Prima Donna</u> in English, though none of the titles really matters), first acted before an audience of three persons in Paris in 1950. This "anti-play" as Ionesco himself called it, inspired by Ionesco's study of English-language primers, presents two English couples speaking nonsense through a long evening; their words, and those of others who enter, make no sense at all. Their message to the audience is that in this absurd world people's conversation generally makes no sense at all.

The non-sense (not necessarily nonsense) play of Ionesco brought drama in 1950 to the point reached by painting and sculpture a generation earlier. These twin arts had very early origins, and once belonged to the mass of the people. In the nineteenth century in western and central Europe, they became largely the domain of specialists living in artists' colonies. As this phenomenon took place, other changes came also, following rather rapidly one upon the other, and affecting art life in North America in the twentieth century and the entire world after 1945. The new turn that took place a generation before Ionesco's play was the beginning of what is called "expressionism" -- the painter or sculptor expressing the emotion he feels as he looks at an object rather than attempting to portray it in correct visual detail. Expressionism, itself divisible into several tendencies, constituted only one of a number of developments which together provide the history of "modern art."

The term modern for history generally takes in the last five hundred years, the period during which European people have traversed the globe. Modern art in European painting goes back only one hundred years, in sculpture even less. It is characterized by honesty in the development of its themes; as an example, before modern art beautiful feminine figures in the nude had had to be portrayed as nymphs or goddesses, while in modern art they appeared as contemporary women. Modern art is also distinguished by a stream of almost restless experimentation in the application of new techniques. The quality of honesty

301

surviving the creation of many new movements has not necessarily carried with it great powers of discernment. Hundreds of modern painters and sculptors have remained true to their own vision, as they lived isolated in colonies, without becoming cognizant of a wider view of humanity.

Famed novelist André Malraux of France discussed the position of modern art in three volumes called <u>Psychologie de l'art</u> (1947-50), translated as <u>The Psychology of Art</u>. He then began to reduce the hodgepodge of provocative essays contained therein to a more smoothly proportioned book, which he titled <u>Les voix du silence</u> (<u>The Voices of Silence</u>). " . . . Every artist starts off with the pastiche," Malraux said. " . . . It is not the sight of a supremely beautiful woman, but the sight of a supremely beautiful painting that launches a painter on his career. . . ." For this reason, all of painting (and of sculpture as well) represents to some extent a heritage of the past; modern art constitutes no exception. The characteristic that differentiates the great artist from other persons "is not the intensity of his responses to what he sees, nor . . . that of his responses to others' works of art; it is the fact that he alone, amongst all those whom these works of art delight, must seek, by the same token, to destroy them." The artist starts with the pastiche; he finishes with a product expressing his own personality. Modern art is itself a metamorphosis of the Christian art from which it streamed, though with the influence of many worlds of non-Christian art brought to bear upon it. It is to be valued highly because, like some but not all earlier art traditions, it grants the artist freedom to be himself, to capture the world in his creations rather than being captured by his subject.

Malraux saw no fault in artists' colonies, which became commonplace with the growth of modern art. " . . . In so far as he is a creator," Malraux said, "the artist does not belong to a

302

social group already molded by a culture, but to a culture which he is by way of building up." When art schools of the past "broke with appearances," however, as modern art has done, they did so with an eye to investing the thing seen with a certain quality; "whereas our modern artists . . . would be hard put to it to say what higher purpose they are serving." Malraux supplied this purpose, in a period of postwar pessimism. "All art," he believed, "is a revolt against man's fate." Man's fate, which may seem pitiful, is to have his days end "in a black night of nothingness" -- modern thought had taught him that, Malraux said. But painting for painting's own sake, he continued, will bear witness to the dignity of man, no matter what happens to him thereafter.

Many of the outstanding artists who helped to create early-twentieth-century schools of painting lived past the end of World War II. Most of them had their roots in nineteenth-century impressionism, which tended to portray images as they reached the artist's brain rather than as he knew them concretely. As impressionism began to crumble into a variety of tendencies, Pierre Bonnard of France (died 1947) was one of a group of "intimists" who portrayed common indoor scenes. Henri Matisse, likewise of France, began his career as a "fauvist" or "wild beast," using extravagant, "liberated" colors in 1905. (Matisse later passed through many stages.) Another countryman, Georges Rouault, moved on quickly from the fauvist wave to become one of the early exponents of expressionism. While living in Paris, Pablo Ruiz y Picasso of Spain and Georges Braque of France developed the "cubist" approach in 1907-8, painting in geometric design. Fernand Léger, another French cubist, became interested in depicting the forms of machinery.

Oskar Kokoschka of Austria, an expressionist, helped to develop new emphases during World War I and its immediate aftermath. The "dadaists" of that time, stressing the irrational side of man and taking a negative stand toward all former art, included Marcel Duchamp, a French painter who moved to New York in 1915. Living in France, Marc Chagall from a Jewish family of Russia at the same time ventured into a more positive, often humorous, type of fantasy painting. Joan Miró of a Spanish Catalan family, who also liked to live in Paris, in the 1920's became a leading "surrealist," stretching the world of fantasy into the improbable realm of dreams. José Clemente Orozco of Mexico (died 1949) in the 1930's produced large panoramas of historical and religious content, in both his home country and the United States.

Pablo Ruiz y Picasso, among the most renowned of modern art practitioners, moved to Paris from Spain very early in the twentieth century. Picasso (as he is abbreviatedly known) became an exponent of expressionism at the time of the First World War, and one who dabbled in fantasy well before the Second. In 1946, with distinct contrast to the mood of Malraux, he expressed his good feeling over the ending of the fighting with a whimsical painting of nymph, goats, and centaurs called La joie de vivre. Jean Dubuffet, French artist who began his career during the 1940's, after the war portrayed mad figures of violence, based on drawings by the insane. Stuart Davis from Pennsylvania, well-known painter between the two wars, became intrigued at this time by the associative aspects of abstract lines and words. Meanwhile, Franz Kline of Pennsylvania (after viewing magnified portions of his earlier paintings) moved suddenly in 1949 from representational sketches to the production of large, completely abstract, black-and-white images, accomplished with housepainter brushes and cheap paints.

Modern sculpture emerged more slowly than modern painting, sculpture having passed through a long period in the seventeenth and eighteenth centuries when very few persons took interest. In the nineteenth century, renewed zeal first brought about complete devotion to the traditions of old masters. The twentieth century changed that situation, moving sculptors into paths similar to those of the painters, though in sculpting there remained a greater scope for individualism on the part of each artist. Constantin Brancusi of Romania, who traveled widely, set the pace with his original ideas through most of the first half of the century; he continued to live into the second. Picasso the cubist painter became also Picasso the cubist sculptor and assembler of various materials. Alexander Calder of Pennsylvania and Alberto Giacometti of Switzerland began their careers as surrealists, but by the 1930's were shifting to styles respectively their own.

Picasso, more renowned for his paintings, spent much of his time immediately after World War II fashioning comic animals of bronze. Jean (or Hans) Arp, born in Strasbourg, at that time in Germany, turned from painting to sculpture in Switzerland during World War I and later settled in Paris. His interest after the Second World War lay in what he called "concretions," portrayals in bronze or cast stone (concrete made to look like stone) of objects, especially organisms, which had a history of growth behind them. Alberto Giacometti, whose Swiss father painted, moved to Paris as a sculptor in the 1920's. His postwar depictions of persons' bodies, all of them extremely attenuated (tall and slender), included the noted Composition with Seven Figures and One Head in bronze (1950). David Smith of Illinois, living in rural New York, liked to construct sculpture in a machine shop rather than hewing or molding it. He began in 1950 to produce completely abstract expressions of lines in space, made of steel.

Twentieth-century architecture broke away from the traditions of the past even more slowly than sculpture. Only in the 1920's, with the development of the new "international" style in Europe, came a recognition of the departures that had become possible with modern structural materials. The international school of architecture

305

derived its name from the fact that its proponents from whatever country had put aside national traditions in favor of certain ideas they shared in common. A prime characteristic of the style was that buildings should be supported by inner structures rather than outside walls, which might thus be made more attractive (usually with fine, straight lines) than they had ever appeared before. Walter Gropius and Ludwig Mies van der Rohe of Germany along with Charles-Edouard Jeanneret ("Le Corbusier") of Switzerland played a large role in developing these ideas. Frank Lloyd Wright of Wisconsin, who discarded much of his own national tradition early in the century, also influenced the new school. All four of these men followed postwar careers.

In the quinquennium 1946-50, construction of new buildings revived slowly from the impact of the war. Le Corbusier, who had already won fame as an architect in two hemispheres, nevertheless managed to initiate a new technique in the creation of an apartment house in Marseilles, France, started in 1947. Here he not only emphasized the derivation of the greatest utility from a restricted amount of space, as he had before the war, but also introduced the technique of leaving concrete in a rough state rather than "finishing" it -- to remain true, he stated, to the nature of the material.

Le Corbusier was one of several world architects invited to help plan the buildings of the United Nations headquarters in New York. This team of men brought the international school of architecture to America. The ideas of the school as applied to skyscrapers, such as that housing the United Nations Secretariat, meant the realization of a tall, rectangular structure beautiful in itself, with room at the base where people could breathe and an interior laid out for efficiency. In this example, glass and marble provided a sheath. Hundreds of variations of this simple skyscraper theme would rise throughout the entire world soon thereafter, as impressive symbols of modern government and industry.

The development of the art of photography in the nineteenth century helped to bring about the restless experimentation in painting, which in turn influenced trends in sculpture, though with lesser impact on architecture. Photography, like painting and sculpture in older times, belonged to everyone. A few professionals, however, mastered photographic techniques more completely than most persons, and encouraged others also to become experts. Alfred Stieglitz of New Jersey, who sponsored shows of photography and founded the school of "photo-secessionists" (seceding from painting) in the early twentieth century, lived until 1946. Edward Steichen of Luxembourg, who moved to the United States, joined Stieglitz in his enterprises, and lived through this quinquennium.

The art of photography itself led in very late nineteenth century to the development of the world's first motion pictures. As a new industry developed in Europe and North America, manufacturing films for public viewing, David Wark Griffith of Kentucky (died 1948) directed noted presentations in the United States; René Clair did the same in France, and Sergey Eisenstein (died 1948) in the Soviet Union, while "Charlie" Chaplin of England attained great fame as a film comedian. In the late 1920's, after the "movies" had become a widespread family pastime, sound tracks added to the film enforced its sense of reality. Walt (Walter) Disney of Illinois, producer of animated cartoons, invented his characters Mickey Mouse and Donald Duck as the new "talkies" were enthusiastically received, and moved on to engineer full-length animated films of popular stories before, during, and after the war, somtimes mixing live characters with the cartoons. Jean Renoir of France, an outstanding director of live persons on film in the 1930's, continued to produce notable pictures after the war. The talking cinema, like the theater, could speak quite directly to the condition of man. Of all the art media, only the novel could provide a comparable mixture of simultaneous entertainment and enlightenment. However, as motion pictures in the 1930's became one of the most popular art forms of the world, only an occasional producer showed an awareness of the wealth of potential in the new medium.

In war-torn Italy in 1945, Roberto Rossellini directed the filming of <u>Roma città aperta</u> (Rome Open City) showing both the demoralization and the heroism that accompanied the last days of Nazi rule there. In <u>Paisan</u> (1946), Rossellini tackled the entire tableau of the Italian war during its last two years, using footage from real life as well as invented stories to show the lack of glamor of the time. Vittorio De Sica in <u>Sciuscià</u> (<u>Shoeshine</u>), also in 1946, dealt with the theme of juvenile delinquency in postwar Italy as he portrayed a tragic path taken by two companions. The same hand mastered <u>Ladri di biciclette</u> (<u>The Bicycle Thieves</u> or, less meaningfully, <u>The Bicycle Thief</u>), 1948, in which Rome is seen through the eyes of the young son of a poor worker when the father's bicycle (necessary to his job) is stolen, and when the father attempts to steal another bicycle in his turn. These four Italian films became popular internationally because with great poignancy and strength they spoke of human life, not just Italian life, in certain aspects that touch nearly all people.

Luis Buñuel of Spain in 1950 directed the filming of <u>Los olvidados</u> (<u>The Forgotten Ones</u>, called also <u>The Young and the Damned</u>) in Mexico. Buñuel portrayed only bleakness, misery, and degradation in this slice of slum life in Mexico City. In the same year, <u>Rashomon</u>, directed by Kurosawa Akira in Japan, related four versions of one rape and one murder, told by the three people involved -- a bandit, the one raped (or was she?), the one murdered -- and a passerby. <u>Kind Hearts and Coronets</u>, a ridiculous British comedy directed by Robert Hamer (1949), made its mark through superb caricatures of English life, especially those executed by actor Alec Guinness. Jean Cocteau of France, known before the war as a poet, playwright, and novelist, directed <u>Orphée</u> (<u>Orpheus</u>) in 1950 from a script written by himself, recreating the ancient Greek legend in a Parisian setting, emphasizing the very special position of the poet or the artist in society. None of these four films attempted to depict an across-the-board investigation of any segment of modern culture. Yet each, while holding the attention of the audience, hit very successfully at some underlying bits of truth. In doing so, they and the four from Italy, along with a host of other motion pictures of widely varying expertise and significance, launched postwar cinema on its way with considerable vitality.

In Europe and North America during this quinquennium, the motion pictures came to be supplemented by television. The movies had found their pictures first, and only later their sound. Television developed its sound first, it might be said, with the radio of the 1920's, and after World War II added its pictures. Television quickly showed exciting new possibilities not available with either radio or theater cinema. Both its live picture transmission and its moving film photographs brought a wide public into intimate contact wth the world's news. With television, leaders would have the opportunity to maintain direct personal liaison with their people. In a free society, this might mean a closer accountability for public actions and mass interest in government programs. But television began its career with great problems. In some countries, like the United States, low television entertainment standards proved a discouraging factor from the beginning. The government in these countries restricted itself to a regulatory role, leaving private industry generally free to set the programming as it saw fit, with the object of making fortunes through advertising. In other countries, like the United Kingdom, the government played a strong part in the actual setting up of programs, with a consequent greater regard for sophisticated standards. The distortion of news to favor a particular cause might of course present temptations to either government or private industry; this situation, with its possible threat to freedom of information, posed questions very great in magnitude.

Games, dance, music, and the theater all involved a direct relationship between an audience and participating artists. Painting, sculpture, architecture, and the motion pictures involved a time lapse between the performance of the artist and the impact upon most of the audience; this likewise increasingly became the case with television. Literature, most abstract of all the arts in the form by which it carries its message, is newer to man than his games, dance, music, painting, sculpture, and architecture. For a long time, literature remained the delight of a select few persons scattered very widely in the world. In the last two hundred years, it has become the joy of many. Neither television nor the cinema nor the stage can compete with its attractions in any fargoing way (with the obvious exception that a play may be read), if simply for the reason that a book may be picked up or set down at the reader's will, while the others demand attention at particular times. Thus the postwar generation has kept on reading, and found new, exciting literature for its mind -- some in the form of poetry, more in the prose essay, and a great deal in the novel, which reached the largest numbers of people.

Among the best known of the prewar poets still active after World War II were Robert Frost of California, moved to New England, who wrote of nature and people; Ezra Pound of Idaho, associated with the government of Mussolini in Italy during the war, interested in social comment; W. H. Auden of England; Pablo Neruda of Chile; T. S. Eliot of Missouri; and Dylan Thomas of Wales (the last four are mentioned again in this chapter or the next). The two most ambitious writers of poems during the first postwar quinquennium were Wynstan Hugh Auden, born in England but resident in New York, and Ricardo Eliézer Neftalí Reyes Basoalto, known as Pablo Neruda, from Chile. Auden represented Christianity; Neruda spoke for communism. Both had something important to say, though critics argued as to how effectively they wrapped their ideas in language.

Auden wrote The Age of Anxiety in 1946. During the war he had produced three other long poems depicting various facets of his belief in a Christian type of existentialism. The new work contained the words, thoughts, and imaginings of four persons drinking in a New York City bar, during the course of the recent warfare. Auden believed that neither Hitler nor the Nazis nor all the fascists in the world could be held responsible for the awful conflict or for the sorry state in which the world found itself afterward -- but that all humanity must share the blame, just for being present at the happening. In this, his reasoning ran close to that of Jean-Paul Sartre the atheist. Auden had shown in his earlier works, however, that he believed each individual could find relief from this guilt, through the acceptance on faith of the atonement provided by Jesus. His drunken characters in The Age of Anxiety came close to thinking these matters through, but went on with their old ways of life without change in attitude.

Neruda wrote much of his Canto general (General Song) in 1948-9 while in strong political disfavor in his home land. (He composed in hiding in Chile, and later while traveling widely; the series of 248 connected poems was first published in Mexico in 1950.) Canto general amounted to a song of the Americas, especially those of Latin heritage. First the terrain, including impressions from a visit to the ruins of Machu Picchu in Peru; then the European conquerors, with special attention to the Spanish conquistadores; next the libertadores or workers for freedom, from sixteenth-century Cuauhtémoc to

311

nineteenth-century Abraham Lincoln and twentieth-century Emiliano Zapata and Augusto César Sandino; afterwards, the traitors to freedom, including Latin American caudillos and North American business firms; finally, a great miscellany of places and people, not neglecting the writer himself -- all this Neruda portrayed in verse which, while personal and explicit and devoid of the subtleties of Auden, climbs to heights of dramatic challenge.

In the communist world, the most popular group of poems from Canto general became "Que despierte el leñador" ("May the Woodsman Awake"), invoking the image of Abraham Lincoln to lead the young people of the United States against their modern-day "oppressors." All over the world, great fame was accorded "Alturas de Macchu Picchu" ("The Heights of Macchu Picchu," finished in 1945); here, after marveling at the splendor of this empty stone city upon a mountain, Neruda brooded upon the oppression which he took (ethnocentrically?) for granted had accompanied its building. "Give me your hand out of the depths / sown by your sorrows," he spoke to the ancient Inca peoples:

> Show me your blood and your furrow;
> say to me: here I was scourged
> because a gem was dull or because the
>   earth
> failed to give up in time its tithe
>   of corn or stone.
> Point out to me the rock on which you
>   stumbled,
> the wood they used to crucify your body.

Neruda wished to lead all workers into a happier, even a utopian, society. His politics made him write bitterly at times ("If you are born tonto in Rumania / you follow the career of tonto. . . . But if you are born tonto in Chile / soon they will make you Ambassador"); however, in his

312

stated concern for the common people and his genuine comprehension of their characters, he spoke
for a multitude of modern-day thinkers.

The essay, developed elaborately in modern
times, is generally written in prose requiring
less cleverness of language than poetry. Many
shorter poems courted popularity after the war by
the way they played with words or even letters in
words without regard to thought content. The
high-quality essay is expected to show some expertise in manipulation of the language, but must
additionally provoke thought. Paul Valéry of
France, who wrote essays both thoughtful and sensuous in tone early in the century, lived until
1945; André Gide of France, a moralist who lived
through this time period, and Jorge Luis Borges
of Argentina -- interested in the mysteries of
life, active both before and after the war --
were two of a very few whose essays showed the
same superb dexterity in the use of language.
Book-length essays in prose of lesser artistry
but remarkable thought content became common by
the nineteenth century, and by 1945 any five-year
period boasted a few outstanding prose essays.
This quinquennium witnessed the publication of
Psychologie de l'art of André Malraux, already
discussed; While Time Remains, by United States
journalist Leland Stowe (1947); The West at Bay,
by British economist Barbara Ward (1948); and The
American Democracy, by British political scientist Harold Joseph Laski (also 1948).

Leland Stowe of Connecticut was one of several North American newspapermen who became convinced internationalists during World War II. In
the discomforting sequence of events that began
in 1943, he believed his own nation stood greatly
at fault. Stowe wrote While Time Remains to his
countrymen. In well chosen words and sophisticated thought, he explained the forces then at
work in the world at large, and adjured his readers to think in global terms. Stowe had obtained
his primary education in small-town schools of
his home state. "In patriotism my mark was never

313

less than 100," he said. "In understanding of other nations and the qualities of their peoples, it never could have been much over 5 percent." If the people of the United States could not overcome this miseducation for peace, Stowe believed that the world faced catastrophe.

The immediate postwar scene provided the focus for much of Stowe's discussion. "The cleanup of European feudalism" (agrarian reform in eastern Europe) and "the rattling of Asia's chains" (preparations for Asian independence) comprised subjects for intensive comment; a sub-essay treated the topic "Mr. Churchill brings 'democracy' to Greece." But Stowe also reviewed the questions of what constitutes fascism (one can find it at home), and what are communism, socialism, and democracy. He favored democratic socialism for nations, and the idea of a federal government for the world.

Barbara Ward in The West at Bay set her geographic horizons less high than Stowe. She shared his convincing idealistic realism, however, and exceeded him in speaking directly to the main theme, which for her was a proposed union of 16 nations. Those she wanted to unite were the ones -- all European, all but one democratic -- which had responded favorably to the offer of United States aid through the Marshall Plan. (Political geographer Halford John Mackinder of England had proposed a broader union, resembling NATO in its inclusion of the United States and Canada, after World War I.) Ward spoke chiefly to the theme of economic unity for these 16 countries. An internationally organized government business sector, to include fuel, iron and steel, and basic foodstuffs, would be paralleled by a private unplanned sector for which barriers between the nations would be eliminated. Political unity might follow, but the difficulties inherent therein should not be permitted to hinder the development of economic togetherness. Author Ward believed that the new union would have to be built upon the Christian

tradition found in all 16 nations' backgrounds --
if for no other reason, as a humanitarian response to the emphasis on social justice found in
the Soviet Union. She had little to say, in this
essay, of the great problems that the union would
face with the large areas of the world outside
the Soviet Union and the United States.

The American Democracy of Harold Laski both
praised and criticized the United States of America from the viewpoint of a believer in democratic socialism. Laski thought that early American
democracy, if it could have followed its own natural development, would have led to a series of
modern reforms much needed by the United States.
Such a maturation had been stultified by an American myth that all progress must be achieved
through individualist efforts, that collective
action ought to be avoided. Laski dealt with
United States government, business, education,
religion, and art, showing his comprehension of
the dominant trends of the previous hundred
years, and his appreciation chiefly of the people
who had objected to them.

Laski criticized vehemently some current elements of United States society, such as the American Medical Association in its opposition to a
national health program. "Granted the general
inertia of doctors," he commented, "their fairly
wide-spread ignorance of the social context in
which their problems are set, and the contempt
the Association encourages in them for any lay
opinion on . . . the economic or political aspects of their profession, the outlook of the
Association has nothing unexpected about it."
Laski took care to keep matters in balance, however, pointing out in this instance that American
doctors' attitudes resembled typical overall
American attitudes. He also liked to look for
signs of a "way out" ahead. The European lawyer
and doctor, he observed, bear a close resemblance
to their American colleagues. It merely happens
that the antiquity of the European professional
ritual conceals better its "conditioning to the

315

pecuniary principle." The American professions, being young, are more likely to show "the degree of difference between the outward claim and the inner reality." Thus, because of their youth, "they may be able to revise their foundations more swiftly. . . ."

The union suggested by Barbara Ward showed no sign of coming immediately into being. (The creation of the Council of Europe in the following year was not the kind of activity she had urged.) The two nations for which her union might have constituted a challenge were the Soviet Union and the United States. In the Soviet Union, Laski said, Lenin "succeeded in seizing the State power on behalf of the masses; but the dream he dreamed, with all its nobility, is still far from fulfillment, and it still exacts an almost overwhelming price from those on whose behalf he had his vision." The United States counted more in his opinion: "World history is more likely to be shaped by American history for the next half-century than by any other element in its making. . . . Something in Europe, I say, men can achieve by understanding and self-preparation. But it is within the United States that the final issue is bound to be decided; on nothing else, perhaps, does the outcome depend so much as upon its ability to conquer both inertia and fear." Laski, who taught university classes in the United States, and Leland Stowe, who carried out his studies there, spoke essentially the same message to the strongest nation on earth: "Wake up, North Americans! Lest your lack of understanding and your too great self-concern lose you the opportunity of the century."

The novel, when it is well done, combines some of the best qualities of poetry and the prose essay. Each novel, effective generally at portraying only one hard-hitting truth, may in this matter remain more limited than a book-length essay. The novel can use prose in a particularly satisfying way, however, so that the

316

language itself brings a full sense of reality, whether that may be joyful or disturbing. Among the well known prewar novelists who lived into the postwar period were Herbert George Wells of England, interested in science and the future; Theodore Dreiser of Indiana (died 1945), critic of the private-enterprise system; Thomas Mann of Germany, analyst of the high culture of Europe through its changes during his lifetime; Edward Morgan Forster of England, commentator on middle-class society; William Faulkner of Missisippi, "owner" of the imaginary Yoknapatawpha County in his home state; and Ernest Hemingway of Illinois, traveler and adventurer. Mann, Faulkner, and Hemingway continued to write for a large public after World War II, Faulkner's Intruder in the Dust (1948) dealing with white-black relationships in Yoknapatawpha County. Five important novels of the first postwar quinquennium were The Wall, by John Hersey (1950); Cry, the Beloved Country, by Alan Paton (1948); La peste, by Albert Camus (1947); Nineteen Eighty-Four, by George Orwell (1949); and Al filo del agua, by Agustín Yáñez (1947). The last is presented under the heading "Religion."

The Wall sprang from the same mind that produced the report Hiroshima; author Hersey, a United States journalist born in China, seemed to specialize in empathy with distressed people. Like the earlier report, The Wall spotlighted individuals caught in a situation that offered little escape; their circumstances, though in this case imagined, came from real life. Noach Levinson, purported author of the events, kept careful records 1939-43 of a group of Jews forced to live in the Warsaw ghettos. Schpunt, a comical Jew, made Nazi soldiers and his own people laugh during an interruption of a prayer service, 1940. (The Nazis said, "Who is the rabbi here?" Schpunt answered, "I. I am the rabbi." The soldiers ordered, "Dance! . . . Dance, Rabbi!" Schpunt danced, and the soldiers laughed, and so did some of the Jews, who knew that Schpunt was not the rabbi.) Schlome Mazur, a young man,

317

wanted to be a rabbi, but died in the typhus plague, 1941. ("Lice are on everything, on the money you get in change, on chairs, on shop counters, on friends. People . . . fear the slightest touch of elbow to elbow in the crowded streets; they shut themselves in at home and find lice crawling up their own clean walls.")

Schorr, a Jewish policeman, worked for the Germans outside the wall, and learned, in 1942, that boxcars used to take Jews away, ostensibly to labor camps on the Russian front, actually returned from their trip within one day. ("The transport with the three cars whose numbers he had memorized left at about ten o'clock on the morning of August 5. All three cars were back the same afternoon, empty.") Six days later, the ghetto community read the report of Lazar Slonim, a Jew who could pass as a non-Jew, after he walked the tracks to discover where the boxcars went. Slonim found Treblinka, a "camp" where Jews by the tens of thousands had walked into chambers carrying bars of soap, expecting to take baths, only to be murdered by gas sent through the pipes, and their corpses removed to clear the chambers for the next batch. The people of the ghetto now looked intensively for places to hide; some has already taken to living in abandoned sewers. They began also to prepare for the day when a remnant would do battle with the Germans, even though they knew this could get them nowhere.

Israel in this story was the infant son of Rutka Mazur, quietly smothered by a friend (and handed back to his mother) after his cries within a group's hiding place had endangered the lives of many. Rachel Apt was a young Jewish military leader, as circumstances in the ghetto worked out. Fair of figure though not of face, she found her first sexual fulfillment during two days in which she deserted her own fighters, in the midst of the great battle. Noach Levinson invented neither heroes nor heroines for his papers, except perhaps himself, inoffensively, as the keeper of the archive. But somehow his very human, totally believable characters nearly all became heroes and heroines as John Hersey transcribed what Levinson had "written."

Cry, the Beloved Country spoke of the race problem in South Africa, one of the most race-conscious nations of the world. Its author was a "white" South African who saw fear taking command of men's minds. "Cry the beloved country," he said, "for the unborn child that is the inheritor of our fear. Let him not love the earth too deeply. . . . For fear will rob him of all if he gives too much. . . ." Paton spoke the words many white South Africans were thinking: "Who knows how we shall fashion a land of peace where black outnumbers white so greatly? . . . Who knows how we shall fashion such a land? For we fear not only the loss of our possessions, but the loss of our superiority and the loss of our whiteness. . . . We do not know, we do not know. We shall live from day to day, and put more locks on the doors, and get a fine fierce dog . . . , and hold on to our handbags more tenaciously; and the beauties of the trees by night, and the raptures of lovers under the stars, these things we shall forego. . . ." But for himself and for other white countrymen, Paton spoke as follows: "Yes, God save Africa, the beloved country. God save us from the deep depths of our sins. God save us from the fear that is afraid of justice. God save us from the fear that is afraid of men. God save us all."

Over two-tenths of the South African people, especially the Afrikaner descendants of the Dutch and the persons of "mixed blood," played no role in Paton's novel. The less-than-one-tenth of the people who traced their ancestry to England found expression through the persons of James Jarvis, Esquire, a well-to-do farmer; his son Arthur, viewed only in posthumous perspective; and Arthur's father-in-law Mr. Harrison. The Reverend Stephen Kumalo, an Anglican parson, and his family represented the seven-tenths of the people

319

called "black" (chiefly the Bantu population) --
Stephen attempted to rescue his sister Gertrude
from prostitution; Stephen's brother John became
a propagandist for the cause of the black workers; Stephen's son Absalom killed Arthur Jarvis
and was executed. Stephen himself, the only one
of the group who had stayed at home and close to
a religion, found Gertrude, John, and Absalom
when he went to look for them in the metropolitan
vicinity of Johannesburg. He lost them all, however, and returned home a very broken man.

Mr. Harrison and Arthur Jarvis, both city
men, had disagreed on the race question. Farmer
James Jarvis had continued the nineteenth-century
relationships in his area (which included Stephen
Kumalo's church and home) without ever thinking
much about them. But between Arthur's death and
Absalom's trial, James became acquainted with the
wealth of material Arthur had written in the
blacks' cause. Harrison's persistent conversation about the threats posed by the blacks now
came to seem like prattling. To honor their son,
James Jarvis and his wife planned a magnificent
program to save the black people of their valley
-- the same black people from whom Absalom had
sprung -- from death and the ravages of despair.
Stephen Kumalo, seeing the plan materialize, became overwhelmed by happiness and appreciation.

Napoleon Letsitsi, a young, black agricultural demonstrator who came to live in the Kumalo
home, received his salary from James Jarvis as
part of the new order of things. Napoleon was
not ungrateful for his position. Yet he could
not agree when the parson said, "Where would we
be without all that this white man has done for
us?" Letsitsi replied that "what this good white
man does is only a repayment." Kumalo did not
like such talk, but understood better when Letsitsi said, " . . . We do not work for men, . . .
we work for the land and the people." "Are there
many who think as you do?" Kumalo queried. "I
do not know," replied the young man, "I do not
know if there are many. But there are some."

320

La peste (The Plague) contained the imagined tale of an epidemic of bubonic plague in Oran, Algeria, during one of the years of the war. The book spoke not about Oran, however, nor of Algerian and North African problems, excepting as those places participate in concerns that are common to everyone. It told of a city of people caught in a plight that inspired a spirit of co-operative unity among them, and of the personal reactions of selected individuals who lived through at least part of the ordeal. Algerian-born author Camus said virtually nothing of the majority of the Oran population, who were Arabic-speaking Muslims. The unknowing reader might suppose that French-speaking Roman Catholics, with an occasional apostate, made up the entire city, quarantined by the authorities while the sickness lasted.

Dr. Bernard Rieux, the purported author of this book, played an important role in the medical fight against the plague. Rieux remained ideologically at odds with his close friend the Jesuit Father Paneloux, dissenting when Paneloux preached that the people were being punished for their sins. When Paneloux stated his conviction that he and Rieux had engaged themselves in the same activity, that of saving mankind, Rieux insisted that he did not hope to save people, but only to help them with their health. Father Paneloux died of the plague, later, refusing medical assistance. Jean Tarrou, caught in Oran while visiting there, died of the plague after the epidemic concluded; Rieux' closest companion, Tarrou kept a diary that contributed much to the book. Tarrou had worked as an international organizer for the communists, hoping to save the world from the death penalty which he abhorred. After he witnessed an execution in Hungary, however, he took stock of the number of murders that he, as a cooperator, had helped bring about over a period of years. He now thought of the plague as a blight affecting human society continually, of which capital punishment formed a part. Each person in society, said Tarrou, was a carrier of

321

the plague if he did not cry out against injustices to individuals.

Tarrou, Rieux, and Camus all insisted that the road toward the greatest happiness lay in fighting the plague, whatever forms that struggle might take, with the purpose not of attaining final victory but of having tried. Camus the novelist like Camus the playwright wished to demonstrate that existence, even in an absurd universe, need itself not be totally absurd. Furthermore, he wanted to indicate that one need not be a saint to serve as a helper in causes that are both sensible and worthwhile.

Nineteen Eighty-Four provided a disheartening look at life in London, 35 years into the city's future. Eric Blair, the author (George Orwell, pseudonym), born of European ancestry in British-held Bengal, stood obviously as an Englishman greatly at odds with something in the United Kingdom. That something he clearly named -- English socialism -- though he carefully avoided any discussion of the politics of the time of writing. By 1984, there existed only three important countries in the world by Orwell's account -- Eastasia (apparently with mainland China at its heart), Eurasia (the Soviet Union), and Oceania (the United Kingdom and the United States, apparently dominated by the British). Their socialist governments fought continually over the remainder of the world, each one maintaining itself in power through the nationalistic devices that usually accompany war, along with a regimen of thought control as complete as could be devised. Winston Smith, at 39 years of age a participant in the preparation of a new (eleventh) edition of the Newspeak language offically adopted by Oceania to express the Ingsoc (English socialist) philosophy and attitudes, held a kernel of rebellion in his heart against the thought control regime. He liked to visit that part of London inhabited by the "proles" (the proletariat of another day) who lived in poor conditions but, not holding party membership, were less carefully watched.

Winston Smith delightedly learned one day that a fellow worker and party member, 26-year-old, freckled-faced, lithesome Julia, took an interest in him and the propensity she guessed he showed toward rebellion. They managed to meet alone in the country, Julia showing the way. Julia took off the sash of the Junior Anti-Sex League, in whose programs she participated to show her devotion to the party. (The party wanted sex desires stifled, if this change proved possible, sex having emerged as one of the most difficult of the old practices to eliminate now that artificial insemination made it no longer necessary.) "Have you done this before?" asked Winston. "'Of course. Hundreds of times -- well, scores of times, anyway.' . . . His heart leapt. Scores of times she had done it; he wished it had been hundreds -- thousands. . . . 'You like doing this? I don't mean simply me; I mean the thing in itself?' 'I adore it.' That was above all what he wanted to hear. Not merely the love of one person, but the animal instinct, the simple undifferentiated desire; that was the force that would tear the Party to pieces." Winston and Julia soon came to love each other, and met regularly in a room in the prole district of the city. Here the officers in charge of looking out for their irregularities as party members caught them. After suffering a variety of indignities, they were pronounced "cured" and readmitted to the party, each of them finally having "betrayed" the other's love through a wish, in the face of bodily peril, that the other be hurt if that would diminish the peril to one's self.

To write an important novel is not necessarily to write a successful one. To write importantly, one must have something of consequence to say, and must say it well enough that it is read by significant numbers of people. In their early postwar novels discussed here, Hersey, Paton, Camus, and Orwell all scored well on these points. To write successfully, however, the

323

author must get across the salient something he has to say to those who have become his audience. In this third objective, Camus and Orwell came notably short of the achievement of Hersey and Paton.

Camus distracted his readers' attention with his own bag of characters: (1) Paneloux himself, the priest, appeared chiefly as a phantom representative of medieval obscurantism, even to the point of preferring death to consultation with a physician. Camus had abandoned traditional Catholicism in writings of the war period. Did it nevertheless haunt his mind? (2) Rambert, a young journalist, wanted to leave Oran to rejoin a girl he had left in France. When he finally arranged an exit by stealth, he gave it up to stay with those who had become his friends, to help fight the plague. He survived. But had Camus, despite disclaimers, felt the need for a saint in his account?

(3) Cottard, an old man evidently worried about a crime in his past, felt happier when others became sad at the time of the plague, and went beserk when the plague terminated. Grand, another old man, fought the plague with success when he contracted it during its fading period, and resolved to start what had become a very meager life all over again. Did Camus unintentionally use Cottard and Grand in a scheme of retributions and rewards that ran contrary to what Rieux and Tarrou were saying? Burdened with such characters, bogged down by detailed descriptions of dying rats and people to the point of analyzing their pustules, and short-circuited all the way through by his unwillingness to picture the city of Oran, Camus did well to get his message across even in part. His theme was that the world is not all absurd, as he and other existentialist writers had pictured it during the war period, but has its worthwhile side in struggles like the one against the plague. (The plague could be a political group like the Nazis, or any other threat to mankind.) And individual men, he

proposed, can gain great happiness by being help-
ers in such times of crisis.

George Orwell scarcely communicated his chief
argument at all. His was a preposterous idea, in
the first place -- that the moderate and very
democratic group ruling the United Kingdom in
1949 would somehow resolve itself into a frightening monster ruling the superstate of Oceania in
1984. Ingsoc, English socialism of 1984, he
said, "grew out of" the "earlier" socialist
movement (nowhere did he make the connection
clearer), though it rejected and vilified "every
principle for which the Socialist movement originally stood." (Orwell, himself a socialist, had
quarrelled with the leadership of the Labor
party.) From all appearances, Orwell did not
really feel competent to explain how this change
might have occurred. Winston Smith possessed a
book which gave that information, but before his
arrest he had managed to read only Chapters 3 and
1, dealing with other matters. Could Orwell have
come through with his explanation, he would have
made himself the hero of the large group of
private-enterprise enthusiasts who argue that
"creeping" socialism will strangle all freedom if
it is not stopped. Without these missing pages
of the book within a book, people read Orwell's
production chiefly for its novelty, its refined
descriptions of the workings of a truly ingenious
police state, its one love affair against the
somber background of hate, and its reminder of
what could happen in world affairs, even if the
indicators of Orwell's own time and place made
those developments seem unlikely. That comprised
assignment enough for a man who was ill when he
wrote this his last book, and who died the year
thereafter.

Religion

Sartre and atheistic existentialism . . Gandhi
and satyagraha . . Sheean: Lead, Kindly Light . .

the World Council of Churches in Amsterdam . .
Yáñez, Al filo del agua.

Religion is an expression of man's soul. It
is the theory by which he lives. It forms a
bridge between the world of his experience, gathered in by his spirit and his mind, and another
kind of world which he envisages as the real
one. Religion was important to early man. Interest in it provided an identifying mark for his
species, as did his propensities toward art and
science. By the time people settled down to
farming, they craved sophisticated explanations
concerning the universe and man's role therein.
(See Chapter I for a review of the chief explanations, or "religions," which developed through
time.)

Old beliefs in religion found sharp challenge
in the modern age, like old techniques in the
arts and the ancient unwisdom of science. The
most startling defiance of the old religion came
from the new science of the sixteenth and seventeenth centuries, which showed that man does not
dwell at the center of his physical universe.
Religionists had barely had time to relocate man
in space when the nineteenth-century theory of
evolution indicated he needed repositioning in
time, and probably in physical relationships as
well. Changes even greater than these affected
modern religion, however. Between the old Christianity and the new discussed in Chapter I, and
between the old religion and the new mentioned in
Chapter III, there existed the differences that
one would expect between the style of the old
human being (before modern democracy and socialism) and the style of the new human being entering a new world. No clearcut proclamation of a
new faith took place. But certain trends seemed
quite clearly indicated.

Least of all did the new religionist want a
god to be adored. The adoration of gods seemed
as quaint to him as the adoration of human be-

ings. There appeared no disinclination to accept a leader. The new people, however, preferred a friend they could work with, not a master-mind they should work for. Anything less would smack too strongly of old-fashioned authoritarianism.

The new leader must furthermore refrain from showing favors to one individual over another. Traditional Christianity, Islam, and Judaism all maintained that their gods loved everybody, but in reality everyone understood that some persons had been favored over others. All the old gods differentiated between continents, between countries, between social classes, between families, even between individuals within families. The new leader would have to display a greater imagination than that, now that a whole world of mankind had become one family.

An additional requirement the new religionist tended to attach left little room for legislative command on the part of moral authority. Too many rules on too many subjects would bring a modern movement to ruin, should it indeed be tempted to specify any. The new leader must recognize that modern life is very complex, that it is very difficult to make regulations covering everything, and that each ethical decision is in a sense a new one, with a slightly different set of circumstances from any posed before. Rather than issue orders, the leader will provide the guidelines by which the decision can be made to the greatest benefit of all the individuals concerned therein.

In mid-twentieth century, few people clamored for the emergence of a new faith. However, in effect, it had already emerged for small groups of persons here and there. A far greater number of people (who were being dragged into the new era rather than stepping into it on their own) saw no need for a new religion. But great masses of individuals, especially in Europe and the Americas, deserted the old-fashioned religion in the nineteenth and twentieth centuries without substituting any organized movement in its stead. They did not turn their faces from religion itself, necessarily, but they shifted away from traditional religion. Every one of them -- some greedy, some altruistic in behavior -- tended to have a "scheme of things" in mind -- logical or illogical, sophisticated or primitive -- which constituted a new religion in substitution for the old. With many millions of persons thus religiously unattached, new ideas coming along might receive a fairer share of attention.

A single quinquennium, or even a quarter-century, is too short an interval for the determination or discernment of any religious trend. One can only say, in passing, that such-and-such events fitting this realm attracted attention at a particular time. In the period 1946-50, the atheistic existentialism of Jean-Paul Sartre caused some stir in France; one Hindu personage, Mahatma Gandhi, received wide recognition as a saint; and Protestant and Orthodox churches took a memorable step toward Christian unity on a global basis. The Mexican novel Al filo del agua of 1947 is also presented here as an illustration of the breakdown of traditional religion in a new era, and as a demonstration of two qualities shared by all the major religions to date.

Jean-Paul Sartre, author of the play Les mains sales, emerged from World War II as a literary hero. He had fought in the French army in 1940, only to be captured by the Germans; released from imprisonment, he opposed the Nazis through the underground movement, in the meantime writing plays to make a living. The plays, collectively, carried a finely woven thread of reasoning that Sartre called existentialism. In 1943, he also finished a philosophical treatise explaining his ideas, entitled L'être et le néant (Being and Nothingness). Many French young people admired Sartre; they liked to gather in cafés and night clubs to discuss his thoughts, or to emulate their mentor's nighttime behavior. Sartre himself disowned some of the existentialist faddists, but found himself a continuing object of attention from persons in many countries. Most of them spent little time with his book, but liked to toy with his vocabulary.

Sartre, himself a professed non-believer of combined Catholic-Protestant background, reached back to Søren Kierkegaard, a Danish Lutheran, for methods of explanation and mannerisms in wording. Kierkegaard lived in the nineteenth century, writing extensively of his experiences in the world and acceptance of traditional Christianity. Kierkegaard used the term "existence" to mean "human existence" alone, or those attributes of human existence which make it different from all other existence. Each individual confronted by Christianity, he said, finds himself lonely and in anguish, as he is called to place his faith in something "absurd" (for which there is no rational proof). When he accepts the faith, he must commit himself by "leaping into the darkness," not knowing where he will land.

Sartre like Kierkegaard spoke of existence as a distinctively human condition. He also shared Kierkegaard's strong emphasis on the freedom of the will, as each individual faces up to life's decisions. Sartre took no interest in Kierkegaard's further conclusions about the importance of choosing traditional Christianity, but he did borrow some other portions of Kierkegaard's language. Man finds the whole world absurd, according to Sartre, because none of it makes sense that is appealing to the intellect. Man is faced not with one choice, but with a steady succession of them, leading him to very frequent, nearly constant anguish. (Some of the young followers of Sartre sought to show this anguish through their demeanor.) The choices themselves are bleak ones, with no promise that any of them will lead anywhere, but people should choose to join projects that aid others, in order to help alleviate the total suffering during one's lifetime. Even the freedom of the will, Sartre said, is hardly to be celebrated. Man is condemned by

329

his nature to be free; it would have been easier or more pleasant otherwise.

Sartre was a practicing Marxist, aiding the cause with his pen, while he expounded these theories -- some of which set no better with the reasoning of Marx than they did with the doctrines of Christianity. At times other Marxist writers criticized him, but he never singled himself out in opposition to them. During this period of his life, he seemed to need Marxism to provide him a justification for being, even while he held to all the tenets of his own existentialism as a person holds to a religion. The reason that Sartre did not push on with his new faith, and that the anguished look in night clubs soon disappeared, may be that his network of thought, while interesting to the intellect, provided really nothing morally satisfying, even for Sartre. In one way, however, the philosophy of Sartre fitted a new style for a new era. According to his conception, people cannot blame their misdoings on some higher fate, but must take complete responsibility for making or not making life better for others.

Mohandas Karamchand Gandhi lived more than 78 years after his birth in northwestern India in 1869. (See "Asian Independence" for some presentation of his political life.) His death in 1948, with the words "Hai Rama" on his lips, probably evoked more sympathetic world attention than any other of the immediate postwar years. "Hai Rama" means "Oh Rama;" Rama was one of the several avataras, or reincarnations of the ancient Hindu god Vishnu. Gandhi's devotion to Hindu principles along with his successes in politics made him a great man to millions of fellow Hindus. His devotion to some universally admired principles together with his indomitable pluck won him the high respect of millions of non-Hindus. Mahatma (Man of Great Soul) Gandhi seemed to very large numbers of people a twentieth-century saint.

Gandhi did not found a new religion, though it seems that with all the loyal support he commanded such a goal might have lain within his reach. Had he built in that direction, he would have used an older religion for a foundation, in keeping with repeated precedents from the past. In some respects, Gandhi remained throughout his life a conventional Hindu. He accepted the caste system, working only for somewhat greater mobility between castes and for the abolition of "untouchability," which he believed found no authorization in Hindu scripture. He lived as a vegetarian, respecting all animal life, and during the greater part of his career achieved a high degree of self-discipline in body and mind. As an unusually religious person, he spent much time in prayer and in contemplation of the ancient writings, though he chose political action over the habits of a recluse.

In two respects, Gandhi adopted unconventional religious practice. All through life he explored the literature, even the hymns, of other faiths, choosing certain selections as his own, commenting on them to his immediate disciples. He believed in the validity of other faiths, a principle Hindus generally acknowledged, but beyond that looked to their fountains of thought for inspiration. A more radical unconventionality, however, came with the re-translation and reinterpretation, midway in his life, of one of the most popular selections of Hindu writing, the Bhagavad Gita or Song of Heaven. The Bhagavad Gita had appeared over two thousand years earlier (as part of the Mahabharata, the world's longest poem) just as the present-day pattern of Hinduism was forming, after the separation of Hindus from Buddhists and Jains. The Gita taken literally is chiefly a pre-battle discourse. A warrior disclaims any desire to fight and kill, preferring alternative modes of conduct -- even the destruction of himself, unarmed and nonresisting, by the enemy. Nevertheless, in the denouement, the warrior accepts his obligation to do battle. Gandhi spoke of the battle-narrative as an allegory, showing the constant struggle within man's mind; the details, he maintained, served only to make the poem more alluring in ancient times. Gandhi's _Gita_ could have served as a point of departure for a new religious faith -- whose chief message, it might have been argued, had lain there all the time, waiting for someone to grasp it in its entirety.

Gandhi gave the name satyagraha, or truth-force, to the main principle he found in the Bhagavad Gita. It stood for his technique -- applied in South Africa, later in India -- of proving the validity of one's cause by bringing suffering upon one's self rather than inflicting it upon another. Vincent Sheean, versatile author from Illinois who was with Gandhi when he died, became convinced that satyagraha might lead to a new era in the world. "It may be said," Sheean admitted, "that Gandhi was by temperament, heredity, childhood training and life-long effort so vowed to non-violence that this determined his view of the truth and hence of the Gita. It may also be said . . . that his political genius recognized non-violence as the only possible means for the powerless Indian masses to achieve their freedom and that this influenced him to exalt it as the final fruit and flower of truth." But Sheean himself had concluded otherwise. He wrote his book Lead, Kindly Light (published in 1949, and named for one of Gandhi's favorite Christian hymns) to show his own conviction that satyagraha constituted not a political stance or a temporary justification for action but Gandhi's great will and testament to all mankind.

The terms "civil disobedience" and "passive resistance," used as equivalents, sometimes by Gandhi himself, for a word difficult to translate into the English language, are not firm enough in their description of satyagraha. The participant in a truth-force struggle must be self-disciplined to the point that he will carry his own suffering through even to death if that is neces-

332

sary. Sheean did not believe that many persons in Europe and North America could be persuaded to participate in that kind of action merely to cure the ills of those regions. He hoped, however, that the power of the individual in European and North American society might prove so great that a small group of totally dedicated people could accomplish a grand moral objective (such as the prevention of war) by using non-violent action to win the sympathy of a much larger group of on-lookers.

Satyagraha did not pretend to comprise a new religion. At the most, it could have formed only a part of one, for it lacked the comprehensive-ness of a religion. Its perseverance after the death of Gandhi, whether as a massive or a more individualistic endeavor, would satisfy to some extent the craving of the new religionist for action in place of adulation in man's relation-ship with his god. Satyagraha as a mass struggle also moved its participants toward recognition of other people without unreasoning favoritism. In either of its styles, satyagraha offered a new moral guideline to take the place of old command-ments, and at the same time raised a whole host of new ethical problems.

The World Council of Churches, with 134 in-dependent denominations as members, came into being in Amsterdam, the Netherlands, on August 23, 1948. The Methodist Church of the United States, the Evangelical (Lutheran) Church in Ger-many, and the Church of England made up the three largest entities involved. The national churches of Greece (Orthodox) and of Sweden (Lutheran) stood large compared to most, as did also the National (predominantly Negro) Baptist Convention of the United States of America, the Protestant Episcopal (formerly Anglican) Church of the United States, and the northern Presbyterian Church of the same country (the southern Presby-terians attended also). Large Orthodox churches in the Soviet Union, Romania, Yugoslavia, and

333

Bulgaria declined invitations to join, as did the pope for Roman Catholicism, and the governing bodies of the Southern Baptist Convention of the United States (though the northern and Negro Baptist conventions cooperated) and the Lutheran group denominated the Missouri Synod.

The Council defined itself as a fellowship of "churches which accept our Lord Jesus Christ as God and Saviour." The fellowship expected to discharge specified functions, particularly "to carry on the work of the two world movements, for Faith and Order and for Life and Work." The movements under such titles had appeared in the 1920's, though their antecedents ran back a few hundred years. The Faith and Order emphasis interested churchmen who wanted to work toward greater ecumenicity. The Life and Work orientation, most notable in the United States, favored the involvement of the church in social issues, so that organized Christianity (as distinct from Christian individuals acting on their own) might play a role in finding valid solutions. The Missouri Synod and the Southern Baptist Convention had not relished the Life and Work trend. The Orthodox churches of eastern Europe presumably found the meeting excessively dominated by the United States, the United Kingdom, and West Germany. The Roman Catholic body retained its traditional position, that unity in Christendom could only be achieved through a decision by those outside the Roman fold to come back in again.

"Man's Disorder and God's Design" became the theme of the meeting in Amsterdam. Its development lay in four lines of thought, on each of which the Council released a paper to its denominations for their further study. The authors of the first of these, "The Universal Church in God's Design," found some agreement on the nature and mission of the church, but recognized a basic difference in outlook as to what constitutes the church in the first place. Anglican and Orthodox believers tended to put great stress on "the visible continuity of the Church" (the doctrine of the apostolic succession) while others placed their emphasis on the "response of faith" to the "initiative of the Word of God" (the doctrine of justification by faith). A second study group, assigned the sub-theme "The Church's Witness to God's Design," agreed more enthusiastically on the proposition that "it is God's will that the Gospel should be proclaimed to all men everywhere." This should be done in such a manner that each man "is confronted with the necessity of a personal decision, Yes or No."

The third study, with the title "The Church and the Disorder of Society," attracted the widest attention. It analyzed both communism and capitalism, weighed both in the balances, and found both wanting in superior merit. "Christian churches," the report said, "should reject the ideologies of both communism and _laissez_ _faire_ capitalism. . . . Communist ideology puts the emphasis upon economic justice, and promises that freedom will come automatically after the completion of the revolution. Capitalism puts the emphasis upon freedom, and promises that justice will follow as a by-product of free enterprise. . . . It is the responsibility of Christians to seek new, creative solutions which never allow either justice or freedom to destroy the other." The fourth study group achieved the greatest specificity as it developed the sub-theme "The Church and the International Disorder." "War as a method of settling disputes," it said, "is incompatible with the teaching and example of our Lord Jesus Christ. . . . The greatest threat to peace today comes from the division of the world into mutually suspicious and antagonistic blocs. . . . Our Lord . . . taught that God, the Father of all, is Sovereign. We affirm, therefore, that no state may claim absolute sovereignty, or make laws without regard to the commandments of God and the welfare of mankind."

The World Council of Churches did not intend to serve as a springboard for a new religion. In

a sense, it sought to bolster an old one, since
many of its denominations had grown weak through
the inattention of their own constituencies. The
dignitaries who attended (and who selected Willem
Adolf Visser 't Hooft of the Netherlands as general secretary) derived generally from the
strongest of their particular points of view.
Splits of opinion did not always fall along de-
nominational lines, but on one or both sides of
any disagreement could be found a band of persons
very traditional in their outlook. This is not
to say that no agreements were reached on newer
ways of looking at the world. The Council's
stand on war possessed a determined, mid-twentieth-century flavor. Its position on capitalism
and communism called for something specifically
new. Traditionalism won its battles on matters
more exclusively religious in nature.

To the traditionalist, it remained important
that the "Father" be considered a "Sovereign."
He must furthermore have a "Design" -- that much
was seemingly taken for granted. The Design,
however, even with the strongest anti-war, anti-
communist, and anti-laissez-faire resolutions,
left people reduced in dignity to something less
than many citizens in modern democracies craved.
To the traditionalist, evangelism continued a
first responsibility of Christians, to take their
"good news" (of the atonement) to everyone in the
world. To many, however, this emphasis meant
that someone loved Gandhi's people less, or Mao's
people less, or the cast-offs of more affluent
societies less, in that they had not already
heard the good news. If the mid-twentieth-century traditionalist clung to old words on those
matters, he would certainly feel reluctant to
drop the word "commandments" in favor of newer
"guidelines." Yet, in failing to do so, he neglected the fact that Jesus himself shied away
from pronouncing commandments, while holding to a
very high tone of morality. Except for patterns
of words, the World Council of Churches proved
more revolutionary than many had expected. If
Christianity wished to provide the basis for a

336

new world religion, however, it appeared that individuals within the faith rather than this overall assemblage of Protestant, Anglican, and Orthodox dignitaries would have to provide the initative.

Agustín Yáñez of Mexico in his novel _Al filo del agua_ (_The Edge of the Storm_) showed the difficulties traditional religion may face when confronted with the mobility and iconoclasm of a new age. At the same time, he illustrated two very important qualities inherent in traditional religion. Yáñez, born in the city of Guadalajara, studied law, and assumed a teaching position in the Faculty of Philosophy and Letters at the National Autonomous University of Mexico. There he played an important role in the development of an emphasis on the humanities. His novel, which took its setting from "a village, any village, of the Archdiocese of Guadalajara" during 1909-10, dealt with the fracturing of a very strict Roman Catholic pattern of living as it came into contact with the boisterous, even chaotic Mexican Revolution of the second decade of the century.

The phrase _al filo del agua_, in Mexican peasant usage, generally means the beginning of the rainy season; here it meant the eve of a still more impressive and imperative event. Yáñez' village of western central Mexico matched many hundreds of thousands of others in the nineteenth and twentieth centuries in the near-devastating impact produced by major social change upon patterns of living associated with the religions of the ancient past. Its life, however, should not be equated with that of a hypothetically typical Mexican village, nor with that of other Roman Catholic communities, any more than with that of the many villages identifiable with other traditional religions of modern times. The details may be very different while the patterns run much the same.

"Village of black-robed women. . . . People

337

and streets absorbed in their own thoughts. . .
.The lowliest house has its cross on top. . . .
There are no fiestas in the village; only the
daily dance of myriads of sunbeams. . . . The
whole existence of the village is a never-ending
Lent. . . ."

The annual Retreat for married men of the
village took place March 21-27, 1909. (Other Retreats for young men, young women, older women,
and unmarried men over 16 had already been
held.) This was a time for meditation, for fast-
ing, for devotional readings, for flagellation,
for sermons, for confessions -- all supervised by
Don Dionisio María Martínez, the very serious and
very conscientious parish priest. Don Dionisio
had designed the entire week to strengthen moral
character. Upon its conclusion, as members of
the community are reunited year after year, "one
man publically begs his family to forgive him,
another restores a sum of money; . . . neighbors
who have been the bitterest of enemies are to be
seen embracing each other. . . ."

The Holy Week Festival ran from the Friday of
Dolores to Good Friday, two days before Easter.
It provided the greatest excitement of the year.
People from the neighboring villages and countryside visited to participate in the processions;
others, from more distant, more urbanized communities, came to witness the spirit of the occasion. Victoria, from the city, visited the
Pérez family, and commented rather innocently
upon the sober and devout manner of the only son
of the home, a former seminary student. Luis
Gonzaga Pérez, hurt by the remark and already
estranged from the "ignorant" village and its
old-fashioned parish priest, absented himself
from the closing ceremonies of the week. While
others followed the procession to Calvary, the
removal of the garments, the nailing to the
Cross, the lifting up of the Cross, the sermon on
the Seven Words, the sermon on the Spear Thrust,
the taking down from the Cross, the procession of
the Holy Burial, Luis carried out his own service

of penance on a hillside.

Damián Limón returned home during Holy Week from an interval in the United States. "I won't deny that life can be hard in the United States," he declared to one of the priests. "But you can live in comfort and freedom . . . ; the poorest earns four times as much as he earns here. . . . The Church doesn't deny human nature, does it, or want a man to spend all his time praying?" Unfortunately, Damián found his mother very ill -- she had lived as an invalid for years -- and the shock of his return proved too much for her to survive. The village blamed Damián for his mother's death, while his father Don Timoteo Limón felt guilty for having wished that his wife would die.

Micaela Rodríguez had not quite reached the age by which she would be expected to have joined the Association of the Daughters of Mary Immaculate -- who for an outside garment wore only the black dress with high neck and long sleeves, its skirt reaching to the ankles. Micaela liked to wear less somber dresses she had purchased on a trip to Guadalajara and Mexico City. Micaela felt attracted to Damián Limón, who reciprocated the feeling but tended to take young Micaela's affections for granted. To spite Damián, Micaela followed the mixed policy of flaunting herself before other men (even Don Timoteo) while averring her intention to join the Daughters of Mary. Victoria, who without trying had also brought Damián under her spell, became intrigued not by the "Northerner" but by Gabriel, ringer of the bells, who had been adopted by Don Dionisio at the age of five, his origin unknown to the village.

May 6, two weeks before Ascension Day, Victoria returned home. Gabriel, deeply touched by her attention, went to the bell tower as he saw her leave. As she looked back toward the tower, "the leading bell rang a solemn, measured, unaccustomed melody, followed by a peal of trebles like those for the Hail, Holy Queen, on Saturday afternoons; then came the tones of the big bass, drowning the trebles when Victoria raised one hand. . . ." On Ascension Day, Don Dionisio sent Gabriel away from the village.

St. Bartholomew's Day, August 24, brought tragedy. Damián Limón killed his father and Micaela Rodríguez, though he had intended to carry Micaela away. Damián surrendered, but the court did not convict him of the death of Don Timoteo -- the village would not allow autopsies, and no one had seen the deed. He did receive a sentence of six years in prison for his murder of Micaela, considered a "crime of passion." Damián escaped, however, without serving his sentence.

A friendly competition developed between two of the curates over the celebration of the Festival of the Immaculate Conception, which climaxed December 8, and that of the Festival of Our Lady of Guadalupe, December 12. For the first, to his eventual regret, the priest in charge of the Daughters of Mary invited musicians from Guadalajara. Arriving tired and sleeping poorly, they played and sang very unsatisfactorily at vespers and high mass. The following evening, instead of returning to the city as they had promised, they drank freely and engaged in unchurchly serenading. Their melodies, never heard before in the village, "revealed a world, a new language, to adolescents on that night . . . , a world and language . . . full of celestial and . . . human charm. . . . The vibrant cries, which could suddenly die to trembling murmurs in the surrounding solitude, took old men and adolescents by surprise. . . . No one would have had the music stop, neither the old, whose age it dissolved, nor the young, for whom it built castles in the air."

María, in 1910, the year of Halley's comet, the year the Mexican Revolution began, turned her back on the old age and her face toward a new era -- not for selfish gain, but because she welcomed

340

the new; she believed in it. María and her sister Marta were the nieces of Don Dionisio Martínez, the parish priest, brought up like Gabriel
in his home. Marta, 28 years of age, longed to
marry and to mother her own child (she had
adopted one boy, Pedrito). María, at 22, missed
Gabriel, for whom she felt a tenderness Don Dionisio discouraged, speaking vaguely of a cousin
relationship. María had read many books, and
concluded after the night of December 8-9, 1909,
that the village knew nothing of real love. One
day, when Damián returned to the village, she
defended him against angry neighbors until he
managed to escape. Later, she learned by reading
a letter addressed to her uncle that Gabriel, now
a successful student of music, had asked Don
Dionisio for her hand, and that the priest had
said no without speaking to her. When the first
band of revolutionary soldiers visited the town,
María of her own free will rode off with them.

What did Agustín Yáñez portray in his account? He pictured the life of people who, while
traditionally wayward in habits, remained almost
fanatically devoted to an old church regime.
(Their religion comprised a mixture of that
brought by the Spaniards with various American
Indian influences.) Yáñez demonstrated how those
habits and this devotion would of necessity become modified in the wake of a national social
revolution; how the securities and the distortions inherent in the old pattern would have to
yield to insecurities and new kinds of reasoning,
taking the human element more fully into account.

Yáñez did not attempt to describe a new society that might take the place of the old. Four
decades after 1910, the new regime for such villages remained to be identified. Yáñez suggested
rather plainly, however, that the ancient religion practiced in his village held two features
explaining its longevity. These two characteristics have indeed been shared by all the world's
international religions that lasted for long periods of time. Honored by time and universality,

341

the same qualities would likely be included in any new religion for a new age.

In this barren village, the one live institution -- religion -- made use of nearly all the art forms man had devised. The ringing of the bells in <u>Al filo del agua</u> epitomized the world of art. Nevertheless, the bells constituted but a small portion of the world of the spirit brought to play in the realm of religion. The village heard fine music in the church, watched dramatic theater on Maundy Thursday and Good Friday, and enjoyed elegance in pictorial representation through religious painting, sculpture, and architecture. Eloquence lodged in the mass, in the sermonizing, in the readings heard from the very Word of God. These elements, almost inevitably, tugged at the people's heart strings. Any scheme that removed them without adequate beauty in their place could hardly expect to win permanence.

In this narrow village, the religion furthermore provided a strong impetus toward moral behavior. The inhabitants held little vision of a wider humanity; the norms of social justice achievable in twentieth-century society provoked small interest on their part. The church aided them, however, in the lives they actually led to mold stronger moral character -- involving altruism as against pure selfishness, and thoughtfulness in place of recklessness, in actions affecting the lives of others. The people of this village admitted their own shortcomings, especially at the time of the Retreats, and in doing so laid a base for even-handed interpersonal relationships. Each of the traditional religions has developed its own techniques for the strengthening of high moral character. Any new religion, properly to deserve the name, would strive mightily toward the same objective.

VI. THE COLD WAR CONTINUES --

1951-1955

A prosaic quinquennium deserves a prosaic title. The second five-year period after World War II held less excitement than the first. A few tens of millions rather than hundreds of millions of persons achieved political independence. No sensational switches to communism took place, nor did democracy achieve startling gains. No surprises emerged during the new period in United Nations patterns of behavior. The state of Israel continued offically at war with its neighbors, but changes in its position remained small. Only the Cold War, with its violence in Korea, its unfinished settlement of the German question, its Cominform, and its NATO, rode high in the news for extended periods. While the character of the Cold War gradually changed, its level neither augmented nor diminished decisively. It constituted the most dramatic story of the quinquennium simply because it did continue, and upon its denouement so many other developments hinged.

Other stories of these five years held drama for specific places and peoples without shaking the entire earth during this time. In the Soviet Union, the "cult of personality" ended upon the death of Joseph Stalin. In the United States, McCarthyism received a sharp setback after reaching a high peak. And again in the United States, the Supreme Court announced that racially segregated schooling at the public expense would no longer be tolerated. (These three developments are covered in one section here, as three steps in human dignity.) Ineffectual, shortsighted

343

democracy lost out during this period in South
Africa, Colombia, and Cuba. Revolution against
economic imperialism appeared in Iran, Guatemala,
and South Viet-Nam, only to be snuffed out by the
United States Central Intelligence Agency. Significant revolution found greater beginners' success in North Viet-Nam, Egypt, and Bolivia,
though each developed its course in distinctive
manner. For the individual countries concerned,
of course, these happenings were far from prosaic. Their impact on the world scene, however,
became more evident in retrospect than at the
time they transpired.

The Cold War (Part II)

The greatest chill of the Cold War for the
South Korean-United Nations allies came on
January 4, 1951, as the North Koreans and "volunteer" Chinese forces took Seoul again and continued southward. General Douglas MacArthur had
just seen his entire position in North Korea dissolve, only days after he had prematurely predicted complete victory. United Nations lines
south of Seoul held, however, and the South Korean side retook the city on March 16. Once
again, the question began to arise as to whether
the United Nations should battle on into North
Korea, if indeed they found themselves able to do
so. Since all the allies except India had approved the earlier invasion, little talk took
place at this point of the principles involved,
but only of the convenience in strategy. Most of
the allies now favored an armistice with troops
at or near the 38th parallel. President Syngman
Rhee and general Douglas MacArthur, backed by
many of their countrymen, preferred to continue
the struggle, even attacking mainland Chinese air
bases or asking for aid from Tai Wan, if those
courses of action seemed desirable or necessary.
On April 11, president Harry Truman took a decisive stand on these matters when he dismissed
MacArthur from his command.

Serious fighting took place in April-May, until the opposing sides reached a virtual stalemate. In July, armistice talks began, with the United Nations having pushed a few miles north of the 38th parallel on the eastern end of the line and the North Koreans and Chinese continuing to hold a few miles south of the parallel on the western end of the line. The talks were interrupted in August, but resumed in October at the village of Panmunjom on this line. In November, the conferees decided that the battle line of that month should become the armistice line, as soon as the various parties could agree on other details.

The chief argument holding up the armistice lay over the disposition of thousands of prisoners of war, held by both sides. The United Nations negotiators asked that each prisoner decide whether he wished to return to his home country or go elsewhere to live. The Communists did not wish to accept this idea, which clashed with historical precedents. Interruption followed interruption in the talks, dragging them on until October 1952. General Dwight Eisenhower, Republican candidate for the United States presidency in the election of November, promised to do something about Korea, to end the uncertainty there; the question remained, however, as to what path he might choose, if he did not wish to follow MacArthur's ideas. The impasse finally dissolved soon after Joseph Stalin died in March 1953. The Communists hinted that they might be willing to accept the idea of voluntary repatriation. With the talks resumed, agreements became possible almost all the way around the table by June. President Rhee objected that Korea would continue disunited and his own government in even greater danger, now that Chinese troops had appeared on Korean territory. Rhee had necessarily, however, to defer to the viewpoint of his strongest ally. A new, powerful thrust by North Korean troops into some of the South Korean positions reminded him of that, and helped to speed the final armistice. It took effect July 28, 1953.

The ugly crisis in Korea found an echo in Europe very early in the quinquennium. John Jay McCloy, high commissioner for the United States zone in West Germany, decided in January 1951 to grant amnesty to one of Germany's greatest war criminals -- and to restore to the man, Alfried Krupp von Bohlen und Halbach, his end-of-the-war property holdings. Alfried Krupp was the heir through his mother (his father's name had been changed) of the very profitable Krupp munitions industry aged a hundred years, the support of the German war machine in World War I and the Nazi forces in World War II. Alfried in 1942-5 set up branches of the firm in occupied countries, such as the Ukraine; he employed slave labor from the concentration camps, even setting up units within those camps; he countenanced one unit employing Jewish girls already doomed to be exterminated. For these faults, the Nuremberg tribunal sentenced him to twelve years in prison, and took his property away from him. McCloy, in returning to Krupp both his former property (in Germany) and his freedom, expressed concern for the "rights" of the Krupp heirs. Washington had already shown greater sympathy with former enemies (Germans, Japanese) than with recent allies (the Soviet Union). Now that greater friction had arisen, in regard to the Korean war, amnesty for Alfried Krupp constituted one way of underlining the position.

While the Korean conferences continued, the United States built fences elsewhere. These were the final years in the presidency of Harry Truman, with Dean Acheson serving as secretary of state (1949-53). Truman and Acheson now sought military partners far outside NATO -- at any place in the world, indeed, where communists might move out of their bounds as they already had in Korea. Japan became an ally in September 1951, when a bilateral pact (following a multilateral treaty of peace) "recognized" Japan's needs for an armed force for self-protection. United States land, sea, and air forces concurrently received the right to prolong their stay in Japan. Partly to allay fears about a rearmed Japan, but also (in Washington's thinking) to set up further bulwarks against communism, the United States in addition concluded the ANZUS treaty with Australia and New Zealand and a bilateral pact with the Philippines; the Philippines had already provided United States forces with bases. The inclusion of Greece and Turkey as members of NATO, accomplished in February 1952, proved more difficult than the trans-Pacific negotiations. The United States desired the NATO broadening, as part of its plan to "contain" the communists. The western European powers, in varying degrees, felt unready to commit themselves to help these two nations so far from the North Atlantic. But American money and military might remained most essential to NATO, and Washington's views prevailed. This uneven relationship among allies continued from the term of Truman into the presidency of Dwight David Eisenhower, who took office in January 1953.

Dwight Eisenhower like his predecessor Harry Truman was truly a man of the people. Eisenhower's parents both came from the very strict River Brethren religious group which had migrated to the United States from Germany. Most River Brethren became prosperous farmers, but these two broke with the sect and tried to manage a store, only to fail. They moved from Abilene, Kansas, to Denison, Texas, where Dwight David was born in 1890, while his father held a railroad job. Soon the family returned to Abilene, where the father worked in a creamery for 20 years; the family remained financially poor. Dwight attended elementary and high school, participating in athletics and spending a portion of his time working at odd jobs or doing chores. When he graduated from high school, he took a job in the creamery with his father.

347

Dwight's parents, like the River Brethren, held to a pacifist outlook. A good friend near Dwight's age, however, sought an appointment to attend the school for naval officers in Annapolis, Maryland. Dwight wanted to do likewise, and, finding that at 20 he was too old to be accepted at Annapolis, worked for and received an appointment to the school for army officers at West Point, New York. He graduated in the class of 1915 with middle standing, equipped with military know-how but poorly acquainted with the world's great realm of ideas. Transfers from one post to another took him to Texas (where he met his wife-to-be), to Georgia, to Kansas, to Maryland, to Pennsylvania, but never to the battle lines of World War I in Europe. In 1921, he went to the Panama Canal Zone. Later in the 1920's, he attended staff school, emerging at the head of his class. After a military visit to France, he settled in his nation's capital, where in 1933 he joined the staff of Douglas MacArthur. In 1935, he followed MacArthur to the Philippines; his return home came four years later, two years prior to the acquisition of the islands by Japan.

Promotions came fast to Eisenhower as World War II began and the United States army prepared for the day when it might become involved in the scramble. Chief of staff George Marshall, with the help of Winston Churchill, chose Eisenhower to lead the United States army, and eventually the British and French armies, fighting the Axis in North Africa and Europe. From June 1942, when he took his position, until the war in Europe terminated three years later, Eisenhower earned great esteem among his countrymen. They liked to call him "Ike"; a sincere man, dedicated to his responsibilities, he

served unpretentiously alongside his soldiers. Unlike general Douglas MacArthur
in the Pacific area, he returned home for
a great ovation as a war hero in 1945,
though a month later he returned to Europe
again. From late 1945 until early 1948,
he served in Washington as chief of staff,
appointed to succeed Marshall.

Eisenhower next left army duties for
two years, while he acted as president of
Columbia University. The men who offered
him this academic position, for which he
qualified neither by training nor by experience, had become convinced he would
make a good president for the United
States. In 1948, Eisenhower had been im-
portuned by both Republican and Democratic
politicians to serve as their party's nominee, though in neither case is it certain
that the party's majority favored him.
From 1950 to 1952, when he did accept the
Republican nomination, he held the position of supreme commander of the forces of
NATO in Europe.

John Foster Dulles, the North American who
had carried out the negotiations of 1951 with the
Japanese, became the secretary of state for president Eisenhower. Dulles, far from disagreeing
with the line followed by Acheson in regard to
military partners, constantly behaved as though
the desire to obtain committed friends had become
an obsession. A nation which had long favored a
tradition of peacetime neutrality, without even
the conscription of its young men for military
service, now appeared so frightened that it must
look for friends in every quarter, even if the
friendship had to be purchased. In September
1953, the United States signed an agreement with
the Franco regime in Spain, which had not received an invitation to join NATO because several
European members of NATO considered the Franco
regime an abhorrence. In exchange for military

349

and economic aid, Spain provided the United States air and naval bases.

A hollow triumph for the security program of the United States came with the signing in September 1954 of the South-East Asian Collective Defense treaty; popularly (for no good reason except an obvious parallel), the new pact took on the name of SEATO. Pakistan, Thailand, and the Philippines alone of the Asian nations signed this treaty, since India, Ceylon, Burma, and Indonesia all opposed the idea. To make up for the lack of countries both geographically eligible and interested, the United States, the United Kingdom, France, Australia, and New Zealand became members. The participating countries, going beyond the pattern of NATO, made it their business not only to defend fellow members of SEATO but also to assist non-members in the southeastern Asian area. This would be done with unanimous agreement to designate such countries on a separate list. Immediately, however, the SEATO nations drew up a protocol naming South Viet-Nam, Cambodia, and Laos as their beneficiaries. In effect, these three lands (having become politically independent a few months earlier) would be "protected" by SEATO from the other side in the Cold War -- though Cambodia and Laos, by the terms of Indochinese independence, were to be considered neutral lands, and South Viet-Nam had been scheduled by the same terms to become part of a larger Vietnamese entity. In another respect, however, SEATO amounted to less than NATO; it spawned no military organization, but remained a treaty declaring countries' intentions.

The ring bordering the communist world, designed to keep communism within bounds, lacked a few nations more to make it complete. The largest gap lay between NATO's easternmost member, Turkey, and SEATO's Pakistan. The United States held economic interests in this Middle Eastern area, but not even a grain of territorial claim. The United Kingdom possessed a large stake in the region, both politically and econom-

ically, however, and undertook the task of filling in this gap. Turkey and Iraq agreed to a
mutual defense treaty in February 1955, called
the Baghdad Pact. Great Britain joined in April,
substituting this for a previous arrangement with
Iraq that permitted British air facilities on
Iraqi soil. In September, Pakistan came in, and
in October, Iran, to close the circle of hands
held more or less closely from Norway all the way
around to Japan.

The United States did not become an early
member of the Baghdad Pact. It lent its encouragement for others to join, and secretary of
state Dulles must have sensed great satisfaction
to see the defensive ring completed within a few
years of his taking office. The people of his
own country did not criticize Dulles for making
these arrangements; generally, they stood as
convinced as he that the idea of containment of
the communist powers was a good one. On this
program, after all, he and the Republicans only
finished what the Democrats had begun. An occasional bellicose statement by Dulles, hardly in
keeping with his reputation as a church man, did
however evoke criticism from the political
opposition. Dulles would not only contain the
communists, he said, but would roll communism
back, perhaps in eastern Europe; or his country
would engage in instant massive retaliation in
the face of communist wrongdoing. President
Eisenhower spoke more moderately, setting the
world more at ease. He retained great popularity, far more than his secretary of state; and
had no need to build up his image through tough
talk out of tune with realities.

Both the president and his secretary of state
became involved in still another line of "anti-
communist" activity. They knew about and countenanced the action program of the United States
Central Intelligence Agency, which struck in Iran
in 1953, in Guatemala in 1954, and in South Viet-
Nam in 1955, to further United States official
policy. These moves, in each of which the Cen-

351

tral Intelligence Agency actually chose a new
chief executive for the respective country,
formed a part of the Cold War as envisaged by
Dulles, with Eisenhower giving his assent. They
are placed separately here (see "Three Revolutions Interrupted") because the United States
government, not the people, carried them out; the
people in each case remained in the dark as to
what really happened. Secrecy prevailed, indeed,
to save the government embarrassment before the
world at large and a variegated public at home,
many of whom would not have approved the undertakings.

In the Soviet Union, Georgy Maksimilianovich
Malenkov served as prime minister from the death
of Stalin in 1953 until Nikolay Aleksandrovich
Bulganin succeeded him in February 1955. Vyacheslav Molotov, foreign minister 1939-49, received his old post back in 1953. In February
1954, the first post-Stalin government suggested
that European countries communist and non-communist form a mutual defense treaty of their
own. The idea did not win favor in western Europe; memories of the necessity for the Berlin
airlift in 1949 proved strong enough that most
European non-communists preferred American protection to a Russian connection.

In late March 1954, Moscow revised its plan
and presented it again, this time suggesting that
the United States and the Soviet Union both belong to the same alliance, or to two alliances,
NATO and the suggested European pact. Such revolutionary proposals, though there is little reason to doubt the sincerity of those who submitted
them, sounded like cheap trumpery of some kind
coming from the lips of Molotov, the man who had
served Stalin so long. Especially, they would
receive little attention from leaders engaged
(rather triumphantly at this point) in sewing in
the communists ever more tightly. The United
States and the United Kingdom (the latter ruled
by Conservatives again since 1951) rejected the
proposal completely. They were indeed so ob-

sessed at the moment in building their own defenses even higher, through the admission of their old enemy West Germany as an ally, that they could not imagine such an arrangement as Moscow had proposed. It was "completely unreal," London said, and so it must have seemed to men who had become accustomed to thinking of the Soviet Union as a permanent enemy.

West German participation as an ally in NATO had been desired by Washington from the beginning. In 1949, however, West Germany had not yet become acknowledged a sovereign state with the right to subscribe to such a treaty. And western European countries that had recently been occupied by the Germans for years felt understandably less eagerness than the faraway Americans to see German strength rebuilt. The larger NATO powers nevertheless agreed in 1954 that West Germany should assume sovereign status, should become a member of a new Western European Union sponsoring a western European army, and should likewise join as an equal in NATO, if the West Germans themselves (and the other peoples involved) cared to do so. The Western European Union would be an extension of the Brussels pact of 1948, involving Great Britain, France, the Netherlands, Belgium, and Luxembourg. Italy now joined this company and the new army along with West Germany. The latter's assumption of sovereignty and admission to NATO came in May 1955.

The Soviet Union had an answer for the rebuff to its overtures. For the first time, Moscow organized a defense community of its own. There had really been no need for one in response to NATO, since Soviet armies remained in some states of eastern Europe and close bilateral understandings existed with the others. The new prominent role of West Germany in the undertakings in the west, however, seemed to require some move on the Soviet part which would grant East Germany and several other countries greater recognition as equals. An Eastern Security pact signed in Warsaw in May provided for the mutual defense of the Soviet Union, Poland, Romania, East Germany, Czechoslovakia, Hungary, Bulgaria, and Albania, though no German soldiers were to participate in defense arrangements immediately. The treaty, in keeping with what Molotov had suggested to the western powers the year before, remained open to membership by non-communist lands, according to its specific wording.

While the alliances seemed to make the Cold War split decisive, other negotiations offered some hope for a better understanding ahead. The armistice agreement in Korea, which had been delayed so long, came rather quickly after the death of Stalin. Was there a possibility of other change? For the first time since 1949, the foreign ministers of the United States, the Soviet Union, the United Kingdom and France met in both parts of Berlin in January-February 1954. They discussed German and Austrian peace treaties, as they had five years before, with the same sense of futility. But they did agree to meet again in Geneva in April for two conferences -- one on Korea, to seek a more permanent solution there; the other on Indochina, where the war between the Viet-Minh and the French had approached crisis stage. For the first time, in these Geneva conferences, the four foreign secretaries mentioned would sit with the foreign minister of Communist China. Other ministers of foreign affairs would be invited also.

The Geneva conference on Korea lasted until June. The 16 United Nations members with forces in Korea, all of whom attended, then terminated this exchange of words, since the talks were getting nowhere. They had pressed the theme of a united Korea following free elections, a less-than-novel idea that the North Koreans and Chinese refused to accept. The simultaneous conference on Indochina continued until July. During its sessions (in early May) the French suffered a humiliating defeat in battle, losing the French fortress near Dien Bien Phu, a Vietnamese village at the northern border of Laos. This Geneva conference did reach some conclusions -- that the fighting should stop, that the French should withdraw, that Cambodia and Laos should become independent and neutral states, that a temporary division should be drawn between North and South Viet-Nam (the northern part to be ruled by Ho Chi Minh and his party), and that elections should be held in two years to determine the future of all Viet-Nam. Three countries -- India, Poland, and Canada -- were chosen to supervise the transition period in all three Indochinese lands. The Vietnamese government in South Viet-Nam, however, failed to give formal approval to these terms, receiving support for its policy line from the United States. Washington had treated the Geneva conference with coolness, having already constructed other plans for southeastern Asia. SEATO formed a part of the program the Eisenhower administration had in mind as a substitute mode of action; its creation followed immediately upon the Geneva conference. But SEATO comprised only a part, as Washington began to envisage its own puppet regime in South Viet-Nam to take the place of the one the French were abandoning. (See "Three Revolutions Interrupted" for further happenings.)

In the next several months after the Geneva conferences, while the United States busied itself building SEATO and reinforcing NATO, the Union of Soviet Socialist Republics underwent a transition from one administration to another, without the occasion of a death. After the accession of Nikolay Bulganin to the Soviet premiership in 1955, it gradually became evident that Nikita Khrushchev, first secretary of the Communist party since 1953, had worked his way to a position of supreme power in the Soviet Union. Khrushchev and Bulganin now made several radical moves, in scope considerably less sweeping but in effectiveness much stronger than the proposals of the Malenkov regime. The two Soviet leaders aimed to convince the world that the Soviet Union wanted peace; for this, they proposed to go much farther than had Stalin with his bevies of doves. They made a kind of peace arrangement with Tito of Yugoslavia; they invited prime minister Konrad Adenauer of West Germany over for talks. And most solidly, they took the few steps required to bring consensus with the United States, the United Kingdom, and France on an Austrian peace treaty. The powers actually signed this treaty May 15, 1955, in Vienna; it took effect (after ratifications) the following July.

Even while Malenkov remained premier, Moscow pushed another initiative, the idea of a "summit conference" of chiefs of state. Washington evinced no interest at first; however, secretary of state Dulles had often argued that a compelling reason for getting West Germany into NATO was that the western states could then bargain with the Soviet Union from a position of strength. Actually, though Dulles continued to talk about the liberation of eastern European peoples from communism as though that might be accomplished by intimidating Moscow, there no longer existed any reason to think that one Cold War combatant could triumph over another by force of arms. The Soviet Union had carried out its first thermonuclear test by early 1951; the United States detonated its first hydrogen bomb in 1952. The Soviet Union had run four years behind with its first nuclear bomb, but now suffered from no lag. With both lands in production of the hydrogen bomb, it mattered little whether one or the other had more, since each country held a sufficient number to ruin the other. Not from a position of greater strength, then, but because the effort seemed desired by the peoples of the world, Washington agreed along with Moscow, London, and Paris that there should be two new conferences in Geneva. The first, with a wide-open agenda, would be attended by heads of state -- president Eisenhower, premier Bulganin, prime minister Anthony Eden of the United Kingdom, and premier Edgar Faure of France. The second, a meeting of the foreign ministers, would be scheduled later in the year.

The summit conference met July 18-23, 1955. The Soviet delegation came prepared to talk about a rather sensational plan for disarmament which Moscow had published two months earlier. This plan went far to assuage the suspicion of insincerity in Moscow's talk of peace. There had existed a Soviet reluctance to be inspected; now objections to the Soviet position on that matter stood largely removed, with the real possibility that agreement could be reached on all details. However, the other powers failed to discuss Moscow's plan seriously, taking now the attitude that disarmament remained impractical without a prior settlement of outstanding difficulties between the two sides. Most of all, they insisted upon an agreement concerning German reunification through free elections, an objective reasonable to persons who stressed political democracy, but alarming to those who favored a continuance of the communist East German regime.

President Eisenhower played a somewhat solitary hand when he presented an "open skies" plan, which would permit aerial reconnaissance of United States and Soviet territory by the other side. The reconnaissance would make surprise attacks difficult, thus removing anxieties and opening the way for farther-reaching agreements after some of the tension had subsided. Eisenhower's step was a lonesome one because, though his plan received praise from everyone -- the president's sincere yearning for peace being obvious -- no one, not even his own Department of State, picked up the idea in any real attempt to promote it. In a sense, it received its most appreciative response from the Soviet Union, which nevertheless (and understandably so) felt that it had presented a far more comprehensive suggestion. Indeed, at key points the Soviet plan offered what the United States had requested eight years earlier.

The summit conference ended with no hint that

it had accomplished anything except the development of a feeling of respect between the Soviet leadership and president Eisenhower. In the months that followed, however, as Eisenhower suffered a heart attack (September 24), the British and French did attempt to pick up the pieces, working with the plans submitted, while Washington showed that it had lost interest in discussing disarmament. When the foreign ministers convened in October-November, they had nothing new to talk about. The British, French, and Americans would not discuss disarmament without a concomitant solution to the German problem. The Russians would not take up the "open skies" proposal except as a part of its farther-reaching disarmament plan. The statement of adjournment did not even express the thought that the foreign ministers might meet again.

Chancellor Adenauer's visit to Moscow, in September 1955, resulted in an agreement to establish diplomatic relations between the Soviet Union and West Germany. Moscow also immediately recognized East Germany as a sovereign state on the same level. After these conversations and that of the foreign ministers at Geneva, during all of which Moscow showed its intention to cling to its postwar gains, the now famous team of Bulganin and Khrushchev made an Asian tour proclaiming peace and friendship. Visiting India, Burma, and Afghanistan in November-December, the new Soviet leadership showed ingenuity in Cold War tactics. For the moment, no comparable ingeniousness emerged on the other side. Without sharp change in the Soviet Union's position on some major issues, however, cleverness remained bound by constricting limits. Washington's negative attitude, furthermore, had nipped very effectively in the bud any possibility that one new agreement might follow another in 1954-5, starting with the Soviet move on disarmament. With neither side prepared to yield a substantive point, the Cold War would continue.

Three Steps in Human Dignity

Some persons believe the world is going nowhere. This outlook has become widespread, particularly among people who have lived through two world wars. Other persons follow a very different view, that the world of human beings has a bright future. Before World War I, many educated people had taken this prospect for granted. This book espouses the theme that the human species may get somewhere if it chooses, but that its progress is neither inevitable nor automatic. There is no path down which all humanity must tread toward a common goal, but there are paths that go somewhere. Whether the three events described in this section took place along one or two or three paths depends upon the imagery the reader may prefer. The two nations involved, the Soviet Union and the United States, would not have admitted they walked in the same path, going anywhere. All three happenings, nevertheless, amounted to steps in human dignity, whose motivations and aspirations were the same.

First came the dropping of the "cult of personality" in the Soviet Union upon the death of Stalin. In his last years, Stalin took justifiable pride in what the Soviet Union had accomplished. The country had recovered amazingly from the rude shock of World War II, and continued to move ahead rapidly on many fronts despite the persistence of some problems. Stalin had grown accustomed, however, to identifying himself with the state. Unabashedly he permitted his subordinates to laud and magnify him in an absurdly excessive manner. With the coming on of age -- he reached his 70th birthday in 1949 -- he began to expect adulation from those closest about him, who had done as much as he to promote the Soviet Union's gigantic programs. He furthermore told them they were "blind as baby rabbits" when they could not see new dangers to the state in the actions of some of its people.

Somehow, quietly, before Stalin died, these men, or at least a number of them, resolved that never again would they lock themselves into a position in which one man could physically dispose of persons even at high level who displeased him.

Stalin in his speeches and writings made clear to the end of his days that he intended to follow his old domestic policies unswervingly. In the 1930's, by building heavy industry and by purging the regime of its traitors, he had brought the Soviet Union to the point that it could survive the massive threat of World War II. With capitalist countries remaining in the world, renewed military conflict remained certain, he thought, and eventually his own nation might again be put to the test. Emphasis on heavy industry rather than consumers' delights should continue steadily, then, to prepare for war, and he himself must constantly be on the outlook for new traitors. He needed to give the matter of personal disloyalties his own careful attention, he felt, because even the closest of those about him seemed unaware of the dangers. His advisers seemed very poorly informed on the state of the nation, in fact, seeing problems where none existed (as in agriculture, for example) or failing to observe treachery close at hand. Further investigation might very well indicate, indeed, that some of his former closest companions were implicated.

In January 1953, the Soviet government announced that nine well known Soviet physicians, in league with capitalist and Zionist spies, had planned to take measures to impair the health of certain Soviet military leaders -- but that their plot had been discovered in time to thwart it. Several of the doctors named were sons of Jewish families, as were many others denounced during the next seven weeks; the entire press of the Soviet Union seemed to be preparing the nation for a new wave of executions like that of the 1930's. The press aroused anti-Jewish sentiment through manufactured descriptions which made

these people seem highly contemptible. Non-Jewish individuals came under Stalin's cold disfavor
also, including men as highly placed as Vyacheslav Molotov and Lavrenty Beria.

The expected purge had not yet materialized
when Joseph Stalin suffered a brain hemorrhage on
March 1, 1953. Four days later he died. Georgy
Malenkov, whom Stalin had commended highly during
1952, spoke first at Stalin's funeral. Fifty-one
years of age, Malenkov had spent his adult life
in faithful service to the Communist party, handling a variety of responsible tasks. Lavrenty
Pavlovich Beria, a Georgian like Stalin, delivered the second address; graduate of a technical institute, Beria had headed the ministry of
the interior since 1938, with control of part of
the secret police. Beria should have caught the
doctors' plot, various papers had said, rather
than its having been detected elsewhere; there
were suggestions of laxity in his department.
Third and last spoke Vyacheslav Molotov, son of a
shopkeeper and Stalin's minister of foreign affairs for ten years to 1949, though since retired
(by Stalin) from high office. Molotov was one of
the "old Bolsheviks," who participated in the
communist revolution of 1917; his last name,
which he adopted himself, meant "hammer."

Nikita Sergeyevich Khrushchev, son of a mine
worker, arranged the funeral ceremonies, giving
Malenkov, Beria, and Molotov the platform. The
new government rested especially on Malenkov as
prime minister assisted by four first deputy pre-
miers -- Beria, who would continue in his post
now unconcerned about charges of laxity; Molotov,
restored to his position in foreign affairs; Nikolay Bulganin, a factory clerk's son who had
worked his way up through the Communist apparatus
without making large numbers of enemies; and
Lazar Kaganovich, of a Jewish family, who had
climbed from employment as a tanner of hides to
the highest levels in the party, only subsequently to fall under Stalin's displeasure. At
first, it appeared that Malenkov like Stalin

361

might become the general secretary of the Communist party while he served as premier; but nine days after Stalin's death the man who planned the funeral became the first secretary of the party.

Nikita Khrushchev, soon to become a powerful figure in world affairs, was born in 1894 in a village 300 miles south of Moscow, on the border of the Ukraine. In childhood, he spoke both Russian and Ukrainian. His father, who farmed for a living in the summer and mined coal in the winter, had to leave his family to work in the mines of eastern Ukraine. The lad attended a Russian Orthodox school for a few years, but spent most of his time as a child caring for the domestic animals of the farmers of his town. At the age of 14, Nikita moved with his father and the family to a village near the father's mine, at first taking up familiar duties as a herdsboy. A year later, he began an apprenticeship as a mechanic in a German-owned engineering firm. He stayed with the firm until 18, when he participated in a strike and lost his employment. He soon found another job as a mechanic for a French mining company. His skill in this position presumably kept him from being drafted into the army during World War I.

The Russian war against Germany and Austria-Hungary ended in 1917. Russian civil war, however, continued until 1920. Khrushchev saw his first military action late in 1917, when he fought on the side of the mine workers in his region against an army associated with the mine owners. When a German army opposing Lenin's revolution occupied much of the Ukraine in 1918, Khrushchev returned to live in the village of his birth. There he joined Lenin's party and became a political commissar in the Red Army, trying to instill

362

pro-communist morale into the minds of peasant soldiers. In 1920, Khrushchev returned to the mines, where he served as manager of propaganda, now persuading workers to work as he had previously encouraged fighters to fight. Two years later, he entered a school that provided basic training to young persons who might later be assigned particular tasks in the building of the new Soviet Union. During the next three years, he studied the teachings of Marx for the first time. "When I listened to lectures on political economy," he later said, "it seemed to me that Karl Marx had been at the mine where my father and I worked."

In 1925, following his three years of schooling, Khrushchev became the secretary of a district committee of the Communist party in the mining area he knew so well. Here he obtained a reputation, which followed him through his career, of paying attention to down-to-earth problems rather than remaining aloof from them. In 1928, he moved on to more important districts in the Ukraine, always serving as secretary (general manager) for the Communist party. In 1929, Khrushchev once again returned to classes, at the Academy of Heavy Industry in Moscow. While a student (in a course supposed to last three years), he acted as party secretary, first for the academy and later for higher-ranking districts; in 1934, he became the party leader of the entire region of Moscow. During these years, devotion to the Communist party meant loyalty to Stalin. One project of priority that Stalin had chosen was the construction of a Moscow subway. Khrushchev took personal charge of the task, and handled his duties well.

A still more challenging assignment came to Khrushchev early in 1938. He then

363

received appointment as the party secretary for the entire Ukraine. Stalin had decided the year before to reorganize the party in the Ukraine, killing or causing to disappear most of the older Ukrainian leadership which he believed had turned against him. At the time, Khrushchev himself took credit for carrying out the purge program, although it began before he took over the Ukrainian office. Khrushchev also turned his attention to the ailing program of agriculture in the Ukraine, having considerable success in applying remedies. From 1941 to 1943, he found himself involved in struggles springing from the German invasion of the Ukrainian republic. Some Ukrainians took the side of Hitler against Stalin. Khrushchev for the first time doubted the infallibility of Stalin, who had signed the non-aggression pact with Hitler. After the war, however, leading the Ukraine as both prime minister and party secretary, Khrushchev played an important role in the Soviet recovery from the conflict. By this time, he had developed enemies in the Soviet hierarchy, but they did not include Stalin. When he lost his party post in the Ukraine in 1947, because of "errors" he had made, he remained the Ukrainian prime minister and soon had his other post restored to him.

In late 1949, Khrushchev returned to his former work in Moscow and became a secretary of the Central Committee in the party. Entrusted with duties concerning national agriculture, he launched the idea that farmworkers might live in larger towns with modern conveniences rather than in small peasant villages. Stalin did not accept the plan, though collective farms were being enlarged at the time. Assigned other duties pertaining to party organization, Khrushchev used the opportunity to build his own standing among lesser party officials. He maintained a record of complete loyalty to Stalin while Stalin remained alive, but also that of a person who had genuinely helped the Soviet Union in its many years of need, and who seemed likely not to trust old formulas as a substitute for original thinking.

These, then, were the men of the highest positions -- Khrushchev, Malenkov, Beria, Molotov, Bulganin, and Kaganovich -- who decided that no one of them should immediately replace Stalin in his role as an old-fashioned absolute sovereign. These were the men, with the exception of only one, who looked toward a regime of collective leadership, in which high-placed advisers might with considerable freedom disagree with the top man among them on a particular subject. No one expected magic harmony to prevail. Stalin's successors only hoped that in the differences of opinion lying ahead no one of them would seek to take advantage of the others through the medium of physical force upon which Stalin had so strongly depended. The new team lost no time in breaking with Stalin's ghost. Within a few weeks, its members spoke out against "hero worship" and in favor of their new policy, which they in effect publicly proclaimed. Their most dramatic decision of this early period was to drop the accusations associated with the doctor's plot, exonerating the accused completely. The ministry of Beria announced, April 3, that the whole idea had been fabricated.

Lavrenty Beria turned out to be the one of the new ruling group who had ambitions for power beyond those of his colleagues. At least two others of the group wanted to be premier -- Malenkov (who already held the position) and Khrushchev -- and to exercise the extra authority the job entailed. Each of them had his particular friends among those in high position and in the large world of subordinates. But neither Malenkov nor Khrushchev intended to force his way into power. Beria, the others came to believe, early embarked on such a course. Through one successful stratagem after another, making use of his authority as minister of the interior, Beria seemed to be building strength in those parts of the Soviet Union bordering on the communist satellites in eastern Europe. It is impossible to judge the extent of the Beria threat. His colleagues, it is to be presumed, felt as enraged over the fact that Beria would attempt to build a position which he might use against them as worried over the extent to which the planning had met with success. At any rate, in June they detained Beria, and in December announced he had been tried in secret; guilty of crimes against the state, the announcement stated, he deserved to be executed. (Khrushchev is quoted as having said still later that Beria was killed in June.) Some supporters of Beria were condemned also. If the decision to treat the Beria movement in this fashion had been made by one man seconded only by his sycophants and admirers, one might speak of dictatorial authority exercised through brutality. Brutality formed a part of the process, to be sure, and the judgment of Beria could not have passed as fair in a democracy. But in the group of men who made the decisions in this very critical case, no one felt he must mirror the opinions of another for reasons of personal safety.

Eventually, Georgy Malenkov became persuaded to give up the helm. On February 8, 1955, he resigned the premiership, stepping down to an inferior position on the ruling Council of Ministers. Nikolay Bulganin succeeded to the top position, while Khrushchev remained the first secretary of the party. Within a few weeks, outsiders began to notice that Khrushchev seemed to speak with as great authority as Bulganin. For a while, people referred to them as the "B & K" team. But even by the end of this quinquennium, the "K" part was pulling noticeably harder than the "B."

The Malenkov and B & K regimes stood as fully determined as that of Stalin to maintain the high prestige of the Soviet Union. They expected, whenever they felt it necessary, to drive very forcefully in any bargaining. But none of the successors felt as convinced as Stalin that hardness always proved an advantage. With the capitalist world, they wanted to search for some kind of modus vivendi in which neither side would have to sacrifice an important position gained. With themselves and with their people, once they had disposed of the Beria threat, they preferred to "live and let live" also. They had not, of course, made any decision to settle disagreements through elections. There was no thought of an opposition party. But the man who wanted to get ahead (like Khrushchev, for example) would now have to court popularity in party ranks in order to reach his goal, rather than counting on officials he himself had chosen. And this practice alone would plant a seed of political democracy in the Communist party apparatus, the country's most intensely cultivated garden.

Democracy of a much higher (though not the highest) level meantime functioned in the United States, in a slow and bumbling but successful effort to terminate the threat of McCarthyism. The anti-communist activities of "Joe" (Joseph Raymond) McCarthy have been introduced in "The Political Spectrum," Chapter V. McCarthy remained a little known United States senator during the years 1947-50, paying scarcely any attention to the world communist situation. In his career through 1950-4, there lay implicit the notion that the world communist position of strength constituted his one great concern. Yet, as he continued his public role he did virtually nothing of an anti-communist nature except to continue his probing for subversives in the government and to hurl accusations against persons in authority. His condemnation by the Senate in 1954 came after he had gone rather far in pointing his finger at Republicans as well as Democrats and the military as well as civilians.

McCarthy began as a lone operator in February 1950, speaking with little preparation and little assurance of the truth of his words, but engaging in strong enough statements (about procommunists in the State Department) that he could count on extensive publicity. Apparently, he sought only a platform upon which the people of Wisconsin would want to return him to the Senate two years hence. As the word spread that a politican had been found who wanted to "do something" about communism (that is, root out the communist sympathizers who he said determined United States policy), he received contributions from persons of both large and small fortunes. Especially dear to him were large amounts donated by newly wealthy Texas multimillionaires of arch-conservative outlook, whose (genuine) negative attitude toward communism matched the degree of anti-communism that McCarthy postured. With the help of such friends, McCarthy possessed the means to operate independently. He gloried in his role, cheerfully accepted the epithet "McCarthyism" as a description of his manner of dealing, and told the Wisconsin people that "McCarthyism is Americanism with its sleeves rolled."

McCarthy addressed his scurrility to the highest levels of the Truman administration in 1951. He spoke of secretary of state Dean Acheson and his "lace handkerchief crowd," and again of Acheson and his "crimson crowd," blaming the secretary for the American rout in North Korea at the hands of the Communist Chinese; and added, through the pretended thoughts of a soldier who had lost his hands and feet, "Mr. Acheson, if you want to at long last perform one service for the American people . . . you should remove yourself from this country and go to the nation for which you have been struggling and fighting so long." George Marshall, the secretary of defense, better known and more popular than Acheson, found himself attacked with equal vehemence; at least McCarthy proved he felt no fear in criticizing widely admired people. Marshall was the "mayor of the palace" in Washington, McCarthy said, with allusions to eighth-century politics in France; Acheson, the "captain of the palace guard;" and president Truman "that weak, fitful, bad-tempered and usable Merovingian in their custody. . . ." McCarthy pushed on beyond this point as well: "The President is not master in his own house," he added. "Those who are master there . . . themselves are not free. They belong to a larger conspiracy, the worldwide web of which has been spun from Moscow. It was Moscow . . . which decreed that the United States should execute its loyal friend, the Republic of China. The executioners were that well-identified group headed by Acheson and George Catlett Marshall."

The name of Adlai Ewing Stevenson appeared on McCarthy's list of the disloyal when Stevenson became candidate of the Democratic party for the presidency in 1952. The Republicans won that election, however (as did McCarthy his reelection to the Senate), and suddenly Republicans replaced all the high officials against whom McCarthy had railed. In fear of what might happen in this new order, if McCarthy should be assigned a place on a committee looking for subversives, the Republican leadership made him the chairman of the Senate Committee on Government Operations, which usually concentrated its energies elsewhere. McCarthy, not to be outdone by such strategy, then appointed himself head of a Permanent Subcommittee of Investigations and proceeded to look into a variety of government business, always probing or pretending to probe for "security risks" of one kind or another. Many people became convinced that his genuine interest lay not in the search for disloyal or aberrant persons, but in the publicity he so obviously enjoyed. He dropped his public investigations in the same order he started them, one at a time, as soon as the big headlines had been extracted from them.

With his name already a byword in the entire world, McCarthy spoke in November 1953 in criticism of the president elected by his own party. "Now, a few days ago," he said, "I read that President Eisenhower expressed the hope that by election time in 1954 the subject of Communism would be a dead and forgotten issue. The raw, harsh, unpleasant fact is that Communism is an issue and will be an issue in 1954. . . . Now Democrat office-seekers . . . have been proclaiming that McCarthyism is the issue in this campaign. In a way, I guess, it is, because Republican control of the Senate determines whether I shall continue as chairman of the investigating committee." For whatever reason, the elections of the following year did bring defeat to the Republicans and an end to McCarthy's chairmanship role. But already, before those elections took place, McCarthy's position had deteriorated considerably.

It had been true in the beginning of McCarthy's career that his colleagues were not afraid of him. Individuals from both political parties exposed his great untruths, and deplored his lack of gentlemanliness. However, the one senator, Millard Tydings of Maryland, who did the most to stand in his way met defeat for reelection in 1950 after McCarthy carried untrue charges about Tydings to the Maryland people. No politician desiring to remain in office could take lightly this threat from the unprincipled employment of money to influence public thinking. By the time McCarthy had repeated the performance against several candidates, there remained only a few senators who criticized him openly. If he had not in his wildness attacked fellow Republicans as well as Democrats and soldiers as well as civilians, who knows how much farther his fascist star might have risen?

After the Republican administration took office in early 1953, McCarthy turned his attention to books in the State Department's overseas libraries. Very little interested in books for himself, McCarthy set his own judgment on a list of those to be banned. His best known

370

agents of investigation, young men named Roy Cohn and Gerard David Schine, indeed traveled abroad to aid in ferreting out bad books, and to determine whether other fault might be found. The Voice of America, the State Department's overseas radio programming, came under similar restrictions and inquiries. In October 1953, partly in response to the drafting of his assistant Schine, McCarthy began to hold hearings on accusations of communist infiltration into the army. At first, army officials tended to make concessions to the inquisitor, to persuade him to leave them alone. Most of the concessions remained futile, however, for McCarthy played no games except his own. Such "cooperation" by the military offered striking testimony of the power held by this one agitator, whom even the president seemed to fear.

It took a brigadier general to break the spell, during hearings broadcast by television. (Altogether, 187 hours of programming spread over 35 days, chiefly in February 1954.) In close questioning which verged on disrespect, McCarthy attempted to determine a malicious cause for the routine promotion of a young army officer while the officer formed the subject of a security investigation. Ralph Zwicker, the brigadier general, failed to be intimidated by McCarthy's questioning, or by the rash manner that McCarthy adopted. Soon Zwicker's superiors (the secretary of defense, even the president) made it clear they stood by him. Others too in high places gained encouragement to speak out. In March, the McCarthy subcommittee held hearings without McCarthy as chairman, in which McCarthy found himself at times on the defensive. At the end of July, a Republican senator offered a resolution that McCarthy's conduct be condemned by the Senate.

The Senate action on the resolution took place December 2, 1954. Sixty-seven members voted to condemn a few of McCarthy's actions; 22 voted against any condemnation. The original charges pressed against the senator from Wis-

371

consin had become whittled down until actually only one of them remained, along with a recitation of insults against the special committee charged with this matter. Even the original charges had failed to reckon with the great indignities McCarthy had wrought to innocent persons' lives and minds. Nevertheless, as an outcome of the vote, McCarthy lost his hold on the country and the people. He continued in his position as a United States senator, but one who as at the beginning of his career seldom found his name in the newspapers.

McCarthy the man had had his career as an actor cut short by a meek, almost gentle, Senate resolution. McCarthyism the hysteria had already passed its peak before the public had its say in the elections in November. Nevertheless, the voters said one of two things in the congressional elections in 1954: either (1) "McCarthyism is not the issue in this campaign, as McCarthy himself suggested;" or (2) "McCarthyism is the issue, and we condemn it." There had always existed a large number of people in the country who disliked virtually everything that McCarthy typified. Even the very strongest of them tended to wilt when McCarthy hurled accusations of complicity in treason and high crime. United, in November 1954, they nevertheless spoke thrugh the quiet and security of the ballot box, and their vote became quietly effective.

What would have happened if McCarthy had behaved more discreetly and managed to hold his following? The question poses an improbable situation. If McCarthy had acted less obtrusively in his career, he would have lacked many of his admirers in the first place. Through boldness, he captured people's attention and held it, for a few years, even as time after time he failed to prove the truth of his assertions. Eventually, his shallowness caught up with him. He posed a genuine danger because too many people -- United States people poorly educated for modern living -- accepted his accusations uncritically. The country was saved from him by a deeply imbedded democratic tradition of voting which proved stronger than the hysteria.

Far more entrenched in United States life than the McCarthyite mannerism lay the practice of treating persons of African descent as though they were pariahs. The Supreme Court decision of May 17, 1954, which forbade further segregation in the public schools on the basis of race or color, constituted the first national blow against this practice for persons in civilian life. (Desegregation of the armed services had started earlier). The decision, unabashedly, amounted to a conversion of the mind of the high court, as old words (in the country's constitution) took on new meaning in the light of modern times. Gandhi had similarly found new significance in the ancient Bhagavad Gita to support the philosophy of satyagraha.

Persons called Negroes in the United States, who lived chiefly in that nation's South, were the descendants of Africans who came across the Atlantic as slaves. Their Negroid ancestry had become much mixed with the Caucasoid of the people who had purchased them from slave-dealers. Children of a "white" father and a "black" mother and all their descendants continued to be counted and treated as Negroes, as long as they retained any physiognomic trace of the African link. Their half-brothers and half-sisters born of the same father but a "white" mother were treated as superiors, no matter how lowly their fortune in life. Before the 1860's, this outlook prevailed through most of the United States, in the North where few Negroes lived as well as the South where slavery flourished. After the 1860's, when Negroes received constitutional freedom, their lot improved substantially in every part of the federal union. But in the 1890's and early 1900's a mass of new legislation in Southern states disfranchised the Negro almost completely, and left him subject to segregation in nearly every walk of life. Rich white and poor white alike seemed determined to go farther and farther in isolating the races. The white person gained the advantage in each unequal division of facilities, while the black found it necessary to learn and keep "his place."

A few Negroes here and there made protest against the new order in the 1890's, seeking redress of their grievances in the courts. Homer Plessy (seven-eighths white, one-eighth black, according to his testimony) took all the way to the Supreme Court his claim of denial of his rights as a citizen when forced to sit on a "colored" coach in a train. Plessy had been arrested under a Louisiana law passed in 1890. His case came before the high court in 1896, as Plessy v. Ferguson -- the latter the name of the Louisiana judge who first ruled against him. Plessy argued that the 14th amendment to the United States constitution -- reading, "No state shall . . . deny to any person within its jurisdiction the equal protection of the laws" -- in effect prohibited the segregation law under which his arrest took place. The court in 1896, however, thought otherwise. To separate the races, it declared, did not make one of them lower than the other in any political sense. The 14th amendment, it added, "could not have been intended to abolish distinctions based upon color, or to enforce social, as distinguished from political, equality." The court further assumed the attitude that the alternative to segregation on trains would be "an enforced commingling of the two races" that would not lead to the overcoming of social prejudices. It stated that if the "colored" race could become a dominant power and enact a segregation law, "we imagine . . . the white race . . . would not acquiesce" in the assumption that it had been relegated to an inferior position. Neither, then, should the colored race make such an assumption; if it does, that is its own fault.

374

Such a decision coming from the Supreme Court naturally encouraged a host of decisions by lower courts upholding the segregation laws wherever someone challenged them. "Separate but equal" facilities in transportation, schools, recreational areas, and public places in general became the theoretical practice throughout the South. "Separate but very unequal" constituted the reality in most instances. As an example, in the school year 1939-40, four Southern states spent over three times as much per student for the education of white children than they did for that of the blacks.

World War II made the first small dent in United States unfairness to the blacks, when with the manpower shortage the federal government decided that companies handling its contracts would have to hire blacks in other than menial positions. In 1948, president Truman issued an order that blacks be granted equal treatment in all federal civilian positions, and another that the military services must be desegregated (the process took ten years). Blacks who took their chances on the battlefield deserved the same treatment as whites, and could get it only by placing the two in the same battalions. Such reasoning ran counter to that employed by the Supreme Court in deciding _Plessy_ v. _Ferguson_. But the postwar Court itself, in marginal cases, showed some sign of discomfiture with the separate but equal doctrine. In 1950, it ruled that a Negro law student in Texas was entitled to enrollment in the University of Texas Law School rather than in a new law school at the Texas State University for Negroes. The University of Texas school held superiority in certain physical attributes -- the variety of the courses, the scope of the library, and so on -- but "more important," said the Court, "the University of Texas Law School possesses to a far greater degree those qualities which are incapable of objective measurement but which make for greatness in a law school. Such qualities . . . include reputation of the faculty, experience of the administration, position and influence of the alumni, standing in the community, traditions and prestige." The National Association for the Advancement of Colored People, founded in 1909 to help Negroes battle their way to a better life, decided to test whether the Supreme Court would use some of the same reasoning concerning education at the primary and secondary levels. (William Edward Burghardt Du Bois of Massachusetts, co-founder of NAACP who later turned to Marxism, lived through this time period.)

There existed no shortage of test cases at hand. In the developments of 1950-2, five of them reached the Supreme Court, which decided to group them. Negroes in a county of South Carolina, suffering from very poor educational facilities, protested segregation in a district where they constituted a majority. When they requested admission to the white schools, a court in South Carolina told them to wait while new black schools could be built, from a fund the state legislature had just authorized for that purpose. A similar situation and decision provoked a case from a county of Virginia, with the chief difference that in the Virginia example the Negro plaintiffs spoke for a large minority of students rather than a majority.

In Topeka, Kansas, an eight-year-old Negro girl named Linda Carol Brown wished to attend a "white" school five blocks from home rather than having to travel 21 blocks to "her" school. Her father, Oliver Brown, and other Negro parents with the same problem constituted the "Brown et al" in the title of the case Brown et al v. Board of Education of Topeka et al, which the Supreme Court treated first in its decision. The lower court in Kansas had ruled that substantial equality existed between Negro and white schools in Topeka, and that Linda Carol Brown and her ᵒfriends would have to go the longer distance to get to the right school for them. Negro parents in Delaware in the meantime pressed a case in which their children received permission to at-

376

tend school with whites, but on the limited grounds of the genuine physical inferiority of the Negro schools they would have had to attend. Only the Supreme Court, said their judge, could rule on the further contention that the separate schools of Delaware could never be made equal, even with a planned refurbishment. A fifth case requiring a separate decision, because it came from the nation's capital, the District of Columbia, rather than one of the states, rose from the desire of some Negro youths residing there to attend a new high school constructed for white students only.

The Supreme Court heard argument in all five of these cases December 9-11, 1952. On June 8, 1953, the Court turned back to the litigants and asked them several questions, in effect seeking a re-arguing of the entire matter. What thought did the framers of the 14th amendment to the constitution give to the possibility that its wording might have a bearing on public school segregation? What rights should the judiciary assume in the matter if the thought of the framers of the amendment did not emerge with clarity? If segregation should be abolished, how might that best be accomplished -- gradually or at one blow? And should the Supreme Court try to decide the details or allow the lower courts to have first say in the matter? The reargument on these bases took place December 7-9, 1953; the Court pronounced its decision May 17, 1954.

There could be no certainty, stated the Supreme Court, what the framers of the 14th amendment intended as to its application to the public schools. A few of those men had spoken of such an application; a few others had denied such an application; and the great majority had remained silent on the subject. In the South at the time of the adoption of the amendment (the 1860's), hardly any public schools existed for either Negroes or whites. Up until then, some states had even carried laws forbidding any education for Negroes. Now, as the Supreme Court spoke (in the 1950's), matters had changed: "Many Negroes have achieved outstanding success in the arts and sciences as well as in the business and professional world." And education had become "perhaps the most important function of state and local governments."

The high court went on to answer the question for mid-twentieth-century United States that the nineteenth-century legislators left unanswered. Its very simple basic response, given here after the Court's rephrasing of the question, consisted of only five words: "Does segregation of children in public schools solely on the basis of race, even though the physical facilities and other 'tangible' factors may be equal, deprive the children of the minority group of equal educational opportunities? We believe that it does."

The justices cited their decision of 1950 concerning the University of Texas Law School in regard to "those qualities which are incapable of objective measurement but which make for greatness in a law school." "Such considerations apply," the court said, "with added force to children in grade and high schools. To separate them from others of similar age and qualifications solely because of their race generates a feeling of inferiority as to their status in the community that may affect their hearts and minds in a way unlikely ever to be undone. . . . Any language in Plessy v. Ferguson contrary to this finding is rejected." The decision as it stood called not for the "commingling of the races" frowned upon by the high court in 1896, and not for "integration" of parties who genuinely preferred to remain apart, but only for the end of segregation in the public schools by state law. A second decision on the same day, based on the 5th amendment to the constitution rather than the 14th, repeated the same reasoning for the children who lived in the District of Columbia.

The Supreme Court acted unanimously in its opinions handed down May 17, 1954. Since its decisions flew directly in the face of Southern custom, and seemed to presage an entire tumbling down of the walls of segregation, the court itself apparently believed unanimity desirable as an added assurance of respect for the opinions of the judicial apparatus. The justices found themselves excoriated by many white persons whose fury they had aroused. The one who read the decisions -- chief justice Earl Warren of California, appointed by president Eisenhower -- received the most criticism of all. Warren and the Court stood prepared for hostility but not for the host of problems which arose in the wake of their notable decision. They made no attempt at the outset to go beyond the establishment of the principle of unconstitutionality. A year later, on May 31, 1955, they rendered the decision that local courts, "guided by equitable principles," would handle the details of desegregation in each district, requiring "a prompt and reasonable start toward full compliance," but permitting time for the working out of all the problems. The test cases in Kansas, Virginia, and South Carolina, the court added, should be terminated "on a racially nondiscriminatory basis with all deliberate speed." As the Supreme Court withdrew from the legal battles for a time, it became quickly obvious that its help would again be needed. The phrase "with all deliberate speed," seized upon by everyone as applying to the entire projected revolution in the South, seemed indeed more shrewd as a semantic device than satisfying as a guide. The real problem, however, lay in the fact that not all the local districts, nor even the judges in them, understood the term "equitable principles" in the same fashion as the Supreme Court.

Every one of the three "steps in human dignity" described in this section constituted a faltering step at best. While the heirs of Stalin set their faces toward the goal of collective leadership to take the place of the cult of personality, they found it necessary completely to eradicate one of their number. When the Senate of the United States ended the worst threats of McCarthyism, it failed to anathematize or even define that movement's most dangerous features. While the Supreme Court stood unanimous in its decision that Negroes must not be separated from whites in the public schools on the basis of color or race, it offered only minimal guidance to the thousands of school districts and judges who, though often hostile to the decision, were expected to carry it out.

Nevertheless, all three steps took on great significance. The individuals responsible for each had thought out the issues and decided in a particular fashion on the basis of equity and fairness. In all three instances, the decision-makers showed a higher respect for the people about them than the Stalinists, McCarthyites, and segregationists had achieved in their time. And the steps they took, in the very midst of the Cold War which involved their countries, brought both the Soviet Union and the United States to more distinctly human planes of living than they had known before.

Three Losses for Democracy

Nations cross the threshold of democracy in both directions, departing from as well as entering the premises. Chapter V indicated the manner in which Czechoslovakia and Hungary left the democratic fold for the first quarter of the spectrum, and mentioned the removal of Thailand, Peru, and Venezuela to the fourth quarter. Indeed, it may be said that all democracies in all time remain in a state of flux with the degree of participation constantly rising or falling like the mercury in a thermometer. Generally, when the movement is downward, as in the United States during the onslaught of McCarthyism, a reaction occurs before the tendency becomes catastrophic, and democracy pushes upward again. However, a downward movement in an immature democracy (especially one not deeply rooted in majority rule) may be sufficient to remove the country in question from the democratic category. Such an event occurred in the lives of three nations during this quinquennium -- South Africa, Colombia, and Cuba. In each case, a regime representing all of the people had not yet been achieved, but only the machinery that might have led to such representation if it could have continued to operate.

In the Union of South Africa (population 13-14,000,000 in this time period), the division between those who did and did not rule lay rather strictly along race lines. The majority of the people, the Bantu, represented the Negroid subspecies of mankind. The minority, descended from the Dutch and the British, represented the Caucasoid. This group, with less than one-fourth of the population, effectively held all the power. Still smaller minorities lived here also -- the so-called Colored (a medley of racial mixes of Bantu, white, Hottentot, and Asian) and the Asian Indians who arrived in the nineteenth century. No one could claim living-space priority in South Africa except the Bushmen with their Khoisan languages, who had largely disappeared as separate peoples. The descendants of the Dutch called themselves Afrikaners and their speech Afrikaans; while the Bantu, who like the Dutch had arrived in South Africa in modern times, considered themselves Africans from farther back in the sense of having lived somewhere on that continent.

When the Union of South Africa came into being in 1910, the South Africa Act of the British parliament defined its structure. Two portions of this act referred only to the second in population of four provinces -- the one called Cape of Good Hope or simply Cape -- the home of many British people. One provision served to protect the English language, the other to maintain a small heritage from British liberalism. In Cape province, the Act provided, English would continue to be recognized as an official language (along with Afrikaans) and native Africans who qualified would vote on the same roll (that is, on the same list of delegates) as whites -- unless a two-thirds vote of the combined South African parliament decided to the contrary. In 1931, on the other hand, with the autonomy of the British dominions defined, it appeared that the parliament of each would enjoy all the privilege in its area formerly pertaining to the body in London. The London parliament made all decisions for its realm by a simple majority vote; should not now the practice in South Africa become precisely the same? The matter of the two-thirds vote, as against the simple majority, developed into a prime controversy. The arbitrary manner of its resolution took South Africa across the threshold of democracy in reverse, and led rather abruptly to sharp authoritarianism.

The real argument, of course, lay not in the technicalities, but in the background questions involved. Basically, they all merged into one: Should South Africa be operated as a multiracial entity, or as a white man's country with very separate provisions for its black people? The Bantu, whose future stood most at stake, made up roughly two-thirds of the population. In 1950, nearly half of the Bantu (but preponderantly women and children) lived in "native reserves," whose territory comprised about eleven percent of the nation's area. The remainder (a majority, including three-fourths of the men) lived on the farms of white families or worked in white-owned mining and manufacturing industries. White people did not intend to create a system in which the Bantu would no longer work for them. But those who subscribed to apartheid or apartness, a more drastic segregation than that practiced in the United States, believed they could accomplish this goal while retaining the blacks' labor.

The National party in office after 1948 considered apartheid its basic objective. It took five steps in that direction during its

382

first three years. One act prohibited marriage between whites and all non-whites, broadening a previous ban on matrimony between whites and Bantus. Another forbade sexual relations between whites and all non-whites. The racial identity of marginal persons in such circumstances came very much into question. The government thus designated three main classes of people, describing them as white, Native, and Colored, and required that each individual be classified in one of them. (The Natives equated with the Bantu; Indian families formed a subclass of the Colored.) Further legislation provided encouragement toward separate residential regions, each to be managed by its own residents -- though always under the supervision of white persons.

Meanwhile, in 1949 the province of South West Africa became attached to South Africa by unilateral decision of the South African government. South West Africa had come under the protection of its neighbor as a League of Nations mandate after World War I. Not only South Africa increased in size by this coup, carried out without reference to the United Nations Trusteeship Council to which other mandates had been referred, but the National party benefited also. Though Bantu people speaking five languages composed a majority in South West Africa, and Khoisan-speaking Hottentots and Bushmen also lived there, the Nationalists won all the seats in the South African parliament supposed to represent the new area.

Clearly, the National party lacked enthusiasm for democracy, as the word had come to be understood in the twentieth-century context. Still, through 1950, many consitutitional niceties continued to be preserved in South Africa. The optimist could argue that the situation remained hopeful, even for the Colored and Bantu, simply because whites still held the right to vote, regardless of the drift of their sympathies. The English-speaking United party might again win, as it had prior to 1948, or parties of more liberal sentiment might arise. Even the Bantu, as they became increasingly eligible to vote, could work more effectively against white supremacy. Bantu and Colored political strength would remain less important, however, if separate voting rolls could be maintained. Cape and Natal provinces (Natal had copied Cape on this matter) remained a worry to the Nationalists, who desired complete apartheid in this realm also. They now set themselves the task of reforming Cape and Natal.

Only the last part of the process remained to be accomplished. Already in 1936, the combined South African parliament had acted by a two-thirds majority to remove Bantu voters from the common roll. Their few representatives, required to be white people, from that point spoke only for the Bantu. That move, while undemocratic in spirit, lay within constitutional bounds, and could easily have been reversed with a change in white sentiment. In early 1951, prime minister Daniel Malan introduced legislation to separate Colored voters from the whites. Since on this occasion the United party stood opposed, there existed no possibility of a two-thirds approval for the bill. The administration, however, counted not on the two-thirds vote taken by the two houses in joint session, but on a majority only from each house voting separately. The measure concerning the rolls, the Nationalists argued, like any other before the parliament, needed only a majority to make it the law of the land. The opposition challenged this reasoning, but stood very divided in its concern (some favoring equal rights for the Colored, some insisting on the constitution of 1910, some reluctant to see disappear the differences between provinces), and the bill passed by a final lower house vote of 74-64.

Four Colored voters went to the courts, protesting the unconstitutionality of these procedures. The Appellate Division of the Supreme Court of South Africa agreed with them in March

384

1952, stating that the definition of a dominion of the Commonwealth legislated in 1931 in no way invalidated the guarantees established in the South African constitution. The National party reacted by creating (via majority vote only) a new High Court of Parliament empowered to override the decisions of the Supreme Court in matters involving the constitutionality of parliamentary acts. As might have been expected, the Supreme Court also declared this bill invalid, stating that the establishment of the new High Court would have negated the principle that no body (in this case the parliament) could be a judge in its own case.

Next, the Nationalists concentrated on the elections of 1953, through which they hoped to improve their power position. This they managed to do, obtaining three-fifths of the seats in the lower house, even though their popular vote remained slightly less than half. (The discrepancy, as in 1948, arose from the inequality of the electoral districts, favoring the rural vote over the urban.) Now the possibility of a two-thirds vote proved again enticing, to avoid the constitutional crisis. In September 1953 and June 1954, joint sessions of the two houses of parliament almost yielded the required two thirds, as a few United party members voted for the bill. The measure failed, however, and Daniel Malan resigned as premier. Johannes Gerhardus Strijdom, who favored the use of more drastic measures to reach the apartheid goal, became Malan's successor.

Strijdom introduced two new bills which passed in May-June 1955, and constituted South Africa's departure from democracy. One increased the size of the Appellate Division of the Supreme Court from five judges to eleven, so that the Nationalist government, choosing the new judges, could count on a court majority friendly to its program. The other nearly doubled the size of the Senate, and in effect more than doubled the Nationalist seats in the Senate, enough to provide that party with two-thirds of the seats when the parliament met in joint session. Strijdom had overcome his party's greatest obstacle. No longer could even a majority of white voters stand in his party's way. And the much greater majority of Native and Colored persons would have to accept any program planned for them without even the privilege of questioning the government's aims.

Apartheid for the Bantu grew steadily during this quinquennium, while the parties fought over the voting rights of the Colored. An act of 1951 provided for the establishment of Bantu authorities to administer the lands reserved for blacks, but under the higher control of white officials. A law of 1953, running counter to the trend in North America, stated carefully that segregated public facilities for whites and non-whites in South Africa need not be equal. Another of the same year provided for a separate education program for the Bantu (two-fifths of whom of school age had already enrolled in school) -- though the (white) minister of native affairs who would administer the program declared specifically that "if the Native in South Africa today in any kind of school in existence is being taught to expect that he will live his adult life under a policy of equal rights, he is making a big mistake." (Presumably, he meant to identify the Native's teacher rather than the Native as the person making the mistake.) Also in 1953, the government prescribed a separate procedure for settling labor disputes involving male Bantu workers, barring strikes and leaving no room for trade unions -- though white workers could continue to join unions and strike.

The African National Congress, organized in 1912, spoke for the educated Bantu. During its first three decades it had followed a moderate course. In the 1940's, it took a more aggressive verbal stand, insisting that blacks should be granted full citizenship. In 1952, Albert John Mvumbi Lutuli became president general of the

African National Congress as it joined with the South African Indian Congress to initiate a Gandhi-style passive resistance campaign. (A Christian teacher and local elected Zulu chief, Lutuli came from Zulu parentage in Southern Rhodesia, moving to South Africa at the age of ten.) Legislation of 1953 (supported by both major political parties) cracked down hard on passive resistance, however, holding out the prospect of loss of property and lashes with the whip for those who participated. The police indeed whipped many Bantu persons, as the harsher consequences of the developing <u>apartheid</u> revealed themselves. Individual participation in protests became extremely hazardous, demanding an almost certain surrender of the small liberty people possessed as the price for a dubious future.

In June 1955, as minority-party fascism took the controls in South Africa, representatives of protesting groups met in a large Congress of the People. The African National Congress participated with the South African Indian Congress, the National Union of the Organization of Colored People, and the South African Congress of Democrats (a small group of whites). The police broke up the meeting before the end of its second day. Already, however, the Congress had voted for a Freedom Charter, declaring that "South Africa belongs to all who live in it, black and white" and that "our people have been robbed of their birthright to land, liberty and peace by a form of Government founded on injustice and inequality. . . ."

Colombia, in South America, took a long step away from democracy in 1953, as did the Union of South Africa two years later. In Colombia (population 12-13,000,000), however, race did not enter the problem; indeed, here no clear racial lines existed. Families originally from Africa lived in the lowlands to the north and west, an assortment of American Indians in the lowlands to the south and east, and some persons of unalloyed European lineage in the highlands; but mestizos, mulattoes, zambos, and mixtures of the three constituted three-fourths of the population. The lighter-skinned people tended to possess more money; those of decidedly mixed heritage along with the Indians and the blacks generally inherited the poverty of sixteenth-century conquered peoples and eighteenth-century slaves. Twentieth-century Colombia, however, posed no legal barrier to prevent anyone from rising to the top. Until 1936, Colombian society (like that of most democratic countries) clung to the supposition that people who because of poverty or illiteracy remained ineligible to vote would eventually join the more privileged in management of the nation as they began to "make something of themselves."

Colombia had contained two major parties, the Liberal and Conservative, from far back in the nineteenth century. The Liberals, like those of most of Latin America, maintained the nineteenth-century, laissez-faire liberal stance long after its abandonment elsewhere. They opposed special privileges for the church and the military, and stressed devotion to political liberties; while economic and social justice only very slowly reached the status of bywords. In 1936, however, Colombian liberalism moved into the twentieth century when a Liberal administration introduced the income tax, several guarantees to labor, and the consitutional right for the state to expropriate private property for reasons of "social interest." For the first time, also in 1936, all men received the right to vote without regard to literacy and ownership of property.

Colombia's reputation for democracy among the Latin American states had developed steadily since 1909. It became stronger than ever with a peaceful transition from Conservatives to Liberals in 1930, followed by the social-justice emphasis of the Liberal campaign in 1934. Most of Colombia's Liberal leaders, however, had little conception of genuine social justice for their

388

country. The revolutionary quality of it, indeed, would have frightened them -- and did frighten them when they began faintly to hear it expounded. The happy little world they envisaged needed little more than the mild social legislation adopted in the mid-1930's to render it full of opportunity for everyone. No racial barriers prevented any male from making his way in society. The Colombian economy needed expansion, the Liberals believed, and with the further development of the land's resources, the poor would benefit automatically. As Colombia's economically deprived people began to vote extensively, however, even though many of them chose to cast the ballots they knew their employers wished, a new spirit became quickly manifest. A distinct breed of public figures arose in response to the new demands, promising drastic changes for the betterment of the masses, including land for land squatters, profit-sharing for employees, and public management of the nation's utilities. The strain these leaders introduced into Colombian democracy proved to be more severe than the weak democracy of the country could stand.

By the later 1940's, Colombia contained four political groupings in place of two, both former parties having splintered. No one wished, however, to desert the time-honored political names, so that except for brief periods Liberals remained Liberals and Conservatives Conservatives, with further designation into party wings. The moderate-socialist Liberals supported Jorge Eliécer Gaitán and would probably have won the presidency in 1950, if their leader had not fallen a victim of an assassin. (See "The Political Spectrum," Chapter V.) The milder social-reform-without-socialism Liberals in power 1934-46 lost that position through the division of their party. Twentieth-century Conservatives, resembling nineteenth-century liberals in devotion to laissez-faire, ruled the country under Mariano Ospina Pérez 1946-50, when the startling bogotazo took place. Nineteenth-century Conservatives, little interested in democracy, preferring aristocracy and traditional Catholicism, obtained a dominant position in 1950 with the accession of president Laureano Gómez.

The assassination of Gaitán combined with the post-<u>bogotazo</u> violence in the countryside to produce bitter feelings between Liberals and Conservatives. Liberals complained that government troops protected families calling themselves Conservatives while punishing those who took the name of Liberals. In September 1949, a gun battle took place in the nation's congress, resulting in the death of one Liberal member. In October, the Liberals nominated Darío Echandía for the presidency, but before the month ended withdrew from the race, citing a lack of guarantees for free balloting. In November, police attacked a group including Echandía on a Bogotá street in broad daylight, killing Darío's brother Vicente. The Liberals not only boycotted the presidential elections of that month (making the election of Gómez legal), but refused to run candidates for the congress in 1951.

The Gómez wing of the Conservative party took little interest in any kind of congress, even one dominated by Conservatives. It desired a strong chief executive backed by the church and the military, a genuine reversion to old times. Gómez planned a constitutional assembly to adopt the changes he intended. The president would rule six years rather than four, controlling his own budgets, keeping the press in line, governing Colombia as a "Christian democracy" rather strikingly Roman Catholic authoritarian. Gómez demonstrated the seriousness of his approach by reducing the power of labor, constricting Protestant religious freedom, and combating most fiercely those individuals of his own party not personally loyal to him. Ospina Pérez, when he decided to run for the presidency at the end of Gómez' term, automatically became a bitter enemy.

In November 1951, Gómez became ill to the

390

point that he could no longer carry out the duties of his office. He asked Roberto Urdaneta Arbeláez to fill the post for him until Gómez himself determined otherwise. While Urdaneta ruled, the rural violence (called <u>la violencia</u>) evolved into a contest between government forces on the one hand and bands of fighters denominating themselves Liberals on the other. By September 1952, the bitterness had reached such a level that bands of armed men in the capital city looted and destroyed the homes of Liberal leaders without interference by the police. Some of the threatened persons had favored cooperation with Gómez to get <u>la violencia</u> stopped. Now the same individuals, fearing for their lives, exiled themselves abroad while the Liberal party ceased to function as a corporate enterprise.

The constitutional assembly planned by Gómez materialized very slowly. A study commission of 1952 remained far behind the ailing president in its enthusiasm for his ideas. The assembly, scheduled for April 1953, was postponed until June 15. In the meantime, Laureano Gómez took two actions that changed the character of the enterprise; both happened the same day, June 13. First, Gómez took back from Urdaneta Arbeláez the active direction of the presidency. Second, Gómez decided to dismiss a popular general named Gustavo Rojas Pinilla, who had stated his loyalty to the acting rather than the ailing president. When Gómez attempted to arrest Rojas Pinilla to oust him from his position, Rojas arrested Gómez instead. Then, when neither Roberto Urdaneta Arbeláez nor Mariano Ospina Pérez would assume the presidential powers, saying that to do so would be to act unconstitutionally, Rojas made himself president of Colombia.

The constituent assembly two days later "chose" Rojas Pinilla to fill out Laureano Gómez' term. Rojas made it clear that he would sponsor no constitutional change of the type Gómez had envisaged. The assembly then became his legislative body, doing his will while in session, allowing rule by executive decree during long interims. In 1954, it decided that Rojas would keep the presidency an additional term of four years. Very popular in 1953, in a country relieved to be rid of Gómez, Rojas Pinilla nevertheless managed to alienate many Colombian people by the year 1955. When much of his administration of affairs proved inept, he stood as the central figure to be criticized. Acting like the warrior he was, he sought to intimidate those with whom he disagreed -- especially the university students and newspaper editors -- winning himself a steady accretion of new enemies.

Democracy died in Colombia, however, in the year 1953. It had begun to falter badly another seven years earlier. Conservative president Ospina Pérez won with a popular minority in 1946 because the Liberal majority split. A system of preferential voting, with all votes for a third-runner recounted, would likely have produced a Liberal president in that year, from one wing of the party or the other. A parliamentary type of government would have accomplished the same result, through a Liberal prime minister rather than a president. In 1950, the bogotazo and la violencia having splattered the country with blood, Laureano Gómez obtained the presidential office by default. The Liberals may be blamed for not even trying to defeat him, and the Conservatives for having chosen such a man. Gómez had desired to end Colombia's democracy in 1953, when Rojas Pinilla performed the task in his stead.

The Colombian "strong executive" type of government, patterned after that of the United States, had led to a succession of presidents who stood weak because a majority of their people disapproved of them. Division in the Liberal party, produced by a longing for social revolution, led to Gómez' and Rojas' policies of the iron hand. From 1946 through 1955, the government turned its back completely on significant social reform, leaving the new expectations of

392

the masses unrealized. Colombian democracy had foundered because its foundations remained too slender to stand the strain of more egalitarian living and the sharpness of its demands.

Cuba (population 6,000,000), across the Caribbean Sea from Colombia, also lost its democracy through an uprising, in 1952. Cuban problems, like those of Colombia, pertained more to poverty than to race, though the Negroes and mulattoes of the island, recuperating from the institution of slavery, tended to fare less well economically than the families of chiefly European heritage. Cuba, however, knew no traditional party system of liberals and conservatives encompassing most of the nation's citizenry. Indeed, Cuba had adhered to democratic principles in government for only a short time. In a sense, its experience began in 1939, three decades after that of Colombia.

The Cuban situation of the 1950's extended back to the year 1933 for its roots. At that time, the rule of one of Cuba's caudillos came to an end, when domestic forces of two kinds overthrew him. One, led by an army officer and stenographer, Fulgencio Batista y Zaldívar, emphasized administrative probity, long lacking in Cuba, and relief for the average citizen from the severities of previous regimes. The other, led by civilians, favored the objectives of the Batista group, but added to them a concern for social and economic reform in favor of the masses. Ramón Grau San Martín, physician and university professor, an outstanding personality of the civilian group, became the provisional president of Cuba in late 1933. The nearby United States government, which had intervened often in Cuban affairs since its recognition of the country in 1898, refused to recognize Grau's leadership; instead, it countenanced a succession of men, 1934-40, placed into and removed from office by Batista.

393

The chagrined group which had promoted Grau turned to political organization to fight for its aims. Thus formed the Partido Revolucionario Cubano (Auténtico) -- the Cuban Revolutionary Party (Authentic) -- "Auténtico" serving as a designation for its members. In 1939, when the Cuban people in a fair election chose the membership of a constitutional assembly, Grau and the Auténticos did well. The new document, under their influence, provided not only for individual liberties and guarantees of a political nature, but for maximum working hours, collective bargaining rights, social security, public housing programs, and even state assistance to cooperatives. The form of government changed a little, with provision for a prime minister and a cabinet appointed by the president but with responsibility to the congress, obliged to resign if it lost the legislative body's confidence. This constitution, finished in 1940, stood as the first official recognition in Cuba of a need for social change, though it stayed well within the bounds of twentieth-century liberalism. Many of its "guarantees" remained, of course, to be implemented.

The three presidential elections which followed may all be put in the category of "fair" -- that is, the public could be quite certain in each case that the winner received a majority of the votes. Batista ran in 1940, and served his first term as president rather than president-maker. Grau won in 1944, and another Auténtico, Carlos Prío Socarrás, in 1948. These three men held twelve golden years of opportunity to prove that democracy and liberalism could bring in a new era in their island. Business flourished during their time; individual fortunes accumulated -- some owned by persons from the United States, but many belonging to Cubans. Yet neither Batista nor Grau nor Prío adopted significant measures to broaden Cuba's distribution of wealth. Instead, they concentrated on two lesser, even ignoble, aims: first, to increase opportunities for persons already well supplied with them; second, to make sure that they personally received a full share of the money circulating. They sponsored "progressive" governments, in the sense that they moved ahead along traditional lines and allowed considerable freedom. At the same time, they permitted and even encouraged very corrupt administrations, despite all they had said about the new honesty. The Auténtico administrations, further, were not revolutionary as they claimed to be, seeking to cure the ills of Cuban society.

Cuba's standard of living, despite the comfortable status of some of its city people, remained very low -- especially in contrast to that of its next-door neighbor, the United States. True, only three Latin American countries (Venezuela, Argentina, and Uruguay) enjoyed per capita incomes higher than that of Cuba, and Latin American peoples generally earned more money than those of Asia and Africa. The average mattered less, however, than the amounts that reached the less favored of the people. Three-fourths of Cuban families had no refrigeration in their homes; nearly two-thirds of them possessed no indoor water facilities; two-fifths of the homes contained no electricity; nearly one-third had earthen floors. Rural people lived less well than those who dwelt in the cities. In the countryside, two-thirds lived on earthen floors; fewer than one-tenth enjoyed electricity; and less than one-twentieth owned refrigerators or used running water indoors. The agricultural people lived in such homes from necessity, not because of any ingrained preference for rusticity. They did not eat well (most had neither milk nor meat); they often felt unwell (parasites, malaria, tuberculosis, and typhus afflicted them); and their knowledge of the modern world remained very limited (most had spent less than three years in school). Their city cousins, though on the average better situated, also often lived under miserable conditions. The Auténtico governments of 1944-52 came little closer than the preceding regime of Batista to making any dent in such poverty. Even had Grau, Prío, and their friends remained completely honest, their very moderate reform programs would scarcely have reached the masses of the people.

New leaders organized the Partido del Pueblo Cubano, or Party of the Cuban People, in 1946. Calling themselves Ortodoxos, they claimed to represent the true spirit of the revolution of 1933. Their principal leader, Eduardo (or "Eddy") Chibás, developed a Sunday evening radio program in which he freely excoriated the wrongdoings of the rulers of the country. By the beginning of the 1950's, Chibás made himself the most popular man in Cuba. Immediate denials of his exposures did the perpetrators little good, when Chibás produced strong evidence to support his charges. The Ortodoxos gained ground, not so much on the virtues of their own program as on the failures of others.

The Ortodoxos also adopted a platform clearly revolutionary in tone. They proposed sweeping economic and social reform to hit every stratum of Cuban society. Corrupt men would have to yield government posts to the honest, as Batista and the Auténticos had said before. But so would wealthy investors from abroad have to yield economic power to the Cubans who should replace them. And so would wealthy Cuban landowners have to share with the tenants who had worked the land for them. City people would have to recognize the rights of those who inhabited rural zones. And the individuals whose families had owned slaves would have to make room for those whose ancestors had worked as slaves on this island until 1886. Chibás, evidently valuing his party's program more highly than his own person, dramatically shot himself at the conclusion of his radio broadcast on August 5, 1951, in protest against the hardhitting attacks of his opponents. When he died eleven days later, carrying the sympathies of a large number of Cuban people, his friend Roberto Agramonte, university professor of psychology, took his place as the likely next president of Cuba.

The Ortodoxos joined some allies to nominate Agramonte for the presidency, in elections scheduled for June 1952. The Auténticos and friends chose Carlos Hevia as their candidate, while another party manufactured for the occasion picked Fulgencio Batista for a second term. As the campaign progressed, strong indications developed that Agramonte would win, and that Batista would run a poor third, behind Hevia. Neither the Auténticos nor the Batista group intended, however, to allow the triumph of Agramonte. Though the Ortodoxos favored political democracy along with their proclivities toward socialism, the changes they proposed ran sharply contrary to the wishes of Cuba's ruling clans. On March 10, Batista (head of one clan) seized power in Cuba, through a quiet revolt by the military; he said he did it to prevent a coup by president Prío (head of the other clan) against his own administration, to prevent the elections.

Batista postponed the elections until 1954, when he "won" the presidency without opposition. In the meantime, as acting chief executive, he stifled in its beginning an attempt by working-class people to depose him, on July 26, 1953, and placed the island under severe controls. Batista had once commanded a strong position in Cuba; now, however, he acted from weakness due to his unpopularity, and managed to survive only through repression of ideas. A strong Ortodoxo sentiment prevailed, as one would expect, in the movement to eliminate Batista as president. A young Ortodoxo lawyer, Fidel Castro Ruz, served as the chief leader of the attempt of July 26; sentenced for rebellion, to 15 years in prison, Castro received amnesty after only one year.

Fulgencio Batista had denied Cuba the privileges won in 1939. Those who vainly fought him struggled for the principle that the party with the people's backing should win. Democracy had

397

come to Cuba for a time, almost miraculously in the rough-and-tumble contention between Batista and the Auténticos, and offered a peaceful way for Cuba to embark upon social revolution. But quite obviously, neither Batista nor the Auténticos intended to let democracy go so far as to remove their power completely. Cuba's democracy had come up against a test too demanding for its stage of maturity. Young Cubans and other Latin Americans who sensed the need for social change in the region had some reason to wonder in the light of this experience whether the democratic system had much to offer the cause of social justice.

The leaders of South Africa, Colombia, and Cuba in the early 1950's all preferred the trappings of democracy -- the way of civilized people -- but felt dismay at the implications of full-blown democracy. They entertained some concept of fairness, but one that remained restricted to a very limited group of persons. When the underprivileged parts of their populations began to think of their own rights, the leaders reacted in fear rather than in intelligence. Their reluctance to allow the masses to improve their own standing through democratic means encouraged the masses to attempt other avenues. Many individuals, even among affluent families, frustrated by the blocks these leaders placed in the way of peaceful change, came to believe in the incompatibility of governmental democracy and social upheaval.

Three Revolutions Interrupted

Democracy and nationalism provided twin themes for revolutions in Europe after 1815. For that postwar period, events in the United States of America and France had set the revolutionary pattern. Latin American leaders inspired by the twin themes won national independence from

France, Portugal, and Spain. The European struggle of the same time, however, reached no such positive conclusion. For the individuals who dominated continental Europe stood opposed to the democratic outlook, and determined to preserve what they labeled the "legitimacies" -- the political arrangements they pretended came from heaven, but which they themselves had devised. Time after time, in alliance, these leaders intervened to prevent revolutionary movements from attaining success. They preserved an uneasy equilibrium for a time, postponing the emergence of a more equitable European society.

Revolutionary movements appeared in the world after 1945 as they had in Europe after 1815. Social justice and nationalism, rather than democracy and nationalism, now served as the twin themes. Social justice might stem from democracy, as many revolutionists believed -- or it might come into existence, others thought, through authoritarian means. During 1951-55, persons in Iran, Guatemala, and South Viet-Nam sought to establish social revolutions to provide a better living for their people -- in each instance, on a democratic and nationalist base. No alliance of governments appeared to oppose them, as in Europe after 1815. However, the United States Central Intelligence Agency arose instead, assuming the role of watchdog, and suppressed all three of these revolutions, one at a time. People in the United States knew very little of the actions this Agency took in their name. People elsewhere in the world quickly recognized the CIA, as it was called, as a symbol of determination to oppose social justice, wherever that concept seemed to the leaders in Washington to clash with United States financial or security interests.

A postwar enterprise, the CIA dated from 1947, in company with its parent body, the National Security Council. The CIA was designed to correlate, evaluate, and coordinate the gathering of intelligence having a bearing on the security of the United States. It received an additional charge, however -- "to perform such other functions and duties related to intelligence affecting the national security as the National Security Council may from time to time direct." The president and the secretary of state sat on the National Security Council with a small number of other persons. The CIA began its secret but spectacular career of interrupting revolutions when Dwight Eisenhower became president, John Foster Dulles secretary of state, and Allen Welsh Dulles (John Foster's brother) director of the CIA, all in early 1953. The first involvement, a rather simple one, occurred in Iran (population 17-19,000,000 in this period) after only half a year.

On the surface, Iran's revolution beginning in 1951 had nothing to do with the United States. It concerned the right of the Iranian lower house of parliament, or Majles, to choose the prime minister it wanted, to carry out the radical social legislation it favored, and to nationalize the properties of the Anglo-Iranian Oil Company as it desired. But eventually, because the National Security Council of the United States decided that the right of the Majles to continue its own program in Iran lay in conflict with the best security interests of the United States, these objectives had to be abandoned. To accomplish its opposition program, the CIA needed only some local (Iranian) cooperation, some agents, and some money.

The Majles had first come into existence in Iran in the year 1906. The shahs who ruled until 1941, however, continued either to oppose or to manage the Majles in such a way that Iran in those days could only be labeled an autocracy. The encouragement given by Mohammad Reza Pahlavi after his accession in 1941 brought about a gradual realization of the constitutional power of the Majles. The socialist Tudeh party founded after the war, though it was outlawed in 1949 (see Chapter V, "The Political Spectrum"), gave the more radical leadership of the country its first opportunity for political activity. The so-called Iran party, formed in 1944, catered to the interests of those seeking less sensational reform, generally somewhat short of socialism, but who devoted themselves more strongly than the Tudeh to the excitement of nationalism. The most heralded personality in the Iran party was that of Mohammad Mosaddeq, from a wealthy landholding family; Mosaddeq held a Swiss doctorate in law, and taught in the university. Around his leadership by the year 1950 also clustered a hodgepodge of small parties, each one distinctive in some way but eager to support nationalism to the extreme.

The Anglo-Iranian Oil Company, with which Mosaddeq tangled in 1951, had come into existence as the Anglo-Persian Oil Company in 1909. The British government itself held a majority of its stock after 1914. In the period after World War II, with the petroleum business booming, the British nation derived considerably more income from the company than did the government of Iran. When Iran adopted an expensive seven-year plan of development in 1947, the country's leadership became sharply divided in ideology. One group, centering about the shah, favored friendship with Great Britain and the United States, hoping to renegotiate the oil contract with the former and to obtain loans from the latter, to supply the necessary financing. Another group, focusing around the figure of Mohammad Mosaddeq, followed a harder line of reasoning in devotion to Iran. Neither group leaned toward the Soviet Union; the Majles that adopted the seven-year plan turned down a suggested Irano-Soviet oil company.

Friends of the shah requested a new agreement from the British approximately to double the oil profits for Iran. They also devoted their energies to negotiations to obtain a sizeable American loan. The United States did approve a loan, but for an amount far below that needed for the seven-year plan. This news, of the year 1950, came along with reports that the Arabian American Oil Company had offered Saudi Arabia 50% of the profits from all its export sales of crude oil. The nationalistic grouping in the Majles, pointing out the smallness of the loan and the inadequacy of an oil contract less favorable than the one offered Saudi Arabia, in late 1950 persuaded the Majles to vote against the renegotiated contract. At this point, sentiment in both the Majles and the country turned rapidly to the idea that Iran should nationalize its oil industry. The first bill stating that principle passed in mid-March 1951. In late April, Mohammad Mosaddeq became prime minister.

Great Britain reacted immediately to the possibility of losing its oil company with a threat to use force if necessary to defend the company's properties. That vague set of international agreements widely known as "international law," however, recognized the right of any nation to expropriate properties within its boundaries, if to do so seemed in the national interest, and the Majles had made clear its readiness to enter conversations concerning what would amount to a forced sale. The British Labor government agreed to talks in which it offered compromise, in the form of a marketing Anglo-Iranian Oil Company that would take the entire exported product of the nationalized company to do with it as it pleased, on the payment of a 50% dividend to Iran. The Iranians, however, had become intent upon managing the entire enterprise. The British did not defend their properties by force, but as Iran took possession of the oil refineries virtually no one stood ready to purchase the petroleum.

The United Kingdom took the case to the International Court of Justice, and afterward to the United Nations Security Council. Mosaddeq, in personal appearances before these bodies, persuaded the Council to defer to the Court (October 1951), and then the Court to decide it held no jurisdiction in the matter (July 1952). The latter decision, on a vote of 9 to 5, rested on Iran's argument that the issue lay between a government and a company rather than between two governments. The personal prestige of Mosaddeq among Iranians rose to a tremendous high. In May 1952, he began to initiate social reforms, particularly in the fields of agriculture and labor, which the Majles had often discussed but no minister before had found the strength to implement. He asked for emergency dictatorial powers from the Majles, and received them for six months from August 1952, after a crisis in which the shah took the prime ministership away from Mosaddeq for six days. In addition to the economic strain caused by the British boycott on Iranian petroleum, and to the difficulties involved in forcing landlords to pay new taxes and give up ancient privileges, Mosaddeq had in these days to face the armed opposition of the outlawed Tudeh party, which favored even more radical change.

After the decision of the International Court of Justice, the United States government lent a hand in further talks between Iran and Great Britain. At that time, Washington continued to stand as a friend to both sides in the conflict. United States leadership under president Truman tended to think of Mosaddeq as the man who, whatever his faults, could save Iran from the more terrible threat of "Tudeh communism." When Iran and the United Kingdom severed diplomatic relations in October 1952, friendship from the United States seemed all the more essential. By March 1953, Britain's Conservative government came to agree to the nationalization with a modified form of marketing agreement devised by the United States, in which American oil companies would also participate -- a proposal which, up to this point, remained acceptable to the Iranian government. The attempt foundered, however, as the Iranians insisted that compensation be paid only for properties while the British demanded remuneration for profits they would be denied in the

403

future. Put simply, the British expected more money for their company than Iran offered to pay.

In January 1953, Mosaddeq won a full year's extension of his dictatorial powers. However, the aggregate of new circumstances served now to dim his prestige. The continuation of the economic crisis and the impossibility of maintaining the series of international triumphs hurt him among all Iranians. The implementation of the reform programs caused the desertion of his wealthier friends. The more conservative leaders who had supported him moved gradually over to the group at the side of the shah. A first effort to encourage Mosaddeq to resign failed at the end of February. The prime minister simply held on to his post after organizing street demonstrations in his own favor. In late May, Mosaddeq took a dramatic step toward the solution of the deepening impasse, writing United States president Eisenhower a direct request for aid. The president, however, sent a discouraging reply. Dated June 29, 1953, it said in effect that if Iran wished aid from Washington it should first agree to the terms which the United States government had suggested for the oil treaty. Less than two months after Eisenhower wrote this note, his Central Intelligence Agency took steps to remove Mosaddeq from office and substitute a more compliant man in his place.

As Mosaddeq found himself confronted increasingly by the shah, the prime minister formulated dramatic new plans to secure his own position. Mosaddeq believed that he retained popular backing far exceeding that represented by his decreased support in the Majles. He asked the shah to dissolve the Majles in order to make way for a new one. Failing in this request, he then took a referendum of his own among the people, asking whether the Majles should be dissolved. This vote might have provided Mosaddeq the new triumph he needed. But to make sure he would win, he provided for balloting in the open, getting nearly all the "yes" slips he wanted without

404

convincing anyone.

The referendum took place on August 3 and 10, 1953. When the shah continued to refuse to dismiss the Majles, Mosaddeq took it upon himself to do so, August 15. That night, the shah attempted to dismiss Mosaddeq, appointing commander of the army Fazlollah Zahedi prime minister in his stead. Mosaddeq held firm, however, refusing to accept his discharge from duties on the shah's determination alone. On August 17, Mohammad Reza Pahlavi lost his nerve and fled the country, while Zahedi remained in hiding. When the shah left, radical groups including Tudeh demonstrated for a republic and more drastic social reform, in the direction of a regime pleasing to the Soviet Union. On August 18, Mosaddeq struck hard against the Tudeh and its cooperating people. It seems one of the ironies of history that the very next day Mosaddeq lost his position because of the pro-Soviet proclivities seen in him by the CIA.

The actual happenings of August 19, 1953, were very simple. First, an anti-Mosaddeq demonstration took place; there existed no novelty in this, however, since paid demonstrators for one or another cause had become a very common sight in the capital city Tehran. Second, disorder occurred, of a type not usually permitted street demonstrators. Third, the bulk of the army and police joined the wild party rather than attempt to suppress it, proceeding to intimidate Mosaddeq and his supporters. The CIA had nothing to do except to choose Mosaddeq's successor, Fazlollah Zahedi, and to pay the demonstrators and the armed forces who joined them. The United States National Security Council approved CIA supervision of the day's critical events, while the British government and the absent shah of Iran lent their support. No one consulted the people of any of the three countries concerning their opinions.

The shah returned from Rome after three days,

405

Zahedi took up his tasks as prime minister, and American oil companies joined the British interests in working out a settlement of the petroleum question. Finally, in 1954, all parties agreed to allow Mosaddeq's expropriation to stand (though Mosaddeq now found himself in prison), with the understanding that half of all profits from the oil exports would go to Iran. An international consortium (rather than the British alone) would manage the entire production for a period of 25 years. United States oil companies (which would further remunerate the British), as an added payoff for the diminutive but decisive intervention of the CIA, made up 40% of the new consortium. The British held another 40%, and the Dutch and French the remainder. Zahedi became ill and had already left office in 1955 when the now powerful shah, showing his gratitude for the aid rendered him two years earlier, caused his government to join the Baghdad Pact to help "contain" the Soviet Union.

The second intervention by the Central Intelligence Agency required more dexterity than the first. In June-July 1954, through the joint efforts of the CIA and the United States Department of State, the president of Guatemala (population 3,000,000) lost his position and Carlos Castillo Armas took his place. Castillo completely lacked credentials from the Guatemalan people. Two years of study in the United States, an intense dislike for the government that preceded him, and a strong anti-communist vocabulary nevertheless qualified him in Washington's opinion.

Guatemala had emerged from a nineteenth-century authoritarian cocoon only in 1944. Free elections in 1945 brought Juan José Arévalo, a university professor and authority on pedagogy, to the presidency. Arévalo placed stress on democracy, encouraging a free press and the organization of opposition parties. His program brought a new measure of dignity to a majority of the Guatemalan people -- 15 Indian groups speaking 11 Maya languages -- simply by granting them the right to vote. Arévalo showed himself a friend of the working-class people, whether Indian or mestizo, by sponsoring a labor code and a social security plan. Persons opposed to these measures tried frequently to unseat him before the end of his term, but failed in their endeavors. The United States ambassador took it upon himself to criticize the Arévalo regime in public; eventually, Washington recalled him, at Guatemala's request.

Jacobo Arbenz Guzmán succeeded Arévalo in 1951. Arbenz was a young military man; his father, a pharmacist, had migrated to Guatemala from Switzerland. For two years, Arbenz followed Arévalo's twin plan of democracy and social change. He took special interest in an agrarian reform program which took unused land away from its (usually absentee) owners and made it available to needy families. This activity brought him into conflict with the United Fruit Company, based in the United States, which held wide areas for future plantings of bananas. The United States embassy helped United Fruit, with no concern for the landless peons. Guatemala's new penchant for democracy brought a few alert communists to its congress, where they soon secured the backing of a non-communist but increasingly anti-United States majority. Arbenz, supported by the communists, eventually became exasperated at anti-communist opposition to his measures. In 1953, after attempted revolts against his presidency, he began a season of arbitrary, even harsh, retribution against his opponents.

The United States government formed its anti-Arbenz conspiracy late in 1953. In Iran, it had feared that Mosaddeq might clear the path for communist seizure of the country. In Guatemala, it believed Arbenz had already embraced communism, to the extent that American security stood threatened. This second intervention called for more assistance and more planning, even more money, than the first, because Arbenz held his position directly from the people. John Peurifoy moved to Guatemala as the ambassador of the United States, chosen especially for this particular mission. Carlos Castillo Armas moved to Tegucigalpa, the capital of neighboring Honduras, where the CIA provided him advice and arms. The Somoza regime in Nicaragua provided a base for airplanes, also to be used in the plan. In January 1954, the Arbenz regime announced its discovery of a portion of this conspiracy, but secured little hearing internationally. In March, the Organization of American States, meeting in Caracas, Venezuela, voted an anti-communist resolution urged by Washington and clearly pointed at Arbenz. In May, a shipload of military supplies reached Guatemala from Czechoslovakia, in a vain effort by Arbenz to counter the CIA.

Castillo and his small, rag-tag army entered Guatemala from Honduras June 18, 1954. The same day, planes struck at Guatemala from their bases in Nicaragua. Castillo's force, no match for the troops of the government, did very little fighting on Guatemalan soil. Arbenz complained of the attacks to the United Nations Security Council, where the United States insisted it had nothing to do with the matter. On June 20, the Security Council requested that all members of the United Nations abstain from rendering assistance to Castillo. Two days later, Guatemala returned to report that the bombing had continued; at this point, the United States delegation succeeded in keeping the item off the United Nations agenda. The OAS took up the matter instead, on June 26, and set up an Inter-American Peace Committee to investigate the situation; the committee took three more days to reach the scene. In the meantime, Washington had supplied more planes, while the CIA managed to misinform Arbenz that his army was doing poorly against Castillo's band. Arbenz, following the advice of communist friends, decided to put arms into the hands of the people. Officers in the army disagreed on this course, however, and on June 27 forced Arbenz to resign.

John Peurifoy, the United States ambassador, next stepped into action, turning down one officer suggested for the provisional presidency, but going along with another for a time. As a result of Peurifoy's persistence, Carlos Castillo Armas became first a member of the ruling junta, second the chairman of the junta, and third the provisional president without the accompaniment of a junta. Castillo scrapped Guatemala's constitution by issuance of a simple decree. He held only a yes-or-no plebiscite concerning his continuance in office. He banned all parties of the left, and made difficulties for parties of the right other than the one of his own creation. He turned back to the previous owners, including United Fruit, much of the land earmarked for the agrarian reform. Yet the people of the United States, little interested in agrarian reform and knowing next to nothing of the petty invasion or the role their government had played, tended to regard the change in Guatemala as a "liberation" from communist tyranny.

In Iran in 1953, Mosaddeq stood clearly apart from Iranian communism. In Guatemala in 1954, Arbenz depended on a few local communists along with many other people for the execution of a non-communist reform program. In Viet-Nam, at the beginning of the following year, a Communist leader had good reason to expect that he would soon become president of his country by popular demand. Ho Chi Minh looked toward social change in Viet-Nam far greater than Mosaddeq or Arbenz had contemplated. The interposition of alien CIA strategy obstructed Ho's program for South Viet-Nam, as completely as it had stifled the lesser plans in Guatemala and Iran.

The war between the French-assisted state of Viet-Nam (headed by Bao-Dai) and the Viet-Minh state of Viet-Nam (ruled by Ho) had already dragged on four years when this quinquennium began. (It started before the French recognized the Bao-Dai creation; see "The Political Spectrum," Chapter V.) Military operations spread from Viet-Nam to all of Indochina. Ho held as his immediate objective an independent and unified Viet-Nam, while the French liked to think of Viet-Nam as an associated state in the French Union. Until 1954, the fighting continued without a definitive victory. But in early May of that year, France suffered a full-scale defeat at Dien Bien Phu, at the very time of the Geneva conference that sought an end to the conflict. (See "The Cold War.")

After Dien Bien Phu, the Viet-Minh had every reason to believe they would soon control all of Viet-Nam. True, another Vietnamese government existed, in the city of Sai Gon, but its army had suffered greatly along with the French and showed little evidence of ability to stand alone. Most of the northern party of the country and about half of the southern remained in Viet-Minh hands. Rather than push for a military takeover, however, Ho preferred to wait for an electoral victory, which he felt certain would be his. Most of the powers at Geneva approved the plan for elections in 1956, so that the state of Viet-Nam might unite without further resort to violence. Ho the maximum nationalist leader had fought the Japanese and the French; surely, a great majority of the Vietnamese could be expected to vote for him.

The French prepared to leave Viet-Nam, regardless of what might happen there. In May 1954, however, the United States government (not its people) decided it could not allow that kind of communist victory. Washington would step into South Viet-Nam (population 12,000,000) simultaneously with the French departure. Just as Bao-Dai had served as France's man in Sai Gon (or in Paris, where he actually lived much of the time), so Ngo Dinh Diem would now act as Washington's man, supported at first through the Central Intelligence Agency. Diem (by Vietnamese usage,

410

the given, not the family, name) came from the Roman Catholic minority in the northern part of Viet-Nam. For several years, he lived in the United States, where a number of influential Catholics knew him. By prearrangement, on June 16, Bao-Dai asked Diem to become prime minister in the Sai Gon regime. Diem requested and received dictatorial powers from Bao-Dai, and subsequently flew to his capital, still occupied by the French. France treated Diem's government as completely independent, pursuant to an agreement it had signed earlier in June. Washington liked Diem for his opposition to the French occupation -- for his freedom from colonialist as well as communist taint -- but more than that, for his readiness to do Washington's bidding, which would soon make him a colonialist supreme.

Diem made only the crudest of attempts to show that the South Vietnamese supported him. He held some obvious popularity among Roman Catholics, two-thirds of a million of whom migrated from North Viet-Nam to join his state. Most of the Buddhist majority revealed no enthusiasm, but in keeping with past custom remained passive. Major opposition came from two strong, military-oriented sects, the Cao-Dai (who mixed tenets of the Buddhist, Taoist, Confucianist, and Catholic peoples) and the Hoa-Hao (who followed a nationalistic Buddhism). Diem forced the sects to yield temporarily, after CIA money had bought out the generals who led them. Next Diem announced a plebiscite -- the people could choose whether they preferred a monarchy under Bao-Dai or a republic with Diem. On October 23, 1955, the republic "won" by more than 98%; no one asked whether the South Vietnamese might prefer a third alternative, such as Ho Chi Minh.

Diem clearly intended from the beginning, along with his backers in the United States, to cancel out the decisions that had been made in Geneva. Diem took no interest in free elections; the one scheduled for Viet-Nam would mark the end of his position. Ho Chi Minh, likewise no gen-

411

eral enthusiast for free elections, nevertheless welcomed the one set for 1956. Advice reaching president Eisenhower indicated that Ho would win without any difficulty. Thus the Ho regime pressed for all-country elections as planned by the conferees in Geneva, while the Diem government opposed them in favor of a South Vietnamese dictatorship. In South Viet-Nam as in Guatemala and Iran, the United States supported the less democratic of two opponents, and the one less devoted to social change. And in South Viet-Nam as in the two previous instances, president Eisenhower and the two Dulles brothers showed confidence in the judgment of the CIA, without reference to the United States Congress or people.

Fully as significant as the attitude toward representative democracy, now that the second half of the twentieth century had dawned, stood the position of a government toward social reform. Mosaddeq, Arbenz, and Ho Chi Minh, each with his own quota of personal frailties, strove for very dissimilar programs. They held one factor in common -- a desire to rid their respective countries of feudalistic and colonialist regimes. Mosaddeq had to contend with British interests, Arbenz with those of the United States, and Ho with the claims of the French. When Washington stepped into all three disputes through the agency of its CIA, it set itself up in opposition to Iranian, Guatemalan, and Vietnamese nationalism; it showed little interest in democracy in the three countries concerned; and it acquired the reputation of a self-appointed guardian to save the world from social revolution.

Three Revolutions Inaugurated

The United States Central Intelligence Agency had become an international phenomenon, an object of world attention though not of universal respect. As a worldwide watchdog, however, the CIA

412

had its limits. While British interests retained a hold in Iran, British influence sharply declined in Egypt. While a left-trending regime in Guatemala came to an end, an even more leftist movement gained strength in Bolivia. While South Viet-Nam, dropped by the French, fell into Washington's plans, North Viet-Nam (population 13-14,000,000) remained with Ho Chi Minh.

Ho Chi Minh had made no secret of his devotion to communism. As a young man in France, he chose the Communist party over the Socialist because of the uncompromising Communist stand against colonialism. (See Chapter IV.) Nevertheless, in the earlier stages of the struggle against the French as they returned to Indochina after World War II, Ho and his associates played down the Communist role and cooperated with a wide variety of individuals. In 1951, Ho's group reorganized both the Communist party (renaming it the Workers party) and the front which their party dominated. The Viet-Minh ceased to exist, though the name continued in use by outsiders. The Workers party controlled the Lien-Vet, the new front organization, more closely than the Communist party had the Viet-Minh.

Until 1954, continual fighting prevented Ho from tackling social reform on a wide scale. He and his government remained in the hills while the French held the northern cities of Ha Noi and Hai Phong. The new measures Ho devised under these circumstances lay considerably short of communism, though they did make some impact on the regions he dominated. A rural tax reform placed greater demands on those more able to pay, while Ho began a campaign to rid his territory of illiteracy, and an agrarian reform in one district only, in 1953. Few wealthy landlords lived in this part of the country (unlike the situation in South Viet-Nam) but as an admirer of Mao's agrarian changes in Communist China Ho tended to follow in his mentor's footsteps. The reform in the one district of North Viet-Nam involved the

413

expropriation of farm holdings in excess of <u>two</u>
<u>acres</u>, making the land available to the <u>more</u>
needy. Ho aroused antagonisms through this
severe program, and lost some of his previous
collaborators. However, his reforms by and
large, though they included some use of terror,
made him the "man of the hour" for many North and
South Vietnamese. Popular measures might be
turned into genuinely communist measures, ran
Ho's thinking, once he had claimed his
all-Vietnamese victory.

In 1954, after the victory at Dien Bien Phu
and the conclusion of the Geneva peace conference, Ho enunciated a conciliatory tone. He felt
certain that he would win the all-Vietnamese
election planned for two years in the future.
"Our people from North to South must fight for
the organization of free general elections to
reunify the whole country," he said. He wanted
to "guarantee freedom of conscience;" to "employ
and treat well the employees and officials who
formerly worked with the opposite side and who
now wish to serve the country and the people;"
and in the "newly liberated" areas, to "protect
the lives and property of our compatriots as well
as of foreign residents, including the French."

A year later, in September 1955, Ho spoke
bitterly about the developments in South Viet-
Nam. He accused the Diem regime of harsh terror-
ism, and said that Diem "also feverishly carried
out the U. S. political line with a view of turning South Viet-Nam into a U. S. colony and military base. . . ." As agreed at the Geneva conference, Viet-Nam stood divided temporarily into
North and South at the 17th parallel of latitude,
and the French had withdrawn from the North as
promised. (Ho had also removed his open forces,
though not all his sympathizers, from the
South.) But the second stage of action defined
by the conference at Geneva, "the stage leading
to the reunification of Viet-Nam through general
elections," Ho said, "cannot as yet be started as
a result of Ngo Dinh Diem's deliberate hindrance."

South Viet-Nam had in effect been snatched from Ho Chi Minh after his forces had defeated the French. No one expected a social revolution in the South from Diem and his overseas allies. North Viet-Nam, on the other hand, belonged to Ho's regime in a way it had not before. If social revolution could be expected during the time of a new war which seemed to be foreboding, the impetus would all come from Hanoi. Ho's own preferences meant that revolutionary planning would lie along communist lines. As Ho looked at matters, indeed, the pursuit of the communist dream constituted the chief reason for the existence of his North Vietnamese regime, aside from the reuniting of the Vietnamese nation.

Egypt (population 21-23,000,000) possessed much the same attitude toward the British that the Vietnamese people held toward the French. Egypt formed neither a colony nor a protectorate, however, like the parts of Indochina, but an independent nation with its sovereignty somewhat delimited by a military agreement. The pact with the United Kingdom, made in 1936, allowed the stationing of British troops on Egyptian territory during a period of 20 years. Thus, at the time of World War II, Italian and German armies drove into Egypt to fight the British there, while the British (from their own point of view) "defended" both Egypt and the Suez Canal. A postwar movement to rid all Egyptian soil of British occupation won the wide acclaim of the Egyptian masses. Young military officers led by Jamal Abd an-Nasir took up this cause, attracting wide attention through their fiery nationalism.

The birth of Jamal Abd an-Nasir took place in Alexandria, early in the year 1918. His mother came from a middle-class family of that city; his father from a family of <u>fellahin</u>, or peasants, in a village far up the Nile. Jamal's father left the village to study until he received an appointment as branch postmaster in a poor section of Alexandria. Jamal, as he grew, lived in a village near Cairo, to which his father was transferred; next, with his father's brother, in Cairo; later, with his maternal grandparents, in Alexandria; for a while in a boarding school, not far from Cairo; and finally with a stepmother and his father, in Cairo again. Jamal did poorly in both elementary and secondary studies, and as time passed displayed resentment against parental authority. While in secondary school, he evidenced a flair for rebellion against government authority as well, and received a wound on the head in one scrape with policemen. His father, who worried that Jamal's activities might lead to his own dismissal as postmaster, felt relieved when Jamal won admittance to the royal military academy at the age of 18.

Nasser (as he is generally known in English) began to read extensively while attending the academy, particularly about nineteenth- and twentieth-century Egypt. Nothing that he read shook his allegiance to traditional Islam, the faith of his childhood. He did find, however, a new exciting reason to live -- to build a stronger Egypt for the future. In his class, the first in the academy to include young men from a non-aristocratic background, others shared young Nasser's enthusiasm. Receiving an officer's commission after two years of study, Nasser spent a year far up the Nile River, not far from where his <u>fellahin</u> uncles lived. In 1939-40, the army stationed him still farther south, in the Anglo-Egyptian Sudan. Both experiences offered him much time to speculate upon his country's character.

Nasser and other Egyptian officers,

like the majority of their nation, tended to favor the Germans over the British in the Second World War. Prime minister Winston Churchill of the United Kingdom ordered that Egyptian troops should not be used on the British front lines, because he feared their loyalty. Hence, after his transfer there in late 1940, Nasser in effect sat out the war in northern Egypt, along with many of his friends -- a situation bound to seem to them humiliating. They felt all the more demeaned when the British used force in 1942 to compel Egyptian king Farouk to appoint a pro-British prime minister. Nasser and his closest friends began to think of the time when they themselves might save Egypt from its position of subordination. Nasser spent the last years of the war teaching in the military school from which he had graduated. He came to be known as one who wanted Egypt to become self-dependable and strong.

From 1946 to 1948 Jamal Abd an-Nasir went to school again, to qualify for an appointment as staff officer. On May 15 of the latter year, the birthday of the state of Israel, Nasser graduated with his class. Assigned immediately to the Palestine front, Nasser soon found himself one of 4,000 Egyptian and Sudanese troops caught in a pocket, surrounded by Israelis. Nasser returned home after the armistice, in 1949, convinced that Egypt had itself to blame for its poor battle showing. Particularly, he realized that many Egyptian soldiers had died because they carried deficient or defective arms, a circumstance pointing directly at corruption among private procurers who stemmed from the aristocracy. Nasser was a military man, whose earlier anger concerning corruption focused upon such military factors. During the same war against

417

Israel, however, he had come to a belief not usually associated with militarism, the conviction that most problems cannot be solved by bloodshed.

The desire to bring great change to Egypt, but if possible to do so peacefully, caused a large number of army officers to form a secret association in 1949. They chose to call themselves the Free Officers; they put Nasser at their head. They built quietly for a revolution to come, without trying to create an artificial opportunity. They first tested their strength in 1951, against their king Farouk, when Egypt found itself in the throes of a nationalistic outburst. The Wafd-controlled parliament had declared its unilateral abrogation of the treaty with the British, five years before its termination date. The Anglo-Egyptian Sudan would become the Sudan, with king Farouk as its ruler; British troops both there and in Egypt were simply expected to leave. The British declined, however, to evacuate the Sudan, and reinforced their army in the vicinity of the canal.

In the middle of the excitement, Farouk attempted to insist that a personal friend become president of the Army Officers Club; the friend happened to be one of those implicated in the sale of defective arms. The Free Officers group had decided to support a widely respected general, Mohammad Neguib, for this position. Neguib won the post with majority backing, very early in 1952, and the king had no difficulty in realizing the deeper meaning of the event. The crisis with the British continued until a severe clash on January 25, 1952, brought death to over 70 Egyptians in uniform. The next day, rioters took over the city of Cairo, striking especially at the shops and hotels catering to foreigners. Farouk called upon his army for help, and his army came to his rescue. The Free Officers had already decided that Farouk should be deposed, but they did not wish him to lose in this manner. They needed more time to work out details before they themselves would strike.

The Free Officers finally chose the night of July 22-23, 1952, as the time for the conspiracy to move. They laid plans to accomplish the entire change without bloodshed. Brief fighting, in which two soldiers died, took place in the night at army headquarters, but by morning complete serenity had returned. Mohammad Neguib, who had not participated in the night's events, became the new chief of state as the head of a revolutionary council. Three days later, Farouk, surrounded at a palace in Alexandria, abdicated in favor of his infant son and prepared to sail away to Italy in exile. At this point, the Free Officers began to realize that, once they had accomplished this much, they lacked a precise plan to carry their revolution farther. Nasser wrote, "What is it we want to do? And which is the way to it? There is no doubt we all dream of Egypt free and strong. . . . As for the way to liberation and strength, that is the most intricate problem in our lives."

For a while, the revolutionary council retained the traditional structure of government, minus only the monarch. This phase ended in September 1952, when Neguib became the prime minister. A few days later came the promulgation of an agrarian reform program, providing that farms of more than 200 acres would be broken up to favor the _fellahin_. This was a moderate measure, leaving intact estates one hundred times the size of those permitted in the North Vietnamese reform. It nevertheless provided the Egyptian revolution with a more popular base. Neguib and Nasser followed this legislation with a series of speeches; some of their friends even spoke in the mosques. They wished to curry favor with persons who had supported the Wafd, and to obtain influence with the followers of the Muslim Brethren, a basically religious society. In February 1953, the Neguib regime made an agreement with the British that the Sudanese should decide

419

the future of the Sudan. In June, the monarchy was abolished, and Neguib became the president of an Egyptian republic, retaining also the prime ministership.

The Free Officers supported Neguib, who had never joined their group, as long as he favored their policies. In his new position, however, Neguib emerged as a person who could attract independent popularity. He soon began to express his own ideas, which included a return to civilian rule and constitutionality. Nasser and other members of the revolutionary council disagreed, since they had every intention of claiming supreme power. Under their pressure, Neguib resigned his prime ministership on February 25, 1954. Many protests arose, and he reassumed the position three days later. Wafdists, Muslim Brethren, and others gave Neguib their open backing after these incidents, and waited for the month of June for announced free elections. On March 28, however, the council called off the elections, and Jamal Abd an-Nasir replaced Mohammad Neguib as prime minister. The leaders of all the old parties, including Wafd, heard themselves pronounced ineligible for cabinet positions during the next ten years.

Neguib remained as president, while Nasser carried on the talks initiated with the United Kingdom. In July 1954, the British agreed to evacuate the Suez Canal area. They retained the right to return, however, at any time in the following seven years that Egypt, any other Arab state, or Turkey might come under attack. The British asked for the special provision on the ground that the Egyptian army needed time to prepare to defend the canal. The Muslim Brethren, however, denounced the pact, and called for prime minister Nasser's ouster. In October, some of their number tried to kill Nasser. In November, the government crushed the organization, placing 4,000 of the Brethren in prison. For good measure, the prime minister relieved president Neguib of his position, and placed him under house arrest.

Nasser had not yet consolidated his "way" to Egyptian "liberation and strength." Once secure in power, however, he and his fellow officers looked to mammoth development plans as one salvation for their country. A high dam across the Nile River at Aswan, backing up water into the Sudan, formed the largest of the projects adopted for their agenda. This dam would provide flood control, irrigation, and electricity far beyond that hitherto available from a low dam at the same site. In December 1955, the United States offered help for the Aswan high dam in the form of large loans to help get the construction started. The World Bank for Reconstruction and Development stood ready to invest even larger sums to see the project through.

The plans for new "strength," however, ran athwart the striving for "liberation," equally important in Nasser's thinking. In January 1955, Egypt showed its strong distaste for the new Baghdad Pact, arranged by its recent antagonist Great Britain with the cooperation of Arab Iraq. In February, the Israelis again stung Egyptian pride by a raid into the "Gaza strip" of Palestinian territory, administered by Egypt since 1948. In April, on the other hand, Nasser received much acclaim at a "third world" conference in Bandung, Indonesia; there, delegates recognized him as a leader of the "nonaligned" world, committed to neither Washington or Moscow. When Great Britain and the United States declined to provide him with arms, which he believed necessary for defense against Israel, Nasser turned to arms talks with the Soviet Union. When he announced assistance from Russia and Czechoslovakia in September 1955, the Egyptian nation recognized a new liberation symbol. Nasser remained distant from communism; instead, he made it clear that as a Muslim he could consider no other faith. As a "third-world" leader, he had simply wanted to show that the future of Egypt depended upon no one save the Egyptians alone.

421

"Every nation . . . undergoes two revolutions," a younger Nasser had said. "One is political. . . . The second . . . is social, in which the classes of society would struggle against each other until justice for all countrymen has been gained. . . ." His social revolution derived from Karl Marx, though his statement of it suggested a paucity of reading and thinking along socially revolutionary lines. By the end of 1955, nevertheless, Jamal Abd an-Nasir had shown he possessed attributes not found in the ordinary soldier. As he saw the matter, his own revolution stood at its beginning rather than its conclusion. He stood well aware of the fact that he himself had yet to define it clearly.

Bolivia remained far from Egypt and North Viet-Nam in total count of people. The Quechua, Aymara, and mestizo population of Bolivia amounted to about 3,000,000. In their extremely low scale of living, however, the Indians of this country -- and most of the mestizos as well -- matched the disadvantaged masses in both Egypt and Viet-Nam. When social revolution came to Bolivia in 1952, and survived initially despite all the problems involved, the continent of South America felt the impact of a genuinely new experience.

In Egypt, Nasser's Free Officers led the revolution; in Viet-Nam, the Viet-Minh of Ho; in Bolivia, the Revolutionary National Movement with Víctor Paz Estenssoro at its head. Paz, a specialist in economic history, had held several posts with the Bolivian government and taught in the university. His party, the Movimiento Nacional Revolucionario or MNR, started as a small organization in 1941. Inspired by a high degree of nationalism, it also took an interest in socialism. The middle-class intellectuals who formed most of its early members agreed with Marxist goals as they interpreted them for Bolivia, though they disliked the Marxist program

422

for attaining the goals. MNR sought the backing of educated persons holding the franchise while courting favor among the people at large. In 1943, the party won attention by supporting a non-violent revolution bringing Gualberto Villaroel to power. Villaroel, a military man, was not a member of MNR. Under his administration, however, a first congress of Indians of Bolivia convened, and a large number of Bolivian miners organized a trade union with MNR sympathies. An anti-MNR coup in 1946 resulted in the death of Villaroel and the exile of MNR leaders. Paz found a position as a university professor in Argentina.

A fair election in 1947 brought in a mild reformist regime that ruled the country four years. MNR secured permission to enter the presidential campaign at the end of this term. To gather the strength it needed, it embarked upon a truly revolutionary course, seeking help especially from the now well-organized tin miners and their leader, Juan Lechín Oquendo. MNR announced that should it win, the government would nationalize the tin mines and engage in agrarian reform, and the Quechua and Aymara people would be brought into national life. A provision that only literate males could vote had always disfranchised the majority of the people. Running on such a radical program, and with a very narrow voting base, Paz (without leaving Argentina) won a plurality in the election of 1951, though his vote fell short of a majority. The congress which should have chosen the president in such circumstances, and which would have had to elect either Paz or one of his considerably less popular rivals, found itself blocked from action when a military junta took over the government.

MNR then decided, in company with Lechín's federation of miners, to use whatever force proved necessary to put its candidate into office. The relative unpopularity of the junta made the way easier. The revolutionary violence started on April 9, 1952; largely due to the armed efforts of the miners, it ended in two days with a victory for MNR. Nearly a week passed before Paz Estenssoro returned from Argentina for his inauguration as Bolivian president. He had managed to retain the favor of the party, operating as he did from some distance, by moving significantly to the left on the spectrum in response to his backers' demands. Once in the presidential chair, he found the pressure for reform even stronger than before.

Paz moved at once to dismantle the army that had blocked MNR from power, and to enfranchise the great mass of workers. No bloody reprisals took place against the army officials, though many of them lost their jobs. Country workers (the campesinos) received arms, as did the members of recently formed labor unions; these were the people, like the miners in 1952, who would protect the MNR program if force became necessary. Paz and his friends hoped, of course, that the granting of the franchise to very large numbers of people would keep MNR in power and the revolution in progress without any recourse to violence. Rather than abolish the army completely, they changed its character to that of an agency to help build the revolution, without the strength to override civil authority.

These were dramatic changes. The nationalization of the tin mines, however, carried still greater weight. Minerals accounted for more than 90% of Bolivia's exports, and tin stood by far the most important of the several minerals. The tin mines, developed in the nineteenth century, had brought great wealth to a very few Bolivians. Simón Patiño, one of them who had moved to Europe to live, counted as one of the most affluent individuals in the world. The great majority of Bolivians, however, received no benefit from the sales of the tin. (Investors in Chile owned nearly one-fourth of the production; parties in the United States, Switzerland, and England nearly one-fifth.) On July 2, 1952, the

424

government took over the control of the sales of Bolivian minerals, so that a greater share of the proceeds might be used for Bolivian projects. On October 31, the government nationalized the operations of the three largest tin mining companies, setting up its own Mining Corporation of Bolivia (Corporación Minera de Bolivia or COMIBOL) in their stead.

The miners themselves would choose two of the seven directors of COMIBOL. The new corporation existed only for their sake and that of the country. The old owners would receive payment, but stood completely removed from their strangle-hold on the Bolivian people at large. COMIBOL encountered immediate problems -- with mines too old to render a profit, with high officers lacking the proper experience for their jobs, with social goals for the workers far in excess of their previous experience, and with a declining world interest in tin. In the early years, however, COMIBOL functioned well, even paying off some of the indemnity (with no knowledge of what the total might be), failing only to provide financially for its own future.

On August 2, 1953, after considerable debate on the matter, the Paz government took its biggest step in the establishment of agrarian reform. Most of the organized discussion took place within the ranks of the Bolivian Labor Central, an agency created by the MNR as its contact with all the Bolivian trade unions. One party of workers represented the Communist outlook, and another identified with the Fourth International of Leon Trotsky. Most of the laborers, however, including the miners' segment headed by Juan Lechín, preferred a non-doctrinaire approach. Agrarian reform would come into existence to provide justice to the campesino, nothing more, nothing less -- though the leaders hoped that the nation would become more self-sufficient in its food supply during the process. Former owners would be paid for land confiscated, to be made available to the campesinos

425

on very easy terms. The size of farm permitted previous owners depended upon the region (with varieties of soil and products taken into account) and upon the use made of the land. The owner would receive favored consideration if he himself had participated in agricultural activity.

While officials discussed all these matters, many Quechua and Aymara farm laborers terminated their previous serf-like relationship with landowners through seizures of the land by force. The governmental reform, when it came, often only made legal that which had already become a reality. The campesino, whether through personal or legal action, at this point in Bolivian history became a free man. Before this, ever since the Spanish conquest, he had remained obliged to work for some wealthier individual -- either for nothing, under forced labor laws, or for next to nothing, in the system of debt peonage. Becoming a free man did not mean that the campesino would himself attain riches. His (generally) very small amount of land prohibited any accumulation of wealth. But the government encouraged both cooperatives and reinstitution of old Indian communal lands while offering some education in the use of up-to-date methods and laying plans for the opening of new areas to families willing to colonize.

In its beginnings, this revolution enjoyed tremendous success, despite the judgments of many prophets of doom. Its greatest triumph lay in the feeling it gave so many Quechua, Aymara, and mestizo people that Bolivia belonged to them. Paz and the men around him stood aware of the great difficulties such a financially poor nation faced. To overcome the most immediate ones, they secured in 1953 a friendly and generous hand of assistance from the United States. Why did the government in Washington, so opposed to agrarian reform in Guatemala at this same time, come up with help for the radical activities of Paz Estenssoro? Perhaps United States leaders wanted to indicate to the world that they did not disapprove of social reform in underdeveloped countries, regardless of what happened in Iran, Guatemala, and South Viet-Nam. Perhaps Washington felt more free to move in Bolivia because United States capital held no commanding influence there. Or perhaps president Paz won the aid by stressing the noncommunist nature of his program. Other than the MNR at the moment, there existed no party to which Bolivians might turn save tiny groups adhering to the person of Argentine Juan Perón or to the memory of either Leon Trotsky or Lenin. The MNR with all its drastic reform represented the height of moderate reasoning by comparison to any of these marginal challengers.

Three significant revolutions had passed their inauguration periods. That in Bolivia traveled the farthest in its first few years, though it functioned under generally democratic auspices. North Viet-Nam, doctrinally committed to a much farther-reaching program, found its revolutionary development frustrated by the prospect of resumed warfare. Egypt lacked a commitment to move in a specific direction, but followed a person truly bent on change, wherever that orientation might lead him. The United States government had not attempted to stop the revolutions in North Viet-Nam, Egypt, and Bolivia. Nevertheless, all three regimes faced great perils ahead. The fact that each one remained distinct from the others, and that each had at least beginners' success, meant that each might inspire a school of emulators. The significance of the three revolutions, if they managed to stay alive, lay not only in the changes they would bring to their peoples, but also in the examples they set for others who might follow the same nationalistic and socially revolutionary guidelines.

The Political Spectrum

Countries changed bands on the world spectrum in 1951-55 far less than in the preceding five years. The count of populations under democratic regimes of one degree or another dropped from about 57% of the world's total in independent countries to 53%, largely because of the defection of Egypt, South Africa, and Colombia from the third quarter to the fourth and the emergence of the two non-democratic Viet-Nams. The count of populations under socialist regimes of one degree or another remained close to the 59% figure of 1950, North and South Viet-Nam each balancing the other in this respect. Other shifts between bands and emergences of new nations involved populations too small to produce a significant difference in world totals.

Beginning with this chapter, national populations are mentioned in this section only for countries that become independent; that contain more than 100,000,000 people; or that move through the arbitrary boundaries of 500,000; 10,000,000; and 25,000,000. The population of the world climbed by 1955 to a total greater than 2,700,000,000, over nine-tenths of whom lived in their own nations.

The first band of the spectrum grew a little, from 36% to 37% of the world's non-colonial population, with the adherence of North Viet-Nam. In 1955, it contained 4 countries in the Orient and 9 in Europe. Mainland China (population 533-582,000,000) experienced rather drastic change at the hands of its Communist regime. The agrarian reform of 1950 reached most rural families outside of Tibet by 1952. Then, with famine threatening because of a bad season, as it had many times in the past, the government organized cooperatives on a large scale to increase food production. The nationalization of city industry came about only gradually, with emphasis on new

428

enterprises initiated by the government rather than rapid elimination of existing companies. As the government invested very widely, putting most of its money in large-sized projects, its efforts soon overshadowed the old, even in the construction stage. In 1954, the government began to buy shares in many private companies, thereby establishing joint ownerships.

China instituted its first five-year plan in 1953, modeling after the early experience of Stalin in the Soviet Union. China stood poorly prepared for rapid industrialization, however, and even with extensive Soviet help had to reduce its goals drastically. Widespread Chinese illiteracy proved one of the greater difficulties. The number of elementary students more than doubled and the number of secondary schools more than tripled from 1949 to 1955, but the nation still remained short of the administrative and technical skills demanded by an intensive industrial buildup. A large-scale birth-control program initiated in 1954 aimed to prevent nullification of industrial progress through population growth.

The Communist regime completed its occupation of the Chinese mainland in 1951, through re-institution of close Chinese control of Tibet. During 1912-49, though still considered a part of China, Tibet had largely managed its own business. The transition back to tighter Chinese rule proceeded with the understanding that Buddhist authority in Tibet would not be terminated, and that not all the Communist program would apply there. Xin Jiang Wei Wu Er (Sinkiang Uighur), north of Tibet and forming the entire northwestern corner of the country, became the second official autonomous region of the new China in 1955. Its Wei Wu Er (Uighur) people, about half its population, spoke a language of the Turkic branch of the Ural-Altaic family. Some testing of strength took place between Communist China and Tai Wan, especially in regard to islands lying between them, but Peking made no attempt to invade Tai Wan. Feelings between Peking and Washington remained bitter, even after the signing of the Korean truce.

A more permanent constitution in 1954 placed all the power in Communist hands, despite the continuance of some persons from other parties in prominent positions. Mao Ze Dong (Mao Tse Tung) became the chairman of the People's Republic, and Jou En Lai (Chou En Lai) the premier on the State Council. The "new" government, like that it replaced, remained outside the United Nations because of its role in the Korean warfare, and in other ways remained a stranger to people on other parts of the globe. Because of inadequate statistics, scholars found it difficult to assess developments on the Chinese mainland. (Published figures, not always in accord, tended to take their expression from percentages of growth, lacking any reference to actual volume.) Anticommunists everywhere hoped that China would encounter nothing but trouble. The desire to trade, however, slowly overcame other attitudes, with Japan and British Hong Kong resuming commercial ties even in the face of Washington's displeasure.

North Viet-Nam, North Korea, and Mongolia were the other three communist lands of the Orient. (For the first of these, see "Three Revolutions Inaugurated.") North Korea suffered much more from the war it started than did its southern counterpart, since more than a million North Korean people either died or took refuge in another country. A purge in the Korean Workers party eliminated South Korean elements in 1953. The government of Kim Il Sung instituted a three-year plan for recovery in 1954. Mongolia remained isolated from most of the world, while Soviet and Chinese advisers helped with a second five-year plan.

Developments in the Soviet Union (180-196, 000,000) have already received attention in "The Cold War" and "Three Steps in Human Dignity."

Most Soviet heavy industries reached the goal set for them in the Fifth Five-Year Plan coinciding with this quinquennium. West European and North American comforts and luxuries reached few Soviet consumers by 1955, but leaders believed they could provide some of these with a little more time. The agricultural sector advanced less rapidly than city industry, while leadership remained dissatisfied with its own farming plans. Under Stalin, collective farms continued to increase in size and decrease in number. Khrushchev favored farm decentralization and the opening of new land. Only at the very end of this period did the world fully realize that the Soviet Union had a new master with his own ideas.

In 1951-3, Poland (with its population again over the 25,000,000 mark) became even more firmly than before a communist state following the Soviet pattern as that pattern had developed under Stalin. In 1952, the year before Stalin died, Poland received a new constitution which left no room for party politics. Boleslaw Bierut, as secretary of the United Polish Workers party since 1948, president of the country 1947-52, and premier 1952-4, became the arbiter of Polish affairs as had Stalin in the Soviet Union. The constitution called for no president and no genuine elections, but only a slate of candidates for the parliament subject to the "approval" of the people. In 1953, the new government showed the firmness of its control when it seized the oppositionist archbishop and cardinal, Stefan Wyszynski, and placed him in a monastery. In 1954, while Bierut continued as secretary of the main party, Jozef Cyrankiewicz returned as premier, a concession to the "collective leadership" idea as developed in the Soviet Union. Some sign of a new Polish independence came in 1955, as the government abandoned a drive to collectivize all farms under state control and encouraged the growth of Yugoslav-style cooperatives. In the same year, however, a Polish six-year-plan for development (1950-5) failed in some of its objectives, provoking unrest.

Marshal Tito's emphasis on cooperatives during this period, with most of the state-owned collective farms abandoned, formed only a part of his plan for a truly independent Yugoslavia. Financial aid from the United States, the United Kingdom, and France enabled him to choose a course different from that which Moscow might have preferred for Yugoslavia. For a time, it looked as though Tito had decided to join the democratic socialist portion of the noncommunist camp. He drastically decentralized the country's economic and political structures, and in 1954 engaged in a 20-year mutual defense pact with Greece and Turkey, members of NATO. After extending the first five-year plan to a sixth year, so that it could meet most of its goals, he decided not to inaugurate a second. By 1955, however, with Bulganin and Khrushchev visiting Belgrade and actually offering apologies for the Yugoslav experience with Stalinism, it became clear that Tito did not intend to propel Yugoslavia into a closer relationship with the noncommunist lands, but only strove to maintain a third position in which he could remain on friendly terms with everyone.

In East Germany, premier Otto Grotewohl and party secretary Walter Ulbricht continued their difficult roles. Upon the death of Stalin, they instituted reforms intended to ease life for the East German people in a number of small ways. Apparently, the changes only served as a reminder of the considerable difference in treatment of East Germany and West Germany by their respective occupying powers. The East Germans demonstrated and rioted on June 16-17, 1953, until Soviet troops stepped in to restore order. In Soviet eyes, East Germany remained a defeated enemy, even after it became a Russian-recognized republic in 1954 and after the signing of a Soviet-East German pact in 1955. Grotewohl and Ulbricht still knew where to look for their orders.

Romania experienced considerable change as it

continued to follow the leader. A first five-year-plan, 1951-5, pushed industrialization rapidly and approached collectivization of agriculture more slowly; generally, the plan reached its goals. A shakeup of offices in 1952 placed Gheorghe Gheorghiu-Dej in the prime ministership. He had hitherto served as secretary for the Romanian Workers party, the largest of the groups in the governing coalition, the only one retaining status as a party after 1952. Romania like Poland turned to "collective leadership" in 1954, imitating the new era in Moscow. Gheorghiu-Dej lost his post with the party, but returned to it in 1955 with the appointment of a new premier in his place.

Collective leadership had prevailed in Czechoslovakia since its transition to communism in 1948. President Gottwald and premier Zapotocky continued in their offices until 1953, while other men served in important posts for both the state and the party. In 1951-2, nevertheless, a great reorganization and purge of the party took place, involving a number of hangings. Klement Gottwald died in 1953, after illness struck him when he attended the funeral of Stalin. Antonin Zapotocky then became president and Viliam Siroky premier, as the government turned toward friendlier relations with its people, many of whom had refused to cooperate in a communist-style regime. This nation's first five-year plan for development (1951-5) placed it in the vanguard of the Soviet satellites in regard to industrial production, the communist regime in Czechoslovakia having more than the others on which to build.

Hungary, Bulgaria, and Albania, the remaining communist states, also placed much emphasis on the ubiquitous five-year plans. The death of Stalin made a strong impact on Hungary, where Imre Nagy acted as premier 1953-5. Nagy and his cabinet decided in effect to make a temporary compromise with capitalism, hoping to improve the morale of the Hungarian people and to increase their food supply. Other concessions made to win popularity included the release of cardinal Jozsef Mindszenty from his life imprisonment. Some leaders of the Hungarian Workers party, however, agreed with an attitude in Moscow that Nagy had gone too far; for this reason, he lost his position. Bulgaria passed through no such experience, the leadership of its Communist party and Fatherland Front remaining the same throughout the quinquennium. Albania matched a Soviet example by divorcing the premiership and the secretaryship of its Labor party in 1953. Enver Hoxha retained the latter position as secretary-general and later first secretary.

The largest Communist parties in the non-communist world in 1955 were those of India and Indonesia, where millions of people voted for the first time in their experience. The Communist parties of Italy and France, however, stood the highest in percentage of the total vote in their countries, even though the French party showed less vigor than it had five years earlier. The Japanese Communist party lost so much backing that it no longer seemed a threat to those who followed a more democratic line.

The second band of the spectrum (4 countries in the Orient, 6 in Europe, 3 in the Americas, 2 in the Middle East in 1955) dropped from 23% to 22% of the world's non-colonial population, having changed only through the adherence of Bolivia. India (population 358-387,000,000), the largest of the countries favoring both democracy and socialism, moved slowly in the socialist direction while keeping its democracy intact. The first election under the constitution of 1950, held in 1952, gave Jawaharlal Nehru's National Congress a commanding lead, with nearly three-fourths of the seats in the lower house of parliament. The Communist, Praja (People's) Socialist, and Kisan Mazdoor Praja (Peasants, Workers, and People's) parties received far fewer votes on the national level, though they showed considerable strength in particular states. Praja socialism constituted a left-wing break-off from the National Congress, preferring to shift more rapidly toward socialism than Nehru, but with no less devotion to democracy. The Kisan Mazdoor Praja organization leaned more than the others toward the thinking of Gandhi.

India in 1951 began a five-year plan for the development of its economy, as had most of the communist-dominated lands. This plan differed, in that India's agriculture received first priority and its manufacturing industry second, and that in both realms private initiative constituted part of the planning. The government often initiated new industries or appropriated old ones it found badly mismanaged. It did not bother companies already serving the people in the majority of instances. From the beginning, the nation controlled most of its railroads; in 1953, it nationalized the aviation network; and in 1955, the leading bank of the country. Meanwhile, India made great efforts to feed itself. Real famine occurred in 1951, as it had from time to time in India's past, when crop failures added to the strain of very inefficient farming. Many people died from hunger again in 1952, when some states enjoyed a bumper crop but transportation to needy regions lacked proper management. India's problems at the beginning of this decade remained very difficult ones, and very plain for the world to see, because unlike the situation in the communist countries there existed no cover of secrecy.

Agitation inside India continued strong in regard to Kashmir, India's relationship to Pakistan, the problem of the treatment of the "untouchables" to which Gandhi had given his last strength, and the desire of many Indian people to live in states that would match India's languages. Andhra, comprising a portion of the Telugu-speaking area in the southeast, became the first of several new linguistic states in 1953. Untouchability, outlawed in India's new constitution, nevertheless caused trouble when persons with some caste standing refused to allow the underprivileged to enter temples and engage in wrestling matches. With former untouchables sitting in parliament, and the National Congress committed to the principle of equal treatment for them in regard to civil rights, their more complete entrance into society would depend upon education and time. Prime minister Nehru chose to think of the allegiance of Kashmir as a matter of education and time also, as he continued to prevent the Kashmiri people from engaging in a United Nations-sponsored plebiscite.

India's relations with Pakistan had remained soured from the beginning by the quarrel over Kashmir. Tension between the two nations increased when Pakistan joined SEATO in 1954 and became a large-scale recipient of United States arms. India committed itself to neither side in the Cold War. In 1954-5, Nehru paid friendly visits to Communist China, the Soviet Union, and Great Britain. Nehru hoped somehow to help bridge the gap between the various contenders, providing the world some relief from its Cold War anxieties. With genuine distress he found it necessary, in December 1955, to send Indian troops to a disputed zone on the border with Tibet, just entered by Chinese soldiers.

Efforts in the direction of democratic socialism in Burma continued to be threatened by the violence of minority groups of distinctive ideological or ethnic orientations. Elections held in late 1951 and early 1952 gave a large majority of legislative seats to the Anti-Fascist People's Freedom League, backing Thakin Nu, now U Nu, to continue as prime minister. (Thakin and U are both titles of respect rather than true names, the latter used for persons of greater experience and age.) U Nu sought to put an end to the civil wars by offering guarantees of special privileges to the ethnic minorities and by defeating other groups in combat. Burmese life settled down as Karen and other linguistically separate groups achieved the right to their own states within the Burmese union and representatives in the nation's cabinet. The most difficult of Nu's problems proved the occupation of a part of Burma by Chinese Nationalist troops fleeing China overland. The United States and Thailand helped settle this crisis through an evacuation of many of these soldiers to the island of Tai Wan.

Australia and New Zealand, the remaining second-quarter lands of the Orient, continued their moderate socialist regimes under parties of non-socialist orientation. In Australia, elections of 1954 brought the Labor party to the fore again as the most popular single group, but the Liberals formed a non-socialist governing coalition. In new elections of 1955, the Labor party lost the support of its own less radical wing, allowing the Liberals to triumph again. Actually, the contention in the campaigns in both Australia and New Zealand lay chiefly over cooperation with Washington in a "harder" stand against communism (the program of the Liberals and the right-wing Laborites) as against a "softer" approach favored by nations like India (the program of the Laborite majority).

In the United Kingdom of Great Britain and Northern Ireland, the largest of the European socialist democracies, the Labor party suffered the same inner division as that of Australia. Prime minister Clement Attlee and a majority of the party in this case, however, preferred close cooperation with the United States, while only a vociferous Labor minority wished to assume an independent position in the Cold War. Elections in October 1951, though they showed a considerable lead for the Labor party in the total popular vote, gave Labor only two more seats than the Conservatives, who thus formed a government in coalition with minor parties. Winston Churchill, the wartime prime minister, came back to his previous position. In 1943-5, Churchill had anticipated a strong postwar British role in the

437

game of the balance of power he assumed would continue. Now, until he finally retired at the age of 80, in the year 1955, he hoped to make some contribution toward ending the struggle of the powers, but found that for his active lifetime this would remain impossible. Anthony Eden, who had served with Churchill for many years, became premier in his stead. New elections of 1955 placed the Conservative party clearly in the lead. Another change in the London scene had come with the death of king George VI and the succession of his daughter queen Elizabeth II in 1952.

The Conservative administration of 1951-5 found itself besieged by difficulties. Cooperation with the government of the United States and the democratic nations of Europe often ran into problems. Great Britain had very recently posed as a world power, but could no longer jauntily set out on a course all its own. Troubles arose in nearly every part of the world where the British still held some control. In Iran, petroleum was the issue; in Egypt, the Suez Canal. In British Guiana, a party of Marxists won the elections; in Kenya, Kikuyu tribesmen called for a return of stolen farm lands. In Cyprus, many people favored a union with Greece. Churchill and Eden generally adopted an attitude of resistance to all new situations and demands. The Conservative leadership fared much better with the carrying out of a large program of aid to Commonwealth and former Commonwealth members in south and southeast Asia, the very places where political freedom had replaced British rule in the second half of the previous decade. The Colombo Plan, named for the capital of Ceylon where the mechanism originated in 1951, administered this extensive program. Meanwhile, at home, the Conservatives kept a promise to denationalize the iron and steel industry, reselling portions of it to the previous owners in 1953.

Great economic problems faced the Scandinavian countries, Finland, and Austria during these

438

years, reminding them that democratic socialism provides no guarantee of prosperity when nations remain dependent upon world markets. Sweden's Social Democratic party, taking unpopular anti-inflation measures, found it necessary to prop up its power by entering a coalition with a small non-socialist party. A minority Social Democratic party, whose opponents failed to band together, ruled Denmark after its adoption of a new constitution and unicameral parliament in 1953. Finland, completing its reparations payments to the Soviet Union in 1952, continued to move warily, with the chief socialist and private-enterprise parties nearly equal in strength. The Labor party in Norway maintained its status as the only one of the four socialist groups in these countries to obtain a clear majority of the vote. In Austria, the People's and Socialist parties continued their joint rule, and celebrated their country's peace treaty arranged in 1955.

Mexico, largest of the second-quarter countries of the Americas, showed that its democracy amounted to something more than simple theory when several parties campaigned actively for the presidency in 1952. The overwhelming support of the voters, however, went as usual to the Institutional Revolutionary party, which received about three-fourths of the ballots. Adolfo Ruiz Cortines, the new president, demonstrated that his party had not become dormant because of its near-monopoly position. He felt that his predecessor, Miguel Alemán, had neglected agriculture in favor of city industry and had shown personal friends too many favors. Ruiz Cortines intended to boost agriculture during his term (lands continued to be expropriated in a program begun in the 1930's), and he hoped to eliminate much of the corruption that had crept in since the time of Cárdenas. While maintaining friendship with the United States, Ruiz indicated that Mexico disagreed with Washington policy concerning social revolution in Guatemala, on Mexico's other border.

Bolivia, moving to this band on the spectrum with its revolution in 1952, found it difficult in 1954-5 to keep the revolution intact, when elements of the prior regime attempted to unseat the new government by violence. The Paz regime had also to contend with staggering inflation, as prices from 1950 to 1955 rose to more than eleven times their former (already swollen) level. Uruguay suffered economic difficulties much like those of Scandinavia, and political problems with the Perón regime in Argentina. The presence of many Argentine opponents of Perón as refugees in the Uruguayan capital helped to exacerbate political relations. In the midst of its tribulations, however, Uruguay adopted a new plan of government in 1952, replacing the president of the country with an executive council of nine members. Three of the nine would represent the largest minority party, and the other six speak for the majority. Uruguay had tried the council method of government before, during 1919-34.

Turkey remained the largest of two second-quarter countries in the Middle East. The Democratic party continued its control of Turkey, with Celal Bayar the president and Adnan Menderes the premier, through elections of 1954 in which they won more than nine-tenths of the parliamentary seats. Turkish people became very concerned in 1955 as the Greek population on the island of Cyprus clamored for union with Greece. Though Greece and Turkey were both members of NATO, and both signatories to a pact with Yugoslavia, relations between them became very strained.

Israel also maintained its commitment to democratic socialism. Many Jewish people came to Israel from Arab lands, especially those of North Africa. They searched for homes and jobs not always easy to find; their lives became even more difficult when prices more than doubled. Immigration of Jews from Europe and North America remained at a lower level than Israeli leaders had expected and desired. Financial aid, both

440

public and private, however, came from the United States on a grand scale. Thus Israel obtained the resources to pursue its economic aims, making a sizeable portion of barren countryside blossom, while Arabic countries on all sides did little by comparison. Israel, much criticized and twice censured by the United Nations Security Council for infractions of the cease-fire of 1949, continued in a state of war with all its neighbors.

The picture of the democratic socialist parties not in power during this period changed significantly only in Japan. There the Social Democratic party split in 1951 over support for the peace treaty with the United States. Both wings of the party grew in strength (while the Communist party was losing), and they reunited in 1955 as the Socialist party, with more than triple the former strength. Other second-quarter parties of considerable size were the Social Democratic of West Germany, Labor of Brazil, the Socialist party of France, and a growing left-wing (willing to form a front with the Communists) Socialist party of Italy. Besides these, the Labor party of the Netherlands and the Socialist party of Belgium continued, as well as a growing Socialist party in Switzerland. The Second (democratic) Socialist International reconstituted itself in West Germany in 1951, with most of these parties as members. Thereafter, meetings took place nearly every year.

The democratic private-enterprise countries (7 in the Americas, 8 in the Orient, 8 in Europe, 5 in the Middle East) made up 31% of the world's non-colonial population in 1955, a net loss of 3% during the quinquennium. Iraq, Cambodia, and Laos joined the third quarter of the world spectrum. The losses to the fourth quarter ran heavy: Egypt, South Africa, Colombia, Cuba, Guatemala, and Liberia. Bolivia alone moved from the third to the second quarter.

The United States of America (population 152-

166,000,000) forged its way into world headlines several times during these five years. Much of its story has already appeared in "The Cold War," "Three Steps in Human Dignity," and "Three Revolutions Interrupted." There remain to be explained the dismissal of general Douglas MacArthur from his posts in Korea and Japan, the election of Dwight David Eisenhower to the presidency, and the developing position of labor in the nation's economy.

After the Korean fiasco of late 1950, when the North Koreans and Chinese pushed back United Nations forces and encircled them, many people held general MacArthur responsible, believing he had acted with too great zeal and independence in his conduct of the war. He had obviously misjudged the intentions of the Chinese, and he spoke often of the "necessity" of widening the conflict to include both mainland China and Tai Wan. On April 11, 1951, president Truman removed general MacArthur from his positions, citing insubordination to the commander-in-chief (Truman himself) and an open clash with his own government on matters of foreign policy. The general came home, upon his dismissal, and received a tumultuous welcome by the citizenry, who for the first time had the opportunity to render him homage for his services in World War II. Many said that MacArthur reasoned wisely and the president weakly about extending the Korean conflict. MacArthur himself believed that the people's desire to follow that policy might bring him the presidency in 1953. As matters turned out, however, he could not compete with another general who had said he would do all he could to stop the Korean war.

In 1952, enthusiasm for Dwight Eisenhower as the Republican nominee ran very high while he remained in Europe. The more conservative faction within the party shied away at first (a portion of it supporting MacArthur), but rendered its support after Eisenhower became the candidate. Adlai Ewing Stevenson, the governor

442

of Illinois and nominee of the Democrats, stressed his convictions as a liberal and internationalist in a brilliant series of campaign speeches, and won the support of more votes than ever before accorded a loser. His failure to match the total of Eisenhower may be attributed chiefly to the fact that his opponent had become popular during the war years. Republican propagandists who labeled the conflict in Korea "Truman's war" presumably aided their own ticket, as did the general when he asserted on the last day of the campaign that he would go to Korea in person to attempt to end the war. He did travel to Korea in December, but Stalin's death in March 1953 rather than Eisenhower's inauguration in January provided the catalytic agent needed for a Korean truce.

While much of Eisenhower's attention as president became focused upon matters of the Cold War as he and his secretary of state perceived them, neither he nor anyone else in the United States government could ignore a continuing wave of strikes at home. In 1952 as in the previous quinquennium, cessations of activity took place in the basic coal and steel industries. Other important strikes that followed generally affected one company at a time rather than an entire industry. Labor achieved genuine gains, some of them by way of strikes, and some through quiet bargaining. In 1955, a union of the American Federation of Labor and the Congress of Industrial Organizations gave the skilled and semi-skilled laboring man an added strategic advantage.

The person on wages improved his purchasing power further as the whole economy prospered through war industry. The gross national product in current dollars rose more than 28% per capita. Since the cost of living for working-class people rose 11% during the same years, however (almost all of it in 1950-2, the time of the Korean conflict and general military build-up) the real increase in buying ability as measured in constant dollars amounted to a little over 13%.

Brazil had its economic problems also, while moving at a considerably lower level. Inflation in Brazil ran rampant, with more than a doubling of the cost of living. Getúlio Vargas started his second term as president early in 1951, with a great deal of planning for the laboring man. The business interests of the country, however, took no interest in socially oriented legislation. Their representatives in the congress and their conservative newspapers made out that Vargas' ideas stood close to communism. While McCarthyism flourished in the United States, Brazil experienced its own brand, backed by precisely the same kinds of people. The only congressional backing Vargas received for his program supported a nationally controlled petroleum industry, which came into being at this time. The clamor against Vargas became intense in 1954 when blame focused on the administration for the attempted assassination of Carlos Lacerda, conservative newspaper publisher. Getúlio Vargas committed suicide in August 1954; his vice-president João Café, succeeded him. In late 1955, Juscelino Kubitschek of the (non-socialist) Social Democratic party won the presidency and João Goulart of the Labor party the vice-presidency, running as a team. Labor party strength ran about half of that of the Social Democrats in the congress, the National Democrats also holding more seats than Labor. The Social Progressive (liberal) and Republican (conservative) parties won minor representation.

Canada continued its tranquil course in cooperation with both the United States and the United Kingdom. Louis St. Laurent stayed on as prime minister, backed by the Liberal majority in parliament which passed successfully through the elections of 1953. The Progressive Conservatives held less than one-third as many seats as the Liberals. Canada played a very active role in NATO, and in 1954 made an agreement with the

United States for a "Distant Early Warning" (DEW) line of radar stations to help protect both countries from the threat of Soviet air flights over the Arctic region. Canada retained its individuality, however, as Canadians of all parties became incensed at suggestions from Washington that the Canadian foreign minister, Lester Pearsall, had cooperated with communism. For some reason, Canadians did not succumb to McCarthyism like so many persons in the United States.

Besides Brazil, only four countries of Latin America leaned toward democratic private enterprise in 1955, just half the number of a decade earlier. Chile, distressed with continuing extreme monetary inflation (prices nearly sextupled), elected Carlos Ibáñez del Campo, a dictator of 1927-31, as president for the six-year term beginning in 1952. Some fear existed that Ibáñez might try to establish one-man rule, following his own previous pattern and that of his friend Juan Perón of Argentina; the Chilean parliament, however, survived. Ecuador also chose a former leader as president in a new term from 1952; its congress like that of Chile contained a variety of parties. José Figueres came to rule in Costa Rica through elections in 1953. The several reforms enacted included nationalization of the banks, but Costa Rica remained at a point a little to the right of socialism. Arnulfo Arias, the president of Panama, again lost his office by coup in 1951. Assassination ended the career of the next elected president, 1952-5. The second designee for the position took the dead president's place, the first designee being impeached for involvement in the murder. During this confusion, negotiations produced a new treaty with the United States, providing an increase in the annuity for the Panama Canal.

Japan, the largest country of the Orient in the third quarter of the spectrum, forged close ties with the United States in 1951. First, Washington acting without its allies made an

445

agreement with Japan on peace terms. The countries that had declared war against Japan received invitations to San Francisco in September 1951, not to discuss the terms but to approve them. India, Burma, and Yugoslavia refused to attend this conference with its flavor of pre-ordination, and the Soviet Union refused to sign the treaty, though 47 nations besides the United States and Japan did vote on it affirmatively. The peace treaty gave the United States the right to administer the Japanese Ryukyu Islands, the largest of which is Okinawa. A special security pact signed by only the United States and Japan granted the former the privilege of maintaining air, land, and sea military bases on Japanese territory, and recognized Japan's right to rearm for its own defense. In early 1954, the Japanese recreated their army, navy, and air force.

Yoshida Shigeru, Japan's very pro-Washington prime minister, continued to hold office until late 1954, even though his (nineteenth-century) Liberal party performed less well than formerly in elections of 1953. Through a complex set of shifts involving both ideologies and personalities, Hatoyama Ichiro took Yoshida's place as premier, promising to discuss peace terms with the Soviet Union and expanded trade relations with Communist China. In late 1955, when the split opposition group of Social Democrats reunited as the Socialist party, the Liberal and People's Democratic organizations, both of which preferred private initiative in the economy, decided in self-defense that they should also unite, as the Liberal-Democratic party favoring Hatoyama.

Indonesia moved cautiously during most of this period toward the situation in which a genuine political campaign might be waged. President Sukarno wanted the people to be represented, and for that reason took regular counsel from a cabinet of widely variant views. He also wanted fair elections to determine the composi-

446

tion of a parliament, but feared the disunity that might accompany the campaign. Finally, in late 1955 two general elections took place, both providing proportional representation for parties -- one to choose the membership of a provisional parliament, the other to set up a constituent assembly. Sukarno did not participate in the campaign, and scarcely any persons who won held his democratic socialist views. The Indonesian Nationalist party, the Masjumi or Indonesian Muslim Council (liberal), the Muslim Schoolmen League (conservative), and the Indonesian Communist party won the largest numbers of seats among the approximately twenty political groups. Sukarno nevertheless remained personally popular. In April 1955, his regime joined with those of India, Pakistan, Burma, and Ceylon to sponsor a first Asian-African conference at Bandung, on the island of Java.

Pakistan took even more time to get its democracy organized than did Indonesia. Assassination terminated the regime of Liaquat Ali Khan, prime minister of the provisional government, in October 1951, the nation thus being deprived of the second of the two men who had done the most to secure Pakistan's freedom. Khwaja Nazimmudin, premier 1951-3, and Muhammad Ali, his successor, ruled Pakistan while two constituent assemblies tried to put this nation together. The first one, established since 1947, brought out its constitution in 1954. Under its terms, Pakistan would become a republic rather than a dominion, though retaining the tie to Great Britain through the Commonwealth as had India. The republic would be offically tied to the Muslim faith; West Pakistan and East Pakistan would be represented at parity. The Muslim League, of the struggle for independence, favored these decisions. In East Pakistan, however, the League did poorly in local elections of 1954, while a left-wing coalition of several parties gained a large majority. In 1955, with East Pakistan under military control, Chaudhri Muhammad Ali took Muhammad Ali's place, initiating a new study of

447

the national constitution. In the meantime, Pakistan's relations with India remained difficult, due to India's refusal to change its position on Kashmir and Pakistan's willingness to join both SEATO and the Baghdad Pact.

In the Philippines government, Ramón Magsaysay served as part of the Liberal regime of Elpidio Quirino until 1953, and then switched to become the Nationalist candidate for the presidency. He and the Nationalists won, receiving the support of a smaller Democratic National party which split from the Liberals. Magsaysay, both before and after 1953, worked hard to eliminate the Hukbalahap problem, using both force (against the leaders) and good treatment (for the farmers who followed the leaders) to accomplish his objective. He succeeded well by 1955, and by that time also secured a reputation as a very genuine liberal, engaged in weeding out corruption and establishing an agrarian reform program. His career signified that in the Philippines the individual counted for more than the party.

Thus lay matters also in South Korea, where Syngman Rhee's administration outlasted the war and two elections running on a Liberal ticket. Rhee took every opportunity to prove himself a conservative as the war went on, and would have earned the title of despot had he not maintained popularity with the majority of his people. Rhee lost the confidence of many delegates who had voted to make him president in the first national assembly, and could not count on the second one to reelect him in 1952. He then sponsored an amendment to the constitution to provide for direct election of the president, and insisted by some show of force that the Assembly vote for the amendment. According to official count, nearly three-fourths of the people voted him a four-year term. The Liberal party which supported Rhee won a clear majority in assembly elections in 1954. At that time, he stood on the world scene as the globe's chief proponent of enlarged international warfare. In the meantime, his country's economy suffered the world's worst inflation of this time period, prices rising to 32 times their former levels.

The Orient held three more third-quarter countries in 1955, two of them having become independent only one year earlier. The government of Ceylon continued its generally tranquil and neutral course with the United National party in control, and a succession of prime ministers. Tamil-language and Marxist-oriented minorities expressed much unhappiness, at one point venting their feelings through riots. Cambodia and Laos ceased to be protectorates of France in late 1954, as the result of the French defeat at Dien Bien Phu and the talks at Geneva. Each of the two had its own principal language -- Lao (a Kadai tongue) for Laos and Khmer for Cambodia -- while a minority in Laos spoke the Miao language of southern China. Theravada Buddhism served as the chief religion of both countries. Norodom Sihanouk, the very popular king of Cambodia (population 5,000,000), declared complete independence in 1953 and again in 1955, though France continued to speak of Cambodia and Laos as associated states in the French Union. Norodom abdicated the Cambodian throne in favor of his father in 1955, after which elections resulted in complete victory for his Popular Socialist Community, basically personalist rather than socialist in nature. As Sihanouk, he then became the prime minister, a position he preferred over that of king. Laos (population 2,000, 000), like Cambodia, followed a constitutional, limited monarchy. The Geneva conferees expected both monarchies to remain neutral in the Cold War. Laos, however, found neutrality difficult when the same powers declared that pro-communist Pathet Lao forces might continue to occupy two of Laos' twelve provinces. The cost of living in Laos more than doubled during this period.

West Germany held the largest population of the several European countries subscribing to democratic private enterprise. In 1955, the United States, British, and French governments recognized West Germany completely as a sovereign state, though the industrial district of the Saar remained tentatively in French hands. Political indpendence came accompanied by a great wave of prosperity, West German industry having recovered (with help) from the havoc of the war. Elderly Konrad Adenauer continued as prime minister after elections in 1953 which favored the Christian Democratic party, giving it a slight majority of the seats in the Bundestag. Adenauer retained the coalition with the Free Democrats, however, since the Social Democratic party, with slightly over half the Christian Democratic strength, stood opposed to Adenauer's program for rearming West Germany under the structures of NATO and the Brussels Pact.

Italy's acceptance of rearmament and membership in NATO came earlier than that of West Germany, and rested very uneasily on the less prosperous Italian economy. Christian Democracy in Germany, to augment the contrast, had for its chief opposition the Social Democratic group calling for neutrality; in Italy, the Christian Democrats contended with the Communist party taking its signals from Moscow. Alcide De Gasperi continued as Italian prime minister until 1953, but sponsored no reforms that showed genuine promise of changing the Italian situation. The Christian Democrats received the largest number of votes again in elections of 1953, but lost their clear majority. The Communist vote remained about the same, but the Socialists willing to cooperate with them grew in standing while the Socialists who had cooperated with De Gasperi until 1951 lost strength. The Christian Democratic party, itself divided between liberal and conservative factions, had to find alliances somewhere. Some looked for an "opening to the right," meaning cooperation with the Monarchists and the neo-fascist Italian Social Movement. Others favored an "opening to the left," seeking coalition with the left-wing Socialists. Neither plan materialized, however, and the government limped along with four prime ministers in two-and-a-fraction years (1953-5) supported by the Christian Democrats and some small parties of the center.

France received a new electoral law in May 1951, intended by the center forces which voted for it to modify proportional representation a little, in the hope of strengthening center co-alitions that would be formed. The bill made less difference than expected, however. The largest three parties after elections in June were the Rally of the French People (a group on the far right pledged to Charles de Gaulle) and after them the Socialists and the Communists. The Popular Republicans and Radicals, whose vote ran somewhat smaller, continued to be repre-sented in the cabinets, none of which lasted as long as one year. At first they combined with the Socialists, later with the Independent party (conservative). After the Gaullists split into two organizations (the larger Social Republican party and the somewhat more liberal Group for Republican and Social Action), Pierre Mendès-France served as premier for nearly eight months in 1954-5, backed by a center-right combination of the Radicals, the Independents, and the two Gaullist groups. The quinquennium ended with a cabinet excluding Mendès-France but including these same parties along with the Popular Repub-licans.

The French workingman during these years saw little attention paid to his needs. If he read the papers, he realized that the Germans who so recently held the French homeland had actually gone farther than he in overcoming the stresses of the war period. He may have felt also that his former British and American allies showed more solicitude concerning West German welfare than that of France. Certainly, no show of sympathy for France materialized as the French pulled out of the Viet-Nam conflict; nor did pro-French feeling manifest itself as unrest

451

appeared in Morocco, Algeria, and Tunisia. The French governments which had to face up to these realities, even to the inclusion of German forces in NATO, found little enthusiasm for their decisions among the people of France. A modest program to aid the French workers after an intense wave of strikes in 1953 seemed only to rub salt into wounds that had opened. There existed no viable solutions for anything, because France could control its own destiny only on the domestic front, and on domestic questions the parties within each coalition disagreed.

The Netherlands enjoyed more prosperity than did France. Willem Drees, the Dutch premier since 1948, resigned his position from time to time only to be reappointed. Drees' Labor party and the Catholic People's party possessed nearly even strength, and served together in the governing coalitions. The Dutch held an advantage over the French in that the Dutch had already accepted the loss of most of their previous empire. Indonesia and the Netherlands, however, continued to argue about the status of West New Guinea.

Europe contained four more democratic private-enterprise regimes, each with its own politics and problems. In Belgium, the Social Christian party governed until 1954, when a coalition headed by the second-place Socialists took over. Switzerland in elections of 1951 and 1955 witnessed a slow growth of its Socialist party, though a coalition of non-socialist groups continued to hold the power. Ireland experienced electoral upsets in 1951 and 1954, but neither new regime showed any desire to end Ireland's position as a neutral. Eamon De Valera again served as premier between those dates. Greece held new elections in 1951 and 1952, modifying its proportional representation system in the first and eliminating it altogether in the second. Thus the Populists, reorganizing as the Greek Rally, climbed to a position of undisputed leadership, with 49% of the people's vote but 80%

of the seats in parliament.

Iran became the largest of the third-quarter countries in the Middle East. After the Mosaddeq period and intervention by the CIA (see "Three Revolutions Interrupted"), Iran returned in early 1954 to the forms of democracy without much regard for its spirit. In the election held then, the shah's choices for the Majles won, while party lines became obliterated.

The switch of Iraq from the fourth to the third quarter in 1954 brought about a total of four smaller Middle Eastern countries with some claim to third-quarter standing. Nuri as-Said, a strong man, ruled Iraq, with a king who assumed his duties at the age of 18, in 1953. In an absence of parties, Nuri's followers won more than two-thirds of the seats in parliament, in three elections 1953-4. They spoke of plans for reform, but Nuri had already served as prime minister several times since 1930. Syria slipped back into the fourth quarter as an army colonel seized the reins of power in 1951. Free elections in 1954 proved the end of that regime, but no one party emerged with more than one-fourth of the vote. Lebanon experienced quarrels between its Muslim and Christian people over the matter of a census to determine the nations' religious composition. Assassination came to the king of Jordan in 1951. The state declared his son mentally incompetent in 1952, and made his grandson king in 1953 -- at the age of 18, like his second cousin in Iraq. Delegates from the area that had formed a part of Palestine filled half of the Jordanese parliament.

Sub-Sahara Africa no longer held a roster in the third quarter in 1955, both South Africa and Liberia having moved over to the fourth band. Most of Sub-Sahara Africa remained non-self-governing during this time.

Fascist-type countries made up 10% of the

world's non-colonial population in 1955, a gain of 3% since five years previously. There were 2 of them in Europe, 4 in the Orient, 5 in the Middle East, 3 in Sub-Sahara Africa, and 12 in the Americas. Six of the countries new in the fourth quarter (all but one of them from the third) have received special treatment in this chapter -- Egypt, South Africa, Colombia, newly independent South Viet-Nam, Cuba, and Guatemala. Liberia from the third quarter and newly independent Libya also joined this band.

Spain went through the quinquennium with Francisco Franco and the Falange party again, its people having to yield to continued encroachments on civil liberties even while their government received better treatment internationally. An agreement of 1953 provided naval and air bases to the United States in exchange for financial aid to Spain. Two years later, despite the anti-Franco feeling prevalent in many countries, Spain became a member of the United Nations. In the meantime, the Franco regime abused minority groups, placing in prison and executing anarchists of the Catalan-speaking area, keeping the monarchists under strict control, dismissing a priest-editor for speaking out on freedom of speech, and permitting zealous Spanish Catholics to raid Spanish Protestant places of worship. Portugal remained under the rule of premier António Salazar, who conducted farcical elections in 1953, after intiating in the previous year a six-year plan for industrial development in both country and colonies.

Thailand continued five more years under the prime ministership of Pibul Songgram and the kingship of Bhumibol Adulyadej. A coup against the premier in late 1951 only brought him a return of his position with more power than before, holding the right to appoint half of his legislature in accord with constitutional provisions prior to 1946. Tied to the United States by friendship and the SEATO treaty, and feeling threatened by the formation of a Thai communist

454

"republic" and army in south China, Pibul spent large sums of money preparing to meet the menace. Advised by American counselors that a Thai social security system and agrarian reform might help to counter disaffection among the people, he placed both plans on the books without implementing them. Late in 1955, he invited the SEATO signatories to use Thai territory for war games.

The legislature of Tai Wan extended the presidency and dictatorship of Chiang Kai Shek for a new six-year term from 1954. Prices in Tai Wan (like prices in South Viet-Nam) more than doubled as Chiang received financial aid from Washington, to prepare for renewed war with Communist China and to spur the Taiwanese economy. Land reform on the mainland found its echo in Tai Wan, where during 1952-4 government initiative turned a large percentage of the land over to the peasants who tilled it. King Tribhuvan of Nepal returned home from India in 1951, but found himself unable to follow through with his desire to democratize that mountain kingdom. When he died in 1955, his son Mahendra Bir Bikram succeeded him, ruling at first as his own prime minister.

Egypt fitted the fourth quarter of the spectrum on the basis of its revolutionary program through 1955, though its rulers held very different ideas from those of the four remaining Middle Eastern countries of this band. Afghanistan retained its old-fashioned quality under the rule of Mohammad Zahir, though both sides in the Cold War offered money for the development of the country. Zahir continued propaganda for the formation of a Pashtunistan in the territory of West Pakistan, and in 1955 a mob hauled down the flag from the Pakistani legation; the two nations severed relations briefly. After this incident, very late in the year, the Bulganin-Khrushchev team from the Soviet Union visited Afghanistan.

Saudi Arabia, enriched even more by developments in the petroleum industry (a new pipeline to the Mediterranean, and the sharp cutback on

455

competition from Iran) continued as an absolute monarchy when Abd al-Aziz Al Saud (Ibn Saud) died and a son succeeded him in 1953. In Yemen, the ruler's brother attempted revolt in 1955, only to be arrested and executed. Libya, one more country speaking Arabic and holding to the Muslim creed, received its independence as a federated constitutional monarchy dominated by its king. on December 24, 1951. Libya (population 1,000,000), under the control of Italy prior to World War II, with "freedom" had to negotiate separately with British, French, and United States forces remaining on its territory.

All three independent countries of Sub-Sahara Africa pertained to the fourth quarter in 1955. Ethiopia, not overlooked by the United States in that country's quest for security, signed a mutual assistance pact with Washington in 1953. A year earlier, Eritrea had joined Ethiopia in a federation ruled by Haile Selassie, in accord with the United Nations decision of 1950. The majority of the Eritrean people differed little from those of Ethiopia. They added to Ethiopia's Muslim population, and their languages, about five in number, represented the Semitic and Cushitic stocks and the separate Sudanic family. The Ethiopian people received a new constitution in 1955, stipulating their right to elect a parliament every four years; but since the members of the cabinet remained responsible to Haile Selassie, the monarch's control remained undiminished. South Africa's turn toward one-party control appeared in "Three Losses for Democracy." Liberia continued its True Whig government under William Vacanarat Shadrach Tubman, president since 1944. It regressed from the third to the fourth quarter in 1955, when the parliament declared all other parties illegal.

Latin America contained twelve of the fascist-type countries in 1955, nearly half of the world's total in this band. Argentina remained the largest of the Latin American dozen. There Juan Perón and his Peronista party ruled until

1955, after Perón's election for a second term, as the façade quality of its pretended democracy became ever more obvious. The name of Eva Duarte de Perón became linked with that of her husband as a vice-presidential candidate in 1951. Eva withdrew, however, because the group of generals who had brought Juan to power did not think a woman (and an under-age one at that) should stand for such high office. Juan won the presidency as he had six years earlier, with the Radical party retaining a few seats in the congress, over-whelmed by the Peronistas around them. Less than two months after the new term began in 1952, Eva died of cancer. Since she had won the hearts of Argentina's masses, through her sympathy extended to them in personal contacts day after day, many believed that the Peronista movement would deter-iorate with her death. A great mass of laboring people, however, remained loyal to Juan, if for no other reason than that he decreed new minimum wages each year to help keep them at par with the harsh inflation. The Argentine cost of living more than doubled during this period, like that of Brazil.

Perón initiated a program of stern suppres-sion of disloyal sentiment in 1953. Brushing closely with death from two bombs, he ordered the arrest of oppositionists, and allowed their of-fices to be burned without police intervention. The Catholic hierarchy, which had earlier given Perón its support, became a major source of cri-ticism, especially after difficulties between Peronists and Catholic labor unions. After a mid-term election in 1954, for half of the seats in the congress, Perón held Radical party leaders responsible for "disrespect" shown to him during the campaign. By late 1954, the quarrel with Roman Catholic bishops became very intense, and Perón undertook a number of measures (such as the legalization of prostitution and divorce) that he knew would infuriate the prelates. Elements in the armed forces came to feel that Perón, origi-nally their man, had gone too far in lashing out against those who disagreed with him. After an

457

abortive attempt in June 1955, they succeeded in September in removing him from the presidential chair. In November, they announced that Argentina would return, under army auspices, to free elections and democracy.

The non-democratic regimes of Gustavo Rojas Pinilla in Colombia, Fulgencio Batista with his Progressive Action party in Cuba, and Carlos Castillo Armas with his National Democratic Movement in Guatemala all began in this quinquennium (see "Three Losses for Democracy" and "Three Revolutions Interrupted"). Similarly cast administrations in Peru and Venezuela continued throughout this period. That of Peru held Víctor Raúl Haya de la Torre in enforced residence in the Colombian embassy for five years (1949-54) and would not allow Haya's party (APRA) to enter the campaign for free elections promised for 1956. The military junta of Venezuela, in power since 1948, retained its group hold until 1952, when one of its members emerged as that country's dictator-president.

Either a previous or a new caudillo ruled each of another half-dozen Latin American countries. In Haiti, the regime set up in 1950 stayed in office through this period. Rafael Trujillo asked his brother to occupy the presidency of the Dominican Republic for five years from 1952. El Salvador kept its "progressive" but non-democratic leader who had taken office in 1950. Honduras edged its way toward democracy until 1954, when physician Ramón Villeda Morales, a genuine twentieth-century Liberal, received a high plurality in a three-way presidential election. The opposition parties refused to attend the congress which would have chosen him or a less popular rival as president, and the vice-president assumed power to run the election again. Paraguay went through a more simple process to exchange one dictator for another in 1954, while Paraguayan prices reached more than seven times their former level. Nicaragua remained under the thumb of Anastasio Somoza García.

458

Aside from the attainment of nationhood by North and South Viet-Nam, Cambodia, Laos, and Libya, and the federation of Eritrea with Ethiopia, few significant changes occurred in the colonial world. France ceded its small colonies on the shore of India to the government of India -- the first in 1952, the remaining four in 1954. Portugal, seeing the wave of national aspirations in crescendo, decided to hold its empire more closely than before. The colonies Mozambique, Angola, Portuguese Guinea, Portuguese Timor, Macao, the Cape Verde Islands, and São Tomé-Príncipe all became Portuguese "overseas provinces" in 1951. The Netherlands likewise made over Surinam and the Netherlands Antilles (Curaçao and other isles) from colonies into integral parts of the Netherlands kingdom in 1954. Greenland became a part of Denmark in 1953. Puerto Rico transformed itself into an associated state of the United States when it adopted a new constitution calling itself a "commonwealth" in 1952. The British in 1953 pulled together the colony of Southern Rhodesia and the protectorates of Nyasaland and Northern Rhodesia in the federation of Rhodesia and Nyasaland. France in 1955 organized the overseas territory of French Southern and Antarctic Lands, consisting of tiny islets. With the reconstitution of Indochina in 1954, Nigeria became by far the largest colony in the world, quietly working its way to self-government under the British flag. Violence in British-held Kenya and Cyprus and incipient struggles against the French in Morocco, Algeria, and Tunisia indicated that new moves for independence would materialize very soon.

International organizations and meetings continued to play a role in world history. The Asian-African Conference held at Bandung, Java, April 18-24, 1955, constituted a new type of movement along international lines. India, Indonesia, Pakistan, Burma, and Ceylon extended the invitations. Ali Sastroamidjojo, prime minister of Indonesia, had fathered the idea.

459

Fourteen of the nations of the Orient sent representatives -- all but South and North Korea, Australia, New Zealand, and Mongolia. Eleven delegations came from the Middle East, omitting only Israel in that area. From Sub-Sahara Africa, Ethiopia and Liberia were joined by persons representing the Gold Coast and the Sudan, working their way toward nationhood; South Africa received no invitation. The Bandung conference lay outside developed patterns of ideological orientation. Two delegations represented communist lands; two, democratic socialist regimes; 14, countries which could be labeled democratic private-enterprise; and nine, states of the fascist band. Communist China and North Viet-Nam contrasted with rightist Thailand and South Viet-Nam. Neutralist countries like India and Burma balanced United States allies such as Pakistan and the Philippines. The 29 powers present did hold some attributes in common. They were poor, "underdeveloped" lands (with the exception of Japan); most of them had felt victimized by colonialism; and all contained a majority of "non-white" (though not necessarily non-Caucasoid) people. After a week of consultation and speech-making, they agreed on (1) principles of economic and cultural cooperation, in regard to the former of which they requested more United Nations and World Bank aid; (2) the principle of self-determination of peoples, with particular reference to the rights of North Africans and Palestinian Arabs; (3) the promotion of world peace, with a request that Asian and African countries be better represented on the United Nations Security Council; and (4) the idea that they should all meet again.

The League of Arab States, joined by Libya in 1953, saw all of its members represented in the Asian-African Conference. On its own, during this quinquennium, the Arab League made plans for easier movement of people and goods from one member-state to another. Along with Arab concern about Palestine, there now developed a sympathy for Arabic-speaking North Africans seeking independence from France. When Iraq became a member of the Baghdad Pact in 1955, protest arose from some of the other Arab states. Egypt, Saudi Arabia, and Syria made a pact of their own, in response, and even technically merged their armies under Egyptian command.

The Tenth International Conference of American States met in Caracas, Venezuela, March 1954. The United States introduced a resolution clearly aimed at the Arbenz regime in Guatemala, stating that "the domination or control of the political institutions of any American State by the international communist movement . . . would call for the adoption of appropriate action in accordance with existing treaties." After one amendment, changing "would call for the adoption of appropriate action" to "would call for a meeting of consultation to consider the adoption of appropriate action," and after many speeches explaining that various countries did not consider the resolution a justification for intervention in any state's internal affairs, the resolution passed with only Guatemala voting in the negative and Mexico and Argentina abstaining. When the Arbenz regime fell in Guatemala, the Organization of American States took no stand, and did nothing to save the legitimate government. When troubles arose on the Nicaraguan-Costa Rican border in January 1955, however, the OAS played a major role in obtaining a genuine peace. These two countries joined Guatemala, El Salvador, and Honduras in August of the same year to form an Organization of Central American States. Usually known as ODECA for its official name, Organización de Estados Centroamericanos, the new entity intended to work in the direction of political union.

The Council of Europe, joined by West Germany in 1951, discussed a European Defense Community and a European Coal and Steel Community, each to include only six of the members -- West Germany, Italy, France, the Netherlands, Belgium, and Luxembourg. Through these two de-

461

vices, a democratic West Germany could cooperate with its neighbors on roughly equal terms. The Coal and Steel Community, ending trade barriers on these two items among the countries concerned, came into existence in 1952. France turned down the European Defense Community in 1954, but accepted the Western European Union including the same six countries with the United Kingdom. The Council of Europe emerged from these difficulties to stand once again as an organization looking toward a wider political union.

The United Nations worked its way nearly to the end of this period with a mounting list of countries seeking admission and no acceptance of any of them. The United States objected until 1955 to the inclusion of five communist countries, and the Soviet Union in return vetoed the admission of the rest. On December 14, 1955, the General Assembly completed the action needed to break the logjam. While again deferring the applications of Mongolia and Japan, the Assembly approved the entry of 16 other nations -- ten from Europe (Italy, Spain, Romania, Hungary, Portugal, Austria, Bulgaria, Finland, Ireland, Albania), four from the Orient (Ceylon, Nepal, Cambodia, Laos), and Jordan and Libya representing the Middle East. Thus the total membership in the United Nations rose to 76 countries. Still missing in addition to Japan, among the larger nations, were Communist China and both parts of each of the three divided countries, Germany, Korea, and Viet-Nam.

Communist China, because of its decision to help North Korea in late 1950, became the subject of the United Nations' most emphatic decision of this period of five years. On February 1, 1951, the General Assembly stated that China had engaged in aggression by assisting the North Koreans. Five communist delegations, India, and Burma voted negatively, and nine others abstained, while 44 nations voted in favor of this resolution. On May 18, the Assembly went farther to recommend that every state in the world apply an embargo on shipment of war goods to mainland China. The vote this time emerged 47 to 0, but with India, Indonesia, Pakistan, Egypt, Burma, Afghanistan, Sweden, and Syria abstaining and five communist delegations refusing to participate. Though the warfare involving the Chinese quieted a few months after this resolution, and though armistice came to Korea in 1953, the bad feeling toward Mao's regime continued strong. A resolution of 1955 not to consider the substitution of Mao's delegates for Chiang's delegates in the United Nations for that year passed 42 to 12, with 6 abstentions.

Only twice again during this quinquennium, in resolutions pointed at Israel, did the strength of United Nations language approach that of May 18, 1951. The Palestine question found its way to the United Nations agenda every year. In 1951, the Security Council by a vote of 8 to 0 called upon Egypt to terminate its interference with the passage through the Suez Canal of goods destined for Israel. In 1953, by 9 votes to 0, the Council expressed "the strongest censure" of a retaliatory action against a Jordanese village by the armed forces of Israel. In 1955, by 11 to 0, the Council condemned a "prearranged and planned attack ordered by Israeli authorities" and "committed by Israeli regular army forces against the Egyptian regular army force" in the Gaza strip. Other resolutions during the five years called upon both Israel and some one of its neighbors to desist from infractions of the cease-fire, or from some associated practice.

On June 20, 1954, when the United States, Nicaragua, and Honduras aided the insurrection of Castillo Armas against president Arbenz of Guatemala, the Security Council passed another unanimous resolution, calling for "the immediate termination of any action likely to cause bloodshed" and requesting "all Members of the United Nations to abstain, in the spirit of the Charter, from giving assistance to any such action." Nowhere

463

in the language of this measure were the guilty parties named. One of them, the United States, made a mockery of the United Nations by voting for the resolution while actually increasing its aid to those who were causing the bloodshed. The Security Council five days later decided not to take up the case again, leaving it to the Organization of American States, which failed to reach the investigatory stage before the coup terminated.

A dozen political problems drifted in and out of the United Nations corridors in addition to the greater crises. A few old questions became settled, though chiefly through external means. Thus, problems between Greece and its neighbors grew less worrisome as that nation settled down and made friends with Yugoslavia. The United Nations Special Committee on the Balkans ceased to function in 1951. The Trieste question found its solution in 1954, when the occupying powers agreed on a compromise territorial division, the city proper going to Italy and the larger part of its free zone to Yugoslavia. Libya and Eritrea settled into independence and federation with Ethiopia, respectively, as the United Nations provided the necessary planning. In 1951-3, the world organization attempted without avail to persuade India and Pakistan to accept a program of demilitarization for Kashmir.

New problems came to the attention of the General Assembly, receiving in most cases little more than an airing. Several countries complained about South Africa's policy of apartheid, which the Assembly condemned, though South Africa paid no attention. The Assembly took a stand against the presence of Nationalist Chinese soldiers on Burmese territory, but the United States and Thailand actually solved the problem by conveying the soldiers to Tai Wan. Complaints about French denial of rights to persons in "protected" Morocco and Tunisia met an expression of hope from the General Assembly that matters could be worked out with French assistance. A similar

464

case with Algeria failed to reach the agenda, though preliminary discussion took place. A question concerning the British control of Cyprus received the same treatment, in effect -- as did also an Indonesian complaint about the Dutch presence in West New Guinea, or West Irian.

Dag Hammarskjöld of Sweden took the place of Trygve Lie as the secretary-general of the United Nations in April 1953. Hammarskjöld came from service as a non-partisan minister in the dominantly Social Democratic cabinet of his country. He accepted his new position as one in which he could hold high the moral values of his own character. It seemed fitting that his term of office coincided with the early history of a United Nations Disarmament Commission, founded in January 1952 to replace the Atomic Energy Commission and the Commission for Conventional Armaments; and that Dag Hammarskjöld would prepare the way for the first International Conference on the Peaceful Uses of Atomic Energy, held in Geneva, Switzerland, August 1955.

The political face of the United Nations remained relatively dormant in this period because nations involved in the Cold War chose not to bring their problems to the world assemblage. The embargo on war goods to Communist China constituted the only change from the previous quinquennium as to the extent of involvement the United Nations would attempt. Even the earlier guidelines, to remain clearly discernible, needed a significant challenge from the world political arena.

Economic Change

Modifications of the world economic panorama during 1951-55 are seen in alterations of the statistical data presented in the previous chapter. There is no attempt here to repeat the entire tableau, but only to show significant

change. The panorama mentioned specific countries as they stood in comparison to one another
in averages of the three years 1948-50. The
modifications presented here are from averages of
the three years 1953-55.

Two types of change are shown. One is that
of extraordinary increase or decline in volume,
for the entire world and for individual nations. The device used to avoid an unwarranted
appearance of precision is the expression of
growth or decline in terms of comparison with the
rate of growth of world population. Approximately 9.1% more people lived in the world in
1955 than in 1950. This rate of growth is expressed by the numeral 1. Twice that rate is 2,
thrice is 3, and so on. The figure "2+" indicates an increase of more than 2 units of world
population growth; or, in other words, that the
national or world rate of increase for that
particular item exceeded twice the rate of growth
in world population. The figure "1-" indicates a
rate of decline greater than 9.1%. (This use of
the negative symbol is of course unusual and
arbitrary; it is to be read not as "less than
one," but as "more than one unit of decline.")
The smaller integers presented may generally be
counted as correct. Figures beyond about 5,
however, may be taken as less certain, and those
above about 10 largely as symptomatic of a high
number somewhere in that vicinity. In the last
case, a small error in the base on which the rate
is calculated might affect the unit figure.

In order to avoid a prolixity of numbers, the
more ordinary rates are not mentioned. Any decline of more than 1 unit in world totals is
indicated, and any decline of more than 2 units
in national totals. For 14 items -- rice, wheat,
maize, cotton, sugar, tobacco, cattle, sheep,
coffee, coal, petroleum, iron, cement, and land
motor vehicles -- any growth of more than 2 units
in world totals is indicated, and any growth of
more than 3 units in national totals. For the
remaining 72 items, any growth of more than 4

466

units in world totals is indicated, and any growth of more than 5 units in national totals. These measures are given for all the countries previously listed for each item. Other countries are mentioned as having newly achieved a position among the leaders, without an indication of their rates of increase. Exports are treated only in a few instances where production statistics did not appear.

The other type of change shown is that of the relative standing of leading countries. If one country surpasses another to the point that the lower of the two shows a total less than four-fifths of the higher, that feat is indicated, and a revised list of the countries on that item presented. As in the economic panorama of Chapter V, the cut-off point lies at one-half the world total for most items -- but at two-thirds for rice, wheat, maize, cotton, coal, iron, and cement, and at nine-tenths for petroleum and land motor vehicles. Near-ties as defined in Chapter V are also mentioned whenever a list is revised. A nation is indicated as having lost its place among the leaders only if it has dropped to less than four-fifths of the last on the list, or has remained at less than a near-tie position for two quinquennia in succession.

A longer list of countries for any item indicates that some of the nations not previously mentioned have increased their production or their holdings, at least by comparison with the previous leaders. A shorter list for any item may indicate a relative increase in production or holdings by any nation on the list, or a decline for countries beyond the cut-off point. The reports and estimates on which the lists are based are taken chiefly from United Nations statistical tables.

The rate of increase for world production of agricultural commodities outside the communist nations of Asia stood at about 18.6% from 1950 to

1955, slightly more than twice (or 2+, to use the system of symbols employed here) the rate of world population growth. The addition of the remainder of Asia would have yielded a still higher rate. The Second World War and the political reverberations therefrom, combined with an increase in world population which the war speeded even while so many died, meant that in 1950 there had existed less for each person to eat than ten years previously. At the end of the quinquennium 1951-55, during which so many of the war's reverberations quieted, world per capita agricultural activity regained its prewar level. This did not mean that everyone could eat well, since many persons had remained unable to provide themselves with proper nutriment before World War II began. Unfortunately, also, there continued great contrast between regions, with many persons of the Orient and Latin America suffering from hunger despite surpluses of food elsewhere.

Three major and two minor cereals participated in the renewal. World production of rice (2+) rose more than twice as rapidly as world population, the increase in China standing at 4+. The Soviet Union (3+), France (3+), and India (4+) contributed to higher totals on wheat. China (7+) developed its harvest of maize. China (13+) more than doubled its production of the millet-sorghum combination, while the United States joined China and India on this item. Barley increased at a rapid pace on the world scale (4+), with assistance from China (9+), the Soviet Union (5+), Canada (6+), and Turkey (7+). The United States maintained controls on the production of wheat and maize, to avoid bringing down the world price, and thereby posed a problem between the cereals farmer and the destitute people of the world. The gap between the amount the farmer needed and the amount many families could pay seemed to call for intergovernmental planning.

The vegetable fibers also grew in quantity. The world of harvest of cotton increased (3+) on a very lively scale, especially in the Soviet

Union (3+), China (13+, more than doubling), and India (7+). Hemp production rose rapidly in the Soviet Union (5+) while declining in India (2-) and Italy (3-). The world total for sisal increased (4+) as Brazil overtook Kenya on this item to rank as co-leader with Tanganyika, while Kenya dropped away from the small leading group. The world total for henequen declined (1-).

A United Nations Sugar Conference in 1953 dealt with the intricacies of world trade in sugar, adopting an International Sugar Agreement effective the following year. World production increased (2+) as France overtook Puerto Rico, and West Germany and the Philippines joined the leaders on this item, producing the following revised list: Cuba, the Soviet Union (5+), the United States, Brazil, France (5+), India, West Germany, the Philippines, Australia (3+), and near-tie Poland (3+).

The world totals for tobacco increased (2+) as China overtook the Soviet Union on another revised list: the United States, India, China (9+), and the Soviet Union.

Three of the domesticated animals increased at more than twice the rate of people. World numbers of sheep (2+) depended on new attention to the species in the Soviet Union (5+) and China (5+). The Soviet Union more than doubled (10+) its count of swine, as Brazil (5+) also augmented its inventory. Ethiopia overtook Iran in numbers of goats, producing a revised list for that item: India, China (10+, more than doubling), the Soviet Union, Turkey, Ethiopia (5+), Nigeria, and Iran. Argentina dropped behind China in numbers of horses and mules, and the United States (4-) lost its place among the leaders: the Soviet Union, Brazil, China, Mexico (8+), and Argentina. China joined India as a leader in count of buffaloes.

Some shifts in country rankings occurred in the vegetable oils. China joined the United

States and the Soviet Union as a leader in production of cottonseed. The Soviet Union and India joined the United States as leaders on linseed, as the harvest in Argentina declined (4-). Malaya joined Ceylon as a major exporter of coconut oil. Italy greatly increased (5+) its production of olive oil. China (2-) produced less sesame seed. The Soviet Union (5+) harvested much more, and Argentina (5-) much less, sunflower seed. World castor oil exports more than doubled (12+), as those of India (13+) did likewise and Brazil (7+) also contributed.

World production of coffee increased considerably (2+), and that of tea (4+) even more so. Nigeria joined the Gold Coast and Brazil as a leader in the list for cacao.

Among the more significant vegetables, China (11+) more than doubled its production of sweet potatoes and yams. The world totals on cassava increased notably (4+) as Indonesia overtook Nigeria on this item, revising the list: Brazil, Indonesia (6+), Belgian Congo, and near-tie Nigeria. Italy joined the United States and the Soviet Union as a leader on tomatoes. India overtook the United States in harvests of beans: Brazil, China, India, the United States. The major fruits experienced only one significant change, as Ecuador joined Brazil and India as a leading producer of bananas.

China joined the group of leaders in cuttings of wood. World catches of fish increased at a lively rate (4+) as China also joined the leaders on this item, surpassing the United Kingdom and Canada as they dropped away from the leading list: Japan (7+), the United States, the Soviet Union, China, and Norway.

Mining, like agriculture, needed the time span of this quinquennium to reach the per capita level of its prewar activity. Manufacturing, however, spurred ahead during these five years to the highest per capita levels in history. The great increase in manufactured goods included the products of both chemical and engineering industries. The growth from 1950 to 1955 of mining and manufacturing together for the entire world aside from the communist nations of Asia stood at about 42.2%, more than twice the rate of agriculture, and greater than four times that of the world population (4+, in terms of the symbols employed here). Only rarely in the 1950's did people remind themselves that the mining of particular commodities, unlike the cultivation of food, would someday reach a termination point.

In most countries, the new records made in manufacturing came far from providing most families with the amenities of modern living. In the more affluent societies, however, the supply of many manufactured items became larger than the demand for them by 1955. Advertising then, in the private-enterprise domains, pointed out to families the convenience of owning more than one automobile or telephone, while manufacturers resorted to planned obsolescense to induce more frequent purchases. Thus a greater-than-ever disparity arose between the masses who had too little and others who frequently possessed more than they could use.

China joined the other three largest countries of the world as a leader in the production of cotton yarn, as the output of this item also rose rapidly in the Soviet Union (6+). The Soviet Union joined the leading group on wool yarn, and the United Kingdom and Japan joined the United States as leaders on rayon and acetate filament yarn.

The Soviet Union (5+) mined considerably more coal than before. The world total of lignite advanced (4+) with contributions from East Germany (5+) and the Soviet Union (6+). West Germany (7+) and the Soviet Union (7+) increased their output of coke.

Crude petroleum provided the most impressive consumption record (5+) of the fuels. Due to its political crisis (see "Three Revolutions Interrupted"), Iran dropped (8-) below Saudi Arabia, Kuwait, and Mexico, losing its place among the leaders. Iraq and Canada joined the leaders, Iraq surpassing Iran and Mexico, and Canada overtaking Mexico, producing an extensively revised list: the United States, Venezuela (4+), the Soviet Union (9+), Saudi Arabia (10+, more than doubling), Kuwait (35+, more than quadrupling), Iraq, Canada, Mexico (38+, also more than quadrupling), and near-tie Indonesia. The new position of Iraq sprang from the discovery of new wells by the Iraq Petroleum Company, a combination of British, French, Dutch, and United States interests dating from before World War I.

A specific indicator of the lively increase in manufacturing lay in the statistics for the mining of iron ore, as measured by its content of iron. The world increase (5+) in output of iron felt the effect especially of the development of the industry in the Soviet Union (10+, more than doubling) and France (6+). The world growth in production of crude iron (4+) and of crude steel (4+) likewise showed particularly in the Soviet Union (9+ and 8+ respectively).

The mining of most of the other metals also advanced rapidly. The Soviet Union and Canada joined the leaders on lead as United States production of this item declined (2-). World mining of bauxite more than doubled (10+) in keeping with the new importance of aluminum, as Surinam (6+) and the United States (6+) contributed and Jamaica joined the leaders with a new bauxite industry. The Soviet Union joined the leaders on zinc, and Indonesia joined Malaya and Bolivia on tin. As world production of manganese (7+) notably increased, the Gold Coast (2-) dropped away from the group of leaders, leaving only the Soviet Union (7+) and India (14+, more than doubling).

472

Canada (5+) pushed its production of silver. World output of nickel (6+) rose at a lively pace. Tungsten world totals more than doubled (12+) as the United States overtook the Soviet Union on this item: China (6+), the United States (27+, more than tripling), and the Soviet Union. The world figure for platinum (5+) increased as South Africa joined Canada as a leader on the item. A revolution occurred in the antimony market, as China joined the group of leaders in first position, Bolivia fell below both South Africa and China, and Mexico (4-) dropped behind South Africa and China and lost its place among the leaders. The revised list on antimony ran: China, South Africa (5+), Bolivia (5-), and near-tie Soviet Union. World production of molybdenum (13+) more than doubled along with that of the United States (14+). World output of titanium (6+) also notably increased.

The production of cement may be taken as a sort of approximation-reading of manufacturing-development ferment or fever, due to the fact that most nations have the materials and the "know-how" to produce their own cement. From 1948-50 to 1953-55, when world cement production (7+) increased greatly, positions among the leaders shifted significantly. The Soviet Union and West Germany, in particular, overtook the United Kingdom, while Japan overtook Belgium, and China joined the leading group. The revised list on cement stood as follows: the United States (3+, but still with well over twice the figure of its nearest competitor), the Soviet Union (14+, more than doubling), West Germany (10+, also more than doubling), the United Kingdom (3+), Japan (23+, more than tripling), France (5+), Italy (13+, more than doubling), Belgium (4+), China, and near-tie India.

Among the non-metallic minerals other than cement, diamonds (6+) stood as the fastest-growing item, still chiefly from the Belgian Congo (5+). World production of asbestos (4+) and phosphate rock (4+) also showed notable gains.

473

Japan joined the United States as a major producer of sulphur.

The world output of land motor vehicles increased rapidly (4+) as West Germany joined the leading group, overtaking Canada. The revised list ran as follows: the United States (with a total more than seven times that of its nearest competitor), the United Kingdom (6+), West Germany, France (12+, more than doubling), the Soviet Union (6+), and near-tie Canada (4+). A significant number of countries lacking the raw materials for the manufacture of automobiles and trucks began to assemble them from imported parts.

Six nations registered three or more times on the "plus" or increase side of these listings, even with the exclusion of the smaller numbers as mentioned. A recapitulation of the records of those six reveals their very strong influence in the growth picture for this period. The totality for each nation holds some meaning in a general sense, but is best interpreted through attention to each item. Agriculture and mining are well represented; manufacturing chiefly by indirect indicators.

The Soviet Union registered positively on 19 separate items, showing a 14+ on cement; 10+ on swine and iron; 9+ on petroleum and crude iron; 8+ on crude steel; 7+ on coke and manganese; 6+ on cotton yarn, lignite, and land motor vehicles; 5+ on barley, hemp, sugar, sheep, sunflower seed, and coal; and 3+ on wheat and cotton.

China held second place in this reckoning, with growth rates showing on ten items, chiefly in the agricultural realm: 13+ on millet and cotton; 11+ on sweet potatoes; 10+ on goats; 9+ on barley and tobacco; 7+ on maize; 6+ on tungsten; 5+ on sheep; and 4+ on rice. France registered on five items: 12+ on land motor vehicles; 6+ on iron; 5+ on sugar and cement; 3+ on wheat. The United States appeared four times: 27+ on tungsten, 14+ on molybdenum, 6+ on bauxite, 3+ on cement. India also registered on four lists: 14+ on manganese, 13+ on castor oil, 7+ on cotton, 4+ on wheat. And Canada with three: 6+ on barley, 5+ on silver, 4+ on land motor vehicles.

By 1955, despite the appearance of China and India on this review of growth activity, the split between "haves" and have-nots" in the world showed more plainly than ever. The "have" countries did not possess everything, nor did the "have-not" nations find themselves with nothing. The "haves" held many or all of the raw materials needed for major lines of modern manufacturing, however, and were actually becoming over-supplied with the products of that manufacturing. The "have-nots," on the other hand, contained minorities of affluent families who shared in the world's new comforts and luxuries, alongside great majorities who found it difficult merely to obtain their daily bread. International trade kept nearly everyone involved in what had become a sort of world economy, but almost always to the disadvantage of the countries whose manufacturing remained weak.

In this quinquennium, after nearly imperceptible beginnings in the previous one, there arose a small though significant effort to establish some better balance between the "haves" and the "have-nots." Precedents had been set by the Marshall Plan of assistance by the United States, largely to prewar "haves;" by diverse procedures through which the Soviet Union aided its eastern European communist cooperators, starting in 1947; and by the Colombo Plan channeling United Kingdom assistance to former as well as present colonies. These three nations and a few others now undertook through bilateral agreements to give and lend money to a variety of less-favored peoples, occasionally for relief in emergency situations, but more often to aid in longer-term development. The International Bank for Reconstruction and Development, financed by all its members (including the United States and the United Kingdom but by its own choice not the Soviet Union), provided a multilateral conduit for such aid. Generally, however, persons in the lending and donating countries preferred to receive the plaudits which they believed would spring from bilateral assistance and which they felt such "generosity" deserved.

The United States (counting grants and net amounts on loans, but excluding military assistance) provided the greatest share of aid during these five years, sending its largest amounts to South Korea, South Viet-Nam, Brazil, Tai Wan, India, Iran, and Israel, in that order. The United Kingdom reached outside the Colombo Plan to assist a few nations in the Middle East, and the Soviet Union under Bulganin and Khrushchev made its first commitments (to Afghanistan and India) outside the communist lands. On a per capita basis in 1955, again counting grants and net loans but excluding military assistance, Israel ranked by far the most favored of the recipient nations, though Libya with significant post-colonial aid from both the United Kingdom and the United States came in an interesting, Arabic-speaking second.

The idea of assistance from one nation to another had received little attention before World War II, excepting in the case of imperialist governments spending money on their colonies. The money that flowed during this period consisted of small amounts by the donors' standards, and (as may be judged by the names of the leading beneficiaries) generally expressed a political sentiment of some kind. The international imbalance of trade would not be redressed by small amounts of aid or by aid granted chiefly to political cooperators. In the year 1955, few persons concerned themselves with the inequities, except in the hungrier nations themselves; but an assistance program begun for whatever reasons on such a worldwide scale seemed likely to prove of some value eventually in solving the imbalance problem.

Science

The fission-fusion-fission bomb . . einsteinium,
fermium, and mendelevium . . the antiproton . .
the molecular clock . . the maser . . a doubling
of galaxy distances . . galaxies in collision . .
the conquest of Mount Everest . . turbidity currents . . the solar battery . . the structure of
deoxyribonucleic acid . . the poliomyelitis
vaccine . . the unidentified flying object catalog . . Fromm, The Sane Society . . Coon, The
Story of Man . . Heilbroner, The Worldly
Philosophers . . the ancient Hittite empire . .
Florinsky, Russia . . Chase, America's Music . .
Latourette, A History of Christianity . .
Gunther, Inside Africa . . Wittgenstein on
language.

Most advances in man's acquisition of knowledge during 1951-55 received less attention from
the public than the development of atomic power,
continuing on the foundations laid in the previous decade. The world's first "thermonuclear"
test, however, remained a secret for some time.
Andrey Dmitriyevich Sakharov, chief designer of
the device, made this achievement possible for
the Soviet Union early in 1951. The hydrogen
bomb, using the fission of the earlier atomic or
nuclear bomb to trigger the fusion of hydrogen
and protons into helium, became a publicized
reality in 1952 when the United States set it up
for a test on a coral atoll in the Pacific. Its
thermonuclear explosion displayed 150 times the
energy of the nuclear blast over Hiroshima.
Edward Teller, born in Hungary, the chemist in
charge of developing this bomb, had moved in 1935
to the United States from Germany. An assistant to Enrico Fermi and Robert Oppenheimer
during the wartime work on the first nuclear
bomb, he favored the thermonuclear device when

477

Oppenheimer opposed it on humanitarian grounds. In 1954, Oppenheimer lost his position as adviser to the Atomic Energy Commission, after Teller testified against him as a security risk.

In 1953, nine months after the test in the Pacific, the Soviet Union performed the first fission-fusion experiment with a bomb carried by airplane. The United Kingdom had carried out its first nuclear explosion in 1952. People began to wonder how many nations would want to follow these examples, and whether some private individual might secure possession of a bomb and employ it to menace a city. No one hurried to produce a cobalt bomb to snuff out lives over a wide area. The United States set off a "fission-fusion-fission" bomb, however, in 1954, over Bikini Island in the Pacific. In this one, the fusion ignited by the original trigger served as a trigger itself, providing high-energy neutrons for the fission of an outside blanket of uranium. The Bikini bomb proved itself 750 times more powerful than the one used at Hiroshima.

The United States, the Soviet Union, and the United Kingdom intended to develop the fission-fusion-fission idea further, until even the Bikini bomb would seem an infant. At this point, however, many people began to protest the wave of atomic weapon experiments. The bomb of 1954 had contaminated 7,000 square miles of stratosphere above the earth. The radioactive "fallout" from the stratosphere takes about a year to settle on the oceans and the continents. Some substances hitherto unknown on earth (the worst of them strontium 90) became evident after that year. The danger to the human species, as well as to the animals and plants, might augment considerably with the continuation of such tests. Indeed, atomic weaponry might prove as dangerous to one's self or one's friends as one's enemies.

Properly controlled atomic power presented its own problems (what to do with its radioactive refuse, for example) but remained relatively free of the immediate grave dangers surrounding the atomic explosions. In 1954, the United States launched the first nuclear-powered submarine, and the Soviet Union built the first atomic reactor to provide electric power. In August 1955, a United Nations International Congress on the Peaceful Uses of Atomic Energy attracted an attendance of 72 nations. Fission power became cheaper than that from burning coal, however, only where coal was scarce and expensive. Fusion power held much greater promise for the future, but remained insufficiently controlled. Fusion power boasted the added merit of leaving no radioactive waste.

Nuclear physicists built ever larger proton synchrotons in the United States during this period, hoping to crack further inner-atom secrets. After the identification of transuranium elements 99 and 100 in the refuse of the first United States thermonuclear explosion, 1952-3, proton bombardment of number 99 produced element 101 (in 1955). Teams headed by Albert Ghiorso, and including S. G. Thompson and G. T. Seaborg, performed this labor at the University of California at Berkeley. They named the elements respectively einsteinium for Albert Einstein (died 1955), fermium for Enrico Fermi (died 1954), and mendelevium for Dmitry Mendeleyev, ninteenth-century Russian creator of the periodic table of the elements.

In 1955, Owen Chamberlain of California and Emilio Gino Segrè of Italy, also working at Berkeley, detected the tracks of a number of antiprotons. These new particles shared all the characteristics of protons save that the antiprotons held a negative rather than a positive charge related to an oppositeness of direction of spin. Since positrons (antielectrons) had revealed themselves in 1932, antimatter on the simple level of hydrogen (with one antiproton and one positron substituting for the one proton and one electron) now seemed entirely feasible. Some scientists began to suggest that whole worlds of antimatter, visible or invisible to man's instruments, may reside within his universe.

The inner world of the molecule received as much attention as that of the atom. Diffraction analysis had shown the spatial relationships among atoms within particular molecules. The three atoms of hydrogen in one molecule of ammonia, for instance, lay at the corners of an equilateral triangle. The one atom of nitrogen in the same molecule lay at some distance "above" that triangle -- or, equally as likely, "below" it. Postwar science noted that indeed such a molecule could be made to vibrate, so that the one atom of nitrogen in the illustration would move from "above" to "below" or vice versa about 24,000,000 times in one second. Since such molecular vibrations are very regular in rhythm, their use to control electric currents meant that (by the early 1950's) man possessed a more precise instrument for measuring time than any he had known before. A caesium clock designed for the United States Bureau of Standards in 1955 incorporated accuracy beyond 9,999,999,999 parts of 10,000,000,000.

Molecular oscillations also provided the base for the world's first "masers." Each molecule releases a photon of energy when it drops from a higher to a lower state of energy -- and absorbs a photon of the same size when it moves from a lower to a higher state of energy. Since 1924, scientists had known that a photon of the precise size for a particular molecule would, upon striking that molecule in a higher state of energy, dislodge another photon of equal size, moving in the same direction. If a number of molecules of a substance could be provided with most of them at the higher energy level, one photon introduced into their presence would produce two, four, eight, sixteen, and so on, all moving at lightning speed in the same direction. Charles Hard Townes of South Carolina succeeded in doing this with ammonia (whose photons lay in the microwave

480

portion of the radiation spectrum) in 1953. He called it "microwave amplification by stimulated emission of radiation" -- whose acronym is <u>maser</u>.

The visible universe increased tremendously both in size and complexity during this period. Not only could the Mount Palomar telescope see much farther than any before; it revealed much more distinctly the details of galaxies already visible, and thus pointed up a very large size miscalculation made by pioneers in the 1920's. Astronomers had determined the approximate distance to the sun and its planets in the seventeenth and eighteenth centuries, using the same triangulation methods employed by surveyors on earth. Finer instruments permitted the extension of this system to the nearer stars in the nineteenth century, using opposite positions on the earth's orbit about the sun as observation points. Study of the "proper motion" of other stars -- that is, their own apparent (though slight) movement over a period of years relative to more distant stars "behind" them -- yielded estimates of distance for some known as Cepheid variables. Named for the constellation Cepheus, in which a notable example is found, these stars vary in luminosity through cycles lasting a few earth-days, with the intrinsically brightest of them having the longest periods; astronomers worked out a tight formula for this relationship during the 1910's. Cepheid variables of the same luminosity period, having the same absolute magnitude (the measure of their brightness at its source), would thus reveal their relative distances from the earth by the apparent magnitude of their light as it reached this planet.

The existence of galaxies outside the Milky Way became certain in 1924, when a new telescope showed Cepheid variables in the so-called Andromeda Nebula. Calculation according to the formula indicated that Andromeda lay close to 1,000,000 light-years (5,878,000,000,000,000,000 miles) away. Cepheid-variable computation then led to the understanding that many galaxies ex-

481

isted at much greater distances than this. Beyond the point at which Cepheid variables could be detected within the configuration of a galaxy, other methods (such as the displacement toward the red in the spectrum) filled in with further estimates -- all tied, however, to the formula determined in the 1910's. Walter Baade of Germany, resident in California, studied Andromeda carefully during World War II, his vision of the sky improved by the wartime blackout. He found two types of stars, very different from one another -- blue stars in the spiral arms of the galaxy, reddish stars in the interior. In 1951, William Wilson Morgan of Tennessee found that the Milky Way is a spiral galaxy like Andromeda, with the earth's sun located in one of the arms. Baade next showed, through an examination of variable stars in the Milky Way, that one distance-formula would not function for all of them, and that a blue-star formula would be needed to calculate the distance to Andromeda. It soon turned out that Andromeda lay more nearly 2,000,000 light-years than 1,000,000 away, and that all the other spiral galaxies outside the Milky Way lay at least double the distance hitherto listed for them.

Henry Norris Russell of New York, who lived through this period, worked out the first theory for the evolution of stars during the 1910's and 1920's. The study of that evolution received considerable impetus from the new understanding of the nature of galaxies. Radio astronomy proved of much assistance in a variety of ways. Edward Mills Purcell of Illinois, working at Harvard University, proved a theory propounded by Hendrik Christoffel Van de Hulst of the Netherlands in 1944, that hydrogen in space could be located through the detection of waves emitted on a precise wavelength (about 21 centimeters) whenever collision of hydrogen atoms occurred. Through this "song of hydrogen," the structure of the Milky Way came to be understood, and the relationship between the evolution of stars and the makeup of galaxies began to reveal itself. In

1951, Walter Baade studied from Mount Palomar the first "radio galaxy" reported from England (that is, the first galaxy detected by radio rather than visual means; over 100 "radio stars" had been detected by this time). Baade reached the conclusion that the strong radio signals derived from two galaxies in collision. (The precise nature of such a collision remained a subject of conjecture.) Within a few years, many more radio galaxies appeared. Viktor Amazaspovich Ambart-sumian of the Soviet Union suggested in 1955 that some of these galaxies might be exploding rather than colliding.

The evolution of the earth had attracted scholars' attention more than a century earlier than the evolution of the stars. Norman Levi Bowen of Canada, moved to the United States, studied the transformations of rocks (under laboratory conditions) for four decades running through this period, providing a basic core of knowledge for the earth's history. While adventurers and science-enthusiasts climbed the highest heights and plumbed the lowest depths at this time, a few scientists made significant new discoveries. Edmund Hillary, a beekeeper of New Zealand, and Tenzing Norgay, his guide from Nepal (of Tibetan culture and descent), climbed Mount Everest of the Himalayan range, the highest in the world at 29,028 feet. Tenzing left a Buddhist food offering at the summit, where they paused 15 minutes. Father-and-son Auguste and Jacques Piccard of Switzerland descended in the same year to a point 10,335 feet below sea level in the Mediterranean Sea near Italy, using a pressurized "bathyscaphe" of their own invention, featuring the principles of the balloon. Other, even more daring dives followed, though none began to reach the depth of the Mariana Trench, east of the Mariana Islands in the Pacific, which the British ship <u>Challenger</u> found in 1951 to exceed 35,000 feet in profundity.

Canyons in the ocean at more shallow levels proved fully as intriguing. William Maurice

Ewing of Texas and Bruce Charles Heezen of Iowa stimulated new thinking in connection with them. Some submarine canyons they believed might exist as a result of action by sudden underwater currents, set into motion by an accumulation of sediment. Heavier water flowing under lighter water could produce the same consequences as any strong current of water under only the atmosphere. Vagn Walfrid Ekman of Sweden, who had spent a half-century explaining ocean currents, turned to these "turbidity currents" for study in the last year of his life, 1953-4. Ewing and Heezen also reached the conclusion in 1952-3, through the study of Atlantic Ocean soundings made by a number of ships, that a very different kind of canyon lay in the mid-Atlantic, stretching the length of a north-south underwater ridge discovered in the 1920's. Some force ill understood by man must have created this rather sharp crack in the earth's surface. Submarine earthquakes had taken place in abundance, they soon noticed, in precisely the same vicinity. A number of earth-scientists began to take interest in tracking these manifestations further.

The treated semiconductors that formed the base of the transistor served a new purpose after 1954. In that year, the Bell Telephone Laboratories put together the first solar battery. Built like a modified sandwich transistor, it led electrons in one direction and the gaps to be filled by electrons in the other, subsequent to the freeing of the electrons from their usual places by the sun's action in striking the surface of the sandwich. The electrons could pass directly only from the outside to the inside of the sandwich, the gaps only from the inside to the outside, excepting that each part was tapped. The wire circuit connecting the taps then provided a path for electric current, the electrons traveling it to the outside of the sandwich again. The solar battery remained weak for the expanse of sunlight needed, but showed much promise for the future. Particularly, as the Soviet Union and the United States announced in 1955 that they intended to launch scientific missiles in orbit about the earth, the solar battery seemed to offer the possibility of very-long-term generation of the power needed to facilitate very-long-range study.

The computer developed rapidly during this period, offering other possibilities for study from space, especially as electronics experts developed models much smaller than the earlier ones. Manufacturing industry adopted the computer as an economy in both time and energy. Scientists took particular interest in the extent to which the machine could replace human thinking. Most of all, they wanted computers capable of performing the tedious, time-consuming labor needed for science to continue at a lively pace. In 1954, for the first time, a computer made a rough translation from one language to another, in this case providing a crude English version of some passages in Russian. No one could be certain how long it might take to train the machine to serve as a sophisticated translator. But, as one example of the possible potential, might the day conceivably arrive when computers would not only perform speedily and well the translation tasks assigned to them, but also inspect more closely than the human brain the often-missed ties between languages?

New advances in the study of genetics, in the meantime, revealed more clearly than ever before the vast intricacy of the living creatures on earth who preceded the machine. For the first time, there appeared some prospect that the mechanism by which heredity transmits its strong influence might come to be explained. In the nineteenth century, biologists had learned that the cell, basic building block of all living things, contains a generous portion of "nucleic acid." Early in the twentieth century, scholars ascertained that this acid comes in two varieties --

485

ribonucleic acid (RNA) and deoxyribonucleic acid (DNA), differing only in that the DNA molecule lacks one oxygen atom present in RNA. Both of the two varieties, it developed, are found in all living cells. DNA appeared expecially in the tiny but visible threads called chromosomes, detected in late nineteenth century.

Thomas Hunt Morgan of Kentucky (died 1945) established the close relationship between chromosomes and heredity in the first two decades of the twentieth century. He and others realized, however, that not enough chromosomes existed to explain the great variety of inherited characteristics. They then accepted a theory of the existence of "genes," invisible factors on or in the chromosomes which set the conditions of birth for living creatures. (The proposed functioning of the genes had already received elaborate investigation back in the 1860's.) The fruit flies employed by Morgan in his studies proved useful over a long period of time in the work of two of Morgan's students whose activity continued through this period. Hermann Joseph Muller of New York, who lived in the Soviet Union and Scotland for a time, studied the mutation of genes as they are influenced by radiation, believing that man should steer his own genetic course. Theodosius Dobzhansky of Russia, who moved from the Soviet Union to the United States, emphasized the swiftness with which a species may evolve through changes in gene-directed traits.

The genes remained invisible, however, and while scientists accepted them, the nature of their functions remained pure hypothesis. Many scholars believed that only study at the molecular level could resolve the air of mystery about them. During the war, a study team found that DNA in a test-tube could influence the inherited properties of bacteria. After the war, several scholars interested themselves in the connections among DNA, chromosomes, and genes. A precise knowledge of the molecular structure of DNA would help. Maurice Hugh Frederick Wilkins -- born in

New Zealand, living in England -- studied DNA through diffraction analysis, reporting in 1953 that the atoms in the DNA molecule seemed to be arranged in a helix. In the same year, Francis Harry Compton Crick of England and his colleague James Dewey Watson of Illinois, on the base of an essentially mathematical approach, decided that a double helix (like a spiral staircase with two rails) filled the demanding requirements.

Aleksandr Ivanovich Oparin of the Soviet Union wrote in 1924 that the very origin of life would soon be explained as a consequence of natural causes. Many people throughout the world looked with disquietude toward the proposed eventuality, preferring to believe that only religion could explain such a momentous occurrence. Still, the new interest in DNA and its companion acid stirred excitement in the minds of many scientists. In 1955, Severo Ochoa of Spain, resident in the United States, found that he could form RNA in a test tube from RNA nucleotides (separate portions of the RNA molecule) through the catalytic action of an enzyme he had isolated. That is to say, the RNA nucleotides had in effect reproduced themselves, like the plants and animals in which they are found. Heinz Fraenkel-Conrat of Germany, moved to California, assisted by Robley Cook Williams of that state, separated the nucleic acid in a tobacco virus from the protein that surrounds it in the natural state. He found that neither the acid nor the protein acting alone could infect tobacco cells in quantity he could measure, though they proved fairly efficient when he mixed them again. He had not restored life from dead acid and protein, as some reporters suggested, but revealed the high vivacity of the nucleic acid when accompanied by its protein.

The study and synthesis of important chemicals of the human body proceeded at a rapid pace. In 1951, Robert Burns Woodward of Massachusetts synthesized cholesterol, and proceeded to calculate the composition of cortisone. In

487

1953, Frederick Sanger of England completed an analysis of the structure of insulin, the first of the intricate proteins to yield its secrets. His painstaking study of the sequence of 51 strands of amino acids and the highly complex bonds between them had consumed the major part of a decade. By 1954, Dorothy Crowfoot Hodgkin resolved the basics of the structure of Vitamin B_{12} which she had begun to study six years previously. In 1955, a new type of chemical showed promise of capturing a large market. An oral contraceptive for women, it entered the bloodstream like a hormone, affecting the nervous system in such a way as to prevent ovulation. "The pill," as it quickly came to be known because of the seeming ease with which it avoided undesired pregnancies (one a day keeping babies away when taken as part of a series), had received approval after testing against short-term undesirable side-effects, though the long-range impact of prolonged medication remained unknown.

At the end of this period, the production of a vaccine to combat poliomyelitis caused a popular sensation. This virus-produced malady attacked both children and adults, often leaving them paralyzed for life. Viruses came to the attention of bacteriologists late in the nineteenth century, without becoming visible under the microscope. Before long, scientists established associations between particular viruses and specific diseases; they had already, in a few instances, learned to treat the sickness without understanding its cause through controlled application of serum to effect immunity. Now they spoke in terms of viruses in the serums, and recognized the possibility of "growing" the viruses in some culture more adequate than that provided by cows (for smallpox) or ducks (for rabies). Fertile chicken eggs served as a culture medium in the fight against yellow fever in the 1930's.

The nature and size of the viruses became plain only with new experiments and the development of the electron microscope in the 1930's and

1940's. Very tiny, as had been expected, the viruses nevertheless ranged considerably in size; the polio variety revealed itself as one of the smallest. All viruses contained the nucleic acid and protein with which Fraenkel-Conrat experimented. After the war, the antibiotics -- several new brands of which appeared during this time period -- made it possible to grow a live culture in a test-tube. (The antibiotics attacked the bacteria which had made the process difficult). Jonas Edward Salk of New York isolated the polio virus and bred it successfully in a test-tube in 1952. Two years later, the serum he prepared successfully passed its first mass trial. In 1955, the Salk vaccine became available for vast inoculation programs, and the great threat of poliomyelitis began to subside. During these same years, other scientists established a statistical association between lung cancer and the smoking of tobacco. No one had identified a cancer-producing virus, although many had tried, and the search for an explanation of this disease continued.

Flying saucers and their kin -- or "unidentified flying objects," as the United States Air Force dubbed them in 1953 -- appeared in two impressive waves during this time period. The first, reaching its greatest height in mid-July 1952, attracted much attention in the United States, especially when multiple observers reported objects flying over the nation's capital at speeds far exceeding those of jet airplanes. The second wave, achieving record-breaking proportions early in October 1954, spread more evenly over the earth's surface, causing much excitement in Europe. Scientists generally continued to ignore the manifestation as a topic worthy of study. Not everyone felt inclined, however, to dismiss the subject so lightly. In 1952, the Aerial Phenomena Research Organization in Tucson, Arizona, began to collect useful data on better-authenticated accounts. In 1954, the Flying Saucer Review appeared in England. Both enterprises received support from many educated people, along with a wide range of other enthusiasts.

Serious students of the UFO phenomenon worked in two directions. Near-simultaneous sightings remote from one another geographically raised the question: Might some correlation among them be found? Repetitions of UFO waves at fairly regular intervals posed the query: Might some significance be attached? (A period of 27 1/2 months passed from the wave-peak of late-March 1950 to that of mid-July 1952; 26 1/2 months from mid-July 1952 to early-October 1954.) To work in either of these directions, investigators needed as complete a list of unexplained sightings as possible, not from one country but the world, not from one quinquennium but from decades. Such a catalog became a prime preoccupation of capable students in this field.

A more abstruse consideration led only to speculation, though of a potentially useful brand. UFO sightings on the large scale of those in 1950, 1952, and 1954 constituted a very new experience in the world's annals. They came on the heels of man's achievements in radio communication, his global struggle of World War II, and his development of atomic fission. All of these happenings might very well have been perceived by intelligent beings on some other planet -- particularly some planet revolving about a star not dissimilar to the earth's sun. Might the UFO waves have been prompted by the actual appearance on earth of electronic equipment designed to make careful reconnaissance for creatures interested in the study of earth-life? Alpha Centauri A, for example, one of a set of triplets constituting the nearest "fixed" star to earth, lay at a distance of 4.3 light-years. Its characteristics closely resembled those of the earth's own sun. An unintended message from the earth would take 4.3 years to reach a planet of Alpha Centauri; an inspection in return would take the same amount of time, if traveling at the speed of light. Alpha Centaurians could have detected the atomic blasts of July-August 1945; they could have responded with the global UFO wave of October 1954, about 9.2 years later.

Might such a conjecture be tested? Only, it seemed, if Alpha Centaurians did exist, and did choose to reveal themselves. Some astronomers wished to search for signs of extraterrestrial intelligence through the use of directed radio signals. Generally, however, they held that UFO chronology possessed no significance as a guide.

Modern man, on the verge of exploring other worlds, had begun to interpret his own with a new degree of profundity. Many of his discoveries yielded immediate applications, such as in the battle against disease. Erich Fromm of Germany, living in the United States, suggested in the same year that polio vaccine became available that man does less well with his mental than his physical health. In The Sane Society, 1955, Fromm (trained as a psychoanalyst) stated that many psychiatrists and psychologists "hold that the problem of mental health in a society is only that of the number of 'unadjusted' individuals, and not that of a possible unadjustment of the culture itself." In answer to the question, "Can a society be sick?" he added that most social scientists hold to a position of "sociological relativism," postulating "that each society is normal inasmuch as it functions, and that pathology can be defined only in terms of the individual's lack of adjustment to the ways of life in his society." Fromm believed, instead, that twentieth-century "industrialized" societies are sick, in that they have made men into robots. He proposed turning from the system in which the more affluent societies lived, toward a new one in which man himself is the central object.

Fromm described man's needs as he saw them, "the same . . . in all ages and . . . cultures," stemming from the conditions of man's existence.

491

Altogether, he listed five: (1) The need for relatedness, fulfilled through love. "If I love, I
care," said Fromm; "that is, I am actively concerned with the other person's growth and happiness. . . ." (2) The need for transcendence of
the role of an animal creature. Either creativity or destruction may fill this one; if man does
not create, producing happiness, he will destroy,
engendering suffering. (3) The need of "rooted-
ness." The concept of brotherliness (each individual a "son of man") must replace the "incest"
fixation by which each person not of the same
blood and soil is looked upon with suspicion.
(4) The need of a sense of identity, with individuality replacing the conformity of the herd.
(5) The need of a "frame of orientation and devotion," to which a man's reason impels him.
"The further his reason develops," commented
Fromm, "the more adequate becomes his system of
orientation, . . . the more it approximates reality. But even if man's frame of orientation is
utterly illusory, it satisfies his need for some
picture which is meaningful to him."

Fromm proceeded to analyze the position of
man, showing how far "capitalist society" comes
from meeting the requisites he had listed. Especially, he dealt with the concept of "alienation" -- the alienation of man from himself, by
which he submits to objects he has created, just
as ancient people worshipped idols that they
formed. Fromm believed that "alienation . . . in
modern society is almost total. . . . Man has
created a world of man-made things as it never
existed before. . . . Yet this whole creation of
his stands over and above him. . . . He is owned
by his own creation, and has lost ownership of
himself."

The Stalinist state, Fromm asserted, offered
less promise than capitalism. Democratic socialism, he felt, held some hope for solutions, but
in Great Britain and Scandinavia so far had not
realized its original aim of putting all emphasis
on the development of the individual. In a con-

clusion, turning away from science and indulging in a modern essay, Fromm described some contemporary West European "Communities of Work." He finally stated that man's choice lies "not . . . between Capitalism or Communism, but . . . between robotism (of both the capitalist and the communist variety), or Humanistic Communitarian Socialism."

Carleton Stevens Coon like Erich Fromm specialized in the study of man. Born in Massachusetts, he attended Harvard University there and became an anthropologist. In 1954, after producing a number of other books, he published The Story of Man, dedicating the work "to homo sapiens, wishing him good luck on his next adventure." As the dedication suggested, the book did not rest with primitive man, but drove all the way to the present. Many of its statements concerning earliest man and his relationship to the primates would stand for only a few years without challenge, since the study of fossil men moved relatively fast. The worth of Carleton Coon's book lay not in the dissemination of information that might soon be superseded, but in the integration of general knowledge that came from a variety of sources, explaining many features of the character of man.

Coon portrayed four "phases" of human history. In the first, homo sapiens emerged as a lone creature, fashioning the earliest tools and learning to use fire. In the second, man took over the earth, hunting creatures in all zoological realms, using clothing to combat the cold. During the third, the barnyard animals and cultivated plants appeared, as well as all the amazing inventions leading to modern societies. Human history is now entering the fourth phase, said Coon, when man may destroy the world, or when nature may regain its balance without man, or when man may learn to restore nature's balance and go on with his civilization. Coon believed that the cultures of the earth must be "unified" if this third option is to be realized.

Not all of _homo_ _sapiens_ ran together through these phases. Hunters of the second and all manner of persons of the third survived into the beginning of the fourth. The third consisted of eight "ages," as pictured by Coon -- the Neolithic (late stone), Bronze, Iron, Gunpowder, Coke, Oil, Hydroelectric, and First Atomic. Each came in more rapidly than the one preceding it, bringing great change in the lives of many people. The First Atomic age placed man already close to the dawn of the fourth phase. Coon ended _The Story of Man_ as Fromm did _The Sane Society_ with an essay veering away from social science. In the new phase, Coon suggested, man may build "a world in which everyone is young and beautiful forever." But man will never enter such a paradise if the graybeards of today who decide the destinies of nations cannot develop minds as bold and flexible as that of the second-phase hunter tracking a bear.

Robert Louis Heilbroner of New York, a practicing economist, contributed another impressive social science effort of this quinquennium. His book _The Worldly Philosophers: The Lives, Times, and Ideas of the Great Economic Thinkers_ appeared in 1953. It treated British, French, German, and North American writers of the last two hundred years. Adroitly, Heilbroner managed not to take sides as he dealt with laissez-faire advocates and the prophets of socialism. He only explained, like a guide in a museum, how the ideas of each man found their rationale in the circumstances of the time. He presented both the proponents and the critics of the new systems of thought that interested him.

In his conclusion, rather than dabble like Fromm and Coon in new and untested ideas, Heilbroner discussed the future of "American capitalism" through two approaches. In the first, he held out the possibility of political isolation. "We must recognize," he stated, "that although we produce one half of all the world's goods, we number but eight per cent of its population. . . . The whole turbulent drama which we have followed . . . has been confined to a fraction of the earth's surface, and during all these two hundred years, to countless millions of Chinese, Indians, Arabs, Africans, or South American peons the notion of a fluid and dynamic economy in which new products appeared and disappeared, in which a great chain of transactions bound together man and man, has never been anything but a tangential curiosity -- strange, rude, disturbing, and often exploitative." In his second approach, Heilbroner declared that the people of the United States themselves will be faced, in the future, with the choices posed by the Marxists, the democratic socialists, the "advocates of managed capitalism" (the liberals), and "the economists of the Right-of-Center" (the "hands-off" conservatives). "But an odd thing," Heilbroner added; "these are not new voices. They go back -- all of them -- to the body of economic thought erected by the great economists themselves."

Both The Story of Man and The Worldly Philosophers constituted history books written by social science specialists, each with a very specific frame of reference in mind. A small group of linguists and archeologists busied themselves at this same time in writing a new chapter of world history, significantly revising the picture of the Middle East in ancient times. European persons who could and did read the ancient histories during medieval and modern periods had believed that two foci of power and culture existed in the eastern Mediterranean area during the second millenium before Jesus. One lay in Egypt. where the hieroglyphic form of writing originated, and the other in Mesopotamia (the modern Iraq), whence came the type of notation called cuneiform. Nineteenth-century travelers and scholars found both cuneiform and hieroglyphic characters, however, in what are now eastern Turkey, Lebanon, Syria, and Israel, written in a language or languages they could not understand. One scholar suggested in 1880 that

495

these writings came from the Hittites mentioned by the Hebrews in the Bible. To the end of the nineteenth century, however, the inscriptions remained a mystery.

In 1906, a German expedition found the ancient capital of the Hittites in grand ruin in northeastern Turkey, confirming the belief that the writings belonged to an important ancient people. During World War I, a Czech scholar advanced a tentative decipherment for the Hittite cuneiform, showing that the Hittite language pertained to the Indo-European language family. Other scholars then worked on a solution for the cuneiform, finding themselves in frequent conflict, and putting aside the translation of the hieroglyphs. In 1947, a Turkish expedition at a new site in the southeastern part of the country located a bilingual key to the hieroglyphs, composed in Hittite and Phoenician. The Hittite hieroglyphs helped to solve the arguments concerning the cuneiform. In the early 1950's scholars advanced the decipherment of the hieroglyphs to new levels, published the first Hittite dictionary, and unearthed thousands of Hittite cuneiform tablets. A description of a once-mighty empire emerged, and a people who though they borrowed the idea of writing from Egypt and Mesopotamia possessed a proud culture of their own. The empire lasted through most of the second millenium before the time of Jesus. A group of successor city-states, lasting another five hundred years, included the people known as Hittites by the ancient Hebrews. Several new books of this time told the Hittite story. Kurt Marek of Germany attracted the most attention with his Enge Schlucht und schwarzer Berg (Narrow Gorge and Black Mountain, the two chief excavation sites), 1955, put into English as The Secret of the Hittites by C. W. Ceram (a pseudonym).

Michael Florinsky wrote very successfully of his estranged homeland in Russia: A History and an Interpretation, 1953. Florinsky particularly desired to present a well-rounded account rather than a specialized commentary. Born in the Ukraine, he had studied economics through the attainment of the doctorate at Columbia University. His several books dealt with the problems of the Soviet Union and Europe. Russia, two volumes in length, took nearly two decades in the writing stage. "Thus whatever its shortcomings," commented Florinsky, "they should not be ascribed to hasty workmanship."

Both volumes surveyed not only dynastic and political history, but economic, intellectual, artistic, and religious developments also. The second volume, treating the nineteenth century and the twentieth to 1917, rendered the story in considerable detail. Florinsky especially enjoyed the resolution of problems arising from two sources in disagreement. He decided he could not write the history of the Soviet Union, or of Russia after 1917, though he had originally intended to do so. "It is not suggested that the history of the Soviet Union cannot and should not be written" Florinsky commented, "but merely that information for a broad and comprehensive picture . . . is not, and perhaps will never be, available." At the very end of the Stalinist period, when this Russian in the United States wrote his preface and presumably his epilogue (containing these words), there existed ample reason for such pessimism.

Gilbert Chase contributed another comprehensive, integrated account, entitled America's Music: From the Pilgrims to the Present (1955). Chase, born in Cuba, knew Europe and Latin America well, though he made his home in the United States of America. He had already written books concerning the music of Spain and Latin America, maintaining the depth and breadth of interest that made America's Music (that is, the music of the United States) possible. Chase took careful account of plebeian beginnings. He recognized the Africans along with the Europeans, the amateurs along with the professionals, the eccentrics as well as the trend-followers. He

497

showed that the people's music took considerable time to reach the sophisticated concert stage, but that in the twentieth century certain popular features have affected many "serious" composers. The final chapter of America's Music, called "Composer from Connecticut," paid a fitting tribute to Charles Edward Ives, who pioneered in bringing American tunes into symphonic music, and who died in 1954 as this book went to press.

A History of Christianity by Kenneth Scott Latourette (1953) made a partisan but nonetheless valuable addition to historical studies. The author, born in Oregon, obtained his doctorate from Yale University in Connecticut, where he taught "missions" and oriental history for a long time. After living a few years in China, he wrote books on both China and Japan. He won much acclaim with A History of the Expansion of Christianity, six volumes published 1937-45. The 1500-page History of Christianity (not a condensation) constituted a new endeavor, picturing the world's largest religious faith as having survived more than one period of recession, always to forge ahead. The hundred-year period ending in 1914 Latourette called the great century for Christendom, with "growing repudiation paralleled by abounding vitality and unprecedented expansion." The period after 1914 he labeled "Vigour amidst Storm." The "storm" consisted of many occurrences, including the development of great indifference to Christianity among the people of western and central Europe. Latourette, nearly 70 years of age in 1953, saw "vigour" in the great activity of Christian leaders throughout the world. He believed too that many of the seemingly secular good deeds and good thoughts of the world stemmed in one way or another from Christianity, and that in this respect also Christianity remained very much alive.

Journalism is generally expressed in less formal language than history. Because its reportage frequently takes place before all the factors in a situation become plain, it may be less reliable than the historical tome. It is nevertheless very widely read in the twentieth century, when more and more individuals like to be informed of the everyday happenings in the world. Occasionally, a well-rounded journalist will write an important essay, such as Leland Stowe's While Time Remains (see "Art," Chapter V). John Gunther, born in Illinois and a reporter of daily events in Europe for twelve years, tried another tack when he wrote Inside Europe in 1936. He reviewed the continent he knew so well, country by country, describing anything of interest to outsiders in the contemporary situation. Success suggested repetition of the formula. Gunther proceeded to publish Inside Asia (1939), Inside Latin America (1941), Inside U.S.A. (1947), and Behind the Curtain (1949), dealing with Europe's communist regimes. In 1955, Inside Africa flowed from his pen. Critics had often asserted that no person could become an expert on so many areas in just a few years' time. Gunther, however, demonstrated his expertise in many ways, especially through the device of comparing the lands with one another, placing all of them in bold relief.

Inside Africa emerged with a very personal approach. Gunther employed the pronoun "I" regularly in reference to a personal experience. Very often, "I" gave way to "we," meaning Gunther and his wife Jane. Their extensive trips through Africa took place on the eve of the termination of colonialism in that continent. Wherever they went -- and they traveled to nearly every place of significance -- they interviewed all kinds of people and observed all manner of events. The result, coupled with Gunther's further study of the continent at home, proved an amazingly intricate and extremely well balanced picture of Africa's ingredients. "Almost the whole of the African continent," Gunther observed, "is . . . trembling and astir with acute nationalist uplift. . . . Some danger exists that, if nationalism succeeds too soon, the new governments may be exploited by corrupt <u>African</u> charlatans, underseasoned intellectuals, and illiterate politicians on the make. . . . Why cannot the white man stay forever, without conflict? Because of the temper of the times. Because his record, whether good or bad, calls forth intense resentment. And above all because he is overwhelmingly outnumbered in a continent not his own." Such reasoning, put in print in 1955, may be regarded by some as prophecy. Actually, despite the informal tone of their texts, these conclusions lay in the best social science tradition of generalization after careful observation and analysis.

While the work of John Gunther lay outside the realm recognized as their own by professional social scientists, and while social science generally remained outside the scientific sphere as delimited by natural scientists, Ludwig Wittgenstein had begun to question the very prevalent assumption among scientists that man could strike through to completely objective descriptions. Wittgenstein (mentioned in Chapter V as a foundation-builder for logical positivism) had lived in England and Ireland since 1929, sometimes teaching philosophy at Cambridge University. His teaching came into sharp conflict with views he had earlier expressed, particularly in his treatise written during World War I. Then, he had spoken of a model language, founded on perfect concepts, matching exactly the concrete realities they were intended to represent. Now, he believed that words and sentences are approximate, and that their meaning truly depends upon the circumstances under which they are uttered. Bertrand Russell in <u>Human Knowledge</u> pointed out the limits of science while retaining his faith in the precision of language. Wittgenstein asserted that, for problems of major impact, language could not be treated as mathematics, but must find its strength in a fargoing comprehension of the very complex strands in its construction. Wittgenstein died in 1951; his <u>Philosophische</u>

500

<u>Untersuchungen</u> (<u>Philosophical</u> <u>Investigations</u>), incorporating his later ideas, appeared in 1953.

Art

Viktor Chukarin in gymnastics . . Emil Zatopek in distance running . . Hungary in the Olympics . . West Germany in soccer . . cha-cha-cha and rock 'n' roll . . Hanson, Sinfonia sacra . . Cage, Imaginary Landscape No. 4 . . Britten: Billy Budd; The Turn of the Screw . . Menotti: Amahl and the Night Visitors; The Saint of Bleecker Street . . Sartre, Le Diable et le bon Dieu . . Ionesco, Les chaises . . Adamov, Le ping-pong . . Beckett, En attendant Godot . . Miller, The Crucible . . Williams, Cat on a Hot Tin Roof . . Anouilh, L'alouette . . Davis, Colonial Cubism . . Marini, Portrait of Curt Valentin . . Kurosawa, Ikiru . . Ray, Pather Panchali . . Kazan, On the Waterfront . . De Sica, Umberto D . . Fellini, La strada . . Bergman, Gycklarnas Afton . . Ophüls, Lola Montès . . Visconti, Senso . . Kazan, Viva Zapata! . . Williams, Paterson . . Bowles, The New Dimensions of Peace . . Castro, the Geography of Hunger . . Thomas, The Test of Freedom . . Lamming, In the Castle of My Skin . . Oldenbourg, La pierre angulaire . . Gouzenko, The Fall of a Titan . . Remarque, Der Funke Leben . . Markandaya, Nectar in a Sieve . . Salinger, The Catcher in the Rye.

The Olympic games and international soccer competition stirred world interest in this quin- quennium even more than in the preceding one. Sixty-nine national entities, including Germany (West and East combined) and Japan as well as the Soviet Union for the first time, sent 5,867 athletes to the summer games in Helsinki, Fin- land, July 1952. Viktor Chukarin of the Soviet Union won four gold medals in gymnastics, for the individual and team all-around competitions as well as the long horse and side horse vaults.

Emil Zatopek of Czechoslovakia earned three in distance running -- the 5,000-meter and 10,000-meter races and the marathon -- while his wife Dana Zatopkova took first place in the women's javelin throw. Zatopek had won his first gold medal in the 10,000-meter race in 1948.

In the team games, the United States took the gold medal again in basketball, the Soviet Union winning the silver, and Uruguay the bronze. In soccer, Hungary won the gold, Yugoslavia the silver again, and Sweden dropped from gold to bronze. India maintained its hold on first position in field hockey, the Netherlands moved from third to second, and the United Kingdom from second to third. In water polo, Hungary improved from silver to gold (thus placing as champion in two team sports), Yugoslavia won the silver medal, and Italy dropped from gold to bronze.

By the scoring used in Chapter V for comparisons among the nations (three points for a gold medal, two for silver, one for bronze, none for lower standings), persons or teams from the United States (165 points), the Soviet Union (141), Hungary (83), Sweden (60), Italy (46), Finland (31), France (31), Czechoslovakia (29), and Germany (29) won two-thirds of the points in the Helsinki games. On the more revealing per capita basis, Luxembourg rated first (with 10.0 points per million of population); Hungary (8.7), Sweden (8.4), Jamaica (8.4), and Finland (7.6) followed; and Switzerland (4.6), Trinidad-Tobago (3.0), Australia (2.9), New Zealand (2.5), and Czechoslovakia (2.3) rounded out the highest ten. (The figure for Luxembourg is an inverted one, since that country contained fewer than 1,000,000 persons.) Luxembourg, New Zealand, and Czechoslovakia took the place in this select group of Denmark, the Netherlands, and Norway.

Thirty nations sent 960 athletes to participate in the winter games held at Oslo, Norway, February 1952. Hjalmar Andersen of Norway achieved three gold medals in speed skating, winning the 1,500-meter, 5,000-meter, and 10,000-meter events. A team from Canada again won the gold medal in ice hockey, the United States taking the silver and Sweden the bronze. Athletes from the host country Norway earned the largest number of points (29) on the weighted scale used here, as the United States (25) and Finland (19) rounded out the first half of the point total. Norway (8.7 points per million population), Finland (4.6), and Austria (2.3) led on the per capita basis, Austria replacing Switzerland and Sweden in this group.

The World Cup tourney in soccer, held in 1954 in Switzerland in accord with a revised playing schedule, brought two winning teams from each of four groups into the quarterfinals. Of the chief contenders in 1950, Spain and Sweden had become eliminated in pre-tourney competition, while Brazil lost out in the quarterfinals -- along with the United Kingdom, Yugoslavia, and Switzerland. Further play in the semifinals and finals then brought West Germany the cup, and put Hungary in second place, Austria in third, and Uruguay (the 1950 champion) in fourth.

Dance styles internationally popular during this period remained much the same as in the preceding one, with the addition of a few new ideas from the Caribbean area. The European fox-trot attracted a wide following along with the mambo and the rumba. The Argentine tango and Brazilian samba likewise received wide acclaim. The cha-cha-cha, a variety of the mambo, spread through most of the Caribbean countries and began to appear elsewhere. The Dominican Republic exported the merengue. The jitterbug style popular in the United States in 1955 suddenly burst into a more frenzied stage called "rock 'n' roll" by its youthful devotees.

The composition of new concert music in this time period included most of the varieties discussed in Chapter V. At one extreme in seriousness stood Howard Hanson with his Sinfonia sacra

503

(1954), intended to invoke memories of the first Easter as described in the gospel called John. At the other extreme stood John Cage of California with his Imaginary Landscape No. 4 (1951), which consisted of directions for 24 operators of 12 radios (one to control the volume, the other to select stations, on each set), with the intent of producing a unique set of voice and instrumental sounds at each offering of the program. Between these two extremes, Jean Françaix of France composed opera stressing a personal element, while veteran Ernest Bloch of Switzerland, resident in the United States, offered orchestral work emphasizing nationalistic (in this case Hebraic) inspiration.

The most popular of the new concert pieces combined various techniques, using whatever seemed to be the most appropriate setting for particular passages. Benjamin Britten, of Peter Grimes fame, in 1951 contributed the opera Billy Budd, about an eighteenth-century sailor sentenced to hang for unpremeditated murder. Billy Budd contained little song but much instrumental music accompanied by recitatives, all of them performed by a male chorus. In 1954, Britten orchestrated The Turn of the Screw, an equally sad story of two children, for 15 players and only six voices. Gian Carlo Menotti, earlier the author of The Medium and The Consul, wrote Amahl and the Night Visitors for television in 1951. Amahl, a crippled boy, emulated the example of the Night Visitors (the Three Wise Men), even going farther than they to give to Jesus his crutches, all that he owned. In return, he found himself unexpectedly and miraculously cured. The Saint of Bleecker Street (1954), also by Menotti, revolved about an Italian girl of New York who received the stigmata, or marks of the crucifixion of Jesus, on her hands. In both of these productions, as he had done before, Menotti presented a high degree of musical variety.

The theme of despair continued to run high during this quinquennium in new (non-musical) productions for the theatre. Jean-Paul Sartre concluded in Le Diable et le bon Dieu, 1951 (The Devil and the Good Lord, also known as Lucifer and the Lord), that traditional concepts of both Good and Evil totally lack reality. A general in sixteenth-century Germany, at the time of the rebellion of the peasants, tries paternalistic-ally to do good for a year and a day, setting up a model city for its inhabitants after previous-ly having served le Diable. Encountering noth-ing but setbacks in his new loyalty as in his old, he decides that man is alone in his world (that there is nothing but sky above him), though he finally consents to lead the peasants in their rebellion.

Eugène Ionesco in Les chaises (The Chairs, 1952) emphasized the same theme in absurdist manner. An old man and woman live in a tower surrounded by water, where the man has long held employment as the keeper. They invite a number of persons to hear their final words to human-ity, presented by a hired orator. The (invisi-ble) guests arrive, and are seated in (visible) chairs, after which the couple leap from a win-dow. The orator, a deaf-mute, makes only gut-tural sounds. Absurd the play, and meaningless the life, Ionesco intended to say. Arthur Adamov, born of an Armenian father in Russia but long resident in France, wrote Le ping-pong (Ping Pong, 1955) in similar vein, at the same time directing a specific slap at capitalism. His characters become engrossed in the pinball machine, allowing it to overwhelm their lives, particularly as commercial considerations begin to appeal to them. They all become ruined by the machine, until two of them in their 70's savagely give themselves over completely to ping pong.

Samuel Beckett, who was born in Ireland but like Ionesco and Adamov lived in Paris and wrote in French, produced En attendant Godot (Waiting for Godot) in 1953. In this very popular ab-surdist play, two impoverished men engage in meaningless conversation while they wait for

Godot to come. Godot simply does not come; he is represented in the play only by a messenger who says he will arrive on the morrow. A few other individuals appear, adding notes of reflection and comedy, but at the end the two men remain alone. They plan to hang themselves the next day (they have already tried) unless Godot should come. If he does arrive, they will be "saved." They agree to go, finally, but they do not move.

Meanwhile, in the United States, Arthur Miller and Tennessee Williams depicted other sad worlds. Miller produced The Crucible (1953), a gripping story of the famed "witch trials" in seventeenth-century New England. McCarthyism had brought a twentieth-century search for witches to all the United States, interrogating Arthur Miller in the process. The Crucible, without mentioning the senator's name, reveals the very close parallels between the McCarthy hearings and the seventeenth-century variety, both steeped in intolerance and indignity. Williams wrote Cat on a Hot Tin Roof (1955) about a family situation in which the title of the play stood for determination. The wife of an estranged couple, to qualify for a legacy, declares falsely that she is pregnant by her husband. Admiringly, the husband feels challenged (for the first time) to make her statement come true.

Jean Anouilh, distinguished French playwright from the period before World War II, portrayed another quality of despair in L'alouette (The Lark), presented 1953. This story of Joan of Arc, of fifteenth-century France, portrays her as a simple country girl who ran into trouble not through her own fault, but because the world about her stood contaminated by sin. Anouilh's pessimism lay in his belief that the world will always remain so contaminated.

Painting in the first half of the 1950's rushed madly from one extreme to another, like some unfortunate creature in the throes of mortal agony. René Magritte of Belgium painted figures of "magic realism" reminiscent of his productions in the 1920's and 1930's -- a mammoth apple filling a room, or coffins substituting for people in copies of paintings well known. Stuart Davis, putting aside his portrayals of words, produced <u>Colonial</u> <u>Cubism</u>, a beautiful composition in five colors, remindful of the European cubist movement of the 1910's and 1920's. Jean Dubuffet continued his depiction of mad and violent figures, particularly of people and cows.

A great variety of abstract images produced in New York attracted wide attention. Jackson Pollock, from Wyoming, known for his "drip" paintings in which he splattered paint on a canvas on the floor, posed as a leader of an abstract "school," though each painter remained very much an individualist. Willem de Kooning of the Netherlands, also in the New York group, painted with a brush exclusively, using vigorous strokes to produce the kind of compositions in many colors that Franz Kline did in black and white. Jasper Johns of Georgia, a younger New York artist of this time period, rebelled against the abstract, creating simple images of everyday objects while experimenting with his materials, intending in one way or another to draw attention not to the object but to the image.

Developments in the world of sculpture ran somewhat less jaggedly. Jean Arp's concretions of living organisms in marble tended to converge toward the human feminine torso. Henry Moore, son of a British coal miner and famed as a sculptor before the war, brought out attenuated figures in bronze, half real, half symbolic. Barbara Hepworth, likewise of the United Kingdom, produced figures in both mahogany and marble noted for their simplicity and high finish. Germaine Richier of France made bronze images of Don Quixote from Spanish sixteenth-century literature, exemplifying the varied facets of his character. Marino Marini of Italy depicted var-

507

ious subjects in bronze, including the very expressive though not completely representational Portrait of Curt Valentin. Giacomo Manzù, also of Italy, frequently chose religious themes, looking back to the sixteenth century for his very effective style in bronze.

Architects who had become famous in the 1920's and 1930's continued in high regard. Ludwig Mies van der Rohe, who had fled to the United States at the time of the Nazi regime, planned twin skyscrapers of steel to be used as apartment houses in Chicago, Illinois, as well as an entire new campus for the Illinois Institute of Technology. Le Corbusier, back in France, meanwhile attracted much attention with the fashioning of a chapel in Ronchamp; built of concrete, the edifice possessed an irregular pattern of windows that let in focused slivers of light. Many other architects kept busy during this period designing new skyscrapers to house the offices of postwar city industry.

The motion picture industry engaged itself in the early 1950's to a rather strong element of pathos. The film Ikiru (Living, or by transposition Doomed), directed by Kurosawa Akira of Japan (1952), told the story of an office-worker who, threatened by cancer, learned how to make his life meaningful as it had never been before, only to have his funeral wake attended by persons who failed to understand. Pather Panchali (Song of the Little Road), done by Satyajit Ray of the Bengali-speaking portion of India (1955), showed the poverty-stricken village life of that land, following the activities of a child named Apu. On the Waterfront, directed by Elia Kazan of Turkey, working in the United States (1954), dipped realistically into the gangster-ridden situation of dock workers in the latter country.

Other cinema concentrated on the pathetic position of just one or two individuals. Such was Umberto D, directed by Vittorio De Sica (1952), the portrait of an old man (Domenico

508

Umberto) without money or friends whose life became meaningless for a time. The experience of the director's own father provided inspiration for this picture. La strada (The Road), done by Federico Fellini of Italy in 1954, comprised the story of a simple-minded and innocent young lady and her heartless traveling companion, who performed a strong-man act for a livelihood. Gycklarnas Afton (Night of Juggling, called in English The Naked Night or Sawdust and Tinsel), by Ingmar Bergman of Sweden (1953), dealt with the meager lives of two circus people as they came into bitter circumstances during a one-performance stop.

Three more films of this time dealt with pathos in history. Lola Montès (1955) was an extravaganza directed by Max Ophüls of West Germany. Filmed in France, West Germany, and Austria, it attracted notice for its elaborate camera work. The original Lola Montès, a beautiful courtesan of the nineteenth century, won the rapt admiration of several distinguished men, but finished her career as a beauty on display in the circus. Senso (Sentiment, also called The Wanton Countess), directed by Luchino Visconti in 1954, in contrast to most Italian cinema after the war showed Italian aristocratic society (of the early nineteenth century) at its best as well as at its worst. The story told of a countess who, after a love affair with an enemy officer, tried unsuccessfully to bribe him to stay in Italy with her. In petulance at his refusal, she betrayed his confidence, bringing on his execution and her own insanity. In Viva Zapata!, another film by Elia Kazan (1952), artists of the United States showed that they could if they tried deal sensitively with the ways of another nation. Marlon Brando acted as the Mexican revolutionary hero in Emiliano Zapata's struggle (until his death in 1919) for a greater degree of justice to his country's peasants.

Television broadcasting spread more widely during this quinquennium, to include a few countries each in South America and northern Africa as well as Japan. In the United States, where only commercial television had arisen previously, new "educational" television became available in some cities without advertising. In Great Britain, where only government programming had existed, competitive commercial television began. Networks developed in both North America and western Europe to provide coverage of sports and special events, and in North America to provide a wide audience for regular network programs. Viewers in western Europe counted as one of their highlights the opportunity to watch the world soccer tourney in Switzerland. Color television emerged in 1955, to open new possibilities in what remained a very new industry and form of art.

Few expressions of sustained thought appeared in poetry at this time. William Carlos Williams of New Jersey and Dylan Thomas of Wales (died 1953) attracted much attention as poets. Thomas received applause for the reading of his own and others' poetry in public auditoriums and on television. In 1951, Williams finished Paterson, a four-part work describing life in the city of that name in New Jersey, relating it to the life of a man. (Author Williams' note: ". . . A man in himself is a city. . . .") There existed many detours in this writing; digressions of almost impenetrable thought had become common in postwar poetry. In one of his, Williams stated (in prose) that "American poetry is a very easy subject to discuss for the simple reason that it does not exist." Other poets, however, refused to be dismissed so lightly. In America and throughout the world, short poems of fine quality remained abundant.

Prose essays caught a greater reading audience. Among the most widely discussed during this period were The New Dimensions of Peace, by Chester Bowles of Massachusetts (1955); The Geography of Hunger, by Josué de Castro of Brazil

510

(1952); The Test of Freedom, by Norman Thomas of Ohio (1954); and In the Castle of My Skin, by George Lamming of the British-held island of Barbados (1953). The last of these constituted an essay in autobiographical form, in which the characters said and did what the author wished to convey to the reader.

Chester Bowles served as United States ambassador to India, traveling widely in Africa and southern Asia, before he wrote The New Dimensions of Peace. Like Leland Stowe, he wanted to alert the people of his own country to the wide range of opportunity before them. He carefully reviewed the essence of four revolutions as he saw them -- the communist variety in the Soviet Union and China, the democratic type in India and the United States. He reminded his readers that president Sukarno of Indonesia, opening the Asian-African conference at Bandung, cited the eighteenth-century revolution in the United States rather than any of those that had occurred since. Bowles agreed with Sukarno that to reach a "full measure of human dignity" the Africans as well as the Asians needed "democratic self-government, free of foreign influence."

The conference at Bandung and other events of 1954-5, including the summit conference discussion of disarmament, opened up new possibilities for diplomacy, Bowles argued. The United States should give up the idea of a Pax Americana in which the remainder of the world would be expected to follow that country's lead. Both military and economic power retain importance, Bowles said, as two of the dimensions of peace, but each of the two is strictly limited in its efficacy. Wise diplomacy, recognition of the need for an end to colonialism, an understanding of the importance in the Asian world of both India and Japan, a better United States image abroad, and a genuine readiness to disarm constituted other dimensions of peace immediately in demand. Bowles hoped that his countrymen would "rise with the occasion." However, he added, "It would be less than honest to deny that our society has developed some sobering weaknesses which . . . might cost us dearly. . . . Many of us have become cut off from the hopes and aspirations of a majority of the world's people. Although we are one of the most literate nations on earth, scarcely one American in a hundred has more than a rudimentary knowledge of the history of Asia, Africa and South America, where the bulk of mankind lives and where the shape of the future may largely be decided." After a rather long list of such weaknesses, Bowles added, "The word has got around that we have lost touch with our tradition. Consequently our rediscovery must be genuine."

Josué de Castro, an expert in nutrition and university teacher, wrote "not of human accomplishment, but of human poverty and distress" in his book The Geography of Hunger. "Because of its explosive political and social implications," he said, "the subject . . . has been one of the taboos of our civilization. . . . Like sex, hunger was shameful, indecent, unclean." Starvation, the most striking of its manifestations, might express itself in famine or in chronic malnutrition leading to death. Hidden (or "specific") hungers also afflicted a large percentage of mankind -- hunger for proteins, for minerals, and for vitamins especially. Except for the Soviet Union, for which he lacked data, author Castro found hunger everywhere as he studied the world region by region. Europe had its shortages, like Asia and Africa; North America, like Middle America and South America -- though the regions varied in particulars as well as degree of severity. Some of the problem stemmed from ignorance; people recognized their own nutritional deficiencies less than the animals about them. Much of the difficulty, however, derived from a lack of concern on the part of the world's population that had the food it needed. Castro believed the world had already entered the social revolution required to correct this situation. Both the capitalist and socialist communities seemed prepared, he felt, to give priority to concrete human problems.

The geography of hunger could change to a geography of abundance, said Castro, with the raising of the productive levels of marginal peoples and their integration into the world economic community. "Latin America, Africa and the Far East," he asserted, "constitute enormous potential markets which will begin to take their place in the world economy just as soon as their inhabitants, properly fed, can produce enough to reach a living standard in keeping with the technical possibilities of the modern age." He disagreed with the "neo-Malthusians" (followers of eighteenth-century Thomas Robert Malthus) who prescribed birth control for burgeoning populations. The best way to reduce the birth rate, he argued, consisted in feeding the hungry, rather than attempting to control them, since the hungriest peoples of the world rather consistently brought into life the largest numbers of children. People generally believed that overpopulation of a country led to the starvation of its inhabitants. Author Castro turned the idea around, speaking only of the nutritional deficiencies, with a theory that specific hunger is the cause of overpopulation.

Norman Thomas, before he wrote The Test of Freedom, ran six campaigns as the Socialist candidate (1928-48) for the presidency of the United States. In book after book, in speech after speech, he made clear his devotion to the principles of both democracy and socialism. Unlike Chester Bowles, he criticized "the liberals" for their shortcomings, for his own persuasion took him farther to the left, the middle of the second quarter of the world spectrum. His book The Test of Freedom (1954, but written a year earlier when McCarthyism ran rampant) did not, however, argue for socialism, but pled for good sense in the search for a nation's subversives.

Norman Thomas believed that subversives did

exist, and that congressional committees might properly look for them. He disagreed with physicist Albert Einstein when the latter said "intellectuals" should refuse to answer questions concerning their political beliefs. Thomas asserted that the congressional investigations (including two besides that of McCarthy) had "sinned grievously against fair play to individuals," and he decried the use of the committees for "political grandstanding." He thought of McCarthyism, however, as a manifestation of an aberrance dating from the 1930's -- a peculiarity not of one senator, but of the American people who followed him. "It is," he said, "highly significant that Joseph McCarthy did not enter the Senate as a convinced . . . crusader against a communism he does not understand. He, a shrewd demagogue, . . . made himself the . . . spokesman of a public which finds it . . . more emotionally satisfying to hunt for . . . communist devils than to understand and counteract the forces that make for communism."

George Lamming, writing In the Castle of My Skin, traced the story of his young life on Barbados, ages 8 to 17. His inclusion of fictitious material gave the account some of the characteristics of the novel. Most of these portions, however, served only as a medium for the expression of the author's ideas. Pa and Ma, two ancient characters set up as individuals in Lamming's unnamed village, at times take on all the wisdom of the ages despite the meagerness of their surroundings. To write an autobiographical essay rather than one more direct in form, Lamming created Ma's and Pa's conversation as well as that of other colloquies.

Trumper, a boyhood friend who moved to the United States, spoke when he returned (at the end of Lamming's narration) about his people, meaning those of African descent no matter where they lived. Before Trumper spoke in this manner, the author had never entertained such a concept. Lamming's people, until he reached 17, were those who lived in his village -- some of them more white, some of them more black, in the color of their skin. They held relationships with other people, most conspicuously the English Mr. Creighton on whose land they all lived, but even those who attended primary school knew nothing of a connection with Africa. George Lamming, who went on to secondary school before accepting a teaching position in Trinidad, became nearly an alien in his village by the age of 17, though he had not yet joined the other world with its difficulties and excitement.

In the Castle of My Skin told a large number of stories to illustrate various facets of Barbados village life. One day, some boyhood friends (Trumper, Boy Blue, and Bob) tested the formula of Danish king Canute, about whom they had heard in school -- sitting at the margin of the sea and pronouncing the words, "Sea come no further." Boy Blue recited the tale of Bambi, a man with two common-law wives, named Bots and Bambina. Pressed by an outsider to marry one of them, Bambi flipped a coin and married Bots. ("The white missis tell him . . . he should, 'cause it was better to live in one mortal sin than two. . . .") The boys had ideas about some things, such as words, and wondered about others, such as slavery, which they had not studied in school. Concerning words, they agreed, "You could say what you like if you know how to say it. It didn't matter whether you felt everything you said. . . . And if you were really educated, and you could command the language like a captain on a ship, . . . then you didn't have to feel at all. You could do away with feeling. That's why everybody wanted to be educated." Take Mr. Creighton for an example of a person without feeling, they might have said a few years later -- or Mr. Slime, the teacher who resigned to become a leader of the village people, only eventually to buy their land and evict some of them, in order to make way for "their" progress.

515

Among the significant novels of this time period were La pierre angulaire, by Zoé Oldenbourg of France (1953); The Fall of a Titan, by Russian Igor Gouzenko (1954); Der Funke Leben, by German-born Erich Maria Remarque (1952); Nectar in a Sieve, by Kamala Purnaiya Taylor, pseudonym Kamala Markandaya, of India (1954); and The Catcher in the Rye, by Jerome David Salinger of New York (1951). These five publications dealt, respectively, with early thirteenth-century situations in France and Palestine; with the bitter side of life in Stalinist Russia; with the last days of a German concentration camp; with recent village life in India; and with the struggle of an adolescent to find his identity in a world that seemed to him rather meaningless.

La pierre angulaire, or The Cornerstone, amply demonstrated the key position of religion in the high middle ages of western European history. Its characters, whether persons of malice or individuals of substantial good will, stood subject to temptations that continue common in the twentieth century. Unlike their modern progeny, however, they could not assume an attitude of indifference to Christianity or to its demands upon them. Ansiau, lord of Linnières (near Troyes and the Seine River in France), had already fought in two crusades, and now wished to return to Palestine as a pilgrim. Herbert le Gros, son of Ansiau and father of Haguenier, spat upon the crucifix and engaged in far-going blasphemy; yet neither Herbert nor his half-sister Eglantine, with whom he practiced incest, could escape the wrath of their God.

The old man Ansiau experienced difficulty in reaching Palestine even with the help of his squire, since warfare had robbed him of one eye and now he lost the other. In Palestine, Arabs captured him and sold him to a family with whom he lived as a slave until the night he fled into the desert and died. In Linnières, meanwhile, the very unpopular Herbert le Gros ruled as lord until his own pilgrimage, without leaving France,

516

only to hear scandals about his second wife Aelis upon his return. When in Herbert's wrath he treated Aelis with violence, Haguenier intervened to help his stepmother, giving his father a hard push that turned out to be fatal. After this frightening episode, Haguenier left not only his wife and his young daughter, but his lady love Marie of Mongenost as well, to enter the doors of a monastery. Zoé Oldenbourg, who knew the French middle ages well, brought out the attributes of her assortment of characters in every detail. He who would read <u>La</u> <u>pierre</u> <u>angulaire</u> would comprehend his own century better, even with the cornerstone changed.

<u>The</u> <u>Fall</u> <u>of</u> <u>a</u> <u>Titan</u>, by Igor Gouzenko, dealt with twentieth-century realities far more complex in scope than those examined in <u>The</u> <u>Corner-</u> <u>stone</u>. Life in the castle of Linnières changed little from one generation to another, despite the dramatic episodes. Life in revolutionary Rostov on the Don, in a southern European part of the Soviet Union, altered much more rapidly. Author Gouzenko disapproved of such revolutionary change. Against the wishes of the Russian people, he maintained, "Stalin was imposing collectivization on the country. The horror, the sorrow, the humiliation for millions of peasants and workers which this policy wrought exceeded in awfulness all the calamities that history had ever seen." When Gouzenko was assigned to work in the Soviet embassy in Ottawa, Canada, he seized the opportunity to desert (1946). Then followed his novel, written in Russian but first published in English in the United States.

The "titan" of the book, named Mikhail Gorin, resembled the writer Maksim Gorky (Aleksey Maksimovich Peshkov), who lived in Nizhny Novgorod (now renamed Gorky for him) rather than in Rostov, and made himself defender of the Soviet regime 1928-36. Gorky's death came in suspicious circumstances, which suggested to many a break between him and the Stalinist regime. The supreme humbling of Gorin in the novel came before his murder by academician Feodor Novikov. It occurred when he agreed to write a play about Ivan the Terrible, the sixteenth-century Russian tsar, suppressing those elements concerning Ivan that made him seem odious to a twentieth-century revolutionary. Gorin did so at the subtle behest of the man who eventually killed him.

Despite the title, the story of young Feodor Novikov constituted Gouzenko's chief concern. Novikov became involved with the Soviet regime through his composition of a history of the ancient Slavs, giving a nationalistic interpretation of the emergence of Russian civilization. Delighted when the top leaders in Moscow approved his account, he agreed to accept his very difficult academic assignment with Mikhail Gorin. (The Stalinist leadership felt in the 1930's that it needed the kind of support abroad that Gorin's cooperation could make possible.) Novikov became more and more enmeshed, especially when he committed murder in self-defense; there would be no prosecution, even though he had killed the son of a party figure, as long as he remained faithful to his assignment. Novikov fell in love with Nina Gorin, Mikhail's daughter, but had to give her up lest their love get in the way of his duty. He married Lida Sidorov, a former pupil and Nina's friend, but separated from her also when officials declared her father an "enemy of the people." He lost the friendship of his brother Nikolai, who liked Lida and eventually took her as his wife, becoming a father to Feodor's unborn child.

Alone in the world, though still in the good graces of the party hierarchy, 32-year-old Feodor Novikov made a frank and impassioned confession to Mikhail Gorin before killing him. Speaking further, however, Novikov accused Gorin: "You promised us heavenly bliss -- where is it? We are your despoiled heirs; we hate you. Yes, deprived of love, we can only hate. . . . Evil has become our natural element. Crime is encouraged by the state. . . . Right

518

now I want to cry out to the whole world: 'Give me a reason for living, give me back the soul taken out of me by filthy hands.'"

Could the novel of Igor Gouzenko, appearing soon after Stalin's death, be described as a success in the sense described in Chapter V? If Gouzenko's interest lay in portraying only the evil side of what nearly everyone considered a harsh regime, he performed his task exquisitely. His main characters remained credible, with all their ugly deeds, because Gouzenko took the trouble to explore their misgivings along with their open qualities. Nina, Lida, and Nikolai emerged as engaging young people who did not fit with the regime. High Soviet officialdom, however, Gouzenko unvaryingly portrayed as clever and vicious in the extreme. At one point, Veria (presumably Lavrenty Beria), visiting a plant, listened to complaints of the workers about their living conditions. Suddenly, he shouted to them, "Run into the director's apartment, take everything he has! The furniture, dishes, everything! Bring it all out here. Don't stand on ceremony!" This accomplished, he added, "Now you are real aristocrats. Regular dukes, out-and-out dukes. Well, boys! I'll bet it wouldn't be a great sin if you worked extra after such a reward. Am I right?" The workers of course responded, "Right! Right!"

Gouzenko's hatred of the ruling class to which Veria belonged showed most blatantly in his description of their eyes and faces. Mikhail Gorin, at his daughter's wedding, "looked over the guests slowly. A sea of beasts stormed around him: bearish faces, foxy snouts, wolfish eyes -- they growled, they hooted." Because these officials contained within them the very essence of evil and not a trace of good, Gouzenko lost his opportunity to explain the decade of the 1930's under the Stalin regime.

Der Funke Leben, or Spark of Life, dealt with life and death in a Nazi concentration camp at

519

the end of World II. Its author, German-born Erich Maria Remarque, had written an account from World War I, called All Quiet on the Western Front in translation. He took up residence in the United States in 1939. All the action of Der Funke Leben took place during a few months in 1945, from the first bombing of the imaginary German town of Mellern, adjacent to the camp, to the liberation of those prisoners who had not already died. "Skeleton 509 slowly raised its skull and opened its eyes," began the story. 509 was one of the self-styled "Veterans," men too weak to work any longer but despite malnutrition able to postpone death over a period of years. Der Funke Leben essentially comprised a description of the kind of life these men lived. "509 let his head droop. . . . The sight of the smoking chimneys in the valley made a man only hungrier than usual. . . . In winter it had taken 509 three months to rid himself of the vision of fried potatoes. He had smelled them everywhere, even in the stench of the latrine shed. Now it was bacon. Bacon and eggs."

Only twelve Veterans remained from a much larger number. One of them, mad, thought himself a sheep dog. The youngest at the age of eleven, Karel of Czechoslovakia, had spent most of his life in concentration camps. The oldest, a Jew of 72 years, took pride in his beard, even though it was infected with lice. Ephraim Berger, former physician and now the head of this section of the camp, bore the responsibility of pulling the gold teeth from bodies taken to the crematorium. Leo Lebenthal, who had connections with the black market of the laboring men, found opportunities to procure "cigarette ends, a carrot, sometimes potatoes, leftovers from the kitchen, a bone, and now and again a slice of bread." All about the Veterans lived skeletons weaker than they, men who had lost hope and the ability to reason though they still ate what they could get and visited the latrine.

Neubauer, the director of the camp, kept his

wife and one daughter at their home in town,
where flowers grew (fertilized by ashes from the
crematorium) and pet rabbits resided. Weber, the
leader of the Schutzstaffeln (SS), carried out
the dirty work in the camp. After the first
bombing of Mellern, Neubauer's family wanted to
move in with him at the camp. Neubauer opposed
the move because his family knew little of the
camp horrors. After other bombings, Neubauer's
wife and daughter did move in with him (they left
him later), while Neubauer thought of this and
that measure (such as better food for the prisoners) that would make him appear humane. In the
meantime, laborers in the camp with whom the Veterans maintained liaison prepared for the day
when the American army would arrive and provide
their release. 509 himself received a revolver
smuggled in by the workers. On the final morning, when Weber and his SS men made themselves
drunk and set fire to the Veterans' building, 509
lay outside among the dead bodies that had accumulated in the few days since work had ceased
in the crematorium. Before stray bullets killed
him, 509 had the satisfaction of shooting Weber
down, calling to his friends to come out of the
burning building as the SS men fled, and watching
Weber burn to death from a plank that fell upon
him.

Der Funke Leben, then, was a novel of violence. Its severities, however, constituted but
a reflection of those that took place on a very
wide scale in central Europe only a few years
prior to this book. They showed, more effectively than any other medium -- whether photographs, motion pictures, or painting -- the awful
degredation to which free men (the camp commanders) sank when they lived under the assurance that such was expected of them. Der
Funke Leben served as a reminder not only of the
darkest side of fascism but also of the extremes
to which some individuals have gone in attempting to prove the superiority of one group of
people over another.

521

Nectar in a Sieve, by Kamala Markandaya, told the story of a family in India. The author, herself Indian, lived with her husband in England when she wrote this account, speaking in the first person for Rukmani, the mother of the family. She told of Nathan the father, "a tenant farmer . . . poor in everything but love and care for me, his wife, whom he took at the age of twelve," and of the first child, a daughter named Irawaddy or Ira. Seven years passed, and some medical help came from a "white" doctor named Kennington or Kenny before another child, the boy Arjun, was born. Four more sons then came in as many years -- Thambi, Murugan, Raja, and Selvam -- and finally after another long pause the baby boy Kuti.

Of all the attention-holding episodes in this book, the most impressive related in some manner to the famine. Arjun and Thambi had migrated to Ceylon to find work, and Murugan had moved elsewhere in India, marrying as he did so. The famine derived from a drought that resulted in widespread crop failure. Poor families like this one possessed too small a reserve of either food or money to carry them through. "We fed on whatever we could find: the soft ripe fruit of the prickly pear; a sweet potato or two, blackened and half-rotten, thrown away by some more prosperous hand; sometimes a crab that Nathan managed to catch near the river. Early and late my sons roamed the countryside, returning with a few bamboo shoots, a stick of sugar cane left in some deserted field, or a piece of coconut picked from the gutter in the town." In the midst of these circumstances, Raja was killed by guards as he attempted to steal a calfskin from the local tannery. This was also the time when Ira, without her parents' knowledge, decided to lend her own body to the male passerby in town in return for money. Kuti, sick from undernourishment, became better with the secret aid of Ira -- but Kuti grew worse again and died.

To top everything, Nathan and Rukmani even-

tually became evicted from their land. Since
Selvam's job (helping to build a hospital for
Kenny) yielded too little money for him to support his parents, they decided to take half their
household goods and go to live near Murugan. In
the midst of a very hard trip, they took refuge
in a temple where they could get free food, but
where someone stole their small store of goods
and money. Returning to the temple after learning that Murugan had deserted his own wife and
child, they took up work in a rock quarry. When
the monsoon rains began, and only the poorest of
the workers went to the quarry, Nathan and Rukmani kept on. "I will rest when we are home,"
Nathan said, but Nathan became very ill and died
on the floor of the temple. Speaking of the
great misery the family had endured, Rukmani reasoned, "We are taught to bear our sorrows in silence, and all this is so that the soul may be
cleansed." Kenny, speaking from another era,
disagreed with Rukmani's comment. Those who
suffer in silence, commented Kenny, are really
"acquiescent imbeciles."

The Catcher in the Rye, by Jerome Salinger,
told the simple story of three days in the life
of an imaginary Holden Caulfield. This adolescent, at the age of 16, having just been "kicked
out" of a private school, told his ensuing experiences in his own, impoverished language.
Caulfield stood aware of some of his own shortcomings. "I shook my head," he said on one occasion. "I shake my head quite a lot. . . .
Partly because I have a lousy vocabulary and
partly because I act quite young for my age sometimes." Author Salinger did not suggest that
Holden Caulfield behaved typically for his time.
He did use Caulfield, however, to show the great
emptiness of life for many children of affluent
families, yearning for a genuineness they fail to
find in their immediate surroundings. Caulfield
used the word "phony" to describe most of the
persons he knew. The cinema he found phony also
(all the cinema he had seen), along with most
other forms of entertainment. Only children in

general, and his younger sister in particular, remained exempt, along with possibly two nuns whom he met during his rather sad weekend.

Holden Caulfield decided to leave school on Saturday evening, four days before the Christmas vacation from which he had been told not to return. He took a train to New York City, where his parents lived, but with the resolution not to see them until they had received the letter announcing his expulsion. In the Lavender Room of his hotel, and in another night club, Holden found nothing he really enjoyed. Then, back in the hotel, "I got in this big mess. . . . The elevator guy said to me, 'Innarested in having a good time, fella? Or is it too late for you?' 'How do you mean?' I said. I didn't know what he was driving at or anything." Holden agreed to the offer but became nervous, and finally paid the girl without availing himself of her services.

Sally Hayes, an old friend, went to a theater performance with Holden on Sunday afternoon. Afterward, their conversation deteriorated until Sally went home, alone. Holden turned to Radio City for further diversion; there he saw the annual Christmas show. ("All these angels start coming out of the boxes and everywhere. . . . Big deal. . . . When they were all finished . . . you could tell they could hardly wait to get a cigarette or something. I saw it with old Sally Hayes the year before, and she kept saying how beautiful it was. . . . I said old Jesus probably would've puked if he could see it. . . .") Next came a meeting with Carl Luce, another old friend, in a bar. Carl, three years older than Holden, soon left, wearied with the conversation. Holden tarried until he became very drunk. After walking outdoors, he decided to visit his sister Phoebe without arousing their parents. Since the parents had left home for the evening, conversation with Phoebe turned out easier than he had expected. Phoebe he liked, and Phoebe was good for him, though she remained a child.

524

Phoebe soon guessed that Holden's appearance three days before vacation meant he had been dismissed from the school. "Daddy'll <u>kill</u> you!" she remarked at first. Later she remonstrated, "'You don't like <u>any</u>thing that's happening.' . . . 'Yes I do. . . . Why the hell do you say that?' . . . 'Because you don't,' she said. 'Name one thing.'" Finally, Holden replied, "You know that song 'If a body catch a body comin' through the rye'?" Phoebe corrected: "It's 'If a body <u>meet</u> a body coming through the rye'! . . . It's a poem." Then Holden: "Anyway, I keep picturing all these little kids playing . . . in this big field of rye. . . . And I'm standing on the edge of some crazy cliff. What I have to do, I have to catch everybody if they start to go over the cliff. . . . That's all I'd do all day. . . . I know it's crazy." Monday noon, Holden met Phoebe to say goodbye to her; he planned to go away without anyone else knowing. Phoebe decided to accompany him. Holden then decided to stay at home.

Holden Caulfield, at 16, came far from understanding all the pretensions of the society in which he lived. He remained particularly imperceptive in economic matters; after all, his parents still carried him financially. The political world lay completely outside his grasp. In the worlds of learning, the arts, and religion, on the other hand, this very uneducated individual knew how to make some very telling comments. He did not like, he even hated, the hypocrisies he did understand. He felt, somehow, that a direct correlation should exist between what a person is and what he says he stands for. In putting these concepts into Holden Caulfield's mind, author Salinger portrayed the emptiness that could creep -- indeed, had crept -- into the most affluent society of the new age.

Religion

Graham and world evangelism . . the World Council of Churches in Evanston . . Sixth Great Buddhist Council . . The Interpreter's Bible . . the Dead Sea Scrolls.

Jerome Salinger finished his novel at the age of 32, after ten years spent in its preparation. William Franklin Graham, Jr., of North Carolina, less than two months older than Salinger, provided one answer for the problem Salinger posed. "Billy" Graham, as he became known to most of the English-speaking world by 1955, believed that everyone would cease to be afflicted by emptiness and would find real purpose in their lives if they subscribed to the principles of traditional Christianity. Early in the century, tradition-minded Protestants of the United States had defined the core of these principles, listing five "fundamental" precepts: (1) acceptance of the literal infallibility of the Protestant scriptures; (2) belief in the virginity of Jesus' mother Mary at the time of Jesus' conception; (3) faith in the atoning crucifixion of Jesus as a substitute for ancient sacrifices; (4) the assurance that Jesus rose bodily from the grave; and (5) the expectation that Jesus will "soon" appear again, in a "second coming," in bodily form. Preaching this "fundamentalist" doctrine, Billy Graham attracted large numbers of people, persuading many of them to declare themselves converts. Beginning in California in 1949, he moved to Massachusetts, to South Carolina, and on to other regions, until virtually everyone in the United States became aware of his campaigns. In 1954-5, he made lengthy appearances in England and Scotland, and one-day stops for preaching in much of northwestern Europe.

That many persons' lives came closer to the Christian ideal as a result of Billy Graham's evangelistic meetings seems a well established

526

fact. Because he and the organized team he created depended upon local churches to follow up
the crusades in maintaining contact with converts, it became impossible to assess the number
of those who remained faithful to the new life.
The time-honored formulae that Graham espoused
had assumed significance through the centuries,
however, in millions of persons' lives. Graham
taught, like hundreds of thousands of preachers
before him in both Catholic and Protestant pul-
pits, that when enough people accepted the traditional version of the Christian gospel -- or,
failing that, when Jesus made his return -- the
society, politics, and economy of the world would
become what they should.

The message of Graham contained a stern aspect, as it had for nearly two millenia. God
could not be expected to compromise with sin --
or in the final analysis, with the unrepentant
sinner. More than the evangelists of old, however, Graham accentuated the positive. The hymn
that became the trademark of his evangelism --
and spread widely and rapidly through many other
channels as well -- testified to both the awe-
someness and the graciousness of the divine
personage he preached:

O Lord my God! When I in awesome wonder
Consider all the worlds thy hands have made,
I see the stars, and hear the rolling
        thunder,
Thy pow'r throughout the universe displayed,
        . . .

When through the woods and forest glades I
        wander
And hear the birds sing sweetly in the trees;
When I look down from lofty mountain grandeur
And hear the brook and feel the gentle
        breeze; . . .

And when I think that God, his Son not
    sparing,
Sent him to die, I scarce can take it in;
That on the cross, my burden gladly bearing,
He bled and died to take away my sin; . . .

Then sings my soul, my Savior God to Thee;
How great thou art, how great thou art!

When Christ shall come with shout of
    acclamation
And take me home, what joy shall fill my
    heart!
Then I shall bow in humble adoration
And there proclaim, my God, how great thou
    art!

Persons in both Great Britain and the United
States who lacked interest in Graham's campaigns
often stated that his preaching lacked substance
in meeting the complicated needs of postwar
society. Graham took a specific stand on a few
public issues of his time -- opposing racial
segregation, for instance -- but tended to describe himself as politically neutral. He opposed communism on religious grounds, associating it with atheism, though he refrained from
attacks on other political ideologies. Only an
accumulation of side-remarks made it clear that
he also opposed democratic socialism, and some
contemporary manifestations of liberalism as
well. Graham maintained not that the gospel he
preached held something new for a new era, but
that it contained a nineteen-hundred-years-old
message not yet grasped by a sufficient number of
people.

In some respects, the theme of the Second
Assembly of the World Council of Churches, in
Evanston, Illinois, August 1954, resembled that
of Billy Graham. The membership of the World
Council had grown since 1948, and increased again
during this Assembly, until it reached a total of

160 denominations. The main theme at Evanston took expression in the title "Christ -- the Hope of the World." Six discussion topics, appealing to a variety of interests, related to the main theme and to church unity, evangelism, the "responsible society," international justice and peace, racial and ethnic tensions, and lay responsibility, respectively.

In what sense might Jesus the Christ, born nearly two thousand years before, be considered the hope of the world? In the sense, said the Second Assembly, that he established a kingdom "that both has come and is coming." The Christian believer "both has eternal life and hopes for it. He has the first fruits, and therefore he longs for the full harvest." When the full harvest arrives, "there will be a new heaven and a new earth. We shall all be changed. . . . The agony of the created world will be recognized as the travail of childbirth." However, as to the time of these happenings, the Council added, "God has not disclosed to us just when."

How might the Christian hope be compared with other "hopes" of the postwar world? The Assembly did not attempt to deal with all of them, but spoke at length concerning four: (1) democratic humanism ("Inequality, discrimination, injustice, reliance on naked power, exploitation, and aggression are not absent from democracies; and only man-centred self-righteousness can believe that they are."); (2) scientific humanism ("The hopes of the scientific humanist . . . are more usually characterized by sobriety and hard work. The Christian can welcome a sober humanist as colleague. . . . But the scientific humanist by his very centering of all hopes on man must reject the Christian faith as an enemy."); (3) Marxism ("Its simplest appeal is to the disinherited multitudes everywhere. . . . They are the true proletariat, the chosen people of Marxist theory. But Marxism speaks also to more prosperous workers who feel cramped and dehumanized . . . and to highly trained scientists, soldiers, patriots, and statesmen impatient for a new day. . . . But the Christian must press on to point out the illusions by which the Marxist creed itself is vitiated. First, the denial of God. . . . Second, the Marxist belief in the capacity of proletarian man. . . . Third, the belief that mere stripping away of economic disabilities can abolish the strife and self-seeking that have marked all human history. . . ."); (4) national and religious renaissance, which the Assembly welcomed as a challenge to Christians "to understand the faith and hope by which so many millions in Asia and Africa are seeking to shape their national and personal lives."

For good measure, the Protestant and Orthodox leadership represented at Evanston decided to compare the hope of traditional Christianity to the "hope of the hopeless," including the atheistic existentialists like Jean-Paul Sartre of France. "They are atheists," said the Assembly, "but atheists of a new kind. . . . They do not rejoice in the non-existence of God, but regard it as placing us in a situation of the most terrible solemnity. Each of us is completely alone, surrounded only by meaninglessness, so that if his life is to have any meaning or any value, he must create such meaning and value for himself. . . . Here we have what is the most honest of all forms of anthropocentrism. . . . In its open-eyed realization of the desperate plight of those who are without God . . . , it repeats what is a central Christian affirmation; while its talk of a courage that can emerge only out of the darkness of the complete renunciation of hope seems to echo, even if only in a perverted form, the Christian teaching that only through the darkness of the Cross, with its cry of dereliction, can hope ever be reborn." This recognition of an affinity, made so plain at Evanston, pointed squarely to the further development of a Christian existentialism, the fount from which Sartre had drunk and departed.

While two branches of Christendom deliberated in Evanston, Theravada Buddhists gathered in Rangoon, Burma, for a two-year congress starting May 1954. Three such congresses recognized by Theravada authorities had met in ancient India, and a fourth in Ceylon. At the fifth, held in Mandalay, Burma, in 1871, scholars revised the Theravada scriptures (called the Tipitaka) to eliminate the copying mistakes of centuries, inscribing the corrected text on marble slabs. The sixth, in Rangoon (known as the Sixth Great Buddhist Council), expected to conclude its sessions on the 2,500th anniversary of the death of Gautama the Buddha. The central meetings of the Council took place in a "Great Cave" constructed by the Burmese government of U Nu, modeled after the cave in India where tradition said the First Council had convened not long after Gautama died.

Monks from Burma and Ceylon, working separately, prepared well in advance of the meeting in Rangoon for the chief business of the Sixth Council, another re-editing of the Tipitaka. Thai, Burmese, and Ceylonese monks together prepared a tentative version shortly before the Council met. Distinguished representation from Thailand, Burma (a majority), Ceylon, Cambodia, and Laos would approve the final text in the ancient Pali language as the work of the Council itself. During the two years, the entire Tipitaka would be recited aloud. In 1955, the Burmese government supported the founding, at the Council's site, of an International Institute for Advanced Buddhist Studies, which U Nu and many others hoped might provide an impetus for a new wave of propagation of Theravada Buddhism in many lands.

Protestant Christian scholars, just before the Buddhist Council, completed work on a Revised Standard Version of the English-language Protestant Bible, more nearly correct and for twentieth-century readers more precise than the King James Version of the seventeenth century used by most Protestants to this time. An outstanding side-by-side reprinting of the King James and Revised Standard versions, initiated in 1951, stood three-fourths completed by 1955. Planned for a total of twelve volumes, it took the name The Interpreter's Bible to express its objective of interpreting the Christian scriptures for the great majority of Protestants. One hundred twenty-five scholars participated in the project. Beneath the parallel presentation of the two versions of the Bible itself lay, first, an exegesis, and second, an "exposition," each written by one of these collaborators. Elaborate introductions prefaced each book of the Bible, and general articles also made an appearance.

The literal infallibility of the Bible, so much stressed in the Billy Graham crusades, received no backing from the writer of the first essay as he dealt with the significance and authority of the Christian scriptures. Speaking of the four gospels or narratives of Jesus' life, he stated, "Scholarly research . . . has convincingly shown that they cannot be accepted in detail as they stand. The evidence is clear that they contain inaccuracies, inconsistencies, interpolations, omissions, overstatements, and so forth. . . ." He insisted, however, that this actuality does not mean "that we cannot arrive at assured knowledge of the historical facts." Neither need this assurance, he added, be dimmed by the possibility that we are presented in the gospels "not with the facts as such, but with a religious interpretation of them, an interpretation which may well lead in places to distortion and misrepresentation."

The writers of the twentieth-century portion of The Interpreter's Bible neither rejected nor insisted upon the remaining four precepts of the Protestant fundamentalists. They emphasized as the "essential" Christian belief, however, "the conviction that God himself came, and comes, into human history in the person of Jesus Christ." Neither the style of traditional Christianity nor that of the Christian "liberals" of the nineteenth century particularly appealed to this group of observers. Most of them felt attracted instead to a newer point of view often labeled "neo-orthodox," critical in its acceptance of historical fact yet convinced that ancient "myths" contained much of present-day value. Karl Barth of Switzerland and Reinhold Niebuhr of Missouri, both of whom lived through this quin-quennium, contributed much in the 1920's and 1930's to the development of the neo-orthodox outlook. The Self and the Dramas of History, by Niebuhr (1955), stressed the non-Biblical argu-ments in favor of the description of the human being that neo-orthodoxy provided. Dietrich Bonhoeffer, a German pastor executed in 1945 for conspiracy against the life of Hitler, felt an early attraction toward neo-orthodox emphases, but moved on during imprisonment in the war years to the point of view that Christianity needs to progress in accord with the maturing of mankind.

Fundamentalist Christianity clung to the literal story of Adam and Eve in their "fall" from the Garden of Eden, presented in the third chapter of the Biblical book of Genesis. Nine-teenth-century Christian liberals, accepting the Darwinian theory of the evolution of mankind, believed that humanity had risen rather than fallen, and rejected Adam and Eve completely. The new thought accepted the ancient narrative, bathing it in a new light. "The truth of the wonderful old drama of Eden," commented The Interpreter's Bible, "is not that we are ac-counted evil because somebody before us did evil. The truth dramatized there is this: Hu-man nature, made to go God's way, has an invet-erate tendency to listen to the temptation to go its own way, and this rebellious way must have an evil end. . . ."

Moral guidelines to replace old commandments provided another focus for commentary, at a point of conversation between Jesus and a lawyer, re-cited in the gospel of Luke. The lawyer asked, "Teacher, what shall I do to inherit eternal life?" Jesus queried in return, "What is written in the law?" The lawyer answered, quoting from two sources in the Jewish scriptures, "You shall love the Lord your God with all your heart, and with all your soul, and with all your strength, and with all your mind; and your neighbor as yourself." Jesus agreed, and proceeded to show his understanding of what love for a neighbor could mean. The Interpreter's Bible discussed the lawyer's findings as follows: "The law was computed by the rabbis to contain 613 commandments (365 'thou shalt nots' and 248 'thou shalts'), but even so many rules were not enough to define duty in all the contingencies of existence; and if that was true then, how much more true would it be now in our vastly more complex society. Rules are rough-and-ready, approximate answers; love alone can prescribe precisely for each need and occasion."

While dealing with the matter of commandments, however, The Interpreter's Bible made no serious attempt to deal with another modern discomfiture in regard to the traditional faith -- the uneasiness over the claim of Christianity to a position of exclusiveness among the world's religions. According to "The Acts of the Apostles," written also by Luke, the apostle Peter strongly affirmed this claim. Peter (and Luke) said, speaking of Jesus, "There is salvation in no one else, for there is no other name under heaven given among men by which we must be saved."

The expositor of The Interpreter's Bible first delivered at this point a modern portrait of hell -- that from which people must be saved if possible. "We may well think of it," he wrote, "in terms of . . . a drought that overtakes a man during his life, drying up his resources and his energies, caused by some block between himself and God." Salvation, then, or the act of getting saved, is the removal of that block. "Peter goes on to say, according to our imagery," added the expositor, "that the only person who can remove it is Jesus Christ. Right

534

there the well-educated person begins to protest.
. . . He knows that the religions of the East
have their literature and culture; that they have
produced great characters and noble lives. It
offends him, as it did not offend his fore-
fathers, when an exclusive claim such as Peter's
is made for Christianity. He wants to be fair
and tolerant to all people. It goes against the
grain of his training and habit of thought to
hear the words, There is salvation in no one
else."

The expositor replied to the protest of the
"well-educated person" with the argument that "we
must dispel the popular notion that one religion
is as good as another." He went to great length
to demonstrate the superiority of his own faith.
These reasonings lay beside the point, however,
not only for the well educated Christian but for
many Christians of lesser intellectual attainment, and a host of well educated and little
educated persons of other than Christian persuasion. The major faiths of the world all had
their own reasons for considering themselves
unique. The real question, which no one addressed to Peter, centered about the matter of
godly favoritism. Why would the one line of
truth, if there existed only one, be revealed to
a very small group of people rather than to
everyone equally? The new publication remained
mute on this point.

Faith remained an essential element in the
attitude of most Christians toward Jesus, as in
that of Muslims toward Muhammad and of Buddhists
toward Gautama. Sensational discoveries in
eastern Palestine, however, starting in 1947,
suggested the further unraveling of the historical riddles surrounding the person of Jesus.
Ancient manuscripts, called the Dead Sea Scrolls
because of their proximity to that body of water,
caused a wave of excitement among Jewish and
Christian scholars. The wave spread from
Palestine to western and central Europe, and

caught the attention of a wide reading public when it reached North America. Controversies concerning the meaning of the scrolls approached high intensity. Millar Burrows of Ohio, professor of theology at Yale University, discussed the findings and their significance in The Dead Sea Scrolls, published 1955.

The scrolls and other evidence appeared in various caves near the site of Khirbat Qumran. A Jewish group (now called the Qumran community) left the materials in these caves during the last century before, and the first seventy years of, the Christian era. The Qumran people in many respects fit a description by a few ancient writers of the Essenes, a Jewish sect that differed in outlook from the better known Pharisees and Sadducees. Because of some similarities in modes of thinking and language concepts, Christian circles rather quickly speculated as to whether Jesus himself had participated in the Qumran community -- or John the Baptist who preceded Jesus, or John the author of the most distinct of the four accounts of Jesus. Significant dissimilarities existed also, however, and in any event no one could pin down such theorizing with certainty. The new evidence clearly revealed a more general reality -- that the Jewish background for Christianity contained far more variety than most scholars had supposed.

The Qumran sect formed part of the Jewish scene not long before present-day Judaism became consolidated. Its interest in Iranian ideas (a corporeal heaven and the contest between good and evil) stood strong, as did that of the early Christians, the Pharisees, and the Essenes. (The Sadducees rejected the Iranian influence.) Unlike the Pharisees, however, the Qumran community placed faith in a special revelation going beyond both the law and the prophets. The Qumran believers indeed considered themselves an elect group of the good who would survive the destruction of the wicked at the imminent end of world history. Early Christians, with a wider concept of the elect, also saw themselves in this role.

The Qumran group followed a multitude of rules based on those of their Hebrew forebears, and held to the ancient idea of atonement for one's sins through animal sacrifices. They emphasized the symbolic value of water in the rituals of cleansing from impurity. They stressed, however, that ceremonies without a change of heart held no meaning for the participant: "Everyone who refuses to enter God's covenant, walking in the stubbornness of his heart, shall not attain to his true community. . . . He will not be purified by atonement offerings, and he will not be made clean with the water for impurity; he will not sanctify himself with seas and rivers. . . ."

Like the Christian community after them, the Qumran covenanters taught a predetermination of world events, without noting any discrepancy between that perspective and the exercise of a person's free will. They pictured themselves as humble beings chosen by God for a happy future, in passages such as the following from their so-called Manual of Discipline:

> But I belong to wicked mankind,
> to the company of erring flesh;
> my iniquities, my transgression, my sin,
> with the iniquity of my heart
> belong to the company of worms and those who
>   walk in darkness.
> For the way of a man is not his own,
> a man does not direct his own steps;
> for judgment is God's,
> and from his hand is blamelessness of
>   conduct.
> By his knowledge everything comes to pass;
> and everything that is he establishes by his
>   purpose. . . .

The Qumran group, and probably the Essenes in general, constituted an important bridge between the traditions of Hebrew priests and prophets and a broader Christianity, as well as between the more ancient Hebrew faith and Judaism. The bridge function, however, held no meaning for those who used the Qumran caves. Their isolation from the world about them, causing them nearly to disappear from history, led to some specialization in trivia. At the same time, the matter of highest significance to them -- a very high tone of morality in relationships among people -- they shared with the most successful religions of the world.

VII. MAN REACHES INTO SPACE --

1956-1960

Surprises and great drama marked this third quinquennium after the passage of World War II. In the preceding five years, many statesmen had come to assume that the world turns on a few simple formulae. Self-assurance had arisen from the relative quiet of the international scene. Unexpected events now shattered expectations built rather exclusively upon precedents. New modes of response appeared, though traditional attitudes abounded. A few old styles of diplomacy were startingly resuscitated. The world moved in hops and jumps rather than in smooth procession, until only those individuals who least comprehended its situation felt certain what would happen next.

Two spectacles unfolded almost simultaneously in the auspicious opening year of the period. The leadership of both Poland and Hungary threatened communist fraternity by breaking step with the Soviet Union. (Further controversy between China and the Soviet Union disturbed the fraternity more deeply, widening as it persisted.) The United Nations General Assembly saved Egypt from Israel, the United Kingdom, and France when those three employed hoary tactics of aggression disguised in modern dress. Through the period, 22 African nations emerged, most without previous experience, as united and sovereign peoples. Far-going social revolution appeared in 1958-9 in two Latin American countries, Venezuela choosing the democratic and Cuba the authoritarian path. The arrival of a United States military force in faraway Lebanon and the flight of United States spy-planes over the So-

539

viet Union constituted two of the more astonishing events in the continuing Cold War. The most awesome development of the period, however, the one from which the chapter takes its name, consisted of the launching of a number of rocket-powered vehicles from two countries of earth into space.

Communist Fraternity Broken

"Comrades! In the report of the Central Committee of the party . . . quite a lot has been said about the cult of the individual and . . . its harmful consequences. . . . After Stalin's death the Central Committee . . . began to implement a policy of explaining . . . that it is impermissible and foreign to the spirit of Marxism-Leninism to elevate one person . . . into a superman possessing . . . characteristics akin to those of a god. Such a man supposedly knows everything, sees everything, thinks for everyone, can do anything, is infallible in his behavior. . . . Such a belief about a man, and specifically about Stalin, was cultivated among us for many years." So began the speech of Nikita Khrushchev before the Twentieth Congress of the Communist party of the Soviet Union, at midnight February 24-25, 1956. In three years, Stalin's death had already affected life in various communist countries, and even in noncommunist nations as well. Only after the very frank discourse by Khrushchev, however, did continuing reverberations from the event seem likely.

Khrushchev spared no extremes from his indictment. "Stalin's willfulness vis-à-vis the party and its Central Committee," he said, "became fully evident after the Seventeenth Party Congress . . . in 1934. . . . Of the 139 members and candidates of the party's Central Committee who were elected at the Seventeenth Congress, 98 persons, i.e., 70 per cent, were arrested and shot. . . ." Stalin showed no

540

heroism, Khrushchev added, even in his role as a war leader. Surprised by the German attack, though he had received several warnings, Stalin had no plan to counter the invasion. When the Russian armies reached their nadir, Stalin discouragedly remarked, "All that which Lenin created we have lost forever."

Again, Khrushchev: "I recall the first days when the conflict between the Soviet Union and Yugoslavia began. . . . Once, when I came from Kiev to Moscow, I was invited to visit Stalin who, pointing to the copy of a letter lately sent to Tito, asked me, 'Have you read this?' . . . Not waiting for my reply he answered, 'I will shake my little finger -- and there will be no more Tito. He will fall.' . . . We have dearly paid for this 'shaking of the little finger.' . . . No matter how much or how little Stalin shook, not only his little finger but everything else that he could shake, Tito did not fall."

In his very long statement, Khrushchev spoke of the doctors' plot invented in Stalin's last days, and explained why he and others who survived Stalin had not protested the many wrongdoings while Stalin remained alive. The speech received no mention in the Soviet newspapers, but 1,436 delegates shared the secret. Word of the denunciations of Stalin soon reached other communist countries. In a sense, Khrushchev had already broken communist fraternity through his sharp criticisms of a man lauded for such a long period by so very many people. Poles, Romanians, Czechs, Slovaks, Hungarians, and Bulgarians might furthermore ponder intently the explanation given for Tito's success. "The reason," Khrushchev said, "was that Tito had behind him a state and a people who had gone through a severe school of fighting for liberty and independence, a people which gave support to its leaders."

Boleslaw Bierut, first secretary of the Polish United Workers party since the dismissal

541

of Wladyslaw Gomulka from that post in 1948, attended the Twentieth Congress in Moscow -- though as a foreign guest he received no invitation to Khrushchev's remarkable speech. Bierut fell ill and died on March 12, 1956, before he left Moscow. Polish minds had always associated Bierut with the control the Soviet Union exercised over their country. Gomulka, by contrast, seemed the embodiment of Polish nationalist communism, since his removal from the secretaryship had followed upon his refusal to criticize Yugoslavia for its break with the Soviet Union. Gomulka achieved new popularity while under arrest in 1951-4, accused of deviation from the Moscow-inspired line.

A Polish workers' strike and riot in the city of Poznan June 28-29, 1956, caused by dissatisfaction over corruption, unemployment, and low wages, brought world attention to this nation. Strikes were not permitted in the communist states; the Polish government had to decide very rapidly what it would do with this one. Repression, attempted first, resulted only in injuries and deaths. Abruptly, the regime decided to promise reform instead. It released arrested persons and actually paid money to workers as compensation for "errors" of the past. The willingness of the regime to bend in this instance caused both workers and writers to suggest further and more widespread reform. In this trend of events, the national imagination settled upon Wladyslaw Gomulka as the man who could rescue Poland from the fetters imposed by the Soviet Union. The whole nation would prosper, many Polish people came to believe, if Gomulka could reattain his former position as the first secretary of the United Workers party. While pressure mounted in favor of Gomulka, Polish Catholics demonstrated for the release from detention of cardinal Stefan Wyszynski, and Polish writers urged the supremacy of the parliament over any party leader.

The Central Committee of the United Workers

party met October 19, 1956. Most Polish citizens expected that Gomulka would be named first secretary during the course of this meeting. Early that morning, as a great surprise, a delegation from the Central Committee of the Soviet Communist party arrived in Warsaw by airplane. Nikita Khrushchev himself led the delegation; with him came Vyacheslav Molotov, Lazar Kaganovich, and others. Quite clearly, the uninvited presence of these Soviet dignitaries in Warsaw meant that they intended to block Gomulka's appointment. Soviet troop movements both in and near Poland indicated the seriousness of their aim.

Khrushchev and his companions failed in their mission. Through the day, it became clear to them that the Polish army would fight rather than obey the pro-Soviet orders of the half-Polish, half-Russian minister of defense Konstantin Rokossovsky. They could see also that Gomulka and his close friends, though determined to have their own way in this instance, did not intend to draw away from the Soviet Union in major matters of policy. The Soviet delegation departed in the early morning of October 20, while much of the world breathed easier. Gomulka became first secretary October 21. A week later, cardinal Wyszynski received his freedom and resumed his position as archbishop. On October 29, pro-Russian Konstantin Rokossovsky departed on permanent leave. In November, as Poland requested loans from the United States, the Soviet Union arranged for money on easy terms -- an admission of a sort that prior to 1956 it had acted as a drain on Poland's economy.

Poland contained 28,000,000 inhabitants in 1956; Hungary, another Soviet satellite, somewhat less than 10,000,000. Hungary experienced a series of events with considerable similarity to those in Poland, but leading to a different conclusion. The position of Wladyslaw Gomulka in Poland found its parallel in that of Imre Nagy in Hungary. Nagy had not spent time in a communist

543

prison, but the Hungarian Workers party had kept him distinctly out of favor 1949-51 and again after his premiership of 1953-5. Matyas Rakosi constituted Hungary's parallel to Poland's Boleslaw Bierut, except that Rakosi outdistanced Bierut in longevity. Rakosi had held the first secretaryship of the Hungarian Workers party since its domination of the government in 1948. When Bierut died in March 1956, furthermore, Rakosi continued in his post, more determined to stem the tide of reform than Bierut's successor in Poland.

In June 1956, the Petofi Circle of intellectuals played somewhat the same trigger role in Hungary as the strike of the Poznan workers in Poland. The Petofi Circle, named for a nineteenth-century Hungarian poet, sponsored a series of debates, which at first drew a few hundred persons for an audience, but soon attracted the attention of thousands. In the early programs, speakers took care not to criticize the government. After a few weeks, however, some of them presented arguments that some party leaders had betrayed the communist revolution. In an eighthour session on the night of June 27 (immediately before the Poznan strike in Poland) a few participants actually pled for the dismissal of Rakosi. The Central Committee of the Workers party then condemned the debates, just as the Circle completed its announced program. From the viewpoint of men like Rakosi, freedom of speech had carried too far. The Communist party of the Soviet Union, though it agreed, arranged the dismissal of Rakosi for letting matters get out of hand. Anastas Mikoyan, the representative of the Soviet party, substituted Erno Gero for Rakosi July 18. The switch held no significance for the Hungarian intellectuals, however, since Gero had supported Rakosi.

The men in Moscow, intent at this time upon bringing Yugoslavia back into the Soviet sphere, seem not to have realized the depth of the Hungarian disaffection. While the popular debates resumed, not only in Budapest but throughout the country, they called Gero to the Soviet Union for talks that lasted an entire month. On October 6, the day before Gero returned, a silent procession of thousands of persons honored a home-grown Hungarian communist executed by the government in 1949. On October 14, the Workers party reinstated Imre Nagy as a member, in a concession to public sentiment -- Nagy had walked in the procession. On the same day, Gero left for a friendly visit to Yugoslavia. On October 22 (again a day before Gero returned home), demands arose from several groups among the intellectuals for greater democratization of Hungary's government and economy, the participation of Imre Nagy in the government, and the expulsion of Matyas Rakosi from his remaining party posts. Wladyslaw Gomulka had entered his party position in Poland one day before these demands.

Verbal protest changed to demonstration on the evening of October 23, as the name of Imre Nagy became a symbol. While some demonstrators tore down a statue of Stalin, and others threw bricks at the windows of the national broadcasting headquarters, the largest crowd gathered in front of the parliament building, calling for Nagy to speak. Nagy did speak, but few heard him in the confusion, and he did not assume the leadership at this point. Gero spoke briefly also, on the radio, making clear his intention to retain control. Hungarian police fired upon the crowd by the broadcasting headquarters, who nevertheless seized the building by morning. Gero, in fright, called upon Soviet motorized troops, stationed outside the city, for aid. As Russian forces appeared in Budapest streets, before dawn, the Central Committee of the Hungarian Workers party decided to make Nagy premier.

The city became quiet on the morning of October 24, though the revolution continued to spread like wildfire. City people had favored one communist over another. People in the countryside took a further step, showing their antipathy to communists in general. The official party disintegrated in the country at large while its leaders wavered in the capital. Mikoyan appeared again from the Soviet Union, in time to see Gero dropped as first secretary of his party, immediately after Soviet tanks had killed Hungarian people in a new demonstration in Budapest streets. Except for this episode, on October 25, the Soviet forces had moved carefully. Mikoyan is believed to have reprimanded Gero for having involved Soviet forces unnecessarily. The revolution, after all, lacked real military strength. Janos Kadar, whose communist career had not lain so close to Moscow as those of Rakosi and Gero, became the new first secretary of the party. On October 26 Mikoyan returned home, leaving Budapest and Hungary in the hands of prime minister Nagy and first secretary Kadar. The Soviet troops continued to maintain a semblance of order in Budapest. Revolutionists throughout the country continued to present demands, many of them read over radio stations.

Imre Nagy spoke on October 28, acceding to most of the demands for a cease-fire by government troops and significant economic and political reform. He failed to specify any over-all changes in the political climate, however. Since demand for further clarity continued, Nagy, Kadar, and two others spoke on the radio October 30, promising abolition of the one-party system, announcing immediate negotiations to remove the Soviet army from Hungary, and proclaiming victory for the revolution. As a symbolic gesture, that very evening, the government released cardinal Jozsef Mindzenty from nearly eight years of detention. The following day, Nagy even spoke of negotiations to remove Hungary from the communist Warsaw Pact. The Hungarian revolution had gone well beyond that in Poland, and for a few days longer it seemed triumphant. Nagy indicated the sincerity of his promises, though the people had virtually forced him to deliver them, through the admission of non-communists to the cabinet.

546

Leaders in Moscow possessed little time to reflect upon these changes. Some among them wished to stop the Hungarian revolution in its tracks; others weighed the damage to the Soviet Union in the realm of world opinion. On October 30, the Soviet government announced its readiness to withdraw troops from Hungary. At some time during the period October 29-31, however, it came to the conclusion to put down the Hungarian revolution instead. In the Middle East, on the first of those three days, Israel attacked Egypt. On the second, Great Britain and France presented ultimatums to Egypt. On the third, October 31, Great Britain and France attacked Egypt. Many persons believe that these happenings persuaded the Russians that they would be foolish to appear less resolute than the Israelis, the British, and the French. Whether the Soviet leaders thought in these terms, or reacted only to the new steps taken by Nagy, it appears that Anastas Mikoyan, in Hungary again the evening of October 30, knew of the decision before he left October 31. Soviet troops took over the Budapest airport as Mikoyan left the scene.

The morning of November 1 brought reports of Soviet troop movements into Hungary. Nagy, while asking the Soviet ambassador to explain these movements, proceeded during the day to obtain parliamentary approval of his decision to declare Hungary a neutral country and immediately to abrogate its adherence to the Warsaw Pact. Nagy informed United Nations secretary-general Dag Hammarskjöld of the decision, with the request that the defense of Hungarian neutrality by the "four great powers" be placed on the agenda of the General Assembly. On the evening of November 1, Janos Kadar announced by radio the formation of a Socialist Workers party to replace the former Workers party. Kadar asserted that he would fight with gun in hand against any attempt by the Soviet Union to unseat the Hungarian government. The same evening, however, an unidentified car drove him away from public view. Early in the morning of November 4, it became clear that Kadar

547

had joined the Soviet leaders rather than wait, gun in hand, to combat them.

Nagy made his second and last appeal to the United Nations on November 2. This time he asked that the Security Council concern itself with continued Soviet troop movements into Hungary. As he waited for some response, a military group he had chosen met with properly designated Russians on November 3, to negotiate the withdrawal of the Soviet forces that had remained in the country before the new movements began. The Russians only pretended to negotiate; they had fully decided to upset the Nagy regime by October 31 at the latest. Their tanks entered Budapest streets in considerable force during the pre-dawn hours of November 4.

The United Nations Security Council held a very unusual meeting at 3:00 A.M., New York time. The Soviet delegate said, "We know why the United States, the United Kingdom and France are placing this matter before the Security Council. We know that the purpose is to conceal, behind speeches full of demagoguery, the action that has been taken by Israel, the United Kingdom and France against Egypt." The United States delegate, knowing his country had not helped to plan the attack on Egypt, responded caustically to the Soviet speaker, alluding to a relief operation for Hungarian refugees: "He would apparently have us believe that our American programme, which aims to fill the people's stomachs with food, is somehow inferior to a Soviet programme which fills their stomachs with lead. . . ." This speech-making, which ended with a Soviet veto of a resolution to censure the Soviet Union, stood of little consequence from the beginning, since by 3:00 A.M. (9:00 A.M. Budapest time) the Nagy government had ceased to function.

Janos Kadar became the premier in a new Hungarian government sworn into office November 7. Kadar also led the new party he had announced six days earlier. His regime detained Imre Nagy

548

November 22 when Nagy left the Yugoslav embassy in which he had taken refuge. Nagy had become a real independence hero to the Hungarian people -- a status even more enhanced by his execution in 1958. Cardinal Mindszenty fled to the United States embassy and stayed there. Budapest workers, as a last gesture of resistance to a government they did not like, despite its domination by a self-proclaimed Workers party, carried out a general strike December 11-12. The new premier indicated he would talk with their leaders, but arrested them instead.

The Soviet suffocation of the radical move towards a more democratic communism in Hungary produced repercussions throughout the communist world. In France and Italy, where communists strove to gain control over their governments by peaceful means, non-communists who had expressed willingness to cooperate with the communists now tended to look at them with suspicion. Smaller communist parties in various other countries became rent by schisms, usually involving struggles between local party leaders. The government of Yugoslavia, which happened to hold a seat in the United Nations Security Council in 1956, abstained from voting rather than casting its ballot against the resolution to censure Moscow. Within a year, however, most of the feuding among communists ceased. The one exception to the trend toward calm within the camp sprang from a tension between Moscow and Peking, which also began at this time, and tended to grow through the remainder of the quinquennium.

At first, the bad feeling between the Soviet Union and Communist China rested upon Chinese criticism of Russian attitudes. At the same Twentieth Congress of the Soviet Communist party to which Khrushchev addressed his denunciations of Stalin, a fraternal Chinese representative made a speech lauding Stalin. Khrushchev's attack on the deceased dictator reflected in some way upon all those who had praised Stalin. The Chinese regime had not only participated (quite

549

unnecessarily) in the Stalin hymn-singing; it had also developed a cult of personality around Mao Ze Dong (Mao Tse Tung) very similar to that which Khrushchev denounced. The Chinese party leadership made it clear as a response to Khrushchev's speech that they believed the Soviet leader had erred in moving too fast, especially without consulting Peking ahead of time; and that they believed for the sake of the future of communism Stalin's mistakes needed to be explained rather than simply denounced. It became obvious to the Russians (though not to most of the world) that Peking intended, now that Stalin was dead, to assume a full share with Moscow in the leadership of the world communist movement. The Chinese, according to their own accounts of later years, even intervened in the October collisions in eastern Europe, favoring Gomulka in Poland but opposing Nagy's more radical revolution in Hungary.

Despite the initial bad feeling, the Chinese and Soviet regimes continued to cooperate through the year 1957. Jou En Lai (Chou En Lai) traveled to Moscow in January of that year to consult with Khrushchev. Together they declared, "The facts testify that any questions of the mutual relations of socialist countries can be fully solved on the basis of unity by means of sincere consultations and comradely consideration." In October, Moscow committed itself to share secrets of the manufacture of atomic bombs with Peking. The following month, Mao himself visited Moscow, there to extol the Soviet experience in communist revolution as a pattern all other communist parties needed to study. "The path of the Soviet Union . . . is basically the bright high road of all humanity," he said. Yet in practical matters the Chinese made it clear that they expected to help choose a course for the communist world in the future. At a meeting of the Third International later in November, Mao went so far as to suggest that nuclear war against capitalist countries, if the capitalists started it, might prove beneficial to world communism. Khrushchev did

550

not relish such a possibility, and emphasized the great damage nuclear war would bring to both sides.

Estrangement between Peking and Moscow increased in 1958. This time, Soviet criticism of Mao replaced Chinese complaints about Khrushchev. The Russians felt that the Chinese were appropriating too large a place in the world communist enterprise. Until 1957, Mao's government had retained a reputation for moderation. Not heavily addicted to the severities of Stalin, it remained indisposed to push the principle of collectivization at the expense of continuing progress in the economy. In the last half of 1957, however, some important policy changes made Communist China seem far more revolutionary than the Soviet Union at any point in its history. In early 1958, a "great leap forward" organized by Mao and his associates, along with the very comprehensive organization of Chinese peasants into working communes, encouraged the Chinese to believe that they had chosen a more effective path toward fast realization of the communist dream than any the Russians had devised. Soviet leaders became miffed by what seemed to them the arrogance of the Chinese mood. Khrushchev said to the Twenty-First Congress of the Soviet Communist party in January 1959, "Society cannot leap from capitalism to communism."

The renewed tension expressed itself dramatically in June 1959, when the Soviet Union cancelled its agreement to aid China in the manufacture of atomic weapons. Most of the world missed the drama, since until a few years had passed it had no knowledge of either the agreement or the cancellation. The Chinese leadership, however, coupled this Soviet decision with a visit made by premier Khrushchev to the United States in September, convincing themselves that the Soviet Union and the United States planned an anti-China alliance. Khrushchev visited Peking after his talks with president Dwight Eisenhower but failed to reassure the Chinese when he described Eisenhower as a person who "understands the need to relax international tension."

The aura of good feeling between the Soviet Union and the United States (or, more precisely, between Khrushchev and Eisenhower) terminated very quickly when the Russians shot down a plane from the United States over Soviet territory on May 1, 1960. Before that, however, the Soviet-Chinese split, or at least the angry words deriving therefrom, had become common knowledge. China found itself saying in April 1960, "War is an inevitable outcome of systems of exploitation and the source of modern wars is the imperialist system. . . . Marxist-Leninists absolutely must not sink into the mire of bourgeois pacifism. . . ." The Soviet Union stated a few days later (before the plane incident), "In order to be loyal to Marxism-Leninism today it is not sufficient to repeat the old truth that imperialism is aggressive. The task is to make full use of the new factors operating for peace in order to save humanity from the catastrophe of another war." In June 1960, the controversy erupted anew when both Russian and Chinese fraternal delegates spoke at a meeting in Romania. At this conference, Albania (sharing no common border with the Soviet Union) took a stand along with the Chinese, thereby having to turn to China for economic aid. The Soviet Union after this meeting cancelled its programs of technical aid to China. As the quinquennium ended, a cold war of words between the Soviet Union and China rivaled the other cold war between the Soviet Union and the United States.

Old-Style Diplomacy

Since 1945, despite the interventions of the Soviet Union and the United States in other nations' affairs and the Soviet use of raw force in Hungary, only one clearcut case of aggression by one country against another had arisen. That one took place in 1950, when North Korean forces invaded South Korean territory obviously bent upon total conquest. The United Nations, because of the absence of the Soviet Union and later over Soviet protests, took its most forceful step in meeting the North Korean threat. If the United Nations armies had limited themselves to defending South Korea rather than invading North Korea in turn, the operation might have made its mark as a notable success. Now, in October 1956, at the very time Soviet tanks moved into Budapest, the United Nations stood faced with its second clearcut case of aggression -- not in Hungary, where local collaborators extended Moscow an invitation, but in Egypt, where three democracies attacked a fourth-quarter regime.

The United Kingdom, France, and Israel -- who constituted the aggressors in this instance -- each had its own reasons for disliking Jamal Abd an-Nasir of Egypt. Nasser had disturbed the political situation in the Middle East simply by his advent to power. Nasser did not favor war, despite his military background, but spoke with great passion in addressing the public whenever his nationalistic pride asserted itself. He genuinely desired friendship from both Cold War opponents, and likewise peace with the state of Israel, which had started its national life before he became Egypt's president. When Israeli forces penetrated the Gaza strip administered by Egypt in February 1955, however, taking action there against the Egyptian army, Nasser organized commando-type units of the fellahin, or peasants, who undertook dangerous reprisal raids into Israel beginning in August.

The mood of Israel lay strongly against the attacks by the fellahin. A strong tendency had emerged toward association of any anti-Israel action with the persecutions of the Jewish people that extended over three millenia. Leo Baeck (died 1956), a German reform rabbi who survived a

553

concentration camp and moved to England after the war, provided a theological justification for the separateness of the Jewish people in his _Dieses Volk: Judische Existenz_ (1955-7, known in English as _This People Israel: The Meaning of Jewish Existence_). Men such as Baeck disapproved of the use of force, believing that Judaism made its contribution through its living testimony to truth. David Ben-Gurion, who became the prime minister of Israel a second time in November 1955 (after serving 1948-53), felt differently about such matters. He stood fully determined, in fact, to hit hard against any of Israel's enemies (its neighbors) whenever he himself believed force justified.

President Nasser took steps in 1954-5 (see "Three Revolutions Inaugurated," Chapter VI) that brought his government into new relationships with the United Kingdom, the United States, and the Soviet Union. In October 1954, he persuaded the British to withdraw their last occupation forces from Egyptian territory. Some British units had resided in Egypt since 1882; the last soldiers left the Suez Canal area on June 13, 1956. British leaders held mixed feelings concerning president Nasser. A long British tradition of friendliness toward the Arab world generally found its expression in paternalism. With the departure of British troops from Egyptian territory, some English people retained the feeling that Great Britain held a special responsibility toward Egypt that might find expression in some program of aid. Conservative leadership, however, took special umbrage at the fact that president Nasser tasted international fame as a leader of the "third world" after the Bandung conference of April 1955 -- and also thought of himself as the most outstanding leader of the Arab world, whose opinions could not be overlooked in countries like Jordan and Iraq. Anthony Eden, who replaced Winston Churchill as the Conservative prime minister in April 1955, stood primarily responsible for attitudes of the United Kingdom in late 1955 and early 1956.

Neither the United States nor the Soviet Union held any special relationship with president Nasser in the beginning. Many people in the United States favored Israel over any of the neighboring Arab states, either because of sympathy for the Jewish people under Nazi persecution or because of the fundamentalist Protestant outlook that God had intended a national home for the Jews in Palestine. The Democratic administration of Harry Truman had catered more to the pro-Israel attitude, however, than that of president Eisenhower, which inclined toward a neutral posture between Arabs and Jews. The anti-Soviet feeling of the United States, strong under both Truman and Eisenhower, remained the chief determinant of the Washingtonian outlook toward president Nasser. The Egyptian-Russian-Czech arms deal of September 1955 posed the question to secretary of state John Foster Dulles (president Eisenhower remained partially out of touch after a heart attack) whether the United States should attempt to vie with the Soviet Union for Nasser's favor, or whether Washington should oppose Nasser because of his new friends.

The events that followed focused upon the Egyptian Suez Canal and Nasser's projected Aswan "high dam." The British had built a "low" dam across the Nile River at Aswan in 1898-1902. The new dam, so fondly cherished by Nasser, would actually be constructed across the lake created by the older one; it would back Nile waters across the border with Sudan. It would in fact constitute the most mammoth engineering feat in history, providing a new life for millions of Egyptian people. The Suez Canal, also a wonder for its time, dated from 1854-69; Egyptian labor, international financing, and French engineering skill had made it possible. British ships used the canal more frequently than those of any other nation. When an Egyptian ruler found himself near bankruptcy in 1875, the British government purchased his 44% of the shares of the Suez Canal Company. The British occupation of Egyptian territory began seven years later, and endured longest in the Suez Canal area.

Shortly before the arms deal of September 1955, the Soviet Union suggested, in noncommital fashion, that it might be willing also to help Nasser with the building of the Aswan high dam. President Nasser, however, had no desire to be drawn deeply into the communist camp; he had always dealt harshly with the small communist movement in Egypt. In any event, greater financial resources existed elsewhere, including those of the World Bank for Reconstruction and Development, in whose decisions the United States played a strong role; the Soviet Union had never become a member of the Bank. After talks in November-December 1955, the United States agreed (subject to an authorization by Congress) that it would grant about $56,000,000 over a period of approximately five years to help get the Aswan dam under way, with the understanding that the United Kingdom would free $14,000,000 of Egyptian-owned funds that it had blocked, and that the World Bank would come into the agreement later. Eugene Black, president of the World Bank, reached an accord with Nasser in February 1956 for a loan of $200,000,000 to be made available when the need arose, with the expectation that Washington and London would provide a total equivalent sum. Egypt would have to find another $900,000,000 on its own.

Even by the time of the Black-Nasser accord, Washington seems to have lost whatever enthusiasm it had engendered for the project. Secretary of state Dulles knew that, in the climate of United States opinion, he would not easily get the money from Congress. Undersecretary of state Herbert Hoover, Jr., acquainted with engineering but naive in international diplomacy, had persuaded Dulles to take some interest in the dam. When Hoover met Nasser, however, he disliked him and began to cool toward the project. Washington pushed a secret mission seeking peace for Israel through mediated talks, and failed in that endeavor. Friends of Dulles began to say that he had lost interest in the dam.

On March 1, 1956, prime minister Anthony Eden (physically ill at the time) reacted with great anger when the government of Jordan dismissed a long-time British adviser. Eden, blaming Nasser for the deed, remarked (according to his foreign secretary), "What's all this nonsense about isolating Nasser or 'neutralising' him, as you call it? I want him destroyed, can't you understand?" Dulles reacted less emphatically but his feeling may have run the same when on May 16 Nasser extended formal recognition to Communist China.

President Nasser had originally objected to conditions which Washington and London tied to their aid. While in the view of the governments lending assistance the conditions only served to ensure the financial soundness of the dam project, to Nasser's nationalistic pride they seemed over-humiliating, allowing for the management of the Egyptian economy by the countries lending aid. Nasser did not cut his bridges behind him on this account. He communicated his thoughts on the matter to Washington and London. As the months passed by without any response from Eden and Dulles, he naturally began to anticipate a final negative decision on the money. As a last measure, he instructed the Egyptian ambassador to Washington that he stood ready to accept all the conditions. On July 19, 1956, when Dulles received this message, he replied that Washington had changed its mind about the agreement. The decision to withdraw the offer, Dulles' office said, came because "the ability of Egypt to devote adequate resources to assure the project's success has become more uncertain than at the time the offer was made." Though Eugene Black had not been consulted by Dulles, this meant the end also of the prospect of World Bank aid.

President Nasser maintained public silence for five days. On July 24, appearing at a village five miles from Cairo, he spoke briskly:

"When Washington sheds every decent principle on which foreign relations are based and broadcasts the lie, snare, and delusion that Egypt's economy is unsound, . . . then I look them in the face and say: Drop dead of your fury for you will never be able to dictate to Egypt." In the city of Alexandria, on July 26, Nasser announced the nationalization of the Suez Canal. "We dug the Canal with our lives, our skulls, our bones, our blood," he said. The profits made from tolls for passage through the canal would no longer accrue to holders of the Suez Canal Company stock. The canal would have reverted to Egypt in 1968 anyhow, with the ending of the 99-year agreement. By appropriating the waterway twelve years early, the Egyptian government would receive the money needed for the Aswan high dam without resort to international financing. To put punch into his words, Nasser ordered his army to seize the canal facilities while he finished his speech.

The day after Egypt nationalized the Suez Canal, Anthony Eden turned away from cooperation with Washington, substituting secret planning with France. Guy Mollet, a Socialist, had become the French premier in January 1956. His cabinet contained a few small parties and a group of Radical Socialists who did not hold socialist views, along with members of the Socialist party occupying 6 of 13 posts. France had not moved from the third to the second quarter of the spectrum.

Guy Mollet as premier inherited the French struggle against independence for Algeria. Many individuals of the Socialist party favored Algerian independence, but Mollet expressed more concern for the French people living in Algeria than for the Algerian people themselves. President Nasser, granting some military aid to the Algerian independence movement and strongly favoring that cause on the Egyptian radio, had made himself as much of an irritant to Mollet as to Eden. On July 27, 1956, Great Britain and France thus began secretly to plot a war of extermination against this one Arabic person they loathed. On the same day president Eisenhower, only twelve days back in his office after an operation for ileitis, took up a campaign to save the world from that war. Though the British and French did not apprise him of their preparations, private messages from London and Paris made him sense them.

Three efforts appeared during the following three months to find some solution to the general disgruntlement provoked by Nasser's seizure of the canal. They all failed because too few of the quarreling nations evinced any willingness to compromise. First, Eisenhower and Dulles suggested a conference in London, to which 24 governments received invitations. Egypt refused to attend -- as did Greece, which felt indisposed toward the United Kingdom over the status of the island of Cyprus. Of the 22 delegations that did participate, August 16-23, a majority of 18 voted for an international board to run the canal. (Ten of the 18 were European; the others were the United States, Pakistan, Japan, Turkey, Iran, Ethiopia, Australia, and New Zealand.) The remaining four -- India, the Soviet Union, Indonesia, and Ceylon -- preferred an acknowledgement of Egypt's right to operate the canal, in consultation with a committee of the canal users. Nasser rejected the majority plan September 9, and the next day suggested a conference of all canal users, to contrast with the selective nature of the meeting in London.

When it became apparent that the first conference might not achieve success, secretary of state Dulles developed a plan for a second one. He suggested a body later called the Suez Canal Users Association, which would regulate traffic on the canal with or without Nasser's consent. If necessary, ships would be placed at each end of the canal to "aid" in its administration. Nasser said of this rather far-fetched plan, "By the same token we should be able to get together a number of countries and say we are forming an association of the users of the Port of London and all ships bound for London would pay to it." Nevertheless, Anthony Eden presented the idea to his parliament September 12-13, and 15 nations adopted it in a second London conference of September 19-21. (These were the 18 who had agreed with one another in the first conference, less Pakistan, Japan, and Ethiopia.) Eden failed to win endorsement of the Labor party for this plan, which he favored and Labor opposed because it might easily lead the countries to war. On September 13 and October 2, however, Dulles made it clear that the United States did not intend that the Suez Canal Users Association should shoot its way through the canal. The Association came into being but did not attempt to operate the Suez Canal.

The efforts of August-September, made largely at Washington's behest, could not have succeeded while London and Paris, though participating in them, remained bent upon removing Nasser from office. Both nations prepared for war with Egypt while they negotiated. Their last pilots left the Suez Canal on September 15. When they took their complaints over the canal to the United Nations on September 23, Egypt countered with a note to the same body, declaring that Great Britain and France threatened war.

For a few weeks, the remainder of the world, not knowing how far preparations for war had advanced, found it possible to believe that the Security Council might come up with an answer to the conflict. In private talks, the United Kingdom, France, and Egypt agreed on six principles for the management of the canal. Three days after their agreement, however, on October 13, the British and French attempted to attach to the resolution in favor of the six principles a statement that the 18-nation agreement of the previous August fulfilled them. The Security Council voted unanimously for the six principles, but the British-French addition failed. Egypt opposed it, though not a member of the

560

Council at the time; the Soviet Union vetoed it, and Yugoslavia also voted in the negative.

After this vain attempt, if indeed it may be called that, London and Paris moved swiftly toward war. A French emissary to London October 14 brought an idea that Eden accepted. Two days later, in Paris, the idea became a plan. On October 24, Anthony Eden, Guy Mollet, and David Ben-Gurion signed it in secret accord. Israel would attack Egypt in the Gaza strip and on the Sinai peninsula. The British would then have an excuse for landing troops near the Suez Canal, since their treaty of 1954 with Egypt specified that they might return to protect the canal at any time during a seven-year period that Egypt became the object of an attack. France would aid both Israel and Great Britain. British and French forces near the canal would then be used to reach Cairo and depose Nasser. The three nations had no plan as to what might happen next.

On October 29, Israeli forces moved into territory that the armistice of 1949 had defined as Egyptian. Israeli paratroopers dropped at a point only 20 miles east of the Egyptian city of Suez, at the southern end of the Suez Canal. On October 30, the British and French governments issued communications to Egypt and Israel, calling for "withdrawal" of their forces to positions ten miles from the canal. If they would not both agree to this stipulation, within twelve hours, London and Paris requested Egypt "to accept the temporary occupation by the Anglo-French forces of key positions at Port Said, Ismailiya, and Suez" along the canal.

The interposition of British and French troops between the Israelis and Egyptians at the canal meant that the Egyptians would have to retreat and the Israelis might occupy the Gaza strip and Sinai peninsula, which they had not even seized at the time the ultimatum was issued. Nasser rejected the "request." That evening, the United Nations Security Council con-

561

sidered two resolutions, submitted by the United States and the Soviet Union, each calling upon Israel to retire its forces behind the seven-year armistice line. Each received seven votes, but failed under the combined veto of the British and the French.

The ultimatum expired on October 31. The British and French began open hostilities by bombing Egyptian airports, preventing the Egyptians from using their air force over the Sinai peninsula. President Nasser ordered the retreat of his entire army to points west of the Suez Canal. The Security Council, stymied by the vetoes, requested the first emergency special session of the General Assembly, on a procedural resolution submitted by Yugoslavia and supported by six others including the Soviet Union and the United States. The bombing fulfilled a promise to Israel, in return for its agreement to provide a pretext for British reoccupation of the canal area. Anthony Nutting, the British foreign secretary, resigned on October 31, full of misgivings but without making public his reasons.

The bombing continued on November 1, with attacks on Egyptian airplanes as well as the air fields where they lay. The Suez Canal, whose safety the British and French had taken as their object of solicitude, lay blocked to traffic when the Egyptians sank several ships in the channel. The Israelis cut off the Gaza strip and continued to occupy the Sinai peninsula. The United Nations General Assembly met, and adopted by a vote of 64 to 5 a resolution drafted by the United States. "The General Assembly," it read, "Noting the disregard on many occasions by parties to the Israel-Arab armistice agreements of 1949 . . . , and that the armed forces of Israel have penetrated deeply into Egyptian territory . . . , Noting that armed forces of France and the United Kingdom . . . are conducting military operations against Egyptian territory, Noting that traffic through the Suez Canal is now interrupted to the serious prejudice of many nations, Expressing its

grave concern over these developments, 1. Urges
. . . that all parties now involved in hostilities in the area agree to an immediate cease-fire
and . . . halt the movement of military forces
and arms into the area; 2. Urges the parties to
the armistice agreements promptly to withdraw all
forces behind the armistice lines . . . ; 5.
Requests the Secretary-General to observe and
report promptly on the compliance with the present resolution . . . ; 6. Decides to remain in
emergency session pending compliance. . . ."

The Assembly had debated through the evening. The vote came at two o'clock on the morning of November 2, New York time. The United
Kingdom, France, Australia, New Zealand, and
Israel provided the opposition. Canada, South
Africa, the Netherlands, Belgium, Portugal, and
Laos abstained. The 64 votes in favor included
all the remainder of the world membership of the
United Nations, excepting Luxembourg. This resolution did not stop the invasion by the Israelis, British, and French. It did cause them to
relinquish their first aim, the elimination of
Nasser.

From this point on there began a new game.
The British and French forces had to occupy the
Suez Canal area to make good their contention
that such a move constituted the full extent of
their original intention. Israeli forces had to
occupy all of Sinai to maintain the farcical
threat that had necessitated the British-French
landings. In response to the resolution of the
General Assembly, Egypt and Israel declared they
would accept a cease-fire, in each case providing that the other did. Great Britain and
France announced that they felt compelled to go
through with landings in the canal area until
both sides might agree to a United Nations force
to keep the peace.

The General Assembly discussed the Suez Canal issue through the night and early morning of
November 3-4, New York time, adopting two new

563

resolutions. One, worded by 19 Asian and African nations led by India, reaffirmed the decision of November 2. Canada (whose flag still carried the British ensign) voted with the 59 countries in favor; 5 delegations again voted no, and 12 abstained. Canada submitted the second resolution, drawing the vote of 57 to 0 with 19 abstentions. It requested the secretary-general to submit a plan for an "emergency international United Nations force" to "secure and supervise the cessation of hostilities." The United Kingdom, France, and Israel joined the abstainers on this vote -- along with the Soviet Union, which took the position that the General Assembly had no right to establish such a force. The United Nations Charter (Article 11) had specified that the Security Council would deal with such a matter. (And the Soviet Union during these very hours had used force on its own initiative in Hungary; a second emergency special session of the General Assembly convened later in the day to discuss that situation in retrospect.)

To uninformed persons -- and that category included most of the population of the world -- November 5 seemed the most dangerous day for the peace of the planet since the year 1945. British and French paratroops dropped on the airport of Port Said. The Soviet Union sent notes to London, Paris, and Tel Aviv, threatening to use force against the three invading armies. The United States government had made it clear that, while it opposed the invasion of Egypt, it did not intend to make any switch in allies. During the same day, however, the General Assembly provided for the emergency force planned since the day before, stipulating that recruitment for the force should not include the five permanent members of the Security Council. Numerically, the vote remained the same as that of the Canadian resolution of the 4th.

At an evening meeting of the Security Council, requested by Moscow, the Soviet delegation proposed that, if the combined forces would not cease action against Egypt within twelve hours and leave Egyptian territory within three days, all members of the United Nations should render assistance to Egypt -- particularly the Soviet Union and the United States, which had great air and naval forces at their disposal. During the same meeting, however, secretary-general Dag Hammarskjöld reported the readiness of all four combatants to cease their fire, and the apparent willingness of Egypt to allow an international force on its territory. Only three Council members -- the Soviet Union, Yugoslavia, and Iran -- voted to place the Soviet resolution on the agenda. The United States, the United Kingdom, France, and Australia voted in the negative, while the four others abstained.

The Israeli army completed its conquest of the Sinai peninsula on the same anxious day of November 5; the Gaza strip had already found itself entirely in Israeli hands. On November 6, the British and French took Port Said, progressing 23 miles farther south before the end of hostilities. No more open fighting took place. The General Assembly now had only to persuade the three armies to withdraw, and to reestablish the Israeli-Egyptian armistice. On November 7, a vote of 64 to 0 with 12 abstentions established a seven-member advisory committee for the United Nations Emergency Force. The same day, only Israel voted against a 19-power Asian-African resolution calling once more for the withdrawal of forces (vote 65 to 1 with 10 abstentions). Of the 24 nations offering to participate in the Emergency Force, the first ten troop units accepted arrived in the Suez Canal area on November 15. By this time, Egypt had formally accepted their presence.

The regular annual session of the General Assembly took up the Suez Canal matter at this point. On November 24, it reiterated the call to the United Kingdom, France, and Israel to withdraw their forces. To that date, none of the British and Israeli troops, and only one-third of the French, had left Egyptian territory. The vote on this occasion ran 63 to 5, with 10 abstentions. On December 22, 1956, the last of the British and French forces left Egypt. Israeli evacuation of the immediate canal area had taken place on December 3.

The Assembly on January 19, 1957, noted "with regret and concern" the failure of Israel to withdraw from all of Sinai, and requested the secretary-general to report within five days the success of further efforts to accomplish full evacuation. The United Kingdom voted for this resolution, and only France and Israel in the negative, in a count of 74 to 2 with 2 abstentions. On February 2, by a numerically identical vote, the Assembly deplored the non-compliance of Israel and asked for complete withdrawal "without further delay." The Israelis finally moved out, and on March 8, 1957, the United Nations Emergency Force took over the administration of all Egyptian territory adjacent to the previous armistice line. Israel did not grant permission for the international force to patrol its side of the line.

The United Nations completed the clearance of obstructions in the Suez Canal April 10, 1957. The nine-month crisis had run its course. Jamal Abd an-Nasir remained the president of Egypt. Anthony Eden had resigned as prime minister of the United Kingdom January 9 on the advice of his physicians, and after much criticism from his countrymen. Guy Mollet remained in office until May 22, 1957, in France, where only the Communists and some of the Socialists had opposed the war. David Ben-Gurion retained his position in Israel, whose people generally favored the invasion, through the remainder of the quinquennium.

Significance attached to the fact that the United Nations by near-unanimous votes (including the United Kingdom after the resignation of Eden) had maintained the pressure on Israel to the point of a complete withdrawal. Even more meaning lay in the decision of the three invading countries, upon the first vote on the crisis in the General Assembly, to give up their intention of unseating president Nasser. These accomplishments had come about without the unanimity of the permanent members of the Security Council, and without the necessity of resort to economic sanctions or arms. As in the case of Indonesian independence, an overwhelming statement of world opinion had provided the vital factor. The world before 1945 had witnessed thousands of examples of the old-style diplomacy, in which a stronger nation took advantage of a weaker one through the use or the threat of force. The world after 1945, the Suez Canal crisis seemed to say, might not experience so much of old-style diplomacy, though the newer-style international intervention on a covert basis might continue for some time.

African Independence (Part I)

While the Egyptian nation struggled to maintain its independence, other African peoples strove to achieve theirs. A multitude of ethnic groups inhabited Africa. Some had organized nation-states for themselves before the nineteenth century. Others had experienced only the more narrow range of existence within tribal identities. Many of them felt the influence of Portuguese commercial ventures on their continent, commencing in the fifteenth century. A few witnessed the arrival of the Dutch at the southern extreme, early in the seventeenth century. All felt the impact of the French, the British, the Germans, the Italians, the Belgians, and the Spaniards who came in the nineteenth century, determined to administer African affairs in a manner serving their own advantage.

The colonies and protectorates the Europeans arranged, in many cases solely for their own con-

567

venience, wished to enter the postwar world with the dignity of sovereign status. Altogether, 22 African countries emerged during this one quinquennium. Sudan, Ghana, Morocco, and Tunisia made the transition in 1956-7. French West Africa, French Equatorial Africa, the French island of Madagascar, and two trust territories administered by the French -- an accumulation of 15 new regimes -- won their independence in 1958-60. The former Italian Somaliland (including its British counterpart) achieved its freedom in 1960, along with the Belgian Congo and British-held Nigeria, the most heavily populated of the lot.

Sudan stood the third largest of the new states in population (11,000,000 at the time of independence) and the most expansive in area. In many respects (though considered in this book as a part of Sub-Sahara Africa), Sudan forms a part of the Muslim world so dominant in the Middle East. In germinal form, it existed as the kingdom of Meroë, which flourished two thousand years ago and whose writing awaits decipherment. From the sixth to the sixteenth centuries, two Christian kingdoms occupied northern Sudan in the place of Meroë. Muslims infiltrating from the north allied with the people of southern Sudan to form a loose confederation for the following three hundred years. Egypt held Sudan next, 1822-85, and an independent sectarian Muslim regime 1885-99. British officers led the Egyptian army that reconquered the country, 1898-9, leading to the establishment of the Anglo-Egyptian Sudan. This unusual condominium, with the British playing the major role, survived officially until January 1, 1956.

Sudanese nationalist movements became active in the 1940's. Some nationalists favored union with Egypt, while others hoped for complete independence. The pro-Egyptian parties snubbed a British-sponsored legislature that initiated sessions in 1948. The Egyptian proclamation of

568

king Farouk as ruler of the Sudan (1951) and the subsequent ouster of king Farouk (1952) helped to resolve the situation, as Egyptian president Neguib agreed with the British that the Sudanese should determine their own destiny. When the Sudan achieved practical autonomy in 1953, the pro-Egyptian group among its leaders retained considerable strength. By January 1, 1956, however, sentiment for complete independence asserted itself, and Sudan gave up the idea of union with Egypt.

Unity within the new nation soon proved its greatest problem. While nearly three-fourths of the people worshipped as Muslims, others (particularly in the southern districts) followed animistic attitudes derived from the ancient past. While half of the people by preference spoke an Arabic dialect, approximately 95 other languages helped to form the Sudanese pattern. One, from the Cushitic branch of the Afro-Asiatic family, lay in the northeast; about 55 of the Sudanic family in pockets scattered through the country, especially in the center and south; and nearly 40 tiny affiliates of the Niger-Congo family (including four Bantu tongues) in the center. Sudan began its life as a parliamentary republic, and managed to hold on as such for nearly three years. Contention between two Muslim sects and the desire of many non-Muslim districts for a high degree of autonomy made the situation of the regime precarious. A quiet revolution in November 1958 brought rule by a military council, with commander-in-chief Ibrahim Abboud at its head.

Ghana, with a population of 6,000,000, became the first of the west African states to achieve its independence. Ghana took its name from an empire whose center lay farther north, important from the ninth to the thirteenth century. The people who created the modern Ghana, whose ancestors may have inhabited the ancient one, spoke over 20 languages of the Kwa and Gur branches of the Niger-Congo family -- including

569

the Akan tongue of Kwa stock, spoken in the southern and central regions.

When the Portuguese arrived on the coast of Ghana in the fifteenth century, they took great interest in the gold found there, to the point that the Atlantic shore received its Gold Coast designation. Later, the same district became a focus for the collection of kidnapped Negro slaves. Other Europeans appeared, and the British declared the Gold Coast their colony in 1874. Ashanti, an Akan-speaking confederacy of the hinterland, fought with the British for a few decades. In 1901, however, the British incorporated the confederacy into the colony, pluralizing its name (the Gold Coast-Ashanti), and for good measure established a protectorate over the Gur-speaking peoples still farther inland. The people of the coast became Christianized, while those away from the ocean maintained their animistic outlook.

British-sponsored primary education in the Gold Coast-Ashanti colony and Akan participation in British military forces overseas helped to bring about the desire for independence in this region. In 1947, when India and Pakistan received their freedom, leaders in this colony founded a United Gold Coast Convention to play the same role here as that of the pre-1947 National Congress in India. In the Gold Coast, however, developments parallel to those in India happened much more rapidly. Kwame Nkrumah, with a college education in the United States, returned to his Gold Coast homeland to serve as secretary of the Convention, but only two years later (1949) led a youth group out of the Convention to form the Convention People's party. Like Gandhi, Nkrumah organized a civil disobedience campaign. His time in prison, however, lasted little more than a year (1950-1). In 1952 he became prime minister of the colony under British supervision, while his party strove for prompt independence and a government leaning toward socialism. Many persons in the colony and

570

protectorate disagreed with Nkrumah's policies, and many did not speak his Akan language. The Convention People's party won decisively in British-sponsored elections of 1956, however, and Ghana attained its independence as an autonomous parliamentary state under the British queen, March 6, 1957. (The word "dominion" for this status had become out-of-date.) A United Nations plebiscite in British Togoland, the trust territory just east of the Gold Coast colony, resulted in a decision that the people of this district would join the new state of Ghana from the beginning. In 1960, a new constitution made Ghana a republic, still within the Commonwealth. Kwame Nkrumah became the first president.

Morocco (10,000,000) and Tunisia (4,000,000), in the African portion of the Middle East, attained their independence from French "protection" on March 2 and March 20, 1956, respectively. The Egyptian revolution of 1952 excited nationalism among the peoples of Morocco and Tunisia as the experience of India moved the people of Ghana. In the seventh century, Arabic-speaking Muslims from the east had overrun the Berber-speaking peoples of Tunisia and Morocco, like those of Algeria between them. Native dynasties ruled the region until the sixteenth century, when Algeria and Tunisia became part of the vast Turkish empire, while Morocco developed a wide northwestern African empire of its own. Local leaders ruled Algeria again within a century, only to have their territory later seized by the French, who declared Algeria an integral part of France in 1834. Tunisia obtained local autonomy from the Turks in the early eighteenth century, only to submit to a French protectorate in 1883. Morocco lost the southern portions of its empire in the eighteenth century, and in 1912 suffered division into three zones, with the major portion to be protected by France and regions on the Mediterranean and the Atlantic by Spain. In 1923, the strategic city of Tangier, of the northern Spanish zone, came under a special "internationalized" regime, with

French influence predominant.

Algeria, where the French treated most of the Arabic- and Berber-speaking population as second-class citizens, developed further problems as Catholic Europeans settled there and about one-eighth of its people came to speak French. Migration from France into Tunisia caused the formation in that area of a nationalist Destour (Constitution) movement in 1920. Neither Destour nor Neo-Destour, a more radical party organized in 1934 with Habib Bourguiba as leader, developed great hostility toward France. Bourguiba spoke fluently the French language of his wife, choosing to remark on more than one occasion, "I do not hate France -- only colonialism." For some time, hope existed that France would relinquish its Tunisian protectorate peacefully. But France held on tightly in North Africa, through the formation of an Istiqlal (Independence) party in Morocco, 1943; through uprisings in Tunisia and Morocco, 1953-4; and through the outbreak of rebellion in Algeria, November 1954, led by a new National Liberation Front. The loss of Indochina in the latter year caused many French citizens to feel even less inclination toward the idea of North African independence.

France tasted defeat in North Africa as in Indochina simply because so many North African individuals came to value the goal of independence more highly than their own lives. To relieve the pressure in Tunisia and concentrate upon Morocco and Algeria, the French granted Tunisia considerable autonomy in August 1955. To concentrate upon Algeria alone, where French "honor" seemed most at stake, France gave Morocco its complete independence on March 2, 1956. To keep the Tunisians quiet, now that Morocco had moved ahead, Paris granted the full measure of freedom to Tunisia on March 20. These measures did not end the French difficulties, however, for the beleaguered Algerian people found loyal allies not only in newly independent Morocco and

Tunisia but in Egypt as well.

Morocco organized itself temporarily as an absolute monarchy with Muhammad V as its sultan. Muhammad's family had ruled, either independently or with "protection," ever since the late seventeenth century. The title of king replaced that of sultan in 1957; the king chose a council to prepare a constitution in 1960. The Spanish-protected area on the Mediterranean and the internationalized zone of Tangier joined the new regime in 1956 and the Spanish-protected area on the Atlantic in 1958, though Spain retained the port cities of Melilla and Ceuta. In Tunisia, the Neo-Destour party and its allies won overwhelmingly in elections on the sixth day of independence. Formerly headed by a bey, Tunisia became a republic in 1957 with Habib Bourguiba as president. A constitution completed in 1959 provided for the presidential type of regime. French forces remained in Tunisia temporarily, at a base near the city of Bizerte.

Despite its other losses in the short space of two years, France continued to hold on with great tenacity in Algeria. Only the Communist party and a small number of Radicals led by Pierre Mendès-France favored the right of Algeria to determine its own destiny. Many French people supported the European population in Algeria, determined to retain its position of privilege. (The Europeans could vote, but most Algerian Muslims could not.) Other French citizens hoped to find a way to keep Algeria a part of France while granting the Muslims greater equality. Guy Mollet, during the preparation of the Suez Canal plan in August 1956, consented to talks in Rome between his own representatives and five from the National Liberation Front. Ahmad ben Bella, one of the Algerian team, had turned to revolution in 1948 after serving in the French army during World War II. Ben Bella and his four countrymen left the conference in Rome to consult with companions in Algeria and allies in Morocco and Tunisia. The French armed forces, however, forced their airplane to the ground, arrested the men, and sent them to prison in France. Mollet, though he had not ordered this kidnapping, failed to free the prisoners. When in January 1957 he suggested a cease-fire to be followed by free elections, no one in Algeria listened to him.

Two men of the Radical party succeeded Mollet as premier (June 1957-April 1958), offering a reorganization of Algeria without a prior cease-fire, but had no more success than Mollet. Ben Bella and his companions remained in prison while French soldiers and Muslim revolutionaries continued to die. On February 8, 1958, French officers in Algeria again asserted their own initiative (as they had in the detention of Ben Bella) by ordering that bombs be dropped on a Tunisian border town. On May 13, the same group, led by Raoul Salan and Jacques Massu, seized the capital city of Algeria (Algiers) when they heard that Pierre Pflimlin would become premier. Pflimlin, a Popular Republican, could be expected to continue to search for a compromise. Salan and Massu did not wish to separate from France, but to pose a threat that would bring to power a French government more distinctly friendly to their interests. Specifically, they believed Charles de Gaulle to be their man.

Charles-André-Joseph-Marie de Gaulle was born in Lille, northern France, in 1890. His parents -- conservative, very nationalistic, and zealously Roman Catholic -- raised him in the city of Paris. Charles' father held the position of lay headmaster in a Jesuit secondary school, where he also taught philosophy and literature. Charles attended this school until 1907, when it closed its doors. He then moved to another Jesuit school near Tournai, Belgium, where he finished his secondary training in 1908. Next he studied in Paris to pass the entrance examination for military officers' school and spent a year as an ordinary soldier (1909-10). He trained as an officer for two years in Paris, and became a lieutenant in the French infantry.

Wounded twice during the first year of World War I, he returned both times to the front, receiving promotion to the rank of captain. A bayonet wound in his thigh and skull injuries from a shell finally put him out of action in 1916. Taken prisoner by the Germans, he attempted several times to escape, though without any success. After World War I, he participated in the Polish war against the Russians as a member of a French mission to assist the Poles. Returning to France in 1921, he taught military history for a year in the academy where he had studied and attended school himself for two years, hoping for further promotion.

Charles de Gaulle made an excellent student of military affairs, though teachers took little notice of him. He shared his parents' enthusiasm for religion and country, but followed tradition less closely than his associates on military matters. Henri-Philippe Pétain, De Gaulle's commander in World War I, liked him despite differences in their outlook; De Gaulle served on Pétain's personal staff, 1925-7. De Gaulle received promotion to commandant in 1927, to lieutenant-colonel in 1933, and to colonel in 1937. He spent the years 1929-31 in the French mandates of Lebanon and Syria.

Slowly, De Gaulle acquired recognition for books he wrote in criticism of the traditional French military outlook. In La discorde chez l'ennemi (Discord among the Enemy, 1924) he showed how fixed ideas had hurt the German effort in World

575

War I. In Le fil de l'épee (The Edge of
the Sword, 1932) he asserted his conviction that officers must sometimes disobey
those above them in authority if they wish
to achieve greatness -- a principle he
applied to civilian leadership also. In
Vers une armée de métier (1934, translated as The Army of the Future), De
Gaulle criticized the static defense line
the French army had designed to stop any
offensive by the Germans, pointing out
that the line by itself, without a complimentary development of mobile warfare,
only provided the French nation a false
sense of security.

Oddly, the fourth of De Gaulle's
treatises to appear -- La France et son
armée (France and Her Army) -- had left
his pen before the others. De Gaulle
wrote it in the early 1920's as a service
to his superior Pétain, who never brought
it to light. Its appearance under De
Gaulle's name in 1938 came as a surprise
to Pétain, who no longer maintained his
friendship for the younger man. Pétain
had paid only lip service to De Gaulle's
arguments concerning the importance of
mobile warfare, while other highly placed
French commanders failed even to go that
far. The Germans, who sensed the value in
De Gaulle's ideas, defeated the French in
1940.

On May 16, 1940, six days after the
beginning of the German offensive against
France in World War II, De Gaulle as a
temporary brigadier-general undertook the
command of a new armored division. On
June 5, he accepted an appointment as
under-secretary for defense. On June 9
and June 16, he flew to London to represent the French government in the painful
decision-making taking place as the Third
French Republic neared its end. After the

formation of the Pétain government the evening before, he returned to London June 17, resolved not to give in to defeat. On June 18, he summoned other sons of France, via a radio speech from London, to rebellion against the German-sponsored Pétain regime. The Free French military group thus initiated remained under De Gaulle's command until France won back its freedom from the Nazis.

The British recognized De Gaulle's group as a cooperating force though the United States maintained ties to the Pétain regime in Vichy. French Equatorial Africa joined De Gaulle's cause, but a joint British-Free French attempt to take over the administration of French West Africa failed in September 1940. The British and Free French cooperated again to defeat Vichy French forces in Syria, July 1941, but the operation produced much friction when the British made decisions without consultation with the Free French command. De Gaulle, without a mandate from the French nation, increasingly thought of himself and his group as a French refugee government. On September 24, 1941, he organized a French National Committee, which dealt with the Soviet Union as well as the United Kingdom. When the resistance against the Germans in France grew appreciably in 1942, many of its leaders sought ties with De Gaulle's organization, renamed Fighting France in July. Many of the resistance leaders stood politically to the left, and for some time De Gaulle maintained more friendly relations with Moscow than with either Washington or London.

When the British and American armies landed in northern Africa in November 1942, the Fighting French played no role in the invasion. Former supporters of

Vichy provided intermediation between the invading armies and the lands they occupied. Charles de Gaulle arrived in Algeria in May 1943, serving as head of a French Committee of National Liberation and gradually taking over responsibility for the Algerian government. On June 3, 1944, the Committee of National Liberation converted itself into a provisional government for France. Three days later, the British and American armies landed in France. De Gaulle followed a week later, but permanently only on August 20. Other refugee governments in London recognized that of De Gaulle, and the Soviet Union, the United States, and the United Kingdom followed by September. In the meantime, the newly liberated population of Paris applauded De Gaulle August 26. De Gaulle took the cheering as a tribute to his person, an outlook not fully justified by the circumstances, and chose to consider it a kind of mandate to return France to its former "greatness."

Charles de Gaulle realized, of course, that not everyone in the provisional government shared his own conception of the program that might lead to greatness. The leadership of the at-home resistance in particular felt little devotion to De Gaulle's ideas, which smacked of conservatism and nationalism and paid scant attention to social reform. Both Socialist and Communist parties participated in the government, and De Gaulle formed an alliance with Joseph Stalin in December. The first constituent assembly chosen by the French people unanimously selected De Gaulle as head of the government, and he included five Communists in his cabinet formed November 21. Suddenly, however, on January 20, 1946, he resigned, giving no satisfactory reason for his decision. De Gaulle cared little for the squabbling and compromise inherent in party politics; it seems certain that he fell quickly out of patience with the constituent assembly. He preferred to sit this one out, believing the country would find it needed him, and expecting then to reorganize France with a strong central executive.

In June 1946, after the nation had rejected the first constitution prepared for it, De Gaulle outlined his own proposals for the government. Other ideas prevailed, however, in the constitution adopted in October. In April 1947, De Gaulle and his friends organized a Rally of the French People to fight for his program, as De Gaulle began to make speeches derogating the parliament and posing a specter of communism. For a short time, it appeared that the Rally of the French People might catch the voters' imagination; more than any other party, it placed the emphasis on nation-enthusiasm. It showed considerable strength in municipal elections of October 1947, but began to fade thereafter.

Gradually, as popular backing for his party subsided, Charles de Gaulle became embittered and isolated. He castigated all international efforts involving the French government -- the Marshall Plan, the North Atlantic Treaty Organization, the European Coal and Steel Community -- as instruments that assisted other nations at the expense of France. In 1953, De Gaulle disowned his own party in the parliament simply because it played a role in the Fourth French Republic that he had come to loathe. In July 1955, he announced his own retirement from public life. Except for a visit to French islands in the Pacific, he spent most of his time during three years (1955-8) in his home in the village of Colombey-les-Deux-Eglises, east of Paris. Here he busied himself writing his memoirs, waiting still -- many people felt -- for the moment that would yet be his in national life.

Pierre Pflimlin became the premier of France May 14, 1958. The parliament granted him emergency powers to handle the Algerian crisis. In actuality, however, he could do nothing without the backing of the French armed forces. When army personnel friendly to the Salan-Massu group in Algeria took over the French island of Corsica, and when a segment of the French navy declared its sympathy for the same cause, Charles de Gaulle made known his willingness (under certain conditions) to serve his country again. Little choice remained for Pflimlin but to resign. De Gaulle became premier May 31, 1958, with emergency powers from the beginning. He expected to submit a new constitution to the French people and to modify the French Union on the basis of popular referenda in the overseas territories.

De Gaulle moved swiftly to assure himself full power, though he exercised great caution in respect to Algeria. Nearly two-thirds of the people of France, and a higher percentage than that (of those who voted) in the territories, said yes to the new constitution, and the Fifth French Republic came into existence on October 4. De Gaulle would act as president rather than premier (elections gave him the position December 21), with powers similar to those of the president of the United States. He also enjoyed one privilege that extended his power further -- the right to determine for himself the existence of an emergency during which he alone might rule by presidential decree. All these changes appealed to the French-speaking community in Algeria as long as they thought of De Gaulle as their man, who would never consent to the separation of Algeria from France. In December, however, De

Gaulle quietly removed Salan and Massu from their positions of authority in Algiers. In September, the Algerian National Liberation Front had organized a provisional government residing in Cairo, Egypt, with Ferhat Abbas as premier. The warfare between the Algerian Muslims and the French continued into its fifth year.

Without any declaration concerning Algeria, De Gaulle arranged a French Community to replace the French Union, permitting overseas territories to secede from the French association if they so desired. The colonial portion of the voting on the creation of the Fifth French Republic also constituted a plebiscite whereby each territory decided its adherence to the French Community. Adherence meant a recognition of French leadership, allowing some measure of autonomy. Only the territory of French Guinea, a part of French West Africa, voted against the French Community in 1958. Its people, Muslim and animistic in their religion, and speaking nine languages of the West Atlantic and Mande branches of the Niger-Congo family, had come under French domination during 1849-98 (the colony dated from 1893). Virtually all of them (97%) chose independence, at the behest of the Marxist-oriented Democratic party and its leader, trade unionist Sékou Touré. The republic of Guinea came into being October 2, with a population of 3,000,000. Touré served as provisional president, joining Ghana (and in 1960 a new republic of Mali) in a federation that remained only a compact. Guinea became offically a one-party state in December 1958, as Touré insisted that no difference existed between his Democratic party and the body of Guinean people. Touré received aid from both the Soviet Union and the United States, though the French deserted him from the beginning.

Charles de Gaulle had not anticipated that any African colony would vote for independence, nor did he intend to give up French rule in Algeria. Continued strife in Algeria, however, coupled with growing indications of pro-Algerian world sentiment, led him to a fresh declaration in September 1959. With the negotiation of a cease-fire, he promised, the Algerian people could decide their own destiny within a period of four years. He rejected, however, a proposal of Ferhat Abbas (made in November) that Ahmad ben Bella and his four prison-mates serve as the Algerian negotiators for a cease-fire. When the French-speaking community in Algeria rose again, January 24-February 1, 1960, freshly arrived units of the French army forced them to desist. Many Muslims welcomed president De Gaulle when he visited Algeria in early December 1960, while those who had rebelled to bring him into power demonstrated against him. Later the same month, the United Nations General Assembly without the participation of France called for the right of self-determination for the Algerian people.

France lost its political hold on nearly all the remainder of French Africa while the Algerian question remained unresolved. The two trust territories that France administered for the United Nations became independent in early 1960. Cameroun, the larger of these, included speakers of about 60 Bantu and a half-dozen Bantu-related languages, of more than 15 other Niger-Congo tongues, and of yet another half-dozen of the Chad branch of the Sudanic family. These people had become part of a German protectorate in 1884. The British took one-fifth and the French four-fifths of the protectorate from the Germans during World War I. The League of Nations then placed the two portions in the care of the British and French, as mandates with the goal of independence; the League of Nations mandates became United Nations trust territories. Though the inhabitants lacked cultural as well as linguistic uniformity (those living near the coast having adopted Christianity, those far inland adhering to Islam, a good half remaining animistic in outlook), they developed an interest in the examples of Ghana and Guinea. Those of the French territory (3,000,000 in number) organized the parliamentary-type republic of

Cameroun on January 1, 1960, allowing considerable power also to the presidency. Those under the British administration, even more linguistically diverse, moved somewhat more slowly toward the same destination.

The people of the French-administered portion of Togoland became the next to achieve independence. Speaking about ten languages of the Kwa and Gur branches of the Niger-Congo family, they had formed a part of the German protectorate of Togoland established in 1885. The British and French both received League of Nations mandates here as in the Cameroons. Some of the people became Christians, while others remained Muslims and animists. When the mandates became trust territories, a movement rose to unify them. Ghana, immediately to their west, suggested a three-way union, since the Kwa and Gur language stocks gave them all something in common. As a result of a United Nations plebiscite, British Togoland did join independent Ghana from the beginning. When the French sector decided in French-sponsored elections of 1956 to assume a closer relationship with France, the United Nations Trusteeship Council declined to approve the step. Togo leaders then requested the total independence, separate from both France and Ghana, which came about on April 27, 1960. The new republic of Togo (1,400,000), with a parliamentary regime, boasted several political parties.

From this point on, African independence spread like a contagion. Senegal and the French Soudan, the next territories to achieve their freedom, formed two of the eight divisions of French West Africa. Senegal lay at Africa's extreme western tip. Its people spoke a half-dozen languages of the West Atlantic branch of the Niger-Congo family. The French had come to the coast of Senegal in the seventeenth century, and urban peoples of the coastal zone had become Europeanized to a greater degree than in most colonies. They secured representation in the

French parliament from 1848; the later colony of (all) Senegal appeared in 1920. The French Soudan lay inland from Senegal, its larger but sparsely settled territory inhabited by a variety of peoples. Here, at the southern edge of the Sahara desert, had lain the seat of the ancient empire of Ghana, as well as those of an empire of Mali from the thirteenth to the sixteenth century and Songhai in the fifteenth and sixteenth. After the beginning of French influence in the late nineteenth century, the Soudan became a part of the colony of Upper Senegal-Niger (1904) until it achieved separate colonial status in 1920. The languages included eight of the Mande and Gur stocks, two of the Sudanic family, and a representation of the Afro-Asiatic family (both Arabic and Berber). A majority of the people in the Soudan worshipped as Muslims, some of the coastal inhabitants of Senegal became Christianized, and many in both colonies remained animistic in their outlook.

After World War II, African leadership in the Soudan sought self-rule for a major portion of French West Africa. Four of the eight overseas territories there after 1947 -- Upper Volta, the Soudan, Senegal, and Dahomey -- together wrote a constitution for a federation they called Mali in 1959, and pressed for French recognition of complete autonomy inside the French Community. The De Gaulle government in an ongoing mood of concession to the inevitable reorganized the French Community on a contractual basis June 4, 1960, opening the possibility of new arrangements. The Mali federation, limited to Senegal and the Soudan by the withdrawal of Upper Volta and Dahomey, negotiated complete independence on June 20, 1960. The leaders of the former French Soudan, however, held less enthusiasm for the French connection than those of Senegal, so that even the limited federation soon dissolved. On August 20, Senegal (3,000,000) seceded and set up a semi-parliamentary republic of its own, within the French Community. On September 22, the former Soudan separated itself from that Community and organized the presidential republic of Mali (4,000,000), looking toward the compact with Guinea and Ghana arranged by the end of the year. Senegal started its life with a moderate socialist regime, led by poet-president Léopold Senghor and his Progressive Union. Mali began as a one-party state under president Modibo Keita and his Soudanese Union, employing Marxist language and ideas.

The island of Madagascar, off the eastern coast of Africa, achieved its independence soon after the federation of Mali. The Mongoloid racial strain of faraway eastern Asia had met the Negroid from nearby Africa in Madagascar, along with a little of the Caucasoid from the Arab world. Through most of the nineteenth century, one kingdom united the island, while the Malagasy language of the Malayo-Polynesian family became dominant. The French, who had first appeared on the island in the seventeenth century, established a protectorate in 1885, transforming it into a colony in 1896. Two-fifths of the people became Christians, while the others remained animists. Madagascar became the independent Malagasy Republic (5,000,000) within the French Community on June 26, 1960. President and prime minister Philibert Tsiranana, pro-French and Catholic, led the nation along with his moderately socialist Social Democratic party.

Four more territories of French West Africa and all four of French Equatorial Africa concluded negotiations for independence in August, according to a neatly synchronized timetable. Dahomey, on the Atlantic coast immediately east of Togo, had become a French protectorate in 1892, and a colony in 1894. Its people, most of whom remained animists, spoke only a few languages of Gur and Kwa stock. Their republic, proclaimed independent August 1, 1960, took a parliamentary form, dominated by a Party of Unity. Like Niger, Upper Volta, and Ivory Coast to follow, Dahomey (2,000,000) chose not to remain a part of the French Community.

The French had entered Niger, an inland area north and northeast of Dahomey, very late in the nineteenth century; they included it in a larger colony in 1904, granting it separate identity in 1922. Its widely scattered peoples spoke three languages of the Sudanic family, one each of the Berber and West Atlantic stocks, and Hausa of the Chad stock. Most of the population adhered to Islam. The presidential-type republic of Niger (3,000,000), proclaimed August 3, 1960, permitted only the Progressive party to operate from the beginning.

Upper Volta also lay inland, west of Niger, north of Ghana and Togo. It contained over 20 languages of Gur stock (Gur is sometimes called Voltaic) and a few of the Mande branch. The Mossi ethnic group, speaking a Gur language, held control over this region from the sixteenth century until 1896, when it suffered defeat by the French. A part of the Upper Senegal-Niger colony 1904-19, Upper Volta then secured separate colonial status, interrupted again 1932-47. Islam claimed some converts here, as well as Christianity, but most of the people remained animists. The Voltaic Republic (4,000,000), organized August 5, 1960, provided a presidential-type regime except that the legislature would designate the president. The Voltaic Republic started its existence as a one-party state, under the so-called Democratic Union.

The French had come to the Ivory Coast, between Liberia and Ghana, in 1843, but occupied the entire region only in 1914. They established a protectorate in 1889, a colony in 1893. The people of the Ivory Coast -- chiefly animists, with Muslim and Christian minorities -- spoke some 30 languages of the Kwa, Gur, and Mande stocks. Félix Houphouët-Boigny, a physician, helped organize a Democratic party here in 1946, along with an African Democratic Rally with branches in several colonies. The French Communist party, at that time a part of the French government, aided him in his early efforts, but Houphouët-Boigny later adopted a moderate tone. Ivory Coast (3,000,000) proclaimed its republic August 7, 1960. In November, it adopted the presidential style of government with Félix Houphouët-Boigny as the first president and the Democratic party dominant.

The four colonies of French Equatorial Africa, unlike the four of West Africa immediately preceding, all decided to remain within the French Community on the achievement of independence. Chad, in the heart of northern Africa (east of Niger, south of Libya), stretched into the vast Sahara Desert from the south. The French moved into the region in late nineteenth century, including it in a larger colony in 1906 and granting it separate colonial status in 1920. The people spoke over 20 languages of the Chad branch of the Afro-Asiatic family, some 20 more (widely variant) of the Sudanic family, and a few of the Niger-Congo family. The inhabitants of the northern part adhered to Islam, while those of the south remained chiefly animists. Chad (3,000,000) became a parliamentary republic August 11, 1960, with its Progressive party in majority control.

Oubangui-Chari lay immediately south of Chad. Containing five languages of the Sudanic family and 15 of the Niger-Congo (nine Bantu tongues included), it became a French colony in 1906. Most of its people clung to the animistic outlook. They established the Central African Republic (1,200,000) on August 13, 1960. The leadership of the parliamentary regime tended toward moderate socialism.

Moyen-Congo reached from Oubangui-Chari to a foothold on the Atlantic. Its people spoke about 25 Bantu languages, and remained largely animist in religious outlook after their organization into a French colony in 1910. They organized the Congo Republic (800,000) on August 15, 1960, choosing the parliamentary-style regime. (The nation is labeled the Congo Republic, arbitrarily, in this study, to distinguish it from a much larger neighboring country, which also took the name of Congo in 1960.)

Gabon, the smallest of the new African nations of this quinquennium, lay on the Atlantic shore immediately west of Moyen-Congo. Entered by the French in 1841, and established as a French colony in 1903, its people spoke about 20 Bantu languages. One-third of them became converts to Christianity, while the others remained animists. The republic of Gabon came into being with 450,000 inhabitants August 17, 1960. Like the other portions of the former French Equatorial Africa, it adopted a parliamentary regime within the French Community.

Of the eight territories of French West Africa, only Mauritania continued French. On the Atlantic coast north of Senegal and south of Morocco, its territory consisted largely of desert. Mauritania had become a French protectorate in 1903, a French colony in 1921. Its population, largely Muslim, spoke Arabic and Berber tongues. Mauritania (1,000,000) became independent of French rule on November 28, 1960, organizing itself as a parliamentary republic, officially Islamic. Morocco held a claim to the Mauritanian territory, however, and for that reason opposed its formation as a state. Egypt, Ghana, Mali, Guinea, and Libya supported the Moroccan claim. Mauritania remained friendly to France and continued to house French troops, though it chose not to remain officially within the formal French Community.

In Africa's eastern extreme, far across the continent from Mauritania and Senegal, lived the Somali people speaking the Somali tongue of the Cushitic branch of the Afro-Asiatic family. Adhering to Islam, they lived in settlements scattered over a wide area. The French, the British, and the Italians all invaded their territory in the decade of the 1880's, establishing protectorates over separate regions. After World War II, the United Nations decided that Italy should rule its prewar protectorate as a trust territory for ten years dating from 1950. The British set their protectorate free on June 26, 1960, five days before the termination of that decade. The former British and Italian regions then united as the republic of Somalia (2,000,000) on July 1, choosing a parliamentary-type regime. Contention arose immediately with all three of the new country's neighbors -- French Somaliland, Ethiopia, and the British colony of Kenya -- each of which contained some Somali population.

The Belgian Congo, occupying a large section of south-central Africa with a very small footing on the Atlantic coast, experienced the most precipitous transition to independence of all the African territories. The people here spoke some 150 Bantu languages (one of them Swahili) as well as another dozen of the Niger-Congo family and ten of the Sudanic. European people entered the region in the 1870's, and in 1885 organized the so-called Congo Free State, ruled by the king but not the nation of Belgium. A wave of complaint abroad concerning the mistreatment of the Congolese people under this regime resulted in 1908 in the transfer of the territory to Belgium as a colony. Demands for independence in the Belgian Congo remained muffled until 1959, when local riots occurred. In the meantime, one-third of the 14,000,000 people had become converts to Christianity from the more prevalent animism, and the Congolese economy had developed further than that of neighboring lands.

The riots of 1959 brought an invitation to Congolese leaders to attend conversations in Belgium. Those more hostile and those more friendly to a continuing Belgian influence in the Congo united in a demand for immediate independence. Congo thus managed to proclaim itself a republic June 30, 1960, in the presence of the Belgian king. The ceremony proved, however, the beginning of trouble rather than of national freedom.

Violence broke out after only two days between the supporters of president Joseph Kasa-Vubu and those of premier Patrice Lumumba. According to the constitution, the premier would wield the executive power, backed by a majority in the legislature. Kasa-Vubu, who favored considerable autonomy for the six provinces of Congo, had desired the position of premier, however, and chose not to allow Lumumba, who stood for a strong central government, to administer the country. Fighting between the two groups of supporters, complicated by some inter-tribal warfare and mutiny in sectors of the army, endangered the lives and properties of the small minority of Europeans present and brought renewed intervention by Belgium.

President Kasa-Vubu and premier Lumumba joined in a protest to the secretary-general of the United Nations (which Congo had not yet joined) asking for that organization's help against the Belgians in uniform. They felt particular concern about an announcement by Moïse Tshombe -- pro-Belgian leader of Katanga, the country's richest province -- of the secession of Katanga from the Congolese government. The United Nations Security Council, at the suggestion of the secretary-general, voted a resolution the night of July 13-14, 1960, calling for the withdrawal of Belgian troops from Congo and authorizing the secretary-general to render military assistance to the Congolese regime. The Soviet Union moved that the Council label Belgium an aggressor, but this the Council refused to do. The vote on the adopted resolution stood 8 to 0, with the United Kingdom, France, and Tai Wan abstaining. Secretary-general Dag Hammarskjöld acted quickly, so that foreign troops (almost all from Africa and Asia, none from the Council's permanent members) landed in the Congolese capital of Leopoldville without delay. Nevertheless, the Belgian troops withdrew slowly, and especially remained in Katanga, lending credence to the idea that the secession movement there constituted an endeavor by Belgian interests to remain in control of the mines in that province. The Soviet Union said it would back the Congolese effort to keep the country united, acting unilaterally if necessary. The Security Council on the night of July 21-22 commended the secretary-general for his prompt action, called for a speedy Belgian withdrawal, and requested that all states refrain from any action that might impede the restoration of Congolese law and order. This resolution passed unanimously.

Dag Hammarskjöld reported to the Security Council August 6 that United Nations forces had replaced those of Belgium everywhere except in Katanga. Moïse Tshombe, newly elected "president" of Katanga, had advised Hammarskjöld, however, that the United Nations troops would encounter armed opposition if they tried to enter that province. The Soviet Union submitted a resolution (not brought to a vote) stating that the secretary-general should take "decisive measures" and use "any means" to eliminate Belgian troops from Congo. A resolution adopted August 9 (by 9 to 0, with France and Italy abstaining) called upon the government of Belgium specifically to remove its forces from Katanga, and declared that the entry of the United Nations Force into Katanga was necessary, though the United Nations would not intervene in the solution of Congolese internal conflicts. On August 12, Hammarskjöld himself flew to Elizabethville, the capital of Katanga, taking with him a group of Swedish troops in the United Nations Force. The secretary-general made this trip, which included talks with Tshombe, on his own initiative rather than in consultation with the central government which the United Nations had originally set out to aid. Prime minister Lumumba, taking a stand against negotiations with the leader of a province in rebellion, refused to talk with Hammarskjöld two days later. The latter argued that he had undertaken the trip to Elizabethville only after he had informed the Congolese delegation in New York, and that the delegation had raised no objections. Patrice

Lumumba turned away from the United Nations at this point, and looked to the Soviet Union for aid.

On September 5, new difficulties arose when president Kasa-Vubu announced the deposition of premier Lumumba, only to have the latter request that the nation back him in a removal of the president; Lumumba accused Kasa-Vubu of treason. The lower house of parliament two days later rejected both dismissals, while the upper house by a narrow vote the following day rejected only Kasa-Vubu's dismissal of Lumumba. The head of the army, Joseph Mobutu, moved September 14 to solve all these complications by ejecting Lumumba from office and placing himself at the head of the state for the remainder of the year. Mobutu recognized Kasa-Vubu as president, but since neither Kasa-Vubu nor Lumumba recognized Mobutu's move, the young republic of Congo came close to anarchy. In the midst of this scene, Congo became a United Nations member September 20. On the same day, a fourth emergency special session of the General Assembly appealed to all the Congolese factions to seek a peaceful solution to their conflicts with the assistance of African and Asian representatives.

Lumumba held the weakest position. Only the protection of the United Nations Force prevented his capture by Mobutu. Kasa-Vubu increased his prestige for the moment when he addressed the United Nations General Assembly November 8, requesting the approval of the credentials of his delegation rather than that of Lumumba. On November 22, he achieved his point when the Assembly voted 53 to 24, with 19 abstentions, to favor his group. Besides the 10 communist votes and that of Cuba in the negative, however, 7 Asian and 6 African states voted no. On November 27, Lumumba left Leopoldville, only to be captured by the troops of Mobutu four days later. His former vice-premier and friend Antoine Gizenga then announced a new government for Congo, with its capital at Stanleyville. The communist governments and those of Egypt, Morocco, Ghana, Mali, Guinea, and Togo in Africa recognized the regime of Gizenga. At the end of the year 1960, the future status of Congo remained very much in question.

Nigeria, the British colony and protectorate whose southern edge lay on the Atlantic coast, held 43,000,000 people in 1960, as many as all the French areas in Africa liberated during this quinquennium. Nigeria contained a number of ethnic groups with separate historical traditions. The Hausa language of the north, of the Chad branch of the Afro-Asiatic family, represented the heritage of a number of Muslim states prominent in the region from the fourteenth to the eighteenth century. In the early nineteenth, people speaking Fulani, of the West Atlantic branch of the Niger-Congo family, occupied a portion of the Hausa region, ruling the kingdom of Sokoto 1809-1903. In the northeast, the Muslim state of Bornu (whose leaders spoke a Sudanic tongue) lasted some 500 years until the early twentieth century. The Yorubu and Ibo languages of the Kwa branch of the Niger-Congo family, each the heritage of advanced cultures in their regions, dominated the southwest and southeast of Nigeria respectively. The Yoruba, Ibo, and Hausa groups stood about equal in strength, each somewhat more numerous than the Fulani. Altogether, Nigeria contained over 60 languages of the Chad stock, about two dozen Bantu and 160 Bantu-related, about one dozen of the Kwa branch, 20 from other divisions of the Niger-Congo family, and two from the Sudanic family.

The British entered Nigeria from the southwest in 1861 and established a protectorate over the southeastern district in 1885. They formed the "colony and protectorate" of Nigeria, including the northern district, in 1914. (Frederick John Dealtry Lugard, born in India of British parents, in effect created this unification of Nigeria, and lived until 1945.) From

1939, the British divided the area administratively into the Western Provinces (where lived the Yoruba), the Eastern Provinces (containing the Ibo), and the Northern Provinces (including both the Hausa and Fulani peoples). Christianity grew chiefly in the Eastern (really southeastern) Provinces, and less in the Western (really southwestern) Provinces, while Islam held the devotion of a majority of the Northern Provinces and exerted some influence in the southwest. Animism assumed a smaller role in north and southwest, but continued a major influence in the southeast.

Nigerian political parties developed along regional lines as several groups began to work toward self-government. First appeared the National Council of Nigeria and the Cameroons, organized in 1944. (The British administered their portion of the Cameroons as a part of Nigeria.) The Ibo leadership came to dominate the National Council, though many minor groups remained allied to it. A Hausa-Fulani partnership led by Abubakar Tafawa Balewa commenced activities in 1949 to balance Ibo strength in the colony at large. The so-called Action Group, constituted in 1951, found its greatest strength among the Yoruba. Nigeria became a "federation" with limited powers in 1954, headed by a governor-general. Its divisions were the Northern Region, the Eastern Region, the Western Region, and the capital of Lagos. On October 1, 1960, the federation received full power to manage its own affairs as a member of the Commonwealth. The head of the National Council, an Ibo, became the first governor-general under the new regime. Hausa-speaking Balewa, whose Northern People's Congress had nearly won a majority in elections of 1959, became the new prime minister. The National Council had run second and the Action Group third in the voting, which took on a strong regional flavoring, though each of the three large parties commanded some following in all of the districts. At the dawn of independence, the parties stood willing to cooperate, and since in any event each of the three outlying districts

594

retained considerable self-rule within the federation, the outlook for Nigeria as the largest African nation seemed favorable at the outset.

During the quinquennium 1956-60, virtually all of French Africa, most of Belgian Africa, and much of British Africa had received its political freedom, along with Italian Somaliland and Spanish Morocco. Most of the new countries lacked the resources and strength to stand alone. Indeed, many of them on their own volition had chosen to cling in some fashion to the European states that previously held sway over them. Others looked toward some kind of African or Sub-Saharan unity. In the meantime, at the end of this period, other African territories remained in European hands. Their future, as well as that of the fledgling new nation-states, so monetarily poor and so divided into peoples who could not understand each other's languages, remained a great question mark in history.

Two American Revolutions (Part I)

New Year's Day, at the head of the calendar, seems a psychologically appropriate moment for the beginning of a new way of life. Individuals frequently resolve to alter their patterns of behavior in what may come to be a superior mode of living. On January 1, 1958, in Venezuela a large majority of the people resolved to replace a dictatorial regime with one dedicated to liberty and a new livelihood for the people. On January 1, 1959, in Cuba one dictator stepped down and another took command, resolving to bring nutrition, schools, and housing to the less favored families of the island. Venezuela and Cuba both started this five-year period under harsh and cruel autocracies which left little room for personal freedom or the betterment of the economically destitute. Venezuela had experienced no very genuine democracy except for a period of nine months in 1948. Cuba had participated in free elections 1940-8, only to experience great disappointment from them. (See "Three Losses for Democracy," Chapter VI.) Venezuela after New Year's Day of 1958 engaged in democratic and socialist revolution simultaneously. Cuba after New Year's Day 1959 settled for socialism without the democracy, but in doing so created much excitement, attracting a sizeable share of world attention.

Venezuela (6-7,000,000 population in this time period) stood as the richest country of Latin America in per capita income, though most of its people shared little in the wealth. The money that existed, in the hands of a few, came chiefly from the petroleum industry established in 1918. Juan Vicente Gómez, who ruled as a dictator 1909-35, granted oil concessions to his family and friends, who sold them to foreign companies. The companies, the family, and the friends thus reaped the profits, which touched the lives of a relative few among the population at large. When Gómez died, his son-in-law and a man chosen by his son-in-law succeeded him, extending their combined terms to a decade. These two presidents took away the lands and fortunes of many formerly favored individuals, but retained the lands for the government and created no revolutionary program for distribution of the income. Their willingness to move in the direction of democracy, though without really crossing the threshold, spurred the efforts of younger men who had hated Gómez and wanted to go all the way in repudiation of his programs.

Jóvito Villalba and Rómulo Betancourt, two of these young men, had led a group of university students in a futile rebellion against Gómez in 1928. The government exiled both Villalba and Betancourt, affording them an opportunity to study the alternatives available to them. In 1936, back in Venezuela, they organized the National Democratic party, with Villalba as sec-

596

retary-general and Betancourt as secretary of organization. The regime denied legal status for the party, and early in 1937, when Villalba and other critics ran successfully for the congress as independents, swiftly exiled most of them again. Rómulo Betancourt escaped the police on this occasion, remaining in hiding in Venezuela for two and a half years, restructuring and continuing to build the clandestine party, eliminating rival leaders who followed Marxist ideas. Villalba, on the other hand, remained in Colombia well past his year of exile, and chose not to rejoin the National Democratic party when he did return home. The police finally captured Betancourt, exiling him to Chile.

When the dictatorial regime relaxed its severity in 1941, Betancourt returned to Venezuela to help found a new party. Essentially, the National Democratic party for which he had labored became the legitimized Democratic Action (Acción Democrática, or AD). AD party leaders worked hard for four years to win the friendship of the people for a program of democratic socialist reform. In 1945 they joined a group in the military to overthrow the old regime. The junta which then ruled until February 1948 contained four AD members of a total of seven, with Betancourt as provisional president. Betancourt said he would not run for the office of constitutional president, and AD nominated novelist Rómulo Gallegos in his stead. The Committee of Independent Electoral Political Organization (Comité de Organización Política Electoral Independiente, or COPEI) of liberal Roman Catholic orientation nominated Rafael Caldera to oppose Gallegos. The Democratic Republican Union (Unión Republicana Democrática, URD) of Jóvito Villalba campaigned only for seats in the congress on a platform like that of AD.

Gallegos won the presidency, serving February-November 1948. He made the mistake of appointing as chief of his general staff a colonel named Marcos Pérez Jiménez, whom Betancourt (suspecting his loyalty) had kept on missions outside the country. Pérez Jiménez helped to plan the coup that ousted Gallegos, and became a member of the succeeding junta. The new government outlawed AD, though not URD and COPEI. It sponsored elections in 1952 for members of a constituent assembly, which in turn would choose a new president. With AD voters instructed to lend their support to URD, the party of Villalba won a majority, while that of Pérez Jiménez ran a poor second. When Pérez ordered a recount, however, after terminating the broadcast of election returns, his party somehow achieved the victory. Pérez Jiménez became president for a full term from 1953.

In many ways, Marcos Pérez Jiménez reverted to the style of Juan Vicente Gómez. His regime allowed no freedom; it reacted very swiftly, and with cruelty, toward critics; it gave rich concessions to a favored few; it cooperated enthusiastically with the foreign oil companies. Betancourt and other AD leaders remained in exile throughout the period 1948-58. The regime picked up Villalba and other URD leaders and flew them out of the country as their prize for winning the elections of 1952. Rafael Caldera, the leader of COPEI, went to prison in 1957, accused of encouraging the Catholic hierarchy to speak out against the government. Lesser political opponents often found themselves subjected to torture. In some respects, however, the Pérez Jiménez regime differed from that of Gómez. Caracas, the capital, became a modern city, with a modern university near its center; superhighways came into evidence in places where traffic demanded them; and great housing developments assumed a place on the urban horizon -- the super-bloques of a dozen stories whose number impresses any visitor. The mass of people, nevertheless, remained poorly fed, and the numerous opposition angry.

Gustavo Rojas Pinilla of neighboring Colombia (see "Three Losses for Democracy," Chapter VI) fell from his caudillo role in May 1957, through the joint action of Colombian Conservatives and Liberals. When Marcos Pérez Jiménez the following December allowed only a yes-or-no plebiscite on the continuation of his regime, AD, URD, and COPEI decided the time had come for them to cooperate in the ousting of their dictator. A small band of communists, some of whom had previously cooperated with Pérez, joined in the conspiracy against him. On January 1, 1958, a portion of the Venezuelan military led the way in rebellion. Pressure then mounted for three weeks, as a greater part of the armed forces insisted on changes, and as university students, residents of the super-bloques, and the leadership of four parties joined forces. On January 21, a general strike began. On January 22, the navy threatened to bombard the capital Caracas from the sea. At three o'clock of the following morning, Pérez Jiménez, his family, and his closest friends left the Caracas airport to take refuge in the Dominican Republic.

The three major political groupings participating in the ouster of Pérez held in common the aspiration to seek a high degree of social change along with the institution of liberty. Originally they hoped to organize a government of national unity, but later in 1958 they agreed to nominate separate candidates for president. The caretaker government until elections consisted of three military officers and two business men, with admiral Wolfgang Larrazábal at their head. This junta prepared a new electoral code providing free and direct voting for national positions and proportional representation of parties in the congress. Rómulo Betancourt sought the presidency on the AD ticket, and won with 47.2% of the vote. Wolfgang Larrazábal, nominated by URD and supported by the Communist party, ran second. Rafael Caldera, the candidate of COPEI (now renamed officially the Copei Social Christian party) came in third. Betancourt, taking the oath of office on February 13,

1959, appointed as original members of his cabinet three men from AD, three from URD, and three from Copei along with six independents.

From the outset, the leaders of the Venezuelan revolution sensed the immensity of their task. The fact that Venezuela enjoyed the highest income for its population size of all the Latin American countries and boasted many mineral resources not everywhere available had to be balanced against the intense poverty existing among the Venezuelan people, compounded by widespread ill health and illiteracy. The Betancourt regime, originally supported by all three major parties, took as its keynote the conclusion that in the face of its staggering enterprise it needed all the help it could get. The government itself would undertake much of the labor needed to refashion Venezuela. Private capital, both domestic and foreign, could also make a large contribution, and its participation in the nation's development would be encouraged. The Betancourt regime did not intend to declare class warfare, frightening or forcing investors away, but to ask and at times insist that they use their money for the good of the country -- and for the masses, not for a privileged few, of the people who lived there.

Agrarian reform constituted the most urgent task of the new democratic government. The Gallegos regime had adopted a law for an Instituto Agrario Nacional a month before that administration's demise. Even Pérez Jiménez established a few agricultural colonies under the provisions of that act, which also served as a basis for a division of the estates of Pérez and his friends beginning in 1958. Venezuela needed a more comprehensive program of agrarian reform, however, and after careful study one became available through a bill passed in March 1960. Both government property and private estates, the latter subject to expropriation with compensation to the owners, would supply free plots of land available to needy peasants. The latter would

600

hold title to the lands thus distributed, though the title might be revoked if the new owner failed to make use of the land. Credits and technical assistance would be granted by the government to enable the farmer to make his land productive. Cooperatives would be encouraged where they seemed most desirable, on grazing lands or soil used for truck gardening. The government requested the cooperation of the entire Venezuelan economic community -- business men, landlords, leaders of peasant and urban unions -- to insure the success of the vast program. It envisaged nothing less than a drastic redistribution of Venezuelan income, to emerge over a period of years.

In April 1960, the month after the agrarian reform, the Betancourt administration inaugurated the Corporación Venezolana del Petróleo. The statutory authority for such a government corporation dated from 1938, only three years after the death of Juan Vicente Gómez, but no one had implemented it during a period of 22 years. The state-directed firm started life as an infant set alongside the giant foreign oil companies, a child to be nourished by domestic sales of petroleum products and eventually the exploitation of untapped petroleum resources. In later decades, it would reach full adulthood through the assumption of the role played in 1960 by the outside oil interests.

The Betancourt government did not contemplate immediate expropriation of the holdings of the foreign oil companies. Instead, it followed the reasoning that the companies also should aid in the quickening of the Venezuelan economy. Expropriation might involve, at least temporarily, a diminution of oil sales. The automatic termination of the large concessions, many of which would expire in the 1980's, might be expected to operate more smoothly. In the meantime, the Betancourt administration offered no new petroleum concessions to private companies, instead revising the tax structure to

raise the Venezuelan share of the profits from
50% to near 70%, and inviting the foreign oil
firms (some of which agreed) to invest their
profit in non-petroleum Venezuelan development
plans.

A state-directed company to develop the Venezuelan power supply dated from 1958. Designed
at the outset to provide electricity where it did
not exist in rural and urban areas, it expected
eventually to take over the private companies
already in the business, forming a national power
network. The Venezuelan Development Corporation,
another arm of the state founded in 1946 during
Betancourt's provisional presidency, encouraged
the rapid development of private industry after
1958. Small business firms received special assistance through the offering of government
loans. Most remarkably, the Betancourt regime
managed a change in outlook on the part of a
sizeable segment of the wealthy class in the
country from a state of fright obvious at the
outset to a feeling of respect for the administration's intentions, extending in some cases
even to a revolutionary enthusiasm for participation in a new order of society.

The pragmatic socialism of Betancourt came
most strongly into evidence with the formation of
the Corporación Venezolana de Guayana in late
1960. Guayana, in the sparsely settled eastern
region of Venezuela, contained rich resources of
iron. The new state enterprise aimed to construct a large city there, with an electric power structure large enough to support a number of
heavy industries. The government did not contemplate the creation of a monopoly in the area.
It planned instead to employ both foreign and
domestic private capital and management skills.
It intended, however, to supervise rapid growth
in Guayana for the good of the nation and all its
people, using public expenditure to move the task
along.

Along with these new projects, the Betancourt

regime spent far more money than Pérez Jiménez to provide schools and well trained teachers for the youth of Venezuela; engaged in significant new health and prison reform campaigns; and greatly encouraged the growth of democratic trade unions, giving them the right to strike but taking measures to promote less militant styles of negotiation. An assessment of all these programs, taking into account the lack of comparable effort by previous dictatorships, leads rather easily to the conclusion that Venezuela had entered a new era in its history. The striking step toward a new nation seemed all the more astounding for its accomplishment through the democratic process, with dissidents allowed full right to criticize until November 1960. A look at the contemporaneous, undemocratic revolution in Cuba aids in the understanding of a change that took place at that time.

The events of New Year's Day 1959 in Cuba (population also 6-7,000,000) are understood best in the context of (1) the disappointment engendered by the democratically elected regimes of Ramón Grau San Martín (1944-8) and Carlos Prío Socarrás (1948-52); (2) the protests of the Ortodoxo party, led by Eddy Chibás until his suicide; (3) the arbitrary rule of Fulgencio Batista (1952-9); and (4) the first major attempt to depose him (1953). ("Three Losses for Democracy," Chapter VI, dealt with these particulars.) Fidel Castro Ruz opposed the Batista dictatorship from its beginning. Ernesto "Che" Guevara of Argentina appeared on the Cuban scene with Castro in 1956.

Fidel Castro, born in 1926, came from Oriente, the easternmost province of the island. His father Angel Castro had come to Cuba from Spain, his mother Lina Ruz from the other end of Cuba. The family owned an estate specializing in sugar cane. The United Fruit Company, from the

United States, operated the nearest town, using it for the production of sugar rather than fruit. About 50 miles to the south of the Castro home lay Santiago, capital of the province. To the west of Santiago lay a chain of mountains named the Sierra Maestra; to the east, the United States naval base of Guantánamo Bay.

Angel Castro paid for Fidel's education in Roman Catholic schools in Santiago and the nation's capital Havana, even giving his son an automobile when he entered the University of Havana, 1945. Fidel studied law while participating in athletics and engaging in student political activity. He became an Ortodoxo, a follower of Eddy Chibás, but also joined student groups involved in conspiratorial activities. In 1947, Castro took part in an aborted mission to depose dictator Rafael Trujillo in the Dominican Republic. In 1948, he attended an "anti-imperialist" student congress in Bogotá, Colombia, sponsored by Juan Perón of Argentina. This meeting coincided with that of the Ninth Conference of American States, though Castro did not participate in the violence of the bogotazo.

Castro graduated with a doctorate in law (1950), becoming a member of a law firm. Suddenly, however, he found himself rather completely out of his element. He had read books concerning revolution, and believed that his destiny included a revolution of some kind, but held few specific ideas about where his revolution might lead. He did know that he stood against criminality in the leadership of Cuba, and that he desired very much to do something to alleviate the plight of poor people. His life as a lawyer in a law office gave him scant opportunity to reach toward these objectives, even though a majority

604

of his clients came from the financially destitute. The coup carried out by Fulgencio Batista afforded Castro his first chance to enter the public arena.

On March 15, 1952, five days after Batista took command in Cuba, Fidel Castro wrote the dictator a letter, denouncing the morality of the coup and predicting that the people would overthrow the new regime. Castro then filed a brief with the Court of Constitutional Guarantees, charging Batista with crimes against the constitution. Castro called the constitution of 1940 "a product of the will of the people," and demanded the punishment of Batista. After these efforts proved vain, an outcome Castro must have expected, he turned to the only alternative open to him, a conspiracy against the regime. Castro and 165 companions planned to seize the Moncada barracks in the city of Santiago, for use in a continuing campaign. On July 26, 1953, when they made their attempt, Castro expected to play on the radio a recording of Chibás' suicide speech, at the same time declaring the "absolute and reverent respect" of the new movement for the constitution of 1940. The attempt at insurrection failed, however, as many of the participants lost their lives both before and after capture. Government forces took others, including Fidel Castro, to prison until their trials could be held.

On October 6, 1953, Castro testified at length in his own defense. A paraphrase of his purported remarks, amounting to a speech, appeared in pamphlet form during his term in prison. According to this text, he delivered a blistering attack on Batista; presented a lengthy review of the miseries of the Cuban people; offered a description of a new Cuba that

605

might appear in the future; continued with a prolonged historical dissertation on the right to overthrow tyrants; and concluded with words that became famous: "Convict me! It doesn't matter! History will absolve me!" The court sentenced Fidel Castro to prison for 15 years, and his younger brother Raúl, another of the band, for 13 years. Batista released both of them in May 1955 as part of a general political amnesty, granted after his managed election to the presidency. This is not to say, however, that the Castro brothers had received a grant of liberty. To stay in Havana meant almost certain death by assassination ordered by the president of the country.

In July 1955, Fidel Castro left for Mexico, where Raúl and other members of the 26th of July Movement (as the group now called itself) had preceded him. From there, he journeyed to Miami and New York looking for exiled Cubans who would back him in a new endeavor. Though Castro had made clear his lack of sympathy for the Auténtico party on many occasions, ex-president Prío Socarrás provided him with funds. Castro's band now attracted discontented Cubans who had fled to more than one country. Some from Guatemala brought with them Ernesto Guevara of Argentina, nicknamed "Che" by his Cuban companions. (Che is an interjection widely used in Argentina to call the attention of a friend.)

Che Guevara, born in 1928, suffered all his life from asthma. In medical training at Buenos Aires, he specialized in allergies. Following a yen for adventure, he traveled widely in Argentina (1949) and to Chile and Peru by land (1951). After employment in a colony of lepers, he moved on to Colombia and Venezuela (1952), even touching at Miami in the United States. Though he came from a middle-class family, Che paid his own expenses on these travels, often living in poverty. After obtaining his doctorate in 1953, he left Argentina again, expecting to work in another leper colony in Venezuela. On the way, a friend persuaded him to go to Guatemala instead.

Guevara felt compassion for the underprivileged in Guatemala as he had for deprived persons elsewhere. He looked with enthusiasm upon the Arévalo-Arbenz program to provide opportunities for the Guatemalan people. He remained in Guatemala through the termination of that program by the United States Central Intelligence Agency (see "Three Revolutions Interrupted," Chapter VI). His experiences in Guatemala convinced him that the United States stood as the chief enemy of the less favored people of the hemisphere. When Guevara moved from Guatemala to Mexico, Raúl Castro served as "best man" at his wedding, and Fidel Castro persuaded him to join the group gathering for a new anti-Batista endeavor.

Training for the expected invasion of Cuba began in rented homes in Mexico City. During the first half of 1956, it continued on a rented estate about 20 miles southeast of the capital. In March, when Castro heard that some Ortodoxo leaders had joined in an (unsuccessful) attempt to persuade Batista to hold fair elections, Castro gave notice that the 26th of July Movement no longer felt bound to the Ortodoxo party -- though he continued to insist that his own group represented the goals of Eddy Chibás. After Mexican police discovered the illegal training program in June, Castro and his men spent part of their time in jail. In September, Castro talked with Prío again, in Texas, thus acquiring significant new financing. During the same month, he agreed to collaborate with José Antonio Echeverría, president of the student body of the University of Havana, and head of a Directorio Revolucionario composed of anti-Batista students.

Castro found a yacht with the (English-language) name _Granma_, near Tuxpan on the Mexican coast, and purchased it with cash. Though it needed repairs and held room for only a small fraction of the 82 men he put on board, he sailed with it for Cuba in the pre-dawn hours of November 25, 1956. Castro intended to reach Oriente province in five days, coincident with an uprising in Santiago. The _Granma_ arrived on the coast of Oriente two days late, however, after the uprising had failed. After three more days, Batista's army met Castro's men and dispersed them. Those not captured or killed found each other in the Sierra Maestra. They numbered less than two dozen, including the Castro brothers and Guevara.

The Batista government announced the death of Fidel Castro and the extinction of his band. To prove the falsity of the announcement, Castro dispatched a courier with instructions to contact the office of some foreign newspaper in Havana. Thus, on February 17, 1957, Herbert Matthews, Latin American correspondent for the New York Times, interviewed Castro in the Sierra Maestra. A week later, when the first installment of Matthews' article appeared, the Cuban government announced that, regardless of whether Castro lived, Herbert Matthews had not interviewed him, and Castro had no force at his command. Matthews had indeed overstated the size of the Castro force, but the outside world felt deeply impressed when the New York Times on February 28 published a photograph of Castro with Herbert Matthews. This event proved the first of many that brought Fidel Castro world attention in a manner shared by few Latin Americans of his century.

Actually, Castro in February 1957 remained

considerably less effective against Batista than the readers of the Matthews interviews realized. Other (equally ineffective) groups plotted against Batista at that time, also depending upon ex-president Prío Socarrás for their financing. On March 13, the Directorio Revolucionario led by José Antonio Echeverría attempted to take the presidential palace and kill Batista. They did seize a radio station, announcing their success, but the attack on the palace had failed. Now Batista like Castro had heard the news of his own death prematurely. Government forces killed Echeverría in the street -- and someone that night murdered the head of the Ortodoxo party, though he had not participated in the uprising. More persons thus became embittered toward Batista, as the police grew suspicious of everyone, until Cuba turned into an island of terror.

Castro, who had no prior knowledge of the attack on the presidential palace, received his first significant body of recruits from Santiago at this time. His group made its first attack on an army barracks in late May 1957, without attempting to linger in the vicinity. When rival anti-Batista leaders (including some volunteer representatives of his own 26th of July Movement) met in Miami Beach, Florida, November 1, Castro denounced their agreement. " . . . While the directors of the other organizations . . . are abroad, carrying out an imaginary revolution," he said, "the directors of the 26th of July Movement are in Cuba, doing the real thing." He made no mention of the financial assistance from Prío which made the Granma expedition possible, nor of the several attacks other groups had launched in vain, nor of his own real lack of accomplishment during the greater part of a year.

Concerning Oriente, Castro observed on this occasion, "The entire population is in rebellion." The difficult months ahead, however, revealed the gross exaggeration in his remark, which must be taken as propaganda rather than as fact. Incensed at the friendliness to Batista shown by the United States government, Castro stated that any revolutionary pact should denounce "foreign interference" -- that is, the sending of "planes, bombs, tanks, and modern arms" to sustain the Batista dictatorship. (The pact of Miami had remained silent on this matter.) Castro proposed judge Manuel Urrutia Lleó for the provisional presidency when Batista should withdraw, because Urrutia at considerable risk to his own person had argued that those involved in the uprising of November 1956 held a constitutional right to attempt to overthrow Batista's illegal regime.

"Let it be understood," Castro added, "that we have renounced the taking of any office in the government; but let it also be known that the 26th of July Movement will never fail to guide and direct the people from the underground, from the Sierra Maestra or from the very graves of our dead. . . . And we will know how to conquer and to die. . . . To die with dignity does not require company." Plainly, Castro had mastered the rhetoric at the age of 31 for which he later became famous. It took him an entire year, nevertheless, and the help of a great number of people, to achieve the position of leadership he had both renounced and claimed.

The Batista regime grew weaker through the year of 1958. In February, old friends such as the leaders of Cuba's small communist party and of Cuba's large Roman Catholic church began to express considerable criticism. In March, the United States government initiated cancelation of shipments of arms. Then also, for the first time, Fidel Castro sent a small group of his followers to carry on resistance outside the Sierra Maestra. Under his brother Raúl's command, they entered northern Oriente, part of which Raúl knew from childhood. Castro achieved scant success in a call for a general strike on the island April 9. Working unilaterally, he found little support even then from trade union and working class people. Whatever small comfort Batista derived from this evidence of the division among his opponents, however, he dissipated entirely in the period May-August through a new effort to strike at Castro. The forces of Castro, small in number but high in morale, defeated the numerically superior army of Batista. Even more significantly, the duration of the conflict impressed a large number of Cuban people, persuading most of the opposition to the Batista regime that it should join in common effort with the Castro command.

New combined-front talks took place in Caracas, Venezuela, now the home of one successful revolution, where a clandestine radio maintained contact with Fidel Castro. A new pact signed July 20, 1958, included the 26th of July Movement and the student-led Directorio Revolucionario (which had sponsored its own group of armed men in the Sierra de Escambray, much closer to Havana than Oriente), along with several trade union leaders and other revolutionary organizations having only their hatred for Fulgencio Batista in common. The union of these disparate groups, according to their statement, took its base in "three pillars, to wit: First: The adoption of a common strategy. . . . Second: To guide our nation, after the fall of the tyrant, to normality by instituting a brief provisional government that will lead the country to full constitutional and democratic procedures. Third: A minimum governmental program that will guarantee the punishment of the guilty ones, the rights of the workers, the fulfillment of international commitments, public order, peace, freedom, as well as the economic, social and political progress of the Cuban people." Fidel Castro (by proxy) became the first signatory to the pact, Carlos Prío Socarrás (in person) the second. No one can say whether either held tongue in cheek as he assented to the second pillar.

The agreement of Caracas failed in its objective of unity among struggling commands. It served rather to yield even greater prestige to the cause of Fidel Castro. In August, Castro felt strong enough to send troops to the center of the island. There, under the leadership of Che Guevara and Camilo Cienfuegos, they operated from the same Sierra de Escambray the Directorio Revolucionario had chosen as a base. In September-October, various acts of bravado (such as the burning of plantations) took place, directed at Batista and his friends. The 26th of July Movement, responsible for many though not all of these acts, resented the fact that a military mission from the United States continued to train Batista's officers (even after the arms embargo) and that the United States ambassador maintained close personal relations with Batista. Everyone expected that Andrés Rivero Agüero, the choice of Batista, would "win" the presidential elections November 3. Very few, however, believed that Rivero would assume his office in February. As the 26th of July Movement received a new volume of enlistments, the communist party decided to ally with Castro as it had for a long time with Batista.

Late in December, Che Guevara, seconded by Camilo Cienfuegos and the Directorio Revolucionario, cut the island of Cuba in two. That action brought the Batista regime to its end before the Castro brothers occupied Santiago. When Batista resigned and flew to the Dominican Republic in the early hours of New Year's Day 1959, Fidel quickly seized Santiago while Guevara and Cienfuegos moved to Havana. The 26th of July Movement aimed to prevent a post-Batista junta of former supporters of the dictator, a plan toward which the United States ambassador had directed his energies. They also wished to prevent other revolutionary groups, especially the Directorio Revolucionario, from placing themselves in positions of influence. They intended to operate not as the pact of Caracas had said they would, in close cooperation with all those who had fought Batista -- the pattern followed the year before by the leaders of Venezuela -- but to place all power in the hands of one leader surrounded by a close circle of friends. The people of Cuba, disillusioned by the electoral contests of the 1940's, and relieved to see the end of near-anarchy and Batista cruelty and bloodshed, turned to the one man who posed as their deliverer. They applauded Fidel Castro as he engaged in a week-long victory parade, January 1-8, from Santiago to Havana.

The Castro regime had very early to formulate a policy toward the many persons who had fought in support of Batista. Some of the richest and most guilty of them had fled; the others found themselves subject to capture and execution. Mass killings commenced on January 2, at first without even the semblance of a trial. Though courts-martial conducted this business after a few days, the vengeful face of the new regime stirred many protests abroad. Fidel Castro asked why hemispheric journals that had never mentioned the atrocities of Batista had become suddenly incensed at the meting out of "revolutionary justice." To prove to foreign news correspondents his contention that judgments including the death sentence had the support of the Cuban people, he extended an invitation to a public trial in the Havana sports coliseum January 21. The invitation backfired, since the trial developed a circus atmosphere, with the large Cuban portion of the audience persisting in interruption of the proceedings with shouts calling for vengeance against the defendants.

More temperate Cubans then joined many of the foreign witnesses in calling for a modification of Castro justice. With the passage of time, a greater degree of calm prevailed in Cuban courtrooms. In early March, however, when a court in Santiago found over 40 of Batista's air pilots innocent of any wrongdoing, Fidel Castro personally rejected the finding, appointed another "more revolutionary" court to retry the men, saw to their imprisonment, and for good measure placed in jail various persons who had testified in the pilots' defense. Castro explained that revolutionary justice stood not on "legal precepts," but on "moral conviction." He did not pause to count how many authoritarian rulers (even Batista) before him had once assumed the same moral stance.

Since the Herbert Matthews interview, Castro had retained much support among liberal and democratic socialist leaders of the American hemisphere. After triumphal parades and speeches all the way beyond Havana to the western end of Cuba, it seemed a natural development for him to visit a neighboring revolutionary regime to continue his celebration. On January 22, 1959, he flew to Venezuela, there to participate in ceremonies jointly honoring his own success and that of the democratic parties of Venezuela the year before. He talked with president-elect Rómulo Betancourt, who had given him some aid early in his career. The two men did not come out of the interview close friends. Betancourt held full credentials as a revolutionary. But to Betancourt, who had worked arduously for years to establish the positive parts of his revolution in the hearts of his people, and who felt that a successful change in society in a nation standing on its own feet required a high degree of careful planning, a man like Castro seemed altogether adventurous, egotistic, and irresponsible.

When José Figueres, ex-president of Costa Rica and another democratic revolutionary, came to Havana for a visit in March, his speech favoring representative democracy and friendship toward the United States met with a negative response. Castro, to whom unsolicited advice verged upon unwelcome criticism, accused Figueres of false friendship upon the latter's departure from the island. Castro had made many statements since his triumph concerning his own anti-communism; he had also suggested elections to be held in a year and a half. Why should persons of good will not trust him to follow these inclinations?

614

For advice, if he needed it, he preferred the counsel of a very few personal friends who had shared with him the dangers of the Sierra Maestra experience.

On January 2, 1959, Manuel Urrutia, the judge whom Fidel Castro had chosen as his provisional president, assumed the office planned for him. José Miró Cardona, another anti-Batista lawyer, received appointment as prime minister. Both men, liberal rather than socialist in their attitudes, immediately found themselves out of step with the boisterousness of the revolution. They stood against the reinstitution of the death penalty, banned by the constitution of 1940. They accepted, but without enthusiasm, the derogation of that constitution on February 7, when a new Fundamental Law placed all power in the hands of the cabinet without a congress. On February 16, Miró resigned and Fidel Castro became prime minister, despite his earlier disclaimers of interest in public office. Urrutia stayed on as president until July, but discontinued his attendance at cabinet meetings.

The Cuban revolution, unlike that of Venezuela, found no time for a careful planning stage. The first of a large number of edicts that together transformed the face of the island appeared in March 1959, while the celebrations continued. The edicts cut rents for urban workers in half; reduced telephone rates; forced owners of vacant lots in the cities to sell them; made tax evasion more difficult; ended the national lottery, instituting government bonds in its stead; and confiscated the property of participants in the Batista regime, even that of members of the Batista congress. Castro personally traveled to the western end of the island, distributing confiscated land to enthusiastic farmers, despite the lack of an agrarian reform to cover the transition. Through this early period of Castro's rule, he spent long hours mixing with and speaking to large crowds of the Cuban people.

From all appearances, Castro had become the idol of the Cuban masses. Some of the more educated, however, found ground for concern in some of the prime minister's remarks. To Cubans as well as foreigners, Castro remained hypersensitive to criticism, reacting very quickly with anger to those who showed skepticism or concern about his intentions for the future. Demanding loyalty to his person, he frowned severely upon any attitude that seemed to him to curb his freedom. Furthermore, Castro talked of a new society in which foreign interests would yield to Cuban interests, the rich would share with the poor, and Cubans of dark skin color would find acceptance on an equal basis. Some individuals on the island and others in the United States believed that only a communist would subscribe to such ideals. Others in both places thought of Castro only as a reformer who needed room for maneuver for a time, but who earnestly sought to return Cuba to its constitutional freedoms following the spirit of 1940. For the time being, Castro clearly ruled as a dictator (though to most Cubans of the time an amiable one) and a person who took great steps before rather than after studying them.

The American Society of Newspaper Editors (an organization in the United States) invited Castro to address its annual meeting in Washington in April. The United States government had made friendly gestures, including the appointment of a new ambassador. Castro left Cuba April 15, and traveled abroad for three weeks. In Washington, he defined an attitude concerning freedom of information: "The first thing dictators do," he said in English, "is to finish the free press and establish censorship. There is no doubt that the free press is the worst enemy of dictatorship." From Washington he moved on to New York, to Montreal in Canada, and from there to the capitals of Brazil, Uruguay, and Argentina. At Buenos Aires, he spoke to a committee of the Organization of American States considering the suggestion of the president of Brazil of a sizeable

616

plan of assistance for Latin America by the United States. Speaking to this group, Castro proposed that Washington extend $30,000,000,000 in economic aid to Latin America over a period of a decade. The Eisenhower administration did not take the proposal seriously.

Prime minister Castro spoke to friendly audiences on this trip, and met with important people. The list did not include Dwight Eisenhower, but Castro did talk with vice-president Richard Nixon. To persistent inquiries in the United States regarding a possible orientation to communism, Castro described his attitude (by the time he reached New York) as a dedication to "humanism." In Montreal he defined his usage of the term -- "that there should not be bread without liberty, but neither should there be liberty without bread." As he arrived back home, Castro knew that the Cuban revolution depended on his moving ahead without waiting for aid from the exterior. He could have used financial assistance, though he had not requested any except as part of a vast Latin American program. Equally as important as money, however, would be the backing of close friends and the mass of the Cuban people.

On May 17, 1959, Castro and his cabinet promulgated an agrarian reform. In certain respects, the plan fulfilled the constitution of 1940, which Batista, Grau, and Prío had all supported vocally -- along with the Ortodoxos, who had never gained the presidency. The measure affected about 40% of the nations' farm lands. To avoid the splitting of large estates and a consequent lowering of production, the reform sponsored cooperatives, with some of them under the management of persons appointed by the state. This radical provision found its offset in the continued existence of large single properties, often in the hands of one family (as much as 3,300 acres for the grower of sugar or rice), untouched by the land redistribution.

617

United States citizens in the cattle and sugar industries lost a large amount of property in this agrarian reform. Both inside and outside Cuba, persons who felt their interests affected spoke of the reform as a "communist" measure, and of Castro as a communist agent. Castro reacted strongly to these accusations, saying in effect that the communists of Cuba should not be accused of dominating him just because they backed what he had done, and that at least their attitude stood preferable to that of the anti-communists who took no interest in his program except to stir up opinion against him.

In late May, Fidel Castro continued to make speeches insisting on his loyalty to the outlook of representative democracy. Labor union elections in May did not favor the communists striving for leadership positions in the workers' movement. Castro had appointed some individual communists to important governmental posts on the basis of their willingness and preparedness to carry out his decisions, supporting rather than criticizing him. Only in June, however, did Castro begin to rely heavily on the advice of his younger brother Raúl and his friend Che Guevara, both of whom had become interested in the tenets of Marxism as the solution for the future of Cuba.

In a note of June 11, the government of the United States expressed "concern" over some provisions of the agrarian reform, emphasizing particularly the necessity, under international law, of "prompt, adequate and effective compensation" for the properties of United States citizens. Two days later, Castro spoke angrily in public of Cuban critics of the reform as traitors, and stated that compensation to previous landowners could come only in the form of bonds. Three mysterious bombs exploded during the course of this speech -- bombs that Castro took as a challenge, whether or not that constituted their real intent. From June 13 on, though his speeches remained mixed in nature over a period of another year, he tended more and more to push the social revolution without attention to political democracy; to fight vehemently against both Cubans and foreigners who criticized his program; and to assert his impatience with those who found fault with his most consistently loyal friends.

Without ample preparation, on June 14, 1959, the Castro regime sponsored an invasion of the Dominican Republic. The attempt repeated the amateur strategies of a host of Caribbean adventurers before Castro's time. The Cubans failed completely in their objective to topple the right-wing dictatorship of Rafael Trujillo. Pedro Díaz Lanz, the head of the Cuban air force, refused to assist the attack on the Trujillo regime. On June 29, Díaz Lanz lost his position, along with other personnel of the air force. On July 1, Díaz Lanz appeared in Miami. The following week, the Internal Security Subcommittee of the United States Senate extended an invitation for him to testify. Díaz Lanz told the senators what some of them wished to hear -- that communists were taking over in Cuba. Castro experienced rage not only at the testimony but at the intervention of a United States legislative committee in Cuban affairs. On July 17, Castro resigned from the position of prime minister. The same night, however, he delivered one of his lengthy speeches on television, attacking president Urrutia for joining in the complaint concerning communism. Urrutia resigned immediately. Osvaldo Dorticós Torrado, chosen by the residue of the cabinet, succeeded as president July 18. Eight days later, on the sixth anniversary of the abortive attack against Batista, the cabinet "persuaded" Fidel Castro to reassume his position as prime minister.

In July, Castro initiated a public works program to decrease unemployment. In August, he began to implement the agrarian reform. In September, he levied high import and liquor taxes in a campaign against alcoholism. An increasing specter of counter-revolution, however, took up most of the energies of the regime after the discovery of a conspiracy in August. The number of political prisoners soon exceeded the numbers held by Batista. During this apprehensive time, airplanes from Florida began to appear in Cuban skies, sometimes dropping propaganda leaflets. On October 11, one plane dropped three bombs on a sugar mill. Pedro Díaz Lanz might be supposed to have organized some of these flights -- but had the CIA, notorious for its interference in the affairs of other nations, now decided to take action against the Castro regime? Wanting to take no chances, Castro appointed his brother Raúl minister for the armed forces October 16. The following day, Havana announced that if Washington would not provide arms for the Cuban government, and would not allow its allies to provide them in its stead, the Castro regime would have to buy them elsewhere.

On October 20, Castro personally arrested Hubert Matos, one of his friends of Sierra Maestra days, who had resigned as military governor of the province of Camagüey the day before, reminding Castro that "great men begin to decline when they cease to be just." A bomber from the United Statres appeared over Havana the evening of Matos' arrest, dropping leaflets prepared by Pedro Díaz Lanz. Nine days later, another of Castro's old companions, the highly loyal Camilo Cienfuegos, successor to Matos in the governorship of Camagüey, disappeared during a flight to Havana. Castro opponents suspected foul play in Cienfuegos' death.

By the end of his first year, Castro had lost many previous friends who stood for some measure of reform but disliked the trend toward authoritarianism. In November, Manuel ("Manolo") Ray lost his post as minister of public works because of his opposition to Matos' arrest. Che Guevara, returning from a long trip abroad with enthusiasm for Egypt and Japan, accepted a position as the head of the Cuban national bank. In November, the Cuban government nationalized several non-agricultural enterprises owned by foreigners. In December, Matos heard his sentence of 20 years in prison for "anti-patriotic and anti-revolutionary conduct."

Castro designated 1960 in Cuba as the Year of the Agrarian Reform. The cabinet devised sweeping health and education measures to bring the peasants who received land more fully into national life. As the year moved along, however, security measures took most of the leaders' attention. Flights from Florida and neighboring states of the United States continued, dropping not only leaflets but many incendiary bombs. Castro's protests to Washington made no impression there. In response, he continued to expropriate the properties of citizens of the United States, and to seek the friendship of another strong power that could pose as a Cuban guardian. Special envoy Anastas Mikoyan came to Cuba in February to sign a pact for economic aid from the Soviet Union. Commercial treaties with other communist countries followed.

Havana and Washington continued to speak to one another, sometimes angrily and sometimes not, until a month later (March 17) when president Eisenhower decided to allow his CIA to plan a military strike against Cuba. The United States agency would train Cuban exiles for the job, scheduled indefinitely for the future. For many months, the project remained a secret to the people of the United States, as news outlets voluntarily cooperated with the Eisenhower administration. The rest of the world heard the truth from Castro's own news agency in April. Guatemala and Nicaragua had decided to cooperate with United States backing in a new Caribbean intrigue, directed at the regime in Cuba.

In March-April-May, Castro felt his regime increasingly threatened by the refugees in Miami and a large number of dissenters at home. He countered by reducing the trade unions to impotence, seizing radio and television stations, putting a clamp on the larger independent newspapers, and moving to dominate the university where he had learned his own lessons in conspiracy against a previous dictatorial regime. The church continued to criticize him as a variety of church youth demonstrated and joined the underground revolutionary organizations. Large numbers of Cubans fled the country, hoping in many cases to fight back. In May, the CIA persuaded five bands of the exiles to join in a Revolutionary Democratic Front. The leaders, including Manuel Antonio de Varona of the Auténticos and Manuel Artime of Catholic orientation, had opposed Batista and now Castro as well, but generally took a negative stand on Castro's more radical reforms as well as his authoritarianism.

During May-June-July, there arose a new showdown with the United States. On May 23, the Cuban regime requested three large oil refineries owned by United States capital to process petroleum imported from the Soviet Union. When they refused, they too found their properties expropriated, on June 30. President Eisenhower, after authorization by his Congress, announced on July 6 that the quota of sugar to be imported from Cuba in 1960 would be reduced by the amount that to that date remained undelivered. On the same day, a Cuban edict nationalized all remaining properties of United States citizens in Cuba. This decision, made by Castro alone, proved too rapid a pace for Castro's communist following, which feared that wholesale nationalization of industry, first the foreign and next the Cuban-owned, would so alienate the Cuban bourgeoisie as to dry up the Cuban economy. These communist forebodings soon turned out to be true. The regime began to implement the edict of July 6 in August, and engaged in large-scale nationalization of properties owned by other foreigners and Cubans until the month of October.

The foreign ministers of the American republics -- including those of Venezuela, Cuba, and the United States -- met in San José, Costa Rica,

August 16-29, 1960. Formally, two consecutive sessions took place, the Sixth and Seventh Meetings of Consultation of Ministers of Foreign Affairs of the Organization of American States. The first dealt with the complaints of democratic Venezuela against the Trujillo dictatorship in the Dominican Republic. The Trujillo regime, Venezuela said, had granted facilities to an airplane that dropped leaflets on Venezuelan territory; issued passports to Venezuelans who plotted against the elected Betancourt regime; and provided assistance to persons involved in an attempt to assassinate president Betancourt. The foreign ministers decided that all members of the Organization should break diplomatic relations with the Dominican Republic and cease to sell arms and implements of war to the Trujillo regime.

Peru had requested the second session to consider "the exigencies of Hemisphere solidarity, the defense of the regional system, and the defense of American democratic principles in the face of threats that might affect them." The United States government wanted a resolution naming the Castro regime as part of the threat to democratic principles. Washington had decided to support the consensus against the Dominican regime in order to remove the most glaring example of its past great difference in attitude toward right-wing and left-wing authoritarianism. The Declaration of San José of August 29, however, made no mention of Castro or Cuba. Instead, it simply stated that the Meeting "1. Condemns emphatically intervention or the threat of intervention . . . from an extracontinental power in the affairs of the American republics and declares that the acceptance of a threat of extracontinental intervention by any American state jeopardizes American solidarity and security. . . . 2. Rejects, also, the attempt of the Sino-Soviet powers to make use of the political, economic, or social situation of any American state. . . . 3. Reaffirms the principle of non-intervention by any American state in the internal or external affairs of the other American states. . . ." While signing the Declaration of San José with its right hand, however, Washington with its left hand continued to prepare an invasion of Cuba precisely counter to point number 3.

Conspiracy against the Castro regime grew more intense in September, and more varied than before. Inside Cuba, Castro evacuated peasants from the Sierra Maestra region who might supply food to his enemies as they once had to him. An organization called the Revolutionary Movement of the People (Movimiento Revolucionario del Pueblo, or MRP), headed by Manolo Ray (whom Castro had dismissed from his cabinet) developed a widespread opposition network in Cuba. The MRP, unlike the other opposition forces, accepted the necessity of drastic social reform in Cuba, but argued that it should be accomplished democratically. The CIA took no interest in Ray's group, despite its strategic situation -- and indeed, as quarrels arose among the refugees in Miami, turned toward the Batista supporters who lived there. CIA agents indeed came to depend on these men, viewing them as reliable anti-communists and the most stalwart of Castro's opponents.

Fidel Castro resided in New York September 18-28, attending (on two days only) the session of the United Nations General Assembly. There he met premier Khrushchev of the Soviet Union in an embrace that symbolized for many onlookers a more intimate relationship between the two than actually existed at the time. Castro spoke for nearly five hours when it came his turn to participate in the general debate with which the Assembly opens. By this time, most news media in the United States had become so outraged by his attitude of hostility that they paid little attention to his words. His concerns made a deeper impression on people of other lands who did not feel the brunt of his attacks.

In the United States, the presidential campaign of 1960 brought out many remarks on Cuba. Vice-president Richard Nixon, Republican, and senator John Kennedy, Democrat, had emerged as the nominees of the two chief parties. Kennedy criticized the Eisenhower administration for its handling of the Cuban question. Asked about his own attitude, Kennedy responded, "The forces fighting for freedom in exile and in the mountains of Cuba should be sustained and assisted. . . ." On October 18, Nixon commented, "I say that our goal must be to quarantine the Castro regime." The following day, Washington imposed an embargo on all shipment of goods to Cuba from the United States except medicines and some food. Kennedy called this action "too little and too late," and refined his former statement to assert that the United States should try "to strengthen the non-Batista Democratic forces in exile and in Cuba itself. . . ."

Nixon replied vehemently on October 21. "Now let's see what this means," he said. "We have five treaties with Latin America, including the one setting up the Organization of American States . . . , in which we've agreed not to intervene in the internal affairs of any other American country. . . . The Charter of the United Nations, its preamble, Article I and Article II, provide that there shall be no intervention by one nation in the internal affairs of another. Now I don't know what Senator Kennedy suggests when he says that we should help those who oppose the Castro regime both in Cuba and without. But I do know that if we were to follow that recommendation that we would lose all of our friends in Latin America, we would probably be condemned in the United Nations, and we would not accomplish our objective. I know something else. It would be an open invitation for Mr. Khrushchev to come in, to come into Latin America and to engage us in what would be a civil war and possibly even worse than that." As he uttered these prophetic words, vice-president Nixon knew that the Eisenhower administration had already approved the action Kennedy recommended. There existed one important difference, however, between the two plans. Kennedy, uninformed of the secret action, specified in October that the non-Batista democratic forces should receive the aid. The CIA leaned more and more heavily on the pro-Batista men whom Kennedy would have excluded.

Kennedy (in public) and Nixon (in private) agreed on aid to Cuban exiles because the Cuban revolution had turned against the United States. Public opinion in the United States easily adopted the conclusion that Moscow had directed the scenario in Havana, just as it once took for granted that Moscow had planned all the changes in Peking. Actually, the communist party of Cuba, called the Partido Socialista Popular, held no seat in Castro's cabinet and constantly had to remind itself of its position as a follower rather than a leader. Unaware of these facts, the people of the United States attributed great significance to the Khrushchev-Castro embrace, and remembered a statement made by Khrushchev the previous July 9, three days after president Eisenhower abridged the sugar quota. "In a figurative sense," Khrushchev had permitted himself to say, "if it became necessary, the Soviet military can support the Cuban people with rocket weapons. . . ." On July 10, Castro took the offer in a concrete rather than a figurative sense.

Khrushchev actually remained wary of recognizing the Cuban revolution as communist. Persons loyal to Moscow had not developed this movement, and could not be trusted to capture it in the future. No one could speak with certainty of the path Castro might choose. Che Guevara traveled to Moscow in October-November -- a convinced Marxist by this time -- but encountered no success in persuading the Khrushchev regime to adopt the Cuban revolution. In Peking, later in November, Guevara met with greater enthusiasm. Peking announced that it would buy 1,000,000 tons of sugar in 1961, and provide technical assistance to Cuba.

President Eisenhower proclaimed on December 16 that the United States would buy no sugar from

Cuba in the first quarter of 1961. The Cuban quota of the United States market in 1958 had amounted to 3,500,000 tons. The United States paid more than the world price for Cuban sugar, while Cuba (since 1934) in return granted import concessions to the products of United States manufacturing industry. Three days after Eisenhower's announcement, the Soviet Union took its first decisive step to keep Fidel Castro on its side, promising to buy over 2,500,000 tons of Cuban sugar in 1961. The Soviet rivalry with China inside the communist camp explained Moscow's decision tardily to pick up a friend that Washington had largely abandoned.

The Castro revolution in Cuba by the end of 1960 had moved past the Venezuelan revolution in two respects. The Cuban government had clearly asserted its independence from subordination to the United States and had shown its readiness to nationalize all property and industry to effect a redistribution of income. Venezuela, proceeding more cautiously along these lines, had done far more toward the immediate prosperity and well-being of the mass of its people. The Castro revolution engendered an excitement, nevertheless, that appealed to many Venezuelan young people as to those of other lands. Thus, in 1960, a group within the Venezuelan Communist party attached itself sentimentally to Havana rather than Moscow. In April, a group from Acción Democrática likewise seceded to form the Revolutionary Left Movement (Movimiento de Izquierda Revolucionaria, or MIR). Later in the year, an element within the Unión Republicana Democrática fell out of step with the government of which URD formed a part.

The foreign minister of Venezuela, a member of URD, refused to vote for the Declaration of San José in August, though pesident Betancourt approved the document. The foreign minister resigned, and in November the remaining URD members of the cabinet followed him. Late that month, young members of the Communist party, the MIR, and the URD rioted in Caracas for four days, calling for a popular insurrection against the Betancourt government. The people did not rise, and the army quelled the disorder as soon as it received a directive to do so. AD and Copei, the two parties continuing in the government, decided to suspend constitutional guarantees of the democratic freedoms in order to deal effectively with those who had taken up arms against the state. The basic democracy of Venezuela remained unimpaired. But the suspension of guarantees in the face of violence made the fact immediately obvious that Castro's authoritarian leftist style in Cuba posed a real threat not only to private-enterprise regimes in the Americas but to those of a democratic socialist orientation as well.

The Cold War (Part III)

"Dear Mr. President," wrote prime minister Nikolay Bulganin to president Dwight Eisenhower on January 23, 1956. "Being deeply convinced that you share my concern over present relations between our countries, I would like to share with you my considerations about possible ways for improving these relations. . . . It cannot be considered as accidental that, with the exception of the period of foreign intervention against the young Soviet Republic, the peoples of our states have never been at war with one another, that there have never been, nor are there now any irreconcilable differences between them, and there are no frontiers of territories that could become the subject of dispute or conflict. . . . That is why the Soviet people received with a feeling of complete understanding the statement you made at the Geneva Conference of the heads of government of the four powers in which you pointed out: 'The American people want to be friends with the Soviet peoples. There are no natural differences between our peoples or our nations. There are no territorial conflicts or commercial rivalries. Historically, our two countries have always been at peace.' . . .

"There can be no doubt," prime minister Bulganin continued, "that the peoples of the Soviet Union and the United States of America are equally interested in stopping the arms drive which compels them to extend energies and resources for unproductive purposes. . . . I am sincerely convinced that improvement in Soviet-American relations is urgent and necessary. . . . In my opinion, this aim would be helped by the conclusion of a treaty of friendship and cooperation between our two countries. . . . With sincere respect, N. Bulganin."

President Eisenhower replied on January 28: "Dear Mr. Chairman: I wish to thank you for your letter. . . . I have given it careful thought. . . . Let me say at the outset that I do indeed believe that the present international situation requires all states, particularly the great powers, to seek to lessen international tension and strengthen international confidence and cooperation." Eisenhower, however, explained, "I first observe that our countries are already bound to each other by a solemn treaty -- the Charter of the United Nations." He then showed how the three terms of the specific treaty suggested by Bulganin in his letter corresponded to agreements already made in the charter. Next the president reviewed the disappointment he had felt from the Geneva summit conference of 1955. He spoke particularly of Germany, of his own "open skies" proposal (which he said Moscow had rejected), and of the "development of contacts between East and West," a matter in which he agreed some improvement had taken place since the conference.

"A further deterioration has taken place," president Eisenhower contended, "because to us it has seemed that your Government had, in various areas of the world, embarked upon a course which increases tensions by intensifying hatreds and animosities implicit in historic international disputes." The president did not specify which of the "various areas of the world" he meant, nor whether Moscow embarked upon this course before or after the summit conference. He then expressed clearly his own basic misgivings, using the phrase "our people" with the same assurance Bulganin had demonstrated: "I share your conviction that an improvement in Soviet-American relations is urgently needed. But frankly, our people find it difficult to reconcile what appears to us to be the purposes of your Government in these areas with your present words. . . . I shall look forward to receiving a further expression of your views. . . . Sincerely, Dwight D. Eisenhower."

The prime minister had used the closing phrase, "With sincere respect;" the president countered with "Sincerely." Two more letters signed "With sincere respect" and one more signed "Sincerely" appeared before the president moved to "I am, Sincerely" and the prime minister replied with the same. The correspondence slowed down as each man and his advisers criticized the other side, and finally concluded at the time of the Hungarian crisis in November. There can be little doubt that Nikolay Bulganin did respect Dwight Eisenhower, just as Eisenhower did speak in sincere language. Bulganin proposed a sincere gesture toward world peace, however incongruous that may have appeared in Washington. Eisenhower did not seize upon the gesture, preferring to stress the misdeeds of the Soviet Union, conveniently ignoring the misdeeds of the United States -- and neglecting to consider the psychological impact toward peace which the treaty proposed by Bulganin might hold even if its terms seemed repetitive. Washington, clothing itself and its people in self-righteousness, had busied itself with a military containment of communism to the point that it could not seriously consider a proposal from new leaders in Moscow looking toward a change in the Cold War climate.

On February 14, 1956, Nikita Khrushchev, the

party leader, spoke to the Twentieth Congress of the Soviet Communist party of a desire for a new world attitude he labeled "peaceful coexistence." His report on this subject came eight months before the troubles in Hungary and ten days before Khrushchev's speech on Stalin (both of them detailed in "Communist Fraternity Broken"). Khrushchev made clear his feeling that only "peaceful coexistence between different states, irrespective of their social systems" could avert "the most destructive war in history." At the time of the Congress, SEATO war games in Thailand sought (according to announcement) to demonstrate the great SEATO military capacity to Peking -- and to help check the spread of neutralist sentiment engendered by the Bulganin-Khrushchev goodwill tour of south Asian countries in November-December 1955.

Before the Hungarian interlude, Soviet officials took three steps toward the peaceful coexistence pattern. On April 17, they dissolved the Cominform along with its worldwide publication. These postwar devices used by Stalin in his attempt to dominate the world communist movement had outlived their usefulness after an existence of nine years. Communist party cooperation would continue, of course, but the announcement took care to emphasize that the parties would take into account "the specific national features and conditions of their countries." Second, during the period April 18-27, the Bulganin-Khrushchev team visited the United Kingdom. At the end of the trip, Bulganin commented to reporters, "Without any risk of revealing any great secret, we can inform you -- confident that our distinguished hosts also hold this opinion -- that the course of the discussions met on their way certain underwater rocks." To the same group, he complained about developments in disarmament negotiations starting with the summit conference of 1955: "On a number of points," he said, "we have proposed the acceptance of the proposals previously made by the western powers. . . . But we now have to defend these proposals

. . . against the representatives of these very powers. As soon as we expressed agreement with their proposals, they at once hastened to renounce them. Perhaps you know what the matter is here. For us it is a riddle."

As its third step toward peaceful coexistence, the Soviet leadership announced the dismissal of Vyacheslav Molotov from the post of foreign minister. The presence of Molotov in post-Stalin cabinets had always constituted one of the prime factors in the encouragement of disbelief in Soviet proposals for peace. Whatever the dismissal of Molotov might have accomplished, however, or any of the other coexistence moves by Moscow, became completely negated by the Soviet use of force in Hungary. The fact that the United States and the Soviet Union voted together against the United Kingdom and France in the Suez Canal dispute made little difference in the Cold War. Immediately afterward, as the influence of London and Paris weakened in the Middle East, Washington moved in quickly to counter a supposed Soviet threat in the area, just as it had in southeastern Asia in 1954. In his hour of peril, president Nasser of Egypt had looked to Moscow rather than to Washington for aid.

In December 1956, the Soviet Union and Japan, tabling their argument over a few small islands, ratified a treaty to end the state of war between them that dated from 1945. This pact did little to change the situation of the Cold War, however, since Japan remained an ally of the United States. Washington, at least, tended to regard each one of its allies as a continuing enemy of the Soviet Union. The theme of perpetual enmity seemed to dominate the thinking of president Eisenhower when he spoke to the United States Congress January 5, 1957. The Soviet use of force in Hungary and the crisis in the Middle East lay very heavily on his mind.

Eisenhower stated his concern for the security of the Middle East. He abstained, however, from rendering a bill of particulars. Instead, he offered words such as these: "The Middle East has abruptly reached a new and critical stage in its long and important history. . . . Russia's rulers have long sought to dominate the Middle East. That was true of the Czars and it is true of the Bolsheviks. . . . The reason for Russia's interest in the Middle East is solely that of power politics. Considering her announced purpose of Communizing the world, it is easy to understand her hope of dominating the Middle East. . . . We have just seen the subjugation of Hungary by naked armed force. In the aftermath of this Hungarian tragedy, world respect for and belief in Soviet promises have sunk to a new low. International Communism needs and seeks a recognizable success." Eisenhower sought from the Congress authorization to extend economic and military assistance to any Middle Eastern "nation or group of nations which desires such aid," and "to include the employment of the armed forces of the United States to secure and protect the territorial integrity and political independence of such nations, requesting such aid, against overt armed aggression from any nation controlled by International Communism."

The government of Syria spoke up on January 12, announcing its "deep conviction that the task of defending peace and security in the Middle East rests with the inhabitants of this area, who alone have the right to defend themselves against all dangers threatening them, no matter whence they come." On January 19, Egypt, Saudi Arabia, Syria, and Jordan affirmed their "faith in the need to maintain solidarity and cooperation" and their appreciation of "the need to participate in the responsibilities resulting therefrom." Indeed, Egypt, Saudi Arabia, and Syria agreed to subsidize the armed forces of Jordan to make up for the allowance the United Kingdom had provided Jordan until 1956. On January 21, the Muslim countries adhering to the Baghdad Pact (Pakistan, Turkey, Iran, Iraq) took a different attitude, noting president Eisenhower's plan with satisfaction. The United States Congress agreed March 9 to grant the president the authority requested. The idea came to be called the Eisenhower Doctrine as a sequel to the Truman Doctrine of 1947. There existed two important differences between the two: (1) The Truman Doctrine specified two countries, the Eisenhower Doctrine an entire region. (2) The Eisenhower Doctrine mentioned a possible employment of the armed forces of the United States.

Arabic people in several lands regarded Moscow as the Arabs' best friend during the darkest days of the Suez Canal crisis. Both Washington and Moscow voted on Egypt's side, but only Moscow of the pair threatened to use its force against the British, French, and Israelis. In early April 1957, the prime minister of Jordan made some preliminary moves toward a program of Soviet aid for his country. The Jordanese king Hussein, however, dismissed his prime minister as well as a like-minded successor. On April 24, as Hussein faced discontent among the Jordanese people, the United States rushed Hussein economic assistance -- and to emphasize the point stationed part of its naval forces in the eastern Mediterranean. In this fashion, though Washington took care not to mention the Eisenhower Doctrine in the matter, American money came to assume importance to Jordan (in place of the British, as once in Greece and Turkey), while Egypt and Syria withdrew from the subsidy agreement they had so recently entered.

Upon invitation, an agent for the United States visited eleven Middle Eastern capitals during March-May 1957. Ranging geographically from Morocco to Afghanistan, they included Israel. Pakistan, Ethiopia, Sudan, and Greece also formed part of the trip. Egypt, Syria, and Jordan, however, remained outside the operation. Of the total of 15 governments contacted, 13 made statements pleasing to Washington. Egypt and Syria, from the point of view of Washington, had joined the Soviet Union, though they had undertaken no military commitments to Moscow but only accepted its aid. Relations between Syria and the United States became severely strained in August, when Syria expelled three of Washington's diplomatic personnel, accusing them of participating in plans for a coup, and the United States in its turn expelled the Syrian ambassador. Reverberations from these actions continued until October, involving movements of the Soviet and American fleets; after that, Middle Eastern tensions relaxed for a time.

On August 26, 1957, the Soviet Union announced that it had successfully fired the world's first intercontinental ballistic missile -- a weapon that could power its own way from one continent to another. The Soviet possession of such a vehicle -- soon labeled an ICBM in English-language usage -- would give it some advantage over the United States, which had to rely upon airplanes for delivery of its nuclear weapons. Many persons expressed skepticism concerning the Russian achievement. Doubts vanished, however, after October 4, as the Soviet Union placed artificial satellites in orbit around the earth, using the same rocket propellant. Washington, intent upon the situation in the Middle East, had not anticipated such developments at this time. Its own scientists, put to hard work on the matter, managed to fire an American ICBM in December. Meanwhile, the United States agreed with Turkey to place ballistic missile installations on Turkish soil, very near the territory of the Soviet Union. On December 30, 1957, in the middle of these preparations for warfare, Washington and Moscow announced agreement on the terms of a cultural exchange, a small dividend from the exchange of correspondence early in the quinquennium.

The Soviet success with its first satellite inspired new suggestions from Moscow for a summit meeting of heads of state to discuss peace and disarmament. Negotiations over a period of months indicated very clearly that the Eisenhower-Dulles team preferred no conference at this time. The United States launched its first successful satellite on January 31, 1958, but remained stung over the fact that the Soviet Union had moved well ahead in the missile game. Adam Rapacki, the foreign minister of Poland, had suggested that the two Germanies, Poland, and Czechoslovakia be considered a central European off-limits zone for nuclear weapons, but Washington turned down the proposal in May 1958. In response to pleas by scientists led by chemist Linus Pauling, who pointed out the rapid growth in pollution of the atmosphere from nuclear weapons testing, the Soviet Union announced a halt in its tests at the end of a series on March 31, 1958. The United States and British governments agreed to call off their experiments for one year after October 31.

In the meantime, the Middle East had developed its most dramatic crisis since 1956. On February 1, 1958, Egypt and Syria announced an intention to combine themselves into a United Arab Republic. On February 14, Iraq and Jordan, whose kings were second cousins, countered with a notice of their agreement to build a (rival) Arab Federation. On February 22, the United Arab Republic came into existence, with Jamal Abd an-Nasir as its elected president. On March 8, the monarchy of Yemen announced its plan to associate with the United Arab Republic in a federal union called the United Arab States. The integration of two or three countries anywhere opened new possibilities for them, but these particular unions posed a new danger. The United Arab States leaned toward the Soviet Union, the Arab Federation toward the United States.

In May 1958, Lebanon, which had become very divided by these moves of neighboring states, began to suffer violence. President Camille Chamoun, a Christian friendly to the United States, accused the United Arab Republic of lending assistance to Lebanese Muslims protesting his rule. Chamoun said that armed bands of Syrians had infiltrated Lebanese territory. The Muslims of Lebanon denied these charges and accused Chamoun of efforts to prolong his term. The Chamoun government took its complaint to the United Nations Security Council on May 22. For a while, the Council postponed its discussion while the League of Arab States attempted to solve the problem, until the League found it could come to no agreement. On June 11, the Security Council decided by a vote of 10 to 0 (the Soviet Union abstaining) to send an observation group to Lebanon -- "so as to ensure that there is no illegal infiltration of personnel or supply of arms or other matériel across the Lebanese borders. . . ." On July 3, the Observation Group reported its inability to that date to ascertain the source of the rebel equipment, but added that Lebanese individuals constituted the "vast majority" of the armed rebels themselves.

Another interim report from the Observation Group, dated July 16, 1958, said it had managed to secure access to all parts of the Lebanese frontier. Two days earlier, however, startling events in Iraq had upstaged the work of the Group. A violent revolution took the lives on July 14 of the king, the crown prince, and premier Nuri as-Said. Iraq became a republic with Abdul Karim Qassim, an army officer, acting as the new premier. Leaders in Washington, shocked by this sudden change at the very seat of the Baghdad Pact, took it for granted without careful investigation that the Soviet Union had engineered the coup.

On July 15, at the invitation of president Chamoun (a large number of whose countrymen disapproved of his action), United States marines began to occupy Lebanon, continuing until 15,000 of them had arrived. He ordered the move, stated President Eisenhower, "to help maintain security and to evidence the concern of the United States for the integrity and independence of Lebanon." Secretary-general Dag Hammarskjöld expressed his hope that the United Nations Observation Group would maintain its own more neutral position. However, on July 17, the day after he spoke, 2,000 British paratroops landed in Jordan at the request of king Hussein. Fifty American planes flew over Jordan in a demonstration of strength while the British operation proceeded. The Middle East had worked itself into an extremely nervous situation, an extension of the climate in London and Washington.

The regime of Qassim in Iraq, it became evident very soon, had risen to power as a homegrown movement, not one sponsored by the Soviet Union. Qassim dissolved the Arab Federation between Iraq and Jordan but made no move to join the United Arab Republic or the United Arab States. Iraq declined to participate further in Baghdad Pact activities, leaving that alliance destitute of its original name, but preferred a neutral course to one distinctly friendly to communism or the Soviet Union. The Arab nations themselves then found a solution to the crisis engendered by the expeditionary forces. The Security Council gave up its debate on the matter, without action, August 7. A third emergency special session of the General Assembly took up the discussion the next day, and on August 21 accepted unanimously a proposal of ten Arab nations including the United Arab Republic, Iraq, Yemen, Jordan, and Lebanon.

Without blaming anyone for anything, the resolution requested the secretary-general to take action "to facilitate the early withdrawal" of United States troops from Lebanon and British soldiers from Jordan. The last of the American force left Lebanon October 25; the British completed their evacuation of Jordan November 2. As a final twist of irony, the Lebanese parliament under the United States occupation chose new persons for president and premier as stipulated in the Lebanese constitution -- in both instances ignoring the preferences expressed by Camille Chamoun. The United Nations Observation Group departed from a quiet Lebanon in December.

638

Many exchanges of diplomatic notes took place while the Middle Eastern crisis lasted. Nikita Khrushchev, since March 1958 the prime minister of the Soviet Union in place of Nikolay Bulganin, proposed July 19 a meeting between himself and the heads of government of India, the United States, the United Kingdom, and France, with the possible attendance also of secretary-general Dag Hammarskjöld. Khrushchev suggested July 22 as a date, and the locale of Geneva, Switzerland. On July 22, he received answers from everyone, ranging from clear acceptance of the idea on the part of prime minister Nehru of India to near-rejection by president Eisenhower of the United States. Khrushchev replied to everyone July 23, accepting the preference of the British to meet in New York and putting forth July 28 as a new date. Few chief executives, however, seconded the enthusiasm of Khrushchev, and the summit meeting did not take place. President Eisenhower spoke to the General Assembly August 13, outlining Washington's hopes for the Middle East, but by this time the danger of war that provided the impetus for Khrushchev's proposals had subsided.

With the Iraqi and Lebanese governments reconstituted and the American and British forces retired from Lebanon and Jordan, Khrushchev looked for something new to move the reluctant president Eisenhower. On November 10, 1958, Khrushchev returned to the theme of Berlin, declaring that if the Soviet Union, the United States, the United Kingdom, and France could not agree on the future of the city Moscow would determine its status in consultation with the East German regime. Notes to Washington, London, and Paris dated November 27 suggested that Berlin might become a free city within the East German zone, and stated that Moscow proposed to make no changes in the rules for military traffic to and from West Berlin during the forthcoming half-year. Moscow regarded this period as "quite adequate for finding a sound basis for a solution to the problems connected with the change in the position of Berlin. . . ." Khrushchev announced the notes as a move to relax tensions in Europe; the press of the United States, however, treated the notes as a sort of ultimatum. Far from relaxing tension, the Soviet declarations made Washington all the more determined that no talks on Berlin should take place during the six-months period.

When Anastas Mikoyan visited the United States as a special envoy from the Soviet Union in January 1959, the Cold War entered a period of moderate thaw from positions that had remained congealed since the time of the crisis in Hungary. By March, Moscow, Washington, London, and Paris had agreed that their foreign ministers should meet again, even before the expiration of the Soviet six-month period. The meeting did convene on May 11 in Geneva. When John Foster Dulles died of cancer, the other four foreign ministers attended his funeral in Washington -- on May 27, the final day of the "ultimatum." The French, British, and United States ministers held steadfast to the idea that German reunification posed the only solution for Berlin. The Soviet delegation continued to speak of a "free" Berlin within East Germany. The conference recessed in a deadlock June 20, resumed sessions July 13, and came to final adjournment August 5 with no inkling of a compromise. From the context of this conference, however, Nikita Khrushchev and Dwight Eisenhower announced August 3 that the premier would visit the United States later in 1959 and would have a personal meeting with the president. Khrushchev hoped, as he had since his coming to power, to use an occasion of this sort for a breaking of Cold War ice.

As preparation for his planned talk with Khrushchev, president Eisenhower traveled to Bonn, to London, and to Paris. Meanwhile, Washington announced that it would not resume nuclear testing during 1959, and Moscow declared that it would hold off its tests as long as others did. Premier Khrushchev, arriving September 15, spoke to the United Nations General Assembly, visited points of interest from New York to California, and finally spent three days in private talks with president Eisenhower at the retreat of Camp David, in Maryland. The two men made no substantive decisions -- neither president nor premier believed that their two countries alone could solve the great problems of the world. They reached agreement, however, on the resumption of talks on Berlin, and on a return visit, by president Eisenhower to the Soviet Union, in 1960. Moreover, the president announced September 28, the day after the talks, that he no longer held to some of his previous objections to a summit meeting. Many people began to speak, hopefully, of the "spirit of Camp David," a genuine contrast to the succession of crises through which they had lived.

The spirit of Camp David did affect the two chief participants in the talks, but reacted on them differently, while scarcely touching many of the president's and the premier's closest advisers. President Eisenhower, with all the caution he continued to exercise because of his basic mistrust of Soviet intentions, felt that his conversations with Khrushchev might lead somewhere. Premier Khrushchev felt excited about the new augury for peaceful coexistence during his tenure in office, believing that Camp David had constituted a genuine break-through. Part of the premier's jubilation sprang from the plan he had submitted to the United Nations General Assembly during the first part of his visit to the United States. It provided for complete disarmament of all the nations over a period of four years. The Assembly passed Khrushchev's ideas, along with a comprehensive British plan submitted one day earlier, to the United Nations Disarmament Commission for study. This action came on November 20, 1959.

President Eisenhower spent much of the month of December visiting other countries, talking over a miscellany of matters and preparing for summit talks to come. On his list stood Italy, the Vatican, Turkey, Pakistan, Afghanistan, India (five days), Iran, Greece, Tunisia, Spain, and Morocco. He also spent three days in Paris with the heads of government of the United Kingdom, West Germany, and France. In February-March 1960, he traveled to Brazil, Argentina, Chile, and Uruguay. Premier Khrushchev likewise went abroad in February-March, visiting India, Burma, Indonesia, and Afghanistan. His sojourn in Paris lasted eleven days, as he made clear the sincerity of his proposals as well as his readiness to negotiate on them. Soon after Khrushchev's visit to Paris, however, the other heads of government meeting in Washington made declarations indicating their unreadiness to negotiate on Berlin in the context of a divided Germany. Khrushchev made it clear that for him some progress on a decision on Berlin remained an essential feature of a summit conference, now scheduled to begin in Paris May 16. Obviously, at least he hoped not only that talks take place but that they acquire genuine substance.

Suddenly, on May 5, 1960, world hopes aroused by the spirit of Camp David plunged again toward the depths of melancholy. Premier Khrushchev spoke to the Supreme Soviet of his nation of an incident that had occurred four days earlier: "Comrades Deputies," he said, "I must inform you of aggressive actions against the Soviet Union. . . . What were these aggressive actions? The United States of America sent its planes, which crossed our state frontiers and invaded the airspace of the Soviet Union. . . . The last but one of these aggressive actions was taken . . . on April 9, 1960. . . . We . . . decided at the time not to take any special measures, . . . because we knew from past experience that this was in fact of no avail. . . . We strictly warned our military men . . . that they must . . . not permit foreign planes to violate our air-space with impunity. . . . The fact that they got away with the incident of April 9 unscathed evidently pleased the American brass-hats, and they decided to repeat their aggressive act. For this purpose, they chose the most solemn day for our people and the working people of all countries -- May Day. . . .

"On that day, early in the morning," Khrushchev continued, "at 0536 hours Moscow time, an American aircraft crossed our frontier and continued flying farther into Soviet territory. . . . The government said: . . . -- bring the plane down! The assignment was carried out -- the plane was brought down! . . . The Soviet Government will protest strongly to the United States. . . . I think that we will also give a most serious warning to those countries which allow their territory to be used by the United States. . . . Imagine what would happen if a Soviet plane appeared, say, over New York, Chicago or Detroit. . . ." But Khrushchev even on May 5 hoped he could preserve the summit talks. "The question is," he said, "who sent that plane which intruded into the Soviet Union? Was it sent with the approval of the Supreme Commander of the United States' Armed Forces, an office which is known to be held by the President? Or was this act of aggression committed by the Pentagon militarists without the President's knowledge?"

Moscow understood more about the plane than Khrushchev revealed. Indeed, it had secured the pilot, air force lieutenant Francis Gary Powers, in its custody. Moscow knew that the plane had flown deep over Soviet territory for military intelligence services. Washington, not sensing that Khrushchev comprehended the mission of the plane, attempted to wriggle its way out of the vehement protest. The State Department announced May 5 the receipt of information that "an unarmed plane, a U-2 weather research plane based at Adana, Turkey, piloted by a civilian has been missing since May 1. During the flight of this plane, the pilot reported difficulty with his oxygen equipment. . . . It is entirely possible that having failure in the oxygen equipment,

643

which could result in the pilot losing consciousness, the plane continued on automatic pilot for a considerable distance and accidentally violated Soviet airspace."

On May 7 the State Department spoke again, declaring that "it has been established that insofar as the authorities in Washington are concerned there was no authorization for any such flight as described by Mr. Khrushchev. . . . Nevertheless it appears that in endeavoring to obtain information now concealed behind the Iron Curtain a flight over Soviet territory was probably undertaken by an unarmed civilian U-2 plane. . . . To reduce mutual suspicion and to give a measure of protection against surprise attack the United States in 1955 offered its open-skies proposal -- a proposal which was rejected out of hand by the Soviet Union. It is in relation to the danger of surprise attack that planes of the type of unarmed civilian U-2 aircraft have made flights along the frontiers of the free world for the past 4 years."

At this point, not only Moscow but much of the rest of the world knew more than Washington had admitted. The question loomed large, not whether the United States had spied on the Soviet Union -- everyone comprehended that both sides carried on secret intelligence activities -- but whether this particular type of "open" spying would be cancelled and the cancellation be made public in time to save the projected summit meeting. Christian Herter, the successor of John Foster Dulles as Eisenhower's secretary of state, implied May 9, just a week before the summit, that the practice of sending spy planes would be continued. "The Government of the United States," he said, "would be derelict to its responsibility . . . to free peoples everywhere if it did not . . . take such measures as are possible unilaterally to lessen and to overcome" the danger of surprise attack by the Soviet Union. "In fact," he continued, "the United States has not and does not shirk this responsibility.

. . . The President has put into effect since the beginning of his administration directives to gather by every possible means the information required to protect the United States and the free world against surprise attack. . . ."

President Eisenhower had thus chosen not to dissociate himself from the airplane spying enterprise, an opportunity that premier Khrushchev had left open to him. A note of May 10 from Moscow to Washington laid out the details of the flight: " . . . A military plane . . . invaded the air space of the Soviet Union to a distance of over 2,000 kilometres. . . . The pilot Powers . . . is alive. . . . In the route map taken from him, the entire route after taking off from Adana (Turkey) is clearly and precisely marked . . . : Peshawar (Pakistan) -- the Aral Sea -- Sverdlovsk -- Archangel -- Murmansk, with a subsequent landing at the Norwegian airfield of Budoe. . . . The Government of the United States, in the first place," the Moscow note proceeded, "admits that its replies to representations of the Soviet Government were made only . . . to evade the essence of the question, and that all the violations by American planes of the state frontiers of the U.S.S.R. have been actions taken in accordance with the policy of the United States. . . . Secondly, and this is the main point, by allowing such actions by American aircraft, the Government of the United States is exacerbating the situation still more."

A near-plaintive quality appeared in this message from Moscow, six days before the scheduled summit conference. In effect, it made the point, "Can you not see that no government can negotiate with another government which deliberately continues a policy of violation of the first government's air space? Can you not see that without a note declaring the policy abandoned the Soviet Union cannot participate in summit talks?" Either Washington failed to comprehend the near-plaintive note or sought to recover a measure of its own dignity when it decided not to announce a decision of May 12 to cancel further flights over Soviet territory. President Eisenhower traveled to Paris for the talks on May 16, prepared to downgrade the significance of the entire U-2 affair. Premier Khrushchev came to Paris very angry.

Khrushchev made only one speech to president Eisenhower, prime minister Harold Macmillan of the United Kingdom, and president Charles de Gaulle of France. "Now that the heads of government of the four powers have come to Paris for the conference," he said, "the question arises of how is it possible to negotiate in a productive way . . . when the Government of the United States and the President personally, far from deploring the provocative act -- the incursion by an American military plane into Soviet territory -- on the contrary, have declared that such actions will continue to be the national policy of the United States. . . . I visited the United States . . . , and I profoundly believe that all sections of the American people do not want war. The only exception is a small and frantic group in the Pentagon and the militarist circles backing it, who line their pockets out of the arms race . . . and who . . . ignore the interests of the peoples of all countries and pursue an adventurist policy. . . . We regret that this meeting has been torpedoed by the reactionary circles of the United States. . . . It will be recalled that President Eisenhower . . . and I agreed on an exchange of visits. Last September I paid such a visit to the United States. . . . The President . . . was to return the visit. We agreed that he would come to the Soviet Union on June 10 and we prepared a hearty welcome for this distinguished guest. . . . I believe that the visit to the Soviet Union by the President of the United States should now be postponed and a date for this visit should be fixed when conditions are ripe for it. . . . I believe that Mr. Eisenhower and the American people will understand me rightly."

Eisenhower's response came too little and too late. "In point of fact," he replied, "these flights were suspended after the recent incident and are not to be resumed." The Paris talks ended the following morning since the president failed to respond to the premier's demand that he "denounce the impermissible provocative actions of the American Air Force. . . ." From one summit conference (1955) to another (1960) the circle had closed.

If president Eisenhower felt any chagrin over the termination of the spirit of Camp David, his distress must have mounted a month later when the government of Japan asked him to "postpone" a visit there. Riots in Japan against a renewal of the Japanese-American alliance prompted the request. The president did visit the Philippines, Tai Wan, and South Korea, all United States allies, in the trip originally intended to include both Moscow and Tokyo. Some observers in the United States believed that Washington had encountered rebuffs because of a failure of aggressive spirit in the face of the "international communist conspiracy." But this viewpoint overlooked several important facts: (1) The United States, not the communists, held the responsibility for the U-2 incident at summit conference time. (2) Japanese conservative attitudes, not those of Japanese communists, produced the riots in Japan. (3) Fidel Castro, not the Cuban communists, had brought about the Havana-Washington impasse through months of interaction with the Eisenhower regime. (4) In Congo, where developments gave no comfort to Washington, the Belgians had caused most of the problem.

In 1959-60, the United States held chief responsibility for one more Cold War crisis, confined to Laos in southeastern Asia. The Geneva accords of 1954 had designated Laos a neutral state, though troops of the communist-oriented Pathet Lao occupied two provinces of the country until a political settlement with them could be reached. However, the United States government, which had not subscribed to the Geneva agreement, followed a course in Laos affecting that nation's neutrality and inviting the kind of pressures in Laos that existed in South Viet-Nam.

Souvanna Phouma served as prime minister of Laos at the time of the Geneva accord. From an aristocratic family, he held engineering degrees from two universities in France. His younger half-brother Souphanouvong, of similar background and training, led the Pathet Lao and the Neo Lao Hak Xat, or Lao Patriotic Front, a political group organized early in 1956. Souvanna Phouma took the idea of Laotian neutrality seriously. In office as prime minister again in 1956, after a lapse of more than a year, he negotiated with Souphanouvong until the two reached an agreement in November 1957. Its terms demobilized most of the Pathet Lao in February 1958, while incorporating the best trained into the Laotian army. The integration of the left-wing troops with the regular army did not in fact take place. In numbers, however, the army far outmatched the remnant of the Pathet Lao.

The Department of State in Washington, concerned about the continued presence of the Pathet Lao, feared that Souvanna Phouma did not understand the threat posed by the new arrangements. Souvanna Phouma planned new elections in which the Neo Lao Hak Xat might participate. The poll held in May 1958 showed the popularity of Souphanouvong and his program. The United States then quickly turned against Souvanna Phouma, who felt he must resign in July. An anti-communist government under Phoui Sananikone lasted a year and a half, while American assistance to the Laotian army increased rapidly. Strangely, while one semi-covert United States agency trained paratroops under the command of an officer Kong Le, another (the Central Intelligence Agency) chose its own strong man, Phoumi Nosavan. Prime minister Phoui Sananikone received arbitrary power for one year, starting in January 1959. In

648

May he delivered an ultimatum to the two battalions of Pathet Lao, to enter the regular army on his terms. One battalion yielded while the other escaped into friendly territory in northern Laos. Souphanouvong and other companions were arrested.

A change of government in December 1959-January 1960 pushed prime minister Phoui, a civilian, aside and brought Phoumi Nosavan, a military man, into a position of influence. The scene remained turbulent, however, throughout the year 1960. Phoumi Nosavan and the CIA rigged elections in April, eliminating the Neo Lao Hak Xat. Souphanouvong and his companions escaped from their prison in May. Kong Le and his paratroops seized the government August 9, turning against the United States agents who trained them. On August 16, Souvanna Phouma became prime minister again with the support of Kong Le. A week later, however, friends of Phoumi Nosavan reentered the cabinet while supporters of Kong Le received minor positions.

In September, Souvanna Phouma quarreled with Phoumi Nosavan over the latter's taking the offensive in warfare against a revived Pathet Lao. Kong Le, on the other hand, moved to ally his forces with the Pathet Lao. In early December, the Soviet Union began to airlift supplies to the Kong Le and Pathet Lao forces. By that time, the United States had extended large-scale assistance to Phoumi Nosavan for a period of about two years (along with its former aid to Kong Le). Starting December 15, 1960, Laos had two governments. Phoumi Nosavan and the CIA dominated the newer one. Kong Le and the Pathet Lao recognized but did not dominate the older one led by Souvanna Phouma. The people of Laos found themselves plunged into a blood-bath by the Cold War antagonisms of two world powers, whose own people lived in domestic tranquility far, far away, almost as though they pulled strings from havens on distant planets.

649

<u>Man</u> <u>in</u> <u>Space</u> (<u>Part</u> <u>I</u>)

    The Soviet, American, and Laotian people did
live far from one another, as judged by popular
attitudes of the year 1960. Significant differences separated them in background, custom, and
outlook, though they also shared much in common.
Three years before 1960, their relationship had
altered, however little they understood the
change. The flight of the first missile into
space outmoded their sentiments of nationalism,
the sum total of distortions of their differences. Just as race, language, and traditional
religion had in recent centuries faded into the
background as possible determinants of the future
of mankind, so nationalism might be expected to
wither in the full development of the space age.
In its place there would surely arise an awareness of the need for interdependence -- first,
among the peoples of the earth; eventually, among
all the species of the planet. These new earthly
ties would become imperative as man reached into
space beyond the earth, at some point making contact with other intelligent creatures -- who, in
awesome numbers and an infinitude of diversity,
must indeed be found to live there.

    A mere half-millenium ago, <u>homo</u> <u>sapiens</u> re-
mained largely unaware of the existence of most
of his own species. Many millions of people in
the Americas, Sub-Sahara Africa, the Orient, and
Europe knew little or nothing of those in the
other regions. When the Europeans undertook
their tremendous voyages of exploration, they
brought increased self-knowledge to all of mankind. As people discovered one another upon the
globe, a few Europeans began to suspect that in
the same manner as their ancient forebears had
erred in counting the Mediterranean Sea as the
center of the earth, so fifteenth-century savants
might be mistaken in assuming that the earth is
the center of its universe.

    Three important steps took place in the development of comprehension of mankind's genuine position in the universe at large -- an understanding bound to remain limited until further advances in the space age. A famed Polish scientist suggested in the sixteenth century that the earth and the planets earth-men see about them revolve about the sun -- rather than the earth forming a hub for both the sun and the planets. A renowned Italian astronomer suggested early in the seventeenth century that the sun served no better than the earth as the center for the entire universe, and that while the earth and other planets revolve about our sun, there are many such suns which in turn bear some kind of relationship to one another. A brilliant English mathematician, later in the seventeenth century, produced a formula to explain all the astronomical movements observable at that time, calling it the principle of "gravity." The orbit of the moon about the earth fitted the admirable new scheme, along with the changing positions of the planets and the sun. At once, it became obvious that human beings might create small moons by projecting missiles above the earth's atmosphere at sufficient speeds, causing them to orbit the globe before returning to its surface. Indeed, with the attainment of even higher speeds, those missiles would depart from earth to wander into space until captured by the gravity of some other heavenly body.

Scientists of the eighteenth and nineteenth centuries, busy catching up with the marvels of this world, found little time to attempt the far more difficult task of attempting to probe beyond it. In the nineteenth century, however, fiction writers played with the idea of flights into and out of space. Late in that century, the idea blossomed in Germany that the counter-thrust propelling force of a large rocket could take a machine above the atmosphere for a journey into space. The Chinese had manufactured small rockets for hundreds of years. Large-scale European experience with them extended less than a century. Now rockets would have to grow to adult-

651

hood, if they were to blast their way through the atmosphere, though the fuel supply needed for that climb would remain little tapped once the vehicle reached the immensities of space.

The first scientific article on space flight appeared in Russia, in the first decade of the twentieth century. It dealt with the practicability of a space rocket burning liquid fuel. In 1919, Robert Hutchings Goddard of Massachusetts (died 1945) demonstrated in writing how a multistage apparatus might reach the moon, with the first-stage rocket dropping aside like an empty fuel tank. In 1926, Goddard fired the first liquid-propellant rocket at a velocity of 60 miles per hour to an altitude of 41 feet, covering a horizontal distance of 200 feet. Scientists in Germany and France, meanwhile, wrote the first scholarly books on interplanetary travel, and Soviet writers compiled an early space encyclopedia. In the 1930's, experiments in the Soviet Union reached record heights of six miles, while engineer Werner von Braun (working with a small group) obtained the patronage of the army for ongoing research in rocketry in Germany. During World War II, while the Soviet Union struggled for survival, Germany developed missiles capable of 100-mile altitudes, using them for precision bombardment of England at distances up to 190 miles. The United States military refused to patronize Goddard's research, though it did approve a program for the development of solid-propellant rocket engines for airplanes, headed by Hungarian-born Theodore von Karman (who lived through this quinquennium).

In 1945, both the Soviet Union and the United States hoped to obtain German rocket secrets to use in their own rocket research. Agents from the United States seized most of the rockets built but not fired, while Soviet authorities found only a few in Poland. Werner von Braun and his top associates surrendered to the United States, while Soviet prisoners included some technical workers of lower rank. The two beneficiaries of Nazi wartime effort then turned to their own programs of rocketry research designed for both military and scientific purposes. These programs remained secret, however, and played no role in the excitement produced by the dramatic new displays of nuclear energy.

The UNESCO-subsidized International Council of Scientific Unions, a federation of 13 world-wide associations in the natural sciences, decided in 1952 to sponsor an International Geo-physical Year from July 1, 1957, to December 31, 1958. Its purpose would be to accelerate the growth of knowledge concerning the earth and its atmosphere. National scientific societies would cooperate in the enterprise. The United States government, followed by that of the Soviet Union, announced in 1955 its intention to add a space probe to the extensive series of observations already planned for the Year. Neither of the two powers offered to share any secrets concerning the rocket programs needed for the space probes. The first efforts of earth creatures to reach into the space beyond them would come from two powerful nations working separately, each of-fering some of their findings as they saw fit to the remainder of mankind.

The Soviet Union sent the first rocket missile into space -- to the great chagrin of scientists in the United States -- and into successful orbit around the earth. Sputnik I (whose name meant "traveling companion" or "satellite") took off from Russian territory October 4, 1957, assisted by three stages of liquid-propellant rockets. An aluminum-alloy sphere weighing 184 pounds, it orbited for three months, with an initial perigee (minimum distance from the earth) of 144 miles and apogee (maximum distance from the earth) of 584 miles. For the first three weeks, it sent back radio messages through which its location could be traced. United States scientists and technicians knew that the missiles they had planned did not compare

with the size of Sputnik I. Some of their countrymen preferred to believe that Soviet society
could not produce such a wonder -- that superior
German technological assistance must account for
the development, or perhaps the entire episode
constituted an elaborate hoax.

New, overwhelming evidence, however, soon
convinced most skeptics. The Soviet Union
launched Sputnik II into orbit -- weighing 1,120
pounds including its final-stage booster mechanism -- November 3, 1957. Sputnik II reached
nearly twice as far into space as its predecessor, with an initial apogee of 1,056 miles. It
sent radio transmissions to the earth for a week,
and remained in orbit more than five months.
Much of the earth's population could see it tumbling in the skies. They knew it contained the
first space traveler from earth, a mongrel fox
terrier named Laika, whose heartbeats came
through on the radio. People generally agreed,
after the second Sputnik, that Moscow had indeed
produced more than a propaganda surprise.

The United States placed its first missile in
space January 31, 1958, naming it Explorer I. A
steel cylinder with aluminum oxide stripes, it
weighed 30.8 pounds including its booster stage,
less than 3% of the mass of Sputnik II. Its appearance at this time, earlier than had been
planned, sprang from the desire of American rocket experts and the government prodding them not
to appear far behind the Soviet Union in the development of a space study program. Explorer I
reached an apogee of 1,585 miles, and carried
instruments to measure radiation.

Vanguard I, an aluminum ball weighing only
3.4 pounds in orbit, took off from the United
States March 17, 1958, with an initial apogee of
2,462 miles. The tiniest of the lot to date, it
nevertheless carried a live radio (powered by
solar energy) through this quinquennium, and instruments that ascertained the correct shape of
the earth, somewhat resembling that of a pear.

Explorer III, launched March 26, resembled Explorer I in most respects. The radiation detection instrument of Explorer I had fallen suddenly silent at 600 miles altitude, after indicating a rise in radiation up to that point. When the radiation counter of Explorer III performed precisely the same, the conclusion seemed certain that the reason lay not with erraticism of the gauge, but in the overwhelming quantity of the radiation encountered. James Alfred Van Allen of Iowa, who had directed this part of the project, took the findings as firm evidence of the existence of a belt of trapped radiation substantially surrounding the earth. Nicholas Christofilos, born in Massachusetts of Greek parents, only the year before had first suggested the idea that charged particles became trapped in magnetic fields.

During the remainder of the Geophysical Year, two more missiles in orbit and two sent far into space added significantly to space science. Sputnik III, May 15, weighed 2,926 pounds without its booster and carried a mass of equipment to measure all aspects of the envelope about the earth from 133 miles perigee to 1,178 miles apogee. Solar batteries provided its power. Explorer IV, July 26, correctly measured part of the radiation belt discovered by its predecessors, raising speculation concerning the danger it might pose to space travelers of the future. In August-September, it also monitored the effects of three nuclear explosiions at altitudes of 300 miles, finding that particles released in such explosions do indeed become trapped, though the effects became minimal within one week. Pioneer I and Pioneer III, October 11 and December 6, lasted only one day each as they soared away from the earth, but revealed the existence of a second radiation belt, named like the first for Van Allen. The lower Van Allen belt reached its peak of intensity at a distance of 1-3,000 miles; the higher at 8-12,000 miles. Both Pioneers traveled over 60,000 miles from their home planet before they fell silent.

On December 18, 1958, the air force of the United States launched a space vehicle outside the scientific program of the Geophysical Year. Weighing 8,800 pounds including its booster, the new missile lifted the morale of United States engineers who chafed under the "burden" of the Soviet lead in space. Their machine reached an apogee of 915 miles, and lasted more than a month. Lacking a scientific payload, its name Score meant "signal communications by orbiting relay equipment." Its fame derived not only from its weight, but from its presentation of the first human voice from space, a pre-taped message of peace from president Dwight Eisenhower.

The Soviet space program recaptured world attention very early in the new year. Luna I, launched January 2, 1959, left earth-orbit after 15 days, following a trajectory close to the path of the moon. One-third of the way there, at about the distance reached by the Pioneers the preceding year, it ejected on command a kilogram of sodium whose reflection could be observed back on earth. Luna I passed within 3,800 miles of the moon and carried its gauges and transmitters on into space, its radio operating through the first 371,000 miles. Taking up orbit about the sun, its aphelion (maximum distance from the sun) lay well beyond the path of the earth, nearly out to the realm of Mars.

Luna II traveled to the moon. Launched September 12, 1959, three days before premier Khrushchev began his visit to the United States, it made impact with the moon 33 1/2 hours later. Its instruments, in operation until the collision, confirmed that the moon carried with it neither radiation belt nor magnetic field such as those surrounding the earth.

Luna I and Luna II provided verification of a theory developed in the 1950's, chiefly by astrophysicist Ludwig Franz Biermann of West Germany. Biermann believed that the tails of comets origi-

656

nated not from pressure of solar light on the gases of the comet, as earlier scientists had supposed, but from reaction to a stream of protons and electrons flowing from the sun. Eugene Newman Parker of Michigan, speculating on the pervasiveness of such a stream of solar radiation to distances far beyond the orbit of the earth, named it the "solar wind." Any solar satellite containing a significant magnetic field would possess a magnetic tail on the side opposite the sun, through which the solar wind could scarcely penetrate. (Beyond that tail, the deflected solar wind would whip with particular fury.) While the two Luna flights encountered the solar wind, the magnetic tail of the earth awaited further study.

Luna III proved a spectacular surpassing all of its predecessors. It left earth October 4, the second anniversary of the original Sputnik. It assumed an extreme initial earth-orbit of 25,500 miles perigee and 294,250 miles apogee, farther into space than the orbit of the moon. On the first passage around the earth, Luna III soared behind the moon itself, passing it at about 4,000 miles, and engaging in the first photography of that side never seen from earth. (Because the moon rotates on its axis in the same time interval as its revolution about the earth, its far side remains either dark or hidden -- turned away from the sun in the one instance, away from the earth in the other.) Luna III snapped 40 minutes of pictures, transmitting them to the earth later. The far side of the moon, the photographs showed, held a greater number of level regions than the near side, though none as large in area, and contained its full complement of the large moon-craters. About 30% of the "back" side remained unphotographed, and the entire task to be done with precision.

Scientific teams in the United States, combining into a cooperative venture on the model followed by the Soviet Union from the beginning, sent eleven missiles into space in 1959. Pioneer

IV (13 pounds) followed Luna I (797 pounds) after two months and a day, in a course taking it close by the moon and into orbit about the sun. Vanguards II and III examined the vicinity of the earth, transmitting the first analysis of the cloud cover and mapping the magnetic field. Explorer VI, launched August 7, reached an apogee of 26,366 miles, contributing the first electronic picture of a portion of the earth's cloud cover. Explorer VII like Sputnik III carried out a number of investigations closer to the earth. Discoverers I, II, V, VI, VII, and VIII, weighing 1,300 to 1,700 pounds, looked toward the American space program of the future. They experimented first with polar orbits in place of the usual east-west trajectories, and later with the ejection of capsules -- either into higher orbit or with the intention of recovery.

The United States launched 17 space missiles in 1960, under nine rubrics covering as many purposes. Pioneer V flew like Pioneer IV into orbit about the sun, sending back data on the solar system for more than three months. Explorer VIII studied the earth's ionosphere. Tiros (television infrared observation satellite) I and II constituted the first stations placed in space for the study of earth's weather. Transits IB and IIA, sent aloft as beacons to help mariners navigate, proved especially useful to submarine crews. Transit IIA carried the first subsatellite, Solrad (solar radiation) I, which entered a separate earth-orbit.

Echo I, the first space balloon, 100 feet in diameter, moved along a path 1,000 miles in space, clearly visible on earth to the naked eye. A "passive" communications satellite, it echoed voice and television signals from earth, bouncing them far beyond the horizon. Courier IB, a more expensive and efficient "active-repeater" communications satellite, itself rebroadcast what it "heard" and "saw" from the earth, yielding sharper beyond-the-horizon sounds and images.

Midas (missile defense alarm system) II had "reconnaissance" (spying upon the Soviet Union) as its mission, but its data processor failed after the first day. Seven more Discoverers experimented like their immediate predecessors with the ejection of capsules. The first successful recovery, from Discoverer XIII, occurred August 11 on the surface of the ocean. The second, from Discoverer XIV, took place August 19 by hook in mid-air. Discoverers XVII and XVIII carried primitive biological specimens. Both the United States and the Soviet Union looked toward human travel in space, with successful recovery an essential ingredient.

The Soviet Union attempted recovery three times in 1960, but experienced success only once. Sputniks IV, V, and VI, each 10,000 pounds with its booster, went into orbit May 15, August 19, and December 1 respectively. Sputnik IV carried a dummy man in a passenger cabin, which separated from the main craft as intended -- but sailed into orbit rather than returning to earth, and eventually disintegrated. Sputnik V, designed as a space ship, carried another dummy, two live dogs, six mice, and other specimens of life. After 17 orbits in one day, the dogs and mice returned safe and sound in a compartment parachuted to the ground, the first mammals to have made the complete journey. Sputnik VI carried two more dogs and other animal and plant passengers -- but all perished when the craft reentered the atmosphere too rapidly and steeply, the day after traveling aloft.

By the end of the year 1960, programs in both the Soviet Union and the United States provided training for manned missions into space. The trainees, future cosmonauts and astronauts of world fame, knew that the fate of the less-than-human passengers of Sputnik VI might also come to them. There could be no guarantee of safety for

the first travelers into such an unknown as
space. Yet no shortage of volunteers existed for
such an exciting mission. Having already reached
into space, man felt determined to travel therein
as an expression of his innate scientific tendencies.

The Political Spectrum

The human population of the world thus reaching into space approached the number of 3,000,
000,000 in the year 1960. Of that total, more
than 2,850,000,000 lived in politically independent states. Their political fortunes during
this five-year period revealed little indication
of the dawning of a new age. Right-wing authoritarianism, indeed, made a remarkable come-back,
to include 17% of the world's inhabitants under
non-colonial regimes.

Countries fitting the two democratic quarters
of the spectrum -- the second and the third --
declined from 53% to 48% of the total. Here the
loss of Pakistan, Indonesia, and Turkey and the
non-inclusion of Congo, Sudan, and Morocco more
than offset the emergence of Nigeria as a democratic regime and the readherence of Argentina,
Colombia, and Peru. Nations of the socialist
allegiance -- the first and second quarters --
dropped in porportion also, from 59% to 56%.
Turkey left this group, but the emergence of
Nigeria, Congo, Sudan, and Morocco as non-
socialist countries constituted the chief reason
for the diminution. At the same time, the re-
strengthening of right-wing authoritarianism took
on less than dramatic proportions, since Pakistan
and Indonesia, with nearly 200,000,000 of the
people involved, had remained very weak in their
attachment to democracy.

The portion of the world's non-colonial population living in countries of the first band of

660

the spectrum dropped from 37% to 35%, though no nation departed from this quarter. (Left to its own devisings in 1956, Hungary might have gone that far.) The formerly all-communist orientation of this band became modified with the inclusion of Cuba, Mali, and Guinea. None of the three considered itself a communist regime at the end of 1960, though all followed socialist programs under essentially one-man regimes. The count in 1960 thus included 4 countries in the Orient, 9 in Europe, 1 in the Americas, and 2 in Sub-Sahara Africa, living under left-wing authoritarianism.

Mainland China (population 582-636,000,000) continued its rapid pace, though not without some setback to the plans of Mao Ze Dong. Mao retained his post as chairman of the Communist party, effectively controlling the nation, though he stepped down from his post as chairman of the republic in 1959. Liu Shao Qi (Liu Shao Chi), a close comrade of Mao since 1932 and generally regarded as Mao's heir apparent since 1956, became the new chairman of the republic. Jou En Lai remained as prime minister. Lin Biao (Lin Piao), the victorious general of 1949, became minister of defense in 1959, instituting tight party influence in the army. The Chinese government recognized two new autonomous provinces (its third and fourth) in 1958. Guang Xi Zhuang (Kwang Si Chuang), the southernmost region of the country, held the Zhuang (Chuang) and other people speaking Kadai languages and a lesser number of Miao and related tongues, along with a majority of Chinese. Ning Xia Hui (Ning Sia Hui), adjacent to the Inner Mongolian autonomous region in the north, protected a Hui (Mandarin-speaking) Muslim community.

Chairman Mao by 1956 had reached a state of exuberance. He had good reason for feeling the exaltation of success. Communist China forces, after defeating Chiang, had fought the United Nations to a stalemate in Korea. Maoist reform had changed the face of China, granting peasants

661

and women a new lease on life, even while communism remained in incipient stages. Most of the
transformation had taken place without a regime
of terror, though Mao himself stated that nearly
1,000,000 persons had died in opposition to his
regime. Many pre-Mao customs persisted among
older people, and some of the more highly educated resisted the ideology of communism, but Mao
felt that most Chinese stood convinced of the
moral rightness and wisdom of the programs he had
begun.

Citing an ancient Chinese metaphor, on May 2,
1956, Mao suggested that Chinese people develop
more of a spirit of criticism. "Let a hundred
flowers bloom, let a hundred schools contend," he
said. Mao sought self-examination within the
guidelines of the system he had established. He
did not expect free thinking outside the range of
his plans. "Marxism is a scientific truth," he
asserted, "and does not fear criticism." Fault-
finding quickly mounted, however, to include not
only procedures but goals and even intentions.
Mao realized within months that the level of
acceptance of his decisions lay much lower than
he had imagined. In 1957, he complained of the
more outspoken statements, labeling them "poison-
ous weeds" rather than flowers. On March 16,
1958, over 10,000 non-communists (including leaders of the democratic parties) found it expedient
openly to "dedicate their hearts" to socialism.
The fact that many of these people lost government positions and some received even harsher
punishment convinced anti-communist observers in
other lands that the entire hundred-flowers campaign constituted an intended snare to trick
anti-communist thinkers in China into revealing
themselves.

An unperturbed Mao showed his exuberance
again in 1958, when the first Chinese five-year
plan ended and a second began. China suddenly
became a most radical communist state, going well
beyond the experiments attempted in the Soviet
Union, when Mao announced a "great leap forward"

662

in which everyone would be considered a soldier and the soldiers would be organized into "communes." An immediate organization of rural communes took place, intended to cover almost all of the country. Even home life broke up for millions of Chinese as men, women, and children lived separately according to a very carefully planned regimen. The government hoped to stimulate production at a sharply improved rate of speed, the first five-year plan having fallen short of its goals because of inherited deficiencies. The great leap forward, Mao believed, would come about through sheer use of imagination and will power.

By 1959, small iron furnaces had begun to spring up in connection with the rural communes, not because they made sense economically -- the quality of their production remained poor -- but simply because China needed iron. By 1960, urban communes on a large scale handled tasks particular to the life of the cities. But by that time, Mao himself realized that he (not his critics on this occasion) had gone too far; that production in many categories, far from leaping forward, lagged far behind the first goals of the program; and that induced enthusiasm on the part of the people could not overcome the great lack of training. China even became hungry as severe droughts hampered agriculture. Extremes in barracks living soon disappeared, and the iron furnaces languished. The communes continued, though many of them had to adjust to take the people's preferred life styles better into account.

Maoist China moved surprisingly in this period to develop a bad relationship not only with the Soviet Union (see "Communist Fraternity Broken") but with India as well. Mainland China, the most populated nation of the earth, thus found itself in conflict by 1960 with the second, third, and fourth most populated nations (the last the United States). The Chinese difficulties with India began in 1957 when the Chinese government constructed a 100-mile road across

663

what India considered the Ladakh district of eastern Kashmir. Obviously, the Chinese considered this district part of their own territory. Two years later, Peking brought Tibet (at one end of this road) under closer Peking control than it had formerly. Of the two Mahayana Buddhist leaders in Tibet, one (called the Panchen Lama) stayed in Tibet to cooperate with the Chinese Communists, while the other (the Dalai Lama) took refuge in India. Later in 1959, Chinese and Indian troops became engaged in border skirmishing. No great fear arose of a war between the two population giants, though the new troubles increased the levels of worldwide apprehension. In 1960, China by contrast turned the other cheek to another neighbor, Burma, relinquishing a great deal of Chinese claim to Burmese territory in a treaty between the two.

In North Viet-Nam, Ho Chi Minh extricated himself in 1956 from criticism of the three-year-old agrarian reform by dismissing those in charge and taking over the chairmanship of the Workers party while retaining the country's presidency. In 1959-60, Ho brought most of the small farms of North Viet-Nam into cooperatives, as a further step toward national direction of the economy. In 1960, a new constitution reorganized the North Vietnamese government, and elections posed 460 candidates for 362 seats in the assembly. Those who won, however, did so with very high percentages of the vote, and Ho continued in both his chairmanship of the Workers party and the presidency.

Ho had already expressed his great disappointment that, because of decisions in Washington and moves in Sai Gon, the national elections for all Viet-Nam as planned at the Geneva conference of 1954 would not be held in 1956 as scheduled. The United States government had simply decided that it would not allow Ho to win control over all of Viet-Nam, even by vote of the people. Ho complained bitterly in 1955. (See "Three Revolutions Inaugurated," Chapter VI.) In

1957, the North Vietnamese government reminded the one in Sai Gon that a year had transpired since the deadline set for elections to unify Viet-Nam, but the Diem regime in Sai Gon did not respond. In 1958, a new Vietnamese war began, in effect, as Ho sypathizers in South Viet-Nam uncovered old caches of arms and resumed the struggle against their enemies, soon taking over considerable sections of South Vietnamese territory. Before 1954, France had stood as the prime enemy; now, the Diem regime and its mentor, the United States, occupied that role.

North Korea, after recovery from the conflict of 1949-53, (the country passed the 10,000,000-mark in population by 1960), moved into a five-year plan for development and socialization of its industry, decreed in 1958 but designated for 1957-61. Kim Il Sung, who continued as premier and as secretary of the Korean Workers Party, expelled members of the party who called for adoption of the Soviet policy of collective leadership, and pressed hard, as had Stalin, toward the nationalization and rapid development of all urban industry and the organization of state-owned and collective farms. Aid came from both the Soviet Union and China, while a "flying horse" movement suggested by Kim emulated the "great leap forward" of Mao Ze Dong. According to announcement, the North Korean regime reached the goals of its five-year plan ahead of time, in 1960. Mongolia instituted a three-year plan for 1958-60, and organized its herdsmen into cooperatives.

The Soviet Union (population 196-214,000,000) provided much of the action of 1956-60 already narrated in the sections "Communist Fraternity Broken," "The Cold War," and "Man in Space." Soviet economic progress continued until the gross national product approached the level of half that of the United States. The Sixth Five-Year Plan, scheduled for 1956-60, gave way early in 1959 to a Seven-Year Plan, 1959-65, designed for still higher goals. Only agriculture lagged, particularly the production of grains. In 1957, the regime decentralized urban industry somewhat, placing more emphasis on guidance within each of 105 industrial regions. Overall decisions remained firmly in the hands of Moscow. Urban working establishments moved toward a shorter working day within the six-day week.

In June 1957, quarrels over the decentralization of industry brought to an end the tentative accord between party leader Khrushchev on the one hand and his colleagues Georgy Malenkov, Vyacheslav Molotov, and Lazar Kaganovich on the other. All three of these dissenters found themselves dismissed from the party council, though they did not disappear from the public eye as they might have under Stalin. Georgy Zhukov, the chief officer who fought the Nazis in World War II, then briefly appeared as a possible counterweight to Khrushchev in the highest party council, until his removal in November. After new "elections" on March 16, 1958, in which 1,378 candidates for the Supreme Soviet "won" without opposition, party leader Khrushchev became premier Khrushchev on March 27. His predecessor Nikolay Bulganin, from this point a distinguished alumnus of the famed B & K team, applauded politely along with the remaining associates.

Poland, it seemed for a short time after the accession of Wladyslaw Gomulka to the secretaryship of the Polish United Workers party on October 21, 1956 (see "Communist Fraternity Broken"), moved in a different direction from that of the Soviet Union. On January 20, 1957, the elections held to determine who would sit in the new parliament offered voters a total of 720 candidates running for 459 seats. The results amply satisfied Gomulka's wishes, but the small (and generally cooperative) Democratic party of the pre-1952 period also found itself the victor in some contests. Poland received international publicity after the elections when some of the new members of parliament voted no rather than yes on a few substantive measures. Economic aid began to flow from the United States in April 1957, as anticommunists hoped to make a real incision in the communist bloc. Polish relations with the government in Washington continued on steady ground. The commitment of party chief Gomulka to the Moscow line became very plain, however, by 1958, along with the solidity of his own position of supreme power in Poland. As if to symbolize the fact that no real break with Moscow had occurred, Jozef Cyrankiewicz, who had become premier in 1954, continued in that position throughout this quinquennium. A five-year plan for Poland, 1956-60, showed considerable success for urban industry -- but less so for agriculture, which remained largely in private hands.

Romania experienced no such turmoil in this five-year period as did Poland and Hungary at its beginning. An expression of unrest came from a Hungarian minority inside Romania in 1959, an echo of discord that long antedated the Romanian communist regime. The government of Romania remained in the hands of the Workers party secretary, Gheorghe Gheorgiu-Dej, and the premier, Chivu Stoica, both of whom had acceded to their positions in 1955. A second five-year plan, 1956-60, greatly increased factory production but yielded less success in agriculture, with about four-fifths of the farm land becoming collectivized. A six-year plan began before the other ended, in 1960.

President Tito of Yugoslavia, who also served as the secretary-general of his country's only (Communist) party, showed clearly in 1956 that he would brook only moderate dissent when he imprisoned Milovan Djilas for his analysis of communism. (See "Art.") Tito returned to half-decade budgeting with a plan to match the period 1957-61. The plan proved a success, achieving its goals in 1960, as Tito continued to receive assistance from the United States. The many diplomatic developments of this quinquennium established Yugoslavia more clearly than before as a leader of the bloc of countries not aligned in

667

the Cold War.

The servile position of the communist regime in East Germany continued through this period, with Otto Grotewohl acting as premier and Walter Ulbricht as secretary of the ruling Socialist Unity party. The statements of premier Khrushchev of the Soviet Union in November 1958 regarding the future of the city of Berlin seemed to indicate plans to grant the East German regime a new measure of dignity, presumably within the mentioned six-month interval. Such plans, if they existed, did not materialize, and Ulbricht followed faithfully on in the course laid down by the Soviet regime. In September 1960, when the president of East Germany died, a constitutional amendment replaced the presidency with an executive council of which Ulbricht became the chairman, though Grotewohl stayed on as premier.

Czechoslovakia, once the home of such intellectually superior statesmen as Eduard Benes and Tomas and Jan Masaryk, showed few signs of sympathy for the dissatisfied intellectuals of Poland and Hungary in 1956. The Czech regime placated university students in June of that year with some easing of former repression. And while the Prague government remained very loyal to Moscow, Czechoslovakia opened itself more than other communist countries to reporters from abroad permitted to write as they pleased. With its second five-year plan (1956-60) an impressive success, and with collectivization of agriculture proceeding rather rapidly, Czechoslovakia indeed seemed a likely object for use as a communist showpiece. Collective leadership continued in Prague, under president Antonin Zapotocky until his death in 1957; Antonin Novotny, first secretary of the Communist party since 1953 and president after 1957; and Viliam Siroky, premier since 1953 and throughout this quinquennium. In a new constitution adopted in 1960, Czechoslovakia became the first of the communist states aside from the Soviet Union to denominate itself a "socialist republic."

The situation in Hungary remained tight for three years after the frustrated liberation movement of 1956. Janos Kadar, as continuing first secretary of the Socialist Workers party and as premier until 1958, remained in complete charge of the country's destiny. He pursued the punishment of the supporters of Imre Nagy while taking measures to relieve the hard-struck Hungarian economy. Following communist procedures, including rapid collectivization of agriculture, and applying the rules with the same vigor he used in ferreting out enemies, Kadar encountered impressive success in increasing production. In 1960, Kadar granted amnesty to most of the political prisoners whom he had not yet executed.

Bulgaria and Albania found their own manner of asserting some small degree of independence in 1958 and 1960, respectively. Bulgaria chose to describe its third five-year plan, whose commencement happened to coincide with the "great leap forward" of mainland China, in terms other than those approved in the Soviet Union. The Bulgarian regime, still dominated by the Fatherland Front, decided it could leap forward also in rather gigantic strides, and did succeed in accelerating production rapidly. Albania under the continued leadership of Enver Hoxha as first secretary of the Labor party, despite the Soviet use of some of its territory as a military base, sympathized with the Chinese ideological position in the dispute between Peking and Moscow. In the United Nations General Assembly, Albania, second-smallest communist state of the world, became a kind of spokesman for Peking, capital of the largest state of the world, in what may be described as one of the international organization's most conspicuous ironies.

Cuba made its own way into the first quarter of the spectrum in 1960, without the full approval of either Peking or Moscow. Cuba did not at this time, however, become a communist state. Fidel Castro followed his own brand of socialism, hazily reminiscent of Marxism. His regime never-

669

theless classified as strictly authoritarian. Mali and Guinea, likewise, from the day of independence dedicated themselves to "African" socialism, authoritarian in nature and Marxist in vocabulary, without accenting the label of communism. Beginning with this chapter, thus, the word "communist" applies more loosely to the first quarter of the spectrum, as has the word "fascist" to the fourth quarter from the start. For the story of Cuba in this five-year period, see "Two American Revolutions." For those of Mali and Guinea, see "African Independence."

By the end of 1960, there remained only two large Communist parties outside the communist countries. The party in India grew slowly and, through a split among non-communists, actually held the executive power in the state of Kerala for a short period through democratic means. The party in Italy retained its strength even though the left-wing Socialist party dropped its friendly attitude in the wake of the Soviet intervention in Hungary. Factionalism following the Hungarian incident hit hard at the Communist party of France, which dropped to a negligible quantity in parliament with the ending of proportional representation. The Communist party of Indonesia lost its independent existence in 1960 as president Sukarno took all Indonesian parties into his own hands.

The second -- democratic socialist -- quarter of the spectrum dropped from 22% to 21% in the count by country of the world's non-colonial population. Five added countries for the second quarter -- Venezuela, Ghana, the Malagasy Republic, Senegal, and the Central African Republic -- did not match the one emigration of Turkey (to the fourth quarter), nor the larger influx of new countries to the third and fourth bands. For the first time, all the regions of the world as used in this book became represented in the second quarter. By the end of 1960, there were 4 countries of this persuasian in the Orient, 6 in

Europe, 4 in the Americas, 4 in Sub-Sahara Africa, and 1 in the Middle East.

India (387-429,000,000) continued under the rule of prime minister Jawaharlal Nehru and his Congress party. New elections in 1957 gave the latter three-fourths of the seats in parliament, while the Communist and Praja Socialist parties combined held a little less than one-tenth. (The Kisan Mazdoor Praja party had merged with the Praja Socialist.) In the new state of Kerala in the far south, the Communist party received a plurality and a Communist prime minister took office. When unrest broke out in Kerala in 1959, however, the national parliament authorized Nehru to intervene in the Kerala government and terminate the Communist administration.

Kerala comprised only one of several new states created in 1956-60 in an attempt to solve some of India's language problems. Most of the revision of state boundaries took place in 1956 with the abolition of rule by maharajas. The president of India would appoint all state governors under the new system, as he had in many states from the beginning. An additional reform in 1960 broke up one state which had continued to harbor two languges, so that the matching of state boundaries with those of major language areas became nearly complete.

The largest princely state, that of Hyderabad, disappeared completely in 1956. Its Marathi-speaking portion went to Bombay, its Telugu-speaking districts to the state of Andhra founded three years earlier, and its Kannada-speaking area to a new state of Mysore. Andhra acquired the city of Hyderabad, which became its capital. To the south of the old state of Hyderabad, other Kannada districts joined Mysore, whose maharaja lost his tenure. Kerala included Travancore, whose maharaja also lost his position, along with other speakers of Malayalam. Madras, which shared the southern tip of the subcontinent with Kerala, widened its borders somewhat to include most of the Tamil language group.

The state of Andhra received the new name of Andhra Pradesh, or Andhra Region. Directly north of Andhra Pradesh after 1956 lay the Hindi-speaking states called (1) Madhya Pradesh (Central Region), the largest in area, incorporating Madhya Bharat, no longer tied to the maharaja of Gwalior; and (2) Uttar Pradesh (Northern Region), by far the largest of the states in population. At the western boundary of Uttar Pradesh lay the small territory of Delhi containing the nation's capital.

To the westward of the three Pradesh states, there existed after 1960 five states and five major languages, running from south to north as follows: (1) Maharashtra, with the Marathi tongue, created from Bombay in 1960; (2) Gujarat (predominantly Gujarati), the remaining portion of Bombay; (3) Rajasthan (Rajasthani) divorced in 1956 from the maharaja of Jaipur; (4) Punjab (Punjabi); and (5) Jammu-Kashmir (Kashmiri), held only partially by India, claimed by Pakistan as well, and free since 1952 from any commitment to the family of the former maharaja.

Eastward from the Pradesh states, there lay after 1956 four states and four major languages besides Hindi, running from south to northeast as follows: (1) Orissa, with the Oriya language; (2) West Bengal (Bengali); (3) Bihar, the second most populated of the states, predominantly Hindi in its language, but containing the Magadhi pocket representing India's most ancient politico-cultural component still identifiable today (see "Asian Independence," Chapter V); and (4) Assam, nearly cut off from the rest of India by East Pakistan, with its predominant language Assamese. At the end of 1960, thus, India contained 15 states and 14 major languages, with only one (Magadhi) of the latter obliged to accept a subordinate role to Hindi at the state level. Seven Indian territories administered by the national government included Delhi and two sets of islands. The combined population of the territories weighed less than half that of Assam, the least populated of the states.

The Indian nation faced the possibility of renewed widespread famine in 1957, with a lower supply of food than at any time since 1951-2. The critical hunger problem and the demands of a second five-year plan, starting 1956, prompted a search for large-scale economic aid. The quest proved difficult, for the loan adequate for a country of a few million population would meet but a small share of India's needs. The middle-of-the-road attitude Nehru had assumed in international matters added to his problems, since he had not endeared himself to either set of Cold War antagonists. Nevertheless, within a few years India received significant loans to avert famine and to develop urban industry. A small percentage of the money came from European communist countries, but a much greater sum from the World Bank and the United States. State and national governments with the cooperation of private capital succeeded in initiating slow economic progress. The states engaged in meaningful agrarian reform by limiting the size of land holdings, while encouraging private rather than collective farming. Both private and national public sectors placed considerable investment in an Indian steel industry.

Those anti-communists who did not like Nehru's neutrality found their antipathy confirmed when Nehru failed to speak out against the Soviet use of force in Hungary. They felt even more convinced when Nehru in 1957 appointed a sharp critic of the United States, Vengalil Krishnan Krishna Menon, as his minister of defense. Later in the quinquennium, however, when Nehru accepted the Dalai Lama from Tibet as a friendly refugee, when president Eisenhower visited India for five days, when Nehru showed by his intervention in Kerala that his friendship with communists abroad did not extend to tolerance for them at home, and when Indian troops

673

found themselves involved in skirmishes with the Communist Chinese, the Indian government established a reputation as a very important outpost of democracy in a most unpredictable world.

Burma entered a new political cycle in 1956 as the National United Front, a communist-oriented group, won nearly one-fifth of the seats in the lower house of parliament. Premier U Nu seemed to some of his colleagues to be overinfluenced by the new group's ideas. U Nu yielded the premiership to one of his critics, U Ba Swe, for nine months in 1956-7. After U Nu resumed the premiership, his Anti-Fascist People's Freedom League broke into two factions, the "Clean" party headed by U Nu and the "Stable" group led by U Ba Swe. "Clean" meant strict adherence to democracy, "Stable" an emphasis on continuing calm and order.

Discord between the two factions itself seemed to some non-participants to threaten Burmese parliamentary life. After the Burmese army engaged in a show of strength, U Nu resigned in favor of general Ne Win as premier (October 1958) until new elections could be held in a quiet atmosphere. In the balloting (February 1960), the Clean branch of the Anti-Fascist People's Freedom League won nearly three-fourths of the seats in parliament, the Stable faction most of the rest, and the National United Front hardly any. U Nu, resuming his position, renamed his group the Union party and proceeded to sign a boundary treaty with Communist China, as one more step in the solution of Burmese marginal problems before the further development of his program of democratic socialism.

Australia, whose population passed the 10,000,000-mark, continued under the rule of a coalition dominated by the Liberal party. The Laborites, many of whom dissented from Australia's support of the United Kingdom in the Suez Canal crisis, found their party torn by internal conflict. Labor received a smaller percentage of the vote in 1958 than it had in 1955. Robert Gordon Menzies, the Liberal prime minister, celebrated ten years in office in 1959, without having either deepened or lightened his country's commitment to socialism. New Zealand chose to be different in 1957 by electing a Labor government, the first since 1949, but voted Labor out of office again in late 1960.

The United Kingdom of Great Britain and Northern Ireland experienced disturbance through most of this period from its relations with other parts of the world. Its deep involvements in Middle East quarrels and participation in Cold War diplomacy have already been explained. (See "Old-Style Diplomacy" and "The Cold War.") Harold Macmillan, who followed Anthony Eden as prime minister on January 10, 1957, led his party to another victory at the polls in 1959, with the Conservatives gaining parliamentary seats lost by the Laborites while the small National Liberal section remained about the same. Macmillan's government granted independence to Ghana, Malaya, Nigeria, and Cyprus, and began to face new racial tensions in the African protectorate of Nyasaland. For the first time, sizeable racial conflicts arose in England itself, as families moved there in considerable numbers from Commonwealth lands in the West Indies, south Asia, and Africa. The United Kingdom tried unsuccessfully to weld the European Coal and Steel Community into a much wider free trade area (to include 13 European members in place of six), and then settled for an agreement called the European Free Trade Association comprising an "outer seven" of nations not included in the Coal and Steel Community.

Great Britain entered the nuclear age during this time period to a degree beyond that of other countries, setting up nuclear power stations as a basic part of its framework of electric power. New dangers to human, animal, and vegetable life appeared in the nuclear waste, making Britishers particularly aware of the perils accompanying the industry. The United Kingdom's first hydrogen bomb, exploded in the Pacific area in 1957, did nothing to alleviate the feeling among many of the British public that they and the rest of the world were living dangerously. The Labor party became wracked with debates over further cooperation with the United States in preparation for war, and left-wing Laborites protested the granting of bases to United States submarines equipped with nuclear missiles.

Other countries of the European northern tier also felt pressures related to the existence of the North Atlantic Treaty Organization and the European Free Trade Association, and experienced domestic problems including labor unrest due to poor economic conditions. In Sweden, the government of premier Tage Erlander, in office ten years in 1956, continued throughout the quinquennium, becoming a minority Social Democratic administration in 1957. Denmark at the same time moved in the other direction, from a Social Democratic minority regime to a coalition with a Social Democratic prime minister. Elections in Finland in 1958 gave a "democratic union" dominated by Communists the largest bloc (one-fourth) in the parliament, but Finland's government remained in the hands of a non-socialist party with a greater number of allies. The Labor party (with Einar Gerhardsen completing a tenth year in the premiership in 1958) continued with its majority in Norway. The coalition between People's and Socialist parties lasted in Austria through elections of 1959, the former holding one more seat in the lower house of parliament and providing the chancellor.

These northern democratic socialist countries did not grow more socialist year by year as did most of the communist lands. The political need to compromise (because of opposition strength) found its match in the moderation of the immediate objectives of the socialist parties themselves. Nevertheless, three of these nations (Sweden, Denmark, and Norway) had made deep com-

676

mitments to a socialist way of life well before
World War II. By 1960, they had also become cognizant of the fact that neither politically nor
economically could they survive alone. More than
most countries, they contributed generously to
worldwide and regional cooperative endeavors.

President Eisenhower, in a speech to a Republican party committee meeting July 27, 1960,
remarked concerning one of the Scandinavian countries that, according to an article he had read,
"their rate of suicide has gone up almost un-
believably," and "lack of ambition is discernible
on all sides." The system of the country, in the
thinking of the president, consisted of an "experiment of almost complete paternalism. . . ."
The Swedish people of whom he spoke (without ever
mentioning their name) might have objected to the
interpretation of their statistics, or disagreed
with the label "paternalism" for the actions of a
democratic state. On the other hand, they might
have agreed that a certain "lack of ambition"
existed, especially in the acquiring of fortunes.

In regard to other charges in the Saturday
Evening Post (December 1959), the U. S. News &
World Report (March 7, 1960), and the Reader's
Digest (March 1960) -- the president had obviously read one of these -- Sweden suffered in
the same manner as more affluent families in the
United States. These statements dealt with high
rates of robbery, drunkenness, and juvenile
delinquency for reasons other than despair and
poverty. People had simply not learned to take
maximum advantage of the leisure and security
available in the 1950's to the great majority of
persons in Sweden and a much smaller percentage
of moneyed families in private-enterprise countries.

Herein lay the possibility of a great emptiness in the new age, as Chapter III has already
stated. Could people on a large scale learn to
substitute new efforts in science, art, and religion for the excitement to be derived from

gaining a material fortune or seeking power over other persons? "They long for something," said one Swedish social worker to the <u>Saturday</u> <u>Evening</u> <u>Post</u> regarding Swedish adolescents. Another Swede explained, "The energy you use for the fight for life is left free here. As yet we haven't found the way to channel this energy. . . ."

Three of the four Latin American countries with some commitment to democratic socialism had not come face to face with the problems of the new age. Mexico continued in rather serene fashion through this period, its Institutional Revolutionary party winning by a large majority as usual in 1958, when Adolfo López Mateos became president to succeed Adolfo Ruiz Cortines. The Mexican economy developed at a rapid rate in both public and private sectors, but the high rate of increase in the population prevented anything more than modest per capita gains each year. In 1960, the left wing of the ruling party declared its solidarity with Fidel Castro. Lázaro Cárdenas, highly regarded by most Mexicans since his administration in the 1930's, became a spokesman for this more radical group, which called for a greater sense of urgency in agrarian reform. López Mateos declared in response that his government represented the far left, that it intended to behave in such manner, and that it would not sever ties with the Castro regime.

Venezuela, which joined the second quarter with a more solid base of democracy than that of Mexico, found itself also faced with enthusiasts for Castro. (See "Two American Revolutions.") Bolivia experienced troubles of an analogous but more complicated nature. Monetary inflation had accompanied Bolivia's social revolution since 1952, as the government printed money without backing. The process reached catastrophic dimensions in 1956 when the <u>boliviano</u> or Bolivian peso, four years earlier quoted at 60 to the dollar, reached the height of 14,000 to the dollar. The United States government and the Inter-

678

national Monetary Fund stipulated that Bolivia, to receive further aid, would have to adopt a National Monetary Stabilization program laid out by George Jackson Eder, a citizen of the United States and representative of the Fund. When the moderate revolutionary leader Hernán Siles Zuazo, vice-president under Víctor Paz Estenssoro, became president in 1956, his name became involved immediately with that of Eder.

Land for the farmers and decent wages for the miners constituted the two great emphases of the Bolivian revolution. Eder, following economic theory popular in the United States, placed a freeze upon wages while allowing prices to rise -- to whatever turned out to be their "natural" level. In more affluent lands, such a policy would lead to worker-consumer distress and complaints. In a country as poor as Bolivia, it meant the end of the revolution for the sizeable bloc of miners and their families. Eder not only controlled wages but abolished the government stores where miners could buy food and produce at cheaper rates than elsewhere. In 1957, Juan Lechín Oquendo, head of the miners, broke with Siles over the implementation of this program. In 1958, ex-president Paz expressed sympathy with Lechín and the miners. By 1960, Eder's program had ended the runaway inflation at the expense of the country's working-class people (prices had more than octupled 1955-60). On August 6, 1960, by an overwhelming majority, Víctor Paz became president and Juan Lechín vice-president of this poverty-stricken land, running again as the candidates of the Revolutionary National Movement.

One segment of the population of Uruguay lay closer to the Scandinavian scene than the other second-quarter countries of Latin America. That portion consisted of the two-thirds classified as urban, of which nearly half lived in the capital city. Uruguay's socialism had never reached its countryside; there large landowners held the farming districts as firmly as in 1911. The proceeds of the farms had paid the country's bills;

for this reason as much as any, presumably, they remained unmolested. When inflation soared (prices nearly tripled) and strikes proliferated during this quinquennium, Uruguay underwent political change. The Blanco party came into power in 1959 after more than half a century of Colorado rule. (The names of the parties are colors chosen in the nineteenth century, having nothing to do with race or communism.) The Blancos combined rural flavor and urban dissatisfaction with a regime that had made urban Uruguay over into a component of the chiefly-north-European new age.

Democratic socialism found its first bastion in Africa in the new state of Ghana. Kwame Nkrumah and his Convention People's party placed the stress on socialism rather than on democracy, however, almost from the beginning, with oppositionist members of parliament falling subject to arrest. The Malagasy Republic, Senegal, and the Central African Republic remained slower in their approach to socialism. For all four of these states, see "African Independence."

When a coup removed Turkey from the second to the fourth quarter in 1960, Israel became a lone socialist state in the Middle East, isolated from its neighbors more than ever by its collusion with the United Kingdom and France against Egypt in 1956. Its situation seemed symbolized by Israeli efforts to make agreements with new African countries on the other side of the Muslim world, and by the spiriting out from Argentina of Adolf Eichmann, prominent Nazi from World War II, for trial in Israel on grounds of "crimes against humanity." Prime minister Ben-Gurion completed his tenth year in office in 1960.

The Socialist party of Japan failed to keep pace with Japanese population growth, but remained the largest functioning socialist party in the non-socialist world. The Social Democratic party of West Germany and the Labor party of Brazil, second and third in size, showed normal growth in this period. In Italy, the left-wing

Socialist party under the leadership of Pietro Nenni criticized the policies of the Soviet Union in Hungary in 1956, and made unsuccessful moves toward affinity with the much smaller and more moderate Democratic Socialist party. The Socialist party of France saw its representation in parliament reduced nearly by half when Charles de Gaulle instituted the Fifth French Republic and changed the voting system. The Labor party of the Netherlands and the Socialist party of Belgium continued important in those countries, while the Social Democratic (formerly Socialist) party of Switzerland lost a little ground in elections of 1959. In Peru, after elections of 1956, members of the aprista movement, basically democratic socialist in ideology, secured some influence in the congress through an Independent Parliamentary Democratic Front.

The third quarter of the world spectrum received the adherence or readherence of Nigeria, Cameroun, Ivory Coast, Chad, Somalia, Dahomey, Togo, the Congo Republic, and Mauritania in Sub-Sahara Africa; of Argentina, Colombia, Peru, Guatemala, Haiti, and Honduras in the Americas; of Malaya in the Orient; and of Tunisia and Cyprus in the Middle East. Those 18 countries (Gabon is not counted here) made no match in population, however, for five lands departing from the third quarter -- Pakistan, Indonesia, Syria (merged into the United Arab Republic), Iraq, and Laos. Thus, the democratic private-enterprise portion of the world's non-colonial population dropped from 31% to 27%. The distribution in 1960 included 13 countries in the Americas, 6 in the Orient, 9 in Sub-Sahara Africa, 8 in Europe, and 5 in the Middle East.

The United States of America (166-181,000, 000) moved through this five-year period under the presidency of Dwight Eisenhower, elected over Adlai Stevenson a second time in 1956. The United States Congress, on the other hand, continued with a Democratic party majority in both houses.

681

The Republican party had in effect chosen a president more popular than itself. President Eisenhower suffered two serious illnesses during this
period, ileitis in 1956 and a minor stroke in
1957, which combined with his heart attack of
1955 caused extraordinary precautions to be taken
as to the welfare of the nation if he should become incapacitated. His physical problems did
not continue, but he did face a difficult world
situation (see "Old-Style Diplomacy," "Two American Revolutions," and "The Cold War"), an embarrassing missiles lag (see "Man in Space"), a very
tight racial problem, and a decelerating economy.
In a period of prosperity at the end of his first
term, Congress passed legislation for a new system of interstate highways, intended to span the
country and connect most of its cities. Alaska
and Hawaii, outside the new highway plan because
of the non-contiguity of their territory, became
states of the United States in 1959.

The Supreme Court school desegregation decisions of 1954-5 had left much racial tension in
their wake. (See "Three Steps in Human Dignity,"
Chapter VI.) Seven states in the southeastern
part of the country made no effort to comply at
the primary and secondary levels. White students
first and the trustees of the institution afterward denied Autherine Lucy, a Negro young woman,
entrance to the University of Alabama. The university itself admitted her under federal court
order, but soon found cause for her expulsion.
In most states where segregation had prevailed,
however, college and university Negro students
began to be admitted to formerly all-white
schools. Desegregation occurred also at primary
and secondary levels in several "border" states,
whose proportion of Negro inhabitants remained
lower than in the "deep south." Little Rock, the
capital of Arkansas, achieved world renown when
Orval Faubus, the governor of that state, used
national guardsmen under his command to prevent
nine Negro children from entering a formerly all-
white school. Three weeks later, after seeming
hesitation on president Eisenhower's part, other

federal troops cleared the way for the admittance of the children.

In 1956, the Supreme Court declared unconstitutional the practice of racially segregated seating on buses. The plight of the Negro bus riders in Montgomery, Alabama, had come to the attention of the world through a boycott organized by Martin Luther King, a Negro pastor. (For the details, see "Religion.") In 1957, Congress passed a mild civil rights law providing for prosecution of persons who denied to others their constitutional right of suffrage. Neither this statute nor the Supreme Court decisions accomplished much during this period in disturbing most facets of segregation in the Southeast. Self-inspired moves in the direction of desegregation by Negroes and white "liberal" friends brought on a wave of bombings by groups of Southern whites newly organized to fight the change. Then, in 1960, Negro students working alone (the first four in Greensboro, North Carolina) began a series of pacific "sit-ins," in which they approached an all-white eating establishment for service, waited if they received no attention, left if required to do so, but continued to return. The Montgomery boycott and the Greensboro sit-ins provided clear evidence that the Negroes of the United States intended to take their own future at least partly into their own hands.

Strikes by labor unions again became common in this period as skilled labor did what it could to keep up with the cost of living. The consumer price index rose 10% as the government, though not involved in warfare, continued to spend heavily for the war that hardly anyone wanted but many believed might come. The country suffered an economic recession in 1957-8, with the gross national product per capita declining. The rise for the entire quinquennium amounted to less than 2% as measured in constant rather than current dollars.

The Democratic party gained a large number of

seats in congressional elections of 1958, so that
the coalition of Republicans and southern Democrats that had kept Congress conservative gave
way to dominance by the Democratic liberal wing.
In 1960, when the Republicans chose vice-president Nixon as their candidate for president and
the Democrats chose John Fitzgerald Kennedy, considerable doubt arose as to who might win. President Eisenhower withheld his blessing for Nixon
until very late in the contest. Kennedy, a Roman
Catholic, had to face the fact that the United
States had never elected a Catholic president.
Kennedy won the race, though with a very narrow
margin of the popular vote. The Democrats also
retained decisive control over both houses of
Congress. Harry Byrd of Virginia, running for
the presidency as a racial segregationist, did
well only in Alabama and Mississippi.

Brazil managed to make its way through this
period with its democracy intact despite a tripling of its cost of living. President Juscelino
Kubitschek, inaugurated early in 1956, performed
the feat without accomplishing anything substantial for his multitude of economically deprived
people. Loans from he United States and the International Monetary Fund helped to stem the tide
of inflationary disaster, but only for a moment
at a time. Kubitschek declined proffered advice
from Washington concerning the cure for inflation
-- the same as that prescribed for Bolivia -- on
the well-founded ground that it might lead to
social revolution.

Kubitschek himself offered three ideas for
which he would be remembered, despite his inability to deal with Brazil's big problems in his
time. Early in his regime, he proposed the
building of a new capital to help focus Brazilian
attention on the country's interior. Traditionally, most national action had taken place within
the territory no more than 200 miles from the
coastline. Despite strong opposition, the very
modern city of Brasília arose more than 600 miles
inland from the old capital Rio de Janeiro. In

684

1958, Kubitschek proposed a vast plan of aid from the United States to Latin America, later dubbed Operation Pan-America. His proposal resulted in the establishment in 1960 of an Inter-American Development Bank. Finally, in 1959 he suggested a new Brazilian agency, the Superintendency for the Development of the Northeast (SUDENE), to change conditions in the hungriest corner of Brazil.

Kubitschek's non-socialist Social Democratic party lost the presidency in the elections of late 1960, but retained the largest bloc of seats in the parliament. The National Democratic Union backed Jânio Quadros, who professed support for the Castro regime in Cuba and declared his interest in social reform. The party did not favor the same ideas but thought Quadros, a colorful personality, might win. Quadros did win, together with vice-president-elect João Goulart of the Labor party (succeeding himself), though no campaign pact existed between them. The Labor party also did well in the lower house of the congress, nearly catching up with the National Democratic Union. The minority Social Progressive and Republican parties remained about the same.

Argentina moved from the fourth quarter of the spectrum to the third in 1958 under the guidance of its military arm. Pedro Eugenio Aramburu, provisional president since November 1955 (two months after the deposition of Juan Perón), declared in 1956 his intention to revoke the Perón-sponsored constitution of 1949 and return to the principles of the previous charter written in 1853. The return to democracy in Argentina, however, remained far from easy. The chief difficulty lay in the fact that the Peronista party, now illegal, represented a large segment of the voters, the working-class people who had admired Perón. The Radicals, who united constituted the strongest force in the country, split on personalities in 1956 into the Intransigent and People's Radical parties. The Peronistas "won" in elections for a constitutional convention in 1957

685

through the medium of over 2,000,000 blank ballots (Juan Perón had suggested the strategy).
The People's Radicals and the Intransigent Radicals came in second and third, and the convention adjourned without agreement.

In 1958 Arturo Frondizi, leader of the Intransigent Radicals, became president while his
party won a majority in the parliament. Frondizi
won, however, only because large numbers of the
peronistas voted for him. Somehow he hoped to
reincorporate them into Argentine political
life. Frondizi's chief immediate difficulty lay
in the fight against severe inflation, as prices
quintupled during this quinquennium. The cure he
adopted resembled the Bolivian program that
Kubitschek rejected in Brazil. The workers
tightened their belts as the government froze
wages while allowing prices to find their "natural" level. Perón, who had done nothing of
structural permanence for the workers, had at
least enforced a rise in wages each year to make
up for the climb in prices. In congressional
elections in 1960, blank ballots cast chiefly by
peronistas again came out first in the tally with
the two branches of the old Radical party taking
second and third place.

In elections of 1957-8, the voters of Canada
changed the complexion of their government. The
Liberal party of Louis St. Laurent lost first
place in parliament in 1957, for the first time
since 1935. Nine months later, it receded into a
role smaller than that formerly played by the
Progressive Conservatives. John Diefenbaker, the
new Progressive Conservative prime minister, took
a strong stand in protecting Canadian economic
interests against those of the United States,
though he cooperated with Washington in matters
of defense. Canada constructed and inaugurated
an important Seaway Route along the St. Lawrence
River. Retiring prime minister St. Laurent had
taken the initiative in this matter after many
years of hesitation by the United States, along
part of whose northern border the St. Lawrence

River lay.

Colombia moved rather tentatively during this period to reenter the realm of democratic private enterprise. Alberto Lleras Camargo, leader of the Liberals, and Laureano Gómez, head of the right-wing branch of the Conservatives, met in Spain in 1956, agreeing to work together to rid the country of its dictator Gustavo Rojas Pinilla. (See "Three Losses for Democracy," Chapter VI.) When Rojas took steps to prolong his tenure in office, elements of the army friendly to Lleras and Gómez deposed Rojas and set up a military junta to supervise new elections. The leadership among Liberals and Conservatives hoped not only to terminate a very willful dictatorship but also to bring to an end what they now termed la violencia, the bloodshed the countryside had experienced ever since the bogotazo of 1948. At the behest of the leaders, the country approved in 1957 a constitutional amendment declaring in effect that anyone running for office in Colombia for a period of twelve years would have to present himself as a Liberal or a Conservative, and that in all branches of the government except the presidency the principle of parity between the two parties would be maintained for the same length of time. The system of proportional representation would prevail within the two parties.

After the leaders chose and the people elected Alberto Lleras Camargo president in 1958, a new agreement specified that the presidency would alternate between the two parties, and that the pact should remain in effect for 16 rather than 12 years. In 1959, these provisions also became a part of the constitution. The Colombian senate tried Rojas Pinilla and stripped him of his political rights as factions within both parties began to suggest changes in the "National Front" arrangements. The government of Lleras Camargo busied itself with plans for social reform, hoping to stave off new disaster.

Peru returned to democracy when Manuel Odría,

who had usurped power in 1948, decided to hold free elections in 1956. Odría did not permit APRA to participate as a party, but some _apristas_ obtained election to the congress as independents while many _aprista_ voters supported Manuel Prado y Ugarteche for president. The Democratic party of Prado, essentially conservative in nature, soon found itself sharing the spotlight with the socialist-oriented, _aprista_-dominated Independent Parliamentary Democratic Front, the second largest group in the congress by 1960. Víctor Raúl Haya de la Torre returned to the country as APRA, legalized by Prado, prepared to nominate Haya for the presidency.

By 1960, democratic private enterprise prevailed in seven smaller Latin American countries. Chile, still greatly troubled by inflation (prices again nearly quadrupled), turned to a businessman for its president in 1958. The (nineteenth-century) Liberals who supported him in Congress held fewer seats than the (middle-of-the-road) Radicals who formed a part of his opposition. Ecuador chose a conservative for president 1956-60, and to follow him José María Velasco Ibarra, who had held the position three times before (1934-5, 1944-7, 1952-6) and professed an interest in social reform, but relied on a largely personalist following. Costa Rica held elections in 1958, in which the divided followers of José Figueres lost to an opponent for the presidency. Panama changed presidents peacefully in 1956 and 1960, but after the Egyptian seizure of the Suez Canal became the scene of demonstrations against sole sovereignty by the United States in the Panama Canal Zone.

Three smaller Latin American countries moved from the fourth quarter to the third. Carlos Castillo Armas, chosen for president of Guatemala by the United States Central Intelligence Agency in 1954, was assassinated in 1957. Demonstrations occurred when a friend of Castillo became the announced winner in elections held later that year. New and more neutrally managed elections

688

in 1958 gave the presidency to a general who until 1944 had served a dictator, but who now possessed his own (conservative) National Democratic
Reconciliation party, nicknamed Redención. When
the dictator-president of Haiti resigned in 1956,
a four-way race for the presidency developed; a
physician won in 1957 in the first fairly free
election Haiti had known. Honduras saw another
dictator ousted and another physician elected
during the same two years. Honduras, however,
had experienced a few fair elections earlier in
its history. Furthermore, the doctor elected in
Honduras turned his attention to social reform,
while the one in Haiti within a year had turned
to fear and intimidation.

The government of Japan continued its devotion to the democratic private-enterprise point
of view, though noisy demonstrations gave ample
indication of disagreement with official policy.
The Liberal-Democratic party supplied all the
prime ministers, Hatoyama Ichiro serving until
late 1956 and Kishi Nobusuke 1957-60. Japan and
the Soviet Union made a joint declaration in
1956, ending the previous state of war but leaving the dispute over Sakhalin and the Kuril
Islands for the future. Japan also made reparations agreements with countries Japanese armies
had occupied.

Premier Kishi, after elections of 1958 that
preserved intact the clear majority of the Liberal-Democratic party in the parliament, proceeded to rewrite the security pact with the
United States. The new version, finished early
in 1960, placed Japan on a more nearly equal
level with the United States than the pact of
1951. Nevertheless, the Socialists and various
youth groups opposed it, favoring neutrality in
its stead. The police not only clashed with the
demonstrating youth groups but prevented the Socialists from voting against the approval of the
pact. Further demonstrations forced the postponement, and effectively the cancellation, of
the planned visit of president Eisenhower to

Japan. Later, fanatics of the far right stabbed premier Kishi three times and assassinated the head of the Socialist party. New elections held in November 1960 left party standings about the same.

President Ramón Magsaysay, popular leader of the Philippines, died in an airplane crash during the last year of his term, in March 1957. His Nationalist vice-president, Carlos García, succeeded him and won election to his own term. Liberal Diosdado Macapagal became the new vice-president, though the Liberals held less than one-third the strength of the Nationalists in the legislature. García followed a more nationalist course than his predecessors, especially in his dealings with the United States, which agreed to give up some of its military reservations in the islands. A return to pre-Magsaysay days came with a regrowth of substantial corruption.

President Syngman Rhee of South Korea during this period added his name to the long list of individuals, once popular in their positions, who refused to give up gracefully with the attainment of considerable age. In 1956, at 81, he secured election for a third term, though Chang Myon of the new opposition Democratic (liberal-conservative) party became vice-president. In 1958, the Liberals supporting Rhee lost their clear majority in the parliament. In 1959, the Democrats protested that the government intended to use a new anti-subversion law against them rather than against Rhee's old enemies, the communists. When elections in March 1960 produced a fourth term for Rhee and the announced victory by a wide margin of Rhee's choice for the vice-presidency over Chang, the Democrats cried fraud and students demonstrated. The army, with support from South Korea's mentor, the United States, sided this time with the students. Syngman Rhee resigned, and his running mate committed suicide. New elections in July produced an assembly that converted South Korea into a parliamentary-style republic, with Chang Myon as its first premier.

With the Liberal party smashed, the Democratic party split into "new" (liberal) and "old" (conservative) wings.

Ceylon and Cambodia continued in the third quarter as smaller states of the Orient. The Sri Lanka (or "Ceylon") Freedom party in 1956 took the majority of seats in the Ceylonese parliament from the United National group. Solomon West Ridgeway Dias Bandaranaike became prime minister, facing a series of riots by persons clamoring for the recognition of Tamil as an official language along with Sinhalese. He retained his position until his assassination in 1959. His widow, Sirimavo Bandaranaike, succeeded him after two elections in 1960. As the world's first woman premier, she held the backing not only of the majority Freedom party, but of some Marxists and most Tamils. Cambodia remained under prime minister Norodom Sihanouk, who angered both sides in the Cold War by his policy of neutrality while accepting aid, but who maintained popularity with his own people through the elections of 1960. His so-called Popular Socialist Community (not really socialist) took over the legislature, and upon the death of his father made Sihanouk "chief of state."

Malaya (population 6,000,000), independent as of August 31, 1957, spoke the Indonesian-Malay tongue it held in common with Sumatra and part of Java, a wide area ruled in the twelfth and thirteenth centuries by a government in Sumatra. Its Muslim faith had come to Malaya with Arabs who wielded influence in the fifteenth century, after the demise of the Sumatra-based empire and its replacement by small states. The Arab influence gave way to that of the Portuguese after 1511, of the Dutch after 1641, and of the British after 1824. British decisions by the time of World War I placed two Malay states inside the colony called the Straits Settlements, four inside the protectorate called the Federated Malay States, and five under separate protectorate arrangements. They all combined in the union (1946) and

691

federation (1948) called Malaya, under British protection -- until independence in 1957 as a parliamentary regime with membership in the Commonwealth, under its own head of government chosen from among the sultans who still ruled the individual states. Communist guerrilla bands posed a serious problem for Malaya upon the achievement of independence, but by the end of 1960 seemed no longer a threat.

West Germany kept Konrad Adenauer on as chancellor throughout this time period, though many persons in and out of the country felt that his stern anti-communist policy needed some revising. Adenauer had reached the age of 81 when elections of 1957 confirmed a slight majority for his Christian Democratic party in the lower house of parliament. Two years later, he came near accepting the honorary position of president, but rejected the idea when he discovered he could not get approval for his own choice for his previous position. In 1956, the Adenauer regime began West German rearmament, with the approval of its NATO allies. During the same year, Adenauer attempted to get rid of proportional representation, to enhance the Christian Democratic majority expected in the elections, but failed when both Social Democrats and Free Democrats opposed him. Most of the Free Democrats then deserted him, breaking his coalition. The Saar, or Saarland, which France had retained after World War II as after World War I, returned to West Germany on the first day of 1957. Continued prosperity helped the Christian Democrats win in the elections of that year. The Social Democrats in 1959-60, hoping soon to break through to victory, moderated their opposition to West Germany's private-enterprise economy and ended their opposition to NATO.

Italy advanced rapidly in industry while its social and political scene remained about the same. A government headed by premier Antonio Segni (1955-7) represented the usual coalition of Christian Democrats with small parties of the center. The following regime, headed by Adone Zoli, constituted minority rule by the Christian Democrats, almost alone. The former standing of parties remained almost unchanged in elections of 1958 -- the Christian Democrats far in the lead but lacking a majority, followed in turn by the Communists, the left-wing Socialists, the Italian Social Movement, and the Democrats (the last-named the Monarchists in disguise). The Christian Democrats continued to provide the prime ministers -- Amintore Fanfani with a coalition cabinet, Antonio Segni (1959-60) with a minority government, and after a few months Fanfani with another minority regime. Neither the "opening to the left" nor the "opening to the right" had yet transpired, and Italy remained a land of privilege for a few and of desperation for many. As if to emphasize the point, in 1957 the government decided not to press charges against members of the aristocracy in the death of Wilma Montesi, a call girl. The victim in this case had participated in an orgy with the accused, who abandoned her on a beach -- to drown -- in 1953.

The Fourth Republic of France became shattered by too many crises in a row. Its last elections, on January 2, 1956, proved as inconclusive as ever. After them, Socialist Guy Mollet (see "Old-Style Diplomacy") served as premier 1956-7 for a minority coalition of Socialists, Radicals, and others. The next three cabinets (see "African Independence") also came from the center, the first as another minority grouping, the second and third representing the Popular Republicans, Radicals and Socialists. Charles de Gaulle, the last premier of the Fourth French Republic, served with a non-political cabinet designed to save the country from civil war over Algeria. The Fifth French Republic came into being October 5, 1958, and De Gaulle became its president January 8, 1959.

De Gaulle's steadiest support in the new lower house of parliament came from a personalist party founded in 1958 -- the Union for the New

Republic, holding the largest number but not a majority of seats. The conservative Independents and Peasants for Social Action (based on the former Independent party), who generally agreed with De Gaulle on domestic matters, held the second largest place. In decreasing order followed the Popular Republicans, Socialists, and Radicals, now all reduced in size, and a Unity of the Republic group favoring a more complete integration of Algeria with France. President De Gaulle had regrouped the assembly this much through his personal popularity and his rejection of the proportional representation in vogue since 1945, though the new regime retained the Third Republic system of a run-off vote. The Communist party became a small minority in the assembly because of these factors and the wrangling over the Soviet intervention in Hungary. The president, however, not the legislature, would determine the policy the Fifth French Republic would follow. In 1958-9, De Gaulle made proposals for a reorganization of NATO and decided that United States fighter planes could no longer be based in France. In early 1960, the parliament gave him authority to legislate by decree for a year in matters affecting national security. In February, despite the objections of the United Nations General Assembly, France exploded its first test atomic bomb in Algeria.

In the Netherlands, Socialist Willem Drees continued as premier until December 1958, with a coalition cabinet of Socialists and the Catholic People's party, nearly even in vote. Indonesia decided to drop its union with the Netherlands early in 1956, as the controversy over the ownership of the western part of New Guinea continued. Elections in early 1959 gave the Catholic People's party a small edge over the Socialists. The latter then entered the opposition while the Catholic People's party formed a new ruling coalition with three minor parties.

Belgium continued under the Socialist-headed coalition in office since 1954 until new elections of 1958 brought about a coalition led by the Social Christians. In 1959-60, the country passed through considerable turmoil over the question of independence for the colony of Belgian Congo. In Greece, elections in 1956 and 1958, making some provision for proportional representation again, nevertheless gave a majority in both instances to the National Radical Union formed to succeed the Greek Rally and to back the personalist rule of Constantino Karamanlis. The United Democratic Left, containing many persons of Marxist orientation, won a protest vote of nearly one-fourth in 1958. The Greek people became upset by the independence of Cyprus, with a Greek-speaking majority among its people, since the cry for union between Greece and Cyprus had run strong. The chief controversy in Switzerland during this time period concerned the matter of woman suffrage, denied at the national level in 1958. Veteran Eamon De Valera acted as prime minister of Ireland again from 1957 to 1959, when he became the president. His party, the Fianna Fail, continued with the majority it won in 1957. The tiny republic of San Marino may be said to have shifted from the second quarter to the third in 1957 when its Communist and left-wing Socialist leadership attempted to remain in office past its term, only to be removed by a Christian Democratic and right-wing Socialist coalition reinforced by Italian strength. The new coalition became a majority by switches in allegiance immediately prior to the crisis.

The adherence of nine nations of Sub-Sahara Africa to the third quarter during this quinquennium meant simply that they carried forward the policies formed before they became independent. Their stories -- that of Nigeria, by far the largest in population; Cameroun, independent in January 1960; Togo, in April; Somalia, in July; Dahomey, Ivory Coast, Chad, and the Congo Republic, in August; and Mauritania, in November -- all received attention in the section "African Independence."

Iran remained the largest of the democratic private-enterprise countries in the Middle East. Its democracy, though not strong, recovered somewhat during this period of time. A seven-year plan for economic development began in 1956. The shah, Mohammad Reza Pahlavi, took measures in 1957 to organize two political parties. In 1958, he declared an interest in social and judicial reform. In 1959, he indicated the seriousness of his intentions concerning agrarian reform by distributing crown and state lands to needy farmers, and placing a maximum on the amount of land wealthy families could hold. In 1960, elections included the two parties given impetus by the shah along with other parties organized independently (though Tudeh remained excluded). When complaints came to the shah about unfair pressures by the party favoring him most, he ordered that the elections be repeated in 1961.

Four smaller countries of the Middle East pertained to the third quarter after Iraq and Syria deserted the band, the former by revolution and the latter by incorporation into the United Arab Republic. For the involvement in international politics of Jordan and Lebanon, see "The Cold War." For the emergence of Tunisia as an independent democratic state, see "African Independence."

The island of Cyprus in the eastern Mediterranean Sea became independent as a presidential-style republic on August 16, 1960. A Greek population had resided on this island for over three thousand years. Turks moved in after 1562, when the island became a part of the Ottoman Empire. The United Kingdom began to administer Cyprus for the Ottoman Empire in 1878, and took it over completely in 1914. In the post-World War II surge of self-determination for colonial peoples, many of the Greek-speaking community on Cyprus wanted union with Greece. The Turkish-speaking people, a minority of one-fourth, objected to the proposed union. The British found themselves caught between two parties, as they had a decade earlier in Palestine. In a compromise solution, Cyprus won its independence with slightly over 500,000 population, under Greek Orthodox archbishop Makarios III as its first president and a representative of the Turkish community as vice-president, as well as Greek-Turkish ratios for the cabinet and legislature.

The fourth -- authoritarian private-enterprise -- quarter of the spectrum increased from 10% to 17% of the world's non-colonial population during this period. The adherence of Pakistan and Indonesia contributed mightily, and that of Turkey substantially, to this change. Iraq, Syria, and Laos also joined the band, Syria by incorporation with Egypt in the new United Arab Republic. The new states of Congo and Sudan joined the fourth quarter after brief experiences with democracy, while Morocco, the Voltaic Republic, and Niger entered at independence. The entry of these countries easily outbalanced the departure of eight Latin American states -- Cuba for the first quarter, Venezuela the second, and Argentina, Colombia, Peru, Guatemala, Haiti, and Honduras the third. At the end of 1960, the fourth quarter held 7 countries in the Orient, 2 in Europe, 8 in the Middle East, 7 in Sub-Sahara Africa, and 4 in the Americas.

Pakistan (with a population increase from 89,000,000 to slightly over 100,000,000) moved rather easily from ineffectual democracy to more energetic authoritarianism. On March 23, 1956, the nation adopted a new constitution, dropping its dominion status and denominating itself an "Islamic republic" within the Commonwealth of Nations. Hussain Shaheed Suhrawardy from East Pakistan, succeeding Chaudhri Muhammad Ali as prime minister in September, made a determined attempt to hold the new republic together. Suhrawardy resigned after little more than a year, however, because of linguistic problems in West Pakistan. His two successors served even shorter terms.

697

On October 7, 1958, the president of Pakistan placed the nation under martial law, stating that he wished to avoid bloodshed. He appointed Mohammad Ayub Khan, the head of the army, to administer the program. On October 27, Ayub made himself president and prime minister, abrogating the constitution of 1956. Ayub professed a desire to lead Pakistan to a more genuine democracy. He began in 1959 with an agrarian reform program, redistributing the lands of some of the largest landholders, and with the election and appointment of persons to serve in "basic democracies" on the strictly local level. In 1960, the representatives of these units gave him an overwhelming endorsement to write a new constitution during a new presidential term of five years. Ayub moved the capital of Pakistan from Karachi to Rawalpindi, near which he intended to construct a new city of Islamabad.

President Sukarno himself took Indonesia into the fourth quarter after a shift in his ideas, confirmed and hardened by action taken by the United States Central Intelligence Agency. Elections for a provisional parliament and a separate constituent assembly, expected to work each in its own sphere simultaneously, had taken place only in late 1955, six years after Indonesian independence. None of the four largest parties successful in the balloting held the same views as Sukarno. Instead, their chief enthusiasms ran respectively to the new nation (the Nationalist party), the Muslim faith (the Muslim Council and the Muslim Schoomen League), and Marxism of the communist brand. While Sukarno also felt enthusiasm for the new nation and religion, the masses failed to comprehend his attachment to democratic socialism.

Sukarno traveled to North America in May 1956, passing more than half a month in the United States. There he saw representative democracy in action but little interest in socialism and very small enthusiasm for Indonesia as a nation. In the same year, he spent half of

698

September in the Soviet Union and half of October in Communist China. Sukarno came away from Moscow and Peking impressed by the vigor of their programs, which seemed to him to suit Indonesian needs. Especially, he admired the freedom of leaders who did not have to contend with a multiplicity of parties each seeking its own ends. Sukarno felt that he must now choose between representative democracy and socialism, and within a few weeks made his new thinking plain.

"Let us be frank about it, brothers and sisters," he said. "We made a very great mistake in 1945 when we urged the establishment of parties, parties, parties. . . . I do not want to become a dictator, brothers and sisters. . . . That is against my spirit. I am a democrat. I am really a democrat. But my democracy is not liberal democracy. . . . What I would like to see in this Indonesia of ours is guided democracy, democracy with leadership, but still democracy." Sukarno thus strove to convince himself of the validity of his position through stress on the reinterpretation of a word. By taking his new stand, he lost the support of the major party closest to his previous policy, the liberal Masjumi (Muslim Council). His strongest backing now came from the Indonesian Communist party. Reactions from the Nationalist party and the conservative Muslim Schoolmen League lay between the extremes.

The Masjumi party, weakest of the four major political groups on the island of Java, held by far the strongest allegiance on the other islands. Disaffection in those islands, a heritage from the days when their leaders dealt separately with the Dutch, mounted after Sukarno's return from China to the point of armed rebellion. A first provisional rebel government appeared on the island of Sumatra in December 1956. Other rebel regimes followed on Sumatra and other islands. President Sukarno, in the meantime, sketched in the details of his plan. His guided democracy would simply retain on a permanent basis the government that had prevailed on a temporary basis -- a cabinet and an advisory council drawn from all points of view, but appointed by the president rather than chosen by the people.

In February 1958, a central rebel regime at Padang, Sumatra, called itself the Revolutionary Government of the Republic of Indonesia. The United States of America extended aid to the rebels through its CIA, providing even planes and pilots to bomb strategic points held by Jakarta. One such plane-and-pilot combination, shot down on May 18, received the acknowledgement of its government only on May 27. (Two more years passed before a similar incident over Soviet territory.) John Foster Dulles, the United States secretary of state, feigned friendship for Jakarta all through this situation, choosing May 20 for new promises of arms and rice. In June 1958, the Sukarno government won a decisive victory. From this point on, however, relations with Washington remained cool.

Faced with inflation that more than doubled food prices in this five-year period, Sukarno issued a five-point program in 1959. It proved a sharp contrast to the goals he had enunciated in June 1945. No longer did Sukarno speak of internationalism, or of belief in one God. Guided democracy and the constitution of 1945 replaced representative democracy, while "Indonesian identity" provided a focus for nationalism. A "guided economy" and "Indonesian socialism" would achieve social justice. In July 1959, Sukarno dissolved the elected constituent assembly and reimposed his original consitution. In March 1960, the elected parliament gave way to an appointed advisory council. In August, the government outlawed the Musjumi party, though the move made little difference, since the parties had already lost their chief function. Sukarno had initiated his new program. Sukarno had built a reputation, however, as a person more adept with broad ideas than with concrete measures to implement them.

700

Thailand sank ever deeper into autocratic rule as quarrels developed with Cambodia and Laos, and as Thailand acquired distinction as an anti-communist crusader nation. Pibul Songgram, who had become prime minister and the strong man of his country through three coups in 1947-51, lost his office through another coup in 1957. The prime minister's prerogative of choosing half the legislature continued through the short terms of the following two men. Still another uprising in 1958 gave Sarit Thanarat the power. Sarit made himself prime minister, abolished the legislature and the constitution of 1932, and set about preparing a new basic charter.

South Viet-Nam received a new constitution in October 1956, as president Ngo Dinh Diem sought to give his regime a more democratic look. The form of government would be that of a republic, with the president given considerable authority. In elections of 1959, however, supporters of Diem made up most of the candidates, his National Revolutionary Movement winning well over half the seats and friendly independents many of the remainder. Diem's chief opponent won election to the parliament, but Diem had him arrested when he entered the chamber. Diem carried out about one-fourth of a planned agrarian reform during this period, following the advice of the United States, taking care to offer compensation to those deprived of their land.

South Viet-Nam returned to a state of turmoil in 1958, as sympathizers with Ho Chi Minh again asserted their hold on a number of regions, resorting to murder and other guerrilla tactics to establish their dominance. Army personnel who believed Diem guilty of inaction made an unsuccessful attempt to depose him in November 1960. In December, the guerrilla opposition organized itself into the National Liberation Front, called incorrectly by its enemies the Vietnamese Communists or Viet-Cong.

Tai Wan remained in the hands of Chiang Kai

701

Shek, who in 1960 entered a new six-year term as "president of the republic of China." In August-October 1958 the mainland Chinese government engaged in large-scale shelling of small islands that pertained to Tai Wan but lay close to the mainland coast. Chiang's partners in the United States spoke belligerently about the matter, as though United States force might be used to prevent Peking's occupation of the islands. Tempers cooled, however, as many persons stopped to think of the staggering factors involved, and the shelling itself decelerated.

The stormy events that swept Laos from the third quarter to the fourth in 1960 have already formed a part of this narrative (see "The Cold War"). Nepal moved briefly to democracy in 1959 with the holding of elections and the designation of a prime minister responsible to the lower house of the parliament. Nepal found itself involved in the bad feeling between Communist China and India, however, and king Mahendra, impatient with the many quarrels within the country at such a difficult time, dismissed the parliament and arrested the prime minister.

The advent of Indonesia and Pakistan to the fourth quarter of the spectrum meant that Spain, which held fewer than one-third the number of people of either of those two countries, had dropped from first to third ranking member of the band by population. Francisco Franco continued to hold power in Spain despite a host of discontented persons, including liberal Catholics, monarchists, communists, democratic socialists, Basques, and Catalans. Franco treated all his opponents about the same, arresting them and throwing them into jail for criticizing the regime, though eventually releasing them again. President De Gaulle of France expressed readiness in 1959 for the admission of the Franco regime to NATO. More democratic European members of NATO disagreed, however, and some of them spoke out against a new German military presence in Spain negotiated by France and chancellor Adenauer.

702

Neighboring Portugal held elections in 1957-8 as premier and strong man António de Oliveira Salazar helped his choices to win by jailing those who had the nerve to stand for office against them.

Turkey joined the fourth quarter through a coup in 1960, as the most populated of the Middle Eastern group in the band. The regime of president Celal Bayar and premier Adnan Menderes had continued through elections of 1957 in which their Democratic party won over two-thirds of the seats in parliament. The Republican People's party campaigned in vain for proportional representation to give its candidates more of a chance. The head of the army engineered the coup in 1960, however, assuming supreme command. Turkey thus entered the lengthening list of right-wing authoritarian regimes allied with the government in Washington. The United States placed guided missiles on Turkish soil, close to the frontier with the Soviet Union, in 1957. The machinery of the Baghdad pact moved from Baghdad to Ankara in 1958, after the revolution in Iraq. When Iraq formally withdrew from the pact in March 1959, the group came to be called the Central Treaty Organization or CENTO, a designation emphasizing the pivotal position of Turkey in the American "containment" of the Soviet Union. The ill fate of the U-2 flight from Turkish territory in 1960 brought world attention to that position.

Egypt received a new constitution in January 1956. Jamal Abd an-Nasir began a new six-year term as president in late June. Four months later, the British and French made their unsuccessful effort to terminate his regime (see "Old-Style Diplomacy"). Nasser on the rebound from this attempt seemed as lively and popular as ever. He talked with the Soviet Union and the United States about financial assistance and received some from both. Moscow agreed in 1959 to help build the high dam at Aswan which Washington, London, and the World Bank had abandoned.

The popularity of Nasser in Arab countries other than his own seemed indicated by the decision of the people of Syria to put aside their own democratically-based regime and accept the rule of Nasser in the United Arab Republic created February 22, 1958. Though not the favorite of all Arabs, Nasser obtained very special treatment from the constitution of the new country, which made him president for a fresh term of six years and allowed him to pick the 600 members of the new assembly from lists drawn up by the people. Syria received one-third of these seats, though it held only one-sixth of the population.

Afghanistan began to emerge from its shell in this quinquennium, as both sides in the Cold War (but particularly the Soviet Union) granted extensive aid, as a first five-year plan commenced in 1956, and as women first appeared in public without veils. The propaganda for a Pashtunistan continued, however, even though the new president Ayub of Pakistan came from the Pashtunistan district. Ruler Mohammad Zahir declared a position of neutrality toward both president Eisenhower, who visited him in late 1959, and premier Khrushchev, who came early in 1960.

Morocco (see "African Independence") began its national life with neither democratic nor socialist trimmings. Saudi Arabia and Yemen, like Afghanistan, felt the liberalizing influence of the outside world during this period. In Yemen, which joined the United Arab Republic in the confederation called the United Arab States and began to protest the British presence in neighboring Aden, the more liberal forces gathered around the crown prince, son of Ahmad who had ruled since 1948. In Saudi Arabia, those who wished to modernize the country supported the ruler's brother, who handled most details of administration 1958-60. Abdul Karim Qassim, who moved Iraq from the third to the fourth quarter by his coup in 1958 (see "The Cold War"), represented other alert forces tied neither to Nasser nor to Moscow. Libya engaged in talks about the military bases remaining on its territory, and became excited over the discovery of large deposits of Libyan petroleum.

Congo and Sudan joined the fourth quarter in 1960 and 1958, respectively, after unsuccessful attempts at democracy as related in "African Independence." Ethiopia rubbed its eyes as these and other countries of Sub-Sahara Africa achieved their independence. Haile Selassie, the emperor, lived in a world apart from the twentieth-century enthusiasms shared by many of the new African leaders. Ethiopia did begin to modernize itself at this time with financial assistance from the richer powers. In December 1960, an unsuccessful coup took place during Haile Selassie's absence, with the intention of placing his son on the throne and more liberal forces in control.

The Union of South Africa regressed from the whiplash to massacre by gunfire in its implementation of the prescribed apartheid. In 1956-7, the government held Albert Lutuli, head of the African National Congress, on charges of treason, though it did not succeed in convicting him. At the town of Sharpeville, in the province of Transvaal, on March 21, 1960, the police killed over 60 non-European individuals and wounded another 180 as they demonstrated against laws requiring them to carry passes when they visited "white" territory. The United Nations Security Council on April 1 voted by 9 to 0 (the United Kingdom and France abstaining) to deplore the loss of life and call upon South Africa to abandon apartheid. Far from complying with this sentiment, the South African regime chose this occasion to outlaw the African National Congress.

When prime minister Johannes Strijdom died in 1958, Hendrik Frensch Verwoerd took his place. Earlier that year, elections in the "white" community gave the National party of Strijdom and Verwoerd nearly two-thirds of the seats in the lower house of parliament, and the United party a

little less than one-third. The government proceeded with its plan to establish "Native" reserves where the majority of the Bantu would live
and gradually assume control -- under the jurisdiction of European South Africa. New industrial
plants arose on the peripheries of the reserves,
expecting to employ the Bantu labor while re-
serving the profits for the white man. In October 1960, after much criticism from other members
of the Commonwealth, white South Africa voted
(but only by about 52%) to cast aside dominion
status and become a republic.

While South Africa moved against the trends
of the continent, Liberia remained impassive,
dutifully electing president William Tubman for a
new term in 1960. The Voltaic Republic and Niger
joined the fourth band as new countries in 1960
(see "African Independence").

The Latin American contingent of the fourth
quarter dropped rather dramatically, from twelve
countries to four, and all of them smaller ones.
In addition, each of the remaining four yielded
some slight indication of evolution away from
old-fashioned caudillism. The Dominican Republic
of Rafael Trujillo found itself increasingly opposed by the Dominican church. After Trujillo
reached into New York for an abduction and murder, the United States rethought its friendly
stance toward the dictator. Washington indeed
voted against Trujillo at the OAS session in
Costa Rica in August 1960, hoping to ensure the
passage of its own anti-Castro measure (see "Two
American Revolutions"). Earlier that month, to
make the Dominican regime a little more palat-
able, Rafael Trujillo dismissed his brother from
the presidency and chose a new puppet in his
stead.

When president Anastasio Somoza García of
Nicaragua was assassinated in 1956, his older son
Luis Somoza Debayle took his place while a younger brother Anastasio Somoza Debayle commanded
the national guard. In several respects, Luis

706

Somoza conducted a milder dictatorship than that of his father. In Paraguay, whose strong man "won reelection" in 1958 and whose prices doubled during this period, a great deal of politico-military skirmishing took place as economically that country (like Ethiopia, Afghanistan, Saudi Arabia and Yemen) began to shake off its isolation from the modern world. The election of 1956 in El Salvador proved another one-party affair managed by the previous administration. Though there followed four years of continued social progress (without basic reform), a coup terminated the regime in 1960. A junta took its place, and made plans for democratic elections to be held the following year.

The establishment of 22 independent nations in Africa and the independence of Malaya and Cyprus left the colonial world at the end of 1960 much reduced from 1955. The most populated of the possessions remaining were Algeria, held by France; Tanganyika, in trust from the United Nations to the British; and Kenya, British colony and protectorate. Aside from the admission of Hawaii and Alaska as states of the United States, the most important colonial change of this period lay in the Caribbean. There the British organized a federation of the West Indies in 1958, to include Jamaica, Trinidad-Tobago, Barbados, the four colonies of the Windward Islands (Grenada, St. Lucia, St. Vincent, and Dominica), and the Leeward Islands, except that the British Virgin Islands remained divorced from the Leeward group and the assemblage. Singapore graduated from its status of a British colony in 1959, becoming a member of the Commonwealth, but remained under British guidance. Nine of the 27 units in the Aden protectorate of the British joined in 1959-60 to form the Federation of Arab Emirates of the South. French Oceania became French Polynesia and Spain made over Spanish Guinea, Ifní, and Spanish Sahara into "African provinces" in 1958.

The high-level Asian-African Conference held in Bandung, 1955, produced no sequel in this quinquennium. Other international meetings of a different sort, however, may be said to have sprung from the spirit of Bandung. In December 1957-January 1958, Cairo acted as host to persons from 45 countries including the Soviet Union and Japan, who organized an Afro-Asian Solidarity Conference. In April 1958, the First Conference of Independent African States met in Accra, the capital of Ghana. The Egyptian part of the United Arab Republic attended with three other lands of the northern tier (Morocco, Tunisia, Libya), two from the northeast (Ethiopia, Sudan), and two from the middle west (Ghana and Liberia) -- all the independent nations of Africa at that time except the uninvited Union of South Africa. This first Accra conference of 1958 based its resolutions on principles enunciated by the United Nations and at Bandung, disregarding the Afro-Asian Solidarity Conference. The last-named held a second meeting at Conakry, Guinea, in April 1960, changing its name to the Afro-Asian Peoples' Solidarity Organization.

A conference of political parties, including some of anti-apartheid persuasion from South Africa, met in Accra in December 1958. Here the All African Peoples' Conference took form, open to any African national political party or federation of labor subscribing to the stated aims. Among other goals, the Conference hoped "to accelerate the liberation of Africa from imperialism and colonialism" and "to develop a feeling of one community among the peoples of Africa with the object of enhancing the emergence of a United States of Africa." The second meeting of this Conference, held in Tunis, the capital of Tunisia, in January 1960, voted resolutions favoring independence for Algeria and dealing with situations in nearly every corner of Sub-Sahara Africa.

The foreign ministers of the eight charter members of the Conference of Independent African

States met with those of Guinea and the provisional government of Algeria, in Monrovia, Liberia, August 1959. New resolutions spoke for the government level on the rapidly evolving situations in Algeria and Sub-Sahara Africa. Presidents Kwame Nkrumah of Ghana and Sékou Touré of Guinea, who on May 1 had announced their own goal of rapid African political union, pressed toward that goal before and after the meeting at Monrovia. However, the Second Conference of Independent African States, at Addis Ababa, June 1960, postponed the subject for a later agenda. Seven new members joined at Addis Ababa, including newly independent Cameroun and Togo along with scheduled-for-independence Nigeria, Congo, the Malagasy Republic, Somalia, and Mali. The focus of the Conference in 1960 lay upon economic and social cooperation, leaving politics to the side.

The African countries disagreed sharply over political affairs in Congo starting in September. Twelve of the countries liberated from French rule -- the Malagasy Republic, Cameroun, the Voltaic Republic, Ivory Coast, Chad, Niger, Senegal, Dahomey, the Central African Republic, the Congo Republic, Mauritania, and Gabon -- met in Brazzaville, the capital of the Congo Republic, in December 1960. The three others -- Mali, Guinea, and Togo -- joined with Ghana and two northern African states to recognize the pro-Lumumba forces in Congo, as related in "African Independence."

The League of Arab States held many meetings during this period, but the Arab political climate prevented close cooperation. Sudan became a member in 1956, Morocco and Tunisia in 1958. Arab unity did bring about the common-sense solution of the Middle Eastern crisis of 1958 (see "The Cold War"), but Arab divisions continued to predominate. The Economic Council of the League in 1959-60 began to search for ways to make itself useful, and sponsored the institution of an Arab Development Bank.

The Organization of American States held no full-fledged Conference, though a great deal of inter-American activity took place. Many political problems arose in the Caribbean area. A major boundary dispute between Honduras and Nicaragua led to mediation by the OAS and the Organization of Central American States and a judgment by the International Court (1960) that favored the claim of Honduras. Petty invasions (without any government's full support) hit Panama, Nicaragua, and the Dominican Republic in 1959, occasioning OAS debate. In 1960, as related in "Two American Revolutions," the American foreign ministers in San José, Costa Rica, passed resolutions concerning the Trujillo regime in the Dominican Republic and any threat that might appear of extracontinental intervention in American hemisphere affairs.

As with the Addis Ababa conference of African states in 1960 and the new emphasis in the Arab League, American hemispheric concern focused in 1959-60 especially on economic and social affairs. An Inter-American Development Bank, created in late 1959, began to operate in October 1960. An Inter-American Fund for Social Development, developed as part of the Bank's operation, provided a means whereby the United States could help Latin America meet its social needs. Cuba did not participate in these proceedings, excepting that it may be said that the existence of the Castro regime helped the United States to "discover" that such large-scale financing, first suggested by president Kubitschek of Brazil in 1958, had suddenly become feasible.

Latin American leadership, however, did not intend to leave all initiative with the United States. In February 1960, Brazil, Mexico, Argentina, Peru, and Chile (the five most populated countries of the region), joined by Uruguay and Paraguay, set up a Latin American Free Trade Association. Over a twelve-year period, they agreed, they would reduce their tariffs upon one another's goods to one-fourth their starting

710

level. In December 1960, Guatemala, El Salvador,
Honduras, and Nicaragua advanced one step farther
by signing an agreement for a Central American
Common Market, inviting Costa Rica and Panama to
join them.

New action by the six of its members that had
formed the European Coal and Steel Community in
1952 overshadowed the Council of Europe during
this period. On January 1, 1958, these six
merged their interests by establishing a European
Economic Community. In twelve years' time, they
expected through this avenue to produce a common
market offering themselves the same advantages
already enjoyed internally by the Soviet Union
and the United States. The new Community would
have a High Authority for administrative purposes, responsible to a European Parliament
(chosen by the parliaments of the six countries
in prescribed ratio), a Council of Ministers to
solve special problems, and even a Court of Justice. West Germany, Italy, France, the Netherlands, Belgium, and Luxembourg thus welded their
economic futures together, providing an inspiring
example. The same six powers formed the European
Atomic Energy Community (called EURATOM) the same
day, for cooperation in developing new power resources.

Other members of the Council of Europe, which
Austria joined in 1956, had worked for a wider
sphere of countries with more modest plans for
free trade. Five of them -- the United Kingdom,
Austria, Sweden, Denmark, and Norway -- joined by
Portugal and Switzerland -- organized a European
Free Trade Association in 1960. Because of their
geographical position in regard to five of the
nations in the Economic Community, the members of
the Association became known as the "outer
seven."

Four new international organizations related
to the United Nations took form during this period. The International Finance Corporation, established in 1956, intended to organize private

711

capital for investment in needy lands. The International Atomic Energy Agency, 1957, assisted in the application of atomic energy to the development of peace, health, and prosperity. Unlike the "specialized agencies" related to the United Nations, as the others were labeled, the IAEA reported to the General Assembly. The Intergovernmental Maritime Consultative Organization, planned a decade earlier, organized itself in 1959 after very slow ratifications. The International Development Association, 1960, offered loans to developing countries on an easier basis than the International Bank for Reconstruction and Development, with which it remained otherwise almost synonymous. The Economic Commission for Africa, established by the United Nations in 1958, joined those created a decade earlier for Europe, Asia and the Far East, and Latin America.

The United Nations membership roll increased impressively during this period. Sudan, Morocco, and Tunisia joined in 1956, as did Japan following the ending of its state of war with the Soviet Union. Ghana and Malaya entered in 1957, and Guinea in 1958. On September 20, 1960, eleven former French holdings became members -- the Malagasy Republic, Cameroun, the Voltaic Republic, Ivory Coast, Chad, Niger, Dahomey, Togo, the Central African Republic, the Congo Republic, and Gabon -- along with Congo, Somalia, and Cyprus. Within a few weeks Mali, Senegal, and Nigeria added to the number. The United Nations thus became more representative of the regions of the world, though several parts of Africa remained unliberated and the largest nation in the world not admitted. The new members would have raised the roll to an even 100, except that the merging of Egypt and Syria made one less, leaving the total at 99.

Each year the General Assembly chose not to put on its agenda the admission of Communist China to the United Nations via the acceptance of its credentials in place of those of Tai Wan for the seat belonging to "China." Negative votes on the matter came from 42 members in 1955, 47 in 1956, 47 in 1957, 44 in 1958, 44 in 1959, and 42 in 1960. With India introducing the question 1956-59 and the Soviet Union in 1960, the positive vote of 12 countries in 1955 grew to 24 in 1956, 27 in 1957, 28 in 1958, 29 in 1959, and 34 in 1960. From 1955 to 1959, abstentions ran from six to nine; in 1960 there were 22 of them. Half of the votes opposed to the admission of Communist China represented countries of the Americas, of which only Cuba voted otherwise.

The Suez Canal crisis in 1956 showed more clearly than ever before the high potential of the United Nations General Assembly for peacemaking. The strength of the United Nations against the collusion of the United Kingdom, France, and Israel rested upon an alignment of the Soviet Union and the United States. When the two strongest powers opposed one another, as in the Lebanon-Jordan crisis of 1958 and the Congo situation of 1960, matters did not go so well. An unusual accord among the Arab countries settled the first of these (though that accord received expression through the medium of the United Nations) while the Congo problem remained acute to the end of the quinquennium.

Early in 1956, before the Suez Canal crisis, the Security Council unanimously condemned the state of Israel for an attack the previous December "against Syrian regular army forces on Syrian territory," despite reported provocation from the Syrian side. On November 4, 1956, after the Soviet Union had blocked a resolution in the Security Council early that morning, the General Assembly, condemning "the use of Soviet military forces to suppress the efforts of the Hungarian people to reassert their rights," called upon the Soviet Union to desist from armed attack and intervention. The vote ran 50 to 8, with India, Indonesia, Egypt, and Yugoslavia among the 15 abstaining. Four more resolutions concerning the Soviet action in Hungary preceded another of

713

December 12, which condemned "the violation of the Charter of the United Nations" by the Soviet Union "in depriving Hungary of its liberty and independence and the Hungarian people of the exercise of their fundamental rights." The vote on this ran 55 to 8, with 13 abstentions. Neither the Soviet Union nor Israel gave any sign that such condemnations produced contriteness. But after 1956, the two countries did nothing new to evoke United Nations censure during this period, all further resolutions applying to them having to do with the events or the vestiges of the events of October-November 1956.

A Special Committee on the Problem of Hungary, initiated in January 1957, failed to receive permission to enter Hungary. A resolution of September 1957 condemned the acts of both the Soviet Union and the Kadar regime in Hungary. Another of December 1958 denounced the execution of Imre Nagy and others. One of 1959 deplored "the continued disregard" by the Soviet Union and Hungary of previous resolutions. The General Assembly took no action on this matter in 1960. The Assembly expressed "grave concern" over French intentions to test nuclear bombs in the Sahara Desert (1959, by a vote of 51 to 16 with 15 abstentions, the United States and the United Kingdom voting in the negative), and recognized "the right of the Algerian people to self-determination and independence" (1960, by 63 to 8 with 27 abstentions, including those of the United States and the United Kingdom). The Security Council, by a vote of 8 to 0 in June 1960, requested the state of Israel "to make appropriate reparation" to Argentina for the impairment of the latter's sovereignty in the seizure of Adolf Eichmann.

Other controversies besides the Hungarian question became perennials of the General Assembly. South Africa became the subject of twin resolutions each year, one on its apartheid policies and one on its treatment of people of Asian Indian origin. South Africa refused to participate in United Nations activities November 1956 - July 1958 because of the attitudes toward its policies. The Kashmir question continued to appear, as did the unsettled factors concerning Korea and Palestine. Cyprus came in for regular discussion until the decisions about its independence. A General Assembly resolution called for "respect for the fundamental human rights of the Tibetan people" in 1959, and Cuba called for Security Council consideration of its case against the United States on July 11 and December 31, 1960.

The United Nations Disarmament Commission founded in 1952 reflected the views of the Soviet Union and the United States disclosed at the summit conference of 1955. Moscow had moved to the general position enunciated by the United States in the Stalin era, while Washington now limited its substantive proposals to the abatement of the immediate crisis atmosphere. When the General Assembly adopted a generally worded plan cosponsored by the United States as a point of reference for the Disarmament Commission in November 1957, at the same time enlarging the Commission from 12 to 26 members, the Soviet Union refused to participate in its work. A resolution of this impasse came in November 1958 with the adoption of the Soviet idea that the Commission should include all members of the United Nations. This very large Commission did no work either, however, and in September 1959 a ten-nation disarmament committee formed outside United Nations channels, representing five communist states and five allied (in effect) against them. The communist countries withdrew from this arrangement in June 1960 after the aborted summit conference of the previous May.

With all the bad feeling in the world in the middle of the year 1960, many of the notable people of the time continued to turn to the United Nations for solace of some kind. Though this organization had often run into frustration in its several attempts at peacemaking, it evidently retained some reputation as a place of hope for the working out of the world's conundrums. At the very least, it provided a forum through which nations could express their feelings. In the session of the General Assembly that began in September 1960 (and had to adjourn much of its work until the following year), an unusual gathering-in of the world's leaders occurred.

From the first quarter of the political spectrum there appeared Nikita Khrushchev, Wladyslaw Gomulka, Gheorghe Gheorghiu-Dej, Josip Broz (Tito), Antonin Novotny, Janos Kadar, Fidel Castro, and Sékou Touré. From the second quarter arrived Jawaharlal Nehru, Harold Macmillan, Robert Menzies, and Kwame Nkrumah. Dwight Eisenhower, Abubakar Tafawa Balewa, John Diefenbaker, Norodom Sihanouk, and king Hussein came from the third quarter. President Sukarno, Jamal Abd an-Nasir, and Joseph Kasa-Vubu represented the fourth quarter. This Fifteenth Regular Session of the General Assembly accomplished less than the Eleventh, which met in 1956. The two together, even with all the angry talk heard in them, seemed to constitute another sign that the world really had entered a new era like none it had known before.

Economic Change

The world economy had recuperated from the disturbances of World War II during the first ten years of the new era, 1946-55. Economists generally believed that productivity would continue to climb during 1956-60. The managers of private enterprise felt keen disappointment when growth indicators in their domain experienced a halt in 1957-8. United States business activity had undergone mild recessions in 1948-9 and 1953-4, attributed to slowdown in demand following two wars. The recession of 1957-8, however, affected all the states noted for privately financed manufacturing activity, including the

716

second-quarter countries with mixed economies. It extended likewise to the countries more noted for their exports of primary products (foods and minerals) than for large-scale manufacturing. It left untouched only the first-quarter communist nations.

The standstill of 1957-8 could not be explained in terms of postwar slump engendered by a sudden halt of the excess of wartime demand. Rather, it seemed to stem from government moves to slow down rates of inflation, actions making it difficult for most people to purchase the products of industry. Prices continually outran wages in the private-enterprise domain. Persons in affluent countries could buy automobiles, but often only through borrowing the money. Most families in less affluent countries could buy no automobile at all, nor many of the other amenities of living. The manufacturers of automobiles and the other conveniences of the modern world thought only in terms of selling to those who had the money or could borrow it, giving no thought to improving the ability to purchase of the great mass of people in the world. International trade almost always gave the price advantage to those nations endowed with money, and shortchanged those who remained less fortunate. When an influential government such as that of the United States chose to make money less available, in order to combat inflation, the restricted nature of the market -- that is, the smallness of the group still able to purchase -- became very plain in the depressing statistics that followed.

If the years 1957 and 1958 proved disappointing in many countries, however, those of 1956, 1959, and 1960 constituted times of growth. Since the communist nations of Europe continued to increase production throughout the entire period, the quinquennium on balance showed progess as had the two before it. Agricultural, mining, and manufacturing industry all reached new high peaks of activity in the world at large,

717

as manufacturing had in the period 1951-55. The changes in various commodities as described in this chapter relate to the three-year interval 1958-60 as compared to the situation already presented for 1948-50 (Chapter V) and 1953-55 (Chapter VI).

Approximately 9.9% more people lived in the world in 1960 than in 1955. This rate of growth is expressed in this chapter by the numeral 1. (Note that a "1" in Chapter VI stood for 9.1%.) Twice the rate of 9.9% is 2, thrice is 3, and so on. The figure "2+" indicates an increase of more than 2 units of world population growth. The figure "1-" indicates a rate of decline greater than 9.9%. (For further discussion of the system, see Chapter VI at this point.)

For all countries previously listed for each item, any decline of more than 2 units is indicated. Any growth of more than 3 units appears on 14 items -- rice, wheat, maize, cotton, sugar, tobacco, cattle, sheep, coffee, coal, petroleum, iron, cement, and land motor vehicles -- and any growth of more than 5 units on all the others. For the world at large, any decline of more than 1 unit is indicated. Any growth of more than 2 units appears on the favored 14 items, and any growth of more than 4 units on all the others.

In the relative standings of leading countries, a revised list appears on any item that reveals one country surpassing another to the point that the lower of the two shows a total less than four-fifths of the higher. The cut-off point remains at one-half the world total for most items -- but at two-thirds for rice, wheat, maize, cotton, coal, iron, and cement, and at nine-tenths for petroleum and land motor vehicles. Near-ties as defined in Chapter V are mentioned whenever a list is revised. A nation is indicated as having lost its place among the leaders only if it has dropped to less than four-fifths of the last on the list, or has remained at less than a near-tie position for two quinquennia in succession. (For further discussion of these lists, see Chapter VI at this point.)

Agricultural growth outside the communist nations of Asia amounted to about 16.9% in 1955-60, compared to the 18.6% of 1950-55. The inclusion of mainland China would have made less difference than in the mid-1950's since that nation after record harvests in 1958 fell drastically on several items in 1959 as the planned "great leap forward" commenced. The slowdown in agricultural increase took on added significance when weighed against the rise in world population. As measured by the units of world population increase employed in this study, agriculture outside the communist nations of Asia stood at a growth index of 2.0 (to the nearest tenth) in 1950-55, but declined to 1.7 in 1955-60. The inclusion of communist China, by making the first but not the second of these indices somewhat higher, would have produced an even greater difference between them.

The three major cereals continued to expand at a lively pace, though none of the minor cereals kept step with them on a global basis. World production of rice (2+) continued to rise more than twice as rapidly as world population. Wheat (2+) matched such growth, assisted by the Soviet Union (4+), as Turkey joined the leaders on this item. An International Wheat Agreement, effective in 1956, regularized international trade in wheat, following the example of sugar in 1954. Maize (3+) did even better than rice and wheat in world totals as the Soviet Union overtook Brazil in production, revising the list for the first time since 1950: the United States, China (3+), the Soviet Union (12+, more than doubling), and Brazil. The United States (20+) nearly tripled its production of sorghum. France joined the list on barley, overtaking India and the United Kingdom as India dropped away from the leaders, revising the group from 1950: China, the Soviet Union, the United States, France, and near-tie

719

Canada.

Cotton advanced less rapidly than rice, wheat, and maize, while other vegetable fibers varied widely. Hemp production declined significantly (2-) in world totals, as the harvest in India slipped behind that of the Soviet Union and Italy dropped from the small list of leaders, revised from 1950: the Soviet Union and India (3-). Sisal harvests continued to increase at a lively pace in Brazil (7+). The world total for abaca declined (1-).

World production of sugar (2+) continued to increase, as India overtook France and Puerto Rico dropped from among the leaders, on the following list revised from 1955: the Soviet Union (7+), Cuba (no longer the pacesetter), the United States, Brazil (5+), India (6+), West Germany (3+), France, Australia, and near-tie Philippines.

China overtook India in the production of tobacco as Brazil joined the four largest countries of the world on this item, revising the list from 1955: the United States, China (6+), India, the Soviet Union, and Brazil.

China also managed to augment its inventory of domesticated animals, including cattle (3+). In numbers of sheep, it surpassed Argentina, India, South Africa, and New Zealand on the list, revised from 1950: Australia, the Soviet Union, China (3+), Argentina, New Zealand, South Africa, and India. China did even better with its inventory of swine (9+). The Soviet Union (5-) dropped behind Turkey, Ethiopia, Nigeria, and Iran and away from the leaders in numbers of goats, as Pakistan joined the leaders on this item, revised from 1955: India, China, Turkey (5+), Nigeria, Ethiopia, Pakistan, and near-tie Iran. The Soviet Union (3-) and Argentina (3-) declined in numbers of horses and mules, while the United States rejoined the leaders on this item. Iran joined the leading group in numbers

720

of donkeys, while India (5+) increased its inventory of camels.

World production of soybeans (4+) increased rapidly as the United States pushed this crop, growing more than half the world total by itself and removing China from the leadership. Argentina surpassed the Soviet Union and India to regain its former position on linseed while Canada joined the leaders on this item, revising the list from 1955: the United States (2-), Argentina (9+), and Canada. The world harvest of rapeseed (3-) diminished with a drastic decrease in the crop in China (6-), as India became a co-leader on this item. World exports of coconut oil (1-) declined as Ceylon dropped behind the Philippines, revising the list from 1955: the Philippines, Ceylon (3-), and Malaya (3-). In 1959, olive oil became the first of the vegetable oils (and the first of the less-than-major world crops) to form the subject of a United Nations commodity agreement like those on sugar and wheat. Sesame seed declined in world totals (1-) as in those of its two leaders, China (4-) and India (2-). Argentina dropped away from leadership status on sunflower seed, leaving the Soviet Union with over half the world figure on that item. Brazil more than doubled (11+) its exports of castor oil, taking more than half the market by itself and dropping India from leadership status.

World harvests of coffee expanded greatly (5+), led by those of Brazil (7+). Nigeria (6+) pushed its production of cacao.

Individual countries registered change on the vegetables and fruits. China joined the Soviet Union and Poland as a leader on potatoes. As the world totals for sweet potatoes and yams greatly increased (7+), Nigeria dropped away from its co-leadership position, leaving China as the sole leader on this item. Italy (5+) increased its yield of tomatoes. India joined China and the Soviet Union as a leader on peas. West Germany

721

(5+) increased its production of apples, as Italy joined the leaders on this item. The world totals on bananas increased (4+) as Ecuador (11+) more than doubled its quantity and Venezuela dropped away from the group of leaders. Turkey joined the leadership in production of grapes.

China surpassed the United States and the Soviet Union in catches of fish, while Peru joined the leaders and Norway dropped away from them, revising the list from 1955: Japan, China (12+, more than doubling), the Soviet Union, the United States, and Peru. The fish meal industry providing fertilizer and animal foods accounted for the enlarged fishing operation in Peru.

Both mining and manufacturing suffered enough from the economic recession of 1957-8 that their total progress through the quinquennium -- though most commodities reached new world highs -- lay considerably below that of the previous five years. The growth rate in mining and manufacturing outside the communist lands of Asia amounted to about 29.7% in 1955-60 compared to 42.2% in 1950-55. Probably the rate for China lay higher, but that nation's manufacturing strength remained too limited to make great impact on the world scene. The slowdown in mining and manufacturing growth, like that in agriculture, took on added significance when weighed against the rise in world population. As measured by the units of world population increase employed in this study, mining and manufacturing outside the communist nations of Asia grew at an index of 4.6 (to the nearest tenth) in 1950-55, but decelerated to 3.0 in 1955-60, less than two-thirds of the former rate per capita.

Several countries changed rank in the production of textile yarns. China with all its difficulties overtook India in the production of cotton yarn, revising the list from 1955: the United States, the Soviet Union, China, and India. The Soviet Union overtook France in output

722

of wool yarn as Italy joined the leaders on this item, revising the list from 1955: the United Kingdom, the United States (2-), the Soviet Union, France, and Italy. Japan overtook the United Kingdom in production of rayon and acetate filament yarn as the Soviet Union joined the leaders, revising the list from 1955: the United States, Japan, the Soviet Union, the United Kingdom, and near-ties Italy and West Germany.

World production of coal (2+) increased considerably, as the Soviet Union and China overtook the United Kingdom, China making its entry into the group of leaders. West Germany dropped away from the leading list, revised for the first time since 1950: the United States, the Soviet Union (4+), China, and the United Kingdom. The Soviet Union overtook West Germany on lignite, as West Germany dropped out of this leadership also, leaving only East Germany and the Soviet Union. Production of coke dropped in the United States (2-).

World production of petroleum (3+) continued to rise rapidly, though at a less furious pace than before. Kuwait overtook Saudi Arabia while Iran, rejoining the leaders, surpassed Canada and Indonesia. Mexico dropped away from the leadership ranks. The new list, revised from 1955, ran as follows: the United States, Venezuela (3+), the Soviet Union (11+, more than doubling), Kuwait (5+), Saudi Arabia, Iran, Iraq (3+), Canada (7+), and Indonesia (7+).

The closure of the Suez Canal in 1956 brought about an increase in world oil prices. Venezuela and the four major Middle Eastern exporters found new money for their budgets, badly needed to meet their development plans. In 1959-60, however, the major international oil companies lowered the prices without consulting the producing nations. The nations found themselves with reduced income at a time of rising prices for the goods they purchased abroad. In self-defense, Venezuela, Kuwait, Saudi Arabia, Iran, and Iraq at a meeting in Baghdad, Iraq (September 1960) created the Organization of Petroleum Exporting Countries (OPEC). Their first aim, to prevent unilateral decisions by the foreign companies that affected their financial status, prepared them for cooperative thinking of a dramatically significant kind, offering the "third world" some real leverage in its relations with the first and second.

World output of iron at the mine (3+) continued to rise, though with the same slackening of pace petroleum had experienced. The Soviet Union, untroubled by the slowdown of 1957-8, overtook the United States for first position on this important item, while China and Venezuela joined the leaders. The new list, revised from 1950, ran: the Soviet Union (4+), the United States (2-), China, France (3+), Sweden, Venezuela, and near-tie Canada. West Germany joined the United States and the Soviet Union as a leader in both crude iron and crude steel.

Only a few of the other metals matched the production rate of iron. Chile (6+) gave renewed impetus to its output of copper. The United States slipped behind Australia and the Soviet Union in production of lead, revising the list from 1955: Australia, the Soviet Union (5+), the United States (2-), Mexico, and Canada. World totals of bauxite (5+) continued to grow rapidly as Jamaica surpassed Surinam and British Guiana, the Soviet Union joined the leadership on this item, and the United States dropped away from it. The new list on bauxite, revised from 1955, ran: Jamaica (18+, nearly tripling), Surinam, the Soviet Union, and British Guiana. The Soviet Union overtook Mexico in production of zinc, revising the list from 1955: the United States, Canada, the Soviet Union (5+), Australia, and Mexico. World output of tin (1-) declined, following that of Malaya (2-), Bolivia (3-), and Indonesia (3-), while China joined these leaders on this item. An International Tin Agreement effective in 1956 attempted to regularize trade in tin in the same manner as the agricultural

724

commodities sugar and wheat. The production of manganese decreased in India (2-).

Peru joined the leaders in the production of silver. World production of tungsten slackened (2-) after its dramatic climb, with the United States dropping back to its position behind the Soviet Union in the list revised from 1955: China, the Soviet Union, the United States (6-), and near-ties South Korea and North Korea. World output of titanium (5+) continued to grow rapidly. The world totals for mercury (4+) also increased significantly, as the United States joined Italy and Spain as a leader on this item.

The manufacturing fever chart as approximated by the output of cement showed continuing fluidity. World production climbed at a rate of 4+, compared to the 7+ of the previous quinquennium. Japan overtook the United Kingdom, while Belgium dropped away from the group of (much more heavily populated) leaders. The new list on cement, revised from 1955, ran as follows: the United States (its lead now considerably reduced), the Soviet Union (10+ more than doubling), West Germany (3+), Japan (8+), Italy (5+), France (4+), the United Kingdom, China (17+, more than doubling), and India (6+).

The Soviet Union joined Canada as a leading producer of asbestos. World production of salt (5+) increased at a lively pace, as China joined the leaders and overtook the Soviet Union on the list, revised from 1950: the United States, China, and the Soviet Union (5+). Phosphate rock (5+) continued to increase rapidly, as the Soviet Union displaced Morocco as co-leader with the United States. The Soviet Union joined the United States and Japan as a leading producer of sulphur.

The automobile and truck industry slowed its pace considerably in this period, though at 2+ its growth continued more than double that of world population. Though the United States pro-

725

duced fewer land motor vehicles than before, its total remained well over triple that of its nearest competitor. Increases for other countries on the list ran as follows: the United Kingdom (5+), West Germany (15+, more than doubling), France (10+, more than doubling), and the Soviet Union (3+). Italy and Japan joined this group of leaders.

As in the previous period, six nations registered three or more times on the plus side of these listings. The Soviet Union again led in this recapitulation, registering positively on eleven items: 12+ on maize, 11+ on petroleum; 10+ on cement; 7+ on sugar; 5+ on lead, zinc, and salt; 4+ on wheat, coal, and iron; and 3+ on land motor vehicles. The Soviet Union had registered on seven of these (petroleum, cement, sugar, wheat, coal, iron, and land motor vehicles) in the preceding period also.

China again held second place in this overview, with growth rates showing on seven items: 17+ on cement; 12+ on fish; 9+ on swine; 6+ on tobacco; and 3+ on maize, cattle, and sheep. Tobacco, maize, and sheep had appeared in the preceding period. West Germany (not included in the previous period) registered on four items: 15+ on land motor vehicles; 5+ on apples; 3+ on sugar and cement. Brazil (also new in the group) scored with four agricultural items: 11+ on castor oil; 7+ on sisal and coffee; 5+ on sugar. France registered on three lists, all continued from the previous period: 10+ on land motor vehicles, 4+ on cement, 3+ on iron. India appeared with three items, all fresh in the present period: 6+ on sugar and cement; 5+ on camels. The United States and Canada, featured in the previous period, registered on only one item each for 1955-60.

United Nations statisticians during this period initiated a system of economic com-

parisons going beyond the production of individual commodities. New tables showed percentages of
overall growth for most nations of the world.
The figures lacked strict comparability, for some
(like that of the United States) showed growth of
the "real gross domestic product at market
prices," while others (such as that of Pakistan)
indicated the growth of "real gross domestic product at factor cost," and still others (such as
those of the Soviet Union and mainland China) the
growth of "real net material product."

The concept of the "net material product,"
used by the communist countries, meant the total
worth of goods produced in the "material" realm
-- agriculture and forestry, mining, manufacturing, construction, transport and communication, trade, and services connected with these
activities. The "gross domestic product at factor cost" included in addition the total worth of
the proceeds derived from banking, insurance, and
real estate, the ownership of dwellings, public
administration and defense, and personal and professional services. The "gross domestic product
at market prices" took in not only the total
worth of the branches of activity, like the other
two, but also the profit made by the seller of
goods, plus the value of indirect taxes levied on
those goods, less the value of government sub-
sidies provided for those goods. To make matters
even more difficult, some countries fitted none
of these categories, but used other descriptions
such as the "net national product at factor cost"
reported by India, which took into account (as
the other measurements did not) the depreciation
of capital.

Percentages of growth did provide greater
comparability than the absolute values from which
they derived, since one of the measurements might
be expected to advance roughly as another. A 1%
growth in a well-developed country, however,
meant much more volume than the same figure in a
less-developed country, because of the larger
base used for the calculation. Furthermore, di-

verse tastes for consumer goods and varying demand for services made it impossible to decide how one economy compared in comfort of living to another even when their "products" totaled about the same. The percentages, despite these deficiencies, held three distinct advantages: (1) They represented average annual rates of growth, so that one bad season would not affect them to the point of distortion.   (2) They dealt with the "real" product in constant prices, eliminating the obfuscation of inflation.   (3) They spoke in per capita terms, revealing whether a nation had achieved something more than merely keeping up with its population increase.

Economic growth for the entire world, excluding only the Asian communist nations and Albania, amounted to 3.2% per capita per year in 1950-60, according to estimates of the gross domestic product at constant market prices.   For the bloc including the Soviet Union and the communist countries of eastern Europe (except Albania), the comparable growth figure stood at 7.4%.   The "developed" non-communist countries showed a figure of 2.7% while the "developing" nations (all of non-communist Latin America, Asia, and Africa except Japan and South Africa) mustered only a 2.3%.   The nations of the European Economic Community in 1950-60 (the Community came into existence only in 1958) progressed at 4.8%; the area included in the new European Free Trade Association, only at 2.6%.

Ten countries and one dependency reported per capita average annual growth rates of 6.0% or better for 1950-60 or some approximating period. Four of the nations held populations of more than 25,000,000:   China (1952-8, cutting off the disappointments of the great-leap-forward years) 11.0%; the Soviet Union 8.3; West Germany 6.7; Japan 6.4.   Four stood in the population bracket 10-25,000,000:   Romania 9.0; East Germany (1955-60) 8.8; Yugoslavia 7.4; Czechoslovakia 6.6.   Two held less than 10,000,000 population: Bulgaria 8.1; Albania 6.1.   The dependency was Jamaica, with 7.2%. Communist regimes ruled eight of the ten nations on this list. All ten had suffered substantially from World War II. Other nations that had also experienced destruction raised themselves more slowly.

International economic aid flowed more freely in this period as the lists of both donors and recipients lengthened. The United States widened its program, sending its largest sums (counting grants and net amounts on loans, but excluding military assistance) to South Korea, India, South Viet-Nam, Pakistan, Turkey, Spain, Tai Wan, and Yugoslavia, in that order. India, Pakistan, Turkey, Spain, and Yugoslavia had all risen in favor. The Soviet Union made its largest commitments to India, Indonesia, and Egypt. The United Kingdom continued to assist some countries outside its former empire, while France embarked upon sizeable programs that included nations leaving the French Community. On a per capita basis in 1960, Jordan received the most generous assistance, followed by Cyprus and Libya. The United States and the United Kingdom supported Jordan and Libya, while the United Kingdom contributed most of the amount for Cyprus.

Science

The strong-focusing proton synchroton . . nobelium . . the antineutron and antineutrino . . challenge to the conservation of parity . . the Mössbauer effect . . laboratory corroboration of the general theory of relativity . . the laser . . the Jodrell Bank radio telescope . . exploration of Antarctica . . the North Pole via submarine . . renewed interest in Gondwana . . the descent into Mariana Trench . . the oceanic ridges . . remanent magnetism and continental drift . . Hess and the sea-floor spreading concept . . the air-cushion vehicle . . the processes of photosynthesis . . Oreopithecus and

729

The magnificent scientific achievement of
this quinquennium was the one for which this
chapter is named, man's first reach into space.
The International Geophysical Year that sparked
two space programs also revealed sensational information concerning the nature of the earth.
Developments in nuclear warfare, so prominent in
the previous two periods, no longer gripped the
world's attention, excepting as many people pled
for a halt to tests. The peacetime development
of fission power proceeded in the Soviet Union,
the United States, West Germany, and France after
the establishment of the first large nuclear reactor in England, 1956. The Soviet Union and the
United States experimented with nuclear power for
ships, but found it economical for the time being
only in submarines.

Proton synchrotons completed during this period surpassed all those preceding in both size
and strength. The prewar cyclotron reached five
feet in diameter and the ability to accelerate
particles to 20,000,000 electron volts. (The
electron volt equals the charge developed by one
electron through a change of one volt in the
field through which it passes.) The synchrotron
of Dubna, Russia, in service in 1957, measured 72
meters (236 feet) across and accelerated protons
to 10,000,000,000 electron volts (10 Bev in American English; 10 Gev in British English, the G
standing for "giant"). The European Organization
for Nuclear Research, representing twelve nations, introduced the "strong-focusing" technique
in its model of 1959, which at 200 meters (656
feet) in diameter reached 28 Bev. The new tech-

nique used magnetic fields of a variety of shapes to prevent its particles from scattering, thus requiring magnets of considerably smaller size. A second strong-focusing proton synchrotron, 257 feet in diameter and producing 33 Bev, reached completion in Brookhaven, New York, in 1960.

A joint team (Swedish-United States) at work in Sweden reported the discovery of element 102 in 1957, naming it nobelium for nineteenth-century Alfred Bernhard Nobel, Swedish founder of the prestigious Nobel prizes. Investigators following the same method in the Soviet Union and the United States failed, however, to confirm the finding. In 1958, the team at Berkeley (including Albert Ghiorso and G. T. Seaborg), produced the element by another process, though the name remained the same.

Two previously postulated atomic particles came to light in 1956. By experiments with an antiproton beam, investigators at Berkeley confirmed the existence of the antineutron, opposite in direction of spin from the neutron but otherwise the same. Clyde Lorraine Cowan of Michigan and Frederick Reines of New Jersey detected the presence of the antineutrino while the neutrino remained to be observed. Physicists had accepted the existence of the two neutrinos in the 1930's, to explain why, as a neutron changes to a proton or a proton to a neutron in radioactive decay, the energy of the electron or positron emitted does not account for the complete loss of mass in the nucleus. The neutrino proper, with presumed zero mass, would bear the remainder of the energy in the proton-to-neutron change, while the antineutrino would do the same in the neutron-to-proton transition. Cowan and Raines saw neither the antineutrinos nor any tracks they left behind them after their creation in neutron breakdown near an atomic fission plant in Georgia. They simply showed their existence through using them to change (supplied) protons into neutrons, reversing the original process.

Each of the atomic particles bore specific characteristics of mass, electric charge, and rate and direction of spin. The quantum mathematics employed to study them took these and other concepts into account. The particles could only be studied and described as they traveled, though the "mass" cited for each of them meant the mass computed for the particle at rest. Both space and time coordinates formed an essential part of the equations indicating change from one particle to another, since distance traveled and time elapsed provided two of the conditions through which the particles might be described. With an inversion of space (represented by the mirror image), some particles would remain unchanged in appearance (like a plain sphere before a mirror) while others would change their aspect (like the hand of a human being before a mirror). If positive and negative space coordinates of a particle appeared the same, that particle possessed "even parity," in the terminology adopted. Another particle, if its positive and negative space coordinates presented distinct images, possessed "odd parity." Until 1956, physicists generally assumed that mathematically valid equations pointed to a balance in parity between the particles prior to a change and the particles subsequent to the change. The presumed balance lay in even-ness and odd-ness, not in numerical values, with even-ness (as in addition of numbers) stemming from even-plus-even or odd-plus-odd, while odd-ness derived from even-plus-odd.

Physicists believed, thus, in the conservation of parity, as they believed in the conservation of mass-together-with-energy. (Prior to 1905, they had believed in the conservation of mass and in the separate conservation of energy.) The conservation of parity implied that in a space-inverted world the same laws of physics would apply as in the world of human experience. In 1956, physicists Chen Ning Yang and Tsung Dao Lee (both born in China and migrated to the United States, their names here Anglicized) challenged the parity-conservation concept, declaring that it seemed not to hold in the weaker of two types of nuclear interactions. (Mesons and other new nuclear particles had shown a marked difference in speed of reaction with other particles, though both "strong" and "weak" interactions took place within a tiny fraction of one second.) Yang and Lee suggested experiments to confirm their theory. Within a year, tests indicated clearly that indentical weak interactions, carried out under extreme care, produced some mesons of odd and some of even parity for no apparent reason. With parity conservation thus no longer credible, physicists began to question two other con-servation "laws" they had assumed. One dealt with "charge conjugation", the relationship be-tween particles and anti-particles; the other with "time reversal", the fourth-dimensional aspect of space inversion.

The first laboratory confirmation of another theory depended upon a discovery made in 1958. Gamma rays (produced by collisions between elec-trons and protons) ordinarily bear a range of wavelengths though emitted by identical atoms, due to the variance of the recoil involved (as with a person firing a gun). Rudolf Ludwig Mössbauer of West Germany learned that the atoms could be arranged in crystal formation so that the gamma rays emitted by them would bear a sharply defined wavelength. This wavelength would then be absorbed, and no other, by atoms of a similar crystal receptive to the addition of electrons. (After absorption, the collision would stand reversed.) The "Mössbauer effect," as the new technique came to be called, held great promise in several fields requiring very minute measurements. Physicists saw in it the possibility of testing Albert Einstein's general theory of relativity in the laboratory.

The "general theory" of relativity proposed by Einstein indicated that gravity could be ex-plained as a distortion-curve in a space-time continuum. (See Chapter V.) The first three tests of the validity of his theory fell in the field of astronomy: observations of the intense gravitational effects of white dwarf stars, measurement of the advance in the perihelion of the planet Mercury as it orbits about the sun, and careful study of the bending effect of the sun's gravitational field on light from the distant stars. Einstein's theory asserted that light emerging from a gravitational field would undergo a slight increase in wavelength, causing a correspondingly slight shift toward the red end of the optical spectrum. In the heavens, only the white dwarf stars held the mass needed to produce the phenomenon to a measurable degree. The Mössbauer effect now made it possible to run an appropriate experiment in the laboratory.

The "Doppler-Fizeau effect," explained in the 1840's, dealt with a shift toward the red in the optical spectrum (denoting an increase in wavelength) whenever a source of light receded from the viewer, and a correlative shift toward the violet (denoting a shortening in wavelength) when the source approached the viewer. In 1960, physicists combined the Doppler-Fizeau effect and the Mössbauer effect to test the Einstein-predicted shift. A crystal emitted gamma rays downward to another crystal that absorbed them. The emitting crystal moved upward at the speed desired. The gamma rays would increase in length (the Doppler-Fizeau effect) as the emitting crystal receded from the absorbing crystal. They could only be absorbed (the Mössbauer effect) if the Einstein-predicted shift occurred in reverse -- a shortening of the rays as they moved toward (rather than away from) the earth's gravitational field -- thus balancing out the Doppler-Fizeau effect. The predicted balance did occur as the experimenters determined the correct speed, yielding a fourth corroboration of Einstein's general theory five years after Einstein himself had died.

Other physicists concerned themselves with the maser, developed in 1953, and its sequel the "laser", a product of this period. The word

<u>laser</u>, meaning "light amplification by stimulated emission of radiation," differed from <u>maser</u> only in the substitution of the word <u>light</u> for <u>micro-wave</u>. Photons in the optical light portion of the radiation spectrum are much shorter in wavelength than those of the already-very-short microwave (the smallest radio-wave) portion. They should behave in the same manner, it seemed, if the amplification process could be initiated. (See Chapter VI.) Theodore Harold Maiman of California managed the problem successfully in 1960 through the medium of an artificial ruby. The first laser, like the first maser, would operate only intermittently. By the end of 1960, models of both operated continuously, the re-preparation of working molecules and emission of the photons taking place simultaneously. The maser served especially as an amplifier of radio waves, the laser for operations requiring ultra-high precision in heating or the conveyance of a very thin stream of light.

Radio astronomy, for which the maser seemed particularly adapted, made significant strides during this period. The Jodrell Bank Experimental Station of England, completed in 1957, held a radio dish antenna 250 feet in diameter. Bernard Lovell, popular writer on radio astronomy, became its first director in time to train it on Sputnik I. Certain "radio stars" came in for particular attention later in this period, as an increasing number of others of that label turned out to be radio galaxies. Visual study of the residue group revealed the existence of faint stars at the indicated points. Their spectra, however, showed lines not easily matched with the spectra of known elements and compounds. The mystery surrounding them had only intensified by the end of the year 1960.

Earth science received far more attention in this period than in the two preceding. The International Geophysical Year of 1957-8, though it provided the impetus for the exploration of space, had as its chief objective the study of the earth. The time period chosen for it, in addition to coinciding with an optimal period for viewing the earth's sun, provided a meaningful anniversary for two previous occasions of international scientific investigation. The First Polar Year of 1882-3 (following the formation of the International Meteorological Organization in 1878) and the Second Polar Year on the 50th anniversary had concerned themselves chiefly with northern polar research. Now the Year of 1957-8 included significant observation of the atmosphere above the earth, of the deep seas surrounding the continents of the earth, and of the continent of Antarctica at the earth's South Pole.

Human beings first saw Antarctica, so far as is known, in the year 1820. At that time, a British expedition viewed land now known as the Antarctic Peninsula, about 600 miles from the southern tip of South America, at approximately 60° West Longitude. A Russian expedition likewise spotted Antarctic mountains near the internationally accepted prime meridian (0° Longitude) and by 1821 circumnavigated what seemed a nearly circular land mass covered with ice. The mass extended about 1,500 miles from the South Pole through nearly half of its range (10° West Longitude to 160° East Longitude) though somewhat less than that for the remainder. Lying west of the Antarctic Peninsula, from about 75° to 95° West Longitude, the Russians discovered a water indentation (now named, for their commander, the Bellingshausen Sea) that reached to about 1,100 miles from the South Pole.

British expeditions in 1822-4 and 1839-40 discovered what are known as Weddell Sea and Ross Sea, respectively, where ships could ply their way to within 900 miles of the Pole. Weddell Sea lay immediately east of Antarctic Peninsula, from 60° to 30° West Longitude, and Ross Sea far to the west, from 140° West to 170° East longitude. Vast ice shelves over the inner portions of these two seas stretched (it developed later) to within 600 and 400 miles of the South Pole. The Antarctic land mass, it became obvious, stood considerably less circular than its ice cap had first appeared. Some persons even suggested a water channel might be found under the ice, connecting Ross and Weddell Seas and separating Antarctica into two land masses.

Separate expeditions reached the South Pole on the ice in December 1911 and January 1912. Richard Evelyn Byrd of Virginia made the first flight over the Pole in 1929. (Byrd remained active in Antarctic exploration until 1956, but died on the very eve of the Geophysical Year in 1957.) The United Kingdom made the first claim to ownership of a slice of Antarctic land in 1917. New Zealand, France, Argentina, Australia, Norway, and Chile followed by the year 1940. One-sixth of the longitudinal range, from the Bellingshausen to the Ross Sea, remained unclaimed. Expeditions from the United States had often visited that region. Permanent stations for scientific investigation became part of the Antarctic scene beginning in 1943. Most of the continent's geography and history nevertheless remained a mystery. The seven claimant powers and the Soviet Union, the United States, Japan, South Africa, and Belgium agreed on a joint effort to explore the South Polar regions during the International Geophysical Year.

The twelve teams encountered results that lay nothing short of sensational. Antarctica, they learned, holds about 95% of the world's ice. If it all melted, the world's oceans would rise by more than 200 feet. The Antarctic land mass underneath the ice had its contours drastically redrawn. Most of the unclaimed portion turned out to be ocean water covered by ice. What had seemed the land edge of a continent in that region resolved into shores of islands. This water-covered-by-ice extended not only from the Ross to the Bellingshausen Sea but to within 200 miles of the Weddell Sea, and possibly even farther. Antarctic Peninsula, which had seemed 800 to 1,000 miles long, now appeared to stretch twice that distance to a tenuous footing on an Antarctic land mass now scarcely more than half a circle about the South Pole. A large chunk of land (30° to 80° East Longitude, 900 miles east-west and 400 north-south) could no longer be included even in that half-circle, as it revealed itself half-water, half-island. Vast expanses of land on the chief mass itself (especially between 90° and 160° East Longitude) lay below sea level. Both those expanses and the large chunk removed, however, would rise above sea level, scientists believed, if the burden of the ice should cease to weigh them down.

The gravimeter and seismic estimates that provided these conclusions offered no conclusive detail (man-made explosions served the seismic method), but sufficed for the broad picture that emerged. A separate British team (not officially connected with the Year) made the first crossing of the continent on ice, from Weddell Sea via the South Pole to Ross Sea. A Soviet team climbed to the Pole of Inaccessibility (the very heart of the Antarctic ice pack), finding on their way mountains 10,000 feet in elevation completely covered by the ice, and an ice-carrying valley about 800 miles in length. French and Australian groups provided many of the estimates on the chief mass of land.

The British and United States teams established with definitude the existence of a mountain chain glimpsed earlier, ranging across the continent from the east side of Weddell Sea to the west side of Ross Sea. An escarpment along the northern edge of these Transantarctic Mountains (as they came to be called) clearly separated the chief land mass, called Greater Antarctica, from the Antarctic Peninsula, islands, and ocean-water-under-ice that altogether comprised Lesser Antarctica. The Transantarctic Mountains lay only about 200 miles from the South Pole, on the South American side.

The excitement of the cooperative study of

Antarctica brought about the signing of an unusual international treaty in 1959. All twelve
of the countries that had participated joined in
wording the agreement. The treaty recognized
that "it is in the interest of all mankind that
Antarctica shall continue forever to be used exclusively for peaceful purposes and shall not
become the scene or object of international discord." Without seeking the renunciation of prior
territorial claims, it stipulated that "no new
claim . . . shall be asserted while the present
Treaty is in force." Scientific investigation in
Antarctica would continue as in the Geophysical
Year, without regard to territorial claims.
Neither plans nor findings would be held in secret, and scientific work would remain open to
inspection by signatory countries. This treaty,
subject to review after 30 years, bore all the
marks of a new age. Someday, when people learned
to cooperate better in other scientific pursuits
-- on their own planet and into space -- they
would likely regard the Antarctic treaty as a
milestone.

The North Polar regions received less attention than Antarctica during the International
Geophysical Year. Two teams of scientists from
the Soviet Union and two from the United States
stationed themselves on drifting packs of ice on
the Arctic Ocean. Aside from these studies, a
submarine crew from the United States became the
first to reach the North Pole under the ice. The
world's first nuclear-powered submarine, the
Nautilus, made the feat possible. With atomic
energy, the Nautilus had no need to surface frequently to recharge batteries as submarines had
always done in the past. An expedition had first
reached the North Pole on the ice in 1909. The
Nautilus dove under the ice cap between Greenland
and the Norwegian archipelago of Spitzbergen in
1957, reaching a point about 180 miles from the
Pole before gyrocompass trouble forced it to turn
back. A combination of threatening ice overhead
and shallow water underneath prevented an entry
through Bering Strait between Siberia and Alaska

in June 1958. Ice conditions changed, however, and the <u>Nautilus</u> moved through Bering Strait July 29, 1958, proceeding to the North Pole August 3 and finding the water there about two-and-a-half miles deep. The ship surfaced two days later on the "other side" of the world as measured longitudinally, between Greenland and Spitzbergen.

Both Antarctica and the deep seas continued to attract wide attention after the close of the Geophysical Year. Geologists made an exciting discovery in the Transantarctic Mountains, well confirmed by the year 1960. A particular combination of Permian fossil leaves and coal deposits with a stratum of glacial rubble underlying them had taken the name Gondwana (Gond-land) from the place it first came to light in 1872, the Gondwana district of the present state of Madhya Pradesh, India. (The remains came from the Permian period, 280-225,000,000 years ago, when seed ferns and fishes remained dominant in the plant and animal kingdoms but conifers and reptiles began to appear.) The same association (of leaves, coal, and glacial rubble) soon appeared in Australia and New Zealand, Africa and Madagascar, and even South America. In 1885, the redundant designation Gondwanaland appeared on maps as a Permian-age feature of the earth's crust -- including India, Australia-New Zealand, Africa-Madagascar, South America, and Antarctica, all situated the same as today, but connected with land bridges. In 1901, the first Permian fossil leaves and coal deposits came to light in Greater Antarctica.

The geologic record of Antarctica continued to take substance until some notion of its history began to take shape. The finding of Permian fossil leaves and coal deposits with as much as 900 feet of glacial rubble underneath spurred new interest in Gondwana by 1960. Most of the new speculation, however, lay not with the theory of land bridges. Alfred Wegener of Germany had suggested in 1912 that Gondwana did exist in Permian times, not as a system of land masses but as a

740

continent that drifted apart. Most earth scientists rejected the idea, since Wegener described great movements of land with little explanation of the mechanics behind the motion. Now, however, the evidence ran strong for some kind of Permian unity among most of the land masses of the southern hemisphere. Lesser Antarctica, it appeared, might provide an exception, since its known history did not extend to the Permian age. The Transantarctic Mountains provided a boundary for two geologic provinces, as distinct as that of India from that of the remainder of Asia.

The probing of the deep seas also continued through this period, producing some truly remarkable surprises for human science, which had long neglected careful study of the floors of the world's oceans. Jacques Piccard, taking employment with the United States navy after its purchase of his bathyscaphe, dived to ever lower depths, finally in 1960 exploring the Mariana Trench at 35,800 feet below sea level. This, the lowest point on the earth's crust known to man, proved still not too deep for some forms of life. (Through their window during the 20 minutes they tarried at the bottom, the two divers saw a flatfish of the sole family and a squid.) Mariana Trench and a number of other deep trenches lay along the western and eastern borders of the Pacific. They took on new and exciting significance at the end of this period, in company with the underwater ridge and canyon ascertained in the mid-Atlantic in the earlier part of the decade.

Bruce Heezen and Maurice Ewing suggested in 1956 that the mid-Atlantic ridge and canyon they had recently pointed out might form a part of a worldwide system. Topographic soundings made during the next few years, partly under the guidance of the Lamont-Doherty Geological Observatory of Columbia University, indicated the existence of such a system, stretching some 40,000 miles. It ran from the Arctic Ocean through the North and South Atlantic, around the southern end of

741

Africa into the Indian Ocean (where an arm reached toward the Gulf of Aden), between Australia and Antarctica to the Pacific Ocean (where another arm pointed toward New Zealand), and finally through the southern and eastern Pacific to the entrance of the Gulf of California. In the eastern Pacific, a ridge (or more gentle "rise") without a canyon stood about 20 miles wide and 5,000 feet in altitude from its base. Elsewhere, widths ranged up to about 30 miles and elevations to as much as 13,000 feet above the base. The canyons (now recognized as "rift valleys" like those sometimes found on land) ran along the crest of the ridges, with depths ranging up to about 5,000 feet. After running a linear course for some distance, both ridge and rift valley might continue on a parallel line either to the left or right of the previous path.

During the course of this study, scientists at the Lamont-Doherty Observatory and at the Scripps Institution of Oceanography of the University of California noticed other characteristics of the deep oceans largely overlooked until this time. Rocks examined from the ocean floor, it appeared, all derived from some age later than the Permian -- their deposit had occurred in the last 200,000,000 years. The sediment of the ocean bottom, far from having accumulated for some 3,000,000,000 years as science had taken for granted, seemed still younger than the oldest rocks. Volcanic islands and submerged volcanoes also revealed in their geology that their ages extended back to periods more recent (never older) than the Permian. Henry William Menard of California, working with the Scripps Institution, discovered hundreds-of-miles-long, straight, east-west "fracture zones" (consisting of ridge and trough) in the eastern Pacific. Victor Vacquier of Russia, emigrated to the United States and also at Scripps, showed in 1960 that patterns of magnetic measurements of bottom rocks continued north-south across these fracture zones, but with displacement to the right or left like the ridges and rift valleys in the mid-Atlantic and mid-Indian Oceans.

Early in this period, two groups of British investigators studied the remanent (remnant) magnetism of continental rocks. To the extent that the rocks show traces of magnetism, their magnetic lines indicate the direction in which the earth's poles lay at the time of the rocks' deposition. A team directed by Patrick Maynard Stuart Blackett of England had already stated (1954) that British rocks of 200,000,000 years age seemed to require a position farther south and rotated counterclockwise 30° from the present location of the British Isles. Now the same group announced an indication from rocks in India that that subcontinent had migrated rapidly to the north during the past 80,000,000 years. Another team headed by Stanley Keith Runcorn of England had studied the possibility of polar wandering from the remanent magnetism of rocks in Eurasia and North America. Runcorn developed smoothly curved paths along which the North Pole seemed to have passed according to the evidence of the rocks. When the North American path turned out to diverge from the Eurasian path as they proceeded backwards in time, Runcorn came to the conclusion (1956) that the two continents had once formed one unit and since separated, carrying their magnetized rocks apart. He thus accepted Alfred Wegener's theory of continental drift.

Harry Hammond Hess of New York proposed a theory in 1960 to account for the revelations of the past several years. Chairman of the department of biology at Princeton University and a specialist on oceanic volcanoes, Hess had studied under Felix Andries Vening Meinesz of the Netherlands (himself active through this period), who first noticed that the earth's gravity measured considerably less over its deep-sea trenches than elsewhere, and believed this fact indicated a downward movement within the earth at the site of the trenches. Hess took up this point, the information on the oceanic ridges and rift valleys,

743

the facts concerning the relative youth of the ocean floors, and a "convection current" hypothesis of movement within the earth (expounded by Arthur Holmes of England in 1928), combining them into a scheme that provided the first reasonable mechanism for an explanation of continental displacement.

Hess suggested that the ocean floors aside from the ridges represented not a part of the earth's crust but the mantle itself, which in continental areas lies underneath the crust. Convection currents within the mantle, he proposed, bring an upswelling of material at the sites of the oceanic ridges. Lava flows at those points produce the ridges. The mantle flows in both directions perpendicular to the ridges, spreading from the rift valleys, and sometimes carrying with it the heavy superstructure of one of the earth's continents. Eventually, the mantle material descends again toward the earth, at the sites of the deep-sea trenches. The pressures built up by the descending mantle cause volcanic eruptions, accounting for the islands very often found alongside the trenches. The oceans as they now exist have formed since Permian times. The ocean floors that existed earlier have returned to the depths of the earth. The proposals of Harry Hammond Hess, submitted in an essay distributed to colleagues, shook the world of geology.

Commercial jet airline service, introduced on a regular basis by the British in 1952, became common between major airports of the world by the year 1960. Jet airline passengers flew higher than they had in propeller-driven planes. In 1959, after its design by Christopher Cockerell of England, the first air-cushion vehicle crossed the English Channel from the United Kingdom to France. The air-cushion vehicle found its niche in flying lower than other machines. Its success over reasonably calm water suggested its possible use on land, where a concrete strip could provide

744

the base on which its operation depended.

The first suggestion that an air cushion beneath a ship might greatly facilitate the ship's progress forward appeared in the 1870's. No one succeeded in designing a concave bottom that would hold the air cushion in place. After World War II, Cockerell as a boatbuilder devoted his talents to the problem. He learned to channel air toward the peripheries of a broad-based craft, so that as the air emerged at the bottom of the craft it created its own curtain to hold itself under the craft. Aware that his principle would permit a not-too-heavy vehicle to hover above the surface of the water, Cockerell suggested that the British government develop such a machine. During three years of further work (1956-9), a rubberized fabric skirt around the hovering craft proved as efficient as the peripheral channeling of the air. The machine that crossed the English Channel weighed four tons, carried three persons, and moved forward at speeds up to 28 miles per hour.

The process of photosynthesis, by which plants appropriate the energy of the sun to manufacture their own substances, remained less a mystery by the end of this period than it had always seemed before. Botanists had understood a hundred years earlier that plants in sunlight removed carbon dioxide from the air, combining it with water from the soil to form their bodies, emitting oxygen into the air in the process. Later in the nineteenth century they learned that these operations took place within tiny structures that formed a part of plant cells. Called "chloroplasts," these structures all contained chlorophyll (isolated in 1817), the substance that seemed to make green plants green. Not until after World War II did scholars succeed in observing an intact chloroplast at work. In 1940, however, Robert Hill of England showed that green material from a broken chloroplast could break water down into its components hydrogen and

745

oxygen in the presence of sunlight and a strong oxidizing agent (willing to accept electrons).

In the later 1950's biochemist Daniel Israel Arnon (born in Poland, resident in the United States) studied the total composition of chloroplasts after obtaining the first one intact from a cell of a spinach leaf in 1954. Melvin Calvin of Minnesota worked out a six-cycle process whereby temperate-climate plants consume carbon dioxide, water, and chemicals from the soil to produce their own substance and oxygen. Robert Hill proposed in 1960 the details of two electronic processes whereby chlorophyll, sunlight, and an oxidixing agent might dissolve water into its components at normal summer temperatures. R. B. Woodward, the synthesizer of cholesterol, managed to synthesize chlorophyll in 1960, as science came apparently very close to the solution of another puzzle.

Two anthropological finds made during this period promised to help solve the mystery of the origins of man. Homo sapiens indeed remained more an enigma than the planet on which he lived. In 1958, two workingmen found a complete though flattened skeleton in a coal mine of central Italy. It received the name Oreopithecus (mountain ape), a label already chosen for scattered bones from the same vicinity. In 1959, Mary Douglas Nicol Leakey of England (in teamwork with her husband Louis Seymour Bazett Leakey, born in Kenya of British parentage) found a skull in Tanganyika, naming it Zinjanthropus or East African man. Scientists considered neither Oreopithecus nor Zinjanthropus an ancestor of modern man. Both, however, seemed to represent offshoots of the Homo sapiens line of descent after that line had separated from another leading to the modern apes.

The idea that man is related physically to the entire animal world of earth, whose creatures have become differentiated through the process of evolution, emerged only in mid-nineteenth century. Four scholars who had contributed much to the development of evolutionary theory remained active through this quinquennium. Alfred Sherwood Romer of New York emphasized comparative anatomy and embryology as keys to relationships among vertebrates. George Gaylord Simpson of Illinois specialized in the very distinctive history of early mammals in South America. Charles Elton of England, developing animal ecology as a science, spoke of the animal as selecting his environment rather than the other way around. Konrad Lorenz of Austria studied animal and human actions in an effort to ascertain the evolutionary roots of the behavior of the several species.

The modern system of classifying plants and animals took form a century before the theory of evolution. When man had to be fitted to the classification scheme, as people gradually accepted the idea of his evolution from lower orders of beings, his designation Homo sapiens included all the living races of mankind. Homo the genus stood structurally distinct from all other genera. Homo sapiens the species constituted a natural group for breeding. Physical anthropologists, in some overeagerness to establish links between modern man and the creatures he most nearly resembled, followed a tendency to apply names to fossil finds suggesting greater remoteness from Homo sapiens than the facts justified.

The fossils of the so-called Neanderthals, first unearthed in Germany in 1856, provided the earliest evidence of an extinct race of man. At first labeled Homo neandertalensis, a name for a new species, they later received the designation Homo sapiens neandertalensis. Not only did the Neanderthals possess intelligence, the evidence indicated, but they likely bred with other races to form the human being of today. Three later finds -- Pithecanthropus (ape man, Java, 1891); Australopithecus (southern ape, South Africa, 1924); and Sinanthropus (Chinese man, 1929) -- at first took these names of separate genera. Later, however, _Sinanthropus_ became _Pithecanthropus pekinensis_ (ape man of Peking) in deference to his relationship to the "ape man" of Java. Still later, most anthropologists recognized all the Pithecanthropi (from Java, China, Africa, and possibly Europe) by the name _Homo erectus_ (man of upright posture), a species described as ancestral to _Homo sapiens_. The Pithecanthropi had moved from "ape man" to "man." Even more recently, the suggestion appeared that not only the Pithecanthropi but also the much earlier Australopithecinae really belong to the genus _Homo_. This is the position taken, by inference, at the beginning of the first chapter of this book.

The Australopithecinae, or a considerable number of them, were the men and women living in South Africa a million years ago. They differed from modern man in some respects, but resembled modern man far more than modern apes. _Zinjanthropus_, found in 1959, seemed related to the Australopithecinae, but apparently constituted no match for many of them in intelligence. As the shaking down from genus to species to race continued in the official nomenclature, _Zinjanthropus_ (along with other less-favored Australopithecinae found since 1938) seemed a likely candidate for the position of the earliest _Homo_ found ineligible for the line of _Homo sapiens_. _Oreopithecus_, as much as 7,000,000 years of age, remained of uncertain classification, though possibly within the Hominidae, or family of man.

A new wave of unidentified flying objects appeared in 1956, reaching its peak in November. The interval between the crests of the waves, 27 1/2 months in 1950-2 and 26 1/2 months in 1952-4, had slipped to 25 1/2 months in 1954-6. Thereafter, the UFO phenomenon showed no regular pattern, new waves appearing every year. The shift came at the time of the first efforts of man in space. Whether or not UFO's possessed some existence other than in people's minds, it seemed obvious that the scanning of the skies induced by the artificial satellites had produced an increased number of UFO reports.

A wide range of persons stated in 1957 that they had witnessed strange objects close to them, on or near the ground. The most substantive of such reports came from Levelland, Texas, the night of November 2-3. There the occupants of seven separate vehicles (automobiles and trucks) -- all within a radius of 15 miles and a time interval of 2 1/2 hours -- encountered a brightly illuminated object sitting on the road, or in one case flying immediately overhead. On each occasion, the electric system of the vehicle failed (motors dying and headlights quenched) in the vicinity of the lighted object, but functioned normally when the object parted. Similar reports, applying to other sightings, came from elsewhere on the planet, adding substantially to the UFO mystery.

With no reference to these close encounters, Carl Gustav Jung of Switzerland in 1958 wrote _Ein moderner Mythus: Von Dingen, die am Himmel gesehen werden_ (translated as _Flying Saucers: A Modern Myth of Things Seen in the Skies_). A psychologist of world renown, Jung placed UFO's in the context of a "collective unconscious" and a series of "archetypes" he had developed in other writings. He believed that humanity shared a memory of previous experiences, deeply buried in the unconscious and dominated by specific archetypes in any particular age. The archetypes, psychic conditioners of a portion of human behavior (such as the tendency toward pugnaciousness), revealed themselves most specifically through abstract images in fantasy, paintings, and dreams.

Jung pointed out that physically real UFO's would provoke human fantasies "like nothing else," though the fantasies could also rise without such stimulation, particularly during the great change expected with a new age. He be-

749

lieved a relationship existed between the shapes reported for UFO's and the symbols he found in selected paintings and dreams. He hoped that this newly established relationship would yield eventual confirmation of a great human search for unity he had postulated, especially unity between "an enigmatic higher world and the ordinary human world." There is a possibility, he added, "that Ufos are real material phenomena . . . , presumably coming from outer space, . . . long . . . visible to mankind. . . . In recent times, . . . unconscious contents have projected themselves on these inexplicable heavenly phenomena and given them a significance they in no way deserve."

With no apparent reference to UFO reports, and motivated instead by developments in radio astronomy, some scientists expressed new interest at this time in the admittedly remote possibility of contact with extraterrestrial intelligence. Advanced civilizations elsewhere in the universe, amply supplied with energy, might have established radio beacons for other creatures who might be listening far out in the immensities of space. If such beacons existed, on what radio frequency might one listen for the best chance of picking up such a broadcast? The recently investigated "song of hydrogen" in space (see Chapter VI) suggested the 21-centimeter (1,420.4056-megahertz) channel as one certain to be universally noticed. Frank Donald Drake of Illinois at the National Radio Astronomy Observatory of Green Bank, West Virginia, listened to this frequency for a total of about 150 hours in April-July 1960, focusing his antenna on two specific stars.

Drake named his enterprise Project Ozma for the mythical land of Oz, created in story form in 1900. His own marvelous and distant places to which he hoped to tune were the stars Epsilon Eridani and Tau Ceti. At 10.7 and 11.9 light years distance respectively, they stood as the 9th and 18th nearest "fixed" stars in space. Astronomers rated the stars according to their spectra, signifying relative temperature and age, on a scale using the letters O, B, A, F, G, K, and M in that order for stars of the same chemical composition as the earth's sun. The letters ran from hot to cold and from young to old, each subdivided by number. (G2 lay closer to F, G8 closer to K.) Any life as known on earth could exist only on planets revolving about stars not greatly dissimilar to the earth's sun, rated at G2. Of the nearest 18 stars, Tau Ceti (G8) and Epsilon Eridani (K2) resembled the earth's sun the most, with only one exception. Alpha Centauri A, at 4.3 light years the nearest in distance (see Chapter VI), rated G2 like the earth's sun. Alpha Centauri, however, was a star of the southern hemisphere of earth's sky, unavailable for observation in West Virginia. Nor did Drake pick up a signal from Epsilon Eridani or Tau Ceti.

While extraterrestrial civilization remained a conjecture and the beginnings of human civilization an enigma, Charles Wright Mills and John Kenneth Galbraith wrote meaningfully of the world in which they lived. Both of them dealt with the United States of America, financially the richest nation of their time. Mills, a sociologist from Texas, taught at Columbia University, somewhat isolated from the realm of action. Since World War II, he had attracted attention as an author who painted in broad strokes with no fear of innovative thinking. Galbraith, an economist from Canada who moved to the United States as a student, taught at Harvard University. Known also as a popular writer, he took time off for political activity, especially as an aide to presidential candidate Adlai Stevenson.

Mills published The Power Elite in 1956, describing the "people at the top" in United States society, whose decisions seemed to mean everything in moments of crisis despite the aura of democracy. Mills did not contend that these people or their families had always held this criti-

751

cal role, nor did he attribute to them the
capacity to determine all history. He believed
only that an elite of power had developed in his
generation, consisting of "those who are able to
realize their will, even if others resist it."
The men in charge of the major institutions --
the "higher politicians and key officials of government," the "admirals and generals," and the
"major owners and executives of the larger cor-
porations" -- held this commanding position.
Deriving from the ranks of "the very rich," they
tended to form an interlocking directorate.
Harry Truman and Dwight Eisenhower, according to
this scheme of things, stood not so much among
the manipulators of power as among the manipu-
lated.

Mills refused to accept the widely held idea
that large numbers of people owned the nation's
wealth through their individual stockholdings.
Only 1.4% of all workers in manufacturing owned
any stock at all, he pointed out. The workers
indeed, far from controlling the wealth, stood in
process of transformation into a "mass society"
in which the individual "does not formulate his
desires; they are insinuated into him." Mills
also recognized the existence of a middle sector
whose opposing tendencies balanced one another.
He believed that the growth of the mass society
and the "stalemate" of the middle sector made
democracy impossible and rule by a power elite
quilty of a "higher immorality" possible. The
"robber barons" of the 1930's, reinterpreted by
historians, had become the "industrial statesmen"
of the 1950's.

"Those who sit in the seats of the high and
the mighty are selected and formed by the means
of power, the sources of wealth, the mechanics of
celebrity, which prevail. . . . A society that
narrows the meaning of 'success' to the big money
and in its terms condemns failure as the chief
vice . . . will produce the sharp operator and
the shady deal." Mills wrote to deplore the many
examples he saw of the sharp operator and the

shady deal in United States history since 1945, and the system he felt had given rise to them. "Blessed are the cynical," he said, "for only they have what it takes to succeed." In his argument, the United States had already moved in spirit from the third to the fourth quarter of the political spectrum. He did not indicate whether the nation's clinging to democratic forms held any hope for change in the future.

Galbraith published The Affluent Society in 1958, inspecting the same scene as Mills and coming up with some ideas about bettering the situation. Galbraith used the concept of "the conventional wisdom" of economic theorists in the United States, the laissez-faire doctrine as modified during two centuries of existence. Productivity, inequality, and insecurity (the last-named that of the entrepreneur as well as the workingman) served as the "ancient" preoccupations of economics, he said. Some economists paid more attention to one than another, but in the concoction of theories felt obliged to take all three into account. In the United States since the 1930's, however, Galbraith argued that productivity had eclipsed the other two preoccupations -- not for any vicious reason but only because inequality and insecurity had diminished in this one country -- which could now be described as an affluent society despite the financial problems of some families.

Galbraith assumed that the income of most people of the United States covered the universal wants of food, clothing, and shelter. If production in those lines amply met the demands of the people, the "conventional wisdom" suggested the nation need feel no concern about economic catastrophe ahead. Galbraith, however, pointed out that "as a society becomes increasingly affluent, wants are increasingly created by the process by which they are satisfied. . . . Increases in consumption . . . act by suggestion or emulation to create wants. Or producers may proceed actively to create wants through advertising and salesmanship." The new wants are just as real as the old ones, and may also cause economic difficulties, especially through the inflation of money. Galbraith accepted the idea (a part of the conventional wisdom) that inflation springs basically from the inability of production to keep up with demand. Inflation before World War II, he pointed out, came generally in moments of national peril, such as wartime. Inflation since World War II had become nearly chronic.

Conservatives generally favored "monetary" measures to combat inflation, such as an increase in the lending rate by national banks to make money more scarce. The higher rate of interest, passed along to lower banks and businesses, would ultimately (ran the theory) discourage demand and stop the price rise. The monetary measures had not prevented inflation in the postwar United States. Liberals, following the lead of John Maynard Keynes, British economist who died in 1946, generally preferred "fiscal" measures to the monetary. Keynes had won fame for his proposal in the 1930's to fight national economic depressions through government spending. The other face of this proposal stipulated that in times of inflation the government should reduce the amount of money available through an increase in taxes until they become greater than its spending. Budget surpluses resulting from this practice would balance out the government deficits caused by its spending in periods of depression. The problem with the Keynes proposal, Galbraith said, lay in the fact that "the policy never looks practical at any particular moment." Demands for government spending in one sector or another of national life produced continuing deficits in the budget, which varied only in size.

Galbraith spoke only briefly in this book of wage and price controls, seeing a possible efficacy for them in conjunction with fiscal measures. He felt that controls need not work great hardship on the majority of business men or the great mass of workers. He expressed more interest in a proposal of his own, a "theory of social balance." Galbraith believed that "by failing to exploit the opportunity to expand public production we are missing opportunities for enjoyment." The nation should recognize that it had put "bigger automobiles" ahead of better schools and parks. Without daring to employ the socialist vocabulary, he stated that public sector spending had fallen far behind that of the private sector in the United States, and that the consequent imbalance needed to be redressed. He spoke of the proposal as a "buying" rather than a "spending" program, a means whereby people would tax themselves to purchase community needs.

"To suggest that we canvass our public wants to see where happiness can be improved by more and better services has a sharply radical tone," Galbraith asserted. Yet to that large portion of the world where public-sector spending included many operations handled by private enterprise in the United States, his proposal seemed moderate indeed. The chief shock administered by Galbraith to liberals among his readers lay not in his proposals for government spending but in the method he chose for financing them. His recommendation for employment of the local sales tax seemed to underline his basic attitude that most United States people enjoyed genuine affluence. Workers had gained during World War II. The gross national product per capita in constant dollars, however, had decreased 7% in 1945-50, increasing only 13% in 1950-55 and considerably less thereafter. Most of them in 1958 lacked financial security of the type Galbraith seemed to take for granted.

Galbraith had worked for Adlai Stevenson in 1952 and 1956. Walt Whitman Rostow acted as confidant to John Kennedy in the campaign of 1960. Rostow, a native of New York and professor of economic history at the Massachusetts Institute of Technology, created the winning Kennedy slogan of "The New Frontier." Rostow published a small book in 1960, The Stages of Economic Growth, styling it "a non-communist manifesto." He used it to embellish a theme from an article of 1956, the "take-off" theory of economic growth. Rostow believed that nations of all quarters of the political spectrum had shared a common experience that profoundly affected their situations.

Most societies of both past and present, and all of them prior to mid-eighteenth century, Rostow classified as "traditional." In them, people generally assumed "that the range of possibilities open to one's grandchildren would be just about what it had been for one's grandparents." In some countries, however, the idea emerged of the possibility of economic progress. This idea and the changes deriving from it in both politics and the economy constituted the "preconditions" for economic take-off. The take-off itself occurred in Great Britain late in the eighteenth century, and in France, the United States, Germany, Sweden, and Japan in the nineteenth. It consisted in each instance of a period of a few decades when old blocks to steady growth were "finally overcome," the "forces making for economic progress" coming to "dominate the society."

After take-off, the nation needed approximately four decades for the next stage, the "drive to maturity." At maturity, "an economy demonstrates that it has the technological and entrepreneurial skills to produce not everything, but anything that it chooses to produce." The "age of high mass-consumption" generally followed maturity, and Rostow expected other stages beyond that he could not yet define.

United States leadership in the year 1960 appreciated the Rostow theory. It offered a convenient rationale for the acceptance of Soviet progress, so obvious since the appearance of Sputnik I. The stages of economic growth as Rostow described them depended not upon devotion to laissez-faire but on allegiance to the idea of progress itself. Take-off seemed as normal for the Soviet Union (or for China, Mexico, or India) as for any of the private-enterprise examples. More excitingly, it offered a new perspective to international aid. The United States could help friendly countries to reach their respective take-offs. The countries could then fly alone.

In actuality, few countries in the world possessed such capabilities. The great majority of national economies lacked the size ever to reach the point of maturity Rostow described, wherein "dependence is a matter of economic choice or political priority rather than a technological or institutional necessity." Flying together, not alone, would most assuredly become for these nations the new world order of progress. Economic growth, after all, remained a far more complicated affair than a treatise as short as that of Rostow could hope to describe. He himself claimed only for his book "that it is possible and, for certain limited purposes, it is useful to break down the story of each national economy . . . according to this set of stages."

Will Durant, Albert Guérard, and William Shirer wrote three extraordinary books of history during this period. That by Durant (1957) constituted the sixth in his story of civilization -- The Reformation: A History of European Civilization from Wyclif to Calvin: 1300 - 1564. The fifth of the series, The Renaissance (1953), had dealt with Italy alone through the same run of time. The Reformation spoke at length, with sympathy for both Catholic and Protestant contenders, of the religious transformation that provided its theme. Excluding Italy, it also treated, like The Age of Faith (see Chapter V), all the other aspects of life among Christians, Jews, and Muslims who lived during its period of time. Durant's Reformation began with the English John Wyclif of the fourteenth century rather than with the German Martin Luther or the French John Calvin of the sixteenth. Afterward, both geographically and ideologically, it followed the current of changing ideas wherever it

757

flowed.

Both Catholic and Protestant spokesmen
defended their outlooks in Durant's epilogue.
The humanist, however, held the last word. "The
real problem for the modern mind," he commented,
"is not between Catholicism and Protestantism,
nor between the Reformation and the Renaissance;
it is between Christianity and the Enlightenment
-- that . . . era which . . . hitched its hopes
to reason, science, and philosophy." For Durant,
the Enlightenment, though "hardly datable," began
in Europe soon after the conclusion date of this
volume.

Albert Léon Guérard, born in France, moved to
the United States in his twenties, before World
War I. He became a distinguished teacher, specializing in French history and thought, and won
respect as a literary critic dealing with a wider
realm. Guérard poured his best skill into his
comprehensive treatise, France: A Modern History,
published in 1959. The word "modern" applied to
this work in several important respects. First,
Guérard started with France's beginnings, accepting the nation's "prehistory" (the part before written records appeared) as an integral
part of the story. Second, he saved half of the
book for France's last century-and-a-half, thus
acknowledging the great transformations that had
transpired since the demise of the nation's absolute monarchy. Third, he wrote of all aspects
of French life, mixing comments on the economy
and society with those of a political nature,
producing a truly integrated account.

Fourth, while indicating complete respect for
the French nation at large, Guérard made clear
his understanding that French individuals could
have shortcomings, even at times selfish intentions, like people from the remainder of the
world. Writing before the solution of the Algerian question, he spoke in favor of the complete
integration of Algeria with France (the original
De Gaulle position) but insisted that "this im-

758

plies that every citizen in Algeria, without distinction of race or religion, must have exactly the same rights and opportunities."

William Lawrence Shirer, born in Illinois, became a newspaper correspondent in Europe. In 1937 he switched to the role of a radio correspondent, stationed in Berlin. His voice became familiar to a very large public in the United States. His Berlin Diary, reaching from 1934 to 1941, attracted much attention during the postwar era. In 1960, he produced The Rise and Fall of the Third Reich: A History of Nazi Germany. Shirer said that "most historians have waited fifty years or a hundred, or more, before attempting to write an account of a country, an empire, an era." The gaining of perspective in this fashion, he argued, nevertheless had to be balanced against the factor that the authors who waited such periods of time "lacked a personal acquaintance with the life and the atmosphere of the times . . . about which they wrote." Actually, many historians preferred also not to wait for such long periods of time to expire, but wrote monographs as soon as some of the documentary evidence became available for the themes they chose.

Shirer wrote his account of Nazi Germany on the basis of the large number of German war documents captured by American armies. His timely text provided informational detail that depicted Adolf Hitler and the men who surrounded him in more human terms than the propaganda of World War II, but left them none the less contemptible in most persons' views. Shirer's story portrayed little happiness, whether in the first astounding half relating prewar events or in the blood-bespattered second half dealing with World War II. His readers could plainly see that Hersey's The Wall and Remarque's Der Funke Leben, as well as Le dernier des Justes by André Schwarz-Bart (1959), dealt not with fantasy but with fact. They could also see in Shirer's text an ocean of human misery resulting from Nazi decisions that the three novels barely began to describe.

Two more books of this period added greatly to public enlightenment without revealing new information. Written by Rudolf Thiel and Loren Eiseley, both were integrating accounts in the history of science. Thiel, a West German student of physics, liked to write popular history. His book Und es ward Licht (And There Was Light: The Discovery of the Universe) appeared in 1956. It presented an account of the history of astronomy -- or more precisely, the story of the main developments in the astrology of ancient times, the astronomy of modern times, and the astrophysics of recent times.

Thiel began by giving the evidence (concerning fortune-telling and the wobble of the earth) that ancient persons studied the heavens with considerable care more than 6,300 years ago. He traced ideas through the "mystic childhood" of ancient and medieval times. He described the "heroic youth" of astronomy in the sixteenth and early seventeenth centuries, explaining the grip held by old ideas on the thinking of noted mathematician-astronomers of that time. Thiel gave proper recognition (more than most science historians) to the imaginative reasoning of sixteenth-century philosopher Giordano Bruno, who first envisioned the universe in terms familiar today. Thiel followed through with the "maturing cosmology" of late seventeenth and early eighteenth centuries, the "adventurous amateurs" of late eighteenth and early-to-middle nineteenth centuries, and the astrophysical "rejuvenation" since 1870.

Loren Corey Eiseley of Nebraska, a distinguished professor of anthropology at the University of Pennsylvania, wrote Darwin's Century: Evolution and the Men Who Discovered It in 1958. Unlike the chronological account of Thiel, this book presented a series of studies analyzing nineteenth-century thinking on evolution in depth. Eiseley showed how the world of science

760

moved hesitantly, almost fearfully, toward the idea of evolution prior to Charles Darwin's time. He portrayed both the magnificence and the shortcomings of Darwin's own reasoning. He stressed more than most writers the late thinking of Darwin, who died in 1882, and of Darwin's contemporary Alfred Russel Wallace, who died in 1913, outlining distinctly the differences between the two men.

Eiseley pointed out that Darwin's emphasis on struggle in nature caused him to neglect the cooperative forces found there, not only among individuals in a society but also among the myriads of cells which selflessly make up the individual. Eiseley, reminding his readers of the tendency of the biologists who first followed Darwin to think in terms of unilinear development of all animals, said that anthropologists remained slow in burying the similarly mistaken concept of a unilinear development of all cultures. And finally, Eiseley believed (as Wallace before him, though not with Wallace's extremism) that the growth of man's brain had introduced a new note of indeterminism in the evolutionary process, that man possessed a power of volition not present in other earth-species.

Eiseley did not take up the matter of scientific nomenclature -- the downgrading of the Neanderthals from species to race, and of the Pithecanthropi from genus to species. These very recent developments did not fit Darwin's century. Like them, however, Eiseley's reasoning pointed toward a greater distinctiveness for man than Darwinists generally had conceded. Man and his fossil bipedal relatives, wherever their remains may be found, fit the separate family called the Hominidae within the order of primates. Darwinists anxious to press the point of man's relatedness to the apes placed them there. Might people, on the basis of their superior brains and the seeming element of volition among them, find scientists willing to accord them the dignity of a separate order? On biological prin-

761

ciples alone, with more advanced studies of the brain, the answer might someday turn to yes. If not, there remained the possibility that factors other than the biological must be taken into account to define man's distinguishing marks.

In the first decade after World War II, with tremendous advance on the frontiers of science, no instrument conveyed a comprehensive picture of the levels at which the various world societies followed in their understanding. In 1957, the United Nations issued a <u>Report</u> <u>on</u> <u>the</u> <u>World</u> <u>Social</u> <u>Situation</u> which, for the first time in this realm, drew some valid comparisons including all the regions of the world. One table of particular worth listed countries and colonies according to the percentage of their children (ages 5 to 14) in school and the annual growth in such percentages in "recent" years (chiefly some portion of the period 1950-55).

Leading countries in population varied greatly in school attendance. China had between 20 and 40% of its children in school, but the enrollment in proportion to the (growing) size of its 5-14 age group increased more than 3% annually. India, in the same general bracket (20-40%), bettered its situation by less than 1% annually. The Soviet Union and the United States both had more than 80% of their children in school. Among other larger countries of the Orient, Pakistan and Indonesia stood in the 20-40% group, as Pakistan's proportion grew less than 1% per year and Indonesia's more than 3%; the Philippines, Thailand, and South Korea ranked in the 60-80% bracket; and Japan in the over-80% group. In Europe, West Germany, the United Kingdom, and France fitted the over-80% category, but Italy, Spain, and Poland remained at the 60-80% level, and advanced at less than one-half of 1% annually. In Latin America, the picture varied widely, with Brazil in the 20-40% position, climbing more than 1% annually; Mexico on the 40-60% level, climbing also more than 1%; and Argentina over

762

80%, climbing still at more than 2%. In Sub-Sahara Africa, Nigeria lay in the 20-40% group, increasing more than 1% annually, while Ethiopia's percentage stood less than 20. In the Middle East, Turkey and Egypt ranked on the 40-60% level as Turkey's proportion grew less than 1% annually while Egypt's increased more than 2%; Iran fell in the 20-40% bracket, climbing less than 1% annually.

Counting all the countries independent at the end of 1955, and paying no heed to size (but with North and South Viet-Nam, North Korea, Yemen, and Europe's tiniest five not recorded), Europe had far the most schooling of the five regions used in this book (eighteen countries over 80%, eight 60-80%, and only Portugal 40-60%). The Americas constituted a far-behind second (four over 80%, four 60-80%, seven 40-60%, and seven 20-40%). The Orient ranked third (three countries over 80%, five 60-80%, one 40-60%, seven 20-40%, and Nepal below 20%). The Middle East came in a rather low fourth (Israel over 80%, two countries 60-80%, two 40-60%, three 20-40%, and Afghanistan, Saudi Arabia, and Libya less than 20%). Sub-Sahara Africa, most of which at the time remained colonial, placed last (South Africa 40-60%, Ethiopia and Liberia less than 20%).

Regrouping the reported countries by position on the political spectrum at the end of 1950 (Iceland, Luxembourg, and newly independent Cambodia, Laos, and Libya are omitted here), the second quarter of the spectrum did the best in school attendance, with nine countries having over 80% of their children in school, Uruguay 60-80%, Mexico and Turkey 40-60%, and India and Burma 20-40% (with Burma's proportion growing more than 3% annually). The first quarter did second best, with three over 80%, six 60-80%, Mongolia 40-60%, and China 20-40% but growing more than 3% annually. The third quarter performed unevenly, with eleven countries over 80%, eight 60-80%, four 40-60%, eight 20-40%, and Liberia less than 20%. The fourth quarter held only Argentina over 80%, but four nations 60-80%, five 40-60%, four 20-40%, and four below 20%.

Recapitulating the same list of countries with the omission of the middle bracket of school enrollment, the political contrast may again be seen. The portion of the list with over 60% of the children in school included 82% of the communist countries, 71% of the democratic socialist, 59% of the democratic private-enterprise, and 28% of those often labeled fascist (Spain, Thailand, Argentina, Tai Wan, and Paraguay). The portion with less than 40% of the children in school, on the other hand, included 9% of the communist nations (that is to say, the one country of China), 14% of the democratic socialist, 28% of the democratic private-enterprise, and 44% of those of the fourth quarter.

Still another picture is obtained in a comparison of populations in 1955. Of the roughly 2,498,000,000 people in independent countries, about 39,000,000 lived in the countries not recorded. Of the remainder, 1,284,000,000 or 52% lived in nations with 20-40% of their children in school. Another 736,000,000, or 30%, lived in countries with over 80% of their children in school. In the countries of the bracket 60-80% there lived 11% of the people, in those of 40-60% just 5% of the people, and in those of less than 20% only 2% of the people. Thus a startling disparity appeared, as more than four-fifths of the people fitted two separated brackets, a little over one-third of that number living in nations of which more than 80% of the children attended school and nearly two-thirds of that number living in nations of which only 20-40% of the children attended school.

The "have-nots" in education, however, faced less a predicament than the have-nots in the economy. Of the 1,284,000,000 people living in countries of the 20-40% bracket, three-fifths (61%) lived with a situation of better than 1% improvement annually, and over one-half (54%)

with an improvement of better than 3% annually. Clearly, the world's store of knowledge would be much more widely disseminated in the future than in the past.

Art

Larisa Latynina, Boris Shakhlin, Agnes Keleti, and Ono Takashi in gymnastics . . Gert Fredriksson in canoeing . . Patricia McCormick in diving . . Yevgeny Grischin in speed skating . . Murray Rose in swimming . . Paul Elvström in yachting . . Australia in two Olympics . . Brazil in soccer . . Nikolais, Totem . . Schuman, New England Triptych . . Illiac Suite . . Blomdahl, Aniara . . Poulenc, Dialogues des Carmélites . . Barber, Vanessa . . Menotti: The Unicorn, the Gorgon, and the Manticore; Maria Golovin . . Britten, A Midsummer Night's Dream . . Ionesco, Rhinocéros . . Genet, Les nègres . . Pinter, The Birthday Party . . Adamov, Paolo Paoli . . Sartre, Les séquestrés d'Altona . . Frisch, Biedermann und die Brandstifter . . Dürrenmatt, Der Besuch der Alten Dame . . Osborne, Look Back in Anger . . Anouilh: Becket, ou L'honneur de Dieu . . Wesker: Chicken Soup with Barley; Roots; I'm Talking about Jerusalem . . O'Neill, Long Day's Journey into Night . . Miró: Night; Day . . Karsh, Portraits of Greatness . . Giacometti, Monumental Head . . Trier, Figur und Raum . . Wright, The Guggenheim Museum . . Le Corbusier, Chandigarh . . Ickikawa, Biruma-na-Tate-goto . . Lean, The Bridge on the River Kwai . . Wajda, Popiol i Diament . . Resnais, Hiroshima mon amour . . Bergman, Det sjunde inseglet . . Stevens, Giant . . Lumet, Twelve Angry Men . . Buñuel, Nazarín . . Ray, Apur Sansar . . Amalle, Les amants . . Godard, A bout de souffle . . Antonioni, L'avventura . . Fellini, La dolce vita . . Visconti, Rocco e i suoi fratelli . . Hitchcock, Psycho . . MacLeish, J. B. . . Perse, Amers . . Lerner, America as a Civilization . . Djilas, The New Class . . Heilbroner, The Future as

History . . Pasternak, Doktor Zhivago . . Castillo, Tanguy . . Schwarz-Bart, Le dernier des Justes . . Michener, Hawaii . . Tomasi, Il Gattopardo . . Doderer, Die Dämonem . . Lee, To Kill a Mockingbird . . Gary, Les racines du ciel.

The political crises of October 1956 affected the summer Olympic games held at Melbourne, Australia, in November-December. Sixty-seven national entities (two less than in 1952) sent only 3,184 athletes to participate. Egypt, Iran, and Lebanon withdrew from the games in protest over the attack on Egypt, and the Netherlands over the occupation of Hungary. Over half of the Hungarian squad refused to return home after the games. An Australian requirement for a six-month quarantine on horses coming from abroad caused the equestrian events (involving another 158 persons) to be held in Sweden.

With all the difficulties, however, the usual Olympic excitement prevailed. Agnes Keleti of Hungary won four gold medals in gymnastics -- on the asymmetrical bars and the balance beam, in the floor exercises, and as a member of a team with portable apparatus -- after having gained her first in floor exercises in 1952. Larisa Latynina of the Soviet Union also gained four gold medals in gymnastics -- the all-around competition for both individuals and teams, the long horse vault, and the floor exercises. Viktor Chukarin won his fifth, sixth, and seventh with the parallel bars and the two all-around competitions. Gert Fredriksson of Sweden earned his fourth and fifth in the 1,000-meter and 10,000-meter kayak singles races after taking them both in 1948 and the shorter in 1952. Patricia McCormick of the United States won first place in both springboard and highboard diving as she had in 1952. Murray Rose of Australia won three gold medals in freestyle swimming, in 400- and 1,500-meter races and the 800-meter relay.

The United States, the Soviet Union, and Uruguay won the gold, silver, and bronze medals in basketball as in 1952. The Soviet Union won the gold in soccer, Yugoslavia the silver a third time in succession, and Bulgaria the bronze. India continued its championship in field hockey, followed now by Pakistan and Germany. Hungary took first place and Yugoslavia second in water polo, as in 1952, the Soviet Union coming in third.

The table of comparisons among nations on the weighted scale used in this study (three points for a gold medal, two for silver, one for bronze, none for lower standings) shows seven nations holding two-thirds of the points in the summer games of 1956: the Soviet Union (with 184 points), the United States (169), the host country Australia (66), Italy (49), Germany (46), Hungary (44), and the United Kingdom (42). On the per capita basis, Iceland led with 12.5 points per million population, the Bahamas followed with 10.0 (both of these inverted calculations), and Australia stood far ahead of others at 7.0. Finland (5.1), Sweden (4.5), and Hungary (4.4) followed as a runner-up group, and Ireland (2.8), Denmark (1.8), Norway (1.4), Romania (1.37), and New Zealand (1.37) farther behind. Iceland, the Bahamas, Ireland, Denmark, Norway, and Romania took the place on this select list of Luxembourg, Jamaica, Switzerland, Trinidad-Tobago, and Czechoslovakia (the tie producing a total of eleven). The lower ratings of the leading squads on the per capita list (1.37 compared to 2.3 in 1952 and 2.8 in 1948) signified that individual competition in the Olympics had lost some of the distortions produced by the Second World War.

Thirty-two nations sent 923 athletes to the winter Olympics at Cortina d'Ampezzo, Italy, January-February 1956. Toni (Anton) Sailer of Austria won three gold medals in alpine skiing -- the slalom, the giant slalom, and downhill. The Soviet Union took first place in ice hockey while the United States again won second, and Canada dropped from first to third. The weighted scale for the winter games of 1956 reveals 32 points for the Soviet Union (the first time it had participated in these events), 22 for Austria, and 18 for Sweden. In per capita terms, the highest-performing squads came from Finland (3.7 points per million population), Austria (3.2), Switzerland (2.8), Norway (2.6), and Sweden (2.5). Switzerland and Sweden had not appeared on this list in 1952.

Eighty-three countries and colonies sent 5,396 athletes to participate in the summer Olympics held at Rome, Italy, August-September 1960. Boris Shakhlin of the Soviet Union won four gold medals in gymnastics -- the all-around individual competition, the parallel bars, the long horse, and the side horse -- after winning in the side horse and all-around team competition in 1956. Larisa Latynina won her fifth, sixth, and seventh with the floor exercises and the all-around individual and team. Ono Takashi of Japan gained three on the all-around team, the long horse, and the horizontal bar, the last a repeat of 1956. Gert Fredriksson earned his sixth in the event for kayak pairs. Murray Rose won his fourth in freestyle swimming, in the 400-meter race, a repeat of one of his three performances of 1956. Paul Elvström of Denmark won in monotype yachting as he had in 1948, 1952, and 1956.

The United States basketball team gained its fourth gold medal in a row, and the team from the Soviet Union its third silver, while Brazil took the bronze. Yugoslavia made it to the top in soccer after achieving second three times, followed on this occasion by Denmark and Hungary. Pakistan moved from silver to gold in field hockey, dropping India from gold to silver as Spain won the bronze. Italy returned as the champion in water polo (as in 1948), followed by the Soviet Union (moving from third to second) and Hungary (from first to third).

The points accrued by six nations on the scale used here amounted to two-thirds of the grand total. The Soviet Union again came out ahead (with 218), followed by the United States (160), Germany (85), Italy (72), Australia (46), and Hungary (41). The ten highest-scoring squads as measured against the populations in their countries were Australia (4.5 points per million population) and Hungary (4.1); followed farther back by New Zealand (3.0) and Denmark (2.8); and still farther by Finland (1.8), Switzerland (1.7), Italy (1.5), Bulgaria (1.5), Czechoslovakia (1.3), and Sweden (1.3). Switzerland, Italy, Bulgaria, and Czechoslovakia took the place on this list of Iceland, the Bahamas, Ireland, Norway, and Romania.

Thirty nations sent 693 athletes to Squaw Valley, California, for the winter Olympics of February 1960. Yevgeny Grischin of the Soviet Union won two gold medals in speed skating -- the 500-meter and 1,500-meter -- as he had in 1956. Competition in ice hockey brought the United States the gold medal (moving up from silver), Canada the silver (moving up from bronze), and the Soviet Union the bronze (dropping back from gold). The Soviet Union won 40 points on the scale used in this book, the United States 20, Germany 19, and Norway, Finland, and Sweden 15 each. On the per capita basis, Norway stood with 4.2 points per million population, Finland second with 3.4, Sweden next with 2.0, and Austria fourth with 1.4. All four countries had appeared on the list in 1956, along with Switzerland.

The World Cup tourney in soccer took place in 1958 in Sweden. Three of the leading four countries of 1954 -- Hungary, Austria, and Uruguay -- failed to reach the quarterfinals on this occasion. Teams from Wales, North Ireland, Yugoslavia, and the Soviet Union met defeat in the quarterfinals. Brazil won the cup in 1958, Sweden achieved second place, France third, and West Germany (holder of the 1954 cup) fourth.

Two of the internationally popular dances introduced in the previous quinquennium became known nearly everywhere in 1956-60. The cha-cha-cha made its way around the world, though by 1960 it showed signs of returning to its home in the Caribbean. Rock 'n' roll in the meantime became popular in many lands among young people. The older generation, many of whom lacked the agility to perform the gyrations rock 'n' roll demanded, tended to frown upon it rather severely. They criticized its music as too raucous, its lyrics as too frankly sensual, and its movements as improper, since they posed a couple facing one another without body contact. Actually, most folk dances in the world involved little body contact. Rock 'n' roll constituted a return to the enthusiasm and lack of restraint characteristic of informal dancing down through the centuries. A new trend in the late 1950's, however, encouraged young people merely to listen rather than to dance the rock rhythms.

Another type of music, the calypso from Trinidad, experienced a round of international popularity during this period. The calypso appealed to persons of all ages, though again there existed a strong tendency to listen rather than to attempt to follow the calypso tempo in dance. Among older people, the fox-trot and waltz remained the most popular of the dances.

More people began to attend performances by trained dance companies, as international visits of ballet teams received great publicity. The ballet of the Soviet Union, superb in the European traditional stylings, visited the United States. A troupe from the United States performed both traditional and modern ballet movements in the Soviet Union. Alvin Ailey of Texas created new modern dance enthusiasm through depictions of Negro moods in both festive and religious occasions. Alwin Nikolais of Connecticut in 1960 choreographed Totem, 15 episodes of modern dance treating the theme of ritual in its widest and most varied aspects, placing emphasis on shape and color along with the music and dance.

Gunther Schuller of New York achieved distinction during this period for his symphonic jazz, combining the classical styles with jazz techniques. Ernst Krenek of Austria, moved to the United States, wrote a very wide variety of music, employing traditional, twelve-tone, and electronic techniques. William Schuman, who had already won fame for his blending of musical types, wrote the New England Triptych in 1956, building upon fuguing tunes and other songs popular when the United States achieved its independence. The same freedom from restraint led to the composition in 1956 of Illiac Suite (for string orchestra), "written" by University of Illinois computers that had been fed data on the composition's characteristics.

Modern opera attracted much attention on the concert stage. One ultra-modern rendition, by Karl-Birger Blomdahl of Sweden (1959) took the name of Aniara, a spaceship in which 8,000 people on their way to Mars learn that because of a collision with an asteroid they are doomed to travel forever in space. Aniara combined tape-recorded sounds with those live on the stage. Francis Poulenc of France looked backward rather than forward in time, without the use of tape but retaining his individuality, when he wrote Dialogues des Carmélites (Dialogues of the Carmelites, 1957), the story of 16 nuns condemned to the guillotine during the eighteenth-century French revolution for refusing to disband their order. Samuel Barber of Pennsylvania wrote the music for Vanessa, produced in 1958, speaking in more romantic vein of the lady Vanessa waiting for the return of her lover, and after 20 years accepting the son of the lover in his stead.

Gian Carlo Menotti, who shared a residence with Barber, wrote the words for Vanessa. Menotti also wrote both words and music for The Unicorn, the Gorgon and the Manticore in 1956, combining seventeenth- and twentieth-century

771

musical ideas. The three mythical animals are the pets of a poet, who becomes annoyed at neighbors attempting to emulate him (literally, to own the same pets). Menotti produced still another opera, _Maria Golovin_, in 1958. Maria, while waiting for the return of her husband, a prisoner of war, accepts the love of a blind friend, who attempts to kill her when her husband returns, but fails and does not realize that the couple have become reunited. Benjamin Britten, who had kept pace with Menotti through all the interval since World War II, in 1960 produced the opera _A Midsummer Night's Dream_, based on the late sixteenth-century play by Shakespeare. In it, as in other work by himself and Menotti, Britten chose the varieties of music suited to his characters, without the restraints of former times.

The absurdist trend in the writing of plays continued during this period, though other drama forms acquired new strength. Eugène Ionesco wrote _Rhinocéros_ (1959), in which one person after another (in a small town) gladly chooses to exchange his human form for that of the once-deemed-ugly beast. The individualist in human society is rare, runs the theme, and even the one who does not go along is unhappy when he finds himself alone. Jean Genet of France, after a quarter-century of life as a criminal, wrote _Les nègres_ (_The Blacks_, 1959). In this complicated play, a group of Negroes demonstrate the murder of a white woman before a court of Negroes masked as white persons. The demonstrators then proceed, with a hint that blacks all over the world are rising, to kill the members of the court. "We are what they want us to be," assert the murderers. "We shall therefore be it to the end, absurdly." Harold Pinter of England produced _The Birthday Party_ (1958), the story of five individuals in a boarding house. Ridiculously, they celebrate the birthday of one whose birthday is not, and speak all manner of calumny about one another without any basis in fact. Thus Pinter introduced to England what Ionesco in _La canta-_

<u>trice</u> <u>chauve</u> had brought to France in 1950.

Arthur Adamov, born in the Russian-held Caucasus but resident in France, presented a play only semi-absurdist in nature in <u>Paolo</u> <u>Paoli</u> (1957). Paolo Paoli, a businessman before World War I, sells objects made of butterfly wings. His attitude of strict attention to trade, caring more for money than for people, multiplied many thousand of times leads to the great tragedy of the war. Jean-Paul Sartre, no writer of absurdist plays himself though he had provided their inspiration, wrote <u>Les</u> <u>séquestrés</u> <u>d'Altona</u> (called imprecisely <u>The</u> <u>Condemned</u> <u>of</u> <u>Altona</u>, or sometimes <u>Loser</u> <u>Wins</u>) in 1959. While his country recovers from the conflict (hence the last title), a German remains hidden in an attic, tormented by his conscience for his treatment of prisoners during World War II. Sartre intended to point a finger at the situation of some of his countrymen in respect to their treatment of Algerians. Max Frisch, author of <u>Die</u> <u>Chinesische</u> <u>Mauer</u> in 1946, produced <u>Biedermann</u> <u>und</u> <u>die</u> <u>Brandstifter</u> (<u>Biedermann</u> <u>and</u> <u>the</u> <u>Firebugs</u>, or simply <u>The</u> <u>Firebugs</u> or <u>The</u> <u>Fire</u> <u>Raisers</u>) in 1958. Biedermann (or "honest man") exercises a kindness to those immediately confronting him that borders on faintheartedness, extending hospitality to two men who actually borrow matches from him to set fire to his house. In this instance, the play did not share the absurdity of the situation. Frisch intended to portray the predicament of Eduard Benes and Jan Masaryk in Czechoslovakia, 1948.

Two more plays of this time period described very unusual, though not absurd, situations. Friedrich Dürrenmatt of Switzerland presented <u>Der</u> <u>Besuch</u> <u>der</u> <u>Alten</u> <u>Dame</u> (<u>The</u> <u>Visit</u> <u>of</u> <u>the</u> <u>Old</u> <u>Lady</u>, or simply <u>The</u> <u>Visit</u>) in 1956. The old lady is a wealthy one who returns to her home town where everyone is poor, and through the charm of her purse slowly persuades the villagers to murder the male one of them who had deserted her in her childhood. John Osborne of England wrote <u>Look</u>

773

<u>Back</u> <u>in</u> <u>Anger</u> (1956), in which a young married couple renounce with vehemence the life of their bourgeois parents without turning to anything better in its stead. Like Holden Caulfield in <u>The Catcher in the Rye</u>, they are put off by what they have seen of the life about them but perceive no resolution of the conflict. This situation, emerging in real life in selected countries, remained unusual for the theater of the late 1950's.

Jean Anouilh, who had dealt with fifteenth-century France in <u>L'alouette</u>, portrayed twelfth-century England in <u>Becket, ou L'honneur de Dieu</u> (<u>Becket, or The Honor of God</u>), 1959. Thomas à Becket, a wordly man in this account, finds the "honor of God" in himself through accepting the archbishopric of Canterbury. King Henry II, Becket's once close friend, pronounces the words of impatience ("Will no one rid me of him?") that bring about Becket's death, then swears that he will find the murderers to defend the "honor of God."

Arnold Wesker of England (1958-60) wrote three plays touching upon the experiences of one working-class family. In <u>Chicken Soup with Barley</u>, the father eats well (on charity) while neighbors feed his daughter. In <u>Roots</u>, a son who has escaped the family background rejects a girlfriend who has not similarly emerged. ("I ent got no roots," she says.) In <u>I'm Talking About Jerusalem</u>, the once-poorly-fed daughter and her husband attempt without success to escape by turning to a model community emphasizing rusticity and creative craftsmanship. Wesker intended to stress his contention that there is no substitute for cultural education and socialism.

Eugene O'Neill, who died in 1953, won renewed attention in 1956 through the posthumous production of <u>Long Day's Journey into Night</u>, an autobiographical play he had finished in 1941 and requested not be presented until 25 years after

774

his death. In one long day of five scenes, Edmund Tyrone (O'Neill himself) finds that he has tuberculosis, while he, an older brother, and his father become whiskey-drunk and his mother returns to an old habit of taking morphine. There is no indication that O'Neill thought of the appropriateness of his theme for his audience; instead, he wrote of one family's tragedy, through whose dense fog of desperation and anger only a few rays of love managed to filter.

Painting and sculpture in these years largely followed directions already established. Joan Miró, famed as a surrealist painter since the 1920's, contributed attractive murals labeled Night and Day for the new headquarters of UNESCO in Paris. Franz Kline attracted continued attention to his bold, abstract strokes in black and white. Mark Rothko (Marcus Rothkovitch of Russia, emigrated to the United States) as another abstractionist painted rectangles upon rectangles, emphasizing the sensuousness of color. On the margins of the field of painting, especially in Japan and the United States, there appeared a phenomenon known as the "happening," not dependent upon witnesses for its "success." In the happening, unrehearsed art activities related in causation and time sequence themselves constituted the art experience. An automobile might be laundered in artistic fashion, for instance. On another margin of painting, Yousuf Karsh of an Armenian family in Turkey, who had taken up residence in Canada, exhibited excellent photographic studies of a variety of the world's most famous people in Portraits of Greatness, 1959.

Three of the leading sculptors of this period appeared earlier in this study. Alberto Giacometti continued producing his attenuated figures in bronze, including among them an impressive Monumental Head, three feet in height. Henry Moore, likewise working in bronze, introduced new and mixed symbolism into figures which grew greater and greater in size. Barbara Hepworth experimented further with sculptural abstractions as she also turned to bronze for outdoor decorations. César Baldaccini, known as César, of France, became noted for a variety of figures built from old parts of machines (such as automobiles), often compressed before he assembled them.

In 1960, Eduard Trier of West Germany wrote <u>Figur</u> <u>und</u> <u>Raum</u> (<u>Form</u> <u>and</u> <u>Space</u>), a book about twentieth-century sculpture. Form, Trier said, is the "living tradition" in modern-day sculpture, while space is the "bold renewal" that makes twentieth-century sculpture different from that of preceding times. Trier used six classifications to sort out the sculpturing art of the century, ranging from preoccupation with form to engrossment with space. They were (1) "kernel sculpture," the traditional pieces of compact mass; (2) the "opening up of solid volume," where spaces or holes begin to appear; (3) the "sign in space," in which disembodiment becomes more complete; (4) "constructions," which give space considerations dominance over form; (5) "sculpture in motion," in which slight forms move through vaster spaces; and (6) "relief," the border where sculpture meets painting, a zone in which space considerations dominate completely.

To discuss the meaning of particular works, Trier grouped them into models of people, of animals, of growth, of miscellaneous objects, and of the landscape, subdividing each group into the classifications of form and space. His group of artists interested in models of people included, of those mentioned in these pages, Manzù (classification 1); Marini, Moore, and Richier (classification 2); Giacometti and Picasso (3); and César (4). The group interested in miscellaneous objects included Arp (also interested in "growth" models, classification 1), Hepworth (2), and Smith (3). Modern sculpture will achieve its purpose, Trier believed, as it finds a natural unity with architecture. In the discussion of this theme, he gave special recognition to Henry Moore of England, who figured not only with

776

sculptures of people (classification 2) but with relief designs incorporated into the very walls of new buildings.

Architecture took new strides in this period as World War II destruction receded even farther into the background. Frank Lloyd Wright made his most remarkable contribution in the design of the Solomon R. Guggenheim Museum in New York City -- completed in 1959, the year of Wright's death. One of the two circular structures that comprised the museum stood much wider at the top than at the bottom, providing exhibition space along circular ramps that narrowed as they descended and offered a continuous view of the ground floor interior. Alvar Aalto of Finland constructed a notable House of Culture in Helsinki, irregular and most pleasing in design, almost all shielded in brick. Pier Luigi Nervi of Italy helped to build sports palaces for the Olympic Games of 1960 in Rome, structures with domes that seemed from the interior to be floating in the air. Philip Johnson, born in Ohio, attracted attention to his designs for skyscrapers and museums as he had already for his modern homes.

It took the imagination of emerging countries in the late 1950's to build entire new cities with the latest architectural ideas. Chandigarh, designed as the capital of Punjab state in India, stood at the base of the Himalaya mountains. Le Corbusier designed the entire city as well as each of its public buildings, a project which he rightly construed as the ultimate in his career, one in which he combined both natural and ferroconcrete beauty with a high degree of functional quality. An architect 20 years younger, Oscar Niemeyer Soares filho of Brazil, designed the government center of Brasília, the new capital of his own country. The plans for Brasília, so far from the districts where most Brazilians lived, constituted the zenith of this decade of futuristic planning, taking for its theme that everything could be made beautiful in a site where man had not dwelt before.

End-of-the-war films with a lesson in each
one took precedence in this period in the motion-
picture industry over the pathos element so
strong in the preceding one. Biruma-na-Tate-goto
(Harp of Burma or The Burmese Harp) directed by
Ichikawa Kon of Japan (1956), told of the surrender of Japanese soldiers to the British in
Burma, and of the decision of one of them (a
musician) to remain in Burma as a Buddhist monk,
making amends for the warfare. The Bridge on the
River Kwai (1957), done by David Lean of the
United Kingdom, showed some British soldiers captured by the Japanese, constructing a bridge on
the railroad from Burma to Thailand, only eventually to see it destroyed by the captured men's
allies. Popiol i Diament (Ash and Diamond or
Ashes and Diamonds, 1958) made the last of three
war pictures directed by Andrzej Wajda of Poland;
it depicted the reactions of a variety of people
to the defeat of the Nazis and the birth of communist Poland. Hiroshima mon amour (1959), done
by Alain Resnais of France, constituted at one
time a love story (a French woman, punished in
1944 for befriending a German, now romantically
involved in Japan) and a sharp documentary reminder of the sadness in the first city to be
blasted by an atomic bomb. Det sjunde inseglet
(The Seventh Seal) by Ingmar Bergman (1957) had
nothing to do with World War II, but spoke of the
return of a soldier from a decade of war (the
medieval crusades) and his experiences in a
plague-ridden Sweden. The title came from the
book of Revelation in the Christian Bible, indicating the time of the end of earth-history
(the crusader played chess with Death throughout
the film) and the divulging of full Reality --
for Bergman a segment of Life devolving about a
few gentle, good, uncomplicated folk.

In the earlier part of this quinquennium,
other films attracting world attention dealt with
a variety of themes. Giant, directed by George
Stevens of California (1956) portrayed three generations of people in Texas, following character-
izations laid down by Edna Ferber of Michigan

778

(1952) in a novel of the same name. Twelve Angry
Men (Sidney Lumet of Pennsylvania, 1957) recited
the narrative of a jury proceeding in which one
juror persuaded all the rest to change a verdict
of guilty for a young man charged with murder.
Nazarín (Nazarene, Luis Buñuel, 1958) told the
story of an early twentieth-century Mexican
Jesus, in trouble with both the church and the
police, who came to realize the hopelessness of
his position. Apur Sansar (The World of Apu,
1958) concluded a trilogy of films by Satyajit
Ray, after Pather Panchali (1955) and Aparajito
(The Unvanquished, 1956). In Apur Sansar, Apu
became a man only to lose his wife in childbirth,
later finding reconciliation with life through
his son and a series of events recalling his own
childhood.

By the mid-1950's, however, the motion-picture industry found itself deserted by millions
of viewers who stayed home to watch television.
To combat the trend, film companies turned their
attention to the production of pictures oriented
toward adult audiences, treating subjects not as
likely to appear on the family screen. Les
amants (The Lovers, 1958) by Louis Amalle of
France exhibited in spirited but tender detail
the one-night rendezvous of a bored wife and a
traveler who happened by. A bout de souffle (Out
of Breath or Breathless, 1959) by Jean-Luc Godard
of France narrated the story of a young man
steeped in senseless crime and the girl who betrayed him. L'avventura (The Adventure, 1960) of
Italian Michelangelo Antonioni portrayed versatile actress Monica Vitti as Claudia, a girl who
sorrows for her best friend lost on an island,
but proceeds to become romantically involved with
the best friend's fiancé -- only to find herself
put aside like her friend, with life simply going
on.

L'avventura spoke of an affluent society, as
did La dolce vita (The Sweet Life, 1959) by Federico Fellini, which emphasized the erotic ennui
of the Italian moneyed class and the hollowness

779

of its pretension to a religion. Rocco e i suoi fratelli (Rocco and His Brothers, 1960) by Luchino Visconti took a close look at a segment of less affluent Italian society with its own version of love, degradation, and crime. Of the traditional types of motion pictures, only the unlikely but cleverly contrived horror cinema of Alfred Hitchcock (such as Psycho, 1960) matched the newer productions in their attraction for adult viewers. Hitchcock, born in England, had started his career there, but moved to the United States.

Television grew greatly in popularity as more transmitters and new programming appeared, as video tape came into common use for the rebroadcast of interesting happenings at convenient times, and as color came increasingly to the screen. Several countries in Asia and Latin America erected their first television stations, as well as a few in Sub-Sahara Africa. West Europeans enjoyed a variety of events carried by their network, while East Europeans began to build their own (connecting in to western Europe as well). The video tape, which made possible an immediate re-run of a film that had been taken for television, meant that public events occurring anywhere in the world could, with the assistance of airplanes, be shown within a short time to the people of any country who took interest in them. Television color developed slowly (chiefly in the United States) after its debut in 1955, plagued by a variety of technical difficulties, and posing the question whether broadcasting companies should develop color transmissions "compatible" with black-and-white (that is, so that both might be watched on the same screen) or should develop "incompatible" color pictures of a superior type.

The role of poetry in the world of literature remained the same in this as in the preceding period. Two examples of poetic narrative attracted considerable attention. Archibald Mac-

Leish of Illinois composed <u>J. B.</u>, a drama written in verse (1957). A modern man caught up in modern circumstances, whose initials happen to be J. B., plays out the role of Job in ancient Hebrew literature, losing his fortune, his children, his health, and his wife, while continuing to insist, "God will not punish without cause. / God is just." His tenacity in faith eventually brings its reward as he enters a new life. His returned wife Sarah points out, "Cry for justice and the stars / Will stare until your eyes sting. . . . You wanted justice and there was none -- / Only love." J. B. insists, "He does not love. He / Is." Sarah responds, "But we do. That's the wonder." Marie-René-Auguste-Aléxis Léger (pseudonym Saint-John Perse), born on the French West Indian island of Guadeloupe, wrote <u>Amers</u>, or <u>Seamarks</u> (also 1957). <u>Amers</u> related various aspects of the lives of both men and cities to pertinent qualities of the sea, emphasizing both the sensuous and the sensual ingredients.

Seven book-length prose essays of this quinquennium made a far greater impact than the narrative poetry. They were <u>America as a Civilization: Life and Thought in the United States Today</u>, completed in 1957 by Max Lerner, Russian-born citizen of the United States; <u>The New Class: An Analysis of the Communist System</u>, by Milovan Djilas of Yugoslavia (also 1957); <u>The Future as History: The Historic Currents of Our Time and the Direction in Which They Are Taking America</u>, by Robert Heilbroner (1959); <u>Figur und Raum</u>, by Eduard Trier (1960, introduced earlier in this section); <u>An Historian's Approach to Religion</u>, by Arnold Joseph Toynbee of England (1956); <u>Die Atombombe und die Zukunft des Menschen</u>, by Karl Jaspers of West Germany (1958); and <u>Konzil und Wiedervereinigung</u>, by Hans Küng of Switzerland (1960). The last three appear under the heading "Religion."

Max Lerner migrated from Russia to the United States while very young. He studied economics and government and became a university teacher, but attracted attention even before the Second World War for his writing. America as a Civilization, begun at the end of the war, culminated as a triumph of careful analysis and workmanship. Lerner wrote that he saw no single key to an understanding of United States civilization, but that the subject must be approached through an intricate "polar pattern" of tendencies. Seemingly opposed to one another, these tendencies nevertheless are the subjects to be investigated. "Americans," he said, "have an idolatry of production and consumption as they have an idolatry of success. But they have not idolized authority . . . and they still cling to individualism, even when it is being battered hard." The United States, he added, has " . . . a loosely planned and indirectly controlled progressive capitalism, whose big prizes continue to go to the rich, but which keeps a prosperous economy going for the nation as a whole. . . ." The life goals of United States people are "success, prestige, money, power, and security," but " . . . what validates these strivings for the American is the idea that he has a natural right to happiness."

"One may guess that America will lead the world in technology and power for at least several generations to come," continued Lerner. "But it is one thing to fill a power vacuum in the world . . . and quite another to offer to the world the qualities of leadership which it requires. . . ." America as a Civilization carried out this kind of balancing with virtually every facet of United States life. Its coverage included virtually all of the praises and criticisms voiced in the United States as well as those of foreigners who had studied the country (such as Harold Laski, 1948). Lerner did not investigate, however, the ideas entertained by other nations for their own satisfaction, such as the importance of minority representation in a democracy. Nor did he examine those aspects of the United States character revealed by the lack of interest in those ideas. How much did the image of the United States as a world leader suffer from its disinterest in other people's aspirations and ideas and its refusal to acknowledge other roads to happiness besides the one the United States had chosen?

Milovan Djilas built a career in the communist party of Yugoslavia, the country of his birth. In 1953, he became one of four vice-presidents of his nation. In early 1954, however, he lost his positions in the party, and in late 1956 found himself in prison, for expression of disillusionment with some of the party's program. The manuscript of his book The New Class, smuggled out of Yugoslavia, first became known through an English translation.

Djilas believed that in the Soviet Union, "Lenin's revolutionary Communism was replaced by Stalin's dogmatic communism, which in turn was replaced by non-dogmatic Communism, a so-called collective leadership or a group of oligarchs." The oligarchs differed from non-communist oligarchs of the past in that those of the past controlled governments to protect their private gains whereas these of the communist present constituted a new class, owning the entire economy and through their control of government protecting that much larger fief. Yugoslavia under one leader Tito, said Djilas, had passed through all three of the stages from revolutionary to dogmatic to non-dogmatic communism, and found itself subject to the new class as much as the Soviet Union.

The communist states, asserted Djilas, "have become uncommonly great physical powers, new and resistant, with a self-righteous and fanatical class which has tasted the fruits of authority and ownership. This development cannot solve any of the questions that were of concern to classic socialism of the nineteenth century, nor even those that were of concern to Lenin. . . ." Despite his negativisms thus expressed, Djilas did not favor a return to capitalism. He argued that

783

in the freer world outside the communist sphere nations like both India and the United States moved of their own volition toward socialism. He stated that in such (democratic) countries the government "cannot be an owner because it is subject to change. . . . All it does is administer and distribute, well or badly, property which does not belong to it."

Robert Heilbroner, author of The Worldly Philosophers (1953) and now of The Future as History, did not dissent from the Djilas outlook on democratic socialism. He emphasized one factor, however, scarcely mentioned by Djilas -- that powerful forces in the United States had assumed a very truculent stand against the emergence of any brand of socialism. The Future as History argued that the United States needed to look at the world about itself. " . . . It is difficult for us," Heilbroner said, "who are absent-mindedly creating our own civilization and . . . convinced of the purity of our international motives, to believe that much of the world sees us as a malign and threatening influence." If the United States would take a look at its place in global history, it would see that "it is in the very nature of a scientific technology that it steadily contracts the boundaries of the self-sufficient person while expanding those of the public particle." Heilbroner did not mean, however, to plead against technology: "The problem is not how to avoid the incursion of science and technology, but how to bring that incursion . . . under deliberate social control."

Heilbroner did not portray socialism as a goal "from which the next stage of development promises to be 'easier' or unambiguously 'better' than the past." Instead, he counted socialism as a step in history, and said that to face the future the United States needed to see it "as part of the sweep of history." Particularly, he pointed out, "There is needed a broad and compassionate comprehension of the history-shaking transformations now in mid-career, of their com-

784

bined work of demolition and construction, of the hope they embody and the price they will exact."

Novels of some significance abounded in this third quinquennium after the Second World War. Among them were <u>Doktor Zhivago</u> (1957), written by Boris Leonidovich Pasternak of Russia; <u>Tanguy:</u> <u>Histoire d'un enfant d'aujourd'hui</u> (1957), by Michel del Castillo of Spain; <u>Le dernier des Justes</u> (1959), by André Schwarz-Bart of France; <u>Hawaii</u> (1959), by James Albert Michener, raised in Pennsylvania; <u>Il Gattopardo</u> (1958), by Giuseppe Tomasi di Lampedusa of Italy, who died in 1957; <u>Die Dämonen</u> (1956), by Heimito von Doderer of Austria; <u>To Kill a Mockingbird</u> (1960), by Nelle Harper Lee of Alabama; and <u>Les racines du ciel</u> (1956), by Romain Gary of France. These novels dealt, respectively, with the life of a lonely poet in a communist revolution; the experiences of an adolescent caught between two extremes; the treatment of Jewish people living in Christian lands; the confluence of four unrelated families into the society of one island; the decadence of a princely family in a republican society; a maelstrom of middle-class activity against a European background; a pattern of racial relationships in the United States; and the importance of elephants, in Africa.

<u>Doktor Zhivago</u>, written by a poet about a poet, reveled in the natural scene. Planned for publication in the Soviet Union, it appeared in Italy instead when the manuscript revealed that poet-author Boris Pasternak lacked enthusiasm for certain aspects of the Communist regime. A widely hailed translation into English appeared in 1958. For both his poetry and this novel, Pasternak won the Nobel prize for literature in 1958, but declined to accept it when the Soviet government frowned upon the award. He died in 1960.

Yurii Andreievich Zhivago, orphaned in early childhood and raised by family friends, as a young man became a doctor of medicine. He married Antonina Alexandrovna Gromeko, or Tonia, the child of his foster parents. In World War I, he served in the Red Cross, behind the Russian lines. Wounded, he later took up duties in a hospital away from the front, where he first conversed with Larisa Feodorovna Guishar, or Lara. Zhivago returned to his family in Moscow between the two revolutions of 1917. For three winters after the revolution led by Lenin, the Zhivagos remained in Moscow, living in a small part of their former home, sharing (on government demand) the remainder with others, and suffering like them from cold and sickness.

Then, in effect, Yurii Andreievich and Tonia endeavored to put the revolution behind them, as they moved to an estate in Siberia once owned by Tonia's grandfather. In Siberia, however, they became caught in the swirl of fighting between "Whites" (anti-communists) and "Reds." Zhivago found Lara again, in the town nearest the estate -- she had gone there searching for her husband -- and began a love affair with her, only soon to be kidnapped and put to work as a doctor for Red partisans. His wife and two children (one of whom he had not seen) returned to Moscow during his absence, and later were deported to Paris. When Zhivago escaped from his captors, he looked for Lara first and his family afterwards. He lived with Lara and Lara's daughter for a while, after which the three of them moved briefly to the estate. Then Lara left with the man who had loved her mother, when he offered both Lara and Zhivago security outside Russian territory.

Zhivago returned to Moscow, taking up an old avocation of writing, but gradually becoming a derelict. He lived for some time, procreating two new children with Marina, the daughter of the former porter of the home where he spent most of his childhood. Zhivago left this new family to live alone, and one day died on the street of a heart attack. In an epilogue, Tania, the daughter of Lara and Zhivago born after the two separ-

786

ated, and brought up as an orphan in far eastern Siberia, appeared as a laundry girl during World War II, about to be taken under the protection of major-general Evgraf Andreievich Zhivago, half-brother of Yurii Andreievich and collaborator with the revolution, who had also protected Tania's father at critical moments during the poet's lifetime.

Non-communist readers acclaimed <u>Doktor Zhivago</u> as a portrayal of the suffering an individualist must endure under a collectivist regime. Pasternak seemed to identify individualism with Christianity in the remarks of one of his characters: "When the Gospel says that in the Kingdom of God there are neither Jews nor Gentiles, does it merely mean that all are equal in the sight of God? No -- the Gospel . . . said: In that new way of living and new form of society, which is born of the heart, . . . there are no nations, there are only individuals." Zhivago himself spoke negatively about communism: "Marxism a science? . . . Marxism is too uncertain of its ground to be a science. Sciences are more balanced, more objective." Another character asserted, "It has often happened in history that a lofty ideal has degenerated into crude materialism. Thus Greece gave way to Rome, and the Russian Enlightenment has become the Russian Revolution.

Yet, Zhivago himself had little to do with the Russian revolution after its first few years. He moved to Siberia, he stated, "in search of quiet, seclusion, and obscurity." Warfare between the Whites (supported by outside powers) and the Reds, not the revolution itself, spoiled the achievement of those objectives. His own lack of attentiveness, not the actions of a revolutionary regime, brought his separation from Tonia, his wife whom he had loved. And if Pasternak allowed Zhivago and others of his spokesmen to speak words contrary to the communist doctrine, he put very different language on the lips of some of his other persons. Lara's hus-

787

band, the night before he committed suicide, declaimed to Zhivago, "None of this can mean anything to you. . . . You grew up quite differently. There was the world of the suburbs, of the railways, of the slums and tenements. Dirt, hunger, overcrowding, the degredation of the worker as a human being, the degredation of women. And there was the world of the mother's darlings . . . ; the world of impunity, of brazen, insolent vice; of rich men laughing or shrugging off the tears of the poor, the robbed, the insulted, the seduced. . . . The night life . . . of the past century . . . existed in every city in the world. But what gave unity to the nineteenth century, what set it apart . . . ? It was the birth of socialist thought."

The interpretation of the novel Doktor Zhivago depended greatly upon the reader. The sophistication made it unacceptable in the Soviet Union, where artists continued to be expected to heap encomia upon the regime. It achieved popularity outside the Soviet Union not for the true depth of its character studies -- Pasternak made real people of his individuals, not half-animals as had Igor Gouzenko -- but because Zhivago evolved as a person who for the love of his individuality set his face squarely against the socialist regime. Pasternak, however, saw more sides to the matter than that. He even understood the very simple outlook of Marina's mother, when she became irritated at Zhivago's running too much water. "All that learning, and where has it got you," she exclaimed.

The true thrust of Pasternak's novel remained only obliquely anti-communist. It is revealed in the final verses he placed in Zhivago's pen. Here Jesus speaks, in the Garden of Gethsemane:

Seest thou, the passing of the ages is like a
        parable
And in its passing it may burst to flame.
In the name, then, of its awesome majesty

I shall, in voluntary torments, descend into my
   grave.

I shall descend into my grave. And on the
   third day rise again.
And, even as rafts float down a river,
So shall the centuries drift, trailing like a
   caravan,
Coming for judgment, out of the dark, to me.

Tanguy: Histoire d'un enfant d'aujourd'hui
(Tanguy: Story of a Child of Today, in translation called Child of Our Time) contained a simple
narrative, matching the experiences of its author
Michel del Castillo. Castillo, born of a Spanish
mother and French father in Spain, lived through
the Spanish civil war of the 1930's with his (republican) mother, later became a prisoner in a
Nazi concentration camp, and still later lived in
an orphanage under the Franco regime. The child
and young man Tanguy did very much the same.

Tanguy and his mother fled to France to seek
financial help from the estranged father, who
disliked the socialist views of his wife. When
the Nazis invaded France the father ("a little
tired of all this Communist scum," he said) denounced his wife and son to the police. Imprisoned by the Vichy regime, they escaped. The
police arrested Tanguy again, however, and the
Nazis took him to Germany when he told part of
the truth about his mother's past and intentions.

Tanguy lived in a special barracks for political prisoners in his camp. He knew, he said,
that "Russian prisoners were treated worse even
than the Jews; . . . that they only got one ra-
tion of bread a day and were dying, one by one,
of starvation and maltreatment." Tanguy fared
reasonably well because he managed to keep working and because his close friend Gunther, a German prisoner older than he, played the piano for
camp officers and received extra food.

789

Returning to Spain at the end of the war, Tanguy turned to the police for aid, only to find himself assigned to a combined orphanage-reformatory. The Brothers, uneducated laymen, ran this institution with the approval of the bishop and the state. ("They turn you into men," said the bishop, "perhaps, shall we say, a little against your will? Of course they sometimes have to beat you. . . .") Tanguy eventually went over the wall with Firmin, a boy who had killed his father when his father beat his mother. For two years, Tanguy found happiness in a Jesuit school; but at 18 years of age sought his parents in Madrid, Barcelona, and Paris.

Tanguy found his father in Paris, and his father decided to help him. Tanguy even took up residence with his father and stepmother. They quarreled, however, over whether Tanguy should keep the company of Monique, a secretary from a poor part of the city. The stepmother tried to calm the father. ("This child can't possibly understand. . . . You mustn't forget he's had to mix with workmen. . . . You've got to be patient. . . . He'll change.") But the father thought otherwise. "Bastard!" he shouted at his son, "I made a gentleman of you. . . . This is the end of it. Out into the gutter with you! Go and find your equals. . . ."

Tanguy at last saw his own mother, in 1955. "They completely failed to understand each other," wrote Michel del Castillo. "For her, the world could still be divided into two camps: comrades and bastards. The bastards were all those who were not on her side. Tanguy did not believe in a world thus split into opposing camps. . . . Because he had learned the value of his brother's blood, he could not bring himself to spill a single drop of it, even in order to build the best of all possible worlds."

A poet wrote Doktor Zhivago about a poet; a young man wrote Tanguy about a young man. André Schwarz-Bart, a son of Polish Jews himself born in France, wrote Le dernier des Justes (The Last of the Just), about a family of Polish Jews who migrated to France, and more particularly about the son named Ernie Levy. The story of Ernie Levy began, stated the author at the outset, in the English city of York on March 11, 1185. On that day, after a powerful sermon by a bishop, the Christian people of the city began to massacre the Jews. Some of the latter fled to an old tower, where the Christians besieged them for six days. On the seventh, rather than die at the hands of the Christians, the Jews submitted to death at the hand of rabbi Yom Tov Levy.

Somehow, the rabbi's son Solomon survived. When he reached maturity, the Eternal approached him in a dream, announcing that to all of Yom Tov Levy's line, lasting through the centuries, there would be granted the favor of one Lamed-Vovnik to each generation. The Lamed-Vov (each of them a Lamed-Vovnik) were the 36 Just Men of each generation upon whom, according to Jewish tradition, the world reposed. " . . . The Lamed-Vov are the hearts of the world multiplied, and into them, as into one receptacle, pour all our griefs."

Solomon Levy lived his adult life out in France, noticed by virtually no one. In the year 1240, however, in a disputation ordered by the French king ("Louis of precious memory," the one called by Christians a saint), Solomon suddenly stepped up to speak to a question concerning the divinity of Jesus. His reasoning condemned Solomon, along with others, "to a Mass, to a sermon, to the wearing of a yellow cloth disc and a sugar-loaf hat and, as well, to a considerable fine." Only Solomon suffered the additional penalty of having his living body cast into the flames.

Manasseh Levy, Solomon's son, in England in 1279 "had to suffer the passion of the wafer by means of a Venetian dagger, thrice blessed and thrice plunged into his throat." Israel, Manasseh's son, died an old man in southern France, of shame, after serving as the recipient of the slap administered annually to one Jew by the local count, at Easter time. Mattathias, next in the Levy line, met death in southern Spain, one of 300 Jews burned alive in a daily quota. Joachim became an exile from Spain, and later from Portugal. Chaim, raised in a Portuguese convent and ordained a Christian priest, nevertheless showed signs of loyalty to the faith of his fathers. He suffered from limbs broken on the rack, and one drop of molten lead each day poured into his eyes, his ears, his mouth, and his anus. A stone thrown in Germany killed Ephraim. A Russian tsar ordered Jonathan tied to a small pony's tail. Nehemiah lost his mind in Poland. Jacob died in a massacre in the Ukraine.

Another Chaim, next in the Levy line, settled in the (imaginary) town of Zemyock in north-eastern Poland. Though friends had to push him in a wheelbarrow because of the amputation of his legs, the townfolk recognized him as one of the Just Men. To everyone's perplexity, however, Chaim had five sons rather than only one (unlike each of his predecessors). He chose the least of them to succeed him, but this one announced on his own death bed that he heard no voice of God. From that time on, the Levys of Zemyock argued over which one of them should be recognized as the Lamed-Vovnik of his generation. Late in the nineteenth century, Mordecai Levy of Zemyock married Judith Ackerman, from another town, who took little interest in the Lamed-Vov tradition. When the Cossacks killed three of their sons, Benjamin remained alive. Mordecai felt that Benjamin, who took no interest in religion, could not be a Lamed-Vovnik -- but looked for a grandson who might fit the role.

Ernie Levy, as matters worked out after the family moved to Germany, was the second grandson, the one whom Mordecai chose to train as a Just Man should be trained. At the age of four, Ernie learned to read the Jewish scriptures and the book of martyrs of the Levy family. But one day

792

he spoke to his grandfather, "If all these stories are true --," and the old man interrupted to answer, "Well, what do you think, my little fledgling, can such things really happen?" And the child replied, "No, of course not."

Little Ernie's education in life lay ahead of him. Once, he was playing with Gentile schoolmates when they decided to act out "the trial of Jesus" and suddenly turned upon Ernie, beating him with rocks. ("It was the year 1933 after the coming of Jesus, the beautiful herald of impossible love," wrote Schwarz-Bart.) Later, a new teacher took the place of one Ernie had liked. The new teacher commanded, on the first day: "Die Hunde, die Neger und die Juden, austreten! Dogs, Negroes and Jews step forward!" -- but no dogs or Negroes were present. And again, trouble arose when Ilse smiled at Ernie, Ilse herself being non-Jewish. First came the taunts -- "I bet you've already kissed her on the mouth! . . . Or stuck his hand in the little basket!" Afterward came the torment -- "We can pull the Devil by his tail."

Ernie tried to commit suicide, in his home, but failed. In 1938, his family moved to France, where Ernie became a stretcher-bearer. The Nazis exterminated his family after they defeated France. Ernie himself went to Marseilles, and there became a derelict, putting aside his Jewish training for a time. Eventually, he found refuge in Paris with some old Jews of Zemyock.

And then Ernie discovered Golda, a Jewish girl, like him alone in the world; Golda limped on a wounded leg. After some time, with the Nazi threat always about the pair, Golda said one day, "Ernie, Ernie, I want to be your wife today." Ernie answered, "Perfect. . . . Excellent. The perfection of excellence. And where will you find a rabbi at this time of day?" Golda: "You know very well . . . that there is no thought of a rabbi in my heart." Ernie: "Perfect. Excellent. Then what is in your heart?" Golda:

"Please." Ernie: "Tomorrow . . . you'll be sorry not to have been . . . before God." Golda:
"Tomorrow . . . it may be too late." And later,
Golda again: "You're as handsome as King David,
do you know that?"

The Nazis did indeed seize Golda the following day, placing her in a camp. Ernie followed
her, and insisted that he be admitted also.
Ernie followed Golda all the way to the gas chambers, where they died together. Mordecai Levy
had made no mistake in regard to Ernie Levy's
place in the world. Four-year-old Ernie had misjudged the facts of the Levy family heritage.

Hawaii, by James Michener, started millions of
years back in history, rather than the hundreds
of Le dernier des Justes. Michener had taken
employment as a teacher and an editor before his
World War II experience with the United States
navy in the Solomon Islands of the Pacific. After the war, he wrote novels of life in the
Pacific islands and elsewhere, appealing to a
wide reading audience. Hawaii constituted a
prose epic of noble proportions, especially
suited for a new era. It suggested a grand path
for art literature of the future, working hand in
hand with new advances in science. For persons
so minded, it even pointed the way toward a
meeting place of art, science, and religion.

Michener's chapter headings (presented here in
their capitalized form) help to explain his
outline. First, he described how Hawaii itself
emerged From the Boundless Deep of the Pacific
Ocean. ("Raw, empty, youthful islands, sleeping
in the sun and whipped by rain, they waited.")
Next, he told of the emigration to Hawaii of Teroro, his wife Marama, and others From the Sun-
Swept Lagoon of an island near Tahiti in the year
817. ("Lacking both metals and maps, sailing
with only the stars and a few lengths of sennit,
some dried taro and positive faith in their gods,
these men accomplished miracles.") Third, he
related the story of Abner Hale From the Farm of

794

Bitterness in New England, his wife Jerusha, and their friends John and Amanda Whipple, on their way to Hawaii as missionaries in 1821. ("Go, spread a Saviour's fame," they sang, "And tell His matchless grace / To the most guilty and depraved / Of Adam's numerous race.")

Hakka-speaking Char Nyuk Tsin came in 1865 From the Starving Village of south China with her Punti (Cantonese-speaking) partner Kee Mun Ki and 299 other men to work in Hawaii's sugar plantations. ("Nyuk Tsin was the last person down the ladder. . . . When it became apparent that the hold was to be completely closed, the Chinese began a loud wail of protest.") Sakagawa Kamejiro came From the Inland Sea village of his parents, near Hiroshima, Japan, with a much larger group of sugar workers imported in 1902. ("The man on the horse is called Wild Whip Hoxworth. If you work good, he is good. If not, he will beat you over the head. So work good.")

Wild Whip Hoxworth was the grandson of sea captain Rafer Hoxworth, and (on his mother's side) of John and Amanda Whipple. Through his paternal grandmother, he could also trace descent from Teroro and Marama through 45 generations. During Wild Whip's time (1857-1927) the Hoxworths, the Whipples, the Hales, and their kin ran the Hawaiian Islands according to their whim. They brought profits into the islands from both sugar and pineapples, but distributed little of the wealth through the wages they paid. Other missionaries came and went, after the original families had turned to business. The Polynesian people they Christianized became fewer and fewer in number, until it could be said that northern Europeans, Chinese, and Japanese -- as well as Portuguese, Koreans, and Filipinos -- had taken over their islands.

By the end of World War II, Hawaii entered a new stage, the era of The Golden Men. ("A new type . . . was being developed . . . , a man wholly modern and American yet in tune with the ancient and the Oriental.") Michener introduced four of them. Hoxworth Hale, great-great-grand-son of Abner and Jerusha Hale, and manager of the business enterprises formerly headed by Wild Whip Hoxworth, understood the subtleties of the other characters well enough to serve as the purported author of the novel. "Hong Kong" or Koon Kong Kee was the grandson of Kee Mun Ki, who had died of leprosy at the age of 28, and of Char Nyuk Tsin, who served as Hong Kong's partner in busi-ness until she died at 106. Shigeo Sakagawa, the son of Sakagawa Kamejiro, became a United States senator and worked for land reform. "Kelly" or Kelolo Kanakoa, a beachboy who entertained divor-cees from the United States, teaching them how to surf, became the husband of Har Lin, or Judy, Kee, the daughter of Hong Kong Kee. Judy made well-to-do night-club entertainers of Kelly and another beachboy.

Kelly Kanakoa spoke both pidgin English and regular English. To his partner on the stage, he said, "More'n hunnerd years ago de missionary come dis rock and find my gradfadder you grad-fadder wearin' nuttin', doin' nuttin', sleepin' under de palm tree, drinkin' okolehau, dey raise hell. Bimeby hunnerd years later you me kanaka we doin' all de work while de missionary kids sleepin' under de palm tree, drinkin' gin, wear-in' almos' nuttin', and doin' nuttin'." (Kanaka is a term of affection between fellow Hawai-ians). To visiting Elinor Henderson (a widow rather than a divorcee), he commented further about the Christian religion, "It's as clear as the mountains at dawn. God loves first white men, then Chinese, then Japanese, and after a long pause he accepts Hawaiians."

Hawaii tied five family histories to the his-tory of one place. It largely omitted the Portu-guese, the Koreans, and the Filipinos who also came to the islands. It explained, however, such diverse phenomena as the relative barrenness be-fore man arrived and the effectiveness of much of the work done by the early missionaries. ("From a mean grass house, in which she worked herself to death, she brought humanity and love to an often brutal seaport," wrote Michener of Jerusha Hale.) It dealt with the water problem in Hawaiian farming, the search for good pineapples suitable to the soil, the labor unions in the sugar industry, and the burning and rebuilding of the local Chinatown.

Hawaii seemed bound to remain for some time a very effective complement to any study designed to explain Hawaii from the vantage point of either natural or social science. Michener in writing this novel pointed up the technique for a new class of literary artists in the future. They would familiarize themselves with the cross-segment of humanity living in a particular place, to explain with the help of science how the people and place came together, developing into whatever they happened to be at the moment the writing takes place. The artist who interlocked these elements with accuracy and skill would assist mankind in the search for new profundities in religion, since those profundities would stem from deeper and more comprehensive analyses of society.

Il Gattopardo (The Leopard) told of the demise of a family within a setting of decadence in nineteenth-century Sicily. Its author Giuseppe Tomasi di Lampedusa, of noble family himself, related the story of Fabrizio Corbera, prince of the house of Salina, which used the gattopardo for its insignia. Don Fabrizio's daughter Concetta played an important role, as did his nephew and ward Tancredi Falconeri, and one Angelica Sedàra, introduced at the age of 17. (" . . . Her skin looked as if it had the flavor of fresh cream . . . ; her childlike mouth, that of strawberries.")

Description rather than action provided this novel's strength. Don Fabrizio, Concetta, and most of their family saw their fortunes subside. Concetta lost out to Angelica in a contest for

797

Tancredi's hand, and lived like both her sisters to an old age unmarried. In the meantime, the bourgeois don Calogero Sedàra, Angelica's father, advanced in wealth and power. Tancredi, allying himself with liberal forces and marrying Angelica rather than Concetta, nevertheless retained the old family ties that led the island to decay. One decade into the twentieth century, the Salina sisters met their final humiliation when they learned that most of the relics in their private chapel held no religious merit, and would not receive the approval of the cardinal of Palermo.

Giuseppe Tomasi felt no optimism about the future of Sicily. Don Fabrizio, asked if he would accept appointment as a senator from Sicily, found it necessary to respond, " . . . Do explain what being a Senator means. . . ." The answer came, " . . . You will represent Sicily . . . , you will make us hear the voice of this lovely country which is now only coming into sight of the modern world, with so many wounds to heal, so many just desires to be granted." Fabrizio preferred not to give his assent, excusing himself with words like the following: "Sleep, . . . sleep, that is what Sicilians want. . . . All Sicilian expression, even the most violent, is really wish-fulfillment: our sensuality is a hankering for oblivion, our shooting and knifing a hankering for death; our laziness, our spiced and drugged sherbets, a hankering for voluptuous immobility. . . ." The only respite from Tomasi's sternness in regard to Sicily and its problems lay in his use of the phrase "in these days," referring chiefly to mid-nineteenth century and leaving some hope for the twentieth.

The life of Austria in the 1920's, as described in Die Dämonen (The Demons), varied considerably from that of nineteenth-century Sicily. In Vienna, the Austrian capital where most of this novel's action took place, the former nobility mixed well with the bourgeois class, as both looked down upon the mass of manual laborers whom they called "the soot." Heimito von

Doderer, the author, born near Vienna, spent several years in Siberia after being captured by the Russians during World War I, and later served as a German air officer in World War II. He held a doctorate in history, but attracted attention with his fiction. He began the rather lengthy Die Dämonen in 1931, electing for his title to copy the German name of the novel published by Russian Fyodor Dostoyevsky in 1871, called in English not The Demons but The Possessed.

Doderer's characters were not demons, but full human beings possessing and sometimes possessed by the frailties that normally affect their kind. Even the narrator, Georg von Geyrenhoff, shared in the weaknesses of his generation. Meisgeier ("the Claw"), a murderer, approached demon-status; but Doderer balanced this single case with the wise and virtuous Kyrill Scolander, who stood for the Austrian philosopher Albert Paris Gütersloh (pseudonym of Albert Konrad Kiehtreiber), whom Doderer admired in real life. Other chief characters (of a total of 142, almost all finely delineated) included Kajetan von Schlaggenberg, who became separated from his wife while engaged in a search for the perfect "fat female;" Charlotte (called Quapp), Kajetan's "sister," who turned out not to be even a half-sister but the illegitimate child of a very wealthy captain Georg Ruthmayr and countess Claire Charagiel; Friederike Ruthmayr, the widow of Georg, who eventually married narrator Geyrenhoff; financier Levielle, who for 13 years kept secret the terms of Georg Ruthmayr's will, which recognized Quapp as his child; and René von Stangeler, a 30-year-old historian who became the archivist of Neudegg Castle, where the countess Claire Charagiel had lived.

No climax appeared in Die Dämonen. It possessed more the quality of an Antonioni motion-picture film, in which life simply goes on. A great fire and general strike (Vienna, July 15, 1927) provided end-of-the-novel connections for many of the characters, but produced little

change in the immediate scene. Doderer believed
that the day of the fire marked the beginning of
the end of Austrian freedom -- that the workers
who started the fire and carried out the strike
(after the murders of two of their number had
gone unpunished) had a hand in bringing in Austria's fascist regime of 1934-8. Doderer chose
not to make this conclusion explicit in his novel, however. Instead, he contented himself with
the investigation of such details as the manuscript (transcribed in full) which Stangeler
found in the Neudegg archives, indicating that
fifteenth-century witch trials sometimes contained strong erotic overtones; or with the application of Scolander's thinking to the problems
of the 1920's. The demons of the twentieth century, in contrast to those of the fifteenth,
Doderer almost surreptitiously pointed out, were
the "rival philosophies" (presumably socialism
and fascism) whose origins he felt had nothing to
do with the progress of humanity.

The meaning of life, said René von Stangeler,
"will not be found in the facts . . . outside
. . . ; it will certainly be found inside
. . . , and will consist in the fulfillment of
one's proper destiny. . . ." (Here, Doderer's
thinking lay close to that of both philosopher
Karl Jaspers and evangelist Billy Graham.)
" . . . In the long run," added another friend
(who attributed the idea to Stangeler, who in
turn often cited Scolander), "true community
cannot rest upon a base that is held in common;
it must rest upon what is not common, upon the
singular, the personal, the noncommunicable
qualities that each possesses. . . ."

To Kill a Mockingbird came from the pen of
Nelle Harper Lee, who had studied law and the
mores of the Deep South of the United States. It
told the story of Jean Louise ("Scout") Finch at
the age of six to eight, as recounted by herself
later. Her older brother Jeremy Atticus ("Jem")
Finch, ages ten through twelve, emerged equally
important in the account, as did lawyer Atticus

800

Finch, Jem's and Scout's father. All action took place during the 1930's in Maycomb, a small (imaginary) town of southern Alabama. The book treated the relations between "ordinary" white people, a poorer class of white people, and the blacks who also inhabited Maycomb. The Finches, included among the "ordinary" whites, showed clear evidence of better education than most of their neighbors.

Three doors from the Finch household lived the Radleys. Arthur ("Boo") Radley, shut in the house by his father during his teens (when he fell into trouble with the law) and now a man in his thirties, provided inspiration for whispered comment and tall tales. Scout, Jem, and a friend felt an irresistible urge to learn more of Boo Radley, though they like everyone else were afraid of the Radley place. Boo, noting their attention, began to leave various objects in a knot-hole of an oak tree where they would find them -- first, two pieces of chewing gum; later, two whittled dolls and a large broken-down watch. Once, when a neighbor's house burned in the middle of a cold night, Boo put a blanket over Scout's shoulders to keep her warm, without her even noticing it.

Atticus Finch, endowed with a conscience, decided to defend Tom Robinson, a Negro accused of raping Mayella Ewell, a member of a poor white family. The court could only balance Mayella's word against Tom's, except that Atticus succeeded in showing that not Tom but Robert Ewell, Mayella's father, had delivered bodily injuries Mayella received. The jury nevertheless found Tom Robinson guilty of rape; officers later shot him dead when he attempted to escape. Robert Ewell, enraged by Atticus' willingness to plead Tom's innocence, attempted to kill Atticus' children as they walked home one night. An onlooker knifed Robert Ewell instead. Sheriff Heck Tate refused to press charges against anyone, insisting Ewell had killed himself. Heck knew, and Atticus eventually understood, that Boo

Radley had saved the children's lives, and did not wish to see him punished.

Earlier in the story, when Atticus presented air-rifles to Jem and Scout as gifts, he had remarked to them, "Shoot all the bluejays you want, if you can hit 'em, but remember it's a sin to kill a mockingbird." A neighbor lady explained, "Your father's right. . . . Mockingbirds don't do one thing but make music for us to enjoy. They don't eat up people's gardens, don't nest in corncribs. . . ." After the death of Robert Ewell, Atticus feebly tried to explain, "Scout, . . . Mr. Ewell fell on his knife. Can you possibly understand?" Jean Louise responded, "Yes sir, I understand. . . . Mr. Tate was right." When Atticus asked, "What do you mean?", his bright young daughter answered, "Well, it'd be sort of like shootin' a mockingbird, wouldn't it?"

Life in Maycomb even without Boo Radley provided ample food for thought for an alert young mind. One day in school, for instance, during the class in Current Events, the teacher Miss Gates told about Hitler and the Jews: "A hand went up in the back of the room. 'How can . . . Hitler just put a lot of folks in a pen like that, looks like the govamint'd stop him,' said the owner of the hand. . . . 'Hitler is the government,' said Miss Gates, and . . . she went to the blackboard. She printed DEMOCRACY in large letters. . . . 'What do you think it means, Jean Louise?' . . . 'Equal rights for all, special privileges for none'" -- the quote came from Atticus. "'Very good, Jean Louise, very good,' Miss Gates smiled. In front of DEMOCRACY, she printed WE ARE A. 'Now class, say it all together.'" But the alert mind remembered that Miss Gates had also once said, as its owner Jean Louise related to Jem, " . . . It's time somebody taught 'em a lesson, they were gettin' way above themselves, an' the next thing they think they can do is marry us." The "they" and the "'em" of this remark referred to the Negroes of Maycomb. "Jem," continued Jean Louise and Harper Lee, "how can you hate Hitler so bad an' then turn around and be ugly about folks right at home -- ".

Les racines du ciel (The Roots of Heaven) referred for its title to the idea "that men needed another company than their own kind, that they craved it desperately, like an almost physical presence, and that nothing on earth seemed big enough to satisfy that urge, those roots of heaven, as Islam called them, which were forever gripping and torturing man's heart. . . ." Romain Gary, born in Moscow of French parentage, a pilot and career diplomat for some time and a novelist since 1945, wrote Les racines du ciel.

French Africa immediately before the political liberation provided the setting. The characters came from an assortment of places and pursued a variety of ends -- Habib, the Lebanese trafficker in arms; Major Forsythe, American "turncoat" in Korea; Father Fargue, Franciscan who worked among lepers; Peer Qvist, on mission for the Danish Museum of Natural History; Duparc, owner of a cotton plantation; Abe Fields, American photographer; Father Tassin, Jesuit conductor of paleontological excavations, who thought of "salvation" as a biological mutation and of humanity as an outdated species still lacking that mutation -- these, and a large assortment of others.

Morel, the chief character, can best be described simply as a lover of elephants. Morel reasoned about Africa's and the world's future in this manner: "Today you say that elephants are archaic and cumbersome, that they interfere with roads and telegraph poles, and tomorrow you'll begin to say that human rights too are obsolete and cumbersome, that they interfere with progress."

Minna, the German-born girl friend of Morel, once she had joined him remained true to the end. Morel, Minna, and their companions traveled far and wide to make their presence felt to persons who treated elephants with brutality. (Monsieur Haas, who worked for zoos and circuses, they shot in the buttocks; Madame Challut, woman champion of big game hunting, they spanked on the buttocks.) Waïtari, an African nationalist who wanted to use Morel in stirring up ill feeling against the French, accompanied Morel and Minna for a time. Waïtari's organization indeed planted as Morel's aide Youssef Lanoto, a non-talkative young man, with instructions to kill Morel when he no longer seemed of service to the nationalist cause.

Waïtari, who had served in the French parliament, complained to Abe Fields in a manner quite different from that of Morel: "We are all the more indignant and outraged because we have had enough of being used by the whole world as its zoo. . . . I can tell you that in our eyes factory chimneys are a thousand times more beautiful than the necks of giraffes which your tourists so much admire." To Peer Qvist, he added: " . . . Do you know what the cost of it is, old man? It is ignorance, leprosy, starvation, elephantiasis, filariasis . . . it's infant mortality and chronic undernourishment of two hundred million people. That's the price our people are paying for . . . the so-called 'natural splendor' by which you set such store."

Morel persisted in his own objectives. To Waïtari's nationalist yearnings, he had this rebuttal: "Nations -- I don't give a damn about them. The old ones, the new ones, mine, yours, the lot of them." After cooperating with three African students in the project involving Madam Challut, only to have the students turn against him in violence, Morel commented, "They've still got a lot to learn. . . . One day they'll have their Stalins, their Hitlers, and their Napoleons, their Führers and their Duces, and then their very blood will cry out to demand respect for nature."

Waïtari went his own way and Morel his. Waïtari knew that if the authorities apprehended Morel everyone would soon comprehend that Morel's audacious outrages had nothing to do with African nationalism. For this reason, 14-year-old Youssef Lanoto held the responsibility of murdering Morel should such a capture by the authorities seem likely. When the moment came, Youssef spared Morel's life by helping him to escape. Youssef, one is led to believe, saw the wisdom in the words of both Waïtari and Morel, and believed their concerns could be harmonized.

Romain Gary sought, however, not to reconcile ideologies but only to present the role of African animals in relation to mankind. His effort complemented that of James Michener, who presented the role of Hawaiian rocks, soil, and plants. As man began to reach into space, Gary's and Michener's novels stressed the affinity of people for the works of earth-nature about them.

Religion

King, Stride toward Freedom . . Toynbee, An Historian's Approach to Religion . . Brunner, Bultmann, Tillich and Christian existentialism . . Jaspers, Die Atombombe und die Zukunft des Menschen . . revival of Buddhism in India . . Ambedkar, The Buddha and His Dhamma . . the rise of Soka-gakkai in Japan . . John XXIII . . Küng, Konzil und Wiedervereinigung.

Neither novel nor, strictly speaking, an essay, one widely appreciated book of this period emerged as a sophisticated personal testimony from a man with deep experience in religion. Martin Luther King, Jr., published Stride toward Freedom: The Montgomery Story in 1958. At the time of the events he described (1955-6), King served as pastor of the Dexter Avenue Baptist Church in Montgomery, Alabama. His father held a Baptist pastorate in Atlanta, Georgia, at the time his son was born. The son received an advanced seminary training and educated himself broadly through reading. The career of Mahatma Gandhi attracted him more than that of any other actor in history. As Martin Luther King, Jr., in 1954 completed residential requirements for his doctorate, he became convinced that his own Negro people could only fight the injustices toward them through the policies Gandhi advocated. His pastorate in Montgomery, which began in that year, provided an unexpected opportunity to test Gandhi's principles.

On December 1, 1955, the driver of a Montgomery bus ordered a Negro lady to surrender the seat she occupied to provide a place for a white man. When the lady refused, she was placed under arrest for violating the city segregation law. Four days later, at the urging of their leaders, virtually all the Negroes of Montgomery refused to ride the buses. Protestant pastors played a strong role in this initial strike for freedom, and in the subsequent boycott lasting more than a year. The blacks demanded courtesy from the bus drivers, seating on a first-come first-served basis (though with blacks seated from the rear and whites from the front), and the hiring of Negro drivers. Legal action proceeded all the way to the United States Supreme Court, which on November 13, 1956, affirmed the decision of a lower court that the municipal segregation law was unconstitutional. On December 21, the day after the mandate to terminate the law arrived in Montgomery, Negroes rode the buses again, treated like other people, except that none of them held jobs as bus drivers immediately.

Martin Luther King presided over the Montgomery Improvement Association whose members saw this project through at considerable inconvenience and a measure of real hardship to themselves. In January 1957, King became president, at a meeting in Atlanta, of a new group called the Southern Christian Leadership Conference with the immediate aim of ending bus segregation in other Southern cities. The SCLC intended to use the same method of nonviolent resistance that had proved effective in Montgomery. The Negro community in that city remained quiet even during that month, when four Negro Baptist churches were bombed, and in February, when the white men responsible for the bombing were acquitted of the crime. They did so not through fear (as in the old days) but through the new dignity they had achieved as a people who refused to strike back with violence when others used violence against them.

"Christ furnished the spirit and motivation" for the campaign, said King, "while Gandhi furnished the method." Concerning the motivation, he quoted the question of disciple Peter, "Lord, how oft shall my brother sin against me, and I forgive him? till seven times? and the response of Jesus, "I say not unto thee, Until seven times: but, Until seventy times seven." When enemies threatened King's life, he experienced fear, but prayed and received assurance. When bombs damaged his house and angry followers appeared in large numbers, he quoted Jesus to them: "He who lives by the sword will perish by the sword." When one pastor spoke out against the movement and sentiment arose against the dissenter, King asked the dissatisfied pastor to appear in the pulpit with him in apology to the congregation, and quoted Jesus again to a restless crowd: "Let him who is without sin cast the first stone."

There are, King said in his summary, three methods by which "oppressed people deal with their oppression." The first way is acquiescence. ("There is such a thing as the freedom of exhaustion. . . . 'Ben down so long that down don't bother me.'") A second way is "resort to physical violence and corroding hatred." The third way is nonviolent resistance which "seeks to reconcile the truths of two opposites -- acquiescence and violence -- while avoiding the extremes and immoralities of both." King portrayed six basic characteristics of nonviolent resistance, all drawn from Gandhi's <u>satyagraha</u> or truth-force: (1) "that nonviolent resistance is not a method for cowards; it does resist;" (2) "that it does not seek to defeat or humiliate the opponent, but to win his friendship and understanding;" (3) "that the attack is directed against forces of evil rather than against persons who happen to be doing the evil," (4) that there "is a willingness to accept suffering without retaliation, to accept blows . . . without striking back;" (5) "that it avoids not only external physical violence but also internal violence of spirit;" and (6) "that it is based on the conviction that the universe is on the side of justice." <u>Satyagraha</u> had truly entered its post-Gandhi phase one in the city of Montgomery.

<u>Stride toward Freedom</u> stemmed from a direct religious experience; the essay called <u>An Historian's Approach to Religion</u>, published in 1956 by British historian Arnold Toynbee, formed by contrast a study based on long years of reflection on the subject. Toynbee, interested in universal history from ancient times to the present, had already won fame for his prolific composition. <u>A Study of History</u>, written by him and presented in eleven volumes (1934-59), spoke appreciatively of the role played by religion in human history, like the story of civilization by Will Durant, but Toynbee unlike Durant adopted certain religious positions as his own, and elaborated upon them in his presentation. In <u>An Historian's Approach to Religion</u>, he spoke of a new historical era that commenced in 1945, and said, "The time has come for us . . . to make a fresh start from the spiritual side."

That fresh start, as Toynbee saw the matter, would follow upon "the task of disengaging the essence from the non-essentials in mankind's religious heritage." This task had become urgent for two reasons: (1) "the West" had returned from an adventure in science and technology "once

808

more, face to face with its ancestral Christianity;" and (2) "technology has brought all the living higher religions . . . into a much closer contact with one another than before." If the religions had not come into intimate contact for the average world person, they had for one like Arnold Toynbee who had studied them extensively.

Toynbee counted seven higher religions in existence today -- Christianity, Islam, Judaism, the modern remnant of Zoroastrianism, Mahayana and Theravada Buddhism, and Hinduism. All of them, he said, agree that "there is a presence in the Universe that is spiritually greater than Man himself." All but Theravada Buddhism hold "that the greatest spiritual presence known to Man has a personal aspect. . . ." Of the six others, all except Hinduism teach that there is a Devil as well as a God, who is "permitted by God to oppose . . . His will." Of the five great religions yet remaining, only two (Christianity and Mahayana Buddhism) hold that "a superhuman being had demonstrated His love for human beings in action," the Buddha (and the bodhisattvas) by refusing nirvana to help others, and the Christ "by taking a menial's form" (that is, a human form) and accepting death on the cross to help others. Toynbee believed that all four of the positions described constituted essential parts of man's religious heritage. The non-essentials, on the other hand, included holy places, rituals, taboos, social conventions, religious myths, and theologies, as well as the self-centeredness that particularly characterizes the three religions founded in or near Palestine.

Arnold Toynbee came close to the thinking of Martin Luther King, Jr., when he added that in Christian and Mahayana Buddhist doctrine "even the extremity of Suffering is not too high a price to pay for following Love's lead; for, in their judgement, Selfishness, not Suffering, is the greatest of all evils, and Love, not release from Suffering, is the greatest of all goods." Mahatma Gandhi, the best known "suffering agent" of Toynbee's own time, however, considered himself a Hindu rather than a Christian or a Mahayana Buddhist. For this reason, or rather for reasons such as this (Toynbee did not cite Gandhi as an example), Toynbee said that the success or failure of a religion must be tested not by its inclusion of his four pieces of essence, but by looking "into the daily lives of its adherents . . . to see how far . . . their religion is helping them to overcome Man's Original Sin of self-centredness." He went on to conclude that no one person alive "is effectively in a position to judge between his own religion and his neighbor's," and that "the missions of the higher religions are not competitive; they are complementary."

Although Toynbee wanted "to make a fresh start from the spiritual side," he gave little indication that he personally stood prepared to do so. The (far-from-novel) spirit of toleration he advocated had yet to become widespread, but seemed inadequate as a sole foundation for a genuinely fresh beginning. Toynbee, though he recognized a new era, continued to think largely in terms of the old one. "Man's true end," he said, "is to glorify God and to enjoy Him for ever." Man, far from being a co-worker, is a servant, a menial, no matter how sophisticated a relationship exists with his master. For man is a victim of "original" sin, the sin of self-centeredness, which Toynbee called a necessity of life. A necessity and a sin for man, that is, but not for the master, since the master is really the center, whereas a man can only strive to occupy, and by his nature must strive to occupy, the master's position. Toynbee listed Christian theology among his non-essentials, but his Study of History, on which the first part of this book took its base, had already made clear that to him certain features of traditional Christian theology remained part of the essence.

Many Protestant theologians during this period adopted a new vocabulary and a new manner of thinking recognized by neither King nor Toynbee in their books. The new manner of thinking depended heavily upon the vocabulary; a modern philosophical approach to traditional Christian thought, it became known as Christian existentialism. It held a few ideas in common with the atheistic existentialism of Jean-Paul Sartre (whose L'être et le néant became available as Being and Nothingness only in 1956), but resembled in much greater degree the thinking of Sartre's predecessor, the Danish Lutheran Søren Kierkegaard (see Chapter V). Edmund Husserl, born of German parents under Austrian rule, provided a complementary philosophical background with the development of "phenomenology" in the 1910's and 1920's. Phenomenology, stressing the importance of observation of matters as they are, nevertheless opposed the claims of logical empiricism (see "Science," Chapter V), stating that truth may be reached through careful reasoning, going well beyond the frontiers of science.

Five non-Protestant thinkers, all but one of whom remained active through this quinquennium, provided additional emphases. Martin Heidegger of Germany, a colleague of Husserl, published Sein und Zeit (Being and Time) in 1927, analyzing the concept of Angst ("anxiety" or "dread"). Karl Jaspers of Germany, a psychiatrist-philosopher and theist who adhered to no specific religion, wrote Vernunft und Existenz in 1935 (translated as Reason and Existenz, last word unchanged) arguing that a person immersed in a state of anxiousness may transcend the normal limits of human experience.

Martin Buber, an orthodox Jew of Austria who later moved to Israel, had produced Ich und Du (I and Thou) in 1923, delineating an "I - It" relationship in which people treat other persons as objects and a preferred "I - Thou" relationship in which the whole of one person interacts with the totality of another. (Science and management employed the I - It outlook, which man

811

should never extend to God.) Nikolay Berdyayev (died 1948), a non-conformist Russian Orthodox believer who moved from the Soviet Union to France, in 1934 spoke in much the same vein in his Ya i mir obyectov (I and the World of Objects, known as Solitude and Society). Gabriel Marcel of France, converted to Roman Catholicism, wrote Etre et avoir (Being and Having) in 1935, contrasting "existential" participation in life with objective observation of life. Man reaches his "true" existence, Marcel stressed, through participation rather than through observation, and through the "grasping" of "mystery" which comes his way.

The "mystery" of Marcel contained the "absurdity" of Kierkegaard. The "grasping" of the mystery equated with the "leap into the darkness" of Kierkegaard and the experience of "transcendence" of Jaspers. This experience would come at the moment of "anguish" of Kierkegaard or during the state of "anxiety" of Heidegger. It stood open to the person described by Marcel, Berdyayev, and Buber who could interreact with other beings rather than merely treating them as objects. Many neo-orthodox Protestants (see Chapter VI) simply applied this language and these ideas to the age-old Christian belief that man should immerse himself in a spiritual existence rather than the material world, that man holds an inborn propensity to do otherwise, but that if man succeeds in bringing himself face-to-face with reality he will have extended to him the free grace of God, which extends far beyond the world man comprehends.

After World War II, three Protestant theologians developed these ideas in grand treatises. Heinrich Emil Brunner of Switzerland contributed three volumes of discussion in Dogmatik (Dogmatics), 1946-60. Rudolf Bultmann of West Germany in his four-part Theologie des Neuen Testaments (Theology of the New Testament, 1948-53) stressed the importance of recognizing the myths of that document not to get at a picture of the historical Jesus but to "know" the Christ the early disciples "knew" through their faith. Paul Tillich of Germany, moved to the United States, published the first of three volumes of Systematic Theology in 1951, the second in 1957. In these and in popular books written during the same decade, Tillich constructed a complete framework for Christian existentialism. Neo-orthodox theologian Karl Barth, on the other hand, argued that existentialism remained a secular philosophy and could only lead to distortion of the Christian message. Others thought of it as a passing vogue, especially meaningful to persons like Jaspers, Marcel, Brunner, Bultmann, and Tillich who had lived close to the anxiety and absurdity of modern warfare.

The existentialist accord that "existence precedes essence" (or, that man's "true" nature lies before him, yet to be realized) fits the traditional Christian concept of heaven, though without specification of details. (The humanist George Santayana of Spain, the United States, and Italy, who died in 1952, stated to the contrary that truth constitutes that part of essence which is illustrated in existence.) The existentialist reasoning concerning "inauthentic" existence applies to the old Christian teaching that man has fallen, or become estranged from God. The agreement among theistic existentialists that man can become attuned to "authentic" existence means that he can put himself in touch with a transcendent God. The Christian existentialist proceeds from this point to declare that in the very moment of anguish, in the very state of despair, one can find God in such a manner that he is saved from his former self. The mold did fit both traditional and neo-orthodox Christianity remarkably. The style, however, seemed rather remote from the more simple language of Jesus, whose teachings often found expression in aphorisms.

Karl Jaspers, who wrote Vernunft und Existenz

in 1935, contributed another treatise on _Vernunft_ (reason) in 1958. He called it _Die Atombombe und die Zukunft des Menschen: Politisches Bewusstsein in unserer Zeit_ (The Atom Bomb and the Future of Mankind: Political Consciousness in Our Time, rendered into English as _The Future of Mankind_). Neither the politics nor the ethics of the late 1950's could lead anywhere in the face of the world's critical circumstances, Jaspers asserted. Only a new moral-political element might present a hope of averting self-destruction. Even this could provide no guarantee of a future for mankind.

Jaspers proposed such a new element, describing it as a "new way of thinking" and defining that as "reason" or "philosophy." The source of reason, for Jaspers, lay "in the true humanity that each of us is given by Transcendence. . . ." Following existentialist style, however, he portrayed the human intellect as predisposed toward a rejection of reason; only by a crisis passage through "existential confusion" could the intellect reach the stage of subordination to reason. Man's perception of "transcendent reality" would provide the motivation for his agonizingly piercing through barriers raised by his intellect to discover the reason that lies there.

Such a process lay not far from the thinking of Brunner, Bultmann, and Tillich -- or even from that of evangelist Billy Graham (whose own planet-wide efforts continued through this period). None of those four individuals, however, saw that process as leading to the discovery of reason. The true thrust of Jaspers' book lay not in the description of this process, but in the possibilities of reason as applied to the world scene. Reason, he observed, is not a system of thought. It is not likely to become a church, a doctrine (like Marxism), or a system; "it is the ever moving freedom of man himself."

The change to follow from reason would com-

814

mence with the individual. "The mischief-maker or secret ill-wisher or slanderer or liar," Jaspers argued, "the adulterer or undutiful son or negligent parent or law-breaker -- by his conduct, which . . . is never wholly private -- keeps peace from the world." Statesmen in particular needed to strive for blamelessness of conduct. High-minded motivations of people in matters of life and death "will work only if they have been working for a lifetime. . . ."

Democracy would provide the channel through which reason might come to play a major role in world affairs. Jaspers listed these theses for the interworking of the two: "1. Reason can prevail reliably only if it guides the people along with their leaders. . . . Democracy . . . requires the whole people to be educated. . . . 2. Reason is not a property but a vehicle. . . . Democracy will last only if it keeps improving. . . . 3. In principle, reason belongs to every human being. . . . Hence, democracy . . . seeks to give everyone equal rights, in the sense of equal opportunities. . . . 4. Reason works by persuasion, not by force. . . . Democracy . . . employs police powers against law-breakers . . . only as authorized by law or in judicial proceedings. . . . 5. . . . . Reason has precedence over all specific laws and institutions. Recognized above any laws are human rights that both bind and free all men. . . . 6. Politically, reason never forgets that it is men who govern. . . . Government even by the best of men needs checking up on."

Jaspers tackled some of the toughest questions that democracy presents -- such as, how the best persons may be brought to power; or, how to prevent democracy from committing suicide (as in Germany, 1933). His answers all took their base in reason, the "new way of thinking" that would bring about a "new politics." He expected no happy millenium to burst upon the world's peoples. "At first," he observed, "the new politics would have to move in the tracks of the

815

old politics."

Karl Jaspers' new way of thinking amounted to
a new religion with certain strong attractions
for modern man. It called for cooperation with,
not the adoration of, a deity. It offered a universal program open to everyone, devoid of godly
favoritism. Most importantly, it exacted a very
high code of ethics, effective on both private
and public levels. It exalted the role of reason, like the "deism" of the eighteenth century,
but accepted none of the "certainties" to which
eighteenth-century deists subscribed. They had
pictured a God unwilling to intervene in the
world, yet disposed to apply rewards and punish-
ments in a life after death. Jaspers pictured a
Transcendent ready to help man find the best in
himself.

Jaspers did not in any comprehensive way attempt to resolve the complexities of modern-day
ethics. Descriptive terms such as "mischief-
maker," "liar," and "adulterer" seemed to present
him no problems. Many of the world's cultures
had already brought much reason into play in
these realms, modifying the inflexibility of
ancient taboos and commandments. Presumably
someone other than Jaspers would build on these
developments. Someone besides this person who
lived so much by his intellect would also have to
take on the task of creating an art image to
bring warmth and tenderness into Jaspers' program.

Jaspers spelled out sparingly some themes for
education to bring about the new politics: (1) a
recognition of the right of specifically gifted
individuals to separate classes; (2) a willingness specifically to train everyone for democracy
-- or, as Jaspers put it, against totalitarianism; and (3) "education proper" as distinct from
specialized training, with a "wide-open approach
to . . . all possibilities of knowledge. . . ."
There seemed some chance that in a world faced
with possible annihilation democratic societies
might at least see the reason for these emphases

in education.

Three activities of wide significance in the Buddhist world took place during this quinquennium. The Sixth Council of Theravada Buddhism in Rangoon, Burma, celebrating the 2,500th anniversary of the death of Siddhartha Gautama the Buddha, came to its conclusion. (See Chapter VI.) One of a few hundred new Buddhist groups in Japan, the Soka-gakkai lay society, rose very rapidly to world attention. (See below in this section.) In India, a few million "untouchables," formerly of the Hindu faith, followed Bhimrao Ramji Ambedkar as converts to Buddhism. India, the land of Buddhist origins, had turned aside from this religion for eight hundred years. Now, it appeared that Buddhism in India held a future as well as a past.

The father of Bhimrao Ambedkar, an officer in the army of India, followed the teachings of fifteenth-century Kabir (the chief precursor of Sikhism) that all religions are one and all men equal. The mother from whom Ambedkar inherited his social position was a Mahar "untouchable" of the old state of Baroda. The Mahars of Baroda, of a wide variety of castes, performed the "polluting" tasks of the communities in which they lived -- the tasks, generally of a menial nature, that traditional Hindu outlook had held made their practitioners "unclean." Most persons of the higher-level castes held that the mere touch of the lower-caste individual made the higher-caste person also unclean. Thousands of smaller Indian groups, with local and occupational names, suffered the same treatment as the Mahars.

Most of the untouchables belonged to castes within the social class called the Shudras, believed to represent the earlier peoples conquered by ancient invaders from Iran. Others, thought by some scholars to represent tribes conquered at later times, held membership in castes considered below the level of the Shudras, performing vocations that brought them even lower esteem. Still others, of tribes remaining unconquered into the twentieth century, even though they had become Hindus in certain respects, found themselves among the untouchables because of non-vegetarian eating habits. The people of unconquered tribes gave little thought to their status. The Shudras and less-than-Shudras, however, stood keenly aware of their low position in life, which they customarily accepted as a role the gods had intended.

All untouchables (as well as the remainder of the Shudras) suffered from two disadvantages in religion. They could neither enter the temples nor study the Hindu scriptures. Those who held these privileges included the male members of castes higher than the social level of the Shudras -- the Brahmins (priests and teachers), the Kshatriyas (warriors and rulers), and the Vaishyas (artisans and gentlemen-farmers). The Shudras and less-than-Shudras could only hope to gain such rights after one or a series of rebirths, bringing them into higher strata of society.

Both the British government and the Congress party stated their concern about the part the untouchables might play in the emerging society of India. Most intellectuals agreed that untouchability would not disappear until the name itself could be banned. Mohandas Gandhi in 1932 proposed the name Harijans (children of Hari or Vishnu, one of two major Hindu divinities) -- a label satisfactory to many high-society persons, but regarded as condescending by Ambedkar and others of the lower castes. After 1935, the government referred to the group as the Scheduled Castes -- those whose names could be found on a long, published list or schedule of castes meriting special attention.

Ambedkar (born 1893) and Gandhi argued much over the nature of the treatment to be accorded the Scheduled Castes. They agreed on a provision for separate voting rights, but not on details of the voting. They agreed that temples and communal wells should be opened for every person's use, but while Ambedkar stressed nationwide legislation to provide these opportunities Gandhi insisted the change could only be accomplished on a well-by-well and temple-by-temple basis. Gandhi, a traditional Hindu in certain respects though very modern in others, could not accept the idea that the Shudras or anyone lesser than they might someday study the scriptures. Ambedkar disagreed violently on this matter, feeling that his own social class deserved every privilege the gods might provide.

Bhimrao Ramji Ambedkar served as minister of law 1947-51, in the first cabinet of independent India. He played a prominent role in the writing of the constitution of 1949, which in the legal sense completely eliminated untouchability and any kind of discrimination based on caste or religion. Ambedkar continued to feel, however, that his triumph contained little substance. Despite his own very broad and solid education, he believed that other highly placed persons resented his physical presence. For a few years, he cast about for a further step to dramatize the situation of some 75,000,000 Indian people who shared his status. On October 14, 1956, at a special ceremony in Nagpur (in the new state of Maharashtra where the Mahars lived), Ambedkar and about 300,000 followers took the vow which changed them from Hindus to Buddhists. "I go to the Buddha for refuge," they declared in both the ancient Pali and modern Marathi languages. "I go to the Dhamma for refuge. I go to the Sangh for refuge." Many millions of Buddhists had repeated the same words before them.

Ambedkar wrote a book about the Buddha, the Dhamma, and the Sangh, emphasizing the two in his title The Buddha and His Dhamma. Dhamma, or dharma, means Doctrine; the Sangh, or the sangha, the religious community. Though Ambedkar himself died on December 6, only 53 days after his initi-

819

ation into Buddhism, his fame and his book survived him. (The book appeared in print in late 1957). Ambedkar left Hinduism because its traditional caste system demeaned his own people. He rejected Christianity and Islam, after a serious look at them, because they had compromised with the caste system in India. He accepted Buddhism because Gautama, its founder, had definitely rejected the caste system some 2,500 years before Ambedkar's lifetime.

In his own depiction of Gautama -- not shared by all the Buddha's following -- Ambedkar presented his leader as one who preferred to be known only as a teacher and a man. "Christ . . . laid down the condition that there was no salvation for a person unless he accepted that Christ was the Son of God," contended Ambedkar. "A seeker after salvation in Islam must accept that Mohammad is the Prophet of God. . . . No such condition was ever made by the Buddha."

The heart of the Buddhist doctrine as perceived by Ambedkar lay in the following progression from Dhamma to Saddhama: (1) Mere Dhamma is the highly structured body of principles defining the reasons for and the conduct of personal morality, accepted generally by Theravada Buddhists as Gautama's basic teaching. (2) However, "Dhamma is Saddhama when it makes learning open to all . . . when it teaches that mere learning is not enough . . . when it teaches that what is needed is Pradnya." Pradnya is wisdom (in contrast to Vidya or knowledge) which includes concern for "the welfare of many folk," the ability to concentrate upon a train of thought, the mastery of one's own intentions, and the attainment of the musings that go with higher thought. (3) "Dhamma is Saddhama only when it teaches that . . . Pradnya . . . must be accompanied by Sila." Sila is "acting aright" as compared with "thinking aright." It means "not to kill; not to steal; nor to tell a lie; nor to indulge in sex immorality and not to indulge in drinking." (4) "Dhamma is Saddhama only when it teaches that

besides . . . Sila what is necessary is Karuna."
Karuna is "love for human beings," exemplified by
the Buddha's readiness to minister to the physical needs of even the most humble person.   (5)
"Dhamma is Saddhamma only when it teaches that
more than Karuna what is necessary is Maitri."
Maitri, going beyond love for human beings, is a
spirit of loving kindness for all living creatures, which brings "freedom of heart."   Maitri
includes the obligation to "bear all insults and
injustices" without resentment or anger.

Finally, Ambedkar maintained, "Dhamma to be
Saddhama must break down barriers between man and
man . . . must teach that worth and not birth is
the measure of man . . . must promote equality
between man and man." In extension of this last
theme, he reasoned, "Is the fittest the best from
the point of society. . . . Equality may help
the best to survive even though the best may not
be the fittest. . . . What society wants is the
best and not the fittest. . . . This was the
viewpoint of the Buddha."

Before his death, Ambedkar expressed a three-
part hope: (1) that a manageable Buddhist bible
would be prepared for use by everyday people; (2)
that the Sangh, the community of Buddhist
priests, would be reformed toward devotion to the
service of the people; and (3) that a Buddhist
world missionary society would be organized.
Whether these goals might eventually be reached
remained a question during this period. Leaders
of the Maha Bodhi society founded in Ceylon,
1891, shared Ambedkar's desire to spread the
Buddhist faith and orient it toward justice for
the suffering. (Maha Bodhi means Great Enlightenment, the experience of Gautama as he became
the Buddha.) The impression made by Ambedkar and
the efforts of Maha Bodhi resulted in the
conversion of about 3,000,000 Hindus to Buddhists
during this quinquennium. Mahars of Maharashtra
provided the bulk of the converts, joined by
former untouchables from Madhya Pradesh and other
states.

821

Soka-gakkai, the Value-Creating Society of Japan, whose growth constituted the third Buddhist development of this period, adhered as a lay religious organization to the Nichiren-sho denomination of Mahayana Buddhism. Nichiren-sho held (in accord with ancient Chinese and Japanese tradition) that Siddhartha Gautama had died 405 years earlier than the Theravada Buddhists believed. The roots of Nichiren-sho reached far back into Buddhist history. Chinese scholars who lived in the sixth century (of the Christian era used in this book) undertook the burdensome task of classifying the already-voluminous Mahayana literature of their time. They aimed to include all of the Buddhist sutras (that is, writings containing discourses attributed to Gautama) in one canon, which would serve as a sure guide for all the Mahayana faithful. They explained differences in the sutras as developments in the teaching of Gautama during a 40-year ministry, in accord with the ability of his disciples to understand new ideas.

The sutras this group of scholars believed more elementary appeared in the early part of their canon. Those they considered more sophisticated appeared toward the end. At the very end came the Saddharmapundarika -- in the ancient Sanskrit language of India literally the Lotus Right Law, or the true law which is like the white lotus in purity and merit. Often called simply the Lotus sutra, it contains 28 chapters covering about 400 pages in English translation. The Buddha appears in the Lotus sutra as a supernatural being with a great ray of light beaming from between his eyebrows. His words are a comfort to those of the Mahayana branch of the religion; the Theravada branch does not accept the Lotus sutra as scripture.

Buddhism came to Japan in the sixth century. The school called Tendai, accepting the arranged canon, remained only one of several sects in Japan. Four new Japanese Buddhist groups arose in the twelfth and thirteenth centuries. One of them maintained the "Pure Land" doctrine already widely accepted in China, teaching that faith in a particular Buddha (named Amida in Japan) could bring salvation (or entrance into nirvana). A second sect, the "True Pure Land," took the more extreme position that faith in Amida formed the only (and a very simple) means of salvation. The True Pure Land teaching saw considerable merit in the mere recitation of the phrase "Adoration to Amida Buddha." A third sect also from China, called Zen in Japan, accented the religious value of meditation. Nishida Kitaro, Japanese philosopher who died in 1945, took Zen as the base for his thinking about the reality of non-self. In the 1950's, some North Americans studied Zen to see what it might hold for them.

The fourth new sect in thirteenth-century Japan took the name of Nichiren, its founder. For years Nichiren studied the literature of the previous groups, finally condemning all except Tendai. From Tendai's exaltation of the Lotus sutra to a high place in Mahayana scripture, he moved on to the position that no other sutra is needed. Like the True Pure Land sect, he found particular merit in the recitation of one short set of words -- in the case of Nichiren, the Japanese phrase "Namu Myoho renge-kyo," meaning "Salutation to the Lotus Right Law Sutra." Indeed, Nichiren taught that faith in this phrase would suffice to procure salvation. Nichiren believed that a special mission devolved upon him to teach true religion and bring salvation to people of his own era. His lifetime fell in the mappo (Latter Law) era beginning 2,000 years after the death of Gautama, in which the latter had prophesied (according to another sutra) that the spirit of his own teaching would die away and be replaced by that of another Buddha.

Nichiren's followers, few in number, quarreled when he died. Nikko, who had served as the master's secretary, taught that Nichiren himself was the third-millenium Buddha of whom Gautama had spoken. Nikko indeed raised Nichiren to the level of a Buddha of an "infinite" past going back beyond the "eternal" past of ordinary Buddhas (including Gautama), while at the same time proclaiming him the leader of the bodhisattvas who (according to the Lotus sutra) would appear in the mappo era. Even Nikko's group of believers in Nichiren became very split. A tiny sub-sect of them held on to the temple at Taiseki-ji, near Mount Fuji, and in 1912 changed its name to Nichiren-sho, meaning True or Orthodox Nichiren. It is generally called Nichiren-sho-shu (True Nichiren Denomination), while its chief rival has the simpler name Nichiren-shu (Nichiren Denomination). Nichiren-sho teaches the importance of the honzon, a tablet containing the sacred phrase; the daimoku, the practice of chanting the sacred phrase; and the kaidan, the altar of a believer and the temple to be built someday when the entire world wishes to come to worship. Other Nichiren sects use the same words (which came from Nichiren) but ascribe to them other meanings.

Makiguchi Tsunesaburo, born in a fishing village in 1871 and raised in a Nichiren home, became a Nichiren-sho convert in 1928. Makiguchi had developed as a writer and teacher. He planned a very lengthy treatise on pedagogy, and published the first four volumes 1930-4. Here he described a new "theory of value," distinguishing the word "value" from "truth." There are three values, he said -- "beauty," "benefit," and "goodness." Benefit is that which contributes to one's own existence, goodness that which contributes to society, and beauty a transient quality in the life of any one person. Effective teaching combined with Nichiren-sho doctrine, Makiguchi believed, could create these values in an individual's life. In 1937, he founded in the city of Tokyo an organization called Soka-kyoiku-gakkai, or Value-Creating Educational Society. In 1943, the state arrested him and his fellow leaders for refusing to participate in the nationally sponsored activities of Shinto. In 1944, Makiguchi died after a year in prison.

A man known after the war as Toda Josei, another teacher from a fishing village, also converted to Nichiren-sho in 1928. He served as the publisher of Makiguchi's books, and found himself likewise under arrest. In prison, Toda began reciting "Namu Myoho renge-kyo" thousands of times a day, and felt after the two-millionth repetition that he had found the "true meaning of life." In 1945, released from captivity, he began to rebuild his publishing business. In May 1946, he and others decided to revive Makiguchi's society with the shorter name Soka-gakkai. Toda became chairman of the board of directors, but neither Soka-gakkai nor his efforts in the publishing business prospered through 1950. Then, on May 3, 1951, Toda became the second president of Soka-gakkai, and vowed to secure the conversion of 750,000 Japanese households to Nichiren-sho before he died.

Soka-gakkai immediately became highly organized. Various groups appeared among the membership, the most important of them the Young Men's and Young Women's divisions. They held as their prime purpose the use of <u>shakubuku</u> methods of conversion (literally "break and subdue," the more forceful of two types described in the sutras) until Nichiren-sho had spread abroad. By the end of 1955, Soka-gakkai had brought in nearly 200,000 families. Two years later, the society announced a membership figure of 750,000 families. Toda died on April 2, 1958. He had made clear his own conviction that Nichiren-sho would bring happiness in the present life -- including both health and wealth -- so that the believer need not wait to enjoy the fullest rewards. Toda did not hesitate, in fact, to portray the <u>honzon</u> as a sort of happiness-machine if prayers offered before it held as their sequel an engagement in <u>shakubuku</u>. If the change in one's life could not be attained until the next reincarnation, he said, he himself would reject Buddhism.

Ikeda Daisaku became the third president of Soka-gakkai on May 3, 1960. Like the first two, he came from a family that had little money; his father was a merchant of seaweed. Raised in Tokyo, while simultaneously attending secondary school and working in munitions manufacture he became ill with tuberculosis. A semi-invalid when he joined Soka-gakkai in 1947, Ikeda nevertheless managed to become very active. In 1954, he became the head of a Youth division encompassing both young men and young women. Toda himself chose Ikeda for the presidency. Toda had inaugurated a Grand Lecture Hall at the temple of Taiseki-ji, basically a place where priests might study, a month before his death. Ikeda planned a companion building, the Grand Reception Hall, for which in 1960 he toured the world in search of varied fine building materials. At the end of that year, Soka-gakkai counted an adherence of 1,720,000 families, but considered these only a beginning.

Soka-gakkai made no claim to the status of a new religion. It formed only a lay organization for Nichiren-sho, itself nearly seven centuries old. Its rapid rise nevertheless resembled the beginnings of many religious movements in history. Like Soka-gakkai, they had first won popularity with a large number of deprived families. Like them, Soka-gakkai offered large rewards while demanding a considerable sacrifice. Japanese households accepting the new outlook abandoned old traditions and patterns of devotion, including all the trappings of Shinto and non-Nichiren Buddhism. Individual converts devoted both their time and their money to the ongoing enterprise. These commitments, however, brought pleasure rather than pain as Soka-gakkai adherents considered themselves a part of something big and new and good. The Soka-gakkai teaching held the added merit of appearing clear and simple, though such description hardly applied to the vast theology attached to Nichiren-sho.

The Roman Catholic church became the focus of attention with the accession of a new pope. Pius

XII, who held the position from 1939 until his death in 1958, had rated as a religious and political conservative. A vehement anti-communist, he stood less clear in his opposition to fascist-type totalitarianism. In 1950, Pius XII pronounced as Catholic dogma the "assumption" of Mary, a belief long held by many Catholics that the mother of Jesus had been taken (assumed) to heaven rather than suffering a normal death.

Angelo Giuseppe Roncalli of an Italian peasant family, the successor of Pius XII elected in 1958, decided to rule under the name John XXIII. (The church had disacknowledged a previous John XXIII, of the years 1410-15.) Cardinal Roncalli had reached nearly 77 years of age before his elevation to the papacy, spending 66 of them in seminary or in service to the church, though he had little experience as a parish priest. He passed the years 1925-44 first as apostolic visitor for the Vatican in Bulgaria, later as apostolic delegate to Turkey and Greece, finding thus the opportunity to become well acquainted with the prelates of Eastern Orthodoxy. His style as pope, much less formal than that of his predecessor, encouraged persons of varying pursuits to think of him as a friend.

On January 25, 1959, only three months after his election, John XXIII announced that a church-wide or ecumenical council would be held at the Vatican. According to the official church count, this would be the 21st council, the first eight having met in the vicinity of Constantinople (today Istanbul) from the fourth to the ninth centuries, and the next eleven in Italy, France, or Switzerland from the twelfth to the sixteenth centuries. The 20th council (1869-70), the first held at the Vatican, proclaimed the pope infallible in official pronouncements he might make in matters regarding morals or faith. Pope John moved in a very different direction in June 1959 as he cited the "irresistible assurance" that "there will be one fold and one shepherd" (John 10:16), describing it as the "compelling motive

827

which led Us to announce publicly Our resolve to call an Ecumenical Council." He hoped that "those who are separated from this Apostolic See" (the Eastern Orthodox and Protestant branches of Christendom) would behold this manifestation of Catholic unity and "derive from it the inspiration to seek out that unity which Jesus Christ prayed for so ardently. . . ."

Pope John took the Christian ecclesiastical world by surprise. Speculation became rife among Protestant and Orthodox thinkers as to what possibilities might lie in the upcoming Vatican Council II. The leaders of several major Protestant denominations, who used the world ecumenical in their own inter-denominational sense and thought much in terms of Protestant or Protestant-Orthodox unity, now began to speak of wider ecumenical vistas lying still farther ahead. Central and northern European Catholic leaders tended also to become excited by the hope for a great Christian reunion. One of them, the liberal theologian Hans Küng, who coming from Switzerland had studied in Rome, London, Amsterdam, Berlin, Madrid, and Paris, and had written his doctoral thesis on a portion of the theology of his countryman neo-orthodox Protestant Karl Barth, in 1960 taught at Tübingen in West Germany. Küng wrote Konzil und Wiedervereinigung (The Council and Reunion, also called The Council, Reform and Reunion) in 1960, to tell what he thought his own church might do to make its position more inviting to those who had become separated.

Because the church is made of human beings with their failures and deformations, and of sinners with their vice and personal guilt, Küng said, renewal of the church is always necessary. Renewal had indeed taken place in the past, both before and after the Protestant break, and renewal might take place again in the immediate future. Catholics and Protestants could come together in a spirit of brotherly love if they approached one another with a kindly openness.

Protestants should note that already the Catholic church had (1) developed an appreciation for the religious values in the Protestant Reformation; (2) shown an increased regard for the use of the Christian scriptures, in accord with the Protestant habit; (3) moved toward a more popular liturgy, in which the mass of communicants might participate; and (4) encouraged an understanding of the doctrine emphasized by Protestants that there is a sense in which every man is his own priest.

Küng hoped that in the matter of theological disputes between Catholics and Protestants an effort to find common territory would take precedence over fear. He felt that in matters of popular piety, such as differing emphases on the position of Mary, a curbing of extremism might accompany a search for middle ground. In regard to the "chief obstacle to reunion," the institution of the papacy, he stressed that the early Protestant rejection of the office derived from the nature of the papacy at that time. The important consideration now, he argued, is the Catholic church and the papacy of today.

Küng spoke specifically of the "new style" of pope John. "He visits the sick in the Roman hospitals, . . . devotes his time to the simple and the poor. He . . . prohibits applause in St. Peters. . . . He . . . makes his way in and out quite simply on foot. . . . Pope John loves the Dialogue Mass, with the whole people . . . saying their responses to the priest out loud and praying the Lord's Prayer with him. . . . He . . . constantly makes expeditions . . . talking informally to people and everywhere radiating a delightful humor, genuine kindliness, simple humanity and, above all, a vast unassuming humility. . . . If even Protestants often show that a Pope of this kind impresses them, this is not because they find such things simply touching in a human way, but because they recognize them as evangelical, springing from the Gospel.

The "restoration of its full value to the episcopal office" -- that is, the return to the bishops of authority that had once belonged to them -- comprised the chief reform Hans Küng thought might issue from Vatican Council II. He hoped that this reform in turn might lead to variety in the performance of the mass in differing localities; to a separate prayer book for secular priests; to dispensation from the clerical obligation of celibacy; to a decentralization of the judging of matrimonial cases, with a liberalization of the rule for "mixed" (Catholic with non-Catholic) marriages; and to a reorganization of book censorship. These changes, if they occurred as a result of Vatican II, would certainly bring Catholics and Protestants closer together, and in some regards the Catholics and Orthodox. But everyone, including Hans Küng, knew that the new style of pope John remained too much an innovation to allow for very early Christian reunification.

INDEX OF COUNTRIES AND DEPENDENCIES

Belgium, 12, 30, 35, 41, 60, 64-65, 85, 133, 193,
    201, 218, 225, 235, 250, 353, 441, 452, 461,
    473, 563, 567-8, 574, 589-91, 595, 647, 681,
    694-5, 711, 725, 737
Belorussia, 28-29, 33, 90-91
Bermuda, 40
Bhutan, 27, 232
Bolivia, 7, 39, 65, 76, 223, 249, 344, 413,
    422-7, 434, 440-1, 472-3, 678, 684, 686, 724
Bornu, 593
Brazil, 7, 12, 19, 37-39, 46, 68, 76, 110, 218,
    221-2, 237, 239, 241-6, 288, 290-2, 441, 444-5,
    457, 469-70, 476, 503, 616-17, 642, 680, 684-6,
    710, 719-21, 726, 762, 768-9, 777
British Guiana, 39, 249, 438, 724
British Honduras, 39
British Solomon Islands, 27, 76, 794
British Somaliland, 41, 244, 568
British Virgin Islands, 707
Bulgaria, 35, 70, 73, 85-87, 98-99, 107-8, 162,
    170-1, 188, 190-1, 193-4, 213-14, 334, 354,
    433-4, 462, 669, 728, 767, 769, 827
Burma, 17, 27, 75, 89, 116, 121, 137, 139-40, 166,
    207, 214, 240, 350, 358, 436-7, 446-7, 459-60,
    462-4, 531, 642, 664, 674, 763, 778, 817

Cambodia, 6, 28, 119, 139, 233-4, 350, 355, 441,
    449, 459, 462, 531, 691, 701, 763
Cameroon, 9
Cameroons, 41, 594
Cameroun, 582-3, 681, 695, 709, 712
Canada, 7, 11-12, 37-38, 45, 63-64, 113, 201,
    208, 222, 232, 240-1, 246, 249-50, 252, 254,
    291, 314, 355, 444-5, 468, 470, 472-5, 503,
    517, 563-4, 616, 686-7, 720-1, 723-6, 768-9
Cape Verde Islands, 41, 459
Caroline Islands, 28, 232
Central African Republic, 587, 670, 680, 709, 712
Ceylon, 11, 27, 116, 137, 139-40, 224, 244-5, 350,
    438, 447, 449, 459, 462, 470, 522, 531, 559,
    691, 721, 821
Chad, 7, 587, 681, 695, 709, 712
Chile, 12, 39, 65, 90, 223, 249, 424, 445, 597,
    606, 642, 688, 710, 724, 737
China, 1-2, 7-8, 10, 16-19, 21, 24-26, 28-29, 66,

China (cont.) 68, 73, 75, 77, 85, 89, 91, 101,
    105-7, 109, 111, 115, 130, 135-6, 141-53,
    155, 166, 170, 173, 180, 185-9, 195, 203-5,
    207-8, 214, 228-9, 240-5, 249, 251, 253, 298-9,
    322, 344-5, 354, 368-9, 413, 428-30, 436-7,
    442, 446, 449, 455, 460, 462-5, 468-71, 473-5,
    495, 498, 511, 539, 549-52, 557, 626-7, 651,
    661-5, 669, 674, 699, 702, 712-13, 719-28,
    747-8, 757, 762-4, 795-6
Cochinchina, 27, 106, 233
Colombia, 7, 12, 19, 39, 65, 76, 222-3, 234, 244,
    344, 381, 387-93, 398, 428, 441, 454, 458,
    597-9, 604, 606, 660, 681, 687, 697
Comoro Islands, 41, 233
Congo, 588-93, 647, 660, 697, 705, 709, 712-13;
    see also Zaire
Congo Republic, 587, 681, 695, 709, 712
Costa Rica, 39, 65, 223, 235, 445, 461, 614, 622,
    688, 706, 710-11
Cuba, 12, 39, 65, 180, 223, 235, 242, 292, 344,
    381, 393-8, 441, 454, 458, 469, 539, 592, 595-6,
    603-28, 647, 661, 669-70, 685, 697, 710, 713,
    715, 720
Curaçao, 40, 459
Cyprus, 43, 191, 438, 440, 459, 465, 559, 675,
    681, 695, 707, 712, 729
Czechoslovakia, 13, 30, 35, 63-64, 79, 83-84, 88,
    99, 170, 188-9, 192-4, 196-9, 207, 213, 291,
    354, 380, 408, 421, 433, 502, 636, 668, 728,
    767, 769, 773

Dahomey, 584-6, 681, 695, 709, 712
Danzig, 30, 35, 64, 88, 168
Denmark, 30, 34-35, 40, 59-60, 91, 111, 193, 202,
    216, 235, 243, 276, 290-1, 439, 459, 502, 676,
    711, 767-9
Dominica, 707
Dominican Republic, 39, 70, 230-1, 235, 458, 503,
    599, 612, 619, 623, 706, 710

East Germany, 154, 160-2, 194, 200-1, 207, 212,
    242, 247, 354, 357-8, 432, 471, 636, 639-40,
    668, 723, 728
Ecuador, 7, 39, 70, 90, 223, 231, 445, 470, 688,
    722

French West Africa, 41, 232-3, 568, 577, 581,
  583-5, 587-8

Gabon, 588, 681, 709, 712
Gambia, 41
Germany, 12, 19, 22, 25, 29-32, 34-35, 37, 44,
  46, 58, 64, 66-67, 73-76, 79, 82-85, 88-90,
  99-100, 109, 111-12, 115, 150, 158-62, 166,
  182, 187-8, 192, 196, 200, 209, 212, 227, 236,
  290, 333, 343, 346-7, 354, 357-8, 362, 364,
  415, 417, 462, 501-2, 516, 520-1, 553, 567,
  575-7, 582-3, 651-2, 654, 747, 756, 759-60,
  767, 769, 789, 792-3, 799; see also East
  Germany, West Germany
Ghana, 9, 568-71, 581-6, 588, 593, 670, 675, 680,
  708-9, 712
Gibraltar, 36, 190
Gilbert and Ellice Islands, 27, 76
Goa, 28
Gold Coast-Ashanti, 41, 245, 249, 460, 470, 472,
  570-1
Great Britain, see United Kingdom of Great
  Britain and Northern Ireland
Greece, 35, 49, 70, 73-74, 81, 85-87, 97, 99, 163,
  170, 180, 190-1, 193, 212, 225, 235, 289, 309,
  314, 333, 347, 432, 438, 440, 452-3, 464, 559,
  634, 642, 695-7, 827
Greenland, 40, 459
Grenada, 707
Guadeloupe, 40, 232
Guam, 28
Guatemala, 7, 39, 70, 111, 223, 235, 344, 351,
  399, 406-9, 412-13, 427, 439, 441, 454, 458,
  461, 463, 607, 621, 681, 688-9, 697, 711
Guinea, 581-2, 585, 588, 593, 661, 670, 708-9,
  712
Gwalior, 27, 119, 126

Haiti, 38-39, 70, 230, 235, 292, 458, 681, 689,
  697
Hawaii, 4, 28, 37, 74, 136, 242, 707, 794-7, 805
Honduras, 39, 70, 231, 245, 408, 458, 461, 463,
  681, 689, 697, 710-11
Hong Kong, 27, 74, 87, 106, 140, 430
Hungary, 35, 58, 70, 73, 85, 87-88, 99, 107, 111,

835

Hungary (cont.) 162, 171, 188, 193-5, 198, 213,
    290-1, 354, 362, 380, 433-4, 462, 502-3, 539,
    543-50, 552-3, 564, 630-3, 640, 661, 667-70,
    673, 681, 694, 713-14, 766-9
Hyderabad, 27, 119, 126, 169

Iceland, 34, 45, 64, 74, 111, 166, 193, 201, 235,
    763, 767, 769
Ifní, 41, 707
India, 3-6, 10-11, 16-19, 21, 26-28, 75, 80, 91,
    103, 115-30, 133, 139-40, 154, 169, 171, 175,
    179-80, 204-5, 207-8, 214, 231-2, 234, 237,
    240-5, 247, 249, 253, 288, 290, 330-2, 350,
    355, 358, 434-6, 446-8, 455, 459-60, 462-4,
    468-70, 472-3, 475-6, 495, 502, 511, 516,
    521-3, 531, 559, 564, 570-1, 593, 639, 642,
    663-4, 670-4, 702, 713, 719-22, 725-7, 729,
    740, 743, 757, 762-3, 767-8, 777, 784, 817-21
Indochina, 27, 73, 105-7, 140, 233-4, 354, 410,
    413, 415, 459, 572
Indonesia, 9, 21, 103-5, 107, 130-5, 140,
    166, 168, 171-2, 207, 224-5, 234, 245, 350,
    421, 434, 446-7, 452, 459, 463, 465, 470, 472,
    511, 559, 567, 642, 660, 670, 681, 694,
    697-700, 702, 713, 723-4, 729, 762
Iran, 8, 10, 13, 16, 18, 20-21, 42, 69, 74, 77,
    91, 111, 167-8, 179-80, 226, 244, 248, 344,
    351, 399-407, 409, 412-13, 427, 438, 453, 456,
    469, 472, 476, 536, 559, 565, 633, 642, 696,
    720, 723, 763, 766, 817
Iraq, 8, 13, 21, 42, 70, 74, 91, 112, 174, 176,
    182, 184, 231-2, 234, 351, 421, 441, 453, 461,
    472, 495, 554, 633, 636-9, 681, 696, 697,
    703-4, 723-4
Ireland, 10, 14, 31, 35, 52, 64-65, 193, 202,
    225, 235, 452, 462, 695, 767, 769
Israel, 8, 20, 116, 166, 174-85, 217, 343,
    417-18, 421, 440-1, 460, 463, 476, 495, 539,
    547-8, 553-6, 561-7, 634, 680, 713-14, 763
Italian East Africa, 41, 74
Italian Somaliland, 41, 168, 229, 244, 568, 595
Italy, 19, 31-32, 34-36, 38, 40-41, 43, 46,
    66-68, 73-74, 76, 79, 81, 89, 107, 111-12,
    154, 162-6, 168, 188-9, 193-4, 201-2, 204,
    207, 214, 218, 224, 229, 235, 237, 239-40,

New Caledonia, 28, 232
New Hebrides, 27-28
New Zealand, 4-5, 11, 27-28, 59-60, 180, 215,
  243, 347, 350, 437, 460, 502, 559, 563, 675,
  720, 737, 740, 742, 767, 769
Newfoundland, 39, 232
Nicaragua, 39, 70, 231, 235, 408, 458, 461, 463,
  621, 706-7, 710-11
Niger, 7, 585-7, 697, 706, 709, 712
Nigeria, 8-9, 21, 41, 233, 244-5, 459, 469-70,
  568, 593-5, 660, 675, 681, 695, 709, 712,
  720-1, 763
North Borneo, 232
North-East New Guinea, 28
North Korea, 136-7, 152, 170, 203-6, 208, 214,
  344-5, 354, 368, 430, 442, 460, 462, 553, 665,
  725, 763
North Viet-Nam, 344, 355, 411, 413-15, 419, 422,
  427-8, 430, 459-60, 664-5, 763
Northern Rhodesia, 41, 249, 459
Norway, 30, 34-35, 59-60, 193, 202, 216, 235-6,
  246, 291, 351, 439, 470, 502-3, 645, 676, 711,
  722, 737, 767-9
Nyasaland, 41, 459, 675

Ottoman Empire, 35, 42, 177, 184, 696
Oubangui-Chari, 587

Pakistan, 11, 13, 21, 24, 121, 124-7, 129-30,
  166, 169, 180, 207-8, 224, 231, 240, 242,
  350-1, 435-6, 447-8, 455, 459-60, 463-4,
  559-60, 570, 633-4, 642, 645, 660, 672, 681,
  697-8, 702, 704, 720, 727, 729, 762, 767-8
Palestine, 16, 18, 43, 112, 169, 171-2, 174-84,
  186, 226, 232, 234, 421, 453, 460, 463, 516,
  535-8, 555, 715, 809
Panama, 39, 65, 74, 111, 223, 445, 688, 710-11
Panama Canal Zone, 37, 39, 348, 688
Papua, 28
Paraguay, 7, 39, 70, 90, 231, 458, 707, 710, 764
Persia, 42; see also Iran
Peru, 7, 12, 39, 65, 90, 223, 230, 380, 458, 606,
  623, 660, 681, 687-8, 697, 710, 722, 725
Pitcairn Island, 27
Philippines, 1-3, 9, 19, 28, 33, 37, 74-75, 85,

839

Philippines (cont.) 89, 91, 116, 137-40, 180,
    207, 224, 242, 244, 347-8, 350, 448, 460, 469,
    647, 690, 720-1, 762, 795-6
Poland, 19, 20, 28-30, 32-34, 68-69, 74, 79-80,
    87-88, 90-91, 98-100, 108, 111, 159, 176, 178,
    184, 188, 191, 193-4, 211-12, 241-2, 245,
    317-19, 354-5, 431, 433, 469, 539, 541-6, 550,
    575, 636, 651-2, 666-8, 721, 762, 778, 791-2
Portugal, 12, 28, 34, 38-39, 41, 70, 118, 131,
    140, 176, 193, 201, 227-8, 399, 454, 459, 462,
    563, 567, 570, 703, 711, 763, 792, 795-6
Portuguese Guinea, 41, 459
Portuguese Timor, 28, 76, 131, 459
Puerto Rico, 37, 40, 242, 459, 469, 720

Qatar, 43

Réunion, 41, 232
Rhodesia and Nyasaland, 459
Romania, 19, 35, 69-70, 73, 85-87, 98-99, 107-8,
    162, 171, 188, 190-1, 193-4, 198, 213, 333,
    354, 432-3, 462, 552, 667, 728, 767, 769
Ruanda, 9
Ruanda-Urundi, 41
Russia, 25-26, 28-29, 32-33, 35, 57-58, 82,
    176-7, 184, 496-7, 652, 736, 792, 799

St. Helena, 41
St. Lucia, 707
St. Pierre-Miquelon, 40, 232-3
St. Vincent, 707
San Marino, 36, 64, 109, 695
São Tomé-Príncipe, 41, 459
Sarawak, 232
Saudi Arabia, 8, 21, 42, 45, 70, 90, 112, 182,
    231, 237, 248, 402, 455-6, 461, 472, 633, 704,
    707, 723, 763
Senegal, 9, 583-5, 588, 670, 680, 709, 712
Seychelles, 41
Siam, 26, 228; see also Thailand
Sierra Leone, 41
Sikkim, 27, 232
Singapore, 232, 707
Sokoto, 593
Somalia, 8, 589, 681, 695, 709, 712

Switzerland (cont.) 510, 639, 681, 695, 711,
    767-9, 827
Syria, 8, 19, 43, 74, 90, 111-12, 167-8, 176,
    182-3, 226, 232, 234, 453, 461, 463, 495, 575,
    577, 633-7, 681, 696-7, 704, 712-13

Tai Wan, 10, 26, 28, 111, 152, 166, 173, 203-4,
    208, 228-9, 344, 429-30, 437, 442, 455, 464,
    476, 590, 647, 701-2, 712-13, 729, 764
Tanganyika, 41, 242, 469, 707, 746
Tannu Tuva, 28, 109
Tanzania, 9
Thailand, 7, 17, 26, 69-70, 74, 106, 166, 228,
    240, 350, 380, 437, 454-5, 460, 464, 531, 631,
    701, 762, 764, 778
Togo, 583, 585-6, 593, 681, 695, 709, 712
Togoland, 41, 571, 583
Tonga, 27
Tonkin, 28, 106-7, 233
Transjordan, 43, 112, 179, 226, 232
Travancore, 27, 119, 126
Trinidad-Tobago, 39, 291, 502, 515, 707, 767, 770
Trucial Oman, 43
Tunisia, 43, 76, 452, 459, 464, 568, 571-4, 642,
    681, 696-7, 708-9, 712
Turkey, 13, 21, 42, 59, 90, 190-1, 193, 217, 235,
    241, 243-4, 347, 350-1, 420, 432, 440, 468-9,
    495-6, 559, 571, 633-5, 642-3, 645, 660, 670,
    680, 696-7, 703, 719-20, 722, 729, 763, 827

Uganda, 7, 41
Ukraine, 28-29, 33, 90-91, 168, 346, 362-4
Union of South Africa, see South Africa
Union of Soviet Socialist Republics, see Soviet
    Union
United Arab Republic, 636, 638, 681, 696-7, 704,
    708
United Arab States, 636, 638, 704
United Kingdom of Great Britain and Northern
    Ireland, 11, 14, 25-28, 30-43, 60-61,
    63-64, 67, 73-77, 79-81, 83-89, 96-101, 106-9,
    111, 115-16, 118-25, 128-9, 131-2, 136, 139-40,
    150, 154-5, 157-60, 162, 167-8, 170, 177-82,
    184-6, 189-96, 200-1, 208, 212, 214-16, 222,
    225-7, 231-5, 237, 239, 241-2, 246-8, 250-2,

842

United Kingdom (cont.) 272, 290, 309, 322, 325,
    334, 348, 350-4, 356, 358, 381-2, 401-4, 406,
    412-13, 415, 417-21, 424, 430, 432, 436-8, 444,
    447, 450-1, 456, 459, 462, 465, 470-6, 478,
    483, 489, 492, 502-3, 510, 526, 528, 539,
    547-8, 553-71, 576-8, 582-3, 588-90, 593-5,
    631-4, 636, 638-40, 642, 674-6, 680, 692, 696,
    703-5, 707, 711, 713-14, 719, 723, 725-6,
    729-30, 736-8, 743-5, 756, 762, 767, 769, 772,
    778
United States of America, 7, 11, 19-20, 28,
    36-37, 39-40, 45, 60-62, 68, 73-77, 79, 81, 83,
    85-89, 91, 94-96, 98-102, 107-9, 111, 130, 133,
    136-8, 150, 152, 154-60, 162, 164-5, 167,
    170-1, 173, 176, 178, 181-96, 200-5, 208-9,
    212, 217-21, 223, 227-9, 231-2, 234, 236-7,
    239-54, 257-8, 272, 277, 286, 290, 292-4, 309,
    314-16, 322, 333-4, 339, 343-59, 367-80,
    398-401, 403-14, 421, 425-7, 430, 432, 437-9,
    441-6, 450-1, 454-6, 459-64, 468-80, 485, 489,
    495, 499, 502-3, 506, 509-11, 513-14, 517,
    523-6, 528-30, 539, 543, 548-9, 551-2, 554-60,
    562, 564-5, 570, 577-8, 581, 607, 610, 612,
    614, 616-30, 632-50, 652-9, 663-5, 667, 673,
    676-9, 681-6, 688-90, 694, 698, 700-3, 706-7,
    710-11, 713-17, 719-27, 729-31, 737-41, 749,
    751-7, 762, 767-71, 775, 777, 780, 782-5, 794,
    796, 800-3, 805-8
Upper Senegal-Niger, 584, 586
Upper Volta, 233, 584-6
Uruguay, 39, 59-60, 90, 217, 291, 395, 440,
    502-3, 616, 642, 679-80, 710, 763, 767, 769

Vatican City, 36, 70, 642, 827-8, 830
Venezuela, 12, 39, 70, 90, 230, 245, 248, 380,
    395, 408, 458, 461, 472, 539, 595-603, 606-7,
    611-15, 622-3, 627-8, 670, 678, 697, 722-4
Viet-Nam, 6, 17, 105-7, 233-4, 354-5, 409-12,
    414-15, 422, 462, 664-5; see also North
    Viet-Nam, South Viet-Nam
Virgin Islands of the United States, 40
Voltaic Republic, 586, 697, 706, 709, 712

West Germany, 19, 154, 160-2, 165, 193, 196,
    199-201, 207, 209, 218, 224, 245, 247, 250,

West Germany (cont.) 334, 346, 353, 356, 358,
432, 441, 449-50, 461-2, 469, 471, 473-4, 503,
509, 636, 640, 642, 680, 692, 702, 711, 720-1,
723-6, 728, 730, 762, 769
West Indies (British), 707
Western Samoa, 28
Windward Islands, 39, 707

Yemen, 21, 42, 45, 70, 112, 166, 184, 232, 456,
636, 638, 704, 707, 763
Yugoslavia, 13, 35, 69-70, 73, 81-83, 85-87, 108,
163, 169, 170, 180, 188, 190, 193-5, 197-9,
203-4, 210, 212-13, 225, 290, 333, 356, 431-2,
440, 446, 464, 502-3, 541-2, 544-5, 549, 561-2,
565, 667-8, 713, 728-9, 767-9, 783

Zaire, 3, 9; see also Congo
Zanzibar, 41
Zimbabwe, 11

INDEX OF PERSONS

Balanchine, George (Georgy Balanchivadze), 292
Baldaccini, César (César), 776
Balewa, Abubakar Tafawa, 8, 594, 716
Balfour, Arthur James, 177
Bandaranaike, Sirimavo Ratwatte Dias, 11, 691
Bandaranaike, Solomon West Ridgeway Dias, 691
Bao-Dai (Nguyen Vinh Thuy), 233-4, 409-11
Barber, Samuel, 294, 771
Bardeen, John, 271
Barth, Karl, 533, 813, 828
Bartok, Bela, 293
Batista y Zaldívar, Fulgencio, 393-8, 458, 603,
  605-15, 617, 624-6
Baudouin of Belgium, 225
Bayar, Celal, 440, 703
Beckett, Samuel, 505-6
Ben Bella, Ahmad, 8, 573-4, 582
Ben-Gurion, David, 183-4, 554, 561, 566, 680
Benes, Eduard, 83-84, 105, 188, 196-7, 668, 773
Berdyayev, Nikolay, 812
Bergman, Ingmar, 509, 778
Beria, Lavrenty Pavlovich, 361, 365-7, 519
Bernadotte, Folke, 182-3
Bernstein, Leonard, 296
Betancourt, Rómulo, 230, 596-7, 599-602, 614,
  623, 627-8
Bethe, Hans Albrecht, 261
Bhumibol Adulyadej, 228, 454
Biermann, Ludwig Franz, 656
Bierut, Boleslaw, 212, 431, 541-2, 544
Black, Eugene, 556-7
Blackett, Patrick Maynard Stuart, 743
Blair, Eric, see Orwell, George
Blankers-Koen, Fanny (Francina), 290
Bloch, Ernest, 504
Blomdahl, Karl-Birger, 771
Bohr, Niels, 259
Bondi, Hermann, 264
Bonhoeffer, Dietrich, 533
Bonnard, Pierre, 303
Bonomi, Ivanoe, 112
Borges, Jorge Luis, 313
Bose, Subhas Chandra, 121
Bourguiba, Habib, 572-3
Bowen, Norman Levi, 483

Dewey, Thomas, 220
Díaz Lanz, Pedro, 619-20
Diefenbaker, John, 686, 716
Dirac, Paul Adrien Maurice, 259-60
Disney, Walter, 307
Djilas, Milovan, 667, 781, 783-4
Dobzhansky, Theodosius, 486
Doderer, Heimito von, 785, 798-800
Dorticós Torrado, Osvaldo, 619
Drake, Frank Donald, 750-1
Drees, Willem, 12, 452, 694
Dreiser, Theodore, 317
Du Bois, William Edward Burghardt, 376
Duarte de Perón, Eva, 457
Dubuffet, Jean, 304, 507
Duchamp, Marcel, 304
Dulles, Allen Welsh, 400, 412
Dulles, John Foster, 349, 351-2, 356, 400, 412,
  555-7, 559-60, 636, 640, 644, 700
Durant, William James, 285, 287, 757-8, 808
Dürrenmatt, Friedrich, 773
Dutra, Eurico Gaspar, 110, 221
Dzhugashvili, Iosif Vissarionovich, see Stalin,
  Joseph

Echandía, Darío, 390
Echandía, Vicente, 390
Echeverría, José Antonio, 608-9
Eckert, John Presper, 269
Eden, Anthony, 356, 438, 554, 557-8, 560-1, 566
Eder, George Jackson, 679
Eichmann, Adolf, 680, 714
Einstein, Albert, 259, 261, 265-6, 479, 514, 733-4
Eiseley, Loren Corey, 760-2
Eisenhower, Dwight David, 345, 347-9, 351-2,
  355-8, 370, 379, 400, 404, 412, 442-3, 551-2,
  555, 559, 617, 621-2, 628-30, 632-6, 639-47,
  656, 673, 677, 681-4, 689, 704, 716, 752
Eisenstein, Sergey, 210, 307
Ekman, Vagn Walfrid, 484
Eliot, Thomas Stearns, 298, 310
Elizabeth II of the United Kingdom, 438
Elton, Charles, 747
Elvström, Paul, 768
Erlander, Tage, 676

Ewing, William Maurice, 483-4, 741

Falla, Manuel de, 293
Fanfani, Amintore, 12, 693
Farouk of Egypt, 417-19, 569
Faubus, Orval, 682
Faulkner, William, 317
Faure, Edgar, 356
Fellini, Federico, 509, 779-80
Ferber, Edna, 778
Fermi, Enrico, 260-1, 477, 479
Figueres, José, 223, 445, 614, 688
Florinsky, Michael, 496-7
Folkers, Karl August, 274
Ford, Henry, 271
Forster, Edward Morgan, 317
Fraenkel-Conrat, Heinz, 487, 489
Françaix, Jean, 504
Franco Bahamonde, Francisco Paulino Hermenegildo
    Teódulo, 12, 33-34, 69, 166, 227, 349, 454,
    702, 789
Frazier, Edward Franklin, 286-7
Fredriksson, Gert, 766, 768
Frisch, Max, 298, 773
Fromm, Erich, 491-4
Frondizi, Arturo, 686
Frost, Robert, 310
Fry, Christopher, 297

Gaitán, Jorge Eliécer, 222, 389-90
Galbraith, John Kenneth, 751, 753-5
Gallegos, Rómulo, 597-8, 600
Gandhi, Mohandas Karamchand, 11, 120-3, 127-9,
    328, 330-3, 336, 373, 387, 435, 570, 806-10,
    818-19
García, Carlos, 690
García Lorca, Federico, 297
Gary, Romain, 785, 803-5
Gaulle, Charles-André-Joseph-Marie de, see De
    Gaulle, Charles-André-Joseph-Marie
Gautama, Siddhartha, the Buddha, 17, 21, 117,
    531, 535, 809, 817, 819-24
Genet, Jean, 772
George II of Greece, 87, 190
George VI of the United Kingdom, 31, 438

Gerhardsen, Einar, 676
Gero, Erno, 544-6
Gheorghiu-Dej, Gheorghe, 13, 433, 667, 716
Ghiorso, Albert, 263, 479, 731
Giacometti, Alberto, 305, 775-6
Gide, André, 313
Gizenga, Antoine, 592-3
Godard, Jean-Luc, 779
Goddard, Robert Hutchings, 652
Goebbels, Joseph, 88
Gold, Thomas, 264
Gómez, Juan Vicente, 596, 598, 601
Gómez, Laureano, 222, 390-2, 687
Gomulka, Wladyslaw, 13, 212, 542-3, 545, 550,
  666-7, 716
Göring, Hermann, 159
Gorky, Maksim (Aleksey Maksimovich Peshkov), 517
Gottwald, Klement, 188, 197, 213, 433
Goulart, João, 444, 685
Gould, Morton, 294
Gouzenko, Igor, 516-19
Graham, Martha, 292
Graham, William Franklin, Jr. ("Billy"), 526-8,
  532, 800, 814
Grau San Martín, Ramón, 393-4, 396, 603, 617
Griffith, David Wark, 307
Grischin, Yevgeny, 769
Gropius, Walter, 306
Grotewohl, Otto, 212, 432, 668
Groza, Petru, 213
Gruen, David, 184; see also Ben-Gurion, David
Guérard, Albert Léon, 757-9
Guevara, Ernesto ("Che"), 603, 606-8, 612, 618,
  620, 626
Guinness, Alec, 309
Gunther, Jane, 499
Gunther, John, 499-500

Hahn, Otto, 260
Haile Selassie, 8, 229, 456, 705
Hamer, Robert, 308
Hammarskjöld, Dag Hjalmar Agne Carl, 12, 465,
  547, 565, 590-1, 637, 639
Hanson, Howard, 294, 503-4
Harris, Roy, 293

Mauchly, John William, 269
McCarthy, Joseph Raymond, 221, 343, 367-73, 380,
  444-5, 506, 513-14
McCloy, John Jay, 346
McCormick, Patricia, 766
McMillan, Edwin Mattison, 262
Mead, Margaret, 283-4, 287
Meitner, Lise, 260
Menard, Henry William, 742
Mendeleyev, Dmitry, 479
Menderes, Adnan, 8, 440, 703
Mendès-France, Pierre, 451, 573
Menon, Vengalil Krishnan Krishna, 6, 11, 673
Menotti, Gian Carlo, 296, 504, 771-2
Menzies, Robert Gordon, 11, 675, 716
Messaien, Olivier, 295
Michael of Romania, 213
Michener, James Albert, 785, 794-7, 805
Mies van der Rohe, Ludwig, 306, 508
Mihajlovic, Dragoljub (Draza), 82-83, 212
Mikolajczyk, Stanislaw, 80, 87-88, 98, 211-12
Mikoyan, Anastas, 544, 546-7, 621, 640
Milhaud, Darius, 294-5
Miller, Arthur, 297-8, 506
Mills, Charles Wright, 751-3
Mindszenty, Joseph, 213, 434, 546, 549
Miró, Joan, 304, 775
Miró Cardona, José, 615
Mobutu, Joseph, 592
Mohammad Reza Pahlavi, 13, 74, 110-11, 400-1,
  403-6, 696
Mollet, Guy, 558, 561, 566, 573-4, 693
Molotov, Vyacheslav, 192, 194, 196, 352, 354,
  361, 365, 543, 632, 666
Montesi, Wilma, 693
Moore, Henry, 507, 775-6
Morgan, Thomas Hunt, 486
Morgan, William Wilson, 482
Mosaddeq, Mohammad, 401-7, 409, 412, 453
Mössbauer, Rudolf Ludwig, 733-4
Muhammad, 20-21, 175, 535
Muhammad V of Morocco, 573
Muhammad Ali, 447
Muller, Hermann Joseph, 486
Mussolini, Benito, 31-32, 34, 68, 76, 89, 162-5,

Mussolini, Benito (cont.) 310
Myrdal, Gunnar, 286

Nagy, Imre, 433-4, 543-50, 669, 714
Nasir, Jamal Abd an-, 8, 415-22, 553-62, 566-7,
    632, 636, 703-4, 716
Nasser, see Nasir, Jamal Abd an-
Nazimmudin, Khwaja, 447
Ne Win, 674
Neguib, Mohammad, 418-20, 569
Nehru, Jawaharlal, 11, 122-8, 434-6, 639, 671,
    673, 716
Nenni, Pietro, 681
Neruda, Pablo, 310-13
Nervi, Pier Luigi, 777
Neumann, John von, 260
Ngo Dinh Diem, 6, 410-11, 414-15, 665, 701
Nguyen Ai Quoc, see Ho Chi Minh
Nguyen Sinh Cung, see Ho Chi Minh
Nguyen That Thanh, see Ho Chi Minh
Nichiren, 823-4
Niebuhr, Reinhold, 533
Niemeyer Soares, Oscar, filho, 777
Nijinsky, Vaslav, 292
Nikolais, Alwin, 770-1
Nishida Kitaro, 823
Nixon, Richard, 617, 624-6, 684
Nkrumah, Kwame, 9, 570-1, 680, 709, 716
Nobel, Alfred Bernhard, 731
Norodom Sihanouk, 449; see also Sihanouk, Norodom
Novotny, Antonin, 668, 716
Nu, 139, 214, 436-7, 531, 674
Nuri as-Said, 453, 637
Nutting, Anthony, 562
Nyerere, Julius Kambarage, 9

Ochoa, Severo, 487
Odría, Manuel, 230, 687-8
Oldenbourg, Zoé, 516-17
O'Neill, Eugene, 297, 774-5
Ono Takashi, 768
Oparin, Aleksandr Ivanovich, 487
Ophüls, Max, 509
Oppenheimer, J. Robert, 261, 477-8
Orff, Carl, 295

Purcell, Edward Mills, 482

Qassim, Abdul Karim, 8, 637-8, 704
Quadros, Jânio, 685
Quirino, Elpidio, 138, 448

Rakosi, Matyas, 544-6
Rapacki, Adam, 636
Ray, Manuel ("Manolo"), 620, 624
Ray, Satyajit, 508, 779
Reines, Frederick, 731
Remarque, Erich Maria, 516, 519-21, 759
Renoir, Jean, 307
Resnais, Alain, 778
Reyes Basoalto, Ricardo Eliézer Neftalí, see
  Neruda, Pablo
Rhee, Syngman, 9, 136-7, 344-5, 448, 690
Richier, Germaine, 507, 776
Rivero Agüero, Andrés, 612
Rojas Pinilla, Gustavo, 391-2, 458, 598, 687
Rokossovsky, Konstantin, 212, 543
Romer, Alfred Sherwood, 747
Roncalli, Angelo Giuseppe, 827; see also John
  XXIII
Roosevelt, Franklin Delano, 37, 75, 77, 81,
  89-90, 94-96, 187, 220, 261
Rose, Murray, 766, 768
Rosenblueth, Arturo, 269
Rossellini, Roberto, 308
Rostow, Walt Whitman, 755-7
Rothko, Mark (Marcus Rothkovitch), 775
Rouault, Georges, 303
Roxas, Manuel, 138
Ruiz Cortines, Adolfo, 12, 439, 678
Ruiz y Picasso, Pablo, see Picasso
Runcorn, Stanley Keith, 743
Russell, Bertrand, 266-8, 288, 500
Russell, Henry Norris, 482
Ruz, Lina, 603

Sailer, Toni (Anton), 767
St. Laurent, Louis, 222, 444, 686
Sakharov, Andrey Dmitriyevich, 477
Salan, Raoul, 574, 580-1
Salazar, António de Oliveira, 12, 228, 454, 703

859

Salinger, Jerome David, 516, 523-6
Salk, Jonas Edward, 489
Sanger, Frederick, 488
Santayana, George, 813
Sarit Thanarat, 701
Sartre, Jean-Paul, 299-300, 311, 328-30, 505,
530, 773, 811
Sastroamidjojo, Ali, 459
Saud, Abd al-Aziz Al, 8, 231, 456
Schaefer, Vincent Joseph, 275
Schine, Gerard David, 371
Schoenberg, Arnold, 295
Schrödinger, Erwin, 259
Schuller, Gunther, 771
Schuman, William, 296, 771
Schwarz-Bart, André, 759, 785, 790-4
Seaborg, Glenn Theodore, 263, 479, 731
Segni, Antonio, 692-3
Segrè, Emilio Gino, 479
Senghor, Léopold, 585
Shakhlin, Boris, 768
Shaw, George Bernard, 215, 296
Sheean, Vincent, 332-3
Shirer, William Lawrence, 757, 759-60
Shockley, William Bradford, 271
Shostakovich, Dmitry, 210, 294
Sibelius, Jean, 293
Sihanouk, Norodom, 6, 449, 691, 716
Sikorski, Wladyslaw, 33, 69, 74, 80
Sikorsky, Igor, 271
Siles Suazo, Hernán, 679
Simpson, George Gaylord, 747
Siroky, Viliam, 433, 668
Smigly-Rydz, Edward, 33, 68-69
Smith, David, 305, 776
Smith, Ernest Lester, 274
Smuts, Jan, 226-7
Somoza Debayle, Anastasio, 706
Somoza Debayle, Luis, 706-7
Somoza García, Anastasio, 231, 408, 458, 706-7
Soong Mei Ling, 143
Souphanouvong, 648-9
Souvanna Phouma, 7, 648-9
Stalin, Joseph, 7, 29-31, 57, 74, 76-81, 83,
86-90, 96, 98-102, 186-9, 192, 195, 200-2,

DATE DUE

GAYLORD			PRINTED IN U.S.A.